always up to date

The law changes, but Nolo is on top of it! We offer several ways to make sure you and your Nolo products are up to date:

1 **Nolo's Legal Updater**

We'll send you an email whenever a new edition of this book is published! Sign up at **www.nolo.com/legalupdater**.

2 **Updates @ Nolo.com**

Check **www.nolo.com/update** to find recent changes in the law that affect the current edition of your book.

3 **Nolo Customer Service**

To make sure that this edition of the book is the most recent one, call us at **800-728-3555** and ask one of our friendly customer service representatives. Or find out at **www.nolo.com**.

please note

We believe accurate, plain-English legal information should help you solve many of your own legal problems. But this text is not a substitute for personalized advice from a knowledgeable lawyer. If you want the help of a trained professional—and we'll always point out situations in which we think that's a good idea—consult an attorney licensed to practice in your state.

8th edition

Plan Your Estate

by Attorneys Denis Clifford & Cora Jordan

Eighth Edition	March 2006
Editor	SHAE IRVING
Book Design	JACKIE MANCUSO
Cover Design	TONI IHARA
Illustrator	MARI STEIN
Production	MARGARET LIVINGSTON
Proofreader	SUSIE SEEFELT LESIEUTRE
Indexer	BAYSIDE INDEXING SERVICE
Printing	DELTA PRINTING SOLUTIONS, INC.

Clifford, Denis.

    Plan your estate / by Denis Clifford & Cora Jordan. -- 8th ed.

      p. cm.

    Includes index.

    ISBN 1-4133-0406-0 (alk. paper)

    1. Estate planning--United States--Popular works. I. Jordan, Cora, 1941- II. Title.

KF750.Z9C59 2006

346.7305'2--dc22

                                                  2005058544

Quantity sales: For information on bulk purchases or corporate premium sales, please contact the Special Sales department. For academic sales or textbook adoptions, ask for Academic Sales. 800-955-4775, Nolo, 950 Parker St., Berkeley, CA, 94710.

ACKNOWLEDGMENTS

Even more than most Nolo books, this one would never have seen the light of day without the generous efforts and contributions of many fine people. So our thanks to all those friends who helped us with this book, both putting it together and with previous editions over the years:

Friends at Nolo, without whose efforts this book wouldn't have existed: Jake Warner, as ever, a great editor, writer, and critic; Mary Randolph, a uniquely gifted and great editor, writer, and organizer extraordinaire; Barbara Kate Repa, another superb editor and writer; Shae Irving, our current editor, at least as talented and as much fun to work with as our previous editors; Stephanie Harolde, who over many years read all of our editing scrawls and turned them into coherent pages, and also did much fine editing as she was preparing yet another draft of the manuscript; and Ella Hirst, for her excellent research.

Mark Peery of Greenbrae, California, a superb estate planning lawyer (and great friend).

All our other friends and colleagues at Nolo. In the past, we've listed everyone, but now we have 80 or more employees, plus more outside writers and an employee manual. Still, Nolo retains the relaxed, friendly atmosphere that makes it such a pleasant (as well as productive) place to work.

Dorcas Moulton, Amanda Cherrin, and Naomi Puro, for their contributions to the cover painting on the original book.

Ken Fischer, Concord, California, a fine insurance agent; Bill Hudspeth, Austin Trust Co., Austin, Texas; Magdelen Gaynor, another fine estate planning attorney, White Plains, New York; Adalene Pettis of State Farm Insurance Co.; and James Wickett of the National Federation of Independent Businesses.

And our continued appreciation to other friends who also helped with other editions of this book: David Marcus; Paul Remack, R.G. Financial Service, San Francisco; Dave Brown; Peter Jan Honigsberg; Robert Wood of Athearn, Chandler & Hoffman, San Francisco; members of the Bay Area Funeral Society; Walter Warner; people who helped prepare the manuscript—Sandy Wieker, Christy Rigg, Cathy Cummings, and Bethany Korwin-Pawloski; and Keija Kimura, Carol Pladsen, and Linda Allison.

And finally, but not leastly, our heartfelt thanks to the many readers who have written us with suggestions, comments, corrections, and other thoughts for improving this book.

TABLE OF CONTENTS

INTRODUCTION: HOW TO USE THIS BOOK

PART I: SETTING YOUR GOALS

1 SELECTING YOUR ESTATE PLANNING GOALS

2 PERSONAL CONCERNS AND ESTATE PLANNING

PART XI: GOING FURTHER

29 USING LAWYERS

30 AFTER YOU COMPLETE YOUR ESTATE PLAN

31 AFTER A DEATH OCCURS

PART XII: SAMPLE ESTATE PLANS

32 SOME ESTATE PLANS

GLOSSARY

APPENDIX: STATE INHERITANCE TAX RULES

INDEX

INTRODUCTION:
How to Use This Book

With this book, you can learn how to sensibly plan for the transfer of your property to your loved ones after you die, with a minimum of fuss and waste. Depending on your situation, this process can be straightforward and simple, involving little more than preparing a will yourself, without ever visiting a lawyer. But if your estate is large or your family needs are complicated, you may need expert help with sophisticated estate tax planning or to create complex legal devices to control what happens to your property after your death. At either end of this spectrum, as well as anywhere in between, this book points you in the right direction.

> ⚠️ **Warning to Louisiana residents:** This book is designed for residents of all states except Louisiana, which has a legal system based on Napoleonic Code, different from the other states. If you live in Louisiana, please return this book to Nolo for a full refund.

Your "estate" is simply all the property you own, whatever it's worth. The "planning" required can be understood by normal, intelligent people—you don't have to be an astrophysicist or even an attorney. Indeed, with the aid of this book and other Nolo resources, you may decide that you can safely do much, or even all, of your estate planning yourself, without professional help.

The word "plan" can be misleading. It doesn't mean you'll have a document that looks like a map, or one that has lots of charts and graphs. And it doesn't have to mean you'll end up with a thick file of papers filled with obscure legalese. Your estate plan will simply consist of the methods and documents you've chosen to handle the matters that concern you.

Plan Your Estate is useful for people with estates of any amount, from relatively modest to many millions. Many of the methods this book covers are equally desirable for small estates as well as large ones. For instance, probate avoidance methods work equally well for estates worth thousands as for those worth millions. Similarly, planning for what happens if you become incapacitated involves substantially the same concerns no matter what the size of your estate. But it's also true that larger estates tend to require more complicated and more in-depth estate planning, particularly tax planning. So we provide thorough discussions of the major ways to save on estate taxes.

While this book focuses on legal and practical issues of estate planning, we want to acknowledge that, viewed from a larger perspective, these are often of minor concern in the face of the overwhelming emotional force and mystery of death. In Chapter 2 we discuss some of the personal realities of estate planning, but this book doesn't attempt to deal with the larger meanings of death; they are appropriately left to philosophers, clergy, poets, and—ultimately—to you. But it's important to recognize that thinking about estate planning touches (at least) on our own mortality—a difficult subject to think about, to talk about, and to plan for. The ancient Greeks believed the inevitability of death could best be faced by performing great deeds. Christian religions offer the promise of eternal life; preparing for death means preparing to "meet your maker." Other cultures have prepared for death in a wide variety of ways, often with elaborate ceremonies.

However you choose to emotionally and spiritually prepare for death—your own or someone you care for—there are also practical consequences that must be handled. In the U.S., if no planning has been done, often a host of highly paid professionals—from lawyers to CPAs, financial advisors, real estate agents, and insurance brokers—consume many thousands of dollars that could have been saved. Estate taxes that might have been reduced or avoided can consume much more. This money, obviously, comes from the estate of the person who died—money that would otherwise be available for family, friends, or charities to inherit. So, in the final analysis, preparing an estate plan is an act of love for your inheritors. Although you don't directly face the consequences of procrastination and avoidance, they will, unless you decide to act.

This book does not present prepackaged estate plans for so-called "standard" situations. With that kind of approach, if a husband and wife have minor children and an estate of approximately $900,000, Plan A is proposed. But a husband and wife with no minor children and an estate over $900,000 should use Plan B. Then there are plans C, D, E, and who knows how many more.

The problem with off-the-shelf estate plans is that, as we all know, real life isn't standardized. There are too many variables in most people's situations to make a one-size-fits-many approach work well. A far better approach is for you to take stock of your own needs and desires, and determine what your personal estate planning goals are. Then, with the broad-based information we present here, you should be able to come up with a good idea of the estate plan you want—one that's geared to your personal situation.

A. How This Book Works

Plan Your Estate covers all major aspects of estate planning, from simple wills to complex estate tax-saving trusts. Estate planning can involve many different factors. Common concerns may include:

- arranging for the care of minor children
- writing a will and avoiding probate
- making sure you get the kinds of medical care you want, if you become incapacitated and can no longer speak for yourself
- naming a trusted person to handle your finances if you become incapacitated and can no longer handle them yourself
- providing for all family members when there has been a second or subsequent marriage, and
- reducing estate taxes.

To prepare the plan that best suits you, you need to understand the different ways of accomplishing each of your particular estate planning goals, as well as how those goals can be connected. This book explains what choices you have, how they work, and the advantages and drawbacks of each.

Unlike many Nolo books, this is not a do-it-yourself law book, with legal forms you can tear out and complete. Rather, the book is divided into parts, each covering a major estate planning concern. Chapter 1 gives you an overview of each part, so you can select only those that concern you. We encourage you to use *Plan Your Estate* as a workbook. Feel free to underline and highlight text or make notes in the margins.

Estate planning is one of the more jargon-ridden areas of law (rather a feat). We've tried to keep this lawyer dialect to a minimum, but it isn't possible to eliminate it entirely. To make this material as comprehensible as possible, we define each important term when it's first used in the text. Also, there's a glossary near the back of the book. Please use it as often as you need to be sure you really understand what you are reading.

LOOK FOR THESE ICONS

We use several icons to alert you to important information:

A caution that there may be some serious risk, or danger, that can arise in this facet of your estate planning.

Indicates where we are definitely offering our own (best) advice, not merely "objective" information.

Lets you know when we believe you need the advice of an attorney, often an estate planning expert.

Refers you to helpful books or other resources.

We believe this book to be the most thorough estate planning manual written for the nonlawyer. But the book doesn't claim to present definitive advice on every aspect of the field. Many subjects covered, such as estate taxes, life insurance, irrevocable trusts, or even wills can get very complicated for people with very large estates or complex family situations. This partially explains why there are volumes of books on each topic in any good-sized law library. Some other subjects are still more esoteric and complex, such as planning when you own property in several countries, or for valuable copyrights or patents.

Also, we do not cover what is often termed "elder law" or retirement issues, which include financial planning for old age, choosing a nursing facility, and protecting assets. Elder law is a separate field from estate planning and this book is big enough. While we do not generally cover pensions or retirement plans, including IRAs or 401(k) plans, we do discuss how any funds left in these plans at your death can best be transferred to beneficiaries.

B. WILL YOU NEED PROFESSIONAL HELP?

Many people worry that estate planning, in reality, means handing thousands of dollars over to lawyers in exchange for mysterious documents. 'Tain't necessarily so. The good news is that you may be able to accomplish all of your estate planning goals without any professional help. By the time you've finished this book you'll be able to make a sensible evaluation of whether or not you need to hire a lawyer or other expert. Make this judgment carefully, of course, but do remember that lawyers, accountants, and other experts aren't magicians. The cost of hiring an expensive estate planner, if you have a moderate estate, is often greater than any savings or certainty you achieve from her.

For most people with moderate estates, the process of estate planning isn't nearly as forbidding as many professionals make it seem. It's our experience, working in this field for over 25 years, that most people who have estates worth less than the federal estate tax threshold and who have clear desires about their property, can safely prepare their own estate planning documents from other Nolo resources, listed in Section C, below.

In some situations, however, even people with modest estates need legal help to do the best estate planning. For example, if you want to provide long-term care for a disabled child, you should see a lawyer to be sure you've best protected any assets you leave for that child's benefit.

Many people with estates exceeding the federal estate tax threshold (explained in Chapter 15, Section A) will conclude that they need the assistance of an experienced lawyer to complete their estate planning. If you do decide you need expert help, the knowledge you gain here should help keep your costs to a minimum. Since you already know the basics, you won't need to purchase this information at $200 (or $500) per hour. Also, if you educate yourself and do much of your initial planning, you're more likely to end up with something that fully expresses your own desires. And you'll be able to better judge whether the attorney is giving you fair value for your money, or simply running up your bill—after all, he knows you have some money.

Finally, some advice about self-help estate planning: Don't back away from preparing your general plan, or even the documents you want, because of derisive comments made by some lawyers. Certain members of the legal establishment have tried to frighten the public with horror stories of disasters that befell some benighted person who prepared her own estate plan. For example, a renowned lawyer once remarked sarcastically that anyone who can take out his own appendix can write his own will. This analogy is just plain false. A more accurate one is that if you can understand a standard tax form, you can determine your estate planning goals and, at least in general terms, choose the best legal methods desirable to accomplish them. The truth is that, with the aid of Nolo resources, hundreds of thousands of people have successfully prepared their own wills and living trusts, without paying a lawyer.

C. OTHER NOLO RESOURCES

As Nolo authors we are, of course, in favor of do-it-yourself law and avoiding lawyers when that's feasible. Throughout *Plan Your Estate,* we alert you when a Nolo book or software program provides more detailed, and how-to-do-it, coverage of an aspect of estate planning than this book does. It may seem self-serving for us to recommend other Nolo products, so let us tell you why we do. Nolo pioneered self-help law, showing people how to safely do it themselves. Our materials have been created and updated with great (often excruciating) care over many years. Literally millions of people have successfully used a Nolo self-help resource. Quite frankly, we believe our resources are by far the best for self-help purposes.

Nolo's estate planning and related resources include:

- *Quicken WillMaker Plus*, software from Nolo that enables you to prepare most or all of the estate planning documents you'll need, including a will, living trust (basic or tax-saving "AB" version), financial power of attorney, health care directive (living will), and documents for your executor, the person who handles your estate after you die.

- *Make Your Own Living Trust*, a complete explanation, including forms, of how to prepare a living trust. The book contains forms and information enabling a married couple with a combined estate over the federal estate tax threshold to prepare a tax-saving "AB" trust.

- *Nolo's Simple Will Book*, an in-depth explanation of how to prepare a will that covers all normal needs, including simple trusts for your minor children. Will forms are available as tear-outs or on a computer disk included with the book.

- *Quick & Legal Will Book*, which enables you to prepare a basic will efficiently.

- *Special Needs Trusts: Protect Your Child's Financial Future,* which shows parents of a disabled child how to provide for the child with a trust, while also preserving eligibility for government assistance.

- *8 Ways to Avoid Probate*, a thorough discussion of all the major ways to transfer property at death outside of a will.

- *Estate Planning Basics*, which concisely explains the essential components of estate planning.

- *Living Wills & Powers of Attorney for California*, which allows Californians to prepare all the documents they need to name a trusted person to handle financial and medical affairs if they become incapacitated and unable to make their own decisions.

- *The Executor's Guide: Settling a Loved One's Estate or Trust*, a comprehensive handbook to help executors and trustees wind up a deceased person's affairs. It can also help you get your estate in shape for your own executor or trustee.

- *How to Probate an Estate in California*, which allows Californians to wrap up a normal estate without an attorney.

- *Get It Together: Organize Your Records So Your Family Won't Have To*, a complete system you can use to organize your legal documents, financial records, and other important personal information for your executor and other loved ones.

- *Deeds for California Real Estate*, which explains how to use deeds to transfer California real estate for estate planning purposes.

- *Long-Term Care: How to Plan & Pay For It*, a practical guide that provides all the information you need to help make the best arrangements for long-term care. It shows how to protect assets, arrange home health care, find nursing and non-nursing home residences, evaluate nursing home insurance, and understand Medicare, Medicaid, and other benefit programs.

- *Social Security, Medicare & Government Pensions*, an invaluable guide through the current maze of rights and benefits for those 55 and over, including Medicare, Medicaid, and Social Security retirement and disability benefits, and age discrimination protections.

- *Nolo's Guide to Social Security Disability*, an in-depth explanation of how to obtain and keep Social Security Disability benefits.

- *Creating Your Own Retirement Plan*, a resource for the self-employed, helping them determine their best retirement plan options, including IRAs, profit-sharing plans, and 401(k)s.

- *IRAs, 401(k)s & Other Retirement Plans*, explaining when you are allowed, or required, to take money out of your retirement plans.

- *Get a Life*, sharing sensible ways for living a fulfilling retirement—ways that have little to do with accumulated wealth and everything to do with quality of life.

You can order any of these resources directly from Nolo. On the website, you'll also find lots of free legal information, including articles on estate planning and many other important topics. ∎

1

SELECTING YOUR ESTATE PLANNING GOALS

There are a number of ways to leave property to those you want to have it after your death. The peculiarities of our system of inheritance mean that substantial amounts of money and time can often be saved if property is labeled and transferred by certain legal methods rather than others. But to choose wisely among these methods, you must first clearly define your estate planning goals.

This book is divided into 12 parts; each part covers a different estate planning goal or purpose. This chapter gives you an overview of each goal, so you can select the ones that matter to you. It also presents a sample estate plan of a couple in their 50s, so you can get a feel for what kinds of decisions you may have to make, and what types of documents you may end up with.

We urge you to read all chapters of every part that concerns you before you actually begin to formulate your own estate plan. Different aspects of estate planning are often intertwined. For example, it just doesn't make sense to decide what property should pass under your will—and so go through probate—until you understand whether some of it might be better left by other probate-avoidance methods. Similarly, if you have a good-sized estate, you'll need to understand how estate taxes work before you can determine the wisest ways to transfer property to your loved ones. The point is that you need a good overview of all the parts of estate planning that concern you before you begin to make your plan.

PART I: SETTING YOUR GOALS

Use Part I to focus on your estate planning goals. After reading the first chapter, you should be able to decide which other parts of the book probably apply to your situation.

You should also take some time to mull over important personal concerns that can arise in estate planning—such as leaving unequal amounts of property to different children or avoiding potential conflicts. Chapter 2 discusses some of these concerns. Unless you're very confident that your personal situation is clear and not conflicted, be sure to check it out.

"Thrift is a wonderful virtue, especially in an ancestor."
                                    —Mark Twain

PART II: LAYING THE GROUNDWORK

This part covers the primary concerns of any estate plan: what you own and whom you want to leave it to.

Obviously, you'll need to be sure of what you own. Also, sensible planning usually requires at least a rough idea of what your property is worth. Chapter 4 contains a worksheet you can use to list all your major items of property or just use as a safety check to make sure you haven't overlooked anything.

Your "estate" includes all the property you own, minus anything you owe (assets minus liabilities). You may find it useful to use the worksheet to make a rough estimate of the dollar value of your estate, which can be helpful both for general planning purposes and to predict whether or not your estate will likely be liable for estate taxes. Of course, your estate will very likely have a different worth when you die, so precise figures aren't necessary.

You can't leave what you don't own. Ownership rules for single people are simple. Except as limited by contract (such as a partnership agreement or other form of shared ownership), you can leave all property you own outright. For these purposes the fact that some institution has a claim on the property, such as a mortgage on a house or a loan lien on a car, doesn't create shared ownership.

Property ownership rules for a married person can be more complex. Read Chapter 3 before you start inventorying your property. Rules affecting ownership of property acquired during marriage may restrict your right to leave property. There are two basic systems that govern a married couple's; which one applies to you depends on what state you live in. The majority of states follow the "common law" system where, in general, the owner of property is the person whose name appears on the ownership document. The other system, applicable in nine states, mostly in the West, is "community property," where most property acquired during a marriage is owned equally by both spouses.

UNMARRIED COUPLES: WHO OWNS WHAT?

Unless an unmarried couple—gay, lesbian, or heterosexual, it makes no difference—agrees to share ownership of specified property, each member of the couple owns only his or her own property. An agreement to own property together must often be in writing to be enforceable. In some states, an oral agreement is effective if it can be proved, but that can often be difficult. In short, it is best for unmarried couples to put any property-sharing agreement in writing.

If you're part of an unmarried couple where each person has kept all property separate (a written agreement to do this, listing the property of each person, is a good idea here as well), each of you is free to give your property to whomever you wish. However, if property ownership is shared, either under the terms of a written contract or in a tenancy in common or partnership, you're free to dispose of your share only, unless the contract or partnership agreement provides otherwise.

Property held by unmarried couples in joint tenancy goes to the survivor automatically.

California, Hawaii, Maine, and Vermont have passed laws that provide gay and lesbian couples with many of the property rights of married couples. (In Massachusetts, gay or lesbian legal residents can marry and so have the rights of any married couple in that state.) To obtain these rights, a lesbian or gay couple must register as domestic partners with the state. However, relying on these laws should never be a substitute for doing your own comprehensive estate planning. It's not wise for any couple, or anyone, to allow the state to do their estate planning for them.

For more information on property ownership problems of unmarried couples and sample property-sharing agreements, see either *Living Together: A Legal Guide for Unmarried Couples*, by Ralph Warner, Toni Ihara, and Frederick Hertz (Nolo), a detailed guide designed to help unmarried couples minimize their entanglements with the law, or *A Legal Guide for Lesbian & Gay Couples*, by Hayden Curry, Denis Clifford, and Frederick Hertz (Nolo).

In common law states, laws limit a spouse's right to disinherit the other spouse. As explained in Chapter 3, in these states a surviving spouse has the right to receive a certain portion of a deceased spouse's property, no matter what that spouse provided or intended. If you plan on leaving your spouse more than half your property, these laws can't affect you.

For most people, the heart of estate planning is deciding who gets what. You may have a very clear idea of who should inherit your property. If so, fine. Still, there are a number of issues that you may want to consider, from naming alternate beneficiaries to leaving shared gifts to forgiving debts. Chapter 5 discusses these and other concerns about your inheritors.

PART III: CHILDREN

If you have minor children, you'll want to plan for what would happen in the unlikely event that you and the other parent (if there is one) die before the children become legal adults. Indeed, for many new parents, concern for their child is what moves them to begin estate planning. Chapter 6 focuses on minor children, because a number of special estate planning issues affect them.

Most likely your first concern is who would raise the children if you couldn't. In your will, you can name someone to serve as the "personal guardian" for your children—the adult who would be responsible for raising them if neither parent could. Your nomination isn't automatically legally binding, but courts normally confirm the person you name if the other parent isn't available. Chapter 6 also discusses what you can do if you do not want the other parent to obtain custody.

The second big issue is who will manage any property you leave to your minor children. Minors cannot legally own more than a minimal amount of property without adult supervision. So leaving property to your minor children requires you to choose a method for adult management. Chapter 6 explains the four legal methods you can use to impose adult supervision over property you leave to minors, and the advantages and drawbacks of each.

Finally, Chapter 6 also addresses estate planning issues pertaining to adult children.

PART IV: WILLS

Everyone should have a will, the most basic estate planning device. Chapter 7 explains why and shows you what you can accomplish in your will.

In your will you name your "executor," the person with legal authority to administer the transfer of your will property. Chapter 7 discusses the responsibilities of an executor, and presents some thoughts on selecting yours.

Wills do have one big drawback: Property left by a will must go through probate. So don't decide what property to transfer by your will until you've looked at transfer methods that avoid probate, which are discussed in Part V.

Whatever you decide about avoiding probate, you still need a will. At a minimum, a will is a backup device essential to transfer any property that somehow wasn't transferred by other methods, such as property you overlooked or that you unexpectedly acquire after setting up your probate-avoidance devices (a surprise inheritance, lottery winnings).

In almost all states, a will is the only document you can use to name a personal guardian for your minor children. Also, a will is best for transferring some types of property, like personal checking accounts or vehicles, that usually aren't convenient to transfer by any other method.

PART V: PROBATE AND HOW TO AVOID IT

Probate is the name given to the legal process by which a court oversees the distribution of property left by a will. The probate process is examined in detail in Chapter 8.

Probate proceedings are generally mere formalities, because there's rarely any dispute about a will, but they are nevertheless usually cumbersome and lengthy. During probate, your assets are identified, all debts and death taxes are paid, fees for lawyers, appraisers, accountants, and for filing the case in court are paid, and the remaining property is finally distributed to your inheritors. The average probate proceeding drags on for at least a year before the estate is actually distributed.

The very word "probate" has acquired a notorious aura. Commonly, it's an institutionalized rip-off of a dead person's estate by lawyers, and sometimes other officials or executors, who get large fees for what in most cases is routine, albeit tedious, paperwork. For example, if a father leaves his estate equally among his three children, and no one contests the will, why should a lawyer be paid a hefty sum to shuffle papers through a bureaucratic maze?

Because probate lawyers are expensive, we've been asked many times by will beneficiaries if they can safely handle probate without an attorney. Unfortunately, except in California and Wisconsin, the answer is normally "no," at least not without considerable difficulty. (In California, probate can be done without an attorney by using *How to Probate an Estate in California*, by Julia Nissley (Nolo). Wisconsin has a simplified probate system, with court clerical assistance for completing the forms. Legally, it's permissible in most states (but not, for example, in Florida) for the executor named in a will to act for the estate, appear in probate court, and handle the proceedings without an attorney. But probate is a technical and tedious area of the law. Without good instructions, which are unfortunately nonexistent outside of lawyer texts (except, to repeat, in California and Wisconsin), the forms can seem very complicated to the uninitiated. Further, in some situations, there are court hearings to attend. In short, learning how to do probate from scratch normally takes considerable time and risks continuing frustration. Worse, the courts and clerks can be unhelpful, or even hostile, to laypeople.

A wiser choice is to reduce or eliminate probate fees by transferring property outside of probate. If you have a moderate estate, you can probably prepare probate-avoidance devices and documents yourself, without an attorney. The next six chapters explain the major probate-avoidance methods:

- Living trusts, which allow you to retain full control over trust property while you live; after your death, your living trust property is transferred quickly to your beneficiaries.

- Joint tenancy, a form of shared property ownership with the key element that the surviving owner of joint tenancy property automatically inherits the share of a deceased owner. No probate is required.

- Pay-on-death designations, which let you name a beneficiary to quickly and easily receive, without probate, assets such as bank accounts or stocks when you die.

- Life insurance, the proceeds of which go directly to the policy beneficiary, without going through probate.

- Individual retirement programs, such as IRAs, profit-sharing plans, or 401(k) plans, where you can leave any money remaining in the account to a named beneficiary. The money is transferred outside of probate.

- State law exemptions from normal probate, which allow smaller estates to go through a simplified probate procedure or avoid probate altogether. These rules apply to estates ranging from less than $5,000 to $150,000, depending on the state. A list of each state's rules is in Chapter 14.

Reading about probate avoidance doesn't mean that you must decide to pursue it. Some people intelligently decide that all the estate planning they want, for now, is a will.

Although you may find it surprising, limiting estate planning to making a will can, in the right circumstances, make good sense. For example, many younger people in good health often sensibly decide to postpone detailed estate planning for later. A will naming a personal and property guardian for minor children and leaving their relatively modest amount of property to a spouse, partner, and perhaps also a few close friends or relatives, is all they want, and need, now. Since probate doesn't happen until death, a younger person should have plenty of time to plan to avoid it later in life.

In contrast, for older people with a reasonable amount of property, or people in ill health, it makes little sense to depend on a will alone. The amount of time and effort it takes to plan to avoid probate is just not that much—certainly far less than will be consumed going through it, not to mention the significant costs saved.

Aside from avoiding probate altogether, if you significantly reduce the value of property transferred by probate, you'll likely reduce the attorney's fee as well. A useful concept here is the "probate estate," the portion of your estate that must go through probate. Anything that is transferred by probate-avoiding methods is not part of the probate estate; it goes directly to inheritors without court proceedings. If you plan wisely, you can reduce considerably the size of your "probate estate" or even eliminate it entirely.

Some reasons for probate. In unusual situations, probate can be useful. If your estate will have many debts or claims by creditors, probate provides a forum for resolving those claims with relative speed and certainty. And if creditors who are notified of the probate do not file claims within a set period (usually a few months), the claims are barred forever.

PROVIDING READY CASH

One goal of estate planning can be to provide ready cash for immediate family needs or, later on, to pay any death taxes or other debts. Particularly if you are your family's main provider, your survivors will need immediate cash for their living expenses, or for the "costs of dying"—hospitalization, funeral, and burial expenses—and other debts and taxes that are due promptly.

If most of your property is transferred by will, your family won't get it while probate moves on. Immediate family members can ask the probate court to release limited amounts for necessities, but it's wiser to plan to have money available without going to court and paying attorneys' fees.

If most of your property will be transferred outside of probate, there is much less reason to worry about arranging for ready cash, since cash is usually accessible promptly. However, if most of your assets aren't "liquid"—that is, cannot easily be converted to cash—you may still need to provide a source of ready cash. For example, if your worth is in real estate and shares of a private corporation that can't readily be sold, your family might have trouble obtaining cash for daily expenses. Traditional sources of cash are life insurance policies or money in a "pay-on-death" bank account.

PART VI: UNDERSTANDING ESTATE AND GIFT TAXES

Most people who engage in comprehensive estate planning want to know about estate and gift taxes. Will your estate be liable for taxes? If so, what can be done to reduce or avoid them? In Chapter 15, you'll learn how both federal and state estate taxes work and whether or not your estate is likely to be subject to tax.

In addition, a handful of states impose inheritance taxes. In theory, these states tax the recipients of a deceased person's property rather than the property itself, but the reality is the same—the taxes are paid out of the deceased's estate. Chapter 15 explains how inheritance taxes work. If your state imposes them, you can find the details in the appendix at the back of this book.

You will likely learn that no federal estate tax will be assessed against your estate. Federal law exempts a certain amount of property from tax. This amount gradually increases from $2 million in 2006 to $3.5 million in 2009. Then it disappears for one year, and one year only, in 2010. (For more details, see Chapter 15, Section A.)

⚠ When couples should consider tax planning. If you're a member of a couple (married or not) with a combined estate exceeding the federal estate tax threshold, you should consider tax planning if each of you plans to leave most or all of your property to the other. Without planning, the survivor could wind up with an estate subject to tax after he or she dies. With sensible planning, this result can often be avoided or reduced. (See Part VII, below.)

Chapter 15 explains this and other major federal estate tax exemptions. Another important exemption is what's called the "marital deduction," which provides that all property left or given to a spouse is exempt from estate or gift tax. However, the marital deduction does not apply to property a citizen spouse gives or leaves to a noncitizen spouse.

Chapter 15 also covers the concept of tax "basis" and how that applies to inherited property. Very briefly, the "basis" of property is the dollar value put on your ownership interest when determining the profit or loss from sale. To simplify here, we can say that the basis of property you own is the purchase price. However, if you inherit property under current federal law, your basis is not the cost to the person who left you the property, but the market value of the property when that person died. This is called a "stepped-up" basis. If you plan to leave property that has significantly increased in value since you purchased it, it's important to understand how this "stepped-up basis" works, and can be used in estate planning.

To get a solid grasp of estate taxes, you also need to understand gift taxes, which are covered in Chapter 16. At first hearing, the phrase "gift taxes" sounds like something Scrooge came up with. How can you tax generosity? But if there were no gift taxes, estate taxes could be avoided simply by giving away property while you live instead of leaving it when you die. So the federal government, and a few states, impose tax on substantial gifts, currently above $12,000 to any person in one year.

DEFINITION OF A GIFT

A "gift" is property you transfer freely (not by sale or trade) to a person or institution. Throughout this book, "gift" is used to describe both property you give away during your lifetime and property you leave at your death. This saves us from having to use the legalese "bequest," "devise," or "legacy."

⚠ Separate taxes and probate. Don't confuse avoiding probate with reducing estate or gift taxes. Unfortunately, avoiding probate doesn't have any effect on estate or gift taxes.

PART VII: REDUCING OR ELIMINATING ESTATE TAXES

Chapters 17 to 23 cover the major methods of estate tax reduction, aside from tax-free gifts. These methods require using some form of irrevocable trust, or, sometimes, a number of trusts. We call these "ongoing" trusts because they function as independent entities for an indefinite time. This is in contrast to a probate-avoidance living trust, which is normally operational only for a brief period, after the death of the person who set it up.

Because an irrevocable trust is an independent legal entity, it must obtain a federal taxpayer ID number. Trustees must keep separate trust financial records and file an annual trust income tax return, paying any taxes due. (See Chapter 17.)

The most common estate tax saving trust is a bypass trust. And by far the most popular bypass trust is one for a couple, commonly called an "AB" trust.

An AB trust can be desirable for couples with a combined estate worth more than the federal estate tax threshold, if each spouse wants to leave everything (or almost everything) to the other. If the property were left outright, the surviving spouse could end up with an estate exceeding the federal tax threshold. An AB trust can eliminate entirely, or, with wealthier estates, significantly reduce, these taxes.

AB trusts should be used only with full knowledge of their limits as well as their advantages. (Chapter 18 spells out the pros and cons.)

Other marital estate tax-saving trusts are covered in Chapter 19. A "QTIP" trust enables a surviving spouse to postpone taxes otherwise due on property worth more than the federal estate tax threshold left in an AB trust.

This chapter also explains what's called a "QDOT" trust, which can be important if you are married to a noncitizen. As we've said, the marital deduction does not apply to property left to a noncitizen spouse. So normally any property over the federal estate tax threshold left by a citizen spouse to a noncitizen spouse is taxable when the citizen spouse dies. A QDOT trust enables the noncitizen spouse to postpone payment of any taxes due until after her or his death.

Whether you're married or not, if you're interested in making a large gift to a charity, and also getting a tax break, you may want to investigate charitable trusts, covered in Chapter 20. With these trusts, you can leave property to charities and simultaneously obtain income tax as well as estate tax benefits. A charitable trust makes sense, from an estate tax perspective, only if your estate exceeds the federal estate tax threshold. However, Chapter 20 also provides useful information about charitable gifts, no matter how large your estate.

Still other kinds of ongoing trusts can be used by anyone, married or not, to save on estate taxes. These trusts, covered in Chapter 21, include:

- Generation-skipping trusts, where you leave property in trust for grandchildren and avoid estate taxes on the trust property when your own children die.

- Irrevocable life insurance trusts, which can, in the right circumstances, save a bundle on estate taxes.

- Grantor-retained interest trusts, which can yield income and estate tax benefits if you transfer your home to a trust for a set period.

One other strategy that can sometimes lower a family's overall estate tax burden is the use of a "disclaimer," which is akin to a trust. A disclaimer is simply a statement that you decline to accept property left to you—a legal way of saying "no thanks." (Chapter 22 explains how to use disclaimers.)

Finally, some people use more than one kind of trust to achieve the most tax savings. (See Chapter 23.)

PART VIII: IMPOSING CONTROLS OVER PROPERTY

For one or more reasons, you may want to impose controls over property you leave—in other words, to legally prevent the beneficiary from gaining unfettered ownership of the property. (Chapter 6 discusses controls you can use over property left to minors. This part covers restrictions on adult beneficiaries.) These types of controls require use of a trust.

You might want to impose such controls if you've remarried and want to balance the interests and needs of your current spouse with those of children from a former marriage. Chapter 24 explains how you can create a trust that leaves the other spouse certain defined rights in the trust property for his or her life, but preserves the principal for your children, who receive the trust property when the surviving spouse dies.

Many issues can come up when trying to balance the rights of the spouse and the children. For example, can the surviving spouse sell trust property? What rights do the children have to see that the trust principal is being preserved? There is no generic solution to these questions. The answers must be worked out individually, fitting your specific desires and needs.

In a number of other situations, discussed in Chapter 25, you may want a property control trust, including:

- **You want to help pay for a child's college or other schooling costs.** Here you'll need to decide whether you want to define what school costs include and what the criteria for being in school are or if you'll let the trustee make those decisions.

- **You want to establish a "special needs" trust for someone with a disability.** Common problems include selecting the trustee, and doing all that's legal to preserve the disabled person's eligibility for government assistance.

- **You want to restrict a beneficiary's access to his or her inheritance.** If you believe an adult beneficiary can't responsibly handle money, you may want to set up a "spendthrift trust." It controls the beneficiary's freedom to use trust property, including the ability to pledge it as a loan.

- **You want to create a trust allowing the trustee to decide how property is distributed to adult beneficiaries.** With what's called a "sprinkling trust," the trustee is authorized to distribute, within any limits set by the trust, unequal amounts of trust income or principal among the beneficiaries. (A "family pot trust" for minor children is a form of sprinkling trust. See Chapter 6, Section C2.)

- **You want someone else to decide what happens to some or all of your property after your death.** This is called a "power of appointment." The person you authorize can select your beneficiaries and decide how much of your property they receive, within any limits you've set.

PART IX: TAKING CARE OF PERSONAL ISSUES

When you're making plans for what happens to your property, don't overlook two important personal concerns that can affect what happens to *you*. First is making arrangements for handling your financial and medical affairs if you become incapacitated and are unable to make these decisions yourself. Second is what you want done with your body after you die. What are your choices, and how can you make your decisions binding?

To be sure your wishes are carried out if you become incapacitated, you need to prepare several documents. For health care, you can prepare documents that specify what type of medical care you want if you become incapacitated and cannot express your wishes, and that authorize someone you've chosen to be sure your wishes for health care are carried out. These documents normally become effective only if you become incapacitated and can't communicate your preferences for treatment.

To handle money matters if you become incapacitated, you can prepare a document called a "durable power of attorney for finances." In this document, you appoint someone to handle your financial affairs and make financial decisions for you. You can include any limits or directions regarding your finances that you wish.

Chapter 26 discusses these issues.

Protecting Assets in Case of Catastrophic Illness. Many people are concerned that if they become seriously ill, all their savings—indeed, all their assets—will be consumed to pay for health care. This is far from an irrational concern. To address it, some people ask for a will clause, or a simple trust, or anything, that will prevent their assets from being used for expensive medical bills. Unfortunately, this is not an easy matter to handle. No simple clause or trust can safely accomplish this. About the best you can do is:

- Seek advice from an expert attorney in your state. The attorney must know applicable federal laws and regulations. He must also be up-to-date on your state's laws.

- If you're a member of a couple, research how you can best protect the assets of the person who doesn't become ill. Many states allow one spouse to shield his or her property from liability for medical bills of the other spouse. This is covered in depth in *Long-Term Care: How to Plan & Pay For It*, by Joseph L. Matthews (Nolo).

- Consider transferring some of your property to trusted family members before you become seriously ill. You need to be careful here, and work with an expert in the field. Federal law prohibits giving away property and then applying for federal medical aid within 36 months of the transfer.

All this can be tricky and even dangerous. Both federal and state legal rules change rapidly. Nevertheless, a lawyer in your state experienced in elder law issues should be able to provide you with some measure of asset protection. This is likely to be less than you want, but the best you can do.

The options you have for disposing of your body after death are covered in Chapter 27. Subjects covered include death notices, donation of body parts for transplants, or your entire body for medical research, funerals, cremation, burials, and how to leave binding written instructions. Doing this kind of planning can be a great gift to your loved ones, freeing them from burdensome tasks immediately after your death and almost always saving significant amounts of money.

Part X: Family Business Estate Planning

Small business owners have special estate planning concerns. Chapter 28 covers some basic issues: operation of the business after an owner's death, planning to reduce or eliminate any possible estate taxes on the business, and avoiding probate of business assets. Business estate planning is a complex field and we can delve into only the most central issues, but at a minimum this chapter should enable you to determine the areas with which you might want more help.

Family Limited Partnerships

Some people believe that, somehow, creating a "family limited partnership" can eliminate all estate taxes, no matter how large the estate and how flimsy the "business." The notion is that the parents can transfer their property into a partnership business entity with their children, and possibly grandchildren, sharing ownership as limited partners. The parents hope that as a result, the partnership will be transferred to younger generations tax free.

For such a plan to succeed, the IRS must be convinced that the limited partnership has a real business purpose. Calling your home or stock investments a business doesn't make them one. But if you own a real business, there can be estate tax advantages to creating a limited partnership for it and transferring minority interests to future inheritors. The pros and cons of this are discussed in more depth in Chapter 28.

Part XI: Going Further

Once you've determined, at least in outline, what your estate planning goals are and how you want to address them, you may want to see a lawyer or other expert.

Chapter 29 discusses the different types of lawyers and other experts that may be helpful, or necessary, for you to pin down the specifics of your plan and prepare the documents you need. The chapter explores how to find a good lawyer, and how to work with one, including making fair and sensible fee arrangements. You may also decide to do some legal research on your own; this chapter gets you started.

After your planning is done and the documents you want have been prepared, you'll need to know what do with them. Chapter 30 covers storing them, making copies, and when to revise your estate plan.

Doing conscientious estate planning while you're alive is a boon to your loved ones—but someone must still complete the process after your death. Chapter 31 gives you an overview of how your property will be transferred, however you leave that property—by will, living trust, joint tenancy, pay-on-death account, or life insurance. It next discusses what happens if your estate owes taxes. The chapter also covers some important matters about ongoing trusts, including how they actually are put in gear, and the responsibility of the trustee to report to the trust beneficiaries.

Part XII: Sample Estate Plans

Now that you've read this first chapter, you should have some focus on the major issues you want to address in your estate planning. Part XII provides several examples of estate plans, to aid your understanding of how different goals and components can be melded into one plan.

In the hope of giving you a clearer notion now of what the end product of your efforts may be, here's one sample estate plan.

Abel Rublestam and Lynn Montgomery are married and in their 50s—he's 58, she's 51. They live in a common law property state. They have two children, Matt and Rebecca. Matt is married and has two young children. Rebecca is in graduate school.

Their property. The couple share ownership of all their property. Their estate consists of a home worth $550,000 ($460,000 equity), securities (stocks and bonds) worth $280,000, money market savings of $350,000, life insurance on each spouse that pays $200,000 on death (for a total of $400,000), and their one-half ownership of the R-S corporation, a family business. It's hard to determine the exact value of their business. As a rough guess, they decide it's worth at least $800,000. The current net worth of each spouse's estate, in 2006, is $1,145,000 and the net worth of their combined estate is $2,290,000.

Their estate planning goals. The couple want to avoid probate. They also realize that their combined estate could be subject to estate tax when the second spouse dies. So they want to eliminate any possible estate taxes.

They consider leaving more property to Matt, because of his family responsibilities. But they decide to leave equal amounts to both children. They don't want to seem to favor one child, or one lifestyle. Also, they don't want to have to revise their plan if a major family event happens to one of their children—say, Matt has a third child or gets divorced, or Rebecca has a child.

Their plan. The couple prepare a living trust to avoid probate. In that trust, they create an AB trust to save on overall estate taxes. Each leaves the other all his or her property. Both name their children as the final beneficiaries of their AB trusts.

They carefully transfer title to their home, R-S stock, securities accounts, and money market funds into the living trust's name, having already checked that the bylaws of their co-op apartment association and the R-S corportion permit this.

Each spouse names the other spouse as beneficiary of their life insurance policy.

When they're older, if their assets increase significantly in value, the couple intend to make tax-free gifts of $12,000 per year each to their children, but decide that they are not ready to do this now.

Each prepares a basic will. Then they prepare health care directives—a declaration and a durable power of attorney for health care for each of them. In their declarations, they each state that they do not wish to be placed on life-support equipment if diagnosed with a terminal illness. In their durable powers of attorney for health care, each names the other as attorney-in-fact, with full authority to make medical decisions and to be sure that all wishes for health care are carried out. Finally, each prepares a durable power of attorney for finances, naming the other as attorney-in-fact. ■

2

PERSONAL CONCERNS AND ESTATE PLANNING

Underlying the creation of any estate plan are profound human concerns: a primal urge for order and the desire to pass on property to loved ones. A good estate plan is an accurate reflection of your deepest personal wishes. Although much of this book is about mechanics, methods, and documents, it's important to remember that no matter how well you deal with legal devices, your estate plan won't succeed unless you take feelings into account, too.

We make no claim to being experts on the psyche. Indeed, we are wary of "experts" (or anyone) who claim precise understanding of something as complex and mysterious as human beings. Happily, you usually won't need an expert to cope with the human realities that can come up in your estate planning. You do need common sense and candor about the strengths, weaknesses, and genuine needs of close family members, and perhaps friends as well. Legal aspects of estate planning are significant, of course (that's why we're here), but should never interfere with what you know in your heart needs to be done.

Many people face no serious personal issues in their estate planning. They know who they want to leave their property to. They do not foresee any possibility of conflict between their beneficiaries, nor threat of a lawsuit by someone claiming they were illegally denied their inheritance. On an emotional level, these people can, happily, focus on the satisfactions they expect their gifts to bring.

Other people's situations are not so clear and straightforward. They must deal with more difficult personal dynamics, such as possibilities of family conflicts, or dividing property unequally between children, or providing care for minor children, or handling complexities arising from second or subsequent marriages.

Before beginning your legal planning, it's vital that you assess your personal circumstances and decide how you want to resolve any difficulties. If you're planning to leave all your property to your spouse or two compatible children, or are otherwise sure you don't face any personal issues, wonderful. You can safely go on to the next chapter that concerns you. If, however, you think you might face complications—or if you're not sure what kinds of problems can come up—read this chapter, which discusses a number of personal concerns drawn from Denis's estate planning practice.

A. Avoiding Conflict

Estate planning involves money—cash or assets that can be sold for cash. Money, as most of us learn as we get older, is strange stuff—or, more accurately, people can do strange things because of the desire for money. (If the love of money isn't *the* root of all evil, it's certainly somewhere under the tree.) So the first step in creating an estate plan is to recognize that if you plan unwisely, your plan may lead to bitterness, strife, and lawsuits rather than the happiness you surely intend. Avoiding conflict after your death to the extent reasonably possible should be a central goal of estate planning.

Start by asking yourself about the potential for conflict in your personal situation. If this potential exists, what can you do to eliminate or at least reduce it? One important thing to remember is that disputes are not always over property that is worth a lot of money. If different family members or other inheritors have deep emotional attachments to heirlooms, or what they stand for, or can't stand the idea of *that person* getting it, fighting can become fierce even if the heirlooms themselves won't make anyone rich.

John Gregory Dunne, in his autobiography *Harp* (Simon & Schuster), gives a telling description of one family's fight over heirlooms. His Aunt Harriet failed to specifically state who got what of her many items of personal property. Dunne wrote:

In legal terms, Aunt Harriet became...."Estate of Harriet H. Burn," appraised and organized, room by room, into "8 carved Hepplewhite mahogany chairs" and "Coalport 'Kings Plate' china service for twelve" and "Repro. Victorian loveseat, blue brocade" and "Light blue upholstered settee, soiled." The house was sold, the belongings apportioned to the surviving children and grandchildren. There is something so metaphorical and final in the act of dividing up the possessions a family has accumulated over several lifetimes and more generations; for the first time I thought there might be a good argument for primogeniture. It was not that the furniture and china and crystal and silver and linens had great worth; it was just that each piece, each object had a private history, a special meaning for one or the other of us. For a family, the process of apportionment is like psychoanalysis or the confessional box; long-buried resentments surface, old hurts and forgotten slights. In the end, a lawyer drew up the order of selection; his ground rules were worthy of Solomon:

"The order of selection will be determined as follows: each of you is requested to pick a number from one to ninety-nine and advise me of it by return mail: the person whose number is closest to the first two numbers of the Connecticut Daily Lottery on Tuesday, October 7, will have first pick, and so forth.... If the first person who selects property picks an item in an amount worth $1,400, the second person will be entitled to pick as many items as he or she wishes up to $1,400 in value. The third person would then have the right to choose property in the amount equal to the value selected by the person who preceded him or her and so forth until all items have been selected. In this way, each family unit will have an opportunity to select property, in turn and essentially of equal value."

The Connecticut State Lottery: God, if there is one, must have a sense of humor.

With some wise planning, the conflicts among the Dunne family could have been avoided. After all, well before Aunt Harriet died, a lawyer could have drawn up this distribution method, complete with the Connecticut State Lottery. So even if you can't, or don't want to, decide before your death exactly who gets what, you can still create a binding method for peaceful and fair distribution of your property after you die.

Let's explore general ways to avoid conflict by looking at three different family situations. Then, we will discuss ways to avoid conflict. But here at the beginning we do want to note that in some cases, there's nothing you can do to prevent disagreements.

EXAMPLE 1: CHOOSING AN EXECUTOR

Patrick and Clara have five children. One, Sean, is a lawyer. Patrick and Clara admit to themselves, though they never reveal it to others, that Sean is their one grasping child, who has always wanted the most, materially, from his parents and the world. Indeed, by sheer persistence, Sean has already managed to acquire a substantial number of family heirlooms. Sean tells his parents he wants to supervise distribution of their property (after both die) as executor of their wills and successor trustee of their living trust, stating that he's obviously the most professionally qualified.

At first, Patrick and Clara aren't sure what to do. Their concern isn't that Sean will violate their wills and distribute their major items of property unequally. Rather, they worry that the personal possessions they have left to all their children won't be divided fairly. After considerable discussion, they decide they don't want Sean to have sole authority to supervise the distribution of their estate. Basically, they conclude that while they love him as they do their other children, they simply can't rely on him to be able to put his own desires aside and distribute their heirlooms impartially. They'd prefer to have their daughter Maude, the kindest and most levelheaded of their kids, be both executor and successor trustee, which will allow her to preside over the division of the personal items. However, they're afraid of offending Sean, something they're determined not to do.

After much thought, they decide to have three executors and successor trustees—Sean, Maude, and another daughter, Maeve. (Patrick, Jr. lives in Europe and isn't interested, and Polly is preoccupied with her medical career.) A majority of executors can decide how the estate is handled. This solution may be a little awkward, and it sets up the possibility that Maude and Maeve may have to combine forces to cope with Sean (as they've had to do for 30 years). But Patrick and Clara feel it has a good chance of success. They plan to talk diplomatically to Maude, Maeve, and Sean to try to achieve some common understanding of what they want. But even if Sean is dissatisfied, the couple believes there is far less risk of serious family strife than if Sean were named sole trustee and executor.

EXAMPLE 2: A CHILD FROM A PREVIOUS MARRIAGE

Sol and Bernice have two children in their late 20s, Abel and Alexis, and a combined estate worth about $730,000. Sol also has a 34-year-old daughter, Lilith, from his first marriage, who he's seen very rarely since his marriage to Bernice. Sol wants to leave Lilith $100,000. "That's absolutely ridiculous," Bernice exclaims. "You're just trying to absolve yourself of the guilt you feel for being unable

to see Lilith all these years." Sol retorts, "Isn't it my money?" Bernice points out that half of it is her money, because their property lists both their names as owners (see Chapter 3). Sol says, "Yes, but half of $630,000 is $315,000, so I can leave $100,000 to Lilith if I want to." But he soon admits that this "divide my estate" approach would mean he would be leaving Bernice $215,000, with nothing for his other two children. In short, Sol realizes that Bernice is right—his children from his present marriage would almost surely feel hurt.

Sol and Bernice decide to work through this problem together. After some lengthy talks, they decide that Sol will leave $40,000 to Lilith, and the rest to Bernice (assuming Bernice survives Sol). When Bernice dies, she will pass on everything that's left to Abel and Alexis. They then check with the two children to see if this seems fair to them as well. Happily, it does. Abel says, "Hey, it's your money, Pa." Their daughter adds, "So enjoy." Both convince Sol and Bernice that they think the gift to Lilith is fair.

EXAMPLE 3: FAMILY HEIRLOOMS

Al is a widower with three children. Although there's no problem dividing his big ticket items among his children equally—they all agree on that—all three children have expressed deep attachment to a number of relatively inexpensive family treasures. Al decides they have to talk it out. He gets all three children together and says, "You're going to have to work it out among you. Come up with something you all agree on and I'll do it. But don't make me guess, and don't leave me worrying that you'll be fighting amongst yourselves when I'm gone."

A family retreat is planned and carried out. It takes longer than any of them anticipate, but the kids stick with it, and eventually, a few flashes of temper and some weary hours later, they've worked out an agreement to divide some items of property and share others. Everyone is in good spirits. Al studies the agreement and secretly concludes that it's more complex than necessary, and in some small ways not completely fair. Still, his kids accept it, and that's what matters to him, so he includes it in his will.

EXAMPLE 4: TROUBLE AHEAD

Freitel is 85 years old and in poor health. She lives in a retirement community in Arizona. She has one son, Hugh, age 57. To her sorrow, she has not been close to Hugh for decades, and has become nearly estranged from him since his third marriage, to Kristin. Freitel believes Kristin dominates Hugh—always rather weak-willed—and that she has encouraged his worst materialistic tendencies.

Freitel has a substantial estate. During her 15 years of retirement, she has been very involved with her church, and also with a program to help poor children. She intends to leave the bulk of her estate to these charities, but worries what Hugh (read Kristin) might do. In one of her calls to Hugh (he almost never calls her), she mentions that she might leave some money to her church. Soon after, she receives calls from Hugh, and even Kristin, suddenly concerned about her health, including, not so subtly, her mental health. Freitel suspects that Hugh and Kristin might contest her will, possibly alleging that the church had gained "undue influence" over her. After talking her worries over with her closest friends, she reluctantly concludes that, given Hugh and Kristin's greed, it's unwise to try to further discuss her plans with them. Better to accept that they may fight her will. She decides to hire a lawyer experienced in will contests, so that she can do everything possible to ensure that her will stands up if attacked in court.

B. LEAVING UNEQUAL AMOUNTS OF PROPERTY TO CHILDREN

Sometimes parents want to leave unequal amounts of property to their children, but don't want to give the impression that they favor the child who is given more. Here are some examples of how people have handled this matter.

EXAMPLE 1: A DISGRUNTLED CHILD

Jim's parents, Mort and Lisa, paid for his college and dental school education and helped him purchase his first house. Melinda, their other child, has always been an independent sort who, while a loving daughter, has prided herself on making it on her own. Now Mort and Lisa want to equalize their gifts by leaving considerably more to

Melinda in their estate plan. Some hints of their thinking are enough to disturb Jim, and he argues that in balance, Melinda will wind up with more than half.

Mort and Lisa talk it over and decide they'll stick to their original plan. They think the dollar figures for each child are close to even overall, and that Jim is being a bit grasping. They also conclude that they won't discuss the subject with Jim again. But in their estate planning documents (a will and a living trust), they'll try to explain why and how they determined the distribution. They'll emphasize that they love both children equally and are determined to treat them equally. Mort and Lisa hope that being fair and firm with Jim will gain his respect in the end.

EXAMPLE 2: THE STRUGGLING MUSICIAN

Ayyad, a widower with a moderate estate, has four grown children. Three are well-established in conventional business careers with excellent future prospects. One is a serious, but impoverished, jazz musician. Because of his greater need, Ayyad considers leaving the musician most of his estate, but decides to confer with his children before finalizing that plan.

To Ayyad's surprise, he learns that two of his children don't agree with his plan. One has never much cared for his musician brother, thinking him irresponsible. (Besides, this child never liked his music, anyway.) Another child points out that she has two children and that, in today's market, neither her nor her husband's jobs are really secure. The musician, she reminds Ayyad, has provided him with no loving grandchildren. The daughter asks whether her children shouldn't receive some "rainy-day" funds from their grandfather.

Ayyad says he'll think this over. He decides he doesn't want to talk it over further with his kids. This is, after all, his decision. He's gotten their input, but it's up to him to decide.

Finally, he decides to divide his total estate by percentages: 50% will go to the musician (Ayyad admires his son and thinks he is sincere, not indulgent), 12.5 % will go to each of his other two children with no children of their own, and 25% to the daughter with children. If any of his other children has a child, or if the musician gains a measure of financial success, Ayyad plans to revise these percentages.

In an effort to soothe feelings, Ayyad writes a detailed letter explaining his decision and expressing his love and good wishes for each child. He attaches the letter to his living trust, where it will be revealed to his children after his death.

EXAMPLE 3: UNEQUAL EARNINGS

Barbara and Barry have two grown children and a substantial estate. Their son is a doctor; their daughter is a part-time college student and environmental activist who wants a career helping make the world a better place, but isn't sure what that career is (or if it exists at all). Barbara and Barry consider leaving the bulk of their wealth to their daughter, figuring that their son is much more secure. But then, on reflection, they decide they don't want such an imbalance. Medicine, they reason, is surely changing, and may not be as lucrative in the future. Also, their son already has one child, with more hoped for. Who knows what his needs may become in the future. And anyway, they've been helping to support their daughter, and expect they may do so for several more years, until she's begun to carve out her niche.

Barbara and Barry decide, for the time being, to divide their estate equally between the two children. But they also agree to periodically review their plan, to see whether they now want to leave more property to one child.

EXAMPLE 4: A DISABLED CHILD

Ruth is a single mother in her late forties with three children: Ben, 20, Liz, 18, and Josh, 14. Josh has a serious physical disability that will require special care for his life. But exactly how much care is not clear when Ruth decides to prepare her estate plan.

Ruth owns a house with about $100,000 equity. She has total savings of roughly $75,000, plus a dwindling 401(k) account, currently worth $40,000. A successful graphic designer, she makes enough money to support her family and put aside modest yearly savings.

Ruth wants to leave all her property in trust for Josh, believing that he has the greatest need for her money. She discusses this with her two oldest children. Liz says honestly that she would like some financial help from home when she goes to college next year—but really, Liz understands and agrees with her mother's decision. Ben, however, proves difficult, indicating (though not clearly) that his mother has always ignored him, and that he should be left at least some of her property, if not a full one-third share.

Ruth, surprised and somewhat hurt, discusses Ben's position with two close friends and Liz. Ruth concludes that Ben is equating money with love (and he's not the first person to do that). She decides on two courses of action: 1) she will leave her estate as she wants to; 2) she will talk to Ben about the two of them going into therapy together (with Ruth paying) over the issue Ben has raised.

KIDS FIRST

Grateful Dead musician Jerry Garcia left a will designed to take care of what was most important to him: his four daughters, ages seven to thirty-one. To accomplish what he wanted, he ignored some sophisticated estate tax-saving strategies that would have delayed his children's inheritance or shifted money to his wife.

Garcia left his wife one-third of his separate property; she already owned one-half of their community property. Legally, property left to a spouse is free of all estate taxes. But Garcia didn't want all the taxes due on his estate to be paid only by his children, so he provided that any taxes due on his estate were to be paid before anyone, including his wife, received any of his property.

One well-known estate planner declared, "Most people make taxes a higher priority. But Garcia did what he wanted, and it was a perfectly reasonable approach." Wow! Even a legal expert agrees that you can do what you think is best for your children, letting tax chips fall where they may.

C. Providing Care for Minor Children

A prime concern of parents of minor children is who will take care of their children if the parents die. If both parents are involved in raising the child (together, or in the case of divorce or separation, with the participation of both), the principal worry is what happens if both parents die. Obviously, if there is only one parent, because the other is dead or has effectively abandoned the child, the sole parent is likely to be even more concerned that his children will be well cared for if he dies.

In either case, the primary issues are who will raise the child and who will be responsible for supervising property the parent(s) leave to the child. These issues are discussed in depth in Chapter 6. Here we want only to indicate some of the emotional concerns that may be raised when trying to resolve them.

EXAMPLE 1: THE BEST CHOICE

A married couple, Taylor and Sondra, have two gradeschool-age children. Taylor and Sondra discuss who will raise their children if they both die before the kids are adults. Taylor strongly promotes his sister, Beth, as the suitable guardian. Sondra thinks Beth is a snob and declares she doesn't want her children raised in that household. She suggests her older brother, Louis. Taylor retorts that Louis may be good with money, but he has a terrible temper and doesn't have the most stable marriage.

Fortunately, Taylor and Sondra are sensitive enough to realize they have to talk seriously to reach an agreement on who would make the best guardian. After considerable discussion, and a fairly successful effort to feel out the kids, they settle on Sondra's best friend, Hilda, who they both trust and respect. Hilda has children about the same age and is willing to accept the responsibility for raising Taylor and Sondra's kids.

But both Sondra and Taylor agree that Hilda is not very sensible with money. They worry that she couldn't sensibly manage the money they would leave for the children. Hilda isn't overjoyed to hear this, but she is goodhearted. She accepts Sondra and Taylor's solution—she will be the children's personal guardian, and Louis will supervise the money left them until they're old enough to get it outright. Louis also agrees to this arrangement.

EXAMPLE 2: SOMEONE WHO'LL ACCEPT THE JOB

Marcie, a single parent, wants her best friend, Shoshana, to be the guardian of Katherine, Marcie's nine-year-old daughter, should Marcie die before Katherine is 18. To Marcie's surprise, Shoshana says she can't accept the responsibility. She has two kids of her own, and that's all she can handle. Marcie is hurt, and worries there's no one she trusts who will do the job. After some reflection and discussion with other friends, Marcie realizes that her brother Alex is willing to be guardian. Marcie is not overjoyed: Alex and she weren't really close as kids and still aren't. But she realizes that Alex is a trustworthy person and that Katherine would be well cared for with him. She concludes that her best estate plan is to stay alive until her daughter is an adult, but if she doesn't, she will rely on Alex.

D. SUBSEQUENT MARRIAGES

People who've married more than once may face problems reconciling their desires for their present spouse and family with their wishes for children from their prior marriages. Individual situations can vary greatly, often depending on whether marriages occurred relatively early or late in life and on how well family members get along. But one thing is obvious—if yours is a nontraditional family, you must carefully consider, and do your best to reconcile, needs that may be competing and conflicting. These issues are covered in more depth in Chapter 24.

EXAMPLE 1: HER KIDS, HIS KIDS

Katerina and Pavel get married when they are in their 50s. Katerina has a son from her prior marriage. Pavel has three children, two daughters and a son. Katerina and Pavel both work. Pavel has a slightly higher income, and savings of $400,000 to Katerina's $130,000. They buy a house, with each spouse contributing half the down payment, and equally sharing the monthly payments. Both spouses want to ensure that, when the other dies, the survivor gets to live in the house for the rest of his or her life. When both spouses die, they want the house to be divided equally, with one share going to Katerina's son and the other share divided between Pavel's three children. Similarly, by use of a marital property control trust (see Chapter 24), each spouse's assets will be left for the "use" of the surviving spouse, with "use" defined to mean the right to receive income the property generates or literal use of some property—for example, a car. Neither spouse can invade the other's principal.

Katerina and Pavel consider the wisdom of discussing their plan with all their children. Since they have chosen Eve, one of Pavel's daughters, to wind up their affairs after their death in the role of the successor trustee of their living trust, they have already discussed it with her. But because Katerina's son, Tad, has never accepted Pavel, and remains hostile to him, Katerina and Pavel sadly decide that talking their plan over with Tad will only provide an occasion for more rancor. So they simply don't tell him what they've agreed upon.

EXAMPLE 2: THE IMPOVERISHED HUSBAND

Angelina, in her 70s, is a wealthy widow with three grown children. She marries Arthur, also in his 70s. They live in Angelina's house. Arthur, who has very little property, has two children from a prior marriage who Angelina does not particularly care for. As she plans her estate, Angelina realizes she wants to allow Arthur to remain in the house if she dies before he does, but doesn't want him to be able to rent out the house, nor be able to sell it and buy another one. She discusses her concerns with him. He is bothered that she doesn't trust him fully. She explains frankly that her children, who are delighted she has married Arthur, are nevertheless concerned that his children might end up with what they see as their inheritance.

Angelina decides to leave much of her property outright to her children. She will create a trust for the house, and leave enough money in the trust to pay for mortgage and upkeep on the house, plus a little extra to supplement Arthur's Social Security and small pension. The trust will be managed by the most responsible of her children. Arthur will have the right to live in the house for the duration of his life and receive the income produced by the trust.

Arthur agrees with this arrangement, but asks what happens if he gets ill and must be hospitalized? Will he be thrown out of the house? His concern prompts Angelina to realize that there are aspects of the trust to pin down. She doesn't want to allow the possibility that Arthur can be thrown out of the house if he's in the hospital for a week. But also, if he moves permanently to a nursing home, she prefers that the house then be turned over to her children rather than remain in trust until Arthur dies. She discusses her concerns with Arthur. He's understanding but concerned, himself, about becoming ill and having to leave the house for a while and then not being able to return to it.

After considerable discussion, Angelina and Arthur agree that he will retain the right to live in, or return to, the house if he's lived away from it for up to eight consecutive months. If he's been away from it for a longer period than that, the house will come under management by the trustee, who can rent it out. But the trustee cannot sell it or live in it or allow other children to live in it while Arthur lives. Any income from the rental is added to the trust income available for Arthur.

Since Angelina is leaving much of her property outright to her children, outside this trust, she feels it is fair for them to wait to inherit the house until Arthur's death. He's in his 70s after all. Anyway, she may well outlive him, and she'll certainly keep the house herself until her death. Angelina then sees a good estate planning lawyer to prepare the trust she wants. With the lawyer's aid, Angelina pins down precisely how the trust will work.

E. LONG-TERM CARE FOR A CHILD WITH SPECIAL NEEDS

Parents of mentally and sometimes physically disabled children may need to provide care and support for those children whether they are minors or adults. Providing this care usually requires preparation of a "special needs trust" to coordinate the parents' contributions with rules on government benefits. This type of trust is discussed further in Chapter 25, Section B. Also, it may well be that, in their estate planning, parents, like it or not, may need to concentrate most of their resources for their disabled child, leaving less for any other children.

EXAMPLE: WORKING IT OUT

The Balfour family has a fifteen-year-old disabled child, Bob, who will need care all his life. They have two other children, both of whom are healthy. The Balfours' primary estate planning concern is doing all they can to arrange for Bob's care after they die. They realize this means leaving Bob most of their modest estate. They discuss this with their 19-year-old daughter, Rebecca, who says "that's fine." Their other son, Jeb, resents Bob a little and isn't so acquiescent. But the Balfours decide that protecting Bob remains their top priority. They hope that, as Jeb matures, he will understand the difficulties Bob faces and that his resentment that Bob got more than his share (as Jeb defines it) of parental attention will fade.

There are many questions the parents must resolve about Bob. Who will be responsible for Bob's personal care after they die? How can they best leave money for his use? How will any money they leave be treated when determining eligibility for government benefits? After all, it makes no sense to leave money to Bob if it means he will be ineligible for government help until it's all used up.

The Balfours must choose a personal guardian to be responsible for Bob until he becomes a legal adult at age 18, and a financial guardian or manager to supervise any money they leave for Bob, as long as Bob lives.

The Balfours discuss these concerns themselves and then broaden their discussion to include Rebecca and other family members and close friends they are considering for these two tasks. Eventually, they choose Mrs. Balfour's younger sister to be Bob's personal guardian if needed. They name their closest friend, William, to be Bob's financial manager, until Rebecca turns 30. After that, she will become Bob's financial manager.

To understand how to dovetail money they leave Bob in trust with government benefits, the Balfours do some preliminary research. They decide to establish a "special needs" trust for Bob. They use Nolo's *Special Needs Trusts*, by Stephen Elias, to prepare a trust that will maintain Bob's eligibility for government assistance programs while establishing a trustee (the property manager) to control trust property used for Bob's benefit.

F.   CONCERNS OF UNMARRIED COUPLES

In almost all states, unmarried couples have no right to inherit each other's property, unless each member of the couple makes a will or legally leaves property to the other. (In California, Hawaii, Maine, and Vermont, lesbian or gay couples registered as "domestic partners" with the state have inheritance rights from each other.) A central concern of most unmarried couples is to be sure they inherit each other's property. Happily, unmarried people— whether lesbian, gay, or heterosexual—have the right to leave their property to whomever they want, as long as they're competent. (Even if one or both has been legally married in the past, they have no obligation to their ex-spouse, unless specific support is still required by the divorce decree.) In case of

serious legal threat by hostile family members, a couple may take action to establish by clear proof that they were competent when they prepared their estate plan.

EXAMPLE 1: VIDEOTAPE EVIDENCE

Ernest and James have lived together for many years. Aside from a few small gifts to friends or family, each wants to leave all their property to the other after death. They're concerned with efficiency and economy, but above all they want to be sure that their estate plan can't be successfully attacked by several close relatives who have long been hostile to their lifestyle. Ernest and James each prepare a living trust leaving their property as they desire. They videotape their signing and the notarization of the living trust to provide additional proof that they were both mentally competent and not under duress or undue influence when they signed.

EXAMPLE 2: THE DOWN PAYMENT

Solveig and Guido have one daughter, Renée, who has lived with Charles for several years. Renée asks her parents for a $50,000 loan for a down payment on a house. Solveig and Guido are not wealthy, but they have sufficient savings to make the loan and they want to help their daughter. They do want the loan repaid (with interest) and they want to be sure they are protected in case their daughter dies; they like Charles, but they don't want him to inherit the house and leave them stuck on the loan. To ease their worries, Renée executes a promissory note to Solveig and Guido for $50,000, plus 6% yearly interest. She also writes a will, expressly leaving her parents the full amount due on the promissory note, including interest.

G. WORRIES ABOUT THE EFFECT OF INHERITING MONEY

Sometimes people worry that someone they want to leave money or property to cannot handle it. In other words, they fear their gifts will have destructive results: the beneficiaries may be too young or too immature, for example. Resolving these concerns always requires a careful examination of both the strengths and weaknesses of the potential beneficiaries. Sometimes it also involves putting one's own worries and prejudices under as objective a personal microscope as possible.

EXAMPLE 1: THE SCHOOL OF HARD KNOCKS

Ely is quite wealthy, and worried about the effects of his wealth on his children and grandchildren. He grew up poor, worked hard all his life and made a small fortune. Shouldn't his kids, now in their 20s and 30s and just making their way in the world, be encouraged to continue to work hard, at least until they're old enough to keep a large inheritance in perspective? If Ely dies soon, and each child inherits over $1 million, will they lose their incentive to strive for goals they might strive for otherwise? Ely is not the type to question whether losing the incentive to strive might be a good thing. He had it, he wants his kids to have it. Ely wonders if his best estate plan wouldn't be to say, "Being of sound mind, I spent all I could and I give the rest to charity"? And what about his grandchildren? Should he give money only to those who join his business? (The fact that none of his children did still rankles.)

No matter how much Ely learns about the intricacies of tax planning and probate avoidance, he needs to do some serious thinking and reflecting on the subject of his money and his family before he can hope to make a sound estate plan. Or put another way, Ely needs to better understand the complicated nature of his own emotions and expectations pertaining to his money. Once over this hurdle, he should be better able to make up a plan to benefit his children and grandchildren.

For example, perhaps Ely will realize that his insistence on making it the hard way is a tad extreme. If so, he may leave (or even give) moderate amounts of property to his children outright to help them cope better with parenting their young children. Ely will leave the rest of his estate in trust for his children. Each child will receive a moderate amount of income for a number of years, only getting the bulk of the property at the age Ely has chosen. (For example, Joseph Kennedy, Sr., established trusts for each of his children that didn't release the trust property until that child became 50 years old.)

Ely decides he doesn't want to hire, or pressure, a grandchild into his business by promises of additional inheritance. Instead, he creates an education trust for each grandchild, leaving each $100,000 for college or other educational costs.

EXAMPLE 2: THE GRASSHOPPER AND THE ANT

Sylvia, a wealthy widow, has two children in their 30s: Yvonne, the sensible one, and Colleen, who's always been improvident and often more than a little self-destructive. Sylvia wants to leave her estate equally to her two daughters. She'll give Yvonne's half to her outright, but she's troubled by the thought of Colleen receiving several hundred thousand dollars. Sylvia decides it's sensible to leave Colleen her money in what's called a "spendthrift" trust, where a trustee, someone other than Colleen, controls the money (principal), and Colleen receives only the trust income. (See Chapter 25.) She can draw on any of the trust principal only if the trustee agrees she needs it for educational, medical, or other essential needs.

Sylvia still faces three important problems: First, who is to be trustee of the trust? Second, should she tell Colleen what she's decided upon? Third, when should the trust end? Sylvia discusses both questions with Yvonne, who convinces her mother that, for reasons having to do with sibling rivalry, she—Yvonne—shouldn't be the trustee. Sylvia reluctantly agrees that, given the personalities involved, and the fact that Colleen will hate not to get the money outright, it's sure to be personally destructive if one sister controls the other's inheritance. So, Sylvia decides to appoint her younger brother as trustee. She also decides the trust will end when Colleen becomes 45, at which point she will get all the money outright. She hopes Colleen will be fully responsible by then. Finally, she decides to tell Colleen her plan, although she's not joyously anticipating that discussion. She softens the blow by also telling Colleen that if, over the coming years, she decides Colleen has matured and can handle money, she will change her estate plan and leave Colleen her money outright.

H. DISINHERITING PEOPLE, INCLUDING CHILDREN

Some parents want to disinherit a child, or children. Other people want to ensure that certain relations or ex-friends get none of their property. Legally, there is no need to disinherit friends or relatives other than your spouse or children—they inherit nothing unless you expressly leave them some property. When it comes to your spouse, he or she normally has rights to a certain percentage of your property. (See Chapter 3.) It is legal to disinherit a child, however, if you take affirmative steps to do so. (See Chapter 6, Section G.) But deciding to disinherit a child is often not easy to do, emotionally.

EXAMPLE 1: THE BAD SEED

Zorba and Kyria have three children—two daughters and a son—and a substantial estate. They are very close to the two daughters, but bitterly on the outs with their son, Nikos. Zorba and Kyria had originally intended to leave most of their property to each other, with some to the two daughters they're close to. Then, when the surviving spouse dies, the remaining property would be divided between the two daughters. But they have second thoughts. Do they really want to cut their son out entirely? This feels too harsh, too rejecting. And if they do cut Nikos out entirely, are they creating any real risk that he will be able to invalidate their estate plan? Although their lawyer tells them that because they are clearly competent, and can legally disinherit Nikos with little danger of him overturning their estate plan, they decide that both parental charity and prudence dictate the same decision. Each will leave Nikos $25,000 and include a "no-contest" clause in their wills. This clause states that if any beneficiary challenges a will, he gets nothing if his challenge is unsuccessful. The parents expect that Nikos will take the certain $50,000 he'll receive from both parents rather than the risk and the cost of a lawsuit he's almost sure to lose. Also, despite the bitterness they feel towards Nikos, both Zorba and Kyria are relieved that they haven't allowed it to cause them to completely disinherit one of their own children.

EXAMPLE 2: THE CHARITY

Peter has two grown children, both very prosperous. Peter decides he wants to leave most of his estate to his favorite charity—a cause he deeply believes in—and the rest to his children. He hints at this to them. One child is supportive; the other is very upset, arguing that property should stay in the family. Peter decides to stick to his plan, accepting whatever disapproval or conflicts it will cause. In his living trust, he states expressly why he has decided that the bulk of his property is best given to the charity, and that even though he has done this, he loves his children deeply.

I. COMMUNICATING YOUR DECISIONS TO FAMILY AND FRIENDS

Many of the examples we've just discussed demonstrate our belief that communication can usually, though certainly not invariably, resolve potential estate planning difficulties with family and friends. Happily, in many families, talking about the older generation's estate planning isn't difficult. Both the parents and the children want the planning to be out in the open, so there will be no surprises down the road. Of course, there are certainly families where raising the subject of the parents' (or grandparents') estate plan may bring up tension, or touch on old conflicts—and others where the response will not be easy to predict. Only you can decide whether, when, and how to talk about your plans, but here are some suggestions that may help with your thinking process:

- Whom do you want to talk to? Obviously, you need to talk to anyone you are naming to have responsibility for your minor children, or for supervising the distribution of your property after you die. But what about some, or all, of your beneficiaries?

- What should you talk about? Do you want to tell people what you've already decided and why, or ask for advice, or state that, within reason, you're open to suggestions? Or do you want to discuss the mechanics of how your estate plan will work with your inheritors? (You should, of course, with your executor and successor trustee.)

- Do you want to give your inheritors copies of your estate plan?

Talking, of course, is not a guarantee of clear sailing. There are occasions when someone doesn't want to hear or talk, or others when communication only reveals a deep and unbridgeable gulf. And from the older generation's point of view, there can be risks involved with communication: if they promise money to beneficiaries, they may feel guilty if a future medical necessity eats up some—or all—of that money. They may also worry that revealing their plans will expose undesirable qualities like greed and hardheartedness in those promised to inherit.

From the younger generation's viewpoint, it can be very difficult to open up estate planning discussions with parents. You certainly don't want to try to force a parent to talk about his or her property or plan. At the same time, you may need or want the reassurance that sensible planning has been done. For instance, you'll probably want to be sure that your parents have arranged for someone to handle their medical and financial affairs if they become incapacitated. There are many decisions to be made concerning this matter alone: Whom will they appoint to serve in this role? How do they each feel about the use of life-prolonging medical procedures, should one of them develop a terminal condition? What happens if they can no longer live independently? Or if maintaining their home becomes too burdensome? Questions can go on here—and it's almost certain that painful subjects will arise when you ask your parents about their estate plan. We can suggest no magic formula that makes broaching the subject easy. All you can do is be tactful and genuinely concerned and see if that opens any doors.

We do think it makes sense for all parents to at least indicate that they have done their estate planning. If not, it's a good idea for communication to be initiated by a child, especially if that child knows or suspects her parent, or parents, have not taken care of even the basics. Saying this is easy, but of course, there can be many barriers to candor, such as:

- a general societal code that death is an unmentionable, especially with one's own parents

- fear that motives can be misunderstood (parent may fear being seen as trying to manipulate

a child by offering inherited money for demonstrations of love; child, in turn, may fear that raising the subject will be seen as pushy or greedy), and

- the sense that honor lies in not caring about a parent's property, or that of any other loved one.

Still, the results of talking openly are usually positive. For example, we know of a situation in which a child who had done very well financially asked her parents to leave a disproportionate share of their estate to the other children. The children's discussion provided the impetus for their parents to do estate planning they'd intended to do for years. They were quite relieved to finally have it accomplished. Even where there are less dramatic results, we feel that communication, particularly among family members, is a healthy process that can aid in preventing later conflicts. ■

3

SPECIAL PROPERTY OWNERSHIP RULES FOR MARRIED PEOPLE

If you are married, special state property ownership laws may affect your estate planning. These laws determine what you own individually and what you own as a member of a couple, and may also give your spouse a right to claim a share of your property after your death.

If you and your spouse plan to leave all, or the lion's share, of your property to each other, it's not of much practical importance to understand who legally owns each item of property. After all, as long as the survivor will get all, or even most, of the property, it's not important how it's labeled. However, if you plan to make substantial gifts of property to someone other than your spouse (especially if your spouse might prefer that you didn't), it's essential that you understand both who owns the property and whether there are any rules in your state which give your spouse the right to at least a minimum portion of it at your death. Otherwise, your decision to give property to someone other than your spouse may occasion a nasty conflict after your death.

IF YOU'RE UNSURE OF YOUR MARITAL STATUS

Most people are quite certain of their marital status. If you're not, here's what you need to know.

The divorce decree. You're not divorced until you have a final decree of divorce (or dissolution, as it's called in some states) issued by a state court in the United States, or under limited circumstances by the legally empowered authorities of a foreign country. (See below.)

If you think you're divorced but never saw the final decree, contact the court clerk in the county where you think the divorce was granted. Give the clerk your name, your ex-spouse's name, and the date, as close as you know it, of the divorce.

Legal separation. Even if a court has declared you and your spouse legally separated, and you plan to divorce, you are still married until you get the divorce decree.

Foreign divorces. Divorces issued to U.S. citizens by courts in Mexico, the Dominican Republic, or another country may not be valid if challenged, especially if all the paperwork was handled by mail. In other words, if you or your spouse got a quickie foreign divorce, you may well be still married under the laws of your state. On the other hand, foreign divorces, where both spouses were present in person or through a representative, may be recognized as valid in the U.S. If you think that someone might make a claim to some of your property after your death based on the invalidity of a foreign divorce, see a lawyer.

Common law marriages. In a few states listed below, a couple can become legally married by living together, intending to be married, and clearly presenting themselves to the world as a married couple. Even in states that allow such common law marriages, most couples who live together don't have common law marriages. Folk law notwithstanding, no magic number of years of living together automatically establishes a common law marriage. If you really do have a valid common law marriage, you must go to court and get a divorce to end it—there's no such thing as a common law divorce.

Common law marriages may legally be created in Alabama, Colorado, District of Columbia, Georgia (only before January 1, 1997), Idaho (only before November 1, 1996), Iowa, Kansas, Montana, New Hampshire (for inheritance only), Ohio (only before October 10, 1991), Oklahoma, Pennsylvania (only before January 1, 2005), Rhode Island, South Carolina, Texas, and Utah.

LESBIAN AND GAY COUPLES

Lesbian and gay couples can register as domestic partners in California, Connecticut, Hawaii, Maine, New Jersey, and Vermont. (The names for these partnerships vary from state to state. For example, Hawaii calls them "reciprocal beneficiary relationships" while in Connecticut and Vermont, they're known as "civil unions.") Lesbian and gay couples who are residents of Massachusetts can marry in that state.

Connecticut, Hawaii, Maine, and Vermont provide inheritance rights for a surviving partner. New Jersey provides no inheritance rights, but it does treat survivors like spouses for inheritance tax purposes. California grants domestic partners the same community property rights and obligations as married couples.

To obtain domestic partnership rights, a lesbian or gay couple must register their partnership with the state. A couple may want to do this for emotional or other reasons, but relying on these laws should never be a substitute for doing your own estate planning. It's not wise for any couple—or individual—to allow the state to do their estate planning for them.

COMMUNITY PROPERTY AND COMMON LAW STATES

COMMUNITY PROPERTY	COMMON LAW
Alaska*	All other states
Arizona	and the District of
California	Columbia
Idaho	
New Mexico	
Nevada	
Texas	
Washington	
Wisconsin (called	
"marital	
property")	

*If agreed to in writing by husband and wife

In community property states, spouses share ownership of most property, even if only one spouse's name is on the title slip or deed. In these states, each spouse is free to leave his or her half of the property as desired, but has no control over the other spouse's half.

In the "common law" states the spouse whose name appears in the ownership document owns that property. However, unlike community property states, these states provide that each spouse has a legal right to claim at least a minimum portion of the other's property at death, even if the deceased spouse left it all to someone else.

Marital property ownership can be confusing. This chapter discusses the basic rules that apply to marital property. It's impossible, short of a ten-volume treatise, to cover every complexity and nuance of marital property law for every state. If you have a question that isn't answered in these pages, you'll need to see a lawyer or research it yourself. (See Chapter 29.)

A. WHAT YOU NEED TO KNOW

In the U.S., there are two major types of marital property law systems. A minority of states, mostly in the West, have "community property" law. (Louisiana, which has a form of community property, originally from French law, isn't covered in this book.) The other states and the District of Columbia follow the "common law" system.

If you think marital property laws could affect your situation, you need to know:

1. Which state is your "domicile," the legal term for where you permanently live, where you have your home.

You can have only one domicile. The state of your domicile governs your marital property—except real estate in another state or country. If you have homes in two or more states, which you choose as your legal domicile can be important, both for property ownership and state inheritance tax purposes. Given a choice, it's usually best to opt for a state that imposes no, or low, property taxes. (See Chapter 15, Section G, for information on state estate and inheritance taxes.)

2. The property ownership laws of your home state, and of any other state or country where you own real estate. Real estate is controlled by the law of the state or country where it is located, no matter where you live.

If you are unsure where you are domiciled. If you own two or more homes in the U.S. or live in both the U.S. and abroad, see a lawyer to discuss how this affects your estate planning. You must determine which state's or country's laws govern your marital property and what, if anything, you can do to change this if you so desire.

Divorce means a new estate plan. If you get divorced, reexamine your estate plan and bring it up to date. In most states, divorce automatically revokes gifts left to your former spouse in your will—but not in all states. Even in states where a divorce invalidates an earlier will's gifts to a divorced spouse, you still need to name a new beneficiary for that property. Also, in almost all states, divorce does not revoke a living trust, even if an ex-spouse benefits from it.

VARYING STATE PROPERTY OWNERSHIP LAWS BY CONTRACT

If you and your spouse don't like the way state law defines your shared ownership of property, you can normally agree to change it at any time. To accomplish this, you and your spouse need to prepare a valid contract. For example, in most states you can agree to change the ownership status of property acquired prior to marriage, which would normally be owned as separate property by the acquiring spouse, to shared ownership. If you make this kind of written agreement before marriage, setting out the terms by which your property shall be owned, it's called a "prenuptial agreement" or "prenup," for short. If you wait until after you're married, you'll make a "postnuptial agreement" or "postnup."

All contracts concerning marital property, including prenuptial contracts, must comply with your state's laws governing them. Generally, this means they must be in writing and that both spouses must voluntarily agree to them after fair disclosure by both spouses of their property ownership and financial obligations. These agreements often explicitly cover inheritance, and property ownership for estate planning purposes.

Help with prenups. To learn more about prenuptial agreements, including how to draft your own contract, see *Prenuptial Agreements: How to Write a Fair & Lasting Contract*, by Katherine E. Stoner and Shae Irving (Nolo).

RESOLVING CONFLICTS OVER PROPERTY OWNERSHIP

It's not crucial to define which spouse owns what property if you and your spouse plan to leave all or most of your property to each other, or in a way the other approves of. However, if you and your spouse discover any conflict over your property ownership that will significantly affect your estate planning, you need to deal with it.

It's best, of course, if you are able to resolve any disagreements between yourselves. If that doesn't work, we urge (parental as we may sound) that you get professional help—from a mediator, lawyer, or therapist. If a mutually agreeable compromise isn't reached prior to death and one spouse tries to leave property the other believes he or she doesn't own, there is real danger of a nasty court fight. After resolving any problems, both spouses should sign an agreement setting forth their decisions.

B. MARITAL PROPERTY IN COMMUNITY PROPERTY STATES

The basic rule of community property law is simple: During a marriage, all property earned or acquired by either spouse is owned in equal half shares by each spouse—except for property received as "separate property" by only one of them through gift or inheritance. This community property concept derives from the ancient marriage laws of some European peoples, including the Visigoths, which passed to Spain and then to many Western states through Spanish explorers and settlers. For estate planning purposes, there are no restrictions on how each spouse can leave his or her half of their community property. Neither is required to leave it to the surviving spouse, although, of course, many spouses do.

In community property states, "separate property" is property owned entirely by one spouse. Property owned by one spouse before a marriage remains separate property even after the marriage, as long as it's kept separate. Also, property one spouse is given or inherits is his or her separate property.

For many couples in long-term marriages, characterizing their property is relatively easy: it's all community property. Any property owned by either spouse before marriage is either long gone or so totally mixed with community property that it has long since lost its separate property status. Neither spouse has inherited or been given any substantial amount of separate property during the marriage, or if they have, it, too, has been mixed into the community pot. Still, even if you believe this to be your situation, read the next few pages to be sure.

1. What Is Community Property?

Unless the husband and wife agree to something different, the following is community property:

- **All income received by either spouse from employment or by other means (except by gift or inheritance to one spouse) during the marriage.** This generally refers only to the period when the couple is living together as husband and wife. From the time spouses permanently separate, most community property states consider newly acquired income and property as the separate property of the spouse receiving it.

  At any time during the marriage, each spouse can arrange to keep his or her own income as separate property. All community property states allow spouses to treat income earned after marriage as separate property if they sign a written agreement to do so and then actually keep their income separate—for example, in separate bank accounts.

- **All property acquired with community property income during the marriage.** For example, if you are married and you use your salary (community property) to buy a car, that car is also community property, even if you take title to it in your name only.

- **All separate property that is transformed into community property under state law.** This transformation can occur in several ways, including when one spouse makes a gift of separate property to both of them. Generally, such a transfer must be done with a signed document.

> **Example:** Ned Terrlin owned a home for five years before he married Sally. He then signed a new deed for the house, listing the new owners as "Ned and Sally Terrlin, as community property." Ned has given one-half ownership of the house to Sally.

Community property can also be transformed into separate property by gifts between spouses. The rules for how to do this differ somewhat from state to state. Normally, if real estate is given, the gift must be in writing. And even for other property, the strong trend is to require that the gift must be made in writing.

Another common example of transformation of separate property is when it gets so mixed together with community property that it's no longer possible to tell the difference between the two. Lawyers call this "commingling."

> **Example:** When she got married, Felicity had a bank account with $14,000 in it, her separate property. During her marriage, now in its 27th year, she maintained this account, depositing money she or her husband earned and making frequent withdrawals. No money in the account is separate property. The original $14,000 has long since been "commingled" with community property funds.

2. What Is Separate Property?

The following property qualifies as separate property:

- all property owned by either spouse prior to marriage

- all property received by one spouse after marriage by gift or inheritance, and

- all property earned or accumulated by one spouse after permanent separation.

As mentioned, separate property stays that way so long as it is not:

- hopelessly mixed (commingled) with community property, or

- transferred in writing to shared ownership by the separate property owner.

3. Pensions

Generally, private pensions and military pensions are considered community property—at least the proportion of them attributable to earnings during the marriage. However, benefits from certain major federal pension programs, including Social Security and Railroad Retirement, aren't community property because federal law classifies them as the separate property of the employee.

4. Distinguishing Community and Separate Property

Most married couples have little difficulty determining what's community property and what is each one's separate property. However, these issues can get complicated. Divorce courts churn out a continual stream of decisions on the fine points of community versus separate property. Here are a few potential problem areas in estate planning:

Appreciated property. In most community property states, when the separate property of one spouse goes up in value, this appreciation is also separate property. However, sometimes one spouse owns separate property before a marriage, but both spouses contribute to the cost of maintaining or improving it during the marriage. The result can be that the property is part community, part separate. If the property substantially appreciates in value over the years, it can be difficult to determine what percentage of the current value of the property is separate property and what is community property.

A common example is a house that was originally owned by one spouse. Then for a length of time, say ten or 20 years, both spouses pay, from community funds, for mortgage, insurance, and upkeep. If the value of the house grew during the marriage, the couple can determine what portion of the present value is community property by agreeing in writing on any arrangement they decide is fair.

Businesses. If a family-owned business was owned by one spouse in whole or part before marriage and grew later, difficult ownership questions can arise. As with home ownership, the basic problem is to figure out what proportion (if any) of the increased value is community property. Again, a married couple can agree on any arrangement they want to. If both spouses work in the business, one sensible approach is to consider all the increase in value from the date of marriage as community property. However, if only the spouse who originally owned the business works in it, resolving ownership percentages can be more difficult. If it's likely the business would have grown in value anyway, much of the increase could reasonably be regarded as separate property.

Monetary recovery for personal injuries. As a general matter, personal injury awards or settlements are the separate property of the spouse receiving them, but not always. In some community property states, this money is treated one way (community property) while the injured spouse is living and another way (separate property) upon his death. Also, the determination as to whether it's separate or community property can vary when the injury is caused by the other spouse. In short, there's no easy way to characterize this type of property. If this issue concerns you, see a lawyer.

Income from separate property. Most community property states hold that income from separate property is also separate property. But a few states say that income from separate property is community property.

Example: Beth and Mike live in Idaho, where separate property income becomes community property. Beth inherits, as her separate property, a herd of 23 Angus cattle from her father. Those cattle go on to breed a herd of more than one hundred cattle. All the descendants of the original 23 animals are considered income from Beth's separate property, and therefore community property.

5. Inheritance Protection for Spouses in California, Idaho, Washington, and Wisconsin

In these four states—and in very limited circumstances—a surviving spouse may be entitled to inherit a portion of the deceased spouse's community or separate property. These laws are designed to prevent spouses from being either accidentally overlooked or deliberately deprived of their fair share of property.

To understand these rules, you need to know just a little bit about "quasi-community property." If you are married and acquire property in a common law state, and then move to California, Idaho, Washington, or Wisconsin, that property will be treated exactly like community property. This property is known as "quasi-community property," except in Wisconsin, where it's called "deferred marital property."

Here's a brief summary of the rules for the community property states that offer statutory protection for surviving spouses.

California. If the deceased spouse made an estate plan before marriage and didn't include the suriving spouse in a will or trust, the surviving spouse can claim *all* of the community and quasi-community property, as well as a share of the deceased spouse's separate property. (Cal. Pro. Code §§ 6560 and following.)

Idaho. In some circumstances, if the deceased spouse gave away quasi-community property, or sold it for less than its value, the surviving spouse can demand that the property be returned to the deceased spouse's estate. The surviving spouse can then claim half of that property. (Idaho Code §§ 15-2-202 and following.)

Washington. If the deceased spouse transferred quasi-community property within three years of death to someone other than the surviving spouse, the survivor can, under certain conditions, claim a half-interest in the property or in the proceeds from the sale of it. However, if the property was sold by the deceased spouse for a reasonable price, or with the consent of the surviving spouse, the surviving spouse cannot make a claim. (Wash. Rev. Code Ann. § 26.16.240.)

Wisconsin. Rather than take what the deceased spouse provided, the surviving spouse can elect to inherit up to one-half of what's called the "augmented deferred marital property estate." This is the total value of the deferred marital property of both spouses, including gifts of deferred marital property made by the deceased spouse during the two years before death. (Wis. Stat. §§ 861.02 and following.)

Spousal protection laws are complicated. If you live in California, Idaho, Washington, or Wisconsin and you wish to learn more about these spousal protection laws, see an experienced estate planning lawyer.

C. MARITAL PROPERTY IN COMMON LAW STATES

Common law states protect spouses and keep them from being left out in the (property) cold when the other spouse dies. But they do it in a different way than community property states.

1. Who Owns What

In common law states, there's no rule that property acquired during a marriage is owned by both spouses. Common law principles are derived from English law, where in feudal times the husband owned all marital property; a wife had few property ownership rights and couldn't even leave any property by will. Still today, in the common law states, the spouse who earns money or acquires property owns it separately and solely, unless, of course, he or she transfers it into shared ownership.

In common law states, the property you own for estate planning purposes, whether you are married or not, consists of:

- everything held separately in your name if it has a title slip, deed, or other legal ownership document (this always includes real estate, vehicles, securities and bank accounts, and your ownership interest in joint tenancy or other shared ownership property), and

- all other property you have purchased from your assets or income.

For example, if you earn or inherit money to buy a house, and title is taken in both your name and your spouse's, you both own it. But if your spouse earns the money to buy it, but somehow title is placed in your name alone, you own it. Similarly, no matter who puts up funds to buy a house, if title is in your spouse's name, he or she owns it.

Despite the general rule stated here, these states have rules that prevent a spouse from disinheriting the other.

2. Family Protection in Common Law States

Common law states give a surviving spouse legal rights to claim a certain portion—usually one-third to one-half—of the other's estate.

Suppose, for example, that one spouse owns the family house, that the car and bank accounts are in his name alone and that he attempts to leave it all to a stranger (or worse, a lover). Can the stranger kick the surviving spouse out of the house, empty the bank accounts and so on? Of course this rarely happens, but just in case, all common law property states prevent the surviving spouse from being completely, or even substantially, disinherited. While many of these protective laws are similar, they do differ in detail.

The methods that common law states use to protect families were developed hundreds of years ago by English courts, which were confronted with the same problem of a few people disinheriting their spouses. In response, they developed legal

concepts called "dower" and "curtesy." "Dower" refers to the rights of a surviving wife; "curtesy" is the share received by a surviving husband. When the United States was settled, most states adopted these concepts. To this day, all common law states still retain some version of dower and curtesy, although many have dropped the old terminology and simply provide for "spousal inheritance rights" or something similar.

In most common law property states, a spouse is entitled to one-third of the property left by the other. In a few, it's one-half or some other standard.

Some states provide that all of the deceased spouse's property, including any that was transferred by means other than a will, is subject to the surviving spouse's claim. Other states take a different approach: they include not only all of the deceased spouse's property, but some or all of the separate property owned by the surviving spouse as well. (The total amount of property used to calculate the surviving spouse's share is called the "augmented estate.")

> **Example:** Alice leaves her husband, Mike, $10,000 and her three daughters $90,000 each in her will. However, Alice also leaves real estate worth $500,000 to Mike by a living trust. The total Mike receives from this augmented estate, $510,000, is more than one-half of Alice's total property, so he has nothing to gain by insisting on his right to make a claim against her will property.

A surviving spouse does not automatically inherit the share that's guaranteed by law; he or she must go to court and ask for it. So if a person leaves nothing to a spouse or leaves less than the spouse is entitled to under state law, the surviving spouse has a choice of either taking what the will or other transfer document provides or rejecting the gift and instead claiming the minimum share allowed by state law. Taking the share permitted by law is called "taking against the will."

Example: Leonard's will leaves $50,000 to his second wife, June, and leaves the rest of his property, totaling $400,000, to his two children from his first marriage. June can take the $50,000 or elect to take against the will and receive her statutory share of Leonard's estate. Depending on the state, this will equal about one-third to one-half of Leonard's total estate.

When a spouse decides to take against the will, the property that is taken must come out of what was left to others. In other words, somebody else is going to get less. In the above example, the children will receive much less than Leonard intended. So, if you don't provide your spouse with at least the statutory share under your state's laws, your gifts to others may be seriously reduced.

 If you want to leave your spouse less than one-half of your estate, see a lawyer. Put bluntly, if you want to leave your spouse little or nothing, and you haven't gotten your spouse's unforced and written consent to your plan, your estate may be heading for a legal mess. See a lawyer.

FAMILY ALLOWANCES

Most states provide additional, relatively minor protections for spouses and children. These vary from state to state in too much detail to discuss here. Generally, however, these devices attempt to ensure that your spouse and children are not left out in the cold after your death, by giving them temporary protection such as the right to remain in the family home for a short period or living expenses while your estate is being settled.

D. MOVING TO A DIFFERENT STATE

A will or living trust valid in one state is, broadly speaking, valid in all. However, problems can develop when married people move from a community property state to a common law property state or vice versa. This is because the property each spouse owns (and is therefore free to leave or give away) may change. If spouses move from one state to another that follows the same property ownership system—for example, New York to Florida, or California to Texas—there is no need to worry about new marital property ownership rules.

Remember, technical property ownership rules are not a worry if spouses plan to leave all or most of their property to each other, or in a way the other spouse approves of.

1. Moving From a Common Law State to a Community Property State

What happens when a husband and wife acquire property in a common law state but then move to a community property state? California, Idaho, Washington, and Wisconsin (community property states) treat the earlier acquired property as if it had been acquired in a community property state. The legal jargon for this type of property is "quasi-community property," except in Wisconsin, where it's called "deferred marital property." Thus, if you and your spouse moved from any common law state into California, Idaho, Washington, or Wisconsin all of your property is treated according to community property rules. (See Section B, above.)

The other community property states don't recognize the quasi-community property concept for estate planning purposes and instead enforce the rules of the state where the property was acquired. So if you moved into any of the other community property states from a common law state, you'll need to assess your property according to the rules of the state where you used to live.

2. Moving From a Community Property State to a Common Law Property State

When spouses move from a community property state to a common law state, each generally retains a one-half interest in the property accumulated during marriage while they lived in the community property state. However, the courts have not been entirely consistent in dealing with the problem in situations where the property is in one spouse's name.

Spousal disagreements. If you have moved from a community property state to a common law state, and you and your spouse have any disagreement or confusion as to who owns what, check with a lawyer. ■

4

INVENTORYING YOUR PROPERTY

Preparing a thorough written inventory of your property is a good idea for thorough estate planning. It helps you:

- remind yourself of what you own

- determine what you owe

- estimate the current net value of your estate as an aid to estate tax planning

- pin down any shared ownership of property

- make a handy list to refer to when leaving gifts to beneficiaries in a will or living trust, and

- have your assets organized in case you later consult an estate planning lawyer.

That said, it's still up to you to decide whether you want to itemize your property in detail or simply estimate its overall worth. For some people, as much precision as possible is an important part of the process—we wouldn't dare say fun—of planning their estate. For others, giving the subject just enough thought to arrive at a decent ballpark estimate suffices. For example:

- If you want to leave all your property to one person, perhaps your spouse, or to your spouse for his lifetime use and then equally to your children, there is far less need to itemize all major items of property than if you wanted to leave separate gifts to a good-sized list of people.

- If you are confident that your net estate is worth less than the federal estate tax threshold, and is likely to remain so, there's no reason to estimate the value of your estate for tax purposes. (See Chapter 15, Section A.)

EXAMPLE: Jane wants to leave all of her woodworking tools and equipment to her friend Alice, her car to her friend Amy, and everything else she owns (stocks, jewelry, money market funds, and personal and household possessions) to her longtime companion Mary. She knows her estate is worth no more than $400,000, well under the federal estate tax threshold, that the state she lives in imposes no estate taxes and that she has no significant debts. Jane decides there's no need for her to list separately each item of property, since with two easy-to-remember exceptions, she's leaving it all to Mary.

One caveat here. If you're a member of a couple, and plan to leave most or all of your property outright to the other member, and your combined estates exceed the estate tax threshold, estate taxes will probably be assessed when the second spouse dies. So you may want to do some tax planning. (See Chapter 15, Section A, and Chapter 18, Section C.)

A. INSTRUCTIONS FOR THE PROPERTY INVENTORY WORKSHEET

Section B of this chapter contains a worksheet to help you inventory your property. As you'll see, you can record a wide range of property. Take a minute to get acquainted with its structure.

The following detailed description of the worksheet and the suggestions for completing it are for those who want or need to be thorough. It's up to you to decide how extensive and detailed your own listings need to be—or if you don't want to use the chart at all.

1. Section I: What You Own

In Section I of the chart, you list your assets—all the property you own. There are four kinds of information to give for each item of property:

- Column 1—a description of the item of property

- Column 2—if ownership of that item is shared, the type of shared ownership

- Column 3—the percentage of any shared ownership property you own

- Column 4—the net value of each item of property (or your share of it) you own.

Now let's take a minute to review the information that should be entered in each column.

YOU MAY BE WORTH MORE THAN YOU THINK

We've been surprised to learn that quite a few people who have worked hard for years, and live a frugal life, find it difficult to admit that their assets could be worth more—sometimes substantially more—than the federal estate tax threshold.

This can occur with owners of appreciated real estate or a successful small business. When asked how much a residence or business is worth, the owner may think in terms of what was paid for it, plus a relatively small markup. We've seen situations where this estimate was hundreds of thousands of dollars off the mark. Or a person may have become so accustomed to the family furniture and paintings he doesn't consider the possibility that the heirlooms are now much sought-after antiques or valuable art.

This lack of fiscal up-to-dateness can mean that a person just doesn't want to admit that he has money. But indulging in denial at the cost of not carefully planning one's estate is no favor to one's beneficiaries, who most likely hope you'll take sensible steps to pass money to them, rather than giving a large amount to the government in taxes. So, be sure your estimates of how much your property is worth are contemporary.

Column 1: Identify and Describe Your Property

Here you identify your property with sufficient detail so there can be no question what it includes. If you include any assets in an individual retirement program, such as an IRA or 401(k), take into account that you may spend some or all of these funds before your death. This worksheet divides your property into four groups:

A. Liquid assets. These include cash, savings, checking, and money market accounts, mutual fund shares, readily tradable stocks and securities, bonds, and certificates of deposit.

EXAMPLES:

- Certificate of Deposit # 10235, Lighthouse Savings and Loan Association, Ventura, CA

- My savings account at Bay Bank (if you have only one savings account)

- My savings account # 18-17411 at Bay Bank (if you have more than one savings account)

- 50 shares Transpacific Corporation common stock.

B. Other personal property. This includes all your property except liquid assets, business interests, and real estate. This catch-all category includes retirement accounts, automobiles, jewelry, furs, precious metals, artwork, antiques, tools, life insurance, collectibles, and so forth.

EXAMPLES:

- $10,000 El Dorado Drainage and Water System, District of Alameda, 1995 bond series C, 5% due June 1, 2010

- My IRA # 442301299 at Wachovia Securities, Santa Barbara, CA

- 2005 Ford Mustang, Michigan License # 123456

- All my fishing equipment

- Gold earrings with the small rubies in them purchased from Charles Shreve and Co. in 1981

- Daumier print captioned "Les beaux jours de la vie"

- Life insurance policy #A106004, You-Bet-Your-Life Insurance Co.

- All my carpenter's tools, including my power saws.

If you are like most people, you have all sorts of minor personal possessions you don't want to bother itemizing. To deal with these, you can group a number of items in one category: "all my tools," "all my dolls," or baseball cards, or records, or machines, and equipment or household furniture—whatever. Of course, some items without large monetary value may have great emotional worth to you and your family: a photo album, an old music box, a treasured chair. List these individually as you desire.

As another alternative, you can conclude your list with one catch-all item such as "all my other personal possessions and furnishings."

FREQUENT FLYER MILES

Here's a new type of personal property that you may be able to leave as part of your estate—frequent flyer miles. Many major U.S. airlines allow you to leave your accumulated miles in your will. Some allow you to leave them to any beneficiary you name but others limit your choice of beneficiaries, so you have to check with your airline to see what they allow. (There go a couple of hours waiting on hold.) Though it's not legally required, it's a good idea to name the airline in your will and specifically state that you leave your frequent flyer miles with that airline to the beneficiary.

C. Business personal property. This includes all business interests, except any real estate used in that business.

EXAMPLES:

- My shares of stock in the Mo-To Corporation

- My business dba Ace Stationery Store, Boca Raton, Florida

- My partnership interest in JTL Partnership Enterprises, Main Office, Detroit, Michigan

- My membership interest in the Gaelic Basketball Lounge Limited Liability Company

- All my copyrights and rights to royalties in the books with the following titles, currently published by Acme Press, Berkeley, California [titles listed]

- All my rights in U.S. Patent #2,230,240: three-way mirror and portable traffic light.

Special estate planning issues for intellectual property. Copyrights and patents are commonly known as "intellectual property." Unique estate planning problems can arise when dealing with this kind of property. Some issues are managerial: Will the beneficiary or beneficiaries be able to manage the asset? For instance, not everyone has the savvy to know how to market copyrighted materials, or develop a patent industrially. If your beneficiaries don't have the knowledge to make smart commercial use of intellectual property, you may be able to put a plan in place to help them. Another issue can be determining the value of intellectual property, especially for estate tax purposes. Sometimes it makes sense to give away intellectual property while you live. Usually, it is tax-wise to give a patent, but not a copyright. (See Chapter 16, Section E.) Because of these kinds of complexities, it's prudent to see a lawyer if your estate includes valuable intellectual property.

D. Real estate. This includes all business real estate, and all houses, co-ops/condominiums, mobile homes attached to land, undeveloped or agricultural land. (The rules on when an attached mobile home becomes "real estate" vary from state to state. If this matters to you, see a lawyer.)

To describe real estate, simply list its address or location. This is normally the street address. If there's no post office address, as with undeveloped land, simply describe the real property in normal language like this: "my 120 acres in Lincoln County near the town of Douglas." You don't need to use the legal description from the deed.

EXAMPLES:

- 126 Oceanview Terrace, Mendocino, California

- My lot on Keeler Street, Middletown, Ohio

- 1001 Main Street (the Fullerton Hardware Building), Moose, New York.

Contaminated property. If you own real estate that may be contaminated by any hazardous substances you could be handing your inheritors a huge headache if you leave them that land. Under federal law, "responsible parties" are liable for the costs of cleaning up contaminated land. Responsible parties include past and current owners of the real estate, whether or not they caused the contamination, or even knew about it when they acquired the land. Federal and state laws contain a long list of contaminants, including petroleum products, dry cleaning solutions, and many other toxins.

Liability for contaminated land cannot be discharged in probate or through any other procedure transferring property to a beneficiary. This liability goes against the land itself, and its current owner, period. So, to help your beneficiaries, as well to be a law-abiding citizen, have an expert check out the condition of any land you own that may be contaminated, and then do what you must to rectify the damage.

Real property often contains items that are properly classified as personal property. For instance, farms are often sold with tools and animals. If you intend to keep both together (as one gift), indicate what this "together" consists of. It's best to specify the large ticket items (tractor, cattle) and refer generally to the rest of the items as "personal property."

EXAMPLES:

- My 240-acre truck farm in Whitman County with all tools, animals, machines, and other personal property located there

- My fishing cabin on the Wild River in Maine with all the fishing gear, furniture, tools, and other personal property that are found there

- My ownership of the mobile home located at E-Z motor camp, and all possessions and furnishings contained in it.

KEEPING GOOD RECORDS

After taking inventory of your property, you might want to take the next step and get better organized for your family. *Get It Together: Organize Your Records So Your Family Won't Have To*, by Melanie Cullen with Shae Irving (Nolo), allows you to organize all your records and important paperwork for yourself and your survivors. You can document important information about everything from estate planning documents to tax records, from financial records to government benefits, and much more. The book's CD-ROM lets you fill out a comprehensive planner that you can readily update if your situation changes.

Column 2: Type of Shared Ownership

You need to be concerned with Columns 2 and 3 only if you own some property with someone else. If you are single and own all your property outright, you can simply skip to the instructions for Column 4. However, if you are married or have entered into personal or business shared ownership transactions, please read what follows carefully. Obviously, before you can sensibly plan your estate, you must clearly understand what you own and therefore have the power to leave.

You probably know whether you own property with others. However you may have to do some investigating to be sure about just how you and the other owners hold title to the property. Never guess. If you're not sure how you own an item of property, take the time to find out. For example, you may have to locate the deed to your house or your stock ownership records to clarify whether you and your spouse own them in joint tenancy. You can check real estate records at the county property recorder's office.

If you are married, live in a community property state, and you and your spouse own both separate and community property, you may have some difficulty determining exactly what you and your spouse own. (We discuss this in Chapter 3.) For example, if you are unsure whether a $23,000 bank account is community property or your separate property, bear in mind that you and your spouse can resolve the confusion by jointly characterizing this account in either ownership category. To do this legally, however, it's important to put your conclusion in writing, signed by both of you.

Below we give you a summary of the different legal forms possible for shared ownership. Some of these concepts may be new to you. If after reading what follows you don't understand exactly what a particular form of shared ownership means, you needn't worry. They are explained in more depth in later chapters. Simply note on your worksheet that the property is held in some form of shared ownership and complete the "Shared Ownership" column later.

Here are the symbols you can use to record the major types of shared ownership:

- **Joint Tenancy (J.T.):** Property held with a written ownership document identifying the owners either as Joint Tenants or Joint Tenants With Right of Survivorship. Under these forms of ownership, each joint tenant owns an equal share of the property. The share of the first tenant to die must go to the survivors, even if there's a will or living trust to the contrary. (Joint tenancy is discussed in detail in Chapter 10.)

Joint tenancy must be created by a written document. If you own property using the phrase "Joint Tenancy With Right of Survivorship," there is no question what type of shared ownership you have. But what about writings that are less clear? For example, suppose your real estate deed says "Tenancy in Common With Right of Survivorship"? In Oregon, this has the same practical effect as joint tenancy; in some other states, it surely doesn't. The point is—don't guess. If you're not clear what kind of legal animal you've got, check it out by doing your own research or checking with a lawyer knowledgeable about real estate law.

Similarly, what if owners are listed simply with an "and" or an "or"? For example, two people own real estate with the title listed as held by "Smith and Jones." Two others own real estate with title listed as "Smith or Jones." Are either of these joint tenancy? The answer is that it depends on

the state in which the property is located. Under most states' laws, neither by itself constitutes joint tenancy, but if you hold ownership with another person with "and" or "or" in the title document, you need to know the specific rules of your state.

JOINT TENANCY

- **Tenancy by the Entirety (T.E.):** This form of ownership, limited to married couples, is recognized in a number of common law states. It is almost identical to joint tenancy and creates a right of survivorship between spouses. It must be created in writing. (See Chapter 10.)

- **Community Property (C.P.):** In the community property states (listed in Chapter 3, Section A), any property spouses earn or acquire during a marriage is shared community property. Even if only one spouse's name is on the title document, if the property was bought with money earned during the marriage, it's community property.

There are a few "separate property" exceptions, discussed below.

Don't overlook the fact that you and your spouse may own partnership interests, corporate shares, or an interest in a tenancy in common that is also community property.

You can leave your one-half share of community property to anybody you wish. Since the other one-half of the community property belongs to your spouse, you obviously have no power to leave it by your will or living trust.

- **Community Property With Right of Survivorship (C.P./S.):** A form of community property that means that the surviving spouse automatically inherits the property when the other spouse dies. In other words, community property that functions like joint tenancy property. Available in Alaska, Arizona, California, Nevada, Texas, and Wisconsin.

- **Separate Property (S.P.):** In community property states, all property that isn't community property is held separately. Property that is given to or inherited by one spouse is his or her separate property. Likewise, property owned by each spouse prior to marriage remains separate property, if it's kept distinct from community property.

  In the common law states (listed in Chapter 3, Section A), separate property means all property that each spouse owns individually, including all property where one spouse's name appears on the title document, unless there is a written contract to the contrary.

- **Partnership (P):** Property owned by business partners, regulated by a partnership agreement (including shares in a limited partnership).

Partnership agreements often contain detailed rules as to what happens to a partner's share at death.

- **Corporate Shares (C.S.):** Shares of a small or closely held corporation (only a few owners) may be freely transferable at death. However, your freedom to transfer them may also be regulated by corporate bylaws or a separate shareholders' agreement.

- **Limited Liability Co. (LLC):** This is a type of business ownership allowing owners advantages of both the corporate and partnership forms. An LLC must be established by formal documents under state law. Your ability to transfer your ownership interest in an LLC is most likely governed by the LLC's operating agreement.

- **Tenancy in Common (T.C.):** Any property held in shared ownership that isn't in another type of ownership—in other words, all shared property not owned in joint tenancy, tenancy by the entirety, community property, partnership, corporation, or LLC. Tenancy in common includes considerable property spouses own together in common law property states. You can own any percentage of tenancy in common property (.005%, 95%, etc.)—owners' shares don't have to be equal, as they must be for joint tenancy property. If the ownership deed doesn't specify the type of shared ownership, it's probably tenancy in common, although, as mentioned above, in some states the word "or" may indicate joint tenancy ownership. Unlike joint tenancy, where there is an automatic right of survivorship for joint tenants, you can leave your portion of property held as tenants in common as you choose, unless restricted by a contract.

Example: Natalie and Jeremy Engels live in North Carolina, a common law property state. They hold several securities, their house and a piece of land with both their names on the title documents, but no joint tenancy designation. They are presumed to own the property as tenants in common, with each owning a 50% share.

Column 3: Percentage of Shared Property You Own

In this column, list the percentage of each item of shared property you own. People who own property as tenants in common, or in a partnership or corporation, should be particularly careful—you can own any percentage of the property. Especially with a partnership, you must check your partnership agreement to be sure. With a tenancy in common, co-owners normally own equal shares (33.3% if you are one of three), unless there is a written agreement to the contrary.

 If you own an interest in a partnership, LLC, or small corporation. Check your operating agreement or corporate documents to see if there are any restrictions on your rights to transfer your interest at death. Often other business owners have an option to purchase your interest or shares. (See Chapter 28, Section A.)

Column 4: Current Net Value of Your Ownership

In this column, estimate the "net value" of each item listed. Net value means your equity in your share of the property. Equity is the market value of your share, less your share of any debts on it, such as a mortgage on a house or the loan amount due on a car.

Making estimates normally doesn't require that you burden yourself seeking exact figures or expert appraisals. After all, the value of your estate will surely change some by the time you die. Here you need only ballpark figures. For example, if you have a reasonable grasp of market prices, and you believe that the net worth of your interest in your house, after you subtract the mortgage, is about $200,000, your car $5,000, and your stamp collection $35,000 if you put an ad in a philatelist's journal, use those numbers. Only with more complex types of property, in particular business interests, may you need expert help.

Example 1: Clay owns a house with a market value of $350,000 as a tenant in common with his sister Ava; each owns half. Clay computes the net value of his share by first subtracting the amount of mortgages, deeds of trust, and liens from the market value to arrive at the total equity in the property:

- Market value: $350,000
- Owed on mortgage: $110,000
- Lien against the property: $10,000
- Total equity ($350,000 minus $120,000): $230,000
- Net worth of Clay's share: $115,000

Example 2: Stacey is sole owner of the Maltese Falcon Restaurant, a successful business she has run for 23 years. She has only a vague notion of its market value since she has never been interested in selling it. To competently plan her estate, she needs a reasonable estimate of the worth of the business. This can be difficult to make, particularly since the market value of her restaurant includes the intangible of "good will." Stacey talks to an accountant to help her arrive at a sensible estimate of the worth of the restaurant.

The last step in Section I of the Property Worksheet is to add up the net value of all your assets, and list that sum in Part E.

2. Section II: What You Owe

In Section II, Liabilities, list any liabilities—debts—you haven't already taken into account in Section I. For example, in Section II, list any significant personal debts—the $10,000 loan from a friend or $5,000 unsecured advance on a line of credit. Also list all other liabilities, such as tax liens or court judgments. Remember, you have taken account of mortgages on your real estate and payments owed on your motor vehicle in Section I, so don't list them here.

Add up your estimate of all your liabilities and list that sum in Part D of Section II.

3. Section III: Your Net Worth

Finally, in Section III of the chart, estimate your current net worth. To get this figure, simply subtract your total liabilities listed in Section II from your total assets listed in Section I.

B. YOUR PROPERTY WORKSHEET

Remember, this chart is purely for your convenience. It can be as messy or as neat as you care to make it. Also, pencil is recommended (unless you're the type who does the *New York Times* crossword puzzle in ink).

PROPERTY WORKSHEET

I. ASSETS

Column 1 Description of Your Property	Column 2 Type of Shared Ownership	Column 3 Percentage You Own	Column 4 Net Value of Your Ownership
A. Liquid Assets			
1. cash			
2. savings accounts			
3. checking accounts			

Column 1 Description of Your Property	Column 2 Type of Shared Ownership	Column 3 Percentage You Own	Column 4 Net Value of Your Ownership
4. money market accounts			
5. certificates of deposit			
6. mutual funds			

Column 1 Description of Your Property	Column 2 Type of Shared Ownership	Column 3 Percentage You Own	Column 4 Net Value of Your Ownership
7. tradable stocks and securities			
8. government bonds			

Column 1 Description of Your Property	Column 2 Type of Shared Ownership	Column 3 Percentage You Own	Column 4 Net Value of Your Ownership

B. Other Personal Property

(all your property except liquid assets, business interests, and real estate: houses, building, apartments, etc.)

Description of Your Property	Type of Shared Ownership	Percentage You Own	Net Value of Your Ownership
1. automobiles and other vehicles, including planes, boats, and recreational vehicles			
2. cameras, computers, and other electronic equipment			
3. precious metals			
4. household goods			

Column 1 Description of Your Property	Column 2 Type of Shared Ownership	Column 3 Percentage You Own	Column 4 Net Value of Your Ownership
5. clothing			
6. jewelry and furs			
7. art works, collectibles, and antiques			
8. tools and equipment			

Column 1 Description of Your Property	Column 2 Type of Shared Ownership	Column 3 Percentage You Own	Column 4 Net Value of Your Ownership
9. valuable livestock/animals			
10. money owed you (personal loans, etc.)			
11. vested interest in profit sharing plan, stock options, etc.			
12. limited partnerships			

Column 1 Description of Your Property	Column 2 Type of Shared Ownership	Column 3 Percentage You Own	Column 4 Net Value of Your Ownership
13. vested interest in retirement plans, IRAs, death benefits, annuities			
14. life insurance			
15. frequent flyer miles (list airlines)			
16. miscellaneous (any personal property not listed above)			

Column 1 Description of Your Property	Column 2 Type of Shared Ownership	Column 3 Percentage You Own	Column 4 Net Value of Your Ownership

C. Business Personal Property

1. patents, copyrights, trademarks, and royalties

_____

_____

_____

2. business ownerships (partnerships, sole proprietorships, limited liability companies, corporations, etc.; list separately and use a separate sheet of paper if you need to elaborate)

name and type of business

_____

_____

_____

3. miscellaneous receivables (mortgages, deeds of trust, or promissory notes held by you; any rents due from income property owned by you; and payments due for professional or personal services or property sold by you that are not fully paid by the purchaser)

_____

_____

_____

Column 1 Description of Your Property	Column 2 Type of Shared Ownership	Column 3 Percentage You Own	Column 4 Net Value of Your Ownership

D. Real Estate

address _____

address _____

address _____

Column 1 Description of Your Property	*Column 2* Type of Shared Ownership	*Column 3* Percentage You Own	*Column 4* Net Value of Your Ownership
address			
address			

E. TOTAL NET VALUE OF ALL YOUR ASSETS $ _____

II. LIABILITIES (what you owe)

Many of your liabilities will already be accounted for because you listed the net value of your property in Part I of this chart. For example, to determine the net value of your interest in real estate, you deducted the amount of all mortgages and encumbrances on that real estate. Similarly the net value of a small business is the value after business debts and other obligations are subtracted. For this reason, the only liabilities you need list here are those not previously covered. Don't bother with the small stuff—such as the phone bill, or what you owe on your credit card this month—which changes frequently. Just list all major liabilities not previously accounted for, so you can get a clearer picture of your net worth.

Column 1 To Whom Debt Is Owed	Column 2 Net Amount of Debt You Owe

A. Personal Property Debts

1. personal loans (banks, major credit cards, etc.)

2. other personal debts

Column 1
To Whom Debt Is Owed

Column 2
Net Amount of Debt You Owe

B. Taxes

(include only taxes past and currently due; do not include taxes due in the future or estimated estate taxes)

_____

_____

_____

_____

_____

C. Any Other Liabilities

(legal judgments, accrued child support, etc.)

D. Total Liabilities

(excluding those liabilities already deducted in Section I)

III. YOUR NET WORTH

Total Net Value of All Your Assets (Section I. E)
minus Total Liabilities (Section II. D)

$ _____

5

YOUR BENEFICIARIES

Deciding which people or organizations you want to receive your property—who will be your beneficiaries—is obviously a main focus of your estate plan. This chapter raises some important concerns about choosing and naming beneficiaries. Even if you are sure who should receive your property and are tempted to skip ahead, we urge you to read at least Sections A through F, which cover important information everyone should take into account. Read the rest of the sections only if the subjects concern you.

Most people know, quite clearly, when they begin their estate planning, who their major beneficiaries will be. You may want to write down the names of all your beneficiaries when you start actually preparing your estate planning documents, like a will or living trust, but that's not necessary now.

SOME THOUGHTS ABOUT GIFT GIVING

What is a gift? That question can be more complex, and interesting, than you might think at first.

In our predominantly commercial culture, gifts, whether they are made during life or at death, are special. They are free, voluntary transfers of property, made without any requirement of receiving anything in return. The essence of gift giving is generosity, an open spirit. To say one makes gifts "with strings attached" is not a compliment.

Much of the satisfaction of estate planning comes from contemplating the positive effects your gifts will have on those you love. Sometimes, this satisfaction is quite focused—you know how much Judith has always liked your mahogany table, and now she'll get to enjoy it. Others are more general—your son can buy a house with the money you leave him, which you hope will relieve some of the financial and emotional pressures that have been weighing on him.

We mention the spirit of giving here because we've learned that it's easy to get entrapped by the details of estate planning and lose sight of your real purpose. So, if technicalities and legalities start to get to you, take a break and remember to whom you're giving your property and why.

If you wish to explore in profound depth what gift giving is, or can mean, read Lewis Hyde's *The Gift* (Vintage/Random House), a brilliant exploration of how gifts work in many cultures.

A. TYPES OF BENEFICIARIES

As you know, the word "beneficiaries" means people or institutions you leave property to. There are different types of beneficiaries; the major types discussed in this book are:

- **Primary beneficiaries.** Those you leave identified gifts of property to.

- **Alternate beneficiaries.** Those named to receive a gift if the primary beneficiary can't receive it.

- **Life estate beneficiaries.** People who receive what's called a "life estate" interest in property, which means some rights to receive income from or use of the property during their life, but who never become legal owners of the property. Life estate beneficiaries have no right to leave this property when they die.

- **Final beneficiaries.** Those named to inherit property after a life beneficiary for it dies.

- **Residuary beneficiaries.** Those named to receive property left under a will or trust that is not expressly left to other beneficiaries. Usually, an alternate residuary beneficiary is also named.

B. PRIMARY BENEFICIARIES

Primary beneficiaries are usually named to receive a specific item of property. For example, a will might state: "I leave my car to my sister Joanne Corbett." Some people name many primary beneficiaries for different items. And some name none at all, simply leaving all their property to their residuary beneficiaries.

1. Simple Beneficiary Situations

If you know you want to leave all your property to one or a few people—say your spouse or children—you still may face some additional complexities. Do you want to name an alternate beneficiary, in case the person you've originally named dies before you do? (See Section D, below.) Suppose you want to name two or more alternate beneficiaries. What happens if they wind up receiving your property? Does each one receive an equal share? If they inherit real estate, must it be sold unless all agree to keep it? In sum, even with a seemingly very simple beneficiary situation, you'll almost always need to go further than just naming one person to receive all you've got.

NAMING BENEFICIARIES IN YOUR ESTATE PLANNING DOCUMENTS DOESN'T REQUIRE A LAWYER

If you are considering preparing your estate planning documents yourself, don't be put off by fears you must hire a lawyer, or use tricky legalese, to identify beneficiaries. You can safely name them in simple, plain English, using the names by which your beneficiaries are normally known.

Even if a beneficiary later changes his or her last name, that's no reason for you to revise your will or trust. For example, if a daughter later marries or divorces and decides to change her last name, you don't need to change her name as listed in your living trust or will. She, and others concerned, will know that you meant to name her.

2. Minors as Primary Beneficiaries

Estate planning issues concerning children are discussed in Chapter 6. Here we briefly summarize the options available if you're considering naming a minor child as primary beneficiary (or, indeed, as any type of beneficiary).

Minor children can own only a small amount of property outright in their own names. This amount, which is set by state law, varies from about $2,500 to $5,000. Any property belonging to a minor above this amount must be legally controlled and supervised by an adult. So if you are contemplating leaving a substantial gift to a minor, you should choose an adult to be responsible for it. Your basic options are:

- A gift for your own children can be left outright to the other parent, who will use it for the children's benefit. If spouses—or even ex-spouses—get along and trust one another to manage money well, this is usually the simplest way to handle the matter.

- Leave the gift to the child, and name an adult to be responsible for supervising it. That adult can be one of the child's parents, but doesn't always have to be. When you have decided who the adult supervisor will be, your next step is to decide what legal form you want to use to make the gift. These issues are covered in Chapter 6.

3. Forgiving Debts

One form of gift is to forgive a debt, essentially leaving a gift to your debtor. Any debt, written or oral, can be forgiven.

Example: Bud loaned his daughter Kathlyn and son-in-law Tyrone $50,000 for a down payment on a house, but doesn't want them to be obligated to repay his estate after he dies. So, in his will, Bud includes a provision stating "I forgive the loan of $50,000 I made to Kathlyn and Tyrone Benson in 2001."

If you're married and forgiving a debt, be sure you have full power to do so. If the debt was incurred while you were married, you may only have the right to forgive half the debt (especially in community property states) unless your spouse agrees in writing to allow you to forgive his or her share of the debt as well.

4. Restrictions on Beneficiaries

There are two possible types of restrictions on gifts to beneficiaries:

- restrictions you, the giver, want to impose, and
- restrictions imposed by law.

a. Personal Restrictions

Most people simply leave their property outright to family, friends, or charities. However, sometimes a person wants to make a gift with restrictions or conditions on it, something like "if such and such happens, then the gift shall go to..." Sometimes called "dead-hand control," the obvious risk is that circumstances are almost sure to change, so you must try to anticipate what is likely—or even possible—to occur in the future, and provide for it. For instance, suppose you left a gift "to John, if he quits smoking." Who could ever tell if John fully quit smoking? He can't be watched around the clock each day. And how long is "quit"? These kinds of restrictions on gifts are probably unenforceable—but they surely can enrich lawyers.

Sometimes, people think that imposing restrictions can be a simple matter of writing a couple of sentences when they name a beneficiary. For instance, some readers have wondered how to "write in a provision" to protect a beneficiary who is disabled, or to place limits on a heavy spender. The unfortunate truth is that to impose controls or restrictions on a gift, you need to create an irrevocable trust, which is not a simple matter. You'll need to hire a lawyer. (See Chapter 25 for a discussion of creating trusts to control property after you die.)

 Restrictions. If you're determined to place restrictions on a gift, see a lawyer.

b. Legal Restrictions

With very few limits, you can leave your property to anyone you choose. While the few existing legal restrictions on beneficiaries rarely apply, let's be cautious and review them briefly.

- Some felons and anyone who unlawfully caused the death of the person who wrote the will (or living trust) cannot inherit under it.

- You cannot attempt to encourage or restrain some types of conduct of your beneficiaries. For example, you cannot make a gift contingent on the recipient's marriage, divorce, or change of religion.

- You cannot validly leave money for an illegal purpose—for example, to establish the Institute to Encourage Minors to Smoke.

5. Pets as Beneficiaries

Legally, pets are property (though many pet owners would, of course, disagree). This means that you can't leave money or property to them, either through a will or trust. Any money you try to leave to a pet will go, instead, to your residuary beneficiary. But that doesn't mean you can't ensure a good home and good care for the animals in your life.

The easiest thing to do is arrange with a friend or family member to care for your pet. Then, in your will or living trust, you leave your pet to that person, along with some money to cover the expenses of your pet's feeding and care.

If you prefer to make more formal arrangements, in roughly half the states you can establish a trust for your pet. The trust is a legally independent entity, managed by a trustee you name. You define the terms of the trust—how your pet is to be cared for—in the trust document. Pet trusts can be desirable for people who feel they'd prefer not to leave their pet (and money for pet care) outright to someone. But creating a pet trust is more costly and complicated than simply leaving your pet outright.

 You'll need an attorney to prepare a pet trust. You can't prepare a pet trust on your own. You'll need to check with an attorney, or do your own legal research, to learn whether you can validly use a pet trust in your state. If you can and want to do so, you should hire a lawyer to draft the document.

These issues are discussed in more detail in *Every Dog's Legal Guide*, by Mary Randolph (Nolo).

C. LIFE ESTATE BENEFICIARIES AND FINAL BENEFICIARIES

As we've said, a life estate beneficiary receives only a limited interest in property. This interest ends when the beneficiary dies. The person who originally left the life estate property names another beneficiary or beneficiaries, usually called the "final beneficiary," to inherit the property outright when the life beneficiary dies.

> **Example:** Mac leaves his brother Sam a life estate interest in Mac's house. Mac names his daughter Gay as the final beneficiary. Mac dies. Sam inherits the life estate interest in the house. (If Mac outlived Sam, the life estate interest would never take effect.) Sam can live in the house, or rent it, but never becomes the legal owner. When Sam dies, the house will go outright to Gay.

Life estates are usually created by a trust. The rights of the life estate beneficiary and the final beneficiaries must be carefully defined in the trust document. Life estate trusts are used for one or both of two purposes:

- to reduce or eliminate estate taxes. (See Chapter 18.)
- to impose controls over property. For example, someone in a second marriage may want to leave her mate a life estate interest in property, with that property then going to her children from a prior marriage when the mate dies. (See Chapter 24.) Or a parent may want to leave property to a disabled child in a long-term managerial trust. (See Chapter 25.)

D. ALTERNATE BENEFICIARIES

Most people name alternate beneficiaries to inherit property if their first choices die before they do. This is especially appropriate if you leave some gifts to older people or people in poor health. Also, you simply might not have the time, or inclination, before your own death, to revise your estate plan if a beneficiary dies before you.

On the other hand, this is one of the many estate planning issues where there are no absolutes. Some people decide they don't want the morbid bother of worrying about their beneficiaries dying before they do. Often, they leave their property to people considerably younger than they are—for example, their children. If a beneficiary dies before they do, they'll probably be able to modify their will, trust, or other document to name a new beneficiary. If they don't, the property will go to their residuary beneficiary (see below), who might, anyway, be the same person they would name as their alternate.

There can be alternate alternates, and indeed, as many layers of alternates as you care to create. Creating a second, third, or more layers of alternates can get quite complicated. There are many "ifs" to work out—"If Joe dies and if Jane dies and if Jack and Jill die..." then what? Usually resolving how to clearly draft a will or trust with layers of alternates requires the assistance of a lawyer.

E. RESIDUARY BENEFICIARIES

Whatever you decide about alternate beneficiaries, you should definitely name a residuary beneficiary or beneficiaries in your will, and in your living trust if you use one. As we've said, a residuary beneficiary receives all property left under a document that isn't received by other beneficiaries, either because no beneficiary was named to get the property, or they didn't survive to inherit it. Your residuary beneficiary is your backup, to be sure your property goes to someone you've chosen

If you prepare a living trust, the residuary beneficiary you name there receives only any remaining trust property not received by other beneficiaries. The residuary beneficiary you name in your will receives all property not left to other beneficiaries by any other method.

Example: Esther receives a surprise inheritance of $23,000 three weeks before she dies. She did not revise her will or living trust to leave this money to a primary beneficiary. The money is inherited by the residuary beneficiary of Esther's will.

A residuary beneficiary doesn't have to serve solely as a backup. Some people leave all of their property to their residuary. Others leave most to the residuary, naming only a few primary beneficiaries for modest gifts.

It's wise, and standard, to name an alternate residuary beneficiary so you have another backup in case your residuary beneficiary dies before you.

F. GIFTS SHARED BY MORE THAN ONE BENEFICIARY

Sometimes people want to leave shared gifts, particularly to their children. A shared gift is one left to two or more beneficiaries; each receives a portion of ownership of the property. This is different from leaving property with directions that it be sold and the profits divided between beneficiaries. With a shared gift, all the beneficiaries own the property itself.

Example: Virginia leaves her house to her three children—Alan, Patsy, and Philip—in equal shares. Each owns an undivided one-third interest in the house.

If you're considering leaving a shared gift, you should resolve some important questions. First, what percentage of ownership does each beneficiary receive? You should spell out the percentages in your will or trust. If you don't, it's generally presumed that you intended equal shares, but this rule isn't ironclad. There's no good reason to be silent on this matter. If you want a gift shared equally, say so.

The next issue is control of the property. Generally, the beneficiaries must agree how to handle their shared ownership. They may all want to keep the property, or decide to sell it and split the proceeds. But if the beneficiaries can't agree how to use the property, they may end up in court. In most states, any co-owner can go to court and force a sale, with the net proceeds divided by percentage of ownership.

If you don't think the beneficiaries can resolve any problems that arise, a shared gift is a bad idea. There's little you can do to forestall serious conflicts. You could try, by putting rules governing what the shared owners can do in your will or trust. For instance, you could specify that "The house cannot be sold unless all three of my children agree to the sale." But often other problems follow. If two kids want to sell the house, but one doesn't, who manages the house? Must it be rented at market value? Can the child who wants to keep the house live in it? If so, must that child pay the others rent? And what happens if one child dies? The difficulties of dealing with these types of complications mean it is rarely sensible to try to impose long-term control on shared gifts.

The final issue to consider is what happens if a beneficiary of a shared gift predeceases you. Here things can become quite complicated. To return once more to the house Virginia wants to leave to her three children, what are her options if she wants to name alternate beneficiaries?

- She can specify that a deceased beneficiary's share is to be divided between her surviving children.

- She can name three separate alternate beneficiaries, one for each child—for example, each of their spouses.

- She can provide that a deceased child's share is to be divided equally between that beneficiary's own children, or, if there are none between her surviving children.

- She can name another alternate beneficiary (a friend or other relative) to receive the interest of any child who dies before she does.

Juggling and resolving these types of contingencies can get confusing, especially if you want two or more layers of alternate beneficiaries. Still, many people want to work out having alternates for shared gifts, which, of course, is fine. If pinning down how it will work gets too tricky, see a lawyer—or consider making your alternate beneficiary plan for shared gifts less complicated.

INFORMING YOUR BENEFICIARIES

Once you've made your estate plan, do you want to tell some or all of your beneficiaries that you've left them property? Do you want to tell them what you've left them? There is no law requiring you to tell your beneficiaries anything. Indeed, if you chose, you can arrange for a dramatic, or melodramatic, reading of your will after your death, just as you've seen in bad movies. At the least, you may sensibly decide there are good personal reasons, such as potential family conflict, for you not to reveal how you're leaving your property. But if there's little or no risk of trouble, why keep your gifts a secret? By informing your beneficiaries of what they'll receive, you can enjoy the pleasures that sharing that knowledge can bring.

G. ESTABLISHING A SURVIVORSHIP PERIOD

A survivorship period requires that a beneficiary must survive you by a specified time period to inherit. The purpose of a survivorship period is to ensure that if the beneficiary dies soon after you do, the property will go to the alternate you've selected, rather than to the people the beneficiary chose to inherit his property.

Survivorship periods are commonly used in wills. Since probate takes months, you're not tying up your property by imposing a short survivorship period—45 to 60 days is common.

Using the same reasoning, establishing a survivorship period of more than a few weeks isn't usually desirable for property transferred by living trust, since a principal advantage of a living trust is that property can be transferred quickly to the new owners. (See Chapter 9.) There's no sense in setting up a living trust to allow quick transfer of property and then frustrating that result by requiring beneficiaries to wait many months to inherit.

H. EXPLANATIONS AND COMMENTARY ACCOMPANYING GIFTS

If you wish, you can provide a brief commentary when leaving a gift in a will or a living trust.

Example: I leave $40,000 to my business associate, Mildred Parker, who worked honestly and competently with me over the years, and cheerfully put up with my sporadic depressions and weirdnesses.

There are times, particularly in family situations, when an explanation of the reasons for your gifts can help avoid hurt feelings or family fights.

Example: I leave my house at 465 Merchant St., Miami, Florida, and all stocks and bonds I own as follows:

- 40% to my son Theodore Stein

- 40% to my daughter Sandra Stein Smith

- 20% to my son Howard Stein

I love all my children deeply and equally. I leave 20% to Howard because he received substantial family funds to go through medical school, so it's fair that my other two children receive more of my property now.

Another approach is to write a letter stating your views and feelings, and attach the letter to your will or living trust. If you have a lot to say, a letter is a better way to go than trying to include it all in your will or living trust. Including lengthy personal explanations in legal documents can render those documents confusing. Further, a will becomes a matter of public record and so would your comments. If you don't want to expose your sentiments to anyone who chooses to look at a probate court file, a letter protects your privacy.

Your letter isn't officially a part of a legal document, and has no legal effect. It is prudent for you to state in your letter that you understand this, to eliminate any possibility someone could claim you intended the letter to somehow modify the terms of your legal documents.

Short of libel, the scope of your remarks is limited only by your imagination. Some writers have expressed, at length and in their own chosen words, their love for a mate, children, and friend. By contrast, Benjamin Franklin left his son William, who was sympathetic to England during our Revolution, only some land in Nova Scotia. Franklin's will stated, "The fact he acted against me in the late war, which is of public notoriety, will account for my leaving him no more of an estate than he endeavored to deprive me of." And the German poet Heine wrote a will leaving his property to his wife on the condition that she remarry, so that "there will be at least one man to regret my death." William Shakespeare cryptically left his wife his "second best bed," a bequest that has intrigued scholars for centuries.

I. DISINHERITANCE

You can disinherit most people simply by not leaving them property. Indeed, "disinheritance" isn't the apt word, since no one except your wife (in common law states) and children (in some situations) have any legal claim on your property.

1. Disinheriting a Spouse

If you live in one of the 41 common law states or the District of Columbia, you cannot disinherit your spouse. (See Chapter 3, Section C.) These states allow a spouse to claim a significant portion of your estate despite your wishes, although many states do allow a spouse to waive these rights in a written marital property agreement.

By contrast, in community property states, a spouse has no legal rights to inherit any of the other spouse's property. Or, put another way, each spouse has the right to leave their one-half of the community property and all his or her separate property as he or she sees fit.

UNMARRIED COUPLES

Unmarried couples living together have no statutory rights to inherit any of each other's property, except lesbian or gay couples registered as domestic partners in Hawaii, Maine, or Vermont. (In California, registered domestic partners are covered by the community property system.) However, in any state, each member of an unmarried couple can leave his or her separate property to anyone he or she wants to, which of course can include the other person.

2. Disinheriting a Child

The rules for disinheriting a minor child are discussed in detail in Chapter 6, Section G. Here we briefly summarize them.

In all states, you have the power to disinherit any or all of your children, if you do so expressly. However, if you fail to mention a child in your will, that child may have a legal right to claim part of your property. Some states laws protect only children born after the will was written. Other states protect any child not mentioned in the will.

The goal of these laws is to prevent children from being unintentionally overlooked. You don't have to leave your children property as primary beneficiaries. The point is to establish that you considered each child when leaving property. Many spouses validly leave all their property to the other spouse, naming their children as alternate beneficiaries. This shows that the children weren't overlooked.

If you want to disinherit a child, you must state that explicitly in your will. There is no legal requirement that you state a reason, but you can if you wish.

LEAVING PEOPLE A MINIMAL AMOUNT

You may have heard that some lawyers recommend leaving a minimal amount, usually one dollar, to certain close relations. This is not legally necessary and is a bad idea. Doing so burdens your executor with trying to track down these beneficiaries, and then get them to sign a receipt for one dollar. And all this when they had no rights to any of your property to begin with.

---

3. No-Contest Clauses

A "no-contest clause" in a will or living trust is a device used to discourage beneficiaries of your estate plan from suing to void the plan and claiming they are entitled to more than you left them. Under a no-contest clause, a beneficiary who unsuccessfully challenges a will or living trust forfeits all his or her inheritance under that document.

No-contest clauses can be sensible if there's a risk that a beneficiary might challenge your will or living trust, claiming that you were incompetent or unduly influenced. The risk of losing all property left to him may by itself deter a potential challenger from suing.

In most situations, a no-contest clause isn't necessary, since there is no reasonable risk of lawsuit by a beneficiary. Also, you don't have to be "fair" when distributing your property. Absent fraud, duress, or mental incompetence, you can leave it however you want to, with the exceptions for your spouse or children noted above.

Potential will/living trust fights. See a lawyer if you fear that a beneficiary might contest your will or living trust. There may be a number of things you can do to establish that you are competent to make your estate plan and to protect your estate from lawsuits, or at least increase the odds that your side will prevail.

J. SIMULTANEOUS DEATH

Many couples, married or not, who leave their property to each other wonder what would happen to the property if they were to die at the same time. (Another common concern—what happens to children if both parents die simultaneously—is discussed in Chapter 6, Section A.) If a survivorship period is imposed on beneficiaries, that includes a spouse, so the issue is taken care of.

Example: Hermancia's and Ed's wills leave their property to each other. Each one's will imposes a 45-day survivorship period on all beneficiaries. Hermancia names their daughter Raquel as her alternate beneficiary. Ed names Raquel and his brother Malachy as his co-alternate beneficiaries, each to receive 50%.

Hermancia dies. Ed dies 25 days after she does. Because Ed did not survive 45 days after Hermancia, he never became owner of her property. It goes directly to Raquel. Malachy does not inherit any of the property originally owned by Hermancia. (He does, of course, inherit half the property owned by Ed.)

If no survivorship period is imposed, and you and your spouse die simultaneously, your property could pass to your spouse or mate, and then immediately to your spouse's inheritors. That might not be the result you want. To eliminate this possibility, you can use a "simultaneous death" clause, which provides that when it's difficult or impossible to tell which spouse died first, the property of each spouse or mate is disposed of as if he or she had survived the other.

How, you may ask, can simultaneous death clauses logically work? How can you be presumed to have outlived your spouse for your will's purposes and she also be presumed to have outlived you for her will's purpose? Yes, it is a logical paradox, but in the real world it works. Under the law, each estate is handled independently of the other. Each spouse's will is read as if the other spouse's will didn't exist. This allows both spouses to achieve the results each wants in the event of simultaneous death. As Oliver Wendell Holmes put it, "The life of the law has not been logic, it's been experience."

K. PROPERTY YOU GIVE AWAY BY WILL OR TRUST THAT YOU NO LONGER OWN AT YOUR DEATH

Before your estate can pay any cash gifts you leave, it must pay all your last debts and taxes, including estate taxes. After that, if your estate doesn't have enough money available to pay your cash gifts, there's trouble. This necessitates what's called an "abatement" in legalese. An abatement means a reduction of gifts when there isn't enough to go around. Specific provisions in your will governing how a shortfall of cash is to be handled will be enforced. Otherwise, the matter is normally resolved by your executor.

There's an obvious way to avoid this sort of nasty post-death mess—don't leave more cash than you're confident you'll have. And if your cash resources drop below this amount, revise your cash gifts. ■

6

CHILDREN

When you're working on your estate plan, the word "children" can have two meanings. The first is "minors"—people who are not yet 18. The second meaning is offspring of any age; parents who live long enough can have "children" who are in their 40s, 50s, or even older. This chapter focuses primarily on minor children because of the special problems inherent in planning for them. We also discuss ways to leave property to a young adult child when you're concerned that the child may not be sufficiently mature to handle money responsibly.

Most parents of minor children are understandably concerned about what will happen to their children if disaster strikes and the parents die unexpectedly. If both parents are raising the children, the major concern is usually simultaneous death of the parents. If you're a single parent and the other parent is deceased, has abandoned the child, or is unavailable for some other reason, you'll want to arrange for someone else to care for, and quite possibly, help and support the child if you die while the child is a minor.

Providing for your minor children if you die involves two distinct concerns:

1. Who will raise the children if you can't—that is, who will be each child's personal guardian?

2. How can you best provide financial support for your children? What money or property will be available? Who will handle and supervise it for the child's benefit? And what legal method is best for managing it?

These concerns are addressed in depth in this chapter.

This chapter does not deal with adult "children" in as much depth because you don't need to appoint a personal guardian for them, nor is a property guardian legally required. However, you may not want to allow your children to receive substantial amounts of property outright while they're still in their 20s or even early 30s. This chapter explains how you can impose mature adult supervision over gifts you leave to young adult children.

Finally, if you want to disinherit a child—not common, but it does happen—this chapter covers special rules you must follow.

REVISE YOUR ESTATE PLAN WHEN A CHILD IS BORN OR DIES

If, after preparing your estate plan, you have an additional child, revise your plan by providing for the new child. If you don't, that child has a legal right to inherit a portion of your property. (The exact percentage depends on state law.) You should also, of course, make sure that all property left to a deceased child is redirected to other beneficiaries.

A. NAMING SOMEONE TO TAKE CUSTODY OF YOUR MINOR CHILDREN

If two biological or adoptive parents are willing and able to care for a minor child, and one dies, normally the other has the legal right to assume sole custody. If the parents are married, or even if they are divorced, as long as both parents are cooperating to raise their children, this rule presents no problem. But what happens if both parents die? Or a sole parent dies?

If no parent is available, some other adult must be legally responsible for raising the child. This adult is called the child's "personal guardian." No personal guardian is required if the child is "emancipated," which means the child has achieved the legal status of an adult; normal grounds are marriage, military service, or factual independence validated by court order.

You must use your will to name your child's personal guardian. Except in a couple of states, you cannot use a living trust or any other document for this purpose. If you have minor children, this is an obvious reason why a will is essential.

It's important to understand that the person you name as a minor's personal guardian in a will doesn't actually become the legal guardian until approved by a court after your death. The judge has the authority to name someone else if the judge is convinced it is in the best interests of the child. In short, children are not property, and naming a personal guardian in a will doesn't have the same automatically binding effect as a provision leaving a lamp to someone. However, if no one contests your choice for your child's personal guardian, a court will almost certainly confirm this person. In practice, a court will reject an unopposed nominee only if there are obvious grave and provable reasons, such as alcoholism, a serious criminal background, or provable child abuse. As a responsible parent, we presume you wouldn't select a guardian with such problems.

1. Choosing the Personal Guardian

You may well know who your child's personal guardian should be. But this isn't always an easy question. We know people who've struggled hard to make the best choice. Keep in mind the obvious: You can't draft someone to parent your kids. Be sure any person you plan to name is ready, willing, and able to do the job.

You should always name an alternate personal guardian as well, in case your first choice is unable or unwilling to serve.

Where two parents are involved in raising their kids, they should agree on the person that they want to appoint—naming different people could result in a nasty conflict if both parents died simultaneously.

It's best not to name a couple as joint guardians, even if they will likely function that way. Doing this raises many potential problems, including what happens if the couple splits up. Better to simply name the member of the couple you rely on the most.

In many families today, children don't all share the same two biological parents, and you may want to name different guardians for different children. Naming different personal guardians for different children is certainly legal. A court would likely follow this arrangement, unless there's persuasive proof that it would be harmful to a child.

Example: Irene is a single parent with two sons, aged 14 and 15, from her first marriage, and a daughter, Bo, age four, from her second. Her first husband has never taken any interest in the children. Her second ex is a decent, though from Irene's view, well below superb, father to Bo, and has also tried to be a decent father to the boys. Irene's brother, Biff, is close to her sons, and she and they feel he would be the best personal guardian for them. But Biff isn't wild about raising a young child. Also, Irene recognizes that if she named Biff as guardian of Bo, and she died while Bo was a minor, the result would probably be a court fight with Bo's father, who would likely prevail. So Irene names her second ex as personal guardian of Bo, and Biff as guardian of her boys. She attaches a statement to her will explaining why she believes this is best for the children.

Choosing a personal guardian does not automatically mean you're also selecting that person to manage any money you leave for your children. Selection of an adult to manage a minor's property is discussed below in Section B. Here we simply want to note that if you're worried that the person you name as personal guardian isn't good with money, you can name someone else for the latter job. There are obvious risks of conflict in having one person have legal authority to raise a child and another to manage money used to support and educate the child. If you decide to divide authority between two people, be sure that both people you want to name are willing to accept their roles. If the two potential guardians genuinely accept this arrangement, your major problem is solved.

2. If You Don't Want the Other Parent to Become Personal Guardian

A parent raising a child may not want the other parent to get custody, for any of a number of reasons. Here are a couple of examples:

- I don't want my ex-husband, who I believe is dangerously mentally unstable, to get custody of my children if I die. How can I prevent him from becoming personal guardian?

- I have legal custody of my daughter and I've remarried. My wife is a far better mother to my daughter than my ex-wife, who mostly ignores her, and is occasionally mean to her. What can I do to try to make sure my present wife gets custody if I die?

There is no definitive answer to these types of questions. Assuming a contested case was presented to a court, a judge's decision would very likely turn on both the facts of each situation and the judge's own beliefs. A general rule is that one parent cannot succeed in appointing someone other than the other natural parent to be personal guardian, unless the second parent:

- has legally abandoned the child, or

- is unfit as a parent.

If the other parent seeks custody after your death, it's usually quite difficult to prove that the parent is unfit, absent serious problems such as

alcohol abuse, a history of child molestation or violence, or mental illness. Your negative opinion of the other parent is never enough, by itself, to prevent custody. If you want to name someone other than the other parent as personal guardian for your children, be sure that person knows that this may lead to a custody fight.

It's unlikely that anyone except the child's other parent would win custody against your wishes. For instance, if you name your best friend Betty to raise your children if you can't and Betty can be proved to be a caring adult, it's unlikely that someone else, such as the child's grandmother, or uncle, could gain custody over your choice.

It can be a good idea to attach a letter to your will explaining your choice for personal guardian. Here's an example of such a letter:

SAMPLE LETTER EXPLAINING YOUR CHOICE FOR GUARDIAN

I have nominated my companion, Peter N., to be the personal guardian of my daughter, Melissa, because I know he would be the best guardian for her. For the past six years, Peter has functioned as Melissa's parent, living with me and her, helping to provide and care for her, and loving her. She loves him and regards him as her father. She hardly knows her actual father, Tom D. She has not seen him for four years. He has rarely contributed to her support or taken any interest in her.

Date: January 15, 2006

[Signed by:] _Juanita R._

It is also possible to explain your choice of guardian in your will.

Potential custody fights. If you don't want the other biological parent to gain custody, it's wise to discuss the details of your situation with a lawyer who specializes in family law. If there's a disputed custody proceeding after your death, a judge has wide discretion in deciding how much weight, if any, to give to a written statement about your child's custody that you make before you die. A good lawyer should help guide you to prepare the most persuasive case you can. This might include preparing your best statement of why the other parent shouldn't get custody, and identifying people who will back up your statement by their court testimony, if necessary.

B. NAMING AN ADULT TO MANAGE YOUR CHILD'S PROPERTY

Minor children cannot own property outright, free of adult control, beyond a minimal amount—usually in the $2,500 to $5,000 range, depending on the state. This means there must be an adult legally responsible for all property owned by a child. This person may be called a "custodian," "trustee," or "property guardian," depending on the method you select for leaving property to your child. (See

Section C, below.) For now, let's simply call this adult your child's "property manager." If you have minor children, a vital part of your estate plan is selecting their property manager.

In addition, you may wish to choose an adult to manage any property you leave your younger adult children. You, like many parents, may not want property to be turned over to children when they become legal adults at age 18. If you wish, you can have that property supervised by a more mature person until the children become 25, or even 35 or older, and are (presumably) more responsible.

TAXATION OF A CHILD'S INCOME

Income received by a minor child age 14 or over is taxed at the normal income tax rate for that child. But income to a child 13 or under can be taxed differently. Under the "kiddie tax," all unearned income over $850 per year that is received by a child younger than 14 is taxed at the highest of the parents' income tax rates. (Unearned income is income from investments, interest, or other sources.) In contrast, earned income (from wages or other work) of a child under 14 is taxed at the child's rate, which is usually 15%. This kiddie tax has eliminated income tax incentives for parents, or others, to transfer income-producing property from themselves, and their own high tax brackets, to a child younger than 14.

---

1. Leaving Property to Your Spouse for the Benefit of Your Children

One alternative for parents of minor or young adult children is for each to leave property outright to the other spouse to be used for their child's benefit. This approach makes sense if the parents trust each other, but obviously isn't a good choice if the other parent is not available or financially imprudent. Even if you leave all property to your spouse, it's always wise to name a backup child's property manager. This takes care of the remote possibility that you and your spouse might die simultaneously.

2. Choosing a Property Manager for Your Child

When deciding on your minor child's property manager, here's a sensible rule: Name the same person you choose to have custody of the children (their personal guardian) unless there are compelling reasons to name someone else. For example, choose a different person if you're concerned that the personal guardian doesn't have sufficient financial or practical experience to manage property prudently.

You should also name an alternate property manager in case your first choice can't serve. Again, name the same person you designated as the child's alternate personal guardian unless there are strong reasons to choose someone else.

The duty of the property manager is to manage the property you leave for your children honestly and in their best interests. This means using it to pay for normal living expenses and health and education needs. If you pick someone with integrity and common sense, your child's property will probably be in good hands. If substantial funds are involved, the property manager can pay for help to handle the more technical aspects of financial management. For instance, it's routine for a property manager to get an accountant's help for complicated tax and accounting matters.

Obviously, it's important to name a property manager who is sincerely willing to do a job that may, depending on the ages of your children, last for many years. It's also wise to choose someone that the other members of your family respect and accept. You want your children to inherit money, not family arguments.

Except as a last resort, don't name a bank or other financial institution to be property manager. Most banks won't manage accounts they consider too small to be worth the bother; as a rough rule, this means accounts worth less than $250,000. And even for larger estates, they charge hefty fees for every little act. In addition, it's our experience that banks are simply too impersonal to properly meet your own child's needs. Far better, we think, to name a human being you trust than a bureaucracy. But if you can't find any adult who's willing and competent to be your child's property manager, normally it's better to name a financial institution than to make no choice at all, which amounts to leaving the matter up to a court. You'll need to check around with different banks and private trust companies to see which ones will accept the job and seem most likely to do it for reasonable fees.

3. Selecting Different Property Managers for Different Minor Children

In some situations, you may want to name different property managers for different minor children. Doing this is legal. And unlike naming a personal guardian, it doesn't require court approval.

C. HOW YOUR CHILDREN'S PROPERTY SHOULD BE MANAGED

Your next task is to choose which legal method you want to use to leave property to your minor or young adult children. There are four basic options for leaving property to minor children:

- a custodianship, under the Uniform Transfers to Minors Act
- a child's trust
- a family pot trust, or
- a property guardianship.

For young adults between the ages of 18 to 25, depending on the state, your only choice is a child's trust.

1. The Uniform Transfers to Minors Act

You can leave gifts to your child (or to any minor) in your will or living trust under what is called "the Uniform Transfers to Minors Act" (UTMA), a law that has been adopted by every state except South Carolina and Vermont. Here your child's property manager is called a "custodian." The custodian's management ends when the minor reaches age 18 to 25, depending on state law.

Here's how leaving a gift using the Uniform Transfers to Minors Act works. In either your will or living trust, you identify the property and the minor you are leaving it to. You then appoint the adult custodian to be responsible for supervising the property until the age the child must receive the property (see the chart on the following page). You provide that the custodian is to act "under the [your state's] Uniform Transfers to Minors Act." You can also name a "successor custodian" in case your first choice can't do the job.

The custodian has great discretion to control and use the property in the child's interest. Among the specific powers the UTMA gives the custodian are the right, without court approval, "to collect, hold, manage, invest, and reinvest" the property, and to spend as much of it "as the custodian considers advisable for the use and benefit of the minor." The custodian must also keep records so that tax returns can be filed on behalf of the minor and must otherwise act as a prudent person would when in control of another's property. A custodian does not,

however, need to file a separate income tax return. The custodian is entitled to be paid reasonable compensation from the gift property. No court supervision of the custodian is required.

Each gift under the Uniform Transfers to Minors Act can be made to only one minor, with only one person named as custodian. A child who reaches the age the Act specifies for termination gets the remaining balance of the gift. The custodian must also furnish an accounting of all funds distributed.

A limitation of the UTMA is that, in most states, custodianships end at age 21, and even at 18 in others. Particularly if your children are already teenagers and your estate is substantial, you may want property management to last longer. If so, you may wish to use child's trusts, which allow you to designate an older age at which property management ends. (See Section 2, below).

STATES THAT HAVE ADOPTED THE UNIFORM TRANSFERS TO MINORS ACT

State	Gift Must Be Released When Minor Reaches Age:		State	Gift Must Be Released When Minor Reaches Age:	
Alabama	21		New Mexico	21	
Alaska	18	(can be extended up to 21)	New York	21	
Arizona	21		North Carolina	21	(can be reduced to no lower than 18)
Arkansas	21	(can be reduced to no lower than 18)	North Dakota	21	
California	18	(can be extended up to 21)	Ohio	21	(can be reduced to no lower than 18)
Colorado	21				
Connecticut	21		Oklahoma	18	
Delaware	21		Oregon	21	(can be extended up to 25)
District of Columbia	18	(can be extended up to 21)	Pennsylvania	21	(can be extended up to 25)
Florida	21		Rhode Island	21	
Georgia	21		South Dakota	18	
Hawaii	21		Tennessee	21	(can be extended up to 25)
Idaho	21		Texas	21	
Illinois	21		Utah	21	
Indiana	21		Virginia	18	(can be extended to 21)
Iowa	21		Washington	21	
Kansas	21		West Virginia	21	
Kentucky	18		Wisconsin	21	
Maine	18	(can be extended up to 21)	Wyoming	21	
Maryland	21				
Massachusetts	21				
Michigan	18	(can be extended upto 21)			
Minnesota	21				
Mississippi	21				
Missouri	21				
Montana	21				
Nebraska	21				
Nevada	18	(can be extended up to 25)			
New Hampshire	21				
New Jersey	21	(can be reduced to no lower than 18)			

STATES THAT HAVE NOT ADOPTED THE UTMA

At present, the UTMA has not been adopted in South Carolina or Vermont.

Even if you live in one of these two states, it is theoretically possible for you to use the UTMA in your will, if the minor or custodian or gift property itself resides in an UTMA state when you die. But for most parents, all these are and will likely remain in the state where they live. Even if one of them is now in an UTMA state, you don't know where it will be when you die. Committing yourself to this kind of updating is an unnecessary burden, because you can easily use a child's trust instead.

2. Trusts for Children

There are two major types of trusts you can use to provide property management for property you leave to your children: a "child's trust" or a "family pot trust." (Other, more sophisticated trusts, such as a "special needs" trust for a disabled child, or a "spendthrift" trust for a child who simply can't handle money, are discussed in Chapter 25.) With a child's trust, you leave specified property to one child; that property is held separately from any property you leave for other children. If you have more than one child, you can create a child's trust for each child. With a family pot trust, you leave property collectively for two or more children in one common fund; any amount of trust property can be spent for any child.

A trust is a legal entity under which an adult, called a "trustee," has the responsibility of handling money or property for someone else—in this case, your child or children. So if you create a trust, your child's property manager is called the "trustee" or "successor trustee." The trust document sets out the trustee's responsibilities and the beneficiary's rights.

A child's trust or family pot trust can be established either by will or living trust. If established as part of a living trust, the property placed in trust avoids probate. If you use your will, the property must go through probate before it's turned over to the trust.

Both a child's trust and a family pot trust are legal in all states. All property you leave to a beneficiary for whom a trust is established will be managed under the terms of the trust document. If you create either type of trust, any property inherited by a minor beneficiary will be managed by the trustee until the beneficiary reaches the age when he or she is entitled to receive the trust property outright.

The trustee's powers are specified in the trust document. Normally, the trustee may use trust assets for the education, medical needs, and living expenses of the beneficiary or, with a pot trust, beneficiaries. With a family pot trust, the trustee doesn't have to spend the same amount on each beneficiary; this flexibility is one of the pot trust's main advantages.

With a child's trust, you can select the age the beneficiary must reach before trust property is turned over to him or her. So child's trusts are commonly used when a large amount of money is left for a child, and the giver doesn't want that child to inherit the property outright before a mature age, perhaps 30 or 35. A child's trust can also be used for property you leave to minors or young adults who aren't your children—your grandchildren, for example.

⚠ **A child's trust shouldn't last a lifetime.** If you want a child's trust to last beyond age 30 or 35, you need to face the likelihood that their problem goes deeper than their youth, and they may never be able to manage their own finances. You may need a more complicated trust. (See Chapter 25.)

Most family pot trusts last until the youngest beneficiary becomes 18. By that age, with all beneficiaries legal adults, it makes less sense to treat them all as one family unit. But you could have a pot trust last until the youngest beneficiary becomes 21, or even older, if you're sure that you want to keep your children's property lumped together this long. Also, some pot trusts are drafted so that they convert to individual trusts when the youngest child reaches 18.

A pot trust is most often used by parents with younger children. These parents want to keep family money together, capable of being spent on any child as needs require. The trustee, like a parent, decides how much money shall be spent on each child. If one child has a serious illness or other extraordinary needs, the maximum family resources possible are there for him or her.

Although family pot trusts clearly have the appeal of flexibility, they can make the trustee's job tougher as compared with a child's trust, where each child's property is legally separate from the trust property of other children. With a pot trust, the trustee may literally be called on to choose between one child's need for expensive orthodonture and another's desire to go to a pricey college.

If there is a wide age gap between children, a pot trust is less desirable. If one child is 16 and another is two, and the trust ends when the youngest becomes 18, the oldest must wait until age 32 to receive any property outright, which may not be what the parents want. Further, it's likely to be harder to balance needs between children of widely varying ages. How much of the pot should be spent for the eldest's college needs? How much retained for the youngest? When children are closer together in age, these types of troubling differences are less likely to arise.

Some parents whose children are young and close in age decide a pot trust is best for the children now. Then, when a child grows older—say the eldest reaches 16—the parents (assuming they are still alive) may decide to pull property for that child out of the pot trust and create a new child's trust or an UTMA custodianship.

> ### IF A CHILD NEVER INHERITS PROPERTY OR RECEIVES IT WHEN OLDER
>
> If you arrange for property management for a minor or young adult, but that person never inherits the property, no damage is done. Likewise, if the beneficiary has already passed the age at which management was slated to end, the management provisions for that beneficiary are simply ignored. For instance, suppose you identify a favorite niece to take property as an alternate beneficiary, and create a child's trust for that property until the niece turns 30. If the niece never inherits the property because your primary beneficiary survives you, no child's trust will ever be established for her. Similarly, if the niece does inherit the property, but is 31 when you die, she will receive the property outright, and the trust provisions will never take effect.

3. Which Is Better for You, the UTMA or a Child's Trust?

We've already discussed some key factors in deciding which method is most appropriate for your family. But because this issue can be so important, let's examine it in more detail.

As a general rule, the less valuable the property involved and the more mature the child, the more appropriate the UTMA is because it is simpler and often cheaper, from a tax point of view, than a trust. There are a several reasons for this.

• Because the UTMA is built into state law, financial institutions know about it and should make it easy for the custodian to carry out property management duties. In states where the UTMA allows for property management until 21 or 25, setting up an UTMA custodianship can be particularly sensible if you leave property worth less than $100,000 to your child. Normally, amounts of this size will be fairly rapidly expended for the child's education and living needs, and are simply not large enough to tie up beyond age 21.

- Another factor can be the age of the child at the time you create your will or living trust. If your daughter is now two years old, it will obviously take far more money to support her until adulthood than if she is currently 17. For instance, $100,000 left to a two-year-old may be used up before she gets to college, but $100,000 left to a 17-year-old should at least cover most, if not all, of her college costs or whatever else she plans to do in the next four years.

- Using the UTMA can also be desirable because trust income tax rates are now higher than individual rates. (See Chapter 17, Section G.) Annual income above $1,500 retained in a child's trust at the close of its tax year is taxed at higher rates than is property subject to the UTMA, which is taxed at the child's individual tax rate. Any trust income spent for the child's benefit during the year will be taxed at the child's rate, not the trust rate. But for income held in the trust, a higher tax rate applies.

- A child's trust is desirable when you want to extend the age at which a beneficiary receives property to well beyond when that child becomes a legal adult. As a rough cutoff point, if you're leaving more than $100,000 to a child, a child's trust is desirable.

Unlike UTMA custodianships, with a child's trust no age limit is imposed by state law. With a family pot trust any termination age is theoretically possible, but as we've discussed, they usually end when the youngest child turns 18, so they also aren't suitable for imposing longer age limits on beneficiaries. By contrast, child's trusts can be, and often are, established for young adults already older than 18 or 21, when a parent (or other older adult) believes the child is not now a good bet for responsibly handling property.

Example: Marilyn, a single parent, creates a living trust leaving her estate, worth $720,000, equally to her two children, Todd, age 25, and Carolyn, age 27. Carolyn has always been frugal, if not parsimonious, with money. She has been saving money from the time of her first allowance. Todd is the flip side of the coin. He runs through whatever cash he has at the blink of an eye and, from Marilyn's perspective, often goes beyond generosity to recklessness with money. So in her living trust, Marilyn leaves Carolyn her half of Marilyn's estate outright. However, Todd's half is left in a "child's trust," with Marilyn's brother—a stable type if ever there was one—as trustee. Todd will not receive any trust property outright until he becomes 35. By that age, Marilyn hopes he will have become sensible enough to manage a large amount of money.

4. Naming a Property Guardian

It is rarely wise to leave property to your children to be supervised by a property guardian. There are several reasons:

- The property must go through your will, which means it will go through probate.

- Property guardians are often subject to court review, reporting requirements, and strict rules as to how they can expend funds. All this usually requires hiring a lawyer and paying significant fees, but in our view does little to guarantee that the property manager will do a good job. And those lawyer fees, of course, come out of the property left to benefit the minor.

- Property guardianship must end at age 18.

All this said, your will should still name a property guardian to serve as a backup to handle any property that for some reason isn't covered by a trust or custodianship.

Specifically, naming a property guardian in your will provides a supervision mechanism in case:

• Your minor children earn substantial money after you die, or receive a large gift or inheritance that doesn't, itself, name a property manager.

• You and your spouse leave property to each other to use for your children, naming the children as alternative or residuary beneficiaries without bothering to add an UTMA designation or establish a child's trust or pot trust. If both spouses die simultaneously, the property will be managed by the property guardian.

• You failed to include in an UTMA custodianship, child's trust, or pot trust some property you want your children to inherit. This can occur because of oversight or, more likely, because you didn't yet own the property when you established your will or living trust and didn't amend that document later.

Creating a child's trust, pot trust, or a custodianship under your state's UTMA is really quite simple to do, so normally the children's property guardian will be used only for the backup purposes listed above. However, if you want to postpone estate planning or keep it to the bare minimum, it is far wiser to name a property guardian than ignore the issue altogether. Having your minor child's property supervised by a property guardian you name in your will is certainly preferable to having a judge appoint someone for the job. So, for example, a young couple, both healthy and unlikely to die for decades, may not want to deal with other supervision methods now. But if they do both die, they don't want a court deciding who'll manage the property they leave for their children. So, they create wills, where each names a property guardian to manage property for their children's benefit if both die simultaneously.

5. Comparison of the Four Major Ways to Leave a Child or Young Adult Property

On the next page is a chart that summarizes the rules for and reasons to use each of the four major methods for leaving gifts to your minor or young adult children.

LEAVING GIFTS TO YOUR MINOR OR YOUNG ADULT CHILDREN

	Gift Under UTMA	Child's Trust Guardian	Property Pot Trust	Family
Availability	All states but SC and VT	All states	All states	All states
Amount of Property	If maximum age for release of gift is 18 in your state, then use is often best for older children or for smaller gifts under $50,000 (depending on current age of child). If age for release is 21 or 25, useful for gifts of $100,000 or more, especially to make sure money will be managed to last through college	Often good for gifts of any amount if UTMA age for release of gift in your state is 18, or if UTMA isn't applicable in your state. Often good for gifts in excess of $100,000 if UTMA applies in your state and age for release of gift is 21 or perhaps even 25	Last resort no matter what the amount	Any amount
Paperwork	No trust tax returns required, but minor must file a yearly return based on money actually received. Custodian must give accounting when property turned over to child	Trustee must file yearly income tax returns for trust. Retained trust income over $1,500 taxed at higher rate than child's individual rate	Usually substantial because reports must be presented to court	Trustee must file yearly income tax return for trust. Trust income over $1,500 kept in trust is taxed at higher rate than any child's individual rate
Court Supervision	None	None	Guardian must make regular reports to court	None
Termination	In most states, custodian must turn over property to child at age specified or by statute, usually 18–21 (25 in CA, AL, NV, OR, RI, TN)	You specify the age at which the minor gets control of the trust property	Guardian must turn property over to child at age 18	Usually, when youngest child reaches age 18 or 21
Uses of Property	Custodian has broad statutory power to use property for child's living expenses, health needs, and education	Trustee normally has power to use any of child's trust property for minor's needs for living expenses, health needs, and education	Heavily limited and regulated by state law	Trustee can spend any trust property for any beneficiary

D. TAX SAVING EDUCATIONAL INVESTMENT PLANS

Federal law provides two different plans you can use to save for a child's education. (You can use them for other young relatives, too.) If you establish one of these plans, future educational expenses should in theory eat up less of your own estate. However, choosing the best plan is not always simple. Both types of plans have drawbacks, and even after you choose the type of plan you'll have some investment decisions to make. To make these choices, you'll need to do some fiscal homework.

1. 529 Plans

A 529 plan is a tax-free investment account established to pay for the higher education expenses of a named beneficiary. The beneficiary must be a "family member," so in addition to your own children, you can use this type of plan for a grandchild, favorite niece or nephew, or other young relation.

a. How 529 Plans Save on Taxes

Income accumulates in a 529 plan free of taxes. Even better, no income tax is assessed on money paid from a 529 plan for the beneficiary's higher education expenses. (Qualified expenses include tuition, books, fees, supplies, and equipment necessary to attend college, graduate school, or an approved vocational institution. Authorized expenses can also include special services for a disabled student.)

For any one beneficiary, you can contribute up to $12,000 per year free from gift tax. (Contributions can be made only in cash.) A couple can give up to $24,000 per year. Any amount over those limits given to one account within a year is subject to federal gift tax. (See Chapter 15, Section A.) However, you can contribute up to $60,000

in one year ($120,000 for both spouses) and face no tax if you live five more years, and make no additional contributions during those five years. If a beneficiary does not attend college, you can name a new beneficiary from the eligible family group. But if you or the beneficiary ever withdraw money from a 529 plan for non-educational purposes, taxes and penalties apply.

b. Choosing a 529 Plan

These plans are called "529" plans because they were created by that section of the Internal Revenue Code. (Sometimes they're also called "qualified tuition programs.") But state law controls the plans, and you can only invest in a state-authorized plan. Each state has a separate plan, managed by an investment company or companies selected by that state. Managers range from TIAA-CREF to Vanguard to J. P. Morgan to various lesser-known financial institutions.

Some state plans allow you to invest only if you live in that state, but most states allow anyone to invest in their plan. (About half the states allow residents to deduct state-plan contributions from their state income tax, which could be an incentive to buy a homegrown plan.) You can invest in more than one 529 plan if you like—and indeed, there is a rather bewildering array of plans to choose from.

Whatever plan or plans you choose, you are basically investing in securities—stocks and bonds. But some states' 529 managers have a far more "aggressive" (risky) investment strategy than do managers of other states' plans. So you'll need to do some homework before selecting a 529 plan that's right for you.

c. Possible Drawbacks of 529 Plans

There can be serious drawbacks to 529 plans. The first of these is high fees. Investors pay annual expenses for management of 529 funds. Many funds' annual administrative charges exceed 2%, significantly higher than for other types of investments. Before you select a 529 plan, investigate all management fees—some can be well hidden. It's also important to check out the plan's disclosure rules: How easy will it be for you to find out how the company is actually handling your money?

Second, each state offers its own plan and these plans vary dramatically. Some state plans exempt withdrawn funds from state income taxes, others do not. Some states penalize its citizens if they invest in another state's plan. Finally, and crucially, the types of allowed investments vary widely among state plans.

For many, the biggest drawback of a 529 plan is limited investment choices. With a 529 plan, you can invest only in the options allowed by the state, which could be just one or two mutual funds. Some people prefer to put money for a young person's education in accounts that allow them to select whatever investments they think are wisest. Commonly, these folks make a gift to a child under The Uniform Transfers to Minors Act (UTMA) and name one parent as custodian (manager) for that gift. (See Section C, above, for more information.) However, money earned in an UTMA account is subject to income tax, and in some circumstances it may also reduce the child's eligibility for other forms of financial aid. So when deciding between a 529 plan and an UTMA gift, you must determine whether investment freedom outweighs other costs. If you need help, a good accountant or other financial adviser can help you with this analysis.

Because 529 plans are essentially securities investments, they come with the stock market pitfalls we've all become aware of. As the legendary Wall Street investor Bernard Baruch observed, the only thing certain about the stock market is that "prices will fluctuate." Still, 529 accounts somehow remain popular; tens of billions of dollars have been placed in these accounts to date.

2. Coverdell Accounts

With a Coverdell account (formerly an Educational IRA), you can contribute up to $2,000 per year, though contribution amounts phase out for folks with six-figure incomes. Further, this $2,000 limit is the total amount that can be set aside in any one year for any one beneficiary. In other words, three different family members cannot each contribute $2,000 per year for one beneficiary. Combined, they can contribute no more than $2,000.

Contributions are not tax deductible when you make them. However, money in the account is not taxed when (or if) it grows, and no tax is due when you make qualified withdrawals from the account to pay for a child's education expenses. (In this way, a Coverdell account functions much like a Roth IRA.)

A parent managing a Coverdell account can use the money for any investment she desires. Investments are not restricted as they are in 529 plans.

While the $2,000 limit restricts the appeal of a Coverdell account, it may be the right plan for some. For example, these accounts can work well for families with young children and not much money: Each year, for each child, the parents put whatever they can afford into a Coverdell account—up to $2,000 per child. At that rate, the total saved could be quite helpful when a child attends college (even if the money wouldn't foot the entire bill for Stanford or Princeton). They can also be useful for grandparents or other relatives who want to contribute something toward a child's education while you invest in a 529 account, or save in other ways for higher education costs.

E. NAMING CHILDREN AS BENEFICIARIES OF LIFE INSURANCE

Some may think we've put the legal cart before the financial horse here—all this discussion about how to leave property to your children before any talk of how to acquire some valuable property to begin with. Well, this is a book on how to dispose of an estate, not about how to acquire one. Indeed, if we were masters of that, maybe we wouldn't have bothered writing the book. So all we can offer here is some general advice.

If you don't have the luxury of putting significant amounts aside, the best way to be sure cash will be available for the children if you die is to purchase some term life insurance. Term is the cheapest form of life insurance. Younger parents can obtain a significant amount of coverage for relatively low cost, for the obvious reason that statistically they are unlikely to die soon, so the risk to the insurance company is low. (Life insurance is discussed in depth in Chapter 12.)

If you name your children as beneficiaries, or alternate beneficiaries, of your policy, and you die while the children are minors, the insurance company cannot legally turn over the proceeds directly to them. If you haven't arranged for another method of adult supervision over the proceeds, court proceedings will be needed to confirm the children's property guardian. This means this property guardian can become enmeshed in the time-consuming court reporting requirements state laws typically impose. It also means the property guardian can only spend money under the terms of state law.

Here are your options for avoiding problems:

- Name the children as policy beneficiaries and name a custodian under the UTMA. Most insurance companies permit this and have forms for it. Essentially, you fill out a separate form for each minor, providing the usual UTMA information—the beneficiary's and the custodian's name, state, and age of termination, if you get to choose. If you want the proceeds to go to more than one child, you'll need to specify the percentage each one receives.

- Leave the proceeds to your child or children using a child's trust or a pot trust as part of a living trust. You name the living trust (or the trustee, if that's what the insurance company prefers) as the policy beneficiary in the living trust. In the trust, you name minors as beneficiaries of any insurance proceeds that trust receives and create the child's or pot trust to handle those proceeds. You'll need to give a copy of your living trust to the insurance company.

It may not be possible to leave insurance proceeds to a child's trust established by a will. Some insurance companies balk at this, on the grounds the trust won't come into existence until you die, and the policy beneficiary must be in existence when named. Rather than try to persuade an insurance company that this can be done, better to use the UTMA or create a living trust to achieve your goals. A living trust avoids this problem because the trust is effective as soon as you create it.

F. LEAVING PROPERTY TO CHILDREN WHO ARE NOT YOUR OWN

If you want to leave property to minor or young adult children who aren't your own, you have the following choices:

- Leave the gift outright to the child's parent or legal guardian, and rely on the parent to use the gift for the benefit of the child.

- Leave the gift in your will or living trust through the Uniform Transfers to Minors Act. (The Act is discussed in Section C, above.) This is best suited for gifts under $100,000.

- Leave the gift through your living trust or will, by creating a child's trust for that gift. You can create a child's trust for any young adult beneficiary who you believe is not presently capable of managing property wisely. You name the trustee of this child's trust, to manage all property in it. Doing this makes sense for large gifts—roughly, above $100,000. This plan can make good sense for gifts to grandchildren, particularly if the trustee is the child's parent and will supervise that child's trust.

Example: John, an elderly widower, wants to leave some antique furniture from his living trust to his 13-year-old grandniece Sally. He decides to make the gift using his state's Uniform Transfers to Minors Act. He names Sally's mother, Mary, to be the custodian. Her husband Fred is the alternate custodian. In his living trust, John makes the following gift: "Sally Earners shall be given the following furniture: my Hoosier cabinet, my two oriental rugs, and my three stained glass lamps; Mary Earners is to be custodian under the Minnesota Uniform Transfers to Minors Act. If Mary Earners is unable to serve, or continue serving, as custodian, the successor custodian shall be Fred Earners."

- The least desirable method is to leave the gift outright in your will. If the child is a minor when you die, court proceedings will be necessary to appoint a property guardian to supervise the gift. And since you are not the child's parent, you can't even appoint or suggest a property guardian for him or her in your will.

G. DISINHERITANCE

To an outsider, it may seem sad that a parent would want to disinherit a child, but it's surely been known to happen. Whatever the reasons, it's legal for a parent to do so.

At the same time, legal rules protect children, and children of a deceased child, from being accidentally disinherited. The legalese for accidentally overlooked children is "pretermitted heirs." In most states, your children have a statutory

right to inherit from you if you unintentionally leave them out of your will or fail to make one. Grandchildren do not have any statutory right to inherit if their parent (your child) is still alive, so there is no need to disinherit them if you don't want them to inherit. However, children of a deceased child (your grandchildren) may have the same inheritance rights as that child.

Special rule for Floridians. The Florida Constitution (Art. 10, § 4) prohibits the head of a family from leaving his residence in his will to someone other than spouse or child, if either exist.

If you want to disinherit a child, you should specifically state that in your will. You can also achieve a functional disinheritance by leaving a child a miniscule amount of property in your will. But do not try to disinherit a child simply by omitting that child's name from your will. If a child's name is omitted, it may not be clear whether you meant to disinherit that child or whether you accidentally overlooked that child. As stated, "overlooked children" have statutory inheritance rights in most states.

Even if you transfer all your property by a living trust and want to disinherit a child, you must use a will to accomplish that. The reason is simple: some state laws require disinheritance to be accomplished by a will, and only by a will.

Similarly, the laws of each state protect your children who are born after your will is made ("afterborn children") by entitling them to a share of your estate. How much a child gets depends on whether you leave a spouse and how many other children you have.

What if you provide for your children outside your will—by leaving them property from your living trust, for example—but didn't mention them in your will? They could, at least in theory, claim to be accidentally overlooked heirs and demand additional shares of your estate. In defining whether a child is overlooked, and therefore entitled to receive a share of your estate, some state's laws specifically refer to omitting a child from a "will." Read literally, these statutes don't allow property left to a child by a living trust (or other method) to be considered to determine if a child has been overlooked. Of course, given the purpose of the pretermitted heir statutes—to protect children from being accidentally disinherited—it's senseless to read the statute so literally. But who says the law can't be senseless?

So, to be absolutely safe, even if you generously provide for your children outside of your will, you should list the names of all your children (and children of a deceased child) in your will and make some provision for them.

Remember, for the "pretermitted heir" issue to become a problem, a child must file a lawsuit contesting your will and estate plan. If you trust that your children aren't going to sue, you don't have to worry about this.

H. CHILDREN CONCEIVED AFTER A PARENT DIES

Rapidly advancing medical technology now makes it possible for a child to be conceived after the biological mother or father dies. (In legal terms, these are known as "posthumously" conceived children.) If sperm or embryos are frozen before a father's death and later used to begin a pregnancy, a child could be born to a father who has been dead for years. Similarly, a fertilized embryo could be carried by another woman well after the embryo donor's death.

Complications from this development have already made it to courts in a handful of states, with inconsistent results. For example, a Massachusetts court ruled that twins conceived through artificial insemination using a late husband's sperm could be entitled to inherit from his estate under the state's

intestacy laws. However, in similar circumstances, an Arizona court ruled that its inheritance laws excluded a child conceived after a father's death.

The rights of a posthumously conceived child may be important for reasons other than inheritance—for instance, the surviving parent may want the baby to qualify for government or other benefits that come only with being the child of the deceased parent.

California has taken the lead in adopting laws governing children conceived after a parent's death. Specifically, California law provides that a child conceived after death will be deemed to be the child of the deceased person and born during his or her lifetime if it is proved by clear and convincing evidence that:

- the decedent specified in writing that his or her genetic material should be used for posthumous conception of a child

- the writing is signed by the decedent and at least one witness

- the person designated by the decedent to use the genetic material was the spouse or registered domestic partner of the decedent (or another person specifically named in the document)

- written notice was given to the decedent's executor, within four months of the decedent's death, that the decedent's genetic material was available for posthumous conception, and

- the child was conceived within two years of the date of issuance of decedent's death certificate.

(Ca. Prob. Code, Section 249.5.)

Clearly, this is a rapidly changing area of law, as well as technology. If you are planning for a posthumously conceived child, you'll want to consider what his or her property rights will be. You'll need to know your state's law (if any) on the subject, as well as figure out what you think is best. It's essential that you consult a knowledgeable estate planning lawyer to discuss these matters. ■

7

WILLS

A will is what many people think of when they first consider estate planning. This makes sense. Everyone should have a will, whether or not they make a more extensive estate plan. And quite a number of people decide that a will is all the planning they need, at least for the time being.

As you undoubtedly know, a will specifies who gets property covered by that document when you die. A will can also serve other vital purposes, such as appointing a personal guardian to raise your minor children if you and the other parent aren't available.

Property left by a will must normally go through probate. As we've mentioned, probate is usually costly and burdensome. So a substantial portion of this book is devoted to explaining how to avoid this process. (Probate is discussed in more detail in Chapter 8.) However, despite the downside of probate, every estate plan should at least include a "backup" will to cover things that probate-avoidance devices don't take care of.

A. A WILL AS THE CENTERPIECE OF YOUR ESTATE PLAN

Many people reasonably decide to make a will the centerpiece—or even, in some cases, the only piece—of their estate plan. They decide that, for the foreseeable future, a will accomplishes their estate planning goals. They can sensibly postpone more complicated, and perhaps more costly, estate planning work. You may be this kind of person if:

- No matter what your age or health, you simply don't want the bother of more extensive estate planning. Quite a few people say, "Yes, I guess I should probably do full-scale estate planning, but I never seem to get around to it, so I'd better at least make a will now and think about the full-scale plan later." After all, a will achieves the basic goal of distributing your property as you see fit, with as little disturbance to you as possible. Sure, a will is likely to lead to probate, but the goal

of probate avoidance, as smart as it is, should never obscure the more important goal of seeing to it that your property goes to the people and organizations you want to receive it.

- You're healthy and, statistically, unlikely to die for decades. If you just want to be certain your basic wishes for your property are carried out in the very unlikely event you die unexpectedly, a will achieves this goal with considerably less paperwork than a living trust. And as you acquire property, and people close to you are born and die, it can be a lot easier to make a new will than to amend a living trust.

- Your primary estate planning goal is to ensure, to the best of your abilities, that if you die, your minor children are well cared for. A will allows you to name a personal guardian (something that, in most all states, can't be done by any other document), while also allowing you to create a method for adult supervision of any property you leave to your children. Years later, of course, if you accumulate considerable property, you may want to engage in more thorough estate planning.

B. A BACKUP WILL WITH A COMPREHENSIVE ESTATE PLAN

If you prepare a thorough estate plan and arrange to avoid probate for all your property do you still need a will? Yes. It's always desirable to have at least a simple will, which we call a "backup" will, as part of your estate plan for one or probably more of the following reasons:

- **To leave property generally best left by will.** Some types of property are not suitable to leave by living trust, and often don't work well with other probate-avoidance devices either. The most common example is your car. Living trusts do not work well for cars, because most insurance companies are unwilling to insure a car owned by a trust; the companies claim they can't tell who is authorized to transfer the car. Occasionally, another probate-avoidance device can be used for a car—owning it in joint tenancy, or holding title in a transfer-on-death registration. (See Chapter 11, Section E.) But most people simply leave their car or cars as part of their will property.

Similarly, if you can leave your frequent flyer miles, you should do so by will. Your miles aren't the type of asset that can be transferred easily to a living trust or left by other means. Of course, first you'll need to check with the airline, to be sure that you can leave your miles to a beneficiary. Most frequent flyer programs do allow this, to the surprise of many flyers. In your will, you simply list the airline and your account number, and name a beneficiary for that property.

- **To dispose of suddenly acquired property.** Anyone may end up acquiring valuable property at or shortly before death, such as a sudden gift or inheritance, poker winings from Texas Hold 'Em, or even a lottery prize. Of course, it's wise to promptly revise your estate plan to name a specific beneficiary to inherit this property. But what if you don't get around to it before you die? If you have a will, that property will go to your residuary beneficiary, who, by definition, takes "the rest of your property"—that is, everything that isn't left to some specific named beneficiary. Unfortunately, there's no easy way to leave leftover property through a living trust, because property must be formally added to the trust for it to be subject to the trust provisions.

- **To dispose of property not transferred by a probate-avoidance device.** If you buy property but don't get around to planning probate avoidance for it—by placing it in your living trust, for example—a will is a valuable backup device, ensuring that the property will go to whomever you want to have it (your residuary beneficiary), and not pass under state law. Similarly, if somehow you've failed to transfer some of your existing property to a probate-avoidance device—for example, because you didn't properly complete transfers of title, a will directs that property to your residuary beneficiary.

- **To name a personal guardian for your minor children.** If you have minor children, you need a will to achieve the vital goal of naming a personal guardian for them. You can't use any other device for this purpose (except a living trust in a couple of states). Also, in your will you can appoint a property guardian for your children, to manage any of their property not otherwise legally supervised by an adult. (See Chapter 6.)

- **To leave property you don't currently own but expect to receive.** If someone has left you property by will, and that property is still enmeshed in probate when you die, you can't arrange to transfer it by a probate-avoidance device such as a living trust, since you don't have title to the property. But under your will, that property goes to your residuary beneficiary. Similarly, if you expect to get money from a lawsuit settlement, only a will can be used to transfer that property. Of course, no one knows what property they might receive shortly before death, which is one reason you always need a will.

- **To disinherit a child or spouse.** You can expressly disinherit a child in your will. (See Chapter 6, Section G.) You can disinherit a spouse in your will only if you live in a community property state. (See Chapter 3, Sections B and C.)

- **To name your executor.** In your will, you name your executor, the person with legal authority to supervise distribution of property left by your will, and to represent your estate. It can be a good idea to have an executor even if you have also set up a living trust and named a successor trustee to manage it when you die, because banks and other financial institutions can be reassured to know an executor exists. The successor trustee and executor are often the same person.

CHOOSING YOUR EXECUTOR

Your executor should be the person you trust the most and who's willing to do the job. If you plan to prepare a living trust, it's generally best that your executor be the same person you choose to be the successor trustee of your trust. If possible, it's best to name an executor who lives in your state, or near it. Some states place extra rules and restrictions on out-of-state executors.

It's simpler to name just one executor, but you can name coexecutors, or even several executors, if you have good reason for it. There can be compelling reasons—family harmony is one common example—for selecting more than one executor.

Some conservative estate planners recommend selecting a bank to be your executor. We strongly recommend against this, unless you have no other option. Your executor is your link to the future, in charge of distributing your property after your death. You want someone human, with genuine concern, not an impersonal institution that charges fees for every small act. If your most trusted friend is your banker, name him as executor, but not the bank itself.

Your executor is responsible for arranging probate and supervising the transfer of your will property to your beneficiaries. This may be simple or complicated. Locating the property may not be easy. More commonly, distributing property can become difficult. For instance, if a will writer leaves general instructions to divide property—such as heirlooms or personal photos—between beneficiaries, the executor may become embroiled in all sorts of personal dramas.

Also, if your estate is over the estate tax threshold, your executor is responsible for filing a federal estate tax return—and also a state one, if it is required. (See Chapter 15.) Of course, the executor doesn't have to actually prepare these tax forms herself. They are complicated forms, and the executor will usually hire an expert to do the work.

What an Executor Does: The Full Picture. For a comprehensive and accessible guide to an executor's duties, see *The Executor's Guide: Settling a Loved One's Estate or Trust*, by Mary Randolph (Nolo). The book covers in depth each legal, financial, or practical matter that an executor may have to handle after a death. It also explains the steps you can take while you are still alive to make your executor's eventual job easier.

- **In case probate is not required.** Some states don't require probate, or greatly simplify probate, for small or modest estates. (See Chapter 14.) If your estate qualifies for simplified treatment, there may be no need to use a series of probate-avoidance devices—a will might do the job. And in some states, even larger estates can make use of simplified probate. For example, California allows estates worth up to $100,000 to be transferred by a will without any probate. Property transferred by probate-avoidance methods doesn't count toward this $100,000 limit. So, in California (and many other states), a will can be a handy method for making small gifts—that treasured antique clock to a niece, or $3,000 to a fondly remembered employee—once you have arranged to transfer the bulk of your estate outside of probate.

C. WHAT MAKES A WILL LEGAL?

Drafting a legal will isn't nearly as complicated as most people fear. The requirements are:

- You must be at least 18 years old.

- You must be of "sound mind." The fact that you're reading and understanding this book is, as a practical matter, sufficient evidence that you meet this test.

- The will must be typewritten or printed on a computer printer. (See Section D, below, for a discussion of handwritten wills.)

- The will must have at least one substantive provision. The most common one leaves some, or all, of your property to whomever you want to have it.

- You must appoint at least one executor.

- You must date the will.

- You must sign the will in front of two witnesses (three in Vermont). Witnesses need only be:

  - Adults (people over 18) and of sound mind.

  - People who won't inherit under the will. Will beneficiaries cannot be witnesses.

Witnesses watch you sign your will and then sign it themselves. They must be told that it's your will they are signing, but they don't have to read it or be told what it contains.

There's no requirement that a will be recorded or filed with any governmental agency. Nor need a will be notarized.

Still you may want to use a notary when signing your will and having it witnessed. In most states, having the witnesses sign a brief statement called a "self-proving" affidavit, which is then notarized, can eliminate any need for a witness to testify at subsequent probate proceedings.

LIVING OVERSEAS

You do not have to live in the U.S. to prepare a will that is valid in this country. To prepare a valid will if you live abroad, you must meet the requirements listed above and maintain legal residence in a U.S. state. If you live overseas temporarily because you are in the armed services, your residence is the Home of Record you declared to the military authorities.

If you live overseas for business, education—or just for the fun of it—you probably still have sufficient ties with a U.S. state to make it your legal home ("domicile" in legalese). For example, if you were born in New Hampshire, lived in New Hampshire, and are registered to vote there, then your residence is New Hampshire for will-making purposes.

⚠ If your choice is not clear. If you do not maintain continuous ties with a particular state, or if you have well-established homes in both the U.S. and another country, consult a lawyer before preparing your will.

WHAT A WILL LOOKS LIKE

Years ago, when Denis was a partner in a small law firm, he learned that some clients were disappointed that their wills didn't look more impressive; a few sheets of typed paper seemed lacking in "gravitas." So he began stapling each will in a blue cover-binder, and attaching a red ribbon and red wax seal. Some clients appreciated these touches—although they were certainly not legally required. If you want extras like these, you can purchase what you need at most stationery stores, for far less than if you buy them from a lawyer.

D. TYPES OF WILLS

There are various types of wills. To help clear up any confusion, we briefly cover the main ones here.

1. Handwritten Wills

A handwritten will (called "holographic" in legalese) must be written, dated, and signed entirely in the handwriting of the person making the will. It does not have to be witnessed. Handwritten wills are recognized by about 25 states. We definitely don't recommend them, even in the states where they're legal.

Handwritten wills aren't recommended because probate courts traditionally have been very strict when examining them after the death of the writer. Since a handwritten will isn't normally witnessed, judges sometimes fear that it might have been forged. Also, a judge may require proof that the will was actually and voluntarily written by the deceased person, which sometimes isn't easy to do. In short, given the tiny bit of extra trouble it takes to prepare a typed will and have it witnessed, it's reckless not to do it.

2. Pour-Over Wills

A "pour-over" will is one that directs that the property subject to it goes to (be "poured over" into) a trust. For example, sometimes people make their living trusts the beneficiaries of their wills. When the will property is poured over to the trust, the trust document controls who receives that property.

a. When a Pour-Over Will Is Undesirable

It's usually not a good idea to use a pour-over will with a basic probate-avoidance living trust. Pour-over wills do not avoid probate. All property that is left through a will—any kind of will—must go through probate, unless the amount left is small enough to qualify for exemption from normal probate laws. Probate is most definitely not avoided simply because the beneficiary of a will is a living trust.

It's generally better to simply use a standard backup will to take care of your leftover (nonliving trust) property. In the backup will, you can name the people you want to get the property, and skip the unnecessary extra step of pouring the property through the living trust after your death.

When used as a backup will, a pour-over will actually has a disadvantage that standard wills don't: It forces the living trust to go on for months after your death, because the property left through the pour-over will must go through probate before it can be transferred to the trust. Usually, the property left in a living trust can be distributed to the beneficiaries, and the trust ended, within a few weeks after the person's death.

b. When You May Want a Pour-Over Will

There are, however, two situations in which you might want to use a pour-over will. The first is if you set up an AB living trust to save on estate taxes. With this device, the spouses want up to the maximum amount of property allowed under the federal estate tax exemption to eventually wind up in the trust of the deceased spouse. (See Chapter 18.) So each spouse writes a pour-over will, leaving his will property to the AB trust. (After one spouse dies, the other spouse should amend her or his will or prepare a new one.)

Also, if you set up, as part of your living trust, a child's trust to provide management for property left to a young beneficiary, you may want any property that child inherits through your will to pour over into that trust. Otherwise, you would create two trusts for the child: one in the will and one in your living trust.

3. Statutory Wills

A statutory will is a preprinted, fill-in-the-blanks, check-the-boxes will form authorized by state law. California, Maine, Michigan, and Wisconsin have statutory wills. In theory, statutory wills are an excellent idea—inexpensive, easy to complete, and reliable. Unfortunately, in practice, statutory wills are so limited in scope they aren't useful for most people. The choices provided in the statutory forms are quite narrow and cannot legally be changed—that is, you can't customize them to fit your situation or, indeed, change them at all. For example, the Michigan form allows you to make only two cash gifts (aside from household property); everything else must go to your spouse or children.

Normally, statutory wills are useful only if you are married and want all or the bulk of your property to go to your spouse (or, if she predeceases you, in trust for your minor children). Because of the limitations of statutory wills, the movement to introduce them in other states has stalled. No state has adopted a statutory will since the late 1980s.

4. Ethical Wills

An "ethical will" is a document or materials in which a person expresses the beliefs and experiences that have mattered most in his or her life. The intent is to communicate core values to loved ones. Such a statement can have real worth to those close to you.

While you could legally include an ethical will statement in your regular will—that is, the one you use to leave your property to others—it's wiser to prepare a separate document. Trying to sum up what's in your soul may turn out to require many pages, and take considerable time. Better not to enmesh that profound searching with the task of preparing your conventional will. More practically speaking, you'll want to avoid including anything potentially confusing or ambiguous in your legal will.

As long as you don't contradict the provisions of your legal will, your options for expressing yourself are limited only by the time and energy you have for the project. You could do something as simple as use your explanatory letter to set out a concise description of your basic values. Or, if you feel inspired, you may leave something much more detailed for your loved ones. Many survivors are touched to learn about important life stories, memories, and events. You might also consider including photographs or other mementos with your letter. If writing things down seems like too much effort, you could use an audio or videotape to talk to those who are closest to you. A little thought will surely yield many creative ways to express yourself to those you care for.

More information about ethical wills. If you want to go beyond writing down some of your experiences and values in your explanatory letter, there is a growing body of websites and literature that can help you explore different ways of making an ethical will. You might begin by visiting www.ethicalwill.com. The site offers some basic free information and sells ethical will-writing kits.

Trying to control behavior. For some, an ethical will means putting provisions in their legal will that attempt to reward beneficiaries for acting in certain ways—or to punish them if they don't. For example, a will writer might want to provide cash incentives to younger beneficiaries if they work for favorite causes. Usually, trying to establish this type of control over others is at best futile, and at worst destructive. If you weren't able to pass on your values and morals by example while you lived, it's very unlikely that you can do so through gifts of your property after your death. Moreover, the mechanics of imposing moral conditions on your gifts are inherently complicated. Among the issues that must be resolved are: Who is to determine whether the beneficiary is fulfilling your moral requirement? How is that to be determined? For how long must the beneficiary do what you want before they receive your gift? Functionally, you must create an irrevocable trust if you want to try to require certain behavior from your beneficiaries. The trustee of that trust would be responsible for determining if your requirements had been met. Setting up this type of trust requires an expert lawyer, and will be a complicated and costly process.

5.   Other Types of Wills

You will almost surely want a formal, witnessed will, either as your primary estate planning device or as a backup to a living trust. But you may also have questions about other types of wills. Here are some wills we have been asked about:

- **Oral wills.** Oral wills (also called "nuncupative" wills) are valid in a minority of states and, even where valid, are acceptable only if made under special circumstances, such as the will maker's perception of imminent death on the battlefield or in some other highly unusual circumstance. Clearly, they are not to be relied on as a serious estate planning device.

- **Electronic wills.** Just one state, Nevada, authorizes what's called an "electronic will." (Nev. Rev. Stat. § 133.085.) An electronic will refers to an original will that is created and stored exclusively in an electronic format—usually, on a computer. The will must use advanced technology to create a distinctive electronic signature and at least one other way to positively identify the will maker, such as a fingerprint, retinal scan, or voice or face recognition technology. While it's true that such technology is developing rapidly, there are currently no readily available or acceptable methods for making an electronic will that's trustworthy and valid. It's likely that Nevada is laying the groundwork for a time when such wills

are easy to prepare. When that time comes, other state laws are sure to follow this one.

- **Video or film wills.** Video or film wills are not valid under any state's law. But films of a person reciting will provisions, such as to whom they are leaving property, can be useful evidence if a will is challenged, to demonstrate that the will maker was of sound mind and didn't appear crazy or under undue influence.

Avoiding lawsuits over your will. If you truly fear a will contest based on your lack of sound mind or the undue influence of a beneficiary, ask a lawyer about using videos or films to help establish that you were thinking clearly when your will was signed.

- **Joint wills.** A joint will is one document made by two people, usually a married couple. Each leaves everything to the other, and then the will goes on to specify what happens to the property when the second person dies. In effect, a joint will can prevent the surviving person from changing his mind regarding what should happen to the survivor's property. We don't recommend joint wills. Even if circumstances change radically, the survivor is prevented from revising or revoking any part of the will. If you want to impose controls over property you leave to your spouse, the sensible way to do it is through a trust. (See Chapter 24.)

- **Living wills.** A living will (commonly called a "health care directive") has no relation to a conventional will at all. Essentially, a living will is a document in which you state whether or not you want your life artificially prolonged by use of life-support equipment. Depending on state law, other issues related to health care can also be covered. They are discussed in Chapter 26.

E. WHAT PROPERTY CANNOT BE TRANSFERRED BY WILL?

In almost all cases, property that is transferred by a binding probate-avoidance device can't also be transferred by will. In other words, once you place property in one of the following forms of ownership, listing that property in your will has no effect:

- Property in a living trust—it goes to the beneficiaries named in the trust document.

- Joint tenancy property—at your death, your share automatically goes to the surviving joint tenants (but if all joint tenants die simultaneously, you can leave your share by will).

- Money in informal bank account trusts or pay-on-death accounts. The person you designate as beneficiary on the account document inherits the funds.

- Life insurance proceeds payable to a named beneficiary or beneficiaries—this money goes directly to the named beneficiaries.

- Funds remaining in retirement plans, including pensions, 401(k)s, IRAs, and profit-sharing plans, payable to named beneficiaries—the beneficiaries in these programs get these assets no matter what your will says.

- Property that is promised to someone in a prenuptial agreement, living-together contract, partnership agreement, corporate shareholder agreement, or other contract.

Washington has passed a law called the "superwill statute" that varies some of the rules above. If you like, you can leave the following types of property in your will:

- your share of joint tenancy bank accounts

- pay-on-death bank accounts

- property in your living trust, and

- money in individual retirement accounts (but not 401(k)s).

If you live in Washington and set up one of these probate-avoidance devices, but later use your will to change the beneficiary, the property goes to the person you name in your will. However, if you designate a new beneficiary after you make your will—for example, by updating the paperwork for a pay-on-death bank account or amending your living trust—the gift in the will has no effect. (Wash. Rev. Code § 11.11.020.)

F.   EXPLANATORY LETTERS ACCOMPANYING YOUR WILL

In addition to preparing your will, you may want to leave a letter explaining your motives and desires in leaving your property. At the beginning of your letter, you should expressly declare that it is separate from your will; this prevents confusion for those who are handling your affairs after death. While the letter has no legal or binding effect, it can give you some peace of mind while you live, and also soothe potential slights or hurts of surviving family members or friends.

We wouldn't attempt to instruct you on how to express the feelings of your heart. What follows are some suggestions of topics you might wish to cover:

1.   Explaining Why Gifts Were Made

You may have thought much about why you're leaving a specific item of property to a beneficiary. In a letter, you can set forth your thoughts. For example, you could write why you've left that boat to your old fishing buddy, or that necklace to your niece.

2.   Explaining Disparities in Gifts

You may wish to explain your reasons for leaving more property to one person than another. This can be particularly valuable if you leave more property to one child than another. Ideally, while you live, you could call together those involved, explaining to them why you plan to leave your property as you do. However, as the ideal may not be (once again) feasible or prudent, explaining your reasons in a letter can be far preferable to silence and mystery. Among the common reasons some people decide to leave different amounts of property are:

- one child has already received more money from a parent than other children—say, for purchase of a house or to cover the costs of education, or
- one family member has greater need than others.

3.   Expressing Positive Sentiments

You may wish to express loving emotions, gratitude or other positive feelings when leaving a gift to a beneficiary. As for negative emotions, we suggest that you leave them out of your will *and* your explanatory letter. The old maxim states, "Don't speak ill of the dead." The wise corollary is that the dead shouldn't speak ill of anybody else. Legally, of course, you can express whatever you like, except that if you libel someone, your estate would be responsible for any damages.

Obviously, there are near-infinite reasons someone might want to express positive feelings in a letter, including:

- appreciating the service and care someone—a doctor, a car mechanic, a teacher, whoever—gave you
- appreciating the fun and love a friend provided, or
- expressing gratitude and respect for someone who aided you when you were in trouble.

4.   Providing Care for Your Pet

As discussed in Chapter 5, Section B, you can't leave property directly to your pets. Usually, the wise thing to do is to use your will to leave your pet and a sum of money to a friend who has agreed, in advance, to take the animal. If you like, you can use a separate letter to express feelings you have about your pet, and how you want it cared for.

Pet trusts. Some states do allow trusts for pets. If your state does, you'll need to see a lawyer to have the trust properly drafted.

G. CAN MY WILL BE SUCCESSFULLY CHALLENGED?

The fact that many people worry about the possibility of lawsuits over their wills shows how fear-ridden estate planning has become. Fortunately, the reality is that will challenges, particularly successful ones, are rare. The legal grounds for contesting a will are limited to extreme circumstances. Basically, your will can be invalidated only if you were underage when you made it, or were clearly mentally incompetent (not of "sound mind"), or the will was procured by fraud, duress, or undue influence.

A person must be pretty far gone before a court will rule that she lacked the capacity to make a valid will. For example, forgetfulness or even the inability to recognize friends don't by themselves establish incapacity. It's important to remember that courts presume that the will writer was of sound mind; a challenger must prove incapacity. Similarly, a will is rarely declared invalid on grounds it was procured by fraud, duress, or undue influence; this requires proof that some evildoer manipulated a person in a confused or weakened mental or emotional state to leave his property in a way the person otherwise wouldn't have. If a will maker is improperly influenced, however, a court is the right place to remedy the injustice.

If you fear a lawsuit. If you think someone might contest your will, it's best to prepare in advance how to prevail against any lawsuit. Or if there are special circumstances, such as a seriously debilitating illness, that you believe might raise questions about your competency and the validity of your will, it's also prudent to see a lawyer. This can mean having the lawyer come to see and perhaps even physically help you. For example, in many states, if you're too ill to sign your own name, you can direct that a witness or an attorney sign it for you. In any unusual physical or mental circumstances, it's prudent to have a lawyer's assistance, especially if substantial amounts of property are involved. Someone could possibly claim that if you were too ill to sign your name, you weren't mentally competent. In any subsequent court challenge to the will, the lawyer's testimony that you appeared to be in full possession of your faculties could be very important.

H. KEEPING YOUR WILL UP TO DATE

If important circumstances change, you may need to revise your will.

1. Does Divorce Automatically Revoke a Will?

In some states, if you get divorced after making a will, the provisions that left property to your former spouse are automatically revoked. But that's not true in all states. In any case, you should always revise your will and bring your estate plan up to date after a divorce. Never rely on a state law for your estate planning, especially for matters concerning an ex-spouse. (See Chapter 30.)

2. What Happens If I Have a Child or Marry After I Make a Will?

If you have a child or get married after you make your will, you must revise your will, and your estate plan, to reflect your new situation. If you don't, your estate may become entangled in laws designed to protect spouses or children. (See Chapter 6.) In any case, you'll probably want to revise your estate plan to provide for the new child or spouse.

3. Is My Will Valid If I Move to a New State?

A will signed in one state remains valid if you move to another state. However, it's often advisable to draft a new will after a permanent move. If you're married and move from a common law property state to a community property state or vice versa, the marital property ownership laws of your new state may affect your will. (See Chapter 3, Section D.) Or your new state may have a different form for a "self-proving" will affidavit than your old one did. (As mentioned in Section C, above, a self-proving affidavit is a statement that your witnesses sign in front of a notary public. It eliminates any requirement that the witnesses personally appear in probate court to testify that it was really you who signed the will.) Or you may want to appoint an executor who lives in your new state. ■

8

PROBATE AND WHY YOU WANT TO AVOID IT

Many people aren't sure what probate actually is, except that it involves lawyers and courts in transferring property after one's death. One thing they do know is they want to avoid it. That's a sound instinct. In most instances probate is a costly and time-consuming business, providing no benefits except to attorneys.

A. WHAT IS PROBATE?

Probate is the legal process that includes:

- Filing the deceased person's will with a local court (depending on the state, the court may be called the "probate," "surrogate," or "chancery" court).

- Identifying and inventorying the deceased person's property.

- Having that property appraised.

- Paying off debts, including estate tax.

- Having the will "proved" valid to the court. (This is almost always a routine matter; indeed, it's so routine that it's done without a formal hearing in many states, unless there is a contest, which is extremely rare.)

- Eventually, distributing what's left as the will directs.

If the deceased person didn't leave a will, or the will isn't valid and the deceased didn't leave the property in any other way, such as through a living trust or joint tenancy, the estate must still go through probate. The property is distributed to immediate family members as state law (called "intestate succession" law) dictates.

People who defend the probate system (mostly lawyers, which is surely no surprise) assert that probate prevents fraud in transferring a deceased person's property. In addition, they claim it protects inheritors by promptly resolving claims creditors have against a deceased person's property. In truth,

however, most property is transferred within a close circle of family and friends, and very few estates face creditors' claims. Whatever bills the deceased had—often not many—are readily paid out of the property left. (According to a study by the American Association of Retired People (AARP), the great majority of creditors' claims are filed by the funeral industry, who have learned to use probate as a collection device.) In short, most people have no need of probate's so-called benefits. The system usually amounts to a lot of time-wasting, expensive mumbo-jumbo of use to no one but the lawyers involved.

The actual probate functions are essentially clerical and administrative. In the vast majority of probate cases, there's no conflict, no contesting parties, none of the normal reasons for court proceedings. Likewise, probate doesn't usually call for legal research, drafting, or lawyers' adversarial skills. Instead, in the normal, uneventful probate proceeding, the family or other inheritors of the dead person provide a copy of the deceased person's will and other needed financial information. The attorney's secretary then fills in a small mound of forms and keeps track of filing deadlines and other procedural technicalities. In some states, the attorney makes a couple of routine court appearances; in others, the whole procedure is normally handled by mail.

There is so much money in the probate business that some lawyers hire probate form preparation services to do all the real work. In most instances, the existence of these freelance paralegal services is not disclosed to clients, who assume that lawyers' offices at least do the paperwork they are paid so well for.

A typical probate takes up to a year or more, often much more. Denis once worked in a law office that was profitably entering its seventh year of handling a probate estate—and a very wealthy estate it was. By contrast, property transfers by other legal means, such as a living trust, can usually be completed in a matter of weeks.

Probate usually requires both an "executor" and someone familiar with probate procedures, normally a probate attorney. The executor, appointed in the will (usually a spouse, relative, or friend of the deceased), is responsible for making sure that the will is followed. The executor hires a probate lawyer to do the paperwork. After that, the executor does little more than sign where the lawyer directs, while wondering why the whole business is taking so long.

B. PROBATE FEES

For their services, the lawyer and the executor are each entitled to a hefty fee from the probate estate. However, many executors don't accept a fee, especially if they inherit much of the property anyway.

A report by the AARP estimated that probate attorneys annually receive fees of $1.5 billion. In many states, the fees can be whatever a court approves as "reasonable." (In 1997, the U.S. Tax Court allowed an attorney's probate fee of $1,600 per hour for a total of $368,100, declaring that the fee "was reasonable under New York law.") In a few states, the fees are a percentage of the estate subject to probate. Either

way, probate attorney fees for an uncomplicated estate with a value of $500,000 (these days, often little more than a home, some savings, and a car) can amount to $10,000 to $15,000 or more. And, in addition, there are court costs, appraiser's fees, and other possible expenses. Moreover, if there are any "extraordinary" services performed for the estate, the attorney or executor can often ask the court for additional fees. Some lawyers even persuade (or dupe) clients into naming them as executors, enabling the lawyers to hire themselves as probate attorneys and collect two fees—one as executor, one as probate attorney.

Is a probate lawyer really necessary? One obvious way to reduce probate fees would be for your executor to appear in court without an attorney ("in pro per") as the representative of your estate. Unfortunately, a few states don't permit the executor to act without a lawyer. And some judges make things difficult for an executor who tries to go it alone. The only states in which it's a reasonable choice for most people are California (see *How to Probate an Estate in California,* by Julia Nissley (Nolo), an excellent self-help book designed for, and used by, thousands of nonlawyers), and Wisconsin, which has an established pro per procedure. In other states where in-pro-per action is theoretically possible, there are no comprehensive published materials, nor is other help available to nonlawyers. Without help, learning to complete the forms, understanding the intricacies of court petitions, estate inventories, "proof of service" declarations, and so on, is likely to be very difficult. To make matters worse, court clerks and judges are likely to be unsympathetic (to put it mildly), so any mistake is likely to cause delay, and possibly embarrassment. Still, handling probate without a lawyer is not impossible. Legal secretaries and paralegals typically copy necessary forms and follow procedures set out in lawyer practice manuals. These are usually available at public law libraries, and many people have successfully used them.

In all states (including California and Wisconsin), rather than trying to save money by having your estate probated without an attorney, it generally makes more sense to see if you can avoid probate at least for the bulk of your property. This approach involves transferring the big ticket items of your property—for example, your house and stock portfolio—outside of probate, leaving only less valuable items to be passed by your will. (As you know, we recommend that you always have a least a backup will. See Chapter 7, Section B.)

If the value of the property transferred by your will is relatively low, probate may not be required. Most states exempt small will estates from probate. The limits vary from state to state. (See Chapter 14.)

Finally, if some of your estate will be subject to probate, you can try to reach an agreement with an attorney to do your probate for less than the conventional fees. If the probate of your estate is routine, it will be sufficiently profitable even at a fee lower than the conventional rate. If you do arrange a reduced fee, put something in writing, even if it's only a letter confirming this arrangement. However, you cannot bind your attorney to handle the probate of your estate for a reduced fee. In fact, you don't have the power to select the attorney at all. The law gives this authority to the executor.

EXCESSIVE PROBATE FEES

Marilyn Monroe's estate offers an extreme example of how outrageous probate fees can be. She died in debt in 1962, but over the next 18 years, her estate received income, mostly from movie royalties, in excess of $1,600,000. When her estate was settled in 1980, her executor announced that debts of $372,136 had been paid, and $101,229 was left as the final assets of the estate, for distribution to inheritors. Well over a million dollars of Monroe's estate was consumed by probate fees.

C. AVOIDING PROBATE

In response to the manifest waste perpetrated by the probate system, a number of legal methods have been developed to avoid probate entirely. Because leaving property in a will usually results in probate, probate-avoidance methods involve arranging, prior to death, to transfer property by other legal means. The major probate-avoidance methods are:

- revocable living trusts (Chapter 9)
- joint tenancy and tenancy by the entirety (for married couples) (Chapter 10)
- "pay-on-death" designations, most often used for bank accounts, but also available for securities (stocks and bonds), vehicles in some states, and real estate deeds in several states (Chapter 11)
- life insurance (Chapter 12)
- retirement accounts that go to a designated beneficiary (Chapter 13)
- state laws that exempt from probate certain amounts of property left by will (Chapter 14), and
- gifts you make while you're still alive (Chapter 16).

Below is a summary chart of the pluses and minuses of each method. Deciding which method, or combination of methods, is best for you is a major part of estate planning. So please read all the chapters on probate-avoidance methods before you make final choices.

TRANSFER DEVICE	AVOIDS PROBATE?	MAJOR ADVANTAGES	DRAWBACKS
Will	No, except in limited circumstances for small estates. (See Chapter 14.)	Simple and easy to prepare; can serve other purposes, such as naming guardian for minor children. Often a good interim device to use until later in life.	Normally puts property in probate where inheritors face attorney's fees and other costs, and time delays.
Living Trust	Yes	Complete control over property while alive; flexibility in providing for beneficiaries. Allows for property management in case of incapacity.	More trouble to establish than a will. Initial attorney's fees can be higher. More trouble to maintain than a will.
Joint Tenancy	Yes	Can be simplest probate-avoidance device to create.	Fine for long-term couples owning property together, but usually not a good substitute for a living trust later in life, because each joint tenant can normally sell their interest. There may be gift taxes involved in creating joint tenancy and putting property in joint tenancy. May mean partial loss of stepped-up tax basis.
Tenancy by the Entirety	Yes	Easy to create.	Available only in some common law states; limited to married couples. Can be a problem if one spouse becomes incapacitated.
Community Property With Right of Survivorship	Yes	Easy to create.	Available only in Alaska Arizona, California, Nevada, Texas, and Wisconsin.
Pay-on-Death Bank Accounts	Yes	Very easy to create; no additional costs.	Limited to bank accounts and some government securities. Not a good idea when small children may inherit, since a property guardian will have to be appointed. (See Chapter 6.)

TRANSFER DEVICE	AVOIDS PROBATE?	MAJOR ADVANTAGES	DRAWBACKS
Transfer-on-Death Car Registration	Yes	Easy to do.	Available only in California, Connecticut, Kansas, Missouri, and Ohio.
Transfer-on-Death Registration for Securities	Yes	Easy to do.	Not available in Texas.
Transfer-on-Death Deeds for Real Estate	Yes	Easy to do.	Available only in Arizona, Colorado, Kansas, Missouri, New Mexico, and Ohio.
Naming Beneficiary to Pension Plan or Retirement Account	Yes	Generally easy to do.	Can be limits imposed by specific policy or plan.
Life Insurance	Yes	Good way to provide quick cash for beneficiaries or to pay estate taxes. Proceeds don't go through probate.	If family members will not need immediate cash (or if they don't rely on you for support), the expense of policy may not be justified.
State Law Exemptions to Normal Probate	Yes	Can work well if state allows this method to be combined with other probate-avoidance methods.	Only relatively small amounts of property qualify. Rules vary for each state. (See Chapter 14.) You have to understand your state's laws; research or hiring an attorney may be required.
Dying Intestate, Without Creating Any Property Transfer Method	No	No effort required.	Usually a terrible choice. Property will be distributed according to state law, which is likely not to be as you wish. Your executor (administrator) will be appointed by a judge. Guardian for your minor children selected by a judge.

1. Informal Probate Avoidance

Some people ask, "Why not just divide up a deceased relative's or friend's property as the will directs, and ignore the laws requiring probate?" Indeed, some small estates are undoubtedly disposed of this way, directly and informally by family members.

Example 1: An older man lives his last few years in a nursing home. After his death, his children meet and divide the personal items their father had kept over the years. What little savings he had were long ago put into a joint account with the children, so there's no need for court proceedings. If the father owned no other property, the children have, in effect, "probated" his estate.

Example 2: Denis's grandmother died in her 80s, a few years after her husband. He doesn't know what formal documents they left regarding their property. But he does know what happened to the household furnishings of their modest home on the outskirts of New York City. He was informed that the house was open to family—indeed, had been open for a couple of days—and he could go and take anything he wanted. Denis took his grandfather's favorite reading chair and their dining room table, both of which he uses to this day. There was never any trouble about where their household furnishings went, nor accounting of it, let alone court proceedings.

For this type of informal procedure to work, the family must be able to gain possession of all of the deceased's property, agree on how to distribute it, and pay all the creditors. Gaining possession of property isn't difficult if there's nothing but personal effects and household items. However, if real estate, securities, bank accounts, or other property bearing legal title papers, such as cars and boats, are involved, informal

family property distribution can't work. Title to a house, for example, can't be changed on the say-so of the next of kin; someone with legal authority must prepare, sign, and record a deed transferring title to the house to the inheritors.

One good rule is that whenever outsiders are involved with a deceased's property, do-it-yourself distribution by inheritors is not feasible. For instance, creditors can be an obstacle. A creditor concerned about being paid can usually file a court action to compel a probate proceeding.

Another stumbling block can be getting family members to agree on how to divide the deceased's possessions. If there's a will, it may not be a problem, since the will acts as a legal blueprint for distribution. If there is no will, things can be trickier. One alternative is for the family to look up and agree to abide by the state intestate succession rules, which specifically cover situations in which there is no will. Or, in either case, the family may simply adopt their own, mutually agreed-on settlement. For example, if, despite a will provision to the contrary, one sibling wants the furniture and the other wants the tools, they can simply trade. All inheritors must agree to the estate distribution if probate procedures are bypassed. Any inheritor who is unhappy with the estate distribution can, like creditors, file for a formal probate.

In sum, informal probate avoidance, even for a small estate, isn't something one can count on. Realistically, probate avoidance must be planned in advance.

2. Planning to Avoid Probate

Because probate has justifiably come to be viewed as an unnecessary device designed to fill lawyers' coffers, some have concluded that probate must be avoided for every last bit of one's property. In our view, this is too rigid. True, most people who take the time to plan their own estate decide they want to avoid probate, at least for the major items of property they own. As we've said, this is fine, but prepare a backup will as well.

But do you want to plan to avoid probate now? Many younger people sensibly elect to put off planning to avoid probate until they are at least in middle age. For example, a younger couple may decide that making wills accomplishes their principal needs, which are to leave most or all property to each other, and to provide money and a guardian for their children if they should die at the same time. They understand that using probate-avoidance methods will require some paperwork now, and perhaps some legal fees. Since it's highly unlikely they will die soon and suddenly (should they become ill, they'll normally have time to plan), and because they haven't yet accumulated a great deal of property, they decide to wait a few decades before engaging in probate-avoidance planning.

D. WHEN YOU MAY WANT PROBATE

If your estate owes a lot of debts, probate may be a good idea. Most estates don't involve complex creditor problems. Most deceased people leave little more than conventional household debts: mortgages, utilities, magazine subscriptions, auto loans, credit cards. Probate is not necessary to handle these debts. But if there's a significant risk that many creditors, especially those owed large sums, will make claims against your estate, probate can be advisable, especially if your executor will contest one or more of these claims.

If you own a failing business, or are involved in complicated financial transactions or complex litigation, probate can provide benefits because it provides a ready-made court procedure for resolving creditors' claims faster than by normal lawsuit. Creditors who are notified of the probate proceeding must file their claims promptly with the probate

court, often within four or six months after probate begins, or they needn't be paid. This is a much shorter deadline than would otherwise apply and can allow beneficiaries to take their property (or what's left) free of anxiety about future creditors' claims.

If you believe someone may challenge your estate plan in court, probate can be the most efficient way to resolve the conflict. Any estate planning device, whether it be a will, living trust, or any combination of legal methods, can be attacked by a lawsuit after your death. Fortunately, the legal grounds for attack are quite limited. The challenger must prove the estate plan is a result of someone's illegal act, such as fraud, duress, or undue influence over the deceased person, or the challenger must establish that the deceased person was mentally incompetent when the documents were signed. These legal theories are hard to prove, although easy to allege. If you believe there's a risk that your estate may be subject to legal attack, even by someone who has little chance of success, probate may be advisable as part of your plan to defeat that attack. Under probate law, only a brief time is allowed for attacking a will, and the people who witnessed the signing of the will should be able to testify that you were of sound mind.

Lawsuit fears. If you're worried about a lawsuit, you should discuss your estate planning with an attorney. Together, you can decide on your best course of action.

E. DEBTS, TAXES, AND PROBATE AVOIDANCE

What about debts? If an estate is probated, debts and taxes are paid before property is distributed to inheritors. If duly notified creditors don't make their claims within the allotted time, they're simply cut off. But if there's no probate, obviously, a probate court can't ensure that debts get paid. However, for most estates, there's no indication that judicial policing is needed. Many people leave no significant debts, and even if some do, they normally leave sufficient assets to pay them. It's important to realize that the primary financial obligations most people do have—mortgages on real estate, or loans on cars—don't need to be paid off promptly after the owner dies. Normally, the person who inherits the asset becomes liable for the mortgage or loan. In other words, mortgages or car loans pass with the property and don't need to be paid off separately.

If no probate occurs to cut off creditors' claims, all the deceased's property remains liable for debts, including any estate tax. This is true even after the property is transferred to inheritors. If only one person will inherit from you, that person will be responsible for paying your debts and any estate tax from the inherited property. If there are several inheritors, the responsibility for paying debts and taxes can, theoretically, become more confusing, but this confusion can be eliminated in advance by earmarking money in your estate plan to pay debts. One way to do this is to allocate, in a living trust, specific assets (a bank account, or a particular stock) to pay debts and taxes. If you don't have a suitable asset available to do this, consider purchasing insurance to provide cash.

If you're concerned about estate taxes, read Chapter 15 to learn whether any federal or state tax will likely be due at your death. If estate taxes seem unlikely, this is, obviously, one less thing to worry about. If estate taxes seem likely, plan to leave enough cash or property that can easily be sold to cover them.

F. PROBATE REFORM

Why is probate so time consuming and expensive? Why is probate court approval required for so many routine actions when there's normally no conflict whatsoever? Aside from the mystique of professionalism and good old greed, the history of probate supplies most of the answer. Probate became legal business through a quirk of English history. In medieval England, wealth and power resided almost exclusively in the ownership of land. It passed, by feudal law, to the eldest son. Inheritance of land was a political matter of direct concern to the king, so land transfers after a death were done through the king's courts.

The proceedings were technical, formal, and costly. Personal property (everything except real estate) was transferred by much simpler ways. When the United States became independent, it followed the traditional British legal system for land inheritance. But instead of distinguishing between land and personal property, our new nation tossed everything into the new "probate" court. Over 200 years later, all types of property can still be transferred through these formal judicial proceedings.

Over the years, there have been countless efforts to reform probate by making it easier or cheaper, or to simply do away with it. But because a complicated probate system means substantial fees for lawyers, the legal profession continues to fiercely defend it.

Lawyers' assurances that probate is necessary sound increasingly hollow. Even the British eliminated tedious, expensive probate proceedings over half a century ago. In 1926, England reformed its probate system to provide that the person named in the will as the executor (normally a nonlawyer) files a simple form listing the estate's assets and liabilities with the local probate office, which appraises the inventory and assesses any death tax due. If the papers are in order, as they should be in all routine probates, a "grant of probate" is issued in as little as seven days. Without any court proceedings, the executor then handles all the estate's problems—paying the bills, collecting assets, and distributing gifts to inheritors. Only if there's a problem, such as a will contest or a contested debt claim, is the matter referred to the Principal Registry, the functional equivalent of our probate courts.

In most countries in Western Europe, probate is even simpler. Wills are presented to a notary when signed. A notary, under this system, is a quasi-judicial official who's responsible for ensuring the validity of documents. Upon death, the deceased person's successor named in the will performs the probate functions without any judicial supervision. If there are disputes such as contests of the will or disputed creditors' claims, they are handled like any other legal conflict.

Will our probate system be reformed soon? Any improvement is likely to be slow and grudging. True, most people favor probate reform, in a vague way. And there's some real pressure on a number of state legislatures to adopt genuine probate reform, on the order of the simplified estate distribution system used in England or other countries. HALT (Help Abolish Legal Tyranny), a Washington, DC-based law reform organization, is one leader in this movement. Unfortunately, though, probate reform isn't a hot, glamorous issue that deeply moves many voters; without lots more public pressure, politicians (many of whom are lawyers, or sensitive to the lobbying of lawyer groups) are unlikely to become seriously interested in it.

Much of what passes currently for probate reform merely simplifies probate procedures for lawyers, but keeps the overall system, particularly the fees, intact. For example, under names like "Independent Administration of Estate Act," or "Unsupervised Administration Law," a number of states have passed laws simplifying probate procedures. But because these laws don't improve nonlawyer access, the result is that lawyers have continued to do the vast majority of probates, charging their same high fees while doing less work.

There's more at work to prevent probate reform than lawyer greed, however. Ours is a society professing devotion to equality, but also to freedom, and that leaves us a little confused about money, especially inherited wealth. We don't have any blood aristocracy, but the grandchildren of wealthy people like Rockefeller, Vanderbilt, or Kennedy and thousands of others inherit money taxed at a far lower rate than any English lord or French duke can.

It's not an exaggeration to say that a principal role for American lawyers is to legitimate wealth. Corporate lawyers are the clergy of money, and present themselves accordingly. They dress in dull garb, display grave demeanors, and occupy somber offices. Wherever the millions originally came from— whether hard, honest toil or robber baron's thievery— lawyers will be standing by. Even if money is filthy to start with, after a couple of generations of lawyers get through with it, it becomes more respectable and, when a few suitable charities are involved, almost holy. And the inheritors receive the money in clear conscience. After all, they didn't have anything to do with any earlier shenanigans.

Probate has been an essential part of this sanctification process. The idea seems to be that if you make the legal process surrounding the transfer of money on death complex and formal, it keeps attention off who decided what the rules are for inherited money anyway.

But despite inertia and greed, there is one real incentive to probate reform, and that's the fact that many middle-class people are learning to avoid the system. An endearing trait of Americans is that they are as good at avoiding rules as economic interests are at inventing them. As we'll discuss in more detail in later chapters, the living trust is currently the most popular of a small flock of safe, easy probate-avoidance schemes—so popular, indeed, that unless lawyers make probate simpler, cheaper, and fairer, Americans may succeed in killing it through almost universal avoidance. ■

9

LIVING TRUSTS

A living trust is an efficient and effective way to transfer property at your death—without probate. Essentially, a living trust is a legal document (a few pieces of paper) that controls the transfer of any property you have placed in the trust; when you die, beneficiaries you've named receive trust property. If this sounds a lot like a will, you're right. A living trust allows you to do the same basic job as a will, with the huge plus of avoiding probate.

One big advantage of living trusts is that they are extremely flexible: You can transfer all your property by living trust, or, if appropriate, use a living trust to transfer only some assets, transferring the rest by other methods. Also, living trusts normally are not made public at your death. Wills, on the other hand, become part of the public record during the probate process.

Living trusts are called "living" (or sometimes "inter vivos," which is Latin for "among the living") because they're created while you're alive. They're also called "revocable" because you can revoke or change them at any time, for any reason, before you die. While you live (as long as you are mentally competent), you still effectively own all property you've transferred to your living trust and can do what you want with that property, including selling it, spending it, or giving it away.

Aside from some paperwork necessary to establish a probate-avoidance living trust and transfer property to it, there are no serious drawbacks or risks involved in creating or maintaining the trust. *You do not need to maintain separate trust tax records or obtain a taxpayer ID number for the trust. All transactions that are technically made by the trust are reported as part of your personal income tax return.*

A basic probate-avoidance living trust can also be combined with other types of trusts. For example, you can create a living trust that first avoids probate and then continues for years after your death to save on estate taxes, control property left to someone with special needs, or provide for your spouse and children from a previous marriage. (Ongoing trusts used to save on estate tax or control property are discussed in detail in Chapters 17 through 25.)

For most people of moderate means, whose estates won't have to pay federal estate taxes, the job is simply to avoid probate. Here's a summary of how a living trust works to accomplish that.

You begin by creating the living trust document. In it, you name yourself as trustee to manage the trust property, and a successor trustee (usually a family member or close friend), to distribute the property when you die. You also name the trust beneficiaries, who receive the property when you die. You then formally transfer property into the trust's name. When you die, the successor trustee simply obtains the property from whoever holds it, and transfers it to the named beneficiaries. No probate or other court proceeding is required.

A. DOES EVERYONE NEED A LIVING TRUST?

Most people who plan their estates eventually turn to a living trust to transfer some, and often the bulk, of their property. If you want to arrange to avoid probate now, because you're elderly, seriously ill, or own lots of valuable property and don't want to risk it going through probate, a living trust is probably the best probate-avoidance device.

But despite our enthusiasm for living trusts, not everyone needs one. The reason is twofold. First, some people don't really need to plan to avoid probate now. Second, other probate-avoidance methods may fit a particular estate planning situation better. Good estate planning can't be reduced to one universal formula. To make good decisions, you need to understand what a living trust can and cannot do and how it can be used with other estate planning methods in devising your overall plan. Norman

Dacey, in his pioneering work *How to Avoid Probate* (Crown), essentially asserted that living trusts should be used by all people in all situations. A number of lawyers now make the same claim in advertisements and seminars. These claims are much too broad.

You may not need a living trust, at least not right now, if you're in one of these categories:

- **You are young, healthy, and unlikely to die for a long time.** People in their 30s, 40s, and sometimes older, usually have the primary goals of seeing that their property will be distributed as they want in the highly unlikely event they die suddenly, and to see that young children are cared for. A will, perhaps coupled with life insurance, often achieves these goals more easily than does a living trust. A will is simpler to prepare and easier to revise than a living trust. While using a will normally means property goes through probate, this occurs only after death. As long as a person is alive, the fact that probate will be avoided is of no benefit. Because very few younger, healthy people die without any warning, it can make good sense now to make and revise a will for a number of years. Later in life, when the prospect of death is more imminent, and the person has (hopefully) accumulated more property, a living trust can be established to avoid probate.

- **You can more sensibly transfer assets by other probate-avoidance devices.** Living trusts aren't the only game in town; joint tenancy, "pay-on-death" bank accounts, and life insurance are among the other methods you can use to leave property outside of probate. And, as we've said, the laws in some states allow certain amounts or types of property (and occasionally property left to certain classes of beneficiaries, such as a surviving spouse) to be transferred without probate even if a will is used. (See Chapter 14.) None of these methods has the breadth of a living trust, which can be used to transfer virtually all types of assets. However, each can be easier to use, and equally efficient, in particular circumstances. For example, adding a pay-on-death designation to a bank account is very simple, and it costs nothing. At your death, the money in the account will go to the person you named, without probate.

- **You have, or may have, complex debt problems.** If you have many creditors, probate provides an absolute cut-off time for notified creditors to file claims. If they don't do so in the time permitted, your inheritors can take your property free of concern that these creditors will surface later and claim a share. A living trust doesn't create any such cut-off period, which means your property could be subject to creditors' claims for a much longer time.

- **There's no one you trust to oversee your trust after your death.** One crucial element in having a living trust work effectively is someone you fully trust who serves as your successor trustee. No court or government agency makes sure your successor trustee complies with the terms of your living trust. So, if you don't have a spouse, child, other relative, friend, or someone else you believe is truly trustworthy to name as successor trustee, a living trust isn't for you.

- **You own little property.** If you don't own much of monetary value, probate fees won't amount to that much anyway. There isn't much point in bothering with a living trust and probate avoidance.

- **You are involved in a divorce proceeding.** To protect the rights of each spouse, your state may have very specific rules about what you can do regarding a living trust after separation but before your divorce is final. For instance, under California law, during a divorce proceeding a spouse cannot transfer property into a living trust.

BE WARY OF "FREE" LIVING TRUST SEMINARS OR HIGH-PRESSURE SALESPEOPLE

There are lots of ads these days for free seminars on living trusts. Usually, these events are nothing more than elaborate pitches for paying a lawyer (or some nonlawyer entity or service) $1,000 or more to write a living trust. Sometimes salespeople contact prospective customers by phone and pressure them to make an appointment to buy a living trust. Is it worth it? Almost invariably, no.

Seminar sponsors try to sell the idea that much of your estate is likely to be gobbled up by estate tax and probate unless you set up trusts now to avoid some of the tax and buy life insurance to pay the rest. In truth, most people don't have estates large enough to owe estate tax. (See Chapter 15, Section A.) Further, there are many ways to avoid probate, and you should evaluate them all before deciding what's best for you.

The sponsors won't tell you this, but instead usually hustle:

- lots of life insurance to pay for supposed estate tax, and

- a fill-in-the-blanks trust that they claim will avoid probate while reducing estate tax—a version of what we call an AB trust.

Sometimes trust seminars and salespeople also push expensive annuities. In 2005, the California Attorney General filed a $110 million dollar lawsuit against one trust mill, alleging that it employed various dishonest practices to lure unsuspecting purchasers, usually older citizens, to purchase undesirable annuities. This trust mill first solicited prospective living trust clients. Then, after obtaining detailed financial information from the client, sales representatives attempted to get the client to convert their assets into costly long-term annuities, which included provisions for high, long-lasting surrender penalties. In other words, once a client realized he'd been taken, it would cost him a bundle to escape the annuity.

Before buying a trust from a salesperson or seminar, ask yourself a few important questions: Do you really need to avoid probate now? Is your estate likely to be liable for estate tax? If so, and you are married, what type—if any—of AB trust makes sense? Is your situation too complex for a standard form? Buying a trust from a seminar is a bit like buying aluminum siding from a door-to-door salesperson. If you really need exactly what the person is selling, you can satisfy yourself by checking references and making certain that the company provides a quality product and that the price is fair. But that takes a lot of work, and there are better ways to find legal help. (See Chapter 29.)

B. LIVING TRUSTS EXPLAINED

Don't let the word "trust" scare you. True, the word can have an impressive, slightly ominous sound. Historically, monopolists used trusts to dominate entire industries—for example, the Standard Oil Trust in the era of Teddy Roosevelt's "trust-busting." And while many people don't know exactly how a trust works, they do know, vaguely, that trusts have traditionally been used by the very wealthy to preserve their riches from generation to generation. (Indeed, isn't one version of the American dream to be the beneficiary of your very own trust fund?) Trusts may even appear to some as a particularly obnoxious form of lawyers' black magic, somehow enabling people to escape tax or other financial obligations. The reality is—as it tends to be—more mundane.

1. What Is a Living Trust?

Living trusts are, in basic concept, simple. You create a legal entity called a trust and transfer something of value to it. You keep control over it while you're alive, and at your death, it goes to the person you've named to inherit it.

To create a trust, you must sign a document that specifies:

1. The "trustee," who has the authority to manage the trust property. You name yourself as the trustee.

2. The "successor trustee," who turns the trust property over to the beneficiaries after your death.

3. The property that is subject to the trust.

4. The "beneficiary" or beneficiaries of the trust, who receive the trust property at your death.

5. Other terms of the trust, including the fact that you can amend or revoke it at any time.

2. How a Living Trust Works

The key to a living trust established to avoid probate is that you, the grantor, aren't locked into anything. You can revise, amend, or revoke the trust for any (or no) reason, any time before your death, as long as you're mentally competent. You appoint yourself as the initial trustee, to control and use the trust property as you see fit. If you become mentally incapacitated, your successor trustee steps in and manages the trust property for your benefit, for as long as you live. If you regain your mental capacity, you regain the authority to manage your living trust property.

And now for the legal magic of the living trust device. Although a living trust is really only a legal fiction during your life, it assumes a very real presence for a brief period after death. When you die, the living trust can no longer be revoked or altered. And because property held in a living trust does not need to be probated, the successor trustee can immediately transfer it to the trust beneficiaries.

A MINI-GLOSSARY OF LIVING TRUST TERMS

The person who sets up a living trust (that's you) is called the **grantor, trustor,** or **settlor.** These terms mean the same thing and can be used interchangeably. You can also set up a trust with your spouse; in that case, you are both grantors.

The grantor creates a written **trust document** or instrument, containing all the terms and provisions of the trust.

All the property you own at death, whether in your living trust or owned in some other form, is your **estate.**

The property you transfer to the trustee, acting for the trust, is called, collectively, the **trust property, trust principal,** or **trust estate.** (And, of course, there's a Latin version: the trust corpus.)

The person who has power over the trust property is called the **trustee.**

The person the grantor names to take over as trustee after the grantor's death (or, with a trust made jointly by a couple, after the death of both spouses) is called the **successor trustee.**

The people or organizations who get the trust property when a grantor dies are called the **beneficiaries** of the trust. (While a grantor is alive, technically he or she is the beneficiary of the trust.)

Some paperwork is necessary to complete transfer of the trust property to the beneficiaries, such as preparing new ownership documents. Still, these matters can normally be handled in no more than a few weeks, without a lawyer. Once the trust property is legally received by the beneficiaries, the trust ceases to exist.

Example: Travis intends to leave his painting collection and his house to his daughter, Bianca, but he wants to have complete control over the house and the collection until he dies, including the right to sell any painting in the collection if he chooses. At the same time, he doesn't want the $450,000 value of this house and the $250,000 value of the collection to be subject to probate. Travis reasons that it's pretty silly to pay thousands of dollars in probate fees just to have his own house and paintings turned over to his daughter.

So Travis establishes a living trust, with the house and paintings as the trust's assets. He names himself as trustee, with full power to control the trust property. Bianca is named as the successor trustee, to take over after he dies. He also names Bianca as the trust beneficiary.

When Travis dies, Bianca, acting as successor trustee, turns the paintings over to the beneficiary, herself, as directed by the terms of the trust. And, as trustee, she prepares and records a deed transferring the house from the trust to herself. The trust then ceases to exist. All probate proceedings, delays, and costs are avoided. And because the estate is worth less than the federal estate tax threshold, no federal estate tax is assessed. (See Chapter 15, Section A.)

3. Living Trusts and Income Taxes

As we've said, during your life, a living trust doesn't exist for income tax purposes. The IRS treats the trust property as it does any other property you own. So, you don't have to maintain separate books, records, or bank accounts for your living trust. And because, while you live, the trust isn't functionally distinct from you, your living trust can't be used to lower your income tax.

SELLING YOUR HOME FROM A TRUST: TAX BREAKS

Many people put their homes—their most expensive asset—into their living trusts. If you do, you won't lose any tax benefits:

- You can still deduct mortgage interest.

- You can sell your principal home once every two years and exclude $250,000 of capital gains from income taxation. A couple can exclude $500,000.

---

4. Living Trusts and Estate Taxes

Let us say it loud, clear, and in capital letters: LIVING TRUSTS DESIGNED TO AVOID PROBATE DON'T REDUCE ESTATE TAXES. We emphasize this because when some people hear the word "trust," they feel it must mean "tax savings."

A living trust designed to avoid probate can, however, be combined with a second trust designed to save on estate tax. A common example of this is when a spouse uses a living trust to first avoid probate and then to establish a trust to pay income to the surviving spouse for his or her life, with the property in the trust going to the children or grandchildren when that spouse dies. This popular estate tax-saving device is called an "AB" trust. (See Chapter 18, Section C.)

5. Living Trusts and Minor Children

You can leave property to minors using a living trust. Many married people name their spouse as beneficiary of their trust, and their minor children as alternate beneficiaries. If you leave minors property in your trust as any type of beneficiary, you impose adult management over that property in the trust document. The different methods of adult management are discussed in Chapter 6.

You can use a living trust to leave life insurance proceeds to minor children. You do not transfer ownership of the policy to the trust, but name it as beneficiary of that policy. In the trust, you name the children as beneficiaries for any insurance proceeds the trust receives. (See Chapter 6, Section E, and Chapter 12, Section D.) As with other types of property, you must set up a method of adult management for the life insurance benefits.

6. Living Trusts for Couples

A living trust can work as effectively for a couple as for a single person. And any couple, married or not, can use one living trust to handle both their shared property and any either owns individually. Because most couples who use living trusts are married, the discussion that follows is cast in terms of "spouses" and "marital property." However, the concepts discussed apply equally to unmarried couples.

The fact that a couple can create a shared living trust to cover the property of both doesn't mean they must. In some circumstances, it may make sense for each spouse to make a separate living trust. For example, if each spouse owns mostly separate property, a combined living trust may make little sense. But if spouses share ownership of much or all of their property, as is usually the case, it's generally preferable that they use one living trust for their property.

If you live in a community property state, in which spouses equally own most property acquired after marriage, you and your spouse almost certainly own property together. Even in the other (common law) states, where one spouse may legally be the sole owner of much property, spouses who have been married for many years typically regard most or all property as owned by both. (See Chapter 3 for a list of common law and community property states and an explanation of both systems of property ownership.) Unmarried couples can also share ownership of property, if they choose, and register any ownership/title document in both their names as co-owners.

Setting up two separate living trusts for shared property owned by a couple is generally undesirable, because ownership of the shared property must be divided. That's a lot of trouble. Worse, it can lead to unfair and undesired imbalances—for example, one spouse's stocks might go up in value while the other's decline.

Fortunately, there is no need for spouses to divide property this way. Instead, a couple can create one trust and transfer the shared property to it. (You can also put individually owned property into the trust.) Each spouse has full power to name the beneficiaries of his or her portion of the property put in trust.

When the first spouse dies, the trust is split in two. One trust contains all property of the deceased spouse. The other contains all property of the surviving spouse. The deceased spouse's property is transferred to the beneficiaries he or she named in the trust document. One beneficiary is commonly the surviving spouse, but children, friends, and charities may also inherit property.

The diagram below shows how this type of marital living trust works. In this example, the husband and wife transfer their shared ownership property into one living trust. The husband is the first spouse to die, the "deceased spouse." The wife is the "surviving spouse."

How a Shared Living Trust Works

1. Husband and wife transfer shared property to trust. (Each spouse can also transfer individually owned property.)

2. Husband dies. Shared trust property is divided in half.

3. Husband's one-half ownership of shared property, and any individually owned property, goes to his beneficiaries. All property owned by wife, including her half of shared property, remains in her trust.

4. Wife's property stays in living trust.

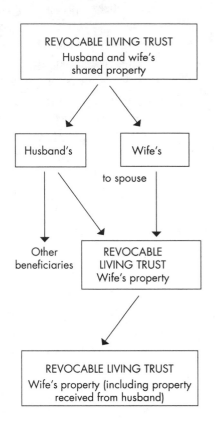

7. Living Trusts and Your Debts

Property in a revocable living trust is not immune from attack by your creditors while you're alive. You have complete and exclusive power over the trust property, so a judge is not going to let you use the living trust (which you can revoke at any time) to evade creditors.

On the other hand, if property is put in a trust that you can't revoke or change (called an "irrevocable trust"), it's a different legal matter. (See Chapter 17.) Property transferred to a bona fide irrevocable trust cannot be reached by your creditors. The key words here are "bona fide." If an irrevocable trust is set up only to defraud creditors, it's not bona fide.

If It Sounds Too Good to Be True...

Some "authorities" have inaccurately stated that property in a revocable living trust can't be grabbed by your creditors during your life. They argue that, for collection purposes, a revocable living trust is legally distinct from its creator. We know of no law or case that supports this position.

 Shielding property. If you're concerned about protecting your assets from creditors, see a lawyer.

C. Major Decisions in Creating a Living Trust

Let's look a little deeper into the key decisions you'll need to make if you want to create a living trust, whether you do it yourself or get help from a lawyer.

Initially, you must make four major decisions:

1. What property will be in the trust?

2. Who will be the successor trustee? (You, or you and your spouse, are the initial trustee or trustees.)

3. Who will be your beneficiaries?

4. If you transfer most or much of the value of your estate by living trust, how will any debts and taxes outstanding at your death be paid?

1. Choosing Property to Put in the Living Trust

You can place all your property in your living trust, or transfer some, or even most, of it by other means, such as a will or joint tenancy. In general, if you decide to use a living trust to avoid probate, it's sensible to transfer all your big-ticket items to it, unless they are covered by another probate-avoidance device. Thus, if you and your spouse already own your house in joint tenancy, you've already arranged to avoid probate of the house.

> **Example:** Mr. and Mrs. Tramsey share ownership of a house with an equity of $150,000, held in joint tenancy, personal possessions worth $20,000, U.S. government bonds worth $80,000, stocks worth $100,000, and a savings account with $60,000 in it. Each wants to leave his or her half of the house, personal possessions, cars, and stocks and bonds to the other. Because the house is already in joint tenancy, the survivor will become the sole owner free of probate. (See Chapter 10.) To take care of the personal possessions, stocks, and bonds, the Tramseys decide to create a revocable living trust.
>
> However, when it comes to their savings account, they both decide that, at death, each will leave his or her half directly to their son, not to the surviving spouse. They learn that the simplest way to transfer bank accounts outside of probate is by using a pay-on-death account. (See Chapter 11, Section A.) So, the Tramseys divide the money in their savings account in half, and each spouse then creates a separate pay-on-death account, naming their son as beneficiary, to receive the money in that account when he or she dies.

Many people do put real estate into their living trust. Some special issues come up when real estate is involved:

- **Property taxes.** In some states, transferring real estate to a new owner can result in property being immediately reappraised for property tax purposes. By contrast, if the property is not transferred to new owners, it usually won't be reappraised for a set period of years, or (in a few states) at all. Because you and your living trust are considered the same basic entity while you're alive, there's no real change in ownership and therefore no reappraisal. If you want to be absolutely sure that this is true in your state and county, check with your local property tax collector.

- **Homestead protection.** State homestead protections, which typically protect your equity interest in a home from creditors up to a designated amount, should not be lost if you transfer real estate to a living trust. If you are not seriously in debt, there is no need to worry about this one. However, if you're in debt and concerned that a creditor may try to force a sale of your house, check your state's homestead rules carefully. (You can find these rules in *How to File for Chapter 7 Bankruptcy*, by Stephan Elias, Albin Renauer and Robin Leonard (Nolo).)

- **Mortgage holder and homeowner's insurance.** Don't bother notifying your mortgage holder or homeowner's insurance company that you have placed your home in your living trust. While you live, you remain the owner of your home for all real-world purposes. Under federal law, your mortgage cannot be called because you transferred your home to a living trust. Also, your insurance policy will still cover your home. But if you tell your bank or insurance company about the transfer, they might raise problems and questions that you'll have to waste time answering. Don't risk the possible hassles.

2. Choosing the Trustees of Your Living Trust

You must make two choices when it comes to naming a trustee to manage the trust property: who will be the initial trustee, and who will take over as the successor trustee when the first trustee dies or becomes incapacitated.

a. Your Initial Trustee

As discussed, the initial trustee of your living trust is usually you, the person who set it up. Serving as trustee is how you continue to absolutely control your trust property.

If you and your spouse (or significant other) set up a trust together, you'll both be cotrustees. When one spouse dies, the other continues as sole trustee.

One spouse as trustee. It's possible, but very unusual, to have only one spouse be the original trustee of a shared living trust. If you're interested in doing this, see a lawyer.

Naming someone else as initial trustee. If you want to name someone besides yourself to be your initial trustee because you don't want to, or cannot, continue to manage your own assets, it greatly complicates matters. You'll probably need much more detailed controls on the trustee's powers. In addition, under IRS rules, if you aren't a trustee of your own living trust, separate trust records must be maintained, and a trust tax return must be filed. However, completing this return need not be particularly onerous; all the IRS requires is filing the face page of the fiduciary return (Form 1041) and a summary listing of items of trust income and expense. These items are actually reported on the trust creator's regular Form 1040 income tax return.

Naming cotrustees. You can name two people (or even more) to serve as initial trustees. This can be desirable if you want or need someone else to manage the trust property for you while you live but you don't want the IRS complications that come with a separate trustee. You name yourself and someone else as trustees and authorize either to act for the trust. Since you are, legally, one of the trustees, the IRS does not require that separate trust records be kept or trust tax returns filed.

b. Your Successor Trustee

It's also essential that you name at least one successor trustee. Your successor is the person who makes your trust work after you die, by distributing its assets to your beneficiaries. With a shared marital trust, the successor trustee takes over after both spouses die. Also, the successor trustee is normally authorized to take over management of the trust if you (or you and your spouse, with a shared marital trust) become unable to handle it yourself.

When you decide on your successor trustee, your job isn't done. You should also name an alternate successor trustee, in case the successor trustee dies before you do or for any other reason can't serve.

c. The Job of the Successor Trustee

The primary job of the successor trustee is to turn trust property over to the beneficiaries you have named. No court's approval is required, and normally this task is not difficult if the property and beneficiaries are clearly identified. Still, some effort is required.

The successor trustee obtains several certified copies of the death certificate of the grantor and presents one, with a copy of the living trust document and proof of her own identity, to financial institutions, brokers, and other organizations that have possession of trust assets. Institutions that deal with financial assets—from title companies to stockbrokers—are familiar with living trusts and how they work. They should not balk at accepting the authority of the successor trustee.

If any documents of title must be prepared to transfer trust property to the beneficiaries, the successor trustee prepares them. For example, to transfer real estate to the beneficiaries, the successor trustee prepares, signs, and records (in the local land records office) the following documents:

- a deed showing the beneficiaries as the new owners, and

- a short statement (declaration) stating that the original trustee (the grantor) has died and the successor trustee has taken over.

In addition to dealing with property subject to formal ownership (title) documents, the trustee supervises the distribution of all other trust assets—household furnishings, jewelry, heirlooms, collectibles—to the appropriate beneficiaries. The trust ends when all beneficiaries have actually received the trust property left to them in the trust document.

d. Notifying Trust Beneficiaries

A number of states have passed laws requiring the successor trustee of a living trust to notify all trust beneficiaries when the trust has become irrevocable—that is, when the grantor dies. Currently Arizona, California, Colorado, Florida, Kansas, Ohio, Maine, Michigan, New Mexico, Nebraska, South Carolina, Tennessee, and Wyoming impose this notification requirement. In many of these states, the successor trustee must also provide a copy of the trust to the trust beneficiaries, at least to those who request a copy.

This notification requirement is based on provisions in the Uniform Trust Code. These provisions are currently being studied by most other state legislatures, meaning that many states will likely adopt similar laws soon.

⚠️ **Successor trustees advised to notify all beneficiaries.** Whatever state you live in, your successor trustee would be wise to notify all trust beneficiaries, in writing, that the trust has become irrevocable, and to provide other basic information about the trust. Here are some facts commonly included in the notice:

- the name and date of death of the trust creator

- the date on which the creator signed the trust

- the name, mailing address, and phone number of the successor trustee, and

- a statement that the recipient (a trust beneficiary) can receive a copy of the trust by notifying the trustee.

It's sensible to send out this type of notice, even if it's not legally required. There's rarely a plausible reason to keep the trust's beneficiaries in the dark about the fact that the trust has become irrevocable, and its basic terms. A successor trustee who keeps the terms of a trust secret is liable to incur suspicion or wrath—or even lawsuits—from the trust's beneficiaries.

e. Choosing Your Successor Trustee

Your successor trustee should be the person you feel is most trustworthy to do the job and who's willing and able to do it. Often a principal beneficiary, such as a spouse or adult child, is named as successor trustee. However, if you believe the beneficiary (much as you love him or her) will be troubled by the practical details and paperwork, it is preferable to name someone else.

When you prepare a backup will, name your successor trustee to serve as executor, too. If a different person fulfilled each function, conflicts could arise.

f. Choosing Cosuccessor Trustees

Legally, you can name as many successor cotrustees as you want, with power divided between them as you specify. However, because of coordination problems and possible conflicts among multiple trustees, it's generally best to name a single successor trustee. This isn't invariably true, however. For example, you might name two or more children as successor cotrustees, to avoid being seen as favoring one child over others. This can be especially appropriate if the children are equal beneficiaries of the trust. And if the children all get along, doing this rarely causes a problem. However, if the children are prone to conflict, you do none of them a favor by having them share power as trustees. It's better just to name the most reliable one and let the chips fall as they will.

g. Choosing a Bank as Successor Trustee

In our experience, it is usually a bad idea to name a bank or financial institution as successor trustee. There are plenty of horror stories involving the indifference or downright rapaciousness of banks acting as trustees of family living trusts. Think of it this way: Your successor trustee is your link with the ongoing life of your loved ones. You want that link to be a human being you trust, not a corporation dedicated to the enhancement of its bottom line. However, if there is no human being you believe will act honestly and competently as your successor trustee, and after reviewing the other probate-avoidance devices discussed in this book, you are still determined to establish a living trust, you'll need to select some financial institution to do the job. Probably the best choice here is a private trust company. These companies generally offer more humane and personal attention to a trust than a bank and can be more reasonable about fees.

3. Naming Trust Beneficiaries

Beneficiaries, of course, are simply the people or organizations you choose to inherit your trust property. You can select anyone you want to be beneficiaries of your living trust. And generally, you can leave each beneficiary whatever trust property you want.

Certain trusts require you to name certain types of beneficiaries. For example, if you set up a probate-avoidance trust combined with an AB estate tax-saving trust, you must name a life beneficiary (your spouse) and final beneficiaries, who receive property after the death of the second spouse. Each spouse can name his or her own final beneficiaries. Commonly, both spouses name the same final beneficiaries—their children—but that's not mandatory. Spouses in second or subsequent marriages often name their children from prior relationships.

If you create a shared living trust with your spouse, each of you can name your own beneficiaries. Commonly, each spouse names the other as the sole beneficiary, with their children as alternate beneficiaries. In other situations, people may wish to divide their property between their spouse and children. And, of course, you can choose other beneficiaries: relatives, friends, or charities.

Example: Malcolm and Ursula create a shared living trust. They have been married for 30 years; neither was previously married. They have one child, Suzanne. Each spouse leaves the bulk of their property to the other. Each also leaves some smaller gifts to relatives, friends, and charities. Both name Suzanne as their alternate beneficiary and residuary beneficiary. They both name Suzanne's husband, Tom, as alternate residuary beneficiary.

You can leave different percentages of different trust properties if you wish, by spelling that out in your trust document.

Example: The grantor's children, John Balesteri, Ellen Balesteri Walsh, and Sophia Balesteri, shall be given the interests stated below in the specified trust properties:

The apartment house at 673 North Maine St., Pittsburgh, PA:

>   40% to John Balesteri;
>
>   30% to Ellen Balesteri Walsh;
>
>   30% to Sophia Balesteri.

The apartment house at 19 Stone St., Pittsburgh, PA:

>   30% to John Balesteri;
>
>   35% to Ellen Balesteri Walsh;
>
>   35% to Sophia Balesteri.

4. Arranging for Payment of Debts and Taxes

Many people don't leave any substantial debts or income or estate tax obligations when they die. (Leaving a house with a mortgage isn't a concern here; the mortgage simply passes with the house.) If you fit into this category, you can go on to other concerns.

When you die, your successor trustee will pay whatever bills you owe, either from property you earmarked in your trust document for this purpose, or from trust property generally. Either way, no beneficiary will suffer a substantial loss.

However, if you transfer the bulk of your property by living trust and will likely have significant debts, including estate taxes, it's best to identify trust assets that you want used to pay off these obligations. First, of course, you'll need to make a realistic appraisal (or at least a decent guess) of what you'll owe, for both regular debts and taxes, at your death. (See Chapter 15.)

D. CREATING A VALID LIVING TRUST

Some people have a lawyer prepare their living trust. If your estate plan calls for combining a living trust with one or more sophisticated ongoing trusts designed to minimize taxes, it's likely you'll need a lawyer to prepare these trusts for you. But other people can safely prepare living trusts themselves, using good self-help materials. In fact, even if you fully intend to pay a lawyer to draft documents, it's still a good idea to educate yourself about living trusts and even to prepare a draft trust.

 Making your own living trust. To learn more about living trusts, or to prepare your own, turn to one of these two Nolo resources:

- *Make Your Own Living Trust*, by Denis Clifford (Nolo). This book contains all the forms and instructions you need to make two kinds of trust: a simple probate-avoidance trust, or a tax-saving trust for couples, called an AB trust.

- *Quicken WillMaker Plus* software (Nolo) allows you to use your computer to generate a probate-avoidance trust or an AB trust.

However you decide to proceed, there are two crucial steps in creating a valid living trust:

1. Preparing the living trust document.

2. Transferring title to property into the name of your trustee (that's you) as trustee of your living trust.

We'll look briefly at each step, to give you an idea what creating a living trust involves.

1. Preparing Your Living Trust Document

No law specifies the form a living trust must take. As a result, there is no such thing as a standard living trust. Indeed, there are a bewildering variety of living trust forms, including some attorney-created forms that contain vast piles of verbiage that serve little real-world purpose, except to generate attorney fees.

Something simple is all you need. Your living trust document must define all the terms of the trust. It names the trustee and successor trustee and your beneficiaries, and lists the trust property. You list the trust property on one or more "schedules" attached to the main trust document. You need only identify each item of property in a way that your successor trustee and beneficiaries unambiguously know what you're referring to. No legal rules require property to be listed in any particular form.

You should sign the trust document in front of a notary public. Unlike wills, no witnesses are required.

FINDING A NOTARY

How do you find a notary, if you don't already know one? Hopefully it won't be hard. Many banks have notaries, as do most real estate offices and title insurance companies. It usually costs less than $20 to have a document notarized. Many law offices have notaries also, but they may charge a heftier fee.

We've received reports that some people have been told that a lawyer must review a living trust (or any legal document) before it can be notarized. This is absolutely wrong. There is no law requiring that a lawyer has to look over a living trust before notarization or at any other time.

⚠ Don't rely on a bank guarantee for your signature. Some banks provide guarantees for customers' signatures on bank and other important documents. Some readers have asked whether they can use a bank guarantee for their living trust, in place of notarization. The answer is no. After your death, it's vital that your living trust be accepted by many institutions, from title companies to county land records offices to stockbrokers. These institutions are not used to seeing living trust signatures validated by a bank guarantee. If any institution refuses to accept your living trust for this reason, there is little or nothing your successor trustee will be able to do about it. Getting a bank guarantee may, for some people, be easier than locating a notary. Unfortunately, this convenience is irrelevant. You must have your signature notarized.

2. Transferring Trust Property Into the Trustee's Name

An essential step in making your trust effective is to transfer ownership (title) of property to the trustee.

If you don't, your successor trustee won't be able to transfer it to your beneficiaries. To achieve this, you register title to trust property, if the item has a title document, in the trustee's name—for example, "Ellen Yurok, as trustee for the Ellen Yurok Trust."

Many estate planning lawyers insist on doing this work. They don't necessarily do it to raise their fees (though that is one result) but because they believe that clients can't be relied upon to do the job right. We think that with clear instructional materials, you can do this work yourself. But even if you decide to let a lawyer do it, you'll benefit from gaining a basic understanding of what's involved.

NAMING THE TRUST AS BENEFICIARY

If you simply name your living trust itself as the beneficiary to receive specified property after you die, you do not have to reregister title to that property. For example, if you want your living trust to receive the proceeds of your life insurance, designate your successor trustee as the policy beneficiary. But do not transfer ownership of the policy or account into the trustee's name. While you live, you, not the trust, are the legal owner of the policy. The trust is simply who you've named to receive benefits payable on your death.

For purposes of transferring title into the trustee's name, there are two types of property: those with ownership (title) documents and those without.

a. Property Without Ownership (Title) Documents

Many types of property don't have title documents, including all kinds of household possessions and furnishings, clothing, jewelry, furs, tools, most farm equipment, antiques, electronic and computer equipment, works of art, bearer bonds, cash, precious metals, and collectibles. You transfer these items to the trust simply by listing them on a trust schedule. In addition, you can use a "Notice of Assignment" form, a simple document that states that the property listed on it has been transferred to the trustee's name. In New York, state law requires that you use such a separate document. (N.Y. Est. Powers and Trusts Law § 7-1.18.)

b. Property With Ownership (Title) Documents

It is vital that all items of trust property that have ownership documents (title papers) be registered in the trustee's name. Your living trust won't affect any property with an ownership document that is not reregistered in the trustee's name.

Property with title documents includes:

- real estate, including condominiums and cooperatives
- bank accounts
- stocks and stock accounts
- most bonds, including U.S. government securities
- corporations, limited partnerships, and partnerships
- money market accounts
- mutual funds
- safe deposit boxes
- vehicles, including cars, most boats, motor homes, and planes.

Note for Colorado readers. In Colorado, if you want to hold real estate in your living trust, state law makes it advantageous to transfer title to the property into the name of the trust itself, rather than the trustee. (Colo. Rev. Stat. §§ 38-30-108, 38-30-108.5.) Colorado law does not require that trust assets be held in the trust's name, but it is becoming the accepted way to proceed. So if you create a living trust and want to transfer Colorado real estate to it, you should take title in the name of, for example, "The John Doe Revocable Living Trust dated January 12, 2004."

Usually, it costs nothing or very little to make these transfers. A very few localities, however do impose hefty transfer and recordation tax. Also, there may be special local forms that must be completed for the transfer to be recorded. For example, in California, transfers of real estate must be reported on a "Preliminary Change of Ownership" form, available at County Recorders' offices. No fee or tax is required to file this form.

GIFT TAX WORRIES

Because your living trust can be revoked at any time before you die, you don't make a gift simply by transferring property to the trust. Therefore, no federal or state gift tax can be assessed. (See Chapter 16 for a discussion of gift taxes.)

---

3. Creating an "Abstract of Trust"

An abstract of trust, sometimes called a "certification of trust," is a kind of shorthand version of your trust document. The purpose of an abstract is to show that your trust exists, without revealing the heart of it—what property is in it and who you've named as beneficiaries. Some people do not want to reveal this information to financial institutions that require proof of the trust's existence before transferring property into the trustee's name. So they submit an abstract instead of a copy of the entire trust document.

In the great majority of states, there's no set form for an abstract. However, a number of states have laws requiring that an abstract contain certain basic information. (These states are California, the District of Columbia, Idaho, Iowa, Kansas, Maine, Michigan, Minnesota, Mississippi, Nevada, Ohio, Oklahoma, Oregon, Rhode Island, South Dakota, Tennessee, Utah, West Virginia, and Wyoming.) The easiest way to find out what form is required, if any, is to ask the financial institution involved.

E. KEEPING YOUR LIVING TRUST UP TO DATE

You need to keep your living trust up to date by making appropriate changes if you acquire or dispose of major items of property or find that, for one reason or another, you want to change your beneficiaries or successor trustees. You can do this kind of work yourself, or you can have a lawyer do it for you. But because a lawyer may not know of changes in your personal life that would result in your wanting or needing to amend your living trust—changes such as divorce, marriage, having a child, selling a major trust asset—it's up to you to keep your trust current.

You can amend or revoke your living trust at any time. However, often a shared living trust document can be amended only by both spouses. This prevents one spouse from pulling a fast one with trust property in the event of a dispute or divorce. When one spouse dies, his or her portion of the trust becomes binding and irrevocable, and the successor trustee distributes the property according to the trust's terms. The surviving spouse can now amend or revoke his or her own portion of the trust, like any other single person.

1. If You Move to Another State

Your living trust remains legal and valid if you move to a different state after establishing it. Revocable living trusts are valid and used in every state.

However, if you're married, and you move from a community property state to a common law state, or vice versa, you may want to check the marital property ownership laws of your new state to make sure that the property you believe is yours really is. (See Chapter 3, Section D.)

2. Amending Your Trust

You must amend your living trust by a signed document and have it notarized. Amendments are usually for simple, clear changes—such as adding a new beneficiary, deleting a beneficiary, changing a successor trustee, or deleting property from the trust. Amendments are not appropriate for making major revisions or wholesale changes in your living trust. In that case, revoke the old trust and prepare a new one.

3. Adding Property to Your Trust

Many living trust forms specifically give you the right to add property to your trust. You can do so simply by listing the new property on the appropriate schedule and transferring title to it (if it has a title document) to the trustee's name.

Just because you've added property to your trust does not mean you've provided for who will receive it after your death. So you may need to amend your trust to name a beneficiary for newly added property.

4. Selling or Refinancing Trust Property

If you decide to sell or refinance property owned by your trust, you can either:

- sell or refinance it directly out of the trust (acting in your capacity as trustee, you sign the title document or otherwise authorize the sale by completing a bill of sale, sales contract, or other document), or

- in your capacity as trustee of the living trust, first transfer title of the trust property back to yourself as an individual (from yourself as trustee), and then sell or refinance the property in your own name.

Use the way that is most convenient. If real estate is involved, what is most convenient is generally what the title company requests.

If you remove property from your trust, be sure to amend the document, so that it doesn't appear to give away property that's no longer in the trust.

5. Revoking Your Living Trust

You can revoke your living trust at any time, for any reason. Revocation must be done in a signed document. A basic shared trust or AB living trust can usually be revoked by either spouse any time. The reason either spouse can revoke a living trust, but it takes both to amend it, is that revocation simply returns both spouses to the status quo. ■

10

JOINT TENANCY AND TENANCY BY THE ENTIRETY

This chapter explains what joint tenancy is and how it works, and explores the advantages and drawbacks of using joint tenancy to avoid probate. The chapter also explains the workings of tenancy by the entirety, which is similar to joint tenancy and available in most, but not all, states for married couples only.

The purpose of joint tenancy is to avoid probate. To simplify and generalize, joint tenancy can be desirable for people, usually a couple, who want to share ownership of property. By contrast, it is rarely sensible for a sole owner to transfer property into joint tenancy with another owner to avoid probate.

A. WHAT IS JOINT TENANCY?

Joint tenancy is one way co-owners, called "joint tenants," can own property together. Under some circumstances, it is a useful probate-avoidance tool, because all property held in joint tenancy carries with it the "right of survivorship." This means that when one joint tenant dies, his or her ownership share of the joint tenancy property is "automatically" transferred to, and becomes owned by, the surviving joint tenant, without the need for probate.

> **Example:** Ron and Linda own their house and a stock account in joint tenancy. At Ron's death, ownership of his half share of the house and stock account automatically goes to Linda, who becomes 100% owner of this property, without probate.

The automatic right of a surviving joint tenant or tenants to inherit is basic to this form of ownership. You cannot leave your interest in joint tenancy property to anyone but the other joint tenants. If you leave it in your will to someone else, that provision has no effect. However, in almost all states, you can easily terminate a joint tenancy ownership while you and all the other joint tenant owners are alive,

changing your share into a form of property called "tenancy in common." You can then transfer or leave your share to whomever you wish.

Other forms of shared ownership, such as tenancy in common or community property, don't create a right of survivorship, and you can leave your share of it by will or living trust.

SIMULTANEOUS DEATH OF JOINT TENANTS

Many joint tenants, as well as married tenants by the entirety, are concerned about what will happen to their property if they die simultaneously. After all, if there's no surviving owner, the right of survivorship that's central to joint tenancy has no meaning. To deal with this highly unlikely but still potentially worrisome possibility, in your will you can name a beneficiary to inherit your share of the property in the event of simultaneous death. Or, if you don't, the property would still pass under your will, to your residuary beneficiary.

Any number of people can own property together in joint tenancy, but they must all own equal shares (except in Ohio and Vermont, where owners can provide otherwise in the deed). The owners share equally in all income, profits, and losses from their property. If an ownership document specifies different percentages or shares of ownership, it's a tenancy in common, not a joint tenancy, and there's no right of survivorship for the co-owners.

UNEQUAL OWNERSHIP OF PROPERTY

If you want to own property in unequal shares, you must do it as tenants in common. For example, two people living together may decide to own property in unequal shares because one person initially has more money to invest in the property than does the other. (Contracts and forms to create a tenancy in common are contained in *Living Together: A Legal Guide for Unmarried Couples*, and *A Legal Guide for Lesbian & Gay Couples*, both published by Nolo.) Property held in tenancy in common does not avoid probate automatically. To avoid probate, each owner can put his or her interest in the property into a living trust. (See Chapter 9.)

STATES THAT RESTRICT JOINT TENANCY

Alaska has abolished joint tenancy for real estate, with the exception for married couples noted below. A few other states restrict joint tenancy, but you can still use it (or an equivalent substitute). Here are the rules you should know:

Alaska	No joint tenancies for real estate, except for husband and wife, who may own property as tenants by the entirety. (See Section D, below.)
Oregon	A transfer of real estate to husband and wife creates a tenancy by the entirety, not joint tenancy. (See Section D, below.)
Tennessee	A transfer of real estate to husband and wife creates a tenancy by the entirety, not joint tenancy. (See Section D, below.)
Texas	A joint tenancy can be created only if you sign a separate written agreement.
Wisconsin	No joint tenancies between spouses after January 1, 1986. If you attempt to create a joint tenancy, it will be treated as community property with right of survivorship. (See Section E, below.)

It's common that real estate is owned in joint tenancy, but any type of property can be owned in this manner and avoid probate. Bank accounts, automobiles, boats, and mobile homes are all routinely held in joint tenancy for just this reason.

B. JOINT TENANCY BANK ACCOUNTS

A joint tenancy bank account can be a useful means of avoiding probate, especially when two people are already a family unit and are sharing income and expenses. Most banks have standard joint tenancy account forms, and all common types of bank accounts, including checking, savings, and certificates of deposit, may be owned in joint tenancy. To open such an account, all people involved sign the account papers as "joint tenants with right of survivorship." (Some banks abbreviate this "JTWROS.") When one joint tenant dies, the other can obtain all the money in the account, with no need to go through probate.

In most joint tenancy bank accounts, any owner can withdraw any or all of the money in the account at any time. If the purpose of the account is for shared expenses—as the family account of a husband and wife—this isn't normally a problem. If it may raise difficulties, ask whether the bank will let you require two signatures for withdrawals on a joint tenancy account. Many will.

A joint tenancy bank account is generally not a good idea if your only purpose is to leave your own money at death to someone else. By changing the ownership document for the account to list the other person as a joint owner, you give that person complete legal access to the account now. The other person can remove all the money in the account at any time while you're alive. As just mentioned, you could try to protect yourself by requiring that both of you must sign to validly withdraw money, but this means you'll have to get someone else's signature each time you want to withdraw your own money from the account.

There's a better way to do it. If your goal is to avoid probate for money in your own account, a pay-on-death account allows you to retain full and exclusive control over your money while you live and still have the account avoid probate. (See Chapter 11, Section B.)

If you're considering creating a joint bank account by adding someone's name to your individual account, you may wonder if you have to concern yourself with gift tax. Happily, no legal gift is made by creating a joint bank account or depositing money in it. However, a gift is made by the depositor

if the other person takes money out of the account. Under current IRS rules, the other person could remove up to $11,000 per year, without there being any gift tax liability. (The rules for gifts and gift taxes are discussed in Chapter 16.)

C. JOINT TENANCY SAFE DEPOSIT BOXES

A joint tenancy safe deposit box can be a good place to keep important papers—wills, funeral instructions, burial or body donation directions, and documents relating to veteran, union, or company pensions or benefits, or individual retirement programs, such as IRAs. This is true because either joint tenant can normally obtain instant access to the documents when they are needed.

If you decide to get a joint tenancy safe deposit box, be sure to specify on the bank account cards whether or not the co-owners share ownership of all contents of the box. This can be particularly important if you keep valuable objects, such as jewelry, in the box. In some states, joint tenancy rental of a safe deposit box gives both joint tenants access to the box, but doesn't necessarily create ownership rights to that box's contents unless it's clearly spelled out. So if you don't want the other person with access to the box to own certain property in it, be sure it's clear that the joint tenancy in the safe deposit box is for access only. And of course, you would also want to leave the property in the box by your living trust or will.

⚠️ **Don't store estate planning documents in a safe deposit box that may be sealed after an owner's death.** In some states with state inheritance tax, safe deposit boxes are sealed by a bank as soon as it is notified of the death of an owner. The contents cannot be released until the box is inventoried by a government official. So if your state has an inheritance tax (see Chapter 15, Section G), check with your bank's officials to see whether the safe deposit box will be sealed upon death of a joint tenant, and how one gets the box unsealed. Usually this can be done reasonably quickly and easily. If not, however, a safe deposit box isn't a good place to store documents that you want to be readily available at your death, including your living trust and will.

D. TENANCY BY THE ENTIRETY

"Tenancy by the entirety" is a form of property ownership that is similar to joint tenancy, but is almost always limited to married couples. (In Hawaii, unmarried couples with registered "reciprocal beneficiary" relationships can take advantage of tenancy by the entirety ownership. In Vermont, the option is available for lesbian and gay couples with registered civil unions.) It has almost the same advantages and disadvantages of joint tenancy, and is most useful when a couple acquire property together. If you do not live in a state that specifically allows tenancy by the entirety, you cannot use it.

STATES THAT PERMIT TENANCY BY THE ENTIRETY

Alaska*	Maryland	Oklahoma
Arkansas	Massachusetts	Oregon*
Connecticut	Michigan	Pennsylvania
Delaware	Mississippi	Rhode Island
District of Columbia	Missouri	Tennessee
Florida	New Jersey	Utah
Hawaii	New York*	Vermont
Illinois*	North Carolina*	Virginia
Indiana*	Ohio**	Wyoming
Kentucky*		

*Allowed only for real estate.

**Only if created before 4/4/85.

Like joint tenancy, property owned in tenancy by the entirety does not go through probate when one spouse dies; it automatically goes to the surviving spouse.

If property is held in tenancy by the entirety, neither spouse can transfer her or his half of the property alone, either while alive or by will or trust. It must go to the surviving spouse. Also, in general, tenancy by the entirety property is better protected than joint tenancy property from creditors of just one spouse. If someone sues one spouse and wins a court judgment, in most states the creditor can't seize and sell the tenancy by the entirety property to pay off the debt. And if one spouse files for bankruptcy, creditors cannot reach or sever the property held in tenancy by the entirety.

⚠️ **The IRS can override tenancy by the entirety protections.** The Supreme Court has ruled that if one spouse owes federal taxes, the IRS can go after that spouse's interest in tenancy by the entirety property. The IRS can impose a lien and force a sale of the property. This is a concern only if you own tenancy by the entirety property and one spouse is in serious tax trouble with the IRS. The overwhelming majority of couples who own tenancy by the entirety property will never have to worry about this.

E. JOINT TENANCY IN COMMUNITY PROPERTY STATES

This section is of interest only to married people who live in or own real estate in a community property state: Alaska (if the couple prepares a written agreement), Arizona, California, Idaho, Nevada, New Mexico, Texas, Washington, or Wisconsin.

Most property accumulated by either spouse during a marriage is the community property of both. (See Chapter 3, Section B, for a discussion of the rules.) Spouses can, and commonly do, hold their community property in joint tenancy with each other to avoid probate when the first spouse dies. Doing this can make good sense. However, for certain important income tax reasons (explained in Section F3, below), it's important to be able to show the IRS that community property held in joint tenancy for probate-avoidance purposes is still community property.

Alaska, Arizona, California, Nevada, Texas, and Wisconsin expressly permit spouses to hold property "as community property with right of survivorship." In other words, in these states you can obtain all the benefits of community property ownership, plus the important advantage that if the deceased spouse's share of community property is left to the surviving spouse, that property doesn't have to go through probate. Instead, the surviving spouse owns it automatically.

Wisconsin law goes even further. It lets married couples avoid probate altogether for their marital property. In a "marital property agreement," they can name a beneficiary to inherit their marital property without probate. The agreement can even provide for the disposition of marital property after the death of the second spouse—although the surviving spouse can amend the agreement, unless that is expressly forbidden in the document.

In the other community property states, there's no statutory authorization for holding community property in joint tenancy. In these states, a standard method of achieving this goal is to hold title in joint tenancy and prepare a separate document, signed by both spouses, declaring that identified property "retains its character as community property, despite our holding title to this property in joint tenancy, which we do solely for convenience, to avoid probate." Why this rigmarole? Because some title companies refuse to permit transfers of real estate into "community property held in joint tenancy,"

maintaining the two legal forms are inconsistent. Because, in the real estate world, it's often sadly true that the law is whatever the title companies say it is, it's safer in these states to go the two-document route: hold title in joint tenancy, and have a separate document stating the property remains community property. Interestingly, neither title companies nor the IRS have any objection to this. It's the all-too-frequent legal story: What you cannot do directly, because of institutions, courts, or misapplication of legal technicalities, you can do indirectly—if you know how.

Although the vast majority of spouses in community property states who hold property in joint tenancy do so with one another, one spouse might wish to place property into joint tenancy with someone else. If the property is the separate property of the transferring spouse, there's no ownership problem, since it's her property to do with as she wishes. (But see Section F, below, for possible tax disadvantages.) However, if the property is community property, serious ownership problems can develop between the surviving spouse and the surviving joint tenant. The reason for this is simple: Each spouse automatically owns one-half of all community property, whether or not his or her name appears on property ownership documents. Thus, the surviving spouse can successfully contend that you have authority to transfer only half of the community property into joint tenancy with someone else. If you do more, you're giving away your spouse's property.

Example: Mrs. Abruzzi, who has one daughter, owns a house as her separate property. She marries Mr. Mykenas. For several years, they use their community property income to pay mortgage payments on the house. Mrs. Abruzzi decides to transfer the house into joint tenancy with her daughter to avoid probate at her death. When Mrs.

Abruzzi dies, Mr. Mykenas could claim that part of the house was community property because community funds were used for mortgage payments. Half of the community property portion of the house is his. Mrs. Abruzzi has no legal right to transfer his portion to her daughter.

F. Tax Concerns Affecting Joint Tenancy

Before deciding whether you want to use joint tenancy in your estate planning, you should understand the possible tax implications. The major concerns are estate taxes, gift taxes, income tax "basis" rules, and property tax reappraisals. We know wading through this probably sounds dreary, but hang in there—you can make it through. And you do need to know this material before you can intelligently resolve whether or not you want to use joint tenancy.

1. Federal Estate Taxes

Owning property as a joint tenant or tenant by the entirety doesn't affect your taxable estate for federal estate tax purposes. The federal government includes the value of the deceased's jointly owned property in the taxable estate. How that value is determined depends on whether the joint tenancy owners were married or not.

a. If You're Married

The tax rule for marital joint tenancies is simple. When a husband and wife own property as joint tenants or tenants by the entirety, one-half of the market value of the property, as of the date of death of the joint tenant, is included in the federal taxable

estate of the first spouse to die. It doesn't matter what amount of money either spouse actually put up to buy the property.

> **Example:** Lou and Isabelle are married and live in New York. During their marriage they purchased real estate as tenants by the entirety. Isabelle actually paid the entire down payment for the property from her savings. Mortgage payments were shared more or less equally by both spouses. Isabelle dies. The IRS rules provide that 50% of the market value of the property on the date of her death is included in her taxable estate. This is true even if she in fact put up more than 50% of the total cost of the property.

Either spouse may transfer separately owned property into joint tenancy with the other spouse without any liability for gift taxes. No gift taxes are assessed against any gift made between a husband and wife (as long as the spouse receiving the gift is a U.S. citizen), no matter how much it is worth.

b. Unmarried Joint Tenancies

The IRS rules defining the worth of a nonmarried joint tenant's share in joint tenancy property are trickier than for married couples. Under the IRS rules, if you own joint tenancy property with someone who isn't your spouse, the value of your interest is based on how much you contributed for the costs of the jointly owned property. If the deceased put up all the money to purchase a piece of joint property, the full market value of the property (at death) is included in the taxable estate. If you paid half the cost of acquiring the property, 50% of its worth is included in your taxable estate.

But here's where matters get sticky. The IRS presumes that the first joint tenant to die contributed all of the money for the purchase of jointly owned property, "less any part that is shown to have originally belonged to ... (another) person." (I.R.C. § 2040.) The IRS also presumes that the first joint tenant to die paid for all capital improvements, if any. The surviving joint tenants can overturn these presumptions by proving that the survivors made cash or other contributions toward buying or maintaining the property. To the extent the surviving tenants can prove that they put up part of the purchase price, mortgage payments, or other expenses, the value of the joint tenancy property interest included in the deceased's taxable estate will be proportionately reduced. Therefore, one risk for unmarried people of holding property in joint tenancy is that, unless they keep good records, the full value of the jointly owned property is subject to death taxes twice: When the first joint tenant dies and then again when the survivor dies.

> **Example:** Decades ago, Phil and his sister Patsy bought a house as joint tenants. They each contributed half the purchase price and paid off the mortgage equally, but any records that can prove that have long since vanished. Patsy dies in 1998. The full 1998 market value of the house is included in her taxable estate, since the IRS presumes she contributed all the purchase price and Phil has no proof to rebut this presumption. Phil, the surviving joint tenant, owns the entire house until he dies in 2002. The full 2002 market value of the house is included in his taxable estate, because he now owns all the property. Had Phil and Patsy kept records, only half the value of the house would have been included in Patsy's taxable estate.

2. Joint Tenancy as a Taxable Gift

If you create a joint tenancy, you may be making a taxable gift (except between married couples). To understand the basics of how gift taxes can affect joint tenancy, all you need to know is that the federal government currently assesses taxes against any gift over $12,000 made to any person, other than one's spouse, in a calendar year. (See Chapter 16.)

Gift taxes can affect joint tenancy because the IRS takes the position that, except for joint bank accounts (discussed below), a taxable gift is made when joint tenancy is created if the owners don't pay equally for the property. So if you put up all the money to purchase property, but list another person as a joint tenant, you've made a legal gift of half-ownership of the property. If the value of that gift exceeds $12,000, you must file a gift tax return and gift taxes are assessed. In other words, if a sole owner of property worth more than $24,000 transfers ownership into joint tenancy with another person, a taxable gift has been made, because the half given away is worth more than $12,000.

> **Example:** Martha transfers her house, worth $300,000 (all equity), into joint tenancy with her son Richard solely to avoid probate. The IRS position is that she has made a taxable gift of one-half the value of the house (less the $12,000 exempt amount).

However, to remind you, if you open a bank account in joint tenancy, with one person actually making all or most of the deposits, there's no taxable gift. Only if a new co-owner actually withdraws money is there a legal gift. This exception also applies to buying a savings bond in joint tenancy. Only when a person takes possession of more than his original contribution (by withdrawing money from the bank account, or selling an interest in the bond) is there a taxable gift.

Normally, no gift taxes must actually be paid when a gift of joint tenancy is made. Any tax assessed is deducted from the giver's estate/gift tax credit. (See Chapter 16, Section C.) In other words, you won't have to spend any cash out of pocket to pay gift taxes, but you must still prepare and file a gift tax return, a hassle to many people.

3. Joint Tenancy and Federal Income Tax Basis Rules

In most cases, someone who inherits joint tenancy property gets a break on income taxes if she eventually sells the property. To understand this, you need to understand the tax concept called "stepped-up" basis.

Put simply, the "basis" of property is the overall dollar cost to you of your interest in that property. To determine the profit or loss if you sell the property, deduct your basis from the selling price. For example, Gus buys stock for $50,000, which is his tax basis for the stock. Two years later Gus sells the stock for $70,000. His taxable profit is sale price ($70,000) less basis ($50,000), leaving $20,000 profit.

The basis is not always simply equal to the owner's original purchase price. For example, the basis of real estate can be its purchase price plus the cost of any capital improvements.

Example: Ardmore buys a house for $200,000 and puts $37,000 into capital improvements. Thus the property's basis is $237,000. If Ardmore sells the house for $350,000, his taxable profit (sales price minus basis) is $113,000.

Under federal law, the basis of inherited property is changed to its market value on the date the owner dies. If the market value has increased from the price the deceased owner paid for the property, the basis to the inheritor is "stepped up" to the higher death-date value. In other words, if B inherits property from A, B's basis in the property is its market value when A died, *not* its basis to A.

Example: Grant's basis in his house was $120,000. Grant dies and leaves the house to Serena under Grant's will. The market value of the house when Grant died was $350,000. When Serena inherits the house, her tax basis for it is stepped up to that market value of $350,000. If Serena sells the house for that amount, she has no taxable gain.

If the market value of property has risen substantially above the original owner's basis, it's clearly desirable for an inheritor of that property to receive a stepped-up basis to the value as of the date of the owner's death. In the above example, if Serena had only received Grant's basis in the house of $120,000 and she then sold the house for the market value of $350,000, she would have a taxable profit (or capital gain) of $230,000. Instead, because of the stepped-up basis, she has no taxable profit.

⚠ Stepped-up basis rules may change in 2010. If the current federal estate tax law remains in effect, the stepped-up basis rules will change in 2010. The new rules will be less helpful to inheritors of large estates. (See Chapter 15, Section F.)

Okay, now to apply this to joint tenancy. The general IRS rule for joint tenancy is that a surviving joint tenant gets a stepped-up basis only for one-half the value of the property, the half owned by the deceased owner. The half owned all along by the surviving joint tenant retains its original tax basis. (A different rule applies to couples in community property states. See Subsection a, below.)

Example: Ellen and Julie buy an investment property (a rental house) for $100,000 and hold it in joint tenancy. Each contributes the same amount to the down payment and operating expenses. When Ellen dies, the property is worth $200,000. The basis of Ellen's half of the property is "stepped up" to $100,000. The basis of Julie's half remains at $50,000, her share of the original purchase price. So Julie's new total net basis becomes $150,000.

This rule does not create any special problem when expenses of buying the joint tenancy were shared equally, or it was created between spouses. But, as we've discussed, if one of the owners did not contribute an equal share to the purchase price (except for spouses), federal tax law includes in the estate of the first joint tenant to die the full market value of the property, less any part the surviving owner can prove he paid for. So if someone transfers solely owned property into joint tenancy as a gift, the entire value of that property will be included in the giver's taxable estate. And because the entire value is included in that estate, all of the property will receive a stepped-up basis.

Example: Mary transfers her house, worth $250,000 (all equity), into joint tenancy with her son, Ed, who pays nothing for his share (it's a gift). When Mary dies, the house is worth $340,000. The full value of the house—$340,000—is included in her taxable estate, because Ed didn't contribute any cash for the property. And because the full value of the house is included in Mary's taxable estate, all of that property receives a stepped-up basis. So Ed's basis is now $340,000.

Sharp-eyed readers may have noticed a problem here. Wasn't Mary supposed to file a gift tax return when she originally transferred the house into joint tenancy with Ed? Yes, that's what the law requires. Since gift tax was assessed, doesn't Ed become the full legal owner of half the property, so that only half of its value is included in Mary's estate, and only half of it receives a stepped-up basis? The answer is no. Despite Mary's filing the gift tax return, the IRS includes all the value of the property in her estate and all the property receives a stepped-up basis. Mary's estate does receive a credit for the gift tax previously assessed.

a. Community Property Held in Joint Tenancy

The stepped-up tax basis rules are different for married couples who live in a community property state. In these states, both shares of community property held in joint tenancy are entitled to a stepped-up basis upon the death of a spouse, no matter what contributions were made to the initial purchase. Thus, if a husband and wife own community property real estate in joint tenancy purchased for $200,000 and worth $2 million at the husband's death, both the husband's and wife's share get a stepped-up basis of $1 million.

But to get the full stepped-up basis, you must be able to prove to the IRS that the joint tenancy property is community property. Otherwise, only the half of the deceased spouse gets the stepped-up basis. So if you're married and do not live in a state that expressly allows community property to be held in joint tenancy (community property with right of survivorship), be sure you can prove it retained its character as community property. (See Section E, above.)

b. Joint Tenancy Property Acquired Before 1977 in Common Law States

If you live in a common law property state and you acquired joint tenancy property before 1977, the tax basis rules were and remain different. Prior to 1977, the full value of joint ownership property is included in the value of the estate of the first owner to die. So the surviving owner received a stepped-up basis for the whole property. (This rule applied to all joint tenants, not only married couples.)

In some circumstances, this can result in significant income tax savings for the surviving joint owner, if subsequently the property is sold.

Example: Rob and Sue bought a farm for $30,000 in 1955, as tenants by the entirety in Iowa. Rob died in 2001. Under the pre-1977 tax law, the full current value of the property, $3,400,000, is included in Rob's taxable estate. However, no estate taxes must be paid because all Rob's interest in the farm goes to his wife, under the rules of tenancy by the entirety, and all property left to a surviving spouse is free of estate tax.

Because the full value of the farm was included in Rob's taxable estate, all of it receives a stepped-up basis to its value at Rob's death. So Sue's basis in the farm is now $3,400,000. If she immediately sells the property for the market value, she should have no taxable gains. By contrast, if Rob and Sue had bought the farm after 1977, and the same figures applied, only Rob's half of the property would get a stepped-up basis, in this case, $1,700,000. Sue's half would retain her share of the original basis, which is one-half of $30,000, or $15,000. So Sue's total basis would be $1,715,000. If she immediately sells the property, her taxable gain would be $1,685,000

The moral: Anyone who bought property in joint tenancy before 1977 has a big tax incentive to keep that form of ownership, rather than transferring the property to a different form of ownership, such as placing it in a living trust.

4. State Income Tax Basis Rules

State tax basis rules can also be quite complicated. However, in general, there's little need to worry about these rules. State income taxes take small enough bites that, in our opinion, they aren't worth bothering about when you're doing estate planning. Also, joint tenancy applies most often to real estate, and land obviously can't be moved from a high-tax state to a low- or no-tax one.

More legal worries. If you have a large estate and want to be extremely cautious and review the impact of your state's basis rules on your estate plan, see a tax lawyer or other tax expert.

5. Local Property Taxes

In some areas of the country, real estate is reassessed for local property tax purposes every time it changes hands. This usually means that taxes go up, sometimes a lot if your property hasn't been reassessed recently.

In general, creating a joint tenancy interest in real property isn't a "change of ownership" if the original owner is one of the new joint tenants. In California, for example, there is no property tax reappraisal if you transfer your property into joint tenancy with yourself and others. However, as a general rule, if the original owner isn't one of the new joint tenants, then any creation of a joint tenancy interest is a change of ownership, and the property will be reassessed. Before relying on this advice, however, contact your local property tax assessor and determine the specific rules for what types of transfers trigger the reassessment of property.

Example 1: Mrs. Jefferson owns two pieces of real estate. She transfers title to the first to herself and her husband, Raymond, as "joint tenants with right of survivorship." She transfers title to the second to herself and her daughter, Lila, also as "joint tenants with right of survivorship." There has been no change of ownership in either of these transfers for reassessment purposes in almost all states.

Also, when Mrs. Jefferson dies, there may be a reappraisal, depending on state property tax rules.

Example 2: Mrs. Jefferson gives a third lot to her son and his wife "Raymond Jefferson and Jane Jefferson, as joint tenants with right of survivorship." There has been a "change of ownership," since the original owner, Mrs. Jefferson, isn't one of the new joint tenants. This is likely to trigger a property tax reassessment.

G. DRAWBACKS OF JOINT TENANCY

As part of deciding whether to use joint tenancy, there are certain possible risks you should consider.

1. Any Joint Tenant Can End the Joint Tenancy

As long as all joint tenants are alive, any of them can terminate the joint tenancy, whether or not the other owners consent to it. (But, to repeat, this is not true for tenancy by the entirety property.) Some states require a joint tenant who wants to end the joint tenancy to go to court and get formal court partition (division) of the property. In other states, any joint tenant has the power to end it without court rigmarole, and can retain his interest, now held as a tenant in common, to do with as he wishes. In either case, if there's a sale, the new owner takes his interest as a tenant in common with the remaining original owners. If the new and old owners can't resolve a conflict, either can ask a court to partition the property into equal halves. If that isn't feasible, the court will order a sale with the proceeds divided in equal shares.

The risk that a co-owner may sell her share of the property may not be serious for couples or close friends who purchase property together with money they each contribute. In this situation, if a divorce, separation, or other reason to end the joint tenancy occurs, each joint tenant simply gets her or his fair share. However, if solely owned property is transferred into joint tenancy by an older person in the form of a gift, the situation is quite different. The older person has given up ownership of half the property. And unlike putting property into a living trust, he can't change his mind later and take it back.

Example: Sid transfers his house into joint tenancy with his nephew Joe. Then the two have a bitter fight. Sid wants to regain sole ownership of the house. Joe says, "Nothing doing. I'm half owner, legally, and there's nothing you can do about it." And there isn't.

So, one question to answer before you transfer property into joint tenancy is: Do you absolutely trust that your joint-tenant-to-be won't sell the property or do anything with the ownership interest that's adverse to you? If you have any doubts, joint tenancy isn't for you.

A living trust may be a better way to transfer property ownership. To eliminate the risk of giving property to someone in joint tenancy who could then sell his interest in the property, or turn into someone you don't get along with, we advise people in Sid's situation to create a living trust. Then name whomever you want as beneficiary for the house. If you have a falling out later, you can simply amend the trust and change beneficiaries.

2. Creditors and Joint Tenancy

Creditors of any joint tenant may go after (legally "attach" or "foreclose") that tenant's individual interest, but not the other joint tenants' interests. But a court may order the whole property sold to reach the debtor's share.

Generally, upon the death of one owner, the surviving owner takes the property free of any responsibility for the deceased's debts. But, in a number of states, a creditor of the deceased owner can go after the property if:

- the deceased person had pledged his interest in the property as security for a loan

- the creditor sued, got a judgment, and initiated legal steps to collect the money before the deceased died, or

- the creditor can show that the joint tenancy arrangement was a scheme set up solely to defraud creditors.

3. Incapacity

Any form of shared ownership can become difficult if one owner becomes incapacitated. The other owners may need someone with legal authority to act for the incapacitated owner, particularly to sell the property or refinance it.

The best way to authorize someone to act for you if you become incapacitated is by use of a durable power of attorney for finances (discussed in Chapter 26). To be secure, owners of joint tenancy property should each prepare a durable power of attorney. Otherwise, a court proceeding may be required if one owner becomes incapacitated.

H. WHEN JOINT TENANCY MAKES SENSE

Don't interpret our comments about the risks of joint tenancy as a damning indictment against using it under all circumstances. In some situations, owning property in joint tenancy certainly does make sense. For people who value simplicity (joint tenancy is easy to create), and whose situations don't involve the drawbacks and risks we've discussed, joint tenancy can work fine.

1. Buying a House

Any two people, most commonly a married couple, can sensibly use joint tenancy to buy a house together if each person wants the other to receive his or her interest in the house on death. Indeed, buying a house in joint tenancy or tenancy by the entirety is probably the most common way this form of ownership is used.

> **Example:** Susan is in her 60s, her mother Kate is in her 80s. They have lived together for four years, and decide to buy a house together. They want to make sure that the survivor has full and exclusive rights to the property when one dies, and that some grasping relations cannot validly contest the survivor's rights. The easiest way for them to achieve their goal is to buy the property in joint tenancy.

INDIVIDUAL GRANT DEED

RECORDING REQUESTED BY

AND WHEN RECORDED MAIL TO

Name **Alfred Smythe**
Address **Easy Street**
City & State **El Dorado Hills, Ca.**

This Order No._____ Escrow No._____

——— SPACE ABOVE THIS LINE FOR RECORDER'S USE ———

MAIL TAX STATEMENTS TO

Name **Alfred Smythe**
Address **Easy Street**
City & State **El Dorado Hills, Ca.**

Individual Grant Deed

~~FOR A VALUABLE CONSIDERATION~~

Alfred Smythe
GRANTS___ to

Anthony Smythe and Alfred Smythe, as Joint Tenants

all that real property situate in the   City of El Dorado Hills

County of   **Dreams**   , State of California, described as follows

(property described and identified)

Said property to be owned in joint tenancy by Alfred Smythe
and Anthony Smythe

Dated____July 1, 1980_____ XXXXXX

_____   /s/ Alfred Smythe_____

_____   /s/ Anthony Smythe_____

STATE OF CALIFORNIA
_____County of _____ } ss.
On_____ 19____ before me, the undersigned,
a Notary Public, in and for said State, personally appeared____
_____
known to me to be the person___ whose name____
subscribed to the within instrument, and acknowledged to me that
___he___ executed the same.

_____
Notary Public

FOR NOTARY SEAL OR STAMP

MAIL TAX STATEMENTS AS DIRECTED ABOVE

2. Transfers Into Joint Tenancy When Death Is Imminent

If a sole owner of property is likely to die soon, transferring that property into joint tenancy can be a useful last-minute probate-avoidance device if no previous estate planning has been done.

> **Example:** Avram, who is old and in rapidly declining health, lives in a co-op apartment in Manhattan. Avram wants the apartment to go to his daughter, Molly, whom he trusts totally—and he wants to avoid probate. He also loathes paperwork and wants the transfer accomplished as simply as possible. Avram can simply transfer ownership of the property into joint tenancy with his daughter. It requires less paperwork than a living trust. He doesn't worry about filing a gift tax return, since by the time it's due, there will probably be an estate tax return instead. And since Molly didn't contribute any cash for the purchase of the co-op, it will all receive a stepped-up basis to the market value at Avram's death.

Transfers of solely owned property into joint tenancy are less desirable if the original owner is likely to live an appreciable time. In this situation, a gift tax return must actually be filed (well, it's supposed to be); then there's more paperwork, and possible subsequent estate tax credit calculations when the original owner dies. For long-term planning with solely owned property, a living trust remains a better method.

I. CREATING A JOINT TENANCY FOR PROPERTY WITH DOCUMENTS OF TITLE

Joint tenancy is commonly used for many types of property with documents of title, including real estate, stocks, vehicles, bank accounts, and safe deposit boxes. There are two ways property with documents of title can be placed in joint tenancy:

- two or more people buy or acquire property and take title in joint tenancy, or
- a person who owns property can transfer title into joint tenancy with another person or people.

1. The Language Required

To create a joint tenancy, the title document must contain words that clearly demonstrate the owners' intention. In most states, joint tenancy may be created by putting the phrase "in joint tenancy" or "as joint tenants" in the ownership document. In some states, it's traditional or required to use the phrase "joint tenants, with right of survivorship," or "in joint tenancy with right of survivorship." This is sometimes abbreviated "JTWROS." Sometimes, the following is used: "Joint tenancy, not as tenants in common, and with right of survivorship." Simply listing the owners' names joined by "and" or "or" is not normally adequate to create a joint tenancy, although a few states allow it.

If you decide to transfer some of your existing property into joint tenancy, you must learn your state's law to learn the exact wording needed. If you're transferring real estate, any reliable title company or lawyer can tell you. You'll find that a few states have special requirements governing how a joint tenancy is created. For example, in Florida, a joint tenancy can be created only in an instrument of transfer—a deed made when property is sold or given away. In Texas, the joint tenancy owners must also sign a separate written contract agreeing to the joint tenancy.

In a number of other states, specific language must be used to create the joint tenancy. In Ohio, for instance, the document must state "for their joint lives, remainder to the survivor of them." In South Carolina, joint tenancy for real estate must use the words "as joint tenants with rights of survivorship, and not as tenants in common." And in Oregon, you can't use the words "joint tenancy," but you can create the functional equivalent by expressly indicating that co-owners have a right of survivorship.

DO YOU ALREADY OWN PROPERTY IN JOINT TENANCY?

You may not remember how you took title to a piece of real estate, or your car, or your bank account. To see if shared ownership property is held in joint tenancy, look on the deed (for real estate) or the title slip (for other kinds of property, such as cars). If it doesn't say the co-owners own the property "as joint tenants" or "with right of survivorship" or similar language, the property isn't held in joint tenancy.

---

2. Real Estate

To demonstrate how simple creating joint tenancy can be, we've included a deed used to transfer solely owned real estate into joint tenancy. (See above.) In this deed, Alfred Smythe has created a joint tenancy in real estate between himself and his son Anthony.

J. CREATING JOINT TENANCY FOR PERSONAL PROPERTY WITHOUT DOCUMENTS OF TITLE

You can also create joint tenancies for property without documents of title, such as valuable paintings, jewelry, or even for your shoes. All you and the other co-owners have to do is declare in a signed document that you all own the property "in joint tenancy" or "as joint tenants." The document doesn't need to be filed with the county land records office, unlike deeds putting real property in joint tenancy. However you should have your signatures notarized.

Example: Guy and Danielle have been together for years. They have acquired a considerable amount of household furnishings, including appliances, furniture, and glassware. Each wants the other to receive all their property when one of them dies. They want to avoid probate and the possibility that a member of either one's family could claim any of their property. So, Guy and Danielle write up and sign a joint ownership document, stating that all the household furnishings listed in it are their joint tenancy property. ■

11

PAY-ON-DEATH DESIGNATIONS:
Bank Accounts, Securities, Stocks and Bonds, Motor Vehicles

With a pay-on-death or transfer-on-death designation, you formally name another person, or persons, to receive certain property, or whatever is left of it, when you die. Property left with a pay-on-death (P.O.D.) designation avoids probate. When you die, the property goes directly to the named beneficiary. (You do not leave pay-on-death property through your will or other transfer device. To accomplish the transfer, you need only the P.O.D. designation.)

Pay-on-death designations have become widely used, particularly for bank accounts and government securities. Most states have adopted laws allowing the use of transfer-on-death registration for securities—stocks, bonds, or stock brokerage accounts. A couple of states, California and Missouri, also allow transfer-on-death registration for motor vehicles. Finally, individual retirement programs, such as IRAs, 401(k)s, or profit-sharing plans, allow you to name someone to receive any funds left in the account at your death; this use of a P.O.D. designation is discussed in Chapter 13.

Pay-on-death accounts avoid probate with a minimum of paperwork. Normally, an institution, such as a bank or the U.S. Treasury Department, provides you with one simple form on which you designate the beneficiary, and that's it. The beneficiary, of course, has no rights to any of the property until your death.

A. CHOOSING BENEFICIARIES

There are few restrictions on whom you can name as a P.O.D. beneficiary (sometimes called a "payee"). But there are some issues that may concern you.

1. Multiple Beneficiaries

You can name more than one beneficiary for a P.O.D. account, except with government securities. (See Section C, below.) You simply list all beneficiaries on the account form. Each will inherit an equal share of the money in the account unless you specify differently.

Be careful when leaving unequal shares. In a very few states—for example, Florida—you cannot change the equal shares rule. If you're concerned about this issue, check your state's laws or open a separate account for each beneficiary.

2. Alternate Beneficiaries

With a P.O.D. account, you cannot name alternate beneficiaries. If you name only one beneficiary and he doesn't outlive you, the P.O.D. designation no longer works, and the funds in the account will pass to the residuary beneficiary of your will. If you name more than one P.O.D. beneficiary, and one dies before you, all money left in the account goes to the surviving beneficiaries. The lesson here is clear: If you're concerned about what happens if a P.O.D. beneficiary doesn't survive you, a P.O.D. account isn't for you, unless you're prepared (and able) to create a new account if a beneficiary does predecease you.

3. Children as Beneficiaries

It's fine to name a minor—a child under 18—as a P.O.D. beneficiary. However, as we've discussed in Chapter 6, if you do this you should consider what might happen if that child is still a minor when you die. Depending on your state's laws, you can choose between the following options:

- You can name an adult "custodian" for the property, under the Uniform Transfers to Minors Act (valid in every state except South Carolina and Vermont). All you need do is name the custodian as the P.O.D. payee of the account. This custodian then has the legal responsibility to manage and use the money on behalf of the child. Then, when the child reaches the age required or permitted under your state's UTMA, the property is turned over to the child. (See Chapter 6, Section C.)

    Example: Mary-Kate wants to make her grandson, Mike, the P.O.D. payee of a bank account. Mike is six years old. So Mary-Kate names Mike's father, Claude, as custodian of the money in the account. On the bank's form, Mary-Kate puts, in the space for the P.O.D. payee, "Claude du Monde, as custodian for Mike du Monde under the Florida Uniform Transfers to Minors Act." If Mike is not yet 21 when his grandmother dies, Claude will be legally in charge of the money until Mike's 21st birthday.

- If you create a child's trust as part of your estate planning, you can name the trustee of that trust as the beneficiary for the P.O.D. account and direct that money from the account be used for the benefit of the child. (See Chapter 6, Section C.)

- If state law allows it, money left to a minor can simply be turned over to the beneficiary's parents. The parents hold the money for the benefit of the child until the child reaches age 18. Unfortunately, at present only five states follow this sensible approach. (See Chapter 6, Section B.)

B. PAY-ON-DEATH BANK ACCOUNTS

Here we look deeper into how pay-on-death bank accounts work. This type of account is called by various names by different banks in different parts of the country. Common names, aside from "P.O.D." account, include "informal trust," "bank trust account," and a "Totten trust" (perhaps from an old New York case, *Re Totten,* although some commentators have suggested the name is derived from the German "Tod," meaning death).

Whatever it's called, it works the same way. You open an account in your name, as depositor, and name your beneficiary—the person you want to receive whatever money is in the account when you die. Sometimes you list yourself as trustee for the benefit of your beneficiary. As long as you live, the beneficiary has no rights to any money in the account. You can spend it freely—indeed, spend it all, if you want to or need to. After your death, the beneficiary can promptly obtain whatever money remains in the account simply by presenting the bank with proof of identity and a certified copy of the death certificate.

Example: Ray Jones wants to leave cash, probate free, to his two daughters. He simply opens a pay-on-death trust certificate of deposit account as "Ray Jones, depositor, as trustee for Michelle and Mary Jones, equal beneficiaries." After he dies, his daughters go to the bank, present a copy of his death certificate and proof of their identities to bank officials, and then withdraw and divide equally all money in the account.

1. Advantages of P.O.D. Bank Accounts

There are normally no risks in creating a P.O.D. bank account. Unlike joint tenancy bank accounts, there's no danger that the beneficiary will withdraw any money from the account while you're alive. In addition, you can close the account any time and can change the beneficiary at any time. You can deposit or withdraw any amount desired (subject, of course, to any penalties the bank applies on early withdrawal, if you have a C.D. account).

Because you retain complete control over the account until death, establishing a pay-on-death account isn't a gift, and therefore doesn't involve gift tax concerns. Only when the beneficiary gets the money at your death does legal ownership of that money change.

2. Opening a P.O.D. Account

An appealing aspect of a P.O.D. account is that it's so easy to open. Most banks, including most credit unions, have standard forms for opening this kind of account; they will do the paperwork for you. A P.O.D. account may either be a newly opened account or an existing account to which you add a beneficiary designation. Banks don't normally charge extra fees for holding your money in a P.O.D. account.

Generally, any regular bank account, including checking, savings, or certificates of deposit accounts, may be used as a P.O.D. account. In practice, these accounts are usually savings accounts, since it's more likely there will be substantial funds in a savings

account at the depositor's death than in a checking account. And because most checking accounts don't pay interest, they aren't suitable places to keep substantial sums.

3. Estate Taxes

The money in a P.O.D. account is included in the taxable estate of the depositor. (See Chapter 15, Section A.) So a P.O.D. account works only as a probate-avoidance device, and will not save on federal or state estate tax, assuming your estate is large enough to owe them.

4. Before You Open a P.O.D. Account

If you decide to open a P.O.D. account, there are a few concerns you should be aware of and ask about at your bank:

- **Early withdrawal penalties.** If the type of bank account you choose for a P.O.D. account requires holding a deposit for a set term, or paying a substantial penalty for early withdrawal—as would be the case, for example, for a six-month certificate of deposit—the penalty is usually waived if the depositor dies before that term expires and the beneficiary claims the funds.

- **Spouse's share of estate.** If you try to disinherit your spouse, the person you name as P.O.D. payee may not get all the money in your account. The reason is simple. In many states, if your spouse goes to court and claims a share of your estate, some funds deposited in a P.O.D. account may be paid to the spouse. (See Chapter 3, Section C.)

- **Special state rules.** A few states—generally those with state inheritance or estate taxes—throw up barriers to collecting a P.O.D. bank account after the depositor dies. For example, Ohio requires that a state estate tax lien form be filled out before releasing any cash to the beneficiary. Ask at your bank if there are any special state rules on collecting a P.O.D. account before you set one up.

C. NAMING A PAY-ON-DEATH BENEFICIARY FOR GOVERNMENT SECURITIES

You can hold U.S. Treasury Department securities (T-bills) in a pay-on-death account form. The Treasury Department, or your investment advisor (if you have one), can provide you with the correct form. In that form, you register ownership of your securities in your (the purchaser's) name, followed by "payable on death to [whomever you name as beneficiary]." If a minor (or incompetent adult) is beneficiary, that status must be stated on the registration.

There can be only one primary owner and one beneficiary for a government security. So a P.O.D. account will not work for government securities if you want the money divided between different beneficiaries.

D. NAMING A BENEFICIARY FOR STOCKS AND BONDS

In every state except Texas, you can add a transfer-on-death designation to brokerage accounts, or to individual securities (stocks and bonds) under the Uniform Transfers-on-Death Securities Registration Act.

If you register your stocks, bonds, securities accounts, or mutual funds in a transfer-on-death form, the beneficiary or beneficiaries you designate will receive these securities promptly after your death. No probate will be necessary. Your broker can provide the forms you'll need to name a beneficiary for your securities account.

⚠️ **Your broker isn't required to cooperate.** Although most stockbrokers and corporate transfer agents offer transfer-on-death registration (where legally permitted), the law doesn't require them to do so; it simply allows them that option. Of course, if they don't offer you that option, you can threaten to switch brokers, or sell your shares, which may well overcome resistance.

Even if you live in one of the few states that haven't authorized transfer-on-death registration, you can use a transfer-on-death registration for securities if any of the following is true:

- The stockbroker's principal office is in a state that has adopted the law.

- The issuer of the stock or the stockbroker is incorporated in a state that has adopted the law.

- The transfer agent's office is located in a state that has adopted the law.

- The office making the registration is in a state that has adopted the law.

If you want to avoid probate but can't use a transfer-on-death designation for your securities, it's usually better to use a living trust rather than joint tenancy. With a living trust:

- the beneficiary of the living trust has no right to the securities while you live, and

- you can change the beneficiary or end the living trust if you wish.

With joint tenancy, you cannot decide to remove the joint tenant as co-owner, and that person is legal co-owner of half of the stock/securities.

E. VEHICLE REGISTRATION

Currently, five states allow you to register cars in transfer-on-death form: California, Connecticut, Kansas, Missouri, and Ohio. If you live in one of these states and want to use transfer-on-death registration for your vehicles, contact your state's motor vehicles agency for the appropriate form. Other states are considering legislation to allow transfer-on-death car registration. It may soon become a widely used probate-avoidance method.

In California, transfer-on-death registration is also available for small boats, called "undocumented vessels," which include the myriad of small pleasure boats that aren't required to have a valid marine document from the U.S. Bureau of Customs. Only one owner and one beneficiary may be listed. (California Vehicle Code § 9852.7.)

SIMPLIFIED VEHICLE TRANSFER

If your state doesn't allow transfer-on-death registration for vehicles, it may still offer a simple method for transferring ownership after a death. Sometimes these streamlined methods are available only to a surviving spouse, or only if the value of the vehicle is below a certain amount. For details and forms, your best bet is to contact your state's motor vehicles agency. To find a link to that agency's website, you can look on the Response Insurance website, at www.response.com/tips_tools/great_links.asp.

F. TRANSFER-ON-DEATH DEEDS FOR REAL ESTATE

In a few states, you can prepare and record a deed now that will transfer your real estate only after you die. The states that allow transfer-on-death real estate deeds are Arizona, Arkansas, Colorado, Kansas, Missouri, Nevada, New Mexico, and Ohio.

The deed should expressly state that it does not take effect until your death, and name the person(s) to receive title to the real estate after your death. A transfer-on-death deed must be written, signed, notarized, and recorded (filed in the county land records office) just like a regular deed. But unlike a typical deed, you can revoke a transfer-on-death deed at any time before your death.

Don't try this unless you know your state law authorizes it. You can't use a deed to transfer real estate at your death unless your state law (or the state law where the real estate is located) specifically authorizes this type of transfer method. If your state law doesn't allow transfer-on-death deeds, you must use a valid transfer device, such as a will, living trust, or joint tenancy. ■

12

LIFE INSURANCE

Life insurance has long been a part of estate planning in the United States. Indeed, one of the reasons some people fear the phrase "estate planning" is that it may be a cover for hard-sell visits by life insurance agents. Life insurance does not need to be a part of every person's estate plan. It can be very useful, however, especially for parents of young children and those who support a spouse or a disabled adult or child. It can also provide cash to pay debts and estate taxes.

A. DO YOU NEED LIFE INSURANCE?

In addition to helping to support dependents, life insurance can help solve several other common estate planning problems. These include:

- **Providing immediate cash at death.** Insurance proceeds are a handy source of cash to pay the deceased's debts, funeral expenses, and income or death taxes. (Federal estate taxes are due nine months after death, so cash to pay them doesn't have to be raised immediately.)

- **Probate avoidance.** Normally, the proceeds of a life insurance policy avoid probate because you name your beneficiary in the policy instead of in your will. This means that the proceeds can be transferred quickly to survivors with little red tape, cost, or delay. (See Section C, below.)

- **Estate tax reduction.** When an insurance policy is not legally owned by the person who is the insured (as explained in Section E), the proceeds are excluded from the insured's taxable estate. This can significantly reduce the estate tax liability of the insured's estate. Obviously, though, this is a benefit only for people whose estates are large enough to owe estate tax in the first place.

Having indicated some of the reasons life insurance can be desirable, let us again emphasize that simply buying some is not an adequate way to plan an estate. Many, if not most, people who have no minor children or financially strapped dependents simply don't need life insurance. Those who decide to purchase insurance should know exactly why they are buying it, the best type of policy for their needs, and of course, should buy no more than they need. As a group, Americans certainly believe in life insurance, holding over two trillion dollars worth—far more, per capita, than any other country.

Here are some questions to ask yourself to help evaluate your life insurance needs.

1. Long-Term Needs

To determine whether it makes sense for you to purchase insurance to provide financial help for family members over the long term, consider these factors:

- How many people are really dependent on your current earning capacity over the long term? If the answer is "no one," it's doubtful that you need life insurance.

- How much money would your dependents really need, and for how long, if you died suddenly? When you determine how much money your dependents will need, subtract the worth of property you leave them and any amounts that will be available from public and any private insurance plans that already provide coverage. Social Security and dependents' benefits may also be available, and you may also be covered by union or management pensions or a group life insurance plan. Don't forget to subtract any other likely sources of income, such as the help reasonably affluent grandparents would assuredly provide for your children in case of disaster. Also, remember that bright kids may get at least partial scholarships, and dependent spouses caring for young children can usually return to work at some point.

2. Short-Term Needs

Now, assess whether you need life insurance for short-term needs.

- How long is it likely to be, after you die, before your property is turned over to your inheritors? If most of your property will avoid probate, there's usually little need for insurance for short-term expenses, unless you have no bank accounts, securities, or other cash assets. By contrast, if the bulk of your property is transferred by will, and therefore will be tied up in probate for months, your family and other inheritors may need the ready cash insurance can provide. While a probate court will usually promptly authorize a family allowance or otherwise allow a spouse or other inheritor access to estate funds, it can still be nice to have insurance proceeds available.

- What other assets will be available to take care of immediate financial needs? Aside from buying insurance, there are other, cheaper, ways of providing ready cash, such as leaving some money in joint or pay-on-death bank accounts, or placing marketable stocks and other securities in joint tenancy.

- Will your estate owe substantial debts and taxes after your death? Lawyers and financial advisors call cash and assets that can quickly be converted to cash "liquid." If your estate has almost all "non-liquid" assets (real estate, collectibles, a share in a small business, jewelry) there may be a major loss if these assets must be sold quickly to raise cash to pay bills, as opposed to what they could be sold for later if there had been enough liquid money from insurance or other sources to meet all pressing bills. Obviously, if your estate has significant funds in bank accounts or marketable securities, you won't need to purchase insurance for this purpose.

Example: Alicia's estate consists of several valuable pieces of real estate and one-half interest in a profitable antique store, but includes very little cash and no life insurance. When she dies, she owes debts of $90,000 (aside from mortgages) and death taxes of $120,000. To raise this money, her beneficiaries (technically, her executor) must sell some of her real estate or her interest in the store. Unfortunately, the country is suffering a recession, and the market value of both antiques and real estate is down. To make matters worse, canny real estate people spread the word that this is a "distress sale" to raise money for estate obligations. As a result the price the beneficiaries receive when they sell one of the pieces of real estate is far below what they would have received if they had the flexibility to choose when to sell the property. Had Alicia purchased an insurance policy with a payoff at death of $210,000 or more, the need to sell the real estate would have been eliminated.

- If you are sole owner of a business, how much cash would it need on your death? Do you want, and expect, that some of your inheritors will continue the business? If so, do you think there will be a sufficient cash flow so the new owners can successfully maintain the business? How much is your death likely to reduce cash flow? How much will it affect the value of the business, if it must be sold? Do you need insurance proceeds to cover any cash flow shortage of the business? (Chapter 28 discusses estate planning for business in more detail.)

  If you don't plan to have your inheritors continue the business, the questions are simpler: Will there be enough cash so the business can stay alive until it is sold? Is there really anything to sell? For many personal service businesses, the answer is no—the business ends when the person providing the service dies.

BUYING INSURANCE

If you don't own life insurance and think you want it, you need to talk to an insurance salesperson or broker. Normally, a salesperson sells for one company only, while a broker can place your policy with one of several. In theory, this would seem to be a reason to prefer a broker, but in practice, the integrity of the person you are dealing with is far more important than is the legal relationship to an insurance company or companies.

If you do contact an insurance salesperson, look for a person who will function as an ally, offering additional information and proposing alternatives—not forcing you. If you get too much quick-sell pressure, contact someone else. And here's one more tip: some salespeople don't recommend that you buy term insurance, or try to talk you out of it, for no other reason than they get a much higher commission from selling you whole life or universal. (See Section B, below, for an analysis of the pros and cons of various types of life insurance.)

Before you contact anyone who sells insurance, you should have a good idea of what kind of policy you need and how much it should cost. The cost of the same insurance can vary considerably from company to company. Often, relatively small mutual companies charge lower rates than some of the giants of TV advertising, and some brokers charge lower "discount" commissions.

Shopping for insurance. For in-depth information about purchasing life insurance, you can turn to *How to Insure Your Life* by Reg Wilson and the Merritt Editors (Merritt). Many states also survey life insurance companies and publish the premiums charged for various policies in different parts of the state. You can find out if your state does this by visiting your state's department of insurance website. To find it, use an Internet search engine such as Google, and type in the term "department of insurance" or "insurance commissioner."

You can also contact a free life insurance rate-shopping service, which will provide information on the costs of different companies' policies. Often free quotes are given only for term insurance policies. Companies that offer free quotes by phone or online include:

- Quicken InsWeb Market
  www.insweb.com

- QuickQuote, 800-867-2404
  www.quickquote.com

- Quotesmith, 800-995-9790
  www.quotesmith.com

Other companies provide online forms you can complete and submit to the quote service. You will usually receive quotes from these companies within a week:

- SelectQuote, 800-963-8688
  www.selectquote.com

- InsuranceQuote Services, 800-972-1104
  www.iquote.com

- MasterQuote, 800-337-5433
  www.masterquote.com

It's often wise to call, rather than contact a company through its website. You can usually get more personalized service from a phone conversation than you can with the constraints of a Web form. Still, the websites can provide information to help you select what type of insurance you want, and how much dollar coverage you need.

These quote-service organizations often make money if you buy a "product" (life insurance) that they recommend, so use any information that they give you as a starting place.

B. TYPES OF LIFE INSURANCE

If you are interested in life insurance, any salesperson will be delighted to explain the bewildering array of policies available to you. But unless you educate yourself first, it's all too easy to get mesmerized by insurance policy lingo and end up paying too much for a policy that may not even meet your needs. Basically, for estate planning purposes, there are two main types of life insurance: term, which provides insurance only for a set period, and some form of "permanent" insurance, which the company can never cancel as long as the premiums are paid. Over time, permanent insurance will build a cash value which produces returns for the policyholder. However, although permanent insurance policies do function as one type of investment, maximizing your investment return is not the purpose of insurance. If that's what you want, look elsewhere.

Permanent insurance includes whole life, universal life, and variable life (discussed below). Any of these types of life insurance can be purchased with one lump sum, called a "single-premium payment," which can be a useful estate planning device if you have sufficient funds and want to lock in your life insurance now. We explain each in the sections that follow.

HOW SAFE IS YOUR INSURANCE COMPANY?

As some surprised and angry insurance policy owners have learned to their dismay, insurance companies can encounter serious financial trouble, and even go broke. For instance, a few insurance companies invested heavily in junk bonds and "go-go" real estate deals during the 1980s, and paid the price of insolvency when glimmers of fiscal (and societal) sanity returned to these economic areas in the 1990s.

There is no national or federal insurance guarantee fund for life insurance companies similar to FDIC insurance for bank depositors. However, all states and the District of Columbia have a state department with some regulatory power over life insurance, as well as some sort of industry-sponsored state guarantee fund. While these funds offer most life insurance policyholders the reasonable hope that they won't lose everything they invested if their insurer goes broke, you still certainly don't want to have to wait for state regulators to take charge of an insolvent company, investigate, and finally—and it can take a while—determine how much money you get back.

To avoid this sad scenario, you can check the reliability of the insurer you plan to buy a policy from. Several major companies rate the financial stability of insurance companies. It's prudent to check

your insurance agency against one—and even better, two—of these rating systems, to be sure the company you're interested in got top grades. You'll probably have to pay a small fee to obtain a specific company's rating.

The names of the major rating companies are:

- Weiss Ratings (the most rigorous of the bunch)
  800-289-8222
  www.weissratings.com

- A.M. Best (Best Insurance Reports)
  800-424-2378
  www.ambest.com

- Moody's Investors Service
  www.moodys.com

- Standard and Poor's
  www.standardandpoors.com

You should be able to locate the reports of these companies at a large public library and online. If not, your insurance agent should be able to assist you with locating their business offices and phone numbers. Each company has a slightly different code for its rating—for instance, Weiss Research's top rating is "A+" whereas Standard and Poor's top rating is "AAA." Each company will provide you its rating code system.

A trustworthy insurance agent is a must.
There are a bewildering number of variations of life insurance policies. Without writing an entire book on the subject, it's impossible to explain the names of every possible option to you here. We can tell you about the basic forms, and offer two pieces of advice: First, many of the variations are of the "bells and whistles" type, with minor differences that don't mean nearly as much as some insurance agents may claim. Second, when it comes to selecting a policy, or fine-tuning your needs, your choice of an insurance agent is crucial. Unless you are prepared to do an immense amount of research yourself, you'll have to rely somewhat on the advice of your agent. So you surely need one you trust. We're fortunate to have fine insurance agents (now friends) and can attest to the value of working with someone you trust and like.

1. Term Insurance

Term insurance provides a preset amount of cash if you die while the policy is in force. For example, a five-year $130,000 term policy pays off if you die within five years—and that's it. If you live beyond the end of the term, you get nothing (except, of course, the continued joys and sorrows of life itself). With term insurance, you pay for only life insurance coverage. The policy does not develop reserves.

Term insurance is the cheapest form of coverage over a limited number of years. As a candid life insurance man once said, "It provides the most bang for the buck, no question—over the short term." There are many types of term insurance, such as policies that have an automatic right to renew for an additional term, but these options don't change the basic fact that term insurance pays off if you die during the policy time period and doesn't pay anything if you live beyond that period.

Term life insurance is particularly suitable for younger people with families, who want substantial insurance coverage at low cost. Since the risk of dying in your 20s, 30s, or 40s is quite low, the cost of term insurance during these years is as reasonable as life insurance prices get. Also, if you need insurance for only a short time, say to qualify for a business loan, term is your best bet. However, the older you are, the more expensive term insurance becomes when you compare how much you have to pay in premiums to the payoff value of the policy. This, of course, is understandable, as the older you are, the greater the chance you will die during the policy term.

As mentioned above, term policies offered by different companies have all sorts of differences, some fairly significant. For example, some policies are automatically renewable at the end of the term without a medical examination, often for higher premiums, and some are not. Some have premiums set for a period of years, but others guarantee a premium rate for only the first year. After that, the rate can go up. Some can also be converted from a term to whole life or "universal" policy during the term, again without needing to requalify. But as we've said, with term insurance you never lock in the right to maintain the policy no matter how old you become. If you want to ensure that insurance will continue in force your entire life, term isn't for you.

2. Permanent Insurance

Permanent insurance is automatically renewable without a new physical examination of the insured. With a permanent policy, your premium payments for the first few (or more than a few) years cover more than the actuarial cost of the risk of death. The excess money goes into a reserve account, which is invested by the insurance company. Unless the company is disastrously managed, these investments yield returns—interest or dividends. A proportion of these are passed along to you. These returns can be used to add to your policy reserves or borrowed against, after a set time. And if you decide to end the policy, you can cash it in for the "surrender value."

Returns that accumulate are not taxable, unless the money is actually distributed to you. Certain partial withdrawals can even be made without paying tax. By contrast, the interest on bank accounts is subject to tax in the year it is paid, even if left untouched in the account.

a. Whole Life Insurance

Whole life (sometimes called "straight life") insurance provides a set dollar amount of coverage that can never be canceled, in exchange for fixed, uniform payments. Because the payments are the same throughout your life, the premiums are comparatively high (versus your statistical risk of death) in the early years of the policy (this is why reserves are built up). Assuming you live a long while after the policy was issued, your payments become low, compared to your risk of death. In other words, insurance companies take in substantially more money on whole life policies during their first few years than they pay out on those policies. The insurance company invests the surplus. Some of the surplus becomes your cash reserve, which grows over time. The cash reserve earns dividends, paid by the insurance company. After a set time, usually several years, you have the right to borrow against the cash reserve. You can also, of course, cancel the policy and receive its cash surrender value.

Whole life often is not desirable for younger people with small children who don't have adequate savings to cope should a main income-provider die. People in this group usually can't afford initially expensive permanent policies.

b. Universal Life Insurance

Universal life combines some of the desirable features of both term and whole life insurance, and offers other advantages. Over time, the net cost usually is lower than whole life insurance. With universal life, you build up a cash reserve, as with whole life. But you can also vary premium payments, amount of coverage, or both, from year to year. In contrast, whole life requires one set payment amount, which cannot be varied, for the life of the policy. Also, universal life policies normally provide you with more consumer information. For example, you are told how much of your policy payments goes for company overhead expenses, reserves, and policy proceed payments, and how much is retained for your savings. This information isn't usually provided with whole life policies.

There can be other significant advantages to universal life; an insurance agent will be glad to explain them to you.

c. Variable Life Insurance

Variable life insurance refers to policies in which cash reserves are invested in securities, stocks, and bonds. In a sense, these policies combine an insurance feature with a mutual fund. Since over the past decade, overall prices on the stock market have risen dramatically, variable life policies have usually produced the best returns. But of course, there's a potential downside to this also. These policies are almost sure to bring unpleasant surprises when financial markets decline.

d. Variable Universal Life Insurance

Variable Universal Life Insurance is a type of whole life insurance that combines the premium payment and coverage flexibility of universal life insurance with the investment opportunity (and risk) of variable life insurance.

3. Single-Premium Life Insurance

With single-premium life, you pay, up-front, all premiums due for the full duration of the policy. Normally, any policy with a savings feature can be purchased with a single premium. Obviously, this requires the expenditure of a large amount of cash— $5,000, $10,000, or often much more, depending on your age and the dollar amount of the policy.

One reason to commit so much cash to buying an insurance policy is that it enables you to give the fully-paid-for policy to new owners. As explained in Section E of this chapter, there can be major estate tax savings if someone other than the insured owns the policy. That way the gift tax obligation is computed on the current—not future—value of the policy. And because there are no more payments to make, a gift of a single-premium policy doesn't involve risks that the new owners will fail to make payments and cause the policy to be canceled.

4. Survivorship Life Insurance

Survivorship life insurance (also called "second to die" or "joint" insurance) is a relatively new type of insurance. It provides a single policy that insures two lives, usually spouses. When the first spouse dies, no proceeds are paid. Indeed, the policy remains in force, and premiums must continue to be paid, as long as a spouse lives. The policy only pays off on the death of the second spouse.

Why would any couple want such a policy? Mainly for use as part of an estate plan for wealthier couples who expect that substantial estate taxes will be assessed on the death of the second spouse. (See Chapter 18.) None of this is of interest to people with moderate-sized estates or smaller, so if you are in this category, you don't need to read this section.

This type of insurance can be particularly desirable when a major family asset is a valuable family business, or real estate interests—assets that aren't liquid, and which the survivors may not want to sell. Or suppose two children inherit a family business, but one doesn't want to keep it going. The other could use her share of the insurance proceeds as an initial buy-out payment, so she could retain ownership of the business.

This kind of insurance can also be desirable if one member of a couple is in less than good health. If the other spouse is in reasonably good health, the couple can usually obtain survivorship life insurance.

Because two lives are insured, premiums for survivorship life policies are comparatively low compared to policies on one person's life. It's those old insurance companies' actuarial tables again: The odds on two people dying in X time period are less than on one. But, of course, cost also depends on the age and the health of the insured couple.

 The federal tax statute governing survivorship life insurance is somewhat ambiguous. Because this is a new and complex area, you need to check with a good estate planning lawyer with current knowledge of the tax rulings on this type of policy. Also, discuss this issue with your insurance agent to ensure your survivorship policy will have the effect you intend. It may be best to have the policy owned by a life insurance trust. (See Section E, below, and Chapter 21, Section B.)

5. "First to Die" Life Insurance

"First to die" life insurance is, as the name indicates, the reverse of survivorship insurance. With a first-to-die policy, two (or occasionally more) people, usually business partners or co-owners, are insured under one policy. Because these policies are usually maintained as a part of a business buyout agreement, usually the company or partnership itself buys and maintains the policy. When the first insured dies, the policy pays off, with the funds typically paid to the company or partnership. Effectively, this means payments go to the other owners of the business.

A first-to-die policy is significantly cheaper than individual policies for two, or several, business owners. Obviously, insuring against only one death exposes an insurance company to lower risks, and lesser proceed payments, than if several people are separately insured for the same amount.

When one business owner dies, the proceeds of a first to die policy can be used to pay off the worth of the deceased owner's interest, under a buyout clause. Or, if the deceased owner's beneficiaries wish to, and are allowed to, participate in the business, the funds can be used for the costs of whatever adjustments and problems the business faces because of the death of an owner.

> **Example:** Paul, Gabe, and Liz are equal partners in a video rental store. Their partnership agreement provides that if a partner dies, the two surviving partners can buy out that partner's interest according to a set valuation formula. The business does not have a great deal of ready cash. Almost all the available cash the partners had was consumed by opening the business, acquiring inventory, and operational costs.
>
> The partnership buys a "first-to-die" policy covering the lives of the three partners. The partners have made a rough guess of how much the business is worth now, and paid for a policy that pays off about half this value. In theory, they need coverage for only one-third of the value, but they hope and expect their business will increase, so want to include some allowance for increased value of a deceased partner's interest.

> If a partner dies, the life insurance pays the proceeds to the partnership. The value of the deceased partner's interest is determined from the formula. The two surviving partners pay this amount to the deceased partner's inheritors. If there are any insurance proceeds left over, the partners can use them however they agree upon. And when everything is wound up, the two surviving partners now own the business 50-50.

6. Annuities

Basically, an annuity is a policy in which an insurance company contracts to pay the policy beneficiary a certain cash amount each year, or month, instead of one lump sum upon death. There are all sorts of annuity policies and combinations of annuity payment plans with cash-value life insurance policies. Some people who don't trust their own ability to hold onto money even purchase an annuity policy when times are good, naming themselves as beneficiary. They thus provide themselves with a set income for life, beginning at a specified age.

An estate planning advantage of an annuity is that you can buy one that will provide periodic payments to someone you believe is unable (too young, or too much of a wastrel) to handle one large lump sum insurance payment. In this sense, annuities work somewhat like a trust.

However, even if you want to arrange for periodic payments to a beneficiary, you should consider other alternatives, including establishing a trust. (See Chapter 17.) Annuity policies tend to be a relatively expensive way to meet your objective. Also, they are not flexible. For example, if special needs of the beneficiary arise, such as an extended illness, the payments often cannot be increased, as they often can be with a well-designed trust. In short, it's usually wiser to buy a more prosaic type of insurance and have the benefits put in trust should you die, to be administered by a trusted friend or family member who can vary pay-outs to meet the needs of the trust beneficiary.

C. LIFE INSURANCE AND PROBATE

The proceeds of a life insurance policy are not subject to probate unless you name your estate as the beneficiary of your policy. If anyone else, including a trust, is the beneficiary of the policy, the proceeds are not included in the probate estate, and the proceeds are paid to the beneficiary without the cost or delay of probate. Except when your estate will have no ready cash to pay anticipated debts and taxes, there is no sound reason for naming your estate, rather than a person or persons, as the beneficiary or beneficiaries of an insurance policy.

⚠ **Think again before naming your estate as a life insurance beneficiary.** In our experience, the problem of a deceased person having substantial debts and no liquid assets is rare. In most instances, estates contain enough cash, or other assets that can be sold for cash, to pay debts and taxes. Unless life insurance proceeds are used for estate costs, they will be distributed to someone, eventually. So it seems foolhardy to reduce the amount inheritors receive from your life insurance because of probate costs—or add to the time your inheritors must wait before they get this money.

D. CHOOSING LIFE INSURANCE BENEFICIARIES

As you know, when you buy life insurance, you name the policy's beneficiaries—those who will receive the proceeds when you die. As long as you own the policy, you can change beneficiaries, provided that you are mentally competent. You can't, however, change an insurance beneficiary by naming someone else in your will or living trust. If one person is named as a beneficiary of a life insurance policy, but another person is named as the beneficiary of the policy in the insured's will or living trust, the first person remains the legal beneficiary. If you want to change a beneficiary, contact your insurance agent, or company, and complete the appropriate form.

1. Special Rules for Community Property States

If you live in a community property state (see Chapter 3, Section A, for a list) and buy a policy with community property funds, one-half of the proceeds are owned by the surviving spouse, no matter who the policy names as the beneficiary. This result can be varied by a written agreement between the spouses, in which one spouse transfers all interest in a particular insurance policy to the other spouse. Again, contact your insurance company for the proper form.

2. Minor Children as Beneficiaries

If you want your minor children to be the beneficiaries of your life insurance policy, you need to arrange some legal means for the proceeds to be managed and supervised by a competent adult. If you don't, and your children are not legal adults at your death, the insurance company would require that a court appoint a property guardian for the children before releasing the proceeds. As discussed in Chapter 6, this is not desirable, since it necessitates attorney's fees, court proceedings, and court supervision of life insurance proceeds left to benefit your children—costs and hassles the children surely won't benefit from. There are two ways to prevent this.

Grandparents or other friends or relatives who name minors as beneficiaries of their life insurance policies can also use these methods.

• Name your living trust (or successor trustee, depending on which the insurance company prefers) as the beneficiary of the policy. In the trust document, you name the minor children as beneficiaries of any money the trust receives from the insurance policy. You also establish within the trust a method to impose adult management over the proceeds, which can be either a child's trust or an UTMA custodianship.

• Leave the proceeds for the benefit of your children simply by using your state's UTMA directly. You name as policy beneficiary an adult "custodian" for your minor child or children.

These two methods are explained further in Chapter 6, Section E.

Finally, you could rethink your plan to name minors as beneficiaries of your life insurance policy. Instead, name a trusted adult beneficiary who you are confident will use the money for the children's benefit.

E. REDUCING ESTATE TAX BY TRANSFERRING OWNERSHIP OF LIFE INSURANCE POLICIES

This section is important only if your estate will likely have to pay federal estate tax. (See Chapter 15.)

Whether or not life insurance proceeds are included in the deceased's taxable estate, and so subject to federal estate tax, depends on who owns the policy when the insured dies. If the deceased owned the policy, the full amount of the proceeds are included in the federal taxable estate; if someone else owned the policy, the proceeds are not included.

Example: Melissa purchases and owns an insurance policy covering her life, with a face value of $200,000, payable to her son, Jeff, as beneficiary. Melissa's business partner, Juanita, owns a second policy, covering Melissa's life for $400,000, payable to Juanita. She will use these proceeds to pay Jeff, Melissa's sole inheritor, the worth of Melissa's interest in the business. Melissa dies. All the proceeds of Melissa's policy, $200,000, are included in her federal taxable estate. However, none of the $400,000 from the policy Juanita owns is part of Melissa's federal taxable estate, because Melissa did not own the policy.

PROCEEDS PAYABLE TO A SPOUSE ARE EXEMPT FROM FEDERAL ESTATE TAX

If a surviving spouse is the beneficiary of a policy owned by the deceased spouse, no federal estate taxes will be assessed against the proceeds, no matter how much they are. This is because all property left to a surviving spouse is exempt from federal tax. (See Chapter 15, Section A.)

There are two ways you can transfer ownership of a life insurance policy. First, you can simply give the policy to another person or persons. Second, you can create an irrevocable life insurance trust, and transfer ownership to that entity. Here we'll primarily focus on the first method. The second we discuss briefly here, and in more depth in Chapter 21, Section B.

If you choose to transfer a life insurance policy, you must do it with the knowledge of, and with forms approved by, the issuing company. The transfer won't be legally effective if the insurance company has no record of it.

You have the right to assign or give ownership of your life insurance policy to any other adult, including the policy beneficiary. (The only exceptions are some group policies, which many people participate in through work, and which don't allow you to transfer ownership.)

INCOME TAXATION OF INSURANCE PROCEEDS

Cash policy proceeds payable to a beneficiary after an insured's death are exempt from federal income taxes. However, if the proceeds are paid in installments, any interest paid on the principal is taxable income to the recipient. Likewise, the proceeds of an insurance policy are exempt from state income tax in most states.

---

1. Transferring Ownership to Other People

Transferring ownership of your policy to another person or persons involves a trade-off: Once the policy is transferred, you've lost all your power over it, forever. You cannot cancel it or change the beneficiary. To make this point bluntly, suppose you transfer ownership of your policy to your spouse, and later get divorced. You cannot cancel the policy or recover it from your now ex-spouse. Nevertheless, in many situations, the trade-off is worth it, as, for example, when you transfer policy ownership to a child (or children) you have a close and loving relationship with.

The IRS has some special rules about determining who owns a life insurance policy when the insured dies. *Gifts of life insurance policies made within three years of death are disallowed for federal estate tax purposes (and often for state death tax purposes, too).* This means that the full amount of the proceeds are included in your estate as if you had remained owner of the policy.

> **Example:** Louise gives her term life insurance, with proceeds of $300,000, payable on death, to her friend, Leon, in 2005. She dies two years later. For federal estate tax purposes, the gift is disallowed, and all the proceeds, $300,000, are included in Louise's taxable estate. If Louise had transferred the life insurance policy more than three years before her death, none of the proceeds would have been included in her taxable estate.

The message here is obvious: If you want to give away a life insurance policy to reduce estate taxes, give the policy away as soon as feasible. (And then don't die for at least three years.)

Another IRS regulation provides that a deceased person who retained any "incidents of ownership" of a life insurance policy is considered the owner. The term "incidents of ownership" is simply legalese for keeping any significant power over the transferred insurance policy. Specifically, the proceeds of the policy will be included in your taxable estate if you have the legal right to do any one of the following:

- change or name beneficiaries of the policy

- borrow against the policy, pledge any cash reserve it has, or cash it in

- surrender, convert, or cancel the policy, or

- select a payment option—decide if payments to the beneficiary can be a lump sum or in installments.

TRANSFERRRING A POLICY WILL NOT AFFECT PREMIUM PAYMENTS

Transferring ownership of a life insurance policy from the insured person to someone else will not change the premium payment amount. The transfer has no effect on the life expectancy of the insured, which is what the insurance company is betting on.

---

2. Gift Tax Concerns

When a life insurance policy is transferred from the original insured owner to a beneficiary, the transaction is regarded as a gift by the tax authorities. So, under current gift tax rules, if a policy with a present value of more than $12,000 is transferred to one person, gift taxes will be assessed. (See Chapter 16.) Even so, the amount of gift tax assessed will be far less than the tax cost of leaving the policy in your estate. This is because the proceeds payable under a policy when the insured dies are always considerably more than the worth of the policy while the insured lives.

Example: In 2006, Eugene transfers ownership of his universal life insurance policy to his son, David. The cash surrender value of the policy when he transfers it is $22,000. Under IRS rules, $10,000 worth of this value is subject to gift tax. Eugene dies four years after giving his son the insurance policy, which pays $300,000. None of this $300,000 is included in Eugene's federal taxable estate. (Nor are the proceeds considered income to David, for federal income tax purposes.)

HOW MUCH IS A LIFE INSURANCE POLICY WORTH FOR GIFT TAX PURPOSES?

If you're considering giving away an insurance policy, you'll want to know the present worth of that policy. If it's over the amount of the annual gift tax exclusion, gift tax will be assessed on the transaction. Under IRS rules, the value of a gift of a life insurance policy for gift tax purposes is its cost (what it would cost to buy a similar policy), not the cash surrender value. For fully paid-up policies, this value is easy to determine, but where further payments will be made, the value of the gift is harder to figure out. Under IRS rules, "all relevant facts and elements of value shall be considered." The IRS regulations use phrases like, "the interpolated terminated reserve as of the date of the gift, plus any prepaid premiums," as a method for determining value. (IRS Reg. 25.2512-1.) Yes, these words are bizarre. All you need do with them, however, is repeat them slowly to your insurance company. They will then give you the dollar value, for gift tax purposes, of your policy.

Fortunately, most insurance companies will provide, on request, an informal estimate of the gift tax value of a policy before you make the actual gift. They will also provide the appropriate forms (usually Treasury Department Form 938) for submission with the gift tax return, if need be.

3. How to Transfer Ownership of Your Policy

You can give away ownership of your life insurance policy by signing a simple document, called an "assignment" or a "transfer." To do this, notify the insurance company, and use its assignment or transfer form. There's normally no charge to make the change. Also, the policy itself will usually have to be changed to specify that the insured is no longer the owner.

After the policy is transferred, the new owner should make all premium payments, unless of course the policy is fully paid up. If the previous owner makes payments, the IRS might contend that the previous owner was keeping an "incident of ownership," so the proceeds of the policy must be included in the deceased owner's federally taxable estate—precisely what you're trying to avoid. If the new owner doesn't have sufficient funds to make the payments, you can give her money to be used for these payments.

If you give a paid-for single-premium policy to a new owner, there's no question about who makes future payments. There aren't any. Because it's paid for in full once it's purchased, single-premium life can be a particularly convenient type of policy to give to a new owner in order to reduce the giver's estate taxes. However, there can be a drawback here, too. The value of the policy, at the time of the gift, may exceed the amount that can be given free of gift tax (currently, $12,000 or less). If so, gift tax will be assessed on all value over the gift tax exempt amount. By contrast, if the giver gives a policy not subject to gift tax, and then every year gives the new owner no more than the gift tax exempt amount to pay for annual premiums, no gift tax will be assessed.

4. Life Insurance Trusts

An irrevocable life insurance trust is a legal entity you create while you live for the purpose of owning life insurance you previously owned. An irrevocable trust is, like a corporation, simply a legal entity, distinct from any human being. (These trusts are covered in more depth in Chapter 21, Section B.)

Once you transfer ownership of life insurance to the trust, it owns the policy, not you. So the proceeds aren't part of your estate.

Why create a life insurance trust, rather than simply transfer a life insurance policy to someone else? One reason can be that there's no one you want to give your policy to. In other words, you want to get the proceeds out of your taxable estate, but you want to exert legal control over the policy and avoid the risks of having an insurance policy on your life owned by someone else—perhaps a spouse or child you don't trust to pay policy premiums. For example, the trust could specify that the policy must be kept in effect while you live, eliminating the risk that a new owner of the policy could decide to cash it in.

Example: Marcie is the divorced mother of two children, in their 20s, who will be her beneficiaries. Neither is sensible with money. Marcie has an estate of $700,000, plus universal life insurance which will pay $1 million at her death. She wants to be sure her estate will not be liable for estate taxes, and so desires to transfer ownership of her policy. However, there's no one Marcie trusts enough to give her policy to outright. With the controls she can impose through a trust, however, she decides it's safe to allow her sister, the person she's closest to, to be the trustee of a life insurance trust for the policy. She creates a formal trust, and transfers ownership of the life insurance policy to that trust. After Marcie's death, her sister will handle the money for the children under the terms of the trust document.

There are strict requirements governing life insurance trusts. If you want to gain the estate tax savings:

- The life insurance trust must be irrevocable. If you retain the right to revoke the trust, you will be considered the owner of the policy, and the proceeds will be taxed in your estate upon death.

- You cannot be the trustee.

- You must establish the trust at least three years before your death. If the trust has not existed for at least three years when you die, the trust is disregarded, for estate tax purposes, and the proceeds are included in your taxable estate.

Get legal help for a life insurance trust. If you want to explore using a life insurance trust, you'll need to see a lawyer. Tax complexities must be considered: How will future premium payments be made? If the person establishing the trust makes the payments directly, or even indirectly, how will that affect estate taxes? Personal concerns also have to be carefully evaluated. Crucially, who will be the trustee? Or, suppose you have a child after the trust becomes operational? Or a child gets divorced? Or marries or remarries? There aren't any standard answers to these questions. You have to carefully work out what you want. ■

13

RETIREMENT BENEFITS

When they retire, most people are entitled to payments from one or more retirement programs, such as Social Security, military plans, private or public employee pensions, union pensions, or an individual retirement plan.

Obviously, when you do your estate planning, you need to take into account any retirement benefits you or other family members have coming. For example, a married couple should consider each spouse's retirement income. If a surviving spouse can expect generous monthly pension checks that will cover living expenses, with a little left over, the other spouse may understandably decide to leave at least some money and property directly to children or friends. Similarly, buying a life insurance policy on the life of a breadwinner makes great sense if there will be little continuing income should he or she die, and much less sense if a generous pension is in the offing.

You probably know what you're likely to have in the way of financial resources on that magic day when you retire—and what your family can expect after your death. If not, be sure to check it out. We know of people who have discovered they were never covered by a pension plan they thought applied to them. And when someone has divorced, the former spouse may have a legal interest in retirement funds that can greatly complicate any distributions.

Planning for a financially comfortable retirement can be complicated, and we don't get into that subject here. This chapter covers the basics of retirement plans as estate planning devices: how common kinds of retirement benefits—Social Security, individual retirement plans, and pensions—are transferred after death, and the impact of choosing beneficiaries to inherit these benefits.

Going beyond finances. While financial planning is essential, a truly successful retirement is about much more than money. *Get a Life: You Don't Need a Million to Retire Well,* by Ralph Warner (Nolo), provides thoughtful advice

on enjoying a fulfilling retirement—emphasizing relationships and personal interests rather than just the accumulation of wealth.

A. SOCIAL SECURITY

The most extensive retirement program in the United States is the federal Social Security system. Despite periodic anxieties that the program will run out of money, it has always managed to make regular payments to millions and continues to do so. Payments usually begin at age 65 (although it's possible to elect to receive smaller payments at age 55, or even younger if you become blind or disabled).

If your spouse is already receiving Social Security and you are at least 62, you may also be eligible to receive a monthly benefit from your spouse's earnings. This is in addition to what your spouse already receives and your own Social Security benefits. (The Social Security Administration usually advises a person approaching age 62 of this benefit. If not, contact your local Social Security office.)

Social Security also provides payments to many surviving relatives of covered wage earners, even if these people are not entitled to payments based on their own earnings record.

These people usually receive some benefits based on a deceased wage earner's record:

- **Surviving spouses.** Social Security provides 100% of a deceased spouse's benefits to a surviving spouse who is 65 or older, depending on the survivor's year of birth. A surviving spouse who is between 60 and 65 gets a smaller amount. Remarriage after age 60 doesn't terminate benefits. A surviving spouse cannot receive double benefits, both on the basis of the deceased spouse and because of his own Social Security contribution. However, the surviving spouse can choose to receive whichever payment is larger.

- **Former spouses.** If the marriage lasted at least ten years, a divorced ex-spouse of the deceased person, who does not remarry before age 60, receives payment for life. It's possible for both a surviving spouse and an ex-spouse to collect Social Security based on the same deceased wage earner. A divorced ex-spouse can receive full benefits at age 65, and reduced benefits from age 60.

- **Unmarried children.** Children up to 18 (or 19, if attending high school full time) receive benefits.

- **Disabled children.** These children can get benefits for as long as they're disabled. This program is of particular interest to parents with a mentally or physically disadvantaged child who will need lifetime care. It means they can create an ongoing trust (see Chapter 25, Section B) to supplement Social Security income; they don't have to start from scratch.

- **Other dependents.** Under certain circumstances, grandchildren, great-grandchildren, and dependent parents age 62 or older may be eligible for payments.

In addition, Social Security pays one lump-sum death payment of $255 to the surviving spouse or child eligible for benefits.

People younger than (roughly) 65 who receive Social Security payments—their own or as the survivor of a deceased worker—may have the payments reduced if they work. If earnings exceed "exempt amounts" set by law, payments are cut. Anyone older than 65, however, can earn an unlimited amount without any reduction in payment.

More information about Social Security benefits. *Social Security, Medicare & Government Pensions*, by Joseph Matthews with Dorothy Matthews Berman (Nolo), explains how to find out exactly what you and your family members can expect to receive in the way of Social Security survivor payments.

B. INDIVIDUAL RETIREMENT PLANS

In addition to depending on Social Security, savings, and investments, many people contribute regularly to one or more individual retirement plans to ensure that they will have enough income when they get older. In fact, retirement plans are becoming major assets of many people. Nevertheless, retirement plans are not primarily designed to be estate planning devices. There may be nothing left in your retirement account when you die. But in case there is money left over, it's important to consider the possible effects on your estate plan.

There are many complex rules governing what you can and can't do with funds in an individual retirement plan. Here we will cover only the basics about using these plans in estate planning.

More information about individual retirement plans. For a thorough explanation of the rules governing retirement plans, particularly how you, or a beneficiary after you die, can withdraw money without getting into trouble, see *IRAs, 401(k)s & Other Retirement Plans: Taking Your Money Out*, by Twila Slesnick and John C. Suttle (Nolo).

1. Traditional Individual Retirement Plans

As you doubtless know, individual retirement plans, such as profit-sharing plans (formerly called Keogh plans), and IRAs (Individual Retirement Accounts) are retirement plans you fund yourself. The money you contribute is tax deductible (within limits); you don't pay tax on the principal or earnings until you withdraw them after retirement. You are in charge of how the money is invested.

A profit-sharing plan is for the self-employed, as is a SEP-IRA. By contrast, any income earner can create a regular IRA by making annual contributions. Currently, annual contributions of up to $4,000 ($4,500 if you're age 50 or older) are tax deductible if you aren't covered by a company retirement plan. The annual tax-deductible amount will rise in coming years, to a maximum of $5,000 ($6,000 for those 50 or older) in 2008. After that, the amount will be indexed for inflation and will periodically rise in $500 increments. (See the chart below.)

If you participate in an employer-sponsored retirement plan, you are entitled to the full tax deduction unless your income is above a certain level. This income ceiling may change each year. Contact your plan administrator to learn the current limit.

Whether or not you participate in an employer-sponsored plan, you can contribute more than the annual tax-deductible amount to an IRA, but you can't take the tax deduction on the overage.

IRA CONTRIBUTION LIMITS

Tax Year	Maximum Tax-Deductible Contribution
2006–2007	$4,000
2008	$5,000
2009+	Indexed for inflation in $500 increments

People age 50 and older can contribute an additional $1,000 per year beginning in 2006.

If you are self-employed, the Tax Relief Act of 2001 raised the contribution amounts for SEP-IRAs according to your income, and also established a catchup program. See your accountant or tax preparer to learn more about these changes.

If you withdraw money early—usually before age 59-1/2—a penalty is imposed, unless you are disabled or the money is used for educational expenses or for first-time home buying (this amount has a limit).

You must begin to take money from your account when you reach age 70-1/2. Then the percentage of the total that you must withdraw each year is determined by your statistical life expectancy. (The IRS determines the withdrawal percentage by using what it calls the "Uniform Lifetime Table.") In theory, this means that all of the funds in the program will be used up by the time you die. And, of course, you can withdraw more than the minimum required amount if you decide to, and deplete the account that way.

Withdrawal amounts are different if your spouse is more than ten years younger. If your spouse is the sole beneficiary of your retirement plan and is more than ten years younger than you, distribution rules are slightly more favorable. Withdrawal percentages are calculated on the basis of both your and your spouse's life expectancies. Because your spouse is younger, your combined life expectancies will be longer than your own life expectancy. Therefore, you will be required to withdraw a lesser percentage from your retirement fund each year than if only your life expectancy were used to determine the percentage. (The IRS determines these percentages by using what it calls the "Joint Life and Last Survivor Table.")

All money remaining in an individual retirement program (if there is any) at the death of the owner goes to a named beneficiary or beneficiaries, free of probate. You simply specify the beneficiary or beneficiaries on the account documents. The money can be paid in a lump sum or in installments. (See Section D, below.)

2. Roth IRAs

A new kind of individual retirement account became available in 1998. (I.R.C. § 408A.) Named after Senator William Roth, the Roth IRA differs from the traditional IRAs just discussed.

You fund a Roth IRA with money that has already been taxed. As in a regular IRA, the money is allowed to grow tax free until it is withdrawn. But when you do withdraw it, no further tax is due as long as the money was in the account for at least five years.

The biggest difference, for estate planning purposes, between regular IRAs (and most retirement plans) and a Roth IRA is that you don't have to start withdrawing money from a Roth IRA when you reach age 70-1/2. In fact, you can still contribute to it after that age and leave the money intact for your heirs.

The tax penalty for withdrawing funds before age 59-1/2, however, does apply to a Roth IRA, with several exceptions. Again, there is no penalty if you are disabled. There is also no penalty if funds are paid to a beneficiary upon the death of the individual. And you may take money out penalty free to buy a first-time house, not only for yourself, but also for a child, grandchild, or parent. You may also use Roth money to pay for education expenses for yourself, your spouse, or children and grandchildren of you or your spouse.

Annual contribution limits are the same as the limits for traditional IRAs. However, individuals who earn over a certain amount are restricted to lesser amounts.

Retirement plan resources from the IRS. If you want detailed (and complex) information about retirement plans, you can download the following publications free of charge from the IRS website: www.irs.gov.

- IRS Publication 590 covers individual retirement arrangements (IRAs).

- IRS Publication 560 covers retirement plans for small businesses, such as profit-sharing plans.

3. 401(k) Accounts

Many employers now offer employees what are called 401(k) plans or 403(b) plans. (The 401(k) is for businesses, the 403(b) for nonprofit corporations and government workers.) Employees defer a portion of their wages, contributing them to the retirement plan. Many employers match these funds or at least make some contribution to the account. It's up to the employees whether or not to participate.

Money in your account is invested, according to your direction, in investments offered by the plan administrator. That money grows (at least you hope it grows) tax free over the years until you withdraw it. In some cases, you can retire at age 55 and take money out without penalty. You must begin withdrawing it at age 70-1/2. At your death, the beneficiary you named receives whatever funds are left in the account. If you are married, the beneficiary must be your surviving spouse unless your spouse signed an agreement giving up this right. (See Section E, below.)

If the money contributed to the plan was never taxed, every withdrawal is subject to income tax. If part of the contribution consisted of money that was taxed previously, a formula will be used to figure out what portion of the withdrawal is subject to income tax. The interest that has been accruing in the account tax free is also subject to income tax.

EDUCATIONAL SAVINGS ACCOUNTS (FORMERLY EDUCATIONAL IRAS)

Two types of tax-saving education accounts— 529 plans and Coverdell Accounts—are authorized by federal law. With each, you name the young people for whom you are saving, and funds you contribute are not considered part of your taxable estate. The beneficiaries are considered the owners of the account, even though you can retain management rights over account investment. These plans are discussed in more detail in Chapter 6, Section D.

C. PENSIONS

A pension, unlike an individual retirement program, is not under your control. Your company sets up a pension plan, and determines what rights you receive. You may acquire the right to receive payments—perhaps generous ones—and this right may extend to your surviving spouse or perhaps other beneficiaries, depending on the pension program. But you don't have any say over how the money in a pension fund is invested, and you have only limited say (at most) over how and when you receive benefits.

SPECIFIC PENSION PROGRAMS

There are many types of pensions: military, railroad, union, and so on. The benefits these programs may provide depend on the specifics of each program. Check the rules of each program that applies to you.

No law requires an employer to offer a pension plan. Some are generous, some are miserly, and some don't even bother to say "tough luck, friend."

 When you are ready to retire, you are indeed fortunate if your pension plan office provides tax assistance. For instance, money contributed during certain years may be taxed at different rates. It is truly necessary to get the tax help you need. A onetime visit to a good accountant will pay off in the long run.

Publications on pension plans. IRS Publication 575 discusses the rules for many pension plans, but it's not easy reading. If you want it, go to www.irs.gov and click on "Forms and Publications."

A number of brochures on pensions, which are easier to understand, are available from The American Association of Retired People (AARP), 601 E Street NW, Washington, DC 20049, 202-434-2277, www.aarp.org, and The Pension Rights Center, 1350 Connecticut Avenue NW, Suite 206, Washington, DC 20036, 202-296-3776, www.pensionrights.org.

If you want help understanding the details of your pension or retirement plan and can't get what you want on your own, you'll need to see a pension-plan expert, or a lawyer knowledgeable in this specialized field.

ERISA Laws

The Employee Retirement Security Act (ERISA), a federal law covering pensions and some other retirement programs, requires that every pension plan spell out who is eligible for coverage. Plans do not have to include all workers, but they cannot legally be structured to benefit only top executives or otherwise discriminate—for example, by excluding older workers.

If you are eligible to participate in your employer's pension program, you are entitled to several documents:

- **A summary plan description.** Explains the basics of how your plan operates. ERISA requires your employer to give you this document within 90 days after you begin participating in a pension plan. It also requires your employer to provide you with any updates to the plan.

  This document will tell you the formula for vesting in the plan, if it is a plan that includes vesting. A vesting plan means that you must work for a certain required period to be eligible for benefits. A formula is used to determine your benefits and the contributions that your employer will make to the plan. The summary will also tell you whether or not your pension is insured.

- **A summary annual report.** Your employer must provide a yearly accounting of your pension plan's financial condition and operations.

- **Survivor coverage data.** If you request it, you should also receive a statement of how much your plan would pay to a surviving spouse or beneficiary should you die. Your plan administrator is also required to give you a detailed, individual statement of the pension benefits you have earned if you request it in writing or are going to stop participating in the plan because, for example, you change employers. You have the right to one such statement per year.

Courts have now expanded ERISA to require that pension benefits go to a surviving spouse after the pension recipient has died. Problems abound in community property states (listed in Chapter 3, Section A) due to remarriage after divorce or death of a nonparticipant spouse. If you are in this situation, you should seek expert advice.

Divorce does not remove a former spouse as beneficiary. For all retirement plans controlled by ERISA, divorce does not automatically remove an ex-spouse as beneficiary of the other spouse's plan. The plan holder must amend the plan and name a new beneficiary. Any state law that automatically revokes a spousal beneficiary designation upon divorce is void for ERISA plans.

D. WHEN YOU RETIRE

Upon retirement, you may have several choices as to how you will receive your retirement benefits.

1. Regular Payments Upon Retirement

After retiring, many people can draw a monthly sum from a pension plan, in addition to any funds they receive from an individual retirement program like an IRA or 401(k). The amount that you can receive from a pension fund depends on many factors defined by the plan, including how long you worked, what your salary was, how much was contributed, your age, and the age of the beneficiary you have named to receive payments upon your death. The payments will continue for your lifetime. If you have named a beneficiary, such as a spouse, to receive payments, the amount of the monthly payment will be slightly adjusted to account for the beneficiary's age.

> **Example:** Jon retires at age 65. His wife, Sita, is six years younger than he is. Their monthly payment from Jon's pension plan is slightly less than if he had been the sole beneficiary of the plan, to account for the extra years of life expectancy for Sita.

2. Lump Sum Payment

Some retirement plans including pensions and 403(b)s allow employees to take the entire amount in their retirement accounts (based on age and amount contributed, plus interest and account earnings) in one lump sum. A number of people choose to do this, believing that they can invest the money and get a greater return than regular payments would bring. Or some may just want the money to buy their dream ship to sail around the world.

Whatever the reason, if you wish to take a lump sum and the plan allows it, you must get tax advice. Again, part of the amount may be taxable, part not, and another part at different rates. In some cases, you are allowed to average the income tax on the amount withdrawn (although it is still due unless you "roll it over" into an IRA—see below).

3. Rolling Pension Funds Into an IRA or Another Retirement Plan

One option available for taking retirement funds, if your plan allows it and if you are not yet 70-1/2, is to roll the money over. You put your funds directly into an IRA and defer income tax until later. The money will continue to grow tax free until it is distributed to you.

> **Example:** Lars takes early retirement at age 62 from the University of California. He has a healthy income from real estate he has bought over the years. He requests his 403(b) funds be rolled over by the University into his IRA at the Able Investment Bank.

You can also roll over money in a company retirement fund if the company discontinues the plan, and you have what's called a "vested interest" in the plan. In other words, you have the right to obtain the money set aside for you in the plan if the company goes broke, or just decides to discontinue the retirement plan, for whatever reason. When you receive your money, you have 60 days to put it into (roll it over to) a new (or existing) IRA in your name. If the money is not rolled over into an IRA within 60 days, the money is then treated as having been distributed to you. You will owe income tax on the money, plus a 10% penalty charge for a premature distribution of retirement funds if you are under 59-1/2 years old.

What if you simply change jobs? Depending on the companies involved, you may have the option of leaving your benefits in the old plan where they will continue to grow tax free. Or you may take them and roll them into your IRA. Or, if both companies allow it, you may roll the old benefits directly into a new pension plan.

Example: Maude has worked for Sunshine Graphics for 15 years. She is offered a position at a higher salary in another city. She checks with both pension plans and discovers that she can have her old benefits directly rolled over into her new pension plan with no tax due until she retires and starts withdrawing money.

E. CHOOSING BENEFICIARIES FOR YOUR RETIREMENT PLANS

Retirement accounts often contain money when the account owner dies. Sometimes, they are a significant part of an estate. Choosing who will inherit these retirement funds may be one of the most important estate planning decisions you make.

You can (and should) always name a beneficiary for an individual retirement plan: an IRA, profit-sharing, or 401(k) account. If you have vested rights in a pension, you may also be able to name a beneficiary to inherit your vested rights.

1. Naming Your Spouse

Many married people name their spouse as the beneficiary of their retirement funds. They want to support their spouses, and in larger estates, defer estate tax. Leaving assets to the surviving spouse postpones tax, under the marital deduction, until the death of the surviving spouse.

If you have a 401(k) plan, you must name your spouse as the beneficiary unless the spouse signs a waiver. Most pension plans follow the same rule, imposed by federal law. Different laws apply to individual retirement programs like IRAs or profit-sharing plans; you can name anyone you choose as beneficiary. However, in community property states, the spouse has a legal interest in money the other spouse has earned unless that spouse signs a document giving up the interest. This can affect both individual retirement plans and pension funds.

Spouses, as retirement plan beneficiaries, get several breaks that other beneficiaries don't. A surviving spouse who inherits the money as beneficiary of an individual retirement plan can have the money paid out over the same period of time she would have had if she had created the plan herself. Another advantage given only to a surviving spouse is the choice of rolling retirement funds over. For example, a spouse can take pension fund money in a lump sum and roll it into his or her own retirement plan. This defers income tax for the surviving spouse and allows the money to continue to grow tax free until the spouse reaches mandatory withdrawal age.

With personal retirement plans like IRAs, if the beneficiary is the surviving spouse, the spouse can elect to treat the IRA as her own.

Example: Oho names his spouse Kia as the beneficiary for his IRA. When Oho dies, Kia is only 55 years old. She converts the IRA into one of her own, and it continues to grow tax free until she reaches the required age for distribution.

If your estate is large enough to face estate tax, you can still leave any funds remaining in your retirement accounts to your spouse. Your personal estate tax exemption can be applied to property left to other beneficiaries.

Example: Randolph dies in 2006, with an estate of $2.5 million, including $700,000 in a profit-sharing plan. His spouse, Rose, is the beneficiary of these funds, so they will not be subject to estate tax because of the marital deduction. Randolph had placed his other assets in an AB trust, with income to go to Rose. Since the amount of these assets is under the personal exemption of $2 million for 2006, no estate tax is due when he dies. (See Chapter 15.)

2. Naming Others as Beneficiaries

For one reason or another, some people name a child or other person as beneficiary. These beneficiaries may have some options regarding how they receive the money over time. In fact, fairly complicated rules can apply to the beneficiary's choice.

In some cases, the beneficiary can elect to take the money remaining in the account in lump sums, sometimes distributed over several years.

Other beneficiaries may receive installment payments based on life expectancy. These options are a complex matter, and it's usually wise to consult a tax expert.

If you are attempting to equalize gifts you leave to your children (as many folks do), and retirement funds seem likely to be part of your estate, remember the income tax consequences. The beneficiary of a retirement program (except funds in a Roth IRA) will have to pay income tax on any money received.

Example: Trish wants to be completely fair and equal to her two children. She leaves her house, worth $300,000, to her son. She designates her daughter as the beneficiary of her SEP-IRA, also worth $300,000 now. The daughter's inheritance is not equal to her brother's even if the SEP-IRA is still worth $300,000 at Trish's death, because it is reduced by the income tax she will pay.

3. Naming Your Living Trust as Beneficiary

If you make a living trust, should you name it as the beneficiary of your retirement plan? Usually, it's not a good idea. Here's why.

No probate benefits. Because no probate is needed to transfer funds in a retirement account to the named beneficiary in the first place, there is no need to name your living trust as beneficiary in an effort to avoid probate.

Possible higher mandatory withdrawals. If your spouse is the sole beneficiary of your living trust and is also more than ten years younger than you, you can spread out withdrawals over a longer period of time. Many people prefer this option, because lower withdrawals mean lower income tax payments.

In addition, IRS provisions that give a surviving spouse favorable rights over a deceased spouse's retirement accounts are not available if a living trust is the beneficiary, even if the surviving spouse is the only primary beneficiary of that trust.

NAMING AN AB LIVING TRUST AS BENEFICIARY

An AB trust is a special type of living trust used by some couples to avoid probate and reduce estate taxes. (See Chapter 15, Section C2.) For many people, a retirement plan is a major asset, and their AB trusts might not be fully funded unless remaining plan assets are placed in the trust. But the law does not allow a trust to "own" a retirement plan while the plan creator lives; it must be owned by an individual. So to fund the AB trust, that trust is named as the beneficiary of the retirement plan. After death, distributions from the plan are directed to the AB trust every year, until the plan funds are depleted. Distributions to trust beneficiaries are made as the trust directs. For more information, see Chapter 18, Section C6.

---

4. Naming an Irrevocable Trust as Beneficiary

Sometimes designating an irrevocable trust to receive what's left in your individual retirement accounts at your death can make sense. You can accomplish this by naming the trustee of the trust as the beneficiary.

One good time to do this is when the beneficiaries are minors and need their money managed by a trustee. The same is true if the beneficiary is incapable—for whatever reason—of managing money. If the trust is properly structured and irrevocable, payments can be received based on the life expectancy of the oldest beneficiary.

F. USING DISCLAIMERS FOR RETIREMENT ACCOUNTS

Disclaimers are explained at length in Chapter 22. Basically, an inheritor can refuse (disclaim) property left to him or her, causing the property to go to someone else. Disclaimers can save on estate tax for people with large estates and substantial sums left in retirement plans.

This is one way it can be done: You set up a formula AB trust that will hold the amount of your personal exemption in the year you die. (See Chapter 18, Section C.) You also designate your spouse as the primary beneficiary of your retirement plans. But you designate the trustee of the trust (usually your spouse) as the alternate beneficiary for these plans. At your death, if the amount in the AB trust isn't enough to take advantage of the entire personal tax exemption, your spouse can disclaim some or all of the retirement benefits and direct them to Trust A. Your spouse, of course, will be entitled to the benefits of the trust.

Example: Lola drafts an AB trust that will pay the income to her husband Riki for his life. She names Riki as the beneficiary of her individual retirement plan. She names the trustee of the AB trust (also Riki) as the alternate beneficiary for her plan. Lola dies in the year 2007, when the personal estate tax exemption is $2 million. The retirement plan contains $600,000, and her other assets are worth $1.9 million. Riki disclaims $100,000 of the benefits, so they go into the trust with her other $1.9 million of assets. The total in the trust is now $2 million, the full exempt amount.

A spousal disclaimer can also send retirement benefits into a trust for the benefit of children or simply outright to others.

Example: Ron and Didi have a combined estate worth $3 million. They have left everything to each other with their children as alternate beneficiaries. Didi is the primary beneficiary of Ron's 401(k) plan, and their children are the alternate beneficiaries. When Ron dies in 2006, Didi disclaims enough of Ron's property, including what remains in his IRA, to equal $2 million, the amount of the personal exemption for that year. All of the disclaimed property goes to the children, and Ron has made full use of his personal estate tax exemption.

G. PROBATE AND TAXES

No matter what the assets in your estate are, you want to avoid probate and minimize any taxes that may be owed to the government when you die. Funds left in your retirement plans at your death are no exception.

1. Probate

Money in an individual retirement plan (such as an IRA, Roth IRA, or 401(k) account) that is left to a named beneficiary at the owner's death does not go through probate. The plan administrator pays the funds directly to the named beneficiary.

If a surviving spouse or other beneficiary is entitled to receive pension payments under the terms of a pension earned by a deceased worker, those don't go through probate either. Again, they're paid directly to the recipient.

2. Estate Tax

The money you leave in an individual retirement plan—for example, the remaining balance in an IRA, profit-sharing account, 401(k) plan, or pension—is subject to federal estate tax for as long as these taxes are imposed (see Chapter 15). It doesn't matter how the funds are paid out, whether in a lump sum or over time. The value in the plan at your death is part of your estate for estate tax purposes.

If the value of your estate exceeds the amount of the personal estate tax exemption, estate taxes will be assessed. Of course, if a surviving spouse inherits the retirement benefits, this money is not taxable, because of the unlimited marital deduction.

3. Income Tax

Generally, no income tax is due on inherited money. For example, if you leave a bank account to your son, he won't have to report it as income. Rules are different for some tax-advantaged retirement plans, however. Someone who inherits the funds in an individual retirement plan, such as a traditional IRA or 401(k) account, must pay income tax on the money. That's because when the money was socked away in the account over (usually) many years, the contributions were tax deductible, and the income accumulated without being taxed.

The money in one of the new "Roth IRAs," however, is not taxed when the beneficiary inherits it. That's because contributions to the Roth IRA are not tax deductible when made. Income from contributions that have been in the account for at least five years is not taxed when it's withdrawn, either before or after the death of the account owner. ∎

14

STATE LAW EXEMPTIONS FROM NORMAL PROBATE

As a general rule, property left in a will must go through probate. However, there are exceptions; many states allow small estates to be transferred free of probate, or under a very simplified probate process. Because of the way the laws are written, however, not only small estates can benefit. Many good-sized estates—worth hundreds of thousands of dollars—legally qualify as "small," and are therefore eligible for special transfer procedures that speed property to inheritors.

There are two basic kinds of probate shortcuts for small estates:

Affidavit procedure—no court required. If the total value of all the property you leave behind is less than a certain amount, the people who inherit your personal property—that's anything but real estate—may be able to skip probate completely. The exact amount varies tremendously—from $5,000 to $150,000 depending on the state.

If your estate qualifies, an inheritor can prepare a short document stating that he or she is entitled to a certain item of property under a will or state law. This paper, when signed under oath, is called an affidavit. When the person or institution holding the property—for example, a bank where the deceased person had an account—receives the affidavit and a copy of the death certificate, it releases the money or other property.

Simplified court procedures. Another option for small estates (again, as defined by state law) is a quicker, simpler version of probate. In some states, these procedures are easy to handle without a lawyer. In other states, you may need a lawyer, so you may face at least some attorneys' fees, court costs, and delays.

Most states have both kinds of procedures; some offer just one. A brief summary of each state's laws is provided in Section C, along with the state statute to help you look up the details yourself. If you want to make your research easier, you can find full details

for each state in *8 Ways to Avoid Probate*, by Mary Randolph (Nolo).

A. WILL YOUR ESTATE QUALIFY?

If you're sure that you will leave behind property worth much more than your state's dollar limit, you probably assume that the simple procedures described in this chapter won't be available to your inheritors. But that might not be true. Even if the value of your estate is much bigger than your state's limit, you may still be able to take advantage of the simpler procedures.

The reason is that when adding up the value of your estate to see whether it is under the dollar limit, many states exclude large chunks of assets. For example, many states don't consider the value of vehicles, real estate, or real estate located in another state. Perhaps more important, many states don't count the value of property that won't go through probate—say, because you've placed it in a living trust or pay-on-death account, or because you own it in joint tenancy with someone else. Considering the many exemptions, it's conceivable that in some states, an estate worth hundreds of thousands of dollars could qualify for "small estate" procedures.

If you plan ahead and learn about your state's rules (keeping in mind, of course, that they may change before your death), chances are good that you can adjust your affairs so that you will leave a "small estate" as your state defines it.

Example: Jerold, a California resident, dies owning a car worth $23,000 and a half-interest in the following assets, worth almost $400,000:

- an IRA worth $75,000
- a pay-on-death bank account with $12,000 in it
- $30,000 worth of stocks

- a house worth $650,000, which he and his wife own as community property with right of survivorship.

The limit for "small estates" in California is only $100,000, but vehicles, payable-on-death accounts, and property that goes to a surviving spouse aren't counted toward that limit. From the list above, only the stocks count, allowing Jerold's estate to qualify for small estate procedures.

IF THERE'S NO DOLLAR LIMIT

When determining which estates qualify for simplified probate, a number of states don't specify a dollar amount as an upper limit. Instead, they grant small estate status to estates that will be used up by paying certain high-priority debts: the family allowance mandated by law, reasonable funeral and burial expenses, and medical costs of the last illness. The reasoning is that if there's nothing left for other creditors, there's no need for a probate court proceeding. Obviously, estates of very different size will qualify, depending on the debts of the deceased person.

B. USING THESE RULES TO PLAN

Understanding your state's definition of a small estate is an essential step in a plan to avoid probate. Once you have that information, you'll know how much effort you need to devote to other probate-avoidance methods.

For example, say you discover that your state allows estates worth up to $70,000 to be transferred by affidavit, and only property that is subject to probate counts toward that limit. You'll know that as long as your most valuable items avoid probate,

your executor will be able to use the small estate procedures for the miscellaneous assets that you leave through your will.

Talk to your executor. Even if your estate qualifies for a simplified probate procedure, it won't do you any good unless your executor knows that the option is available. Too many confused or intimidated executors simply turn everything over to a lawyer, and inheritors pay the price.

C. SUMMARY OF STATE LAW EXCEPTIONS TO NORMAL PROBATE

ALABAMA
Affidavit Procedure: No

Simplified Probate: $3,000 personal property

Statute: Ala. Code § 43-2-690 and following

ALASKA
Affidavit Procedure: $15,000 personal property

Simplified Probate: Up to value of homestead allowance, exempt property, family allowance, expenses of death, and last illness

Statute: Alaska Stat. §§ 13.16.680, 690, 695

ARIZONA
Affidavit Procedure: $50,000 personal property

Simplified Probate: $50,000

Statute: Ariz. Rev. Stat. §§ 14-3971.B, 3971.E, 3973

ARKANSAS
Affidavit Procedure: No

Simplified Probate: $100,000 plus limited amounts for surviving spouse or dependents

Statute: Ark. Stat. Ann. § 28-41-101

CALIFORNIA

Affidavit Procedure: $100,000; special affidavit for real estate worth less than $20,000

Simplified Probate: To surviving spouse, community property petition, no dollar limit; otherwise $100,000

Statute: Cal. Prob. Code §§ 13050, 13100 and following; § 13500 and following; § 13200 and following

COLORADO

Affidavit Procedure: Net estate, $50,000

Simplified Probate: No fixed dollar limit

Statute: Colo. Rev. Stat. §§ 15-12-1201, 1203

CONNECTICUT

Affidavit Procedure: No

Simplified Probate: $20,000 personal property

Statute: Conn. Gen. Stat. § 45a-273

DELAWARE

Affidavit Procedure: $30,000 personal property only. Beneficiaries can only be spouse, grandparents, children, or other specified relations, trustee, or funeral director

Simplified Probate: No

Statute: 12 Del. Code § 2306

DISTRICT OF COLUMBIA

Affidavit Procedure: No (except if entire estate is no more than two cars, and all debts and taxes are paid)

Simplified Probate: $40,000

Statute: D.C. Code § 20-351 and following

FLORIDA

Affidavit Procedure: No (except for very small estates that meet certain requirements)

Simplified Probate: $75,000 property in Florida subject to probate; also available if deceased person has been dead more than two years

Statute: Fla. Stat. §§ 735.101 and following; 735.201 and following; 735.301

GEORGIA

Affidavit Procedure: No

Simplified Probate: No

Statute: None

HAWAII

Affidavit Procedure: $100,000 personal property

Simplified Probate: No

Statute: Hawaii Rev. Stat. §§ 560:3-1201 and following; 560:3-1205 and following

IDAHO

Affidavit Procedure: $75,000 personal property

Simplified Probate: No fixed dollar limit

Statute: Idaho Code §§ 15-3-1201 and following; 15-3-1203 and following

ILLINOIS

Affidavit Procedure: $100,000 personal property

Simplified Probate: $100,000 real and personal property if all heirs and beneficiaries consent in writing

Statute: 755 Ill. Comp. Stat. §§ 5/25-1 and 5/9-8

INDIANA

Affidavit Procedure: $25,000 personal property only

Simplified Probate: $25,000

Statute: Ind. Code §§ 29-1-8-1, 29-1-8-3 and following

IOWA

Affidavit Procedure: $25,000 personal property

Simplified Probate: $50,000 total value of probate and nonprobate Iowa property only to surviving spouse or child; $15,000 to parent or grandchild; $10,000 to relatives

Statute: Iowa Code §§ 633.356, 635.1

KANSAS

Affidavit Procedure: $20,000 personal property

Simplified Probate: No dollar limit on some estates if court and heirs agree

Statute: Kan. Stat. Ann. §§ 59-1507b, 59-3202 and following

KENTUCKY

Affidavit Procedure: No

Simplified Probate: By agreement of all beneficiaries; when spouse receives probate estate under $15,000 (intestate only, or where renunciation of will by spouse)

Statute: Ky. Rev. Stat. §§ 391.030, 395.455

LOUISIANA

This book is not applicable in the state of Louisiana.

MAINE

Affidavit Procedure: $10,000 personal property

Simplified Probate: No fixed dollar limit

Statute: Me. Rev. Stat. Ann. tit. 18-A § 3-1201 and following; § 3-1203 and following

MARYLAND

Affidavit Procedure: No

Simplified Probate: Up to $30,000 of Maryland probate property; up to $50,000 if spouse is sole beneficiary

Statute: Md. Code Ann., Est. and Trusts § 5-601 and following

MASSACHUSETTS

Affidavit Procedure: No

Simplified Probate: $15,000 personal property, for close family only

Statute: Mass. Laws ch. 195, §§ 16, 16A

MICHIGAN

Affidavit Procedure: $15,000 personal property

Simplified Probate: $15,000; also if entire estate does not exceed homestead allowance, family allowance, exempt property, last illness, and funeral costs

Statute: Mich. Comp. Laws §§ 700.3983, 3982, 3987

MINNESOTA

Affidavit Procedure: $20,000 personal property

Simplified Probate: Court can order if certain conditions met

Statute: Minn. Stat. §§ 524.3-1201, 1203

MISSISSIPPI

Affidavit Procedure: No, except that the inheritors of a bank savings account of $12,500 or less may obtain the funds by affidavit

Simplified Probate: No

Statute: Miss. Code Ann. § 81-14-383

MISSOURI

Affidavit Procedure: No

Simplified Probate: $40,000

Statute: Mo. Rev. Stat. § 473.097

MONTANA

Affidavit Procedure: $50,000 personal property

Simplified Probate: No fixed dollar limit

Statute: Mont. Code Ann. §§ 72-3-1101, 1103

NEBRASKA

Affidavit Procedure: $25,000 personal property

Simplified Probate: No fixed dollar limit

Statute: Neb. Rev. Stat. §§ 30-24, 125, and 127

NEVADA

Affidavit Procedure: $20,000 personal property if no real estate owned in Nevada (available only to family members)

Simplified Probate: $200,000 with court approval

Statute: Nev. Rev. Stat. Ann. §§ 146.080, 145.020 and following, 146.070

NEW HAMPSHIRE

Affidavit Procedure: No

Simplified Probate: No dollar limit for surviving spouse or only child

Statute: N.H. Rev. Stat. Ann. § 553:32

NEW JERSEY

Affidavit Procedure: No (only if no valid will, then $20,000 to spouse, or $5,000 to others)

Simplified Probate: No

Statute: N.J. Stat. §§ 3B:10-3, 10-4

NEW MEXICO

Affidavit Procedure: $30,000; also, if married couple owns principal residence worth $100,000 or less as community property and no other assets require probate

Simplified Probate: No fixed dollar limit

Statute: N.M. Stat. Ann. §§ 45-3-1201, 1205, 1203

NEW YORK

Affidavit Procedure: No

Simplified Probate: $20,000 personal property (plus certain types of exempt property, to specified dollar limits)

Statute: N.Y. Surr. Ct. Proc. Act Law § 1301

NORTH CAROLINA

Affidavit Procedure: $10,000, personal property; $20,000 if intestate and spouse is sole beneficiary

Simplified Probate: No

Statute: N.C. Gen. Stat. § 28A-25-1 and following

NORTH DAKOTA

Affidavit Procedure: $15,000 personal property

Simplified Probate: No fixed dollar limit

Statute: N.D. Cent. Code § 30.1-23-01 and following, § 30.1-23-03

OHIO

Affidavit Procedure: No

Simplified Probate: $35,000; $100,000 if spouse is sole beneficiary

Statute: Ohio Rev. Code Ann. § 2113.03

OKLAHOMA

Affidavit Procedure: No

Simplified Probate: $150,000

Statute: 58 Okla. Stat. § 241

OREGON

Affidavit Procedure: No

Simplified Probate: $140,000; personal property up to $50,000, real estate up to $90,000

Statute: Or. Rev. Stat. § 114.505 and following

PENNSYLVANIA

Affidavit Procedure: No

Simplified Probate: $25,000 personal property

Statute: 20 Pa. Cons. Stat. § 3102

RHODE ISLAND

Affidavit Procedure: No

Simplified Probate: $15,000 of personal property if no real estate owned

Statute: R.I. Gen. Laws 33-24-1

SOUTH CAROLINA

Affidavit Procedure: $10,000 personal property (but affidavit must be approved and signed by a judge)

Simplified Probate: $10,000

Statute: S.C. Code Ann. §§ 62-3-1201, 1203

SOUTH DAKOTA

Affidavit Procedure: $50,000 personal property

Simplified Probate: No limit

Statute: S.D. Codified Laws §§ 29A-3-1201 and following, 29A-3-1301 and following

TENNESSEE

Affidavit Procedure: No

Simplified Probate: $25,000

Statute: Tenn. Code Ann. § 30-4-102 and following

TEXAS

Affidavit Procedure: $50,000 personal property if person dies intestate

Simplified Probate: No dollar limit if (1) value of property doesn't exceed what is needed to pay family allowance and certain creditors; or (2) either the will or all inheritors request "independent administration"

Statute: Tex. Prob. Code, §§ 137, 143, 145

UTAH

Affidavit Procedure: $25,000 personal property

Simplified Probate: No fixed dollar limit

Statute: Utah Code §§ 75-3-1201, 1203

VERMONT

Affidavit Procedure: No

Simplified Probate: $10,000 personal property

Statute: Vt. Stat. Ann., tit. 14, §§ 1901-03

VIRGINIA

Affidavit Procedure: $15,000 personal property; benefits, wages up to $15,000

Simplified Probate: No

Statute: Va. Code Ann. §§ 64.1-123, 132.2

WASHINGTON

Affidavit Procedure: $60,000 personal property

Simplified Probate: Available for solvent estates of any kind

Statute: Rev. Code Wash. § 11.62.010 and following

WEST VIRGINIA

Affidavit Procedure: No

Simplified Probate: $100,000

Statute: W.Va. Code § 44-3A-5

WISCONSIN

Affidavit Procedure: $20,000 personal property

Simplified Probate: $50,000, and all to surviving spouse or child; Wisconsin also has an "informal"

probate procedure that doesn't require a lawyer and has no fixed dollar limit

Statute: Wis. Stat. §§ 867.03, 867.01

WYOMING

Affidavit Procedure: $150,000 personal property

Simplified Probate: $150,000

Statute: Wyo. Stat. Ann. §§ 2-1-201, 205

D. CALIFORNIA EXEMPTIONS FROM NORMAL PROBATE

California has two useful simplified probate procedures:

1. The "community property petition" allowing all property left to a surviving spouse to be transferred by summary probate.

2. An affidavit procedure allowing personal property worth less than $100,000 to be transferred entirely outside of probate.

California also allows up to $20,000 worth of real estate to be transferred by filing an affidavit first with the probate court, then with the county recorder. Given the prices of California real estate, this procedure is rarely helpful.

1. The Community Property Petition

By using a community property petition, a surviving spouse can readily obtain the portion of the deceased spouse's property left to him or her. It makes no difference if it's jointly owned community property or the deceased's separately owned property. There's also no dollar limit either on the total amount of the estate or the amount of the property that can be transferred to the surviving spouse by this method. Even if some of the deceased's share of the community property is left to others, the spouse can still obtain his or her portion of it, without the expense of probate.

The community property petition is a simple one-page, two-sided form that can be prepared by a surviving spouse who is entitled to property of a deceased spouse, either from a will or by intestate succession if there was no will. The petition is filed with the local probate court, which sets a hearing date. Notice of the hearing must be given to certain people, including all beneficiaries named in the will. Then the hearing is held, and the property ordered transferred to the surviving spouse unless someone contests the petition, which is very rare. Most surviving spouses should be able to handle the process without a lawyer. All the forms and instructions you need are in *How to Probate an Estate in California*, by Julia Nissley (Nolo).

2. The Affidavit for Personal Property

If a deceased left, by will or intestate, personal property and/or real estate worth less than $100,000 (net), the inheritors can obtain the personal property by filing a simple form, called an "Affidavit for Collection of Personal Property," with the people or organizations holding the deceased's property. In addition, the inheritors can also collect all of the following under the affidavit: all vehicles owned by the deceased, no matter how much they are worth, and up to $5,000 in back pay.

The purpose of the affidavit is to enable beneficiaries of a deceased person who left a small estate to obtain the cash and other assets they inherit immediately without a lot of red tape. The affidavit can be prepared by the inheritors who are entitled to the deceased's estate, either by will or, if there's no will, by the laws of intestate inheritance. If there's more than one beneficiary under a will (or the intestacy laws if there's no will), all the beneficiaries must sign the affidavit. A copy of the affidavit is then presented to people or organizations holding the property left by the will; they must promptly release the assets to the beneficiaries. Forms and instructions are contained in *How to Probate an Estate in California*.

An affidavit doesn't have to be filed with any state agency. No court or other probate proceeding is required. There's no procedure to verify the inheritor's declaration that the deceased's net estate in California is worth less than $100,000. In this one instance, the law appears to go by the honor system.

Example: Harry Billings dies in Los Angeles. Under Harry's will, his sole beneficiary is his adult daughter, Myra. Harry owned no real estate. His estate is worth $108,500: bank accounts and a CD worth $83,000; personal property (stereo, household furniture, two valuable cameras, some rare books) worth $15,000; a car (owned outright by Harry) with a market value of $6,000; and back wages owed Harry (unused vacation pay) of $2,500. Even though Harry's estate, left by his will, exceeds $100,000, all of the property may be collected by Myra by affidavit. His bank CD and personal possessions are worth a total of $98,000, under the $100,000 limit. Separate exemptions allow his car and back wages to be claimed by affidavit.

Myra simply completes the affidavit and attaches one copy of the death certificate. She then gives them, plus her own ID, to Harry's bank; the holder of the personal property (in this case, Harry's landlord); the DMV; and the company that owes Harry the back vacation pay. The bank and the holder of Harry's personal property must release it to her promptly. The Department of Motor Vehicles will reregister the car in Myra's name, and the company will turn over Harry's unused vacation pay to her.

The affidavit must state, under oath, that the total value of the deceased's estate in California is less than $100,000. However, as we've explained, certain items, such as vehicles, no matter how much they are worth, don't count toward the $100,000 limit.

Property in a living trust isn't counted toward the $100,000 limit. Thus, savvy Californians with good-sized estates can use other probate-avoidance methods to pass their valuable items of property and rely on the affidavit procedure to avoid probate on the rest, which they leave by will.

Example: Teresa has an estate consisting of a house in Los Angeles, with equity of $620,000; a summer cottage at Stinson Beach, with equity of $220,000; the furnishings of her two houses worth $40,000; a bank account of $60,000; life insurance with total proceeds of $300,000; and various heirlooms worth a total of $45,000. At her death, she wants her children to receive all her property, except for the heirlooms, which she intends to give to cousins and other relatives. Teresa doesn't think of herself as wealthy…but, in fact, her taxable estate now amounts to $1,285,000. Rather than have all this property subject to regular probate she:

- transfers the houses and furnishings into a living trust, naming her children as beneficiaries

- creates a pay-on-death bank account for her savings, naming her children as beneficiaries, and

- assigns ownership of her life insurance policies outright to their beneficiaries, and gives up all ownership of them.

Now, only the heirlooms, worth less than the $100,000 limit, remain in Teresa's probate estate. She can distribute these by her will, and her inheritors can claim them simply and speedily by using an affidavit.

E. New York Exemptions From Normal Probate

New York law provides a simplified probate procedure for estates of personal property worth less than $20,000. Also, New York entirely exempts certain property of a deceased spouse that is set aside for the surviving spouse, or the deceased's minor children if there is no spouse. The total amount of property that can be set aside for family use is $56,000. All property set aside for family use isn't counted as part of the $20,000 that can be exempted from probate. Thus, in theory, an estate totaling $76,000 could be eligible for New York's affidavit procedure if the maximum amount of exempt property was left to a surviving spouse or minor children.

Under the simplified probate procedure, the deceased's executor acts as a "voluntary administrator," preparing an affidavit listing the property and beneficiaries and filing it with the probate court (called "surrogate court") clerk. The executor then has authority to collect the deceased's personal property and distribute it to the beneficiaries according to the will or the intestacy laws.

The simplified probate procedure can be combined with other probate-avoidance devices. Thus, if someone transfers big-ticket items like houses and stocks by living trust, she could then transfer small personal gifts, with a total value less than $20,000, by her will free from normal probate.

F. TEXAS EXEMPTIONS FROM NORMAL PROBATE

In Texas, regular probate is normally quite easy, though a lawyer is required. An uncontested estate can be heard by a judge within ten days of filing a petition for probate. Nevertheless, Texas also provides for two simplified probate procedures. The first, called "summary probate," is available regardless of the value of the estate if the value of all property does not exceed what is needed to pay the family allowance permitted by law and certain creditors. The second simplified procedure is called "independent administration." It is permitted if either the will or all the inheritors acting together specifically request it.

If using independent administration, the executor files an application to probate the will, exactly as in traditional probate. A hearing is then held on the validity of the will. If the will is proved valid, and it's shown that the estate has no outstanding debts or other problems, the court orders independent administration, dispensing with many of the tedious steps of normal probate. (The Texas statute is silent, however, on whether independent administration means reduced attorney's fees, which means that it's up to your inheritors to negotiate.)

The court order admitting the will to probate authorizes transfer of the deceased's property to those entitled to it under the will. Furthermore, since the will has been proved in court, title to the property transferred in this way isn't open to challenge. However, independent administration does normally require an attorney, so the major drawback of normal probate is still involved and it isn't therefore a fully satisfactory alternative to probate-avoidance techniques.

Texas also has an affidavit procedure allowing personal property worth up to $50,000 to be transferred outside of probate, but the affidavit can be used only for people who die intestate, leaving no valid will. Thus, this affidavit procedure is of no use to people who plan their estates, which includes writing a will.

G. FLORIDA EXEMPTIONS FROM NORMAL PROBATE

Florida law provides two different types of simplified probate.

1. Summary Probate

Florida permits summary probate (called "summary administration") if

- there's a will, and
- the value of the entire estate subject to probate in Florida, less the value of property exempt from creditors, is less than $75,000.

Property exempt from creditors, under Florida law, includes:

- homestead property (basically, a house) exempted under the state constitution
- a "family allowance," specified by statute, for the support of the deceased's family, and
- certain property of a deceased person—household furniture, furnishings, and appliances (up to a net value of $10,000), cars, personal effects not disposed of by will (up to a net value of $1,000)—which can be claimed by the deceased's surviving spouse or minor children.

You can combine the summary administration procedure with other probate-avoidance devices. For example, you could transfer all of your assets by living trust, leaving just $50,000 worth of personal property under your will. The property that passes under your will can be quickly transferred using summary administration.

Summary administration is also available in Florida if the deceased person has been dead for more than two years, regardless of the size of the estate.

2. No Probate Required

For certain very small estates, Florida doesn't require probate. These estates can consist only of personal property (not real estate). All the property must be exempt from creditors' claims except for any amount that is needed to pay funeral costs and two months' last illness expenses. After receiving a letter stating the facts above, the court will authorize the transfer of the property to the people who are entitled to it. ■

15

ESTATE TAXES

All U.S. citizens, and all others who own property in the U.S. are currently subject to federal estate tax. All property you own, whatever the form of ownership, and whether or not it goes through probate after your death, is subject to this tax.

By now, you've undoubtedly heard that Congress has "repealed" the estate tax. Actually, it passed a law that's far more complex and confusing than a simple repeal. Among other things, the current estate tax law:

- increases the size of an estate that can pass free of estate tax from $2 million in 2006 to $3.5 million in 2009 (see the chart below)

- lowers the top estate tax rate from 46% to 45%

- repeals the estate tax entirely for one, and only one year, in 2010, and

- revives the estate tax, with a personal exemption of $1 million, for 2011 and thereafter.

For technical, as well as political, reasons, Congress could not simply do away with estate taxes—and unfortunately, in estate planners' opinions, the new law is a mess. With a law like this, how can anyone with substantial assets sensibly engage in long-range estate tax planning? It would be extremely difficult to create three different plans that are both sensible and valid—one if you die before 2010, another if you die in 2010, and yet another if you die in 2011.

Worse, even if you, with the help of experts, could prepare a tri-part plan, it couldn't cover what would happen if Congress revises the estate tax law—or, more realistically, *when* Congress revises the estate tax law. It's the consensus of estate tax experts that Congress will have to revise the law before 2010. It's ridiculous to repeal the estate tax law in one year, and then bring it back the next year with an exemption reduced to $1 million. Among the other oddities of that situation, it could make wealthy elderly people quite nervous in 2010, when their

inheritors would have an immense financial interest in them dying during that year.

How Congress might revise the estate tax law is uncertain. It will depend upon political and economic realities that cannot be predicted now. For instance, Congress could decide in, say, 2008 to keep the exemption at $2 million, and eliminate further increases or repeal. Or—well, the possibilities are many. We do believe that it's very unlikely that Congress will ever reduce the personal exemption to less than $1 million.

If you have an estate worth more than $1 million, you'd be wise to keep up with any changes in the federal estate tax law. You can find up-to-date information at Nolo's website: www.nolo.com.

For now, what you can intelligently do is devise a plan that makes sense through 2009. You need to understand that you will likely have to revise your plan if you have the good fortune to live to 2009—or if Congress revises the estate tax law before then.

To help you with your planning, this chapter helps you determine several important things:

- whether or not your estate will owe either federal or state estate taxes (a few states still impose them)

- if your estate will owe taxes, how much those taxes are likely to be

- how you can eliminate, or at least reduce estate taxes and still achieve your other estate planning goals, and

- what sources of funds will be used to pay any taxes for which your estate is ultimately liable.

A. FEDERAL ESTATE TAX EXEMPTIONS

Before worrying about federal estate taxes, obviously you'll want to assess whether you're likely to owe them. Most people won't, because their estates aren't large enough to be taxed. Several federal tax law exemptions and deductions allow you to leave substantial amounts of property free of estate taxes. The most important of these are:

The personal estate tax exemption. The personal exemption allows a set dollar amount of property to pass tax free, no matter who inherits it (I.R.C § 2010).

THE INTERNAL REVENUE CODE (I.R.C.)

You'll see a number of references in this and other chapters to the "I.R.C.," which is the legal abbreviation for a set of tax laws known as the Internal Revenue Code. The Internal Revenue Code can be found in Title 26 of the United States Code (U.S.C.), the collection of all the federal statutes.

If your estate is worth more than the amount of the personal exemption for the year of your death—that is, if it is above the estate tax threshold—your estate will owe taxes unless other exemptions or deductions apply.

THE PERSONAL ESTATE TAX EXEMPTION

Year of Death	Amount of Personal Exemption	Highest Death Estate Tax Rate
2006	$2 million	46%
2007	$2 million	45%
2008	$2 million	45%
2009	$3.5 million	45%
2010	Estate tax repealed	N/A
2011	$1 million unless Congress extends repeal	55%

We use the term "estate tax threshold" to mean the amounts of the personal exemption in any and all years. Thus, "estate tax threshold" refers to the existence of the exemption and the range of exempt amounts, from $2 million to $3.5 million.

If you have made taxable gifts during your life, the amount of the personal exemption will be reduced. Currently, you can give away property worth up to $12,000 per recipient in a calendar year free of gift tax. (See Chapter 16.)

The marital deduction. This deduction exempts from estate tax *all* property left to a surviving spouse. (I.R.C. § 2056(a).) The marital deduction is not allowed for property left to noncitizen spouses. But the personal estate tax exemption can be used for property left to noncitizen spouses. (See Section C2, below, for more on leaving property to a noncitizen spouse.)

The charitable deduction. The charitable deduction exempts all property left to a tax-exempt charity. (I.R.C. § 2055(a).)

In addition to these exemptions, several smaller exemptions are briefly mentioned in Section C4, below.

ESTATE TAXES ON PROPERTY OUTSIDE THE UNITED STATES

If you own property or earn income in another country, your estate may well be subject to taxes in that country. But if you are also a U.S. citizen or resident, some or all of the property taxed by the other country may be taxed by the United States as well.

 Get expert advice. International estate tax planning requires a lawyer. If you own property or earn income in another country, you'll definitely need legal help with your planning.

NO INCOME TAXES ON INHERITED PROPERTY

Because quite a number of people worry about this, we want to state directly that someone who inherits property does not have to pay income taxes on the worth of inherited property. There is one exception. A beneficiary who receives funds from a retirement plan with deferred income taxes, such as an IRA or 401(k) plan, must pay income tax on the funds received. Also, after a person inherits property, any income subsequently received from the property is regular income and is subject to income tax.

Special rules for capital gains taxes on the sale of inherited property are discussed in Section F, below.

B. THE BIG PICTURE: ESTATE AND GIFT TAXES

Before we get into the details of federal and state estate taxes, let's pull back and look at the underlying reasons for these taxes.

Whether or not to tax property transferred at death is a decision that every society with private property makes for itself. In the days of "survival of the fittest" capitalism in 19th century America, there were no federal estate taxes. By contrast, in some European countries today, taxes take a very significant portion of larger estates. Until the recent estate tax "repeal," modern America was somewhere in between.

Trying to reduce estate taxes to a minimum through estate planning is sometimes thought of as a form of lawyer's magic, by which taxes can be avoided completely no matter how large the estate. It's certainly true that there is a bit of gimmickry in some schemes of the very rich to avoid estate taxes. Indeed, avoiding or minimizing taxation at death has been criticized. Doubters maintain that it is a game for the rich, and that society would be better off if people couldn't pass immense sums from one generation to the next. Perhaps. Since neither of us stands to inherit big money, we're not zealous to protect estates of billionaires. Still, we've noticed that even many progressives seem to prefer to leave whatever wealth they've acquired to family, friends, or worthy causes rather than turn it over to the government.

Until recently, federal estate taxes were an attempt to balance two conflicting principles: First, everyone should be able to pass on property they've acquired; and second, this is not a land of aristocracy—some of the wealth of the rich should be returned at death to the public for the general welfare. To achieve this balance, estate tax policy attempted to distinguish between property of the middle class, which is exempt, and property of the wealthy. Overall, estate taxes achieved this balance. Fewer than 2% of all estates are currently subject to estate tax. This percentage will get smaller as the estate tax threshold rises.

Currently, it's not clear whether the U.S. government will continue taxing people's estates. In our opinion, Congress must make a decision by 2010. We'll be curious to see if the inheritors of multi-millionaires and billionaires can continue to receive the same support they've garnered from our present political leaders.

Under federal tax law, substantial gifts (currently more than $12,000 per year to any one person) are taxable, to the giver. The gift tax rate is the same as the estate tax rate. This prevents wealthy people from giving away much or all of their estate shortly before death, and thus avoiding estate tax. (See Chapter 16, Section A.)

Example: Marcus makes taxable gifts totaling $295,000 during his life. This amount is deducted from his personal estate tax exemption. When he dies in 2006, his net taxable estate is worth $2,055,000.

To determine the tax owed, first calculate the available exemption.

The personal exemption for 2006	$2,000,000
Subtract taxable gifts–	$295,000
Remaining exemption	$1,705,000

Then determine the taxable amount.

Taxable estate	$2,055,000
Subtract remaining exemption	–$1,705,000
Taxable amount	$350,000

Prior to 2004 the amount of the personal estate tax exemption was the same as the gift tax exemption. For example, the total exemption for taxable gifts and estate taxes for 2003 was $1 million. However, starting in 2004, these two exemptions divide. The gift tax exemption remains at $1 million; the personal estate tax exemption rises from $2 million in 2006 to $3.5 million by 2009. For the very wealthy, this can make it less advantageous to make large gifts during life.

Example: Tess gives away almost all of her estate during her lifetime. Her taxable gifts total $1.4 million dollars. She must pay gift taxes on $400,000. She dies in 2006 with an estate of $500,000.

If Tess had kept her entire estate until her death in 2006, she would have paid no taxes. Her gifts and remaining estate total $1.9 million, below the amount of the estate tax exemption for 2006.

C. WILL YOUR ESTATE HAVE TO PAY TAXES?

Whether or not your estate will owe federal estate tax depends on several factors: the size of your estate, who inherits it, and when you die.

1. Estimating Your Net Worth

You can't, of course, know what the value of your estate will be at your death. The best you can do is make a reasonable estimate of your current net worth (assets minus liabilities). This should be sufficient for estate tax planning purposes.

If you completed the property worksheets in Chapter 4, Section B, you should have a ballpark estimate of your current net worth. If you didn't complete the property worksheet, you'll need to make an estimate now, unless you know what you own is well below the estate tax threshold. In that case, don't worry about estate taxes for the time being. If you later strike it rich, that will be the time for you to learn about estate taxes and ways to reduce them.

Under federal estate tax law, most property is valued at its market value as of the date of the owner's death, less any debts on the property. However, a few types of property can be valued at less than their market value. Family farmland can be valued for its (continued) use as a farm, not at its highest possible market value. So can real estate used in a family business. So even if farmland would be worth more if sold to a developer to build an apartment complex or a shopping center, you don't have to use that higher value. (The specific tax rules on this are discussed in Chapter 28, Section B.)

At your death, the amount in any individual retirement plan you own, such as an IRA, 401(k), or profit-sharing plan, is included in your taxable estate. This amount is not reduced by any income tax that a beneficiary must pay when he or she receives these funds.

Also, it may be hard to determine the value of some types of property, such as royalty rights or stock in a closely held corporation. Make your best guess—or pay for an expert's opinion.

WHO APPRAISES YOUR ESTATE AFTER YOU DIE?

Having the value of your estate determined is the responsibility of the person you appoint to supervise your property. This is the successor trustee if the property is left by living trust, or the executor if the property is left by will. If all property is left by joint tenancy, the surviving joint tenant has the responsibility to see whether an estate tax return must be filed or taxes paid.

The federal government isn't involved in appraising property in an estate. Obviously, though, the IRS can challenge and audit estate tax returns, just as it can audit income tax returns. In some states that impose death taxes, official appraisals are done as part of the death tax system. Most states, however, do not make governmental appraisals.

It may be difficult for an executor, trustee, or probate attorney to establish the market value of many items—works of art, closely held businesses, or stock in small corporations, for example. Saving receipts, bookkeeping records, and other documents stating the actual cost of items can be very useful and can save time and money later. Large estates that have many assets (appreciated real estate, art, interests in small businesses, to name but a few) can afford to, and usually should, hire an expert appraiser.

2. Property Left to Your Spouse

As we stated earlier, property that you leave to your spouse is not subject to federal gift or estate taxes, no matter how much the property is worth. This is called the "marital deduction."

> **Example:** Pedro leaves his wife Rebecca $5,770,000. No estate tax is assessed, no matter what the year of Pedro's death.

UNMARRIED COUPLES DON'T QUALIFY

There are no exemptions similar to the marital deduction for unmarried partners or "significant others." Quite simply, the estate tax laws are written to encourage and reward traditional relationships.

⚠ **No marital deduction for property left to noncitizen spouse.** If your spouse is not a U.S. citizen, property you leave to her or him is not eligible for the marital deduction. The special estate tax rules that apply to noncitizen spouses are discussed below, in Section 2c.

a. How the Marital Deduction Works

To stress the most important point about the marital deduction: It makes no difference how much money or property you give during life or pass at death to your spouse. Whether it's a $500,000 house, $1.2 million in emeralds, or a $500 million collection of Impressionist paintings, it's all exempt from estate tax. And the property's legal form makes no difference either; it can be community property, joint tenancy property, "quasi-community" property, or separate property.

You can use the marital deduction in addition to all other allowable estate tax deductions.

> **Example:** Sue has an estate valued at $6.6 million. She leaves $1 million to her children and $5.6 million to her husband. All Sue's property is exempt from federal estate taxes—the $5.6 million because of the marital deduction and the $1 million because it is below the estate tax threshold.

b. How the Marital Deduction Can Be a Tax Trap

The fact that no federal estate tax is assessed when property is left to the surviving spouse can mislead people into thinking that leaving everything to a spouse must be the best thing to do. It often is not. The marital deduction can have a downside if members of a couple together own assets worth more than the amount of the personal estate tax exemption. That amount, as you know, ranges from $1.5 million to $3.5 million, depending on the year of death. Increasing the size of the surviving spouse's estate can eventually result either in estate tax being assessed, when there otherwise would be none, or in higher estate taxes.

> **Example:** Barbara and Tim are an elderly married couple; each has an estate worth $1.5 million. If Tim leaves all his property to anyone but Barbara, no tax will be owed because his estate is under the estate tax threshold. And if Tim leaves everything to Barbara, no tax will be due because of the marital deduction. However, suppose Tim dies in 2006, leaving all his property to Barbara, and Barbara dies in 2008. Barbara's estate will then be worth $3 million. The personal exemption for 2008 is $2 million. So Barbara's estate will owe tax on $1 million. By contrast, if Barbara died owning only her original $1.5 million, no estate taxes would be due.

This tax trap is particularly dangerous when both spouses are old or in poor health. The survivor isn't likely to live long enough to really benefit from legally owning the deceased spouse's property.

It is often wiser, from an estate tax viewpoint, to use the personal exemptions of both members of the couple, rather than only one, as can occur if the marital deduction is used. The standard, and popular, way to avoid this tax trap is to create what's called an "AB" trust, which allows the surviving spouse to have income from and use of the deceased spouse's property, but never become the legal owner of it. Doing this allows each spouse to use the personal estate tax exemption. (See Chapter 18, Section C, for an explanation of how these trusts work.) Another alternative is for each spouse to leave property directly to children or other beneficiaries. However, this leaves the surviving spouse without income or use of the deceased spouse's property, which many married couples don't want.

c.   Special Rules for Noncitizen Spouses

As we've said, no marital deduction is allowed for property one spouse leaves to the other if the surviving spouse is not a citizen of the United States. It doesn't matter that a noncitizen spouse was married to a U.S. citizen or is a legal resident of the U.S. The surviving spouse must be a U.S. citizen to be eligible for the marital deduction.

In contrast, property a noncitizen spouse leaves to a citizen spouse is eligible for the marital deduction. Congress seems to have feared that noncitizen spouses would leave the U.S. after the death of their spouses, whisking away their wealth to foreign lands, so it would never be subject to U.S. tax. Presumably, Congress thought that citizen spouses will remain here.

Even without the marital deduction, a U.S. citizen can leave a noncitizen spouse a good deal of property free of estate tax. The personal estate tax exemption can be used for property left to anyone, including a noncitizen spouse. So property worth between $2 million and $3.5 million (to say it again, depending on the year of death) can be left tax-free to a noncitizen spouse.

> **Example:** Lucy leaves all her property to her husband Devi, a noncitizen. When she prepares her estate plan, her estate is worth $900,000. Whatever the year of her death, this amount will be under the estate tax threshold. However, in 2006 Lucy unexpectedly inherits $1.3 million and shortly thereafter dies. Her total estate is $2.2 million. The personal estate tax exemption for 2006 is $2 million. Because Devi is not a citizen, $200,000 of Lucy's estate is subject to tax.

There are two ways, however, that a spouse can give or leave property to a noncitizen spouse and obtain additional estate tax benefits. U.S. gift tax law provides that a citizen spouse can currently give the other, noncitizen spouse up to $120,000 per year free of gift tax. (I.R.C. § 2525(i)(2).) Thus, a citizen spouse with an estate of $2.3 million could be sure that her estate would not owe tax by giving the noncitizen spouse $100,000 in each of three years, then leaving him the remaining $2 million at death.

Further, all property left by one spouse to a noncitizen spouse in what's called a "Qualified Domestic Trust" (QDOT) is not subject to estate tax until the noncitizen spouse dies. (See Chapter 19, Section B.)

If a noncitizen spouse becomes a naturalized U.S. citizen before the deceased spouse's estate tax return must be filed (nine months after death), the surviving spouse is then entitled to the full marital deduction. For a prosperous couple residing in the U.S., and who are not both U.S. citizens, obtaining the estate tax advantage of the marital deduction can be one good reason for becoming U.S. citizens.

Tax planning for noncitizen spouses. If you're married to a noncitizen and have an estate worth more than $2 million, you should see a lawyer to ensure that you comply with the special rules that affect noncitizen spouses.

3. Gifts to Charities

All gifts you make to tax-exempt charitable organizations are exempt from federal estate and gift taxes. It doesn't matter whether you make these gifts during your life or leave them at your death. If you plan to make large charitable gifts, be sure you've checked out whether the organizations are in fact tax exempt. The most common way an organization establishes that it's a tax-exempt charity is by obtaining a ruling from the IRS, under Internal Revenue Code Section 501(c)(3). (These organizations are referred to, in tax lingo, as "501(c)(3) corporations.") Many charitable institutions, particularly colleges and universities, provide extensive information about tax-exempt gift-giving and offer a variety of gift plans.

Making substantial gifts to charities through trusts is discussed in Chapter 20.

4. Other Estate Tax Exemptions

There are also federal estate tax deductions for:

- funeral expenses, which can range from minimal to many thousands of dollars

- estate expenses, such as probate fees; again, a wide range of expenses is possible here, up to tens of thousands of dollars or even more, depending on the worth of the probate estate and state probate fee rules

- any claims against the estate, and

- a certain percentage of state estate tax paid, and estate tax imposed by foreign countries on property the deceased owned there.

For most people, these exemptions are relatively minor. It's rarely necessary to estimate them to see whether or not your estate is likely to be liable for estate taxes. If you're close enough to the tax threshold so that these deductions may matter, you're close enough to consider estate tax planning.

CONSERVATION EASEMENTS

If you own undeveloped land that has risen greatly in value and you would like the land to be preserved after your death, rather than, say, be developed for condos, consider creating a conservation easement. Your estate can obtain a sizeable tax break if you do so. Estate taxes on land with a conservation easement are cut by 40%. The maximum tax break here is $500,000. With a conservation easement, limited agricultural and forestry land uses are allowed, but subdividing for development is prohibited. To be eligible for this easement, the land must be within 25 miles of a large metropolitan area, national park, or wilderness area, or ten miles from certain national forests.

Even if you don't create a conservation easement, the inheritors of the land can do so within nine months after your death, and obtain the same estate tax benefits.

D. CALCULATING AND PAYING ESTATE TAXES

Here we discuss when an estate tax return must be filed, property valuation for estate tax purposes, how to calculate the amount of taxes your estate will owe, and when the taxes must be paid.

1. Filing a Federal Estate Tax Return

A tax return, IRS Form 706, must be filed for an estate with a gross value exceeding the amount of the personal exemption for the year of death. That's *gross,* not net. This means that, for purposes of deciding whether a return must be filed, you don't subtract the amount a deceased owed from what he owned. An estate tax return may have to be filed even though no taxes are actually due.

> **Example:** The gross value of Dan's estate is $2.2 million. The personal estate tax exemption for 2006 is $2 million. Because Dan's gross estate is worth more than the exempt amount, his executor must file an estate tax return. However, no tax will be due, because Dan's net estate turns out to be well under the estate tax threshold. It is worth 1,250,000, because of mortgages on his real estate investments.
>
> Here are the gross and net figures for Dan's estate:

Gross Estate	Net Estate
$200,000 cash	$200,000 cash
$50,000 personal property	$50,000 personal property
$250,000 stock investments	$250,000 investments
$400,000 house	$100,000 real estate investments
$1,100,000 real estate investments	$600,000 equity in house
$200,000 summer cottage	$50,000 equity in summer cottage
$2,200,000 total	$1,250,000 total

If an estate tax return must be filed, it is due within nine months of the death of the deceased, but the IRS may grant extensions.

The executor of the deceased's will is legally responsible for filing an estate tax return, if due. If there is no will, but there is a living trust, the job falls to the successor trustee named in the trust.

In perhaps the most common situation, a person creates both a will and living trust and names the same person to serve as executor and successor trustee. If the executor and successor trustee are not the same person, both must cooperate so the executor has sufficient financial information to determine whether an estate tax return must be filed, and what the right figures are if a return is required.

Obtaining and filing a return. If an executor must file a federal estate tax return, he or she will want to hire a tax expert to prepare Form 706. It is not an easy form to complete. *The Executor's Guide: Settling a Loved One's Estate or Trust,* by Mary Randolph (Nolo), includes a thorough discussion of Form 706 and other federal tax forms an executor may be required to file.

You can obtain IRS tax forms in a number of ways. The easiest is to download forms and instructions for free from the IRS website: www.irs .gov. But you can also visit an IRS office, or call 800-829-1040 and enjoy a phone message offering more options than LifeSavers has flavors.

2. Property Valuation

Under federal law, a deceased person's property can be valued either as of the date of death or six months afterwards (referred to in tax lingo as the "alternate valuation date"). This is an all-or-nothing proposition. Your executor cannot value some assets as of the date of death and others six months later. Which valuation date is best for your estate is a matter for your successor trustee and executor to decide with a lawyer, and perhaps a tax adviser as well.

Example: Ellen dies on May 1, 2006. She owned real estate with a net worth of $2.3 million on that date. There's a sudden crash of real estate values in her area. Six months after her death, her real estate is valued at $1.65 million. Her executor takes advantage of the alternate valuation date to value her real estate at the lower amount, and so avoids paying estate tax.

As mentioned, there are special valuation rules for family farms or real estate used in a family business. See Chapter 28, Section B.

3. How to Calculate Federal Estate Taxes

There's probably no reason to try to calculate the precise amount of tax your estate will owe when you die. First, you don't know the year in which you'll die, so you can't know the amount of the personal estate tax exemption that will apply. Second, as we've said, Congress may change the exempt amounts in the coming years. And finally, you can't know now exactly what your property will be worth at your death. However, if you want to understand how estate taxes actually work, read on.

Technically, the personal estate tax exemption works by use of a "unified" tax credit. The credit is called "unified" because the same rates apply to taxable lifetime gifts as to property left on death. The credit is the amount that would otherwise be due on the exempt amount for the year of death. This credit will increase until 2011. However, the total lifetime gift tax exemption will remain at $1 million, and will not rise as the personal exemption amount does. This means it will never be desirable, from a tax standpoint, for a wealthy person to make taxable gifts worth more than $1 million.

Year of Death	Personal Exemption	Highest Estate and Gift Tax Rate	Estate Tax Credit
2006	$2 million	46%	$780,800
2007	$2 million	45%	$780,800
2008	$2 million	45%	$780,800
2009	$3.5 million	45%	$1,255,800
2010	Estate tax repealed	top individual income tax rate (gift tax only)	
2011	$1 million unless Congress extends repeal	55% unless Congress extends repeal	$345,800

UNIFIED FEDERAL ESTATE AND GIFT TAX RATES

Column A	Column B	Column C	Column D
			rate of tax on excess
net taxable estate over	net taxable estate not over	tax on amount in column A	over amount in column A
$ 0	$10,000	$ 0	18%
10,000	20,000	1,800	20
20,000	40,000	3,800	22
40,000	60,000	8,200	24
60,000	80,000	13,000	26
80,000	100,000	18,200	28
100,000	150,000	23,800	30
150,000	250,000	38,800	32
250,000	500,000	70,800	34
500,000	750,000	155,800	37
750,000	1,000,000	248,300	39
1,000,000	1,250,000	345,800	41
1,250,000	1,500,000	448,300	43
1,500,000	2,000,000	555,800	45
2,000,000	2,500,000	780,800	46*
2,500,000	infinity	1,025,800	46*

*These rates drop between 2004 and 2010. See the chart on the previous page.

Here's how you use the estate tax credit to calculate the amount of tax owed.

- First, determine the amount of the net taxable estate, by subtracting all allowable deductions.

- Second, compute the "tentative tax" from the estate tax table above. This is the tax that would be due on the net estate if there were no unified credit (that is, no personal estate tax exemption).

- Finally, subtract the amount of the unified credit for the year of death from the tentative tax. The result is the tax actually owed.

What does all this translate to in reality? It means that if tax is owed, the rates start high. For 2006, the rate may be as high as 46%.

Estate taxes work with estate tax credits so that high rates will apply to any amount subject to estate tax.

Example: Esmerelda dies in 2006 with an estate of $2.1 million. The amount subject to tax is $100,000. The tax rate applied is the rate for $2 million to $2.5 million, which is 46%— not the rate for $100,000, which is 30%. The tax owed is $46,000.

Technically, the tax is calculated by determining the tax due on $2.1 million, which is $826,800. Then the estate tax credit of $780,800 for 2006 is deducted, leaving a tax bill of $46,000.

MORE INFORMATION ON FEDERAL ESTATE TAX LAWS

More detailed information about federal estate and gift taxes can be found in IRS Publication 950, *Introduction to Estate and Gift Taxes*. It's available free at many IRS offices or online at www.irs.gov.

You can also read the relevant federal tax statutes, if you dare to plunge into this morass of legalese. It is dense, even for tax professionals. Federal estate tax laws are found in the Internal Revenue Code, Title 26 of the United States Code, the official collection of all federal statutes.

4. Planning for Payment of Estate Tax

You have two approaches to consider when you're planning for payment of any estate taxes due after your death. The first is to specify, in your will or living trust, assets to be used to pay any taxes. Obviously, you'll need to make sure the assets you've named are worth enough to cover the tax bill. The second approach is to allow your executor/ successor trustee to decide which assets should be used to pay estate taxes. You can also combine these approaches—specify certain assets, and provide that if they don't cover all estate taxes, your successor trustee/executor can choose which other assets to use.

If your estate is over the estate tax threshold, it is unwise to be silent in your will and living trust about how any taxes should be paid. Without direction from you, the IRS will look to the law of the state where you lived (in legalese, your "domicile") to determine how taxes are paid. State laws vary

significantly on this. And some states' laws are extensive and complex. Here, as in other aspects of estate planning, it's far better for you to make a decision than to let the matter rest with state law.

You'll need some foresight when deciding how estate taxes are to be paid. You want to be sure the method you've chosen doesn't risk harming or even destroying your basic goals. Suppose, for example, you leave your house to your son and your stock and cash to your daughter. Any remaining assets pass to your husband. You want your son to receive the house free and clear of estate taxes, so you provide that estate taxes are to be paid out of your daughter's inheritance. To make sure your daughter isn't short-changed, you leave her what you think will be enough extra to pay the estate taxes on the house.

Over the years, the house more than doubles in value, but you've spent quite a bit of your cash and sold some of your stock. Come estate tax time, much of your daughter's inheritance goes to pay the estate taxes on the house. The result is that your son gets your house, which is worth twice what you figured on, and your daughter gets significantly less than you planned on. So, to point out the obvious, keep your estate planning in tune with your current financial situation, especially if you're using the payment of estate taxes to balance inheritances.

E. REDUCING FEDERAL ESTATE TAXES

What can you do to reduce federal estate taxes if you think your estate will be liable for them? Not as much as you might think, although for the very wealthy, high-priced experts do come up with ingenious, pushing-the-edge tax dodges. For the rest of us, aside from making use of the estate tax exemptions and deductions discussed above, there are only a few major ways you can lower estate taxes.

1. Give Away Property While You Live

While you're alive, you can give a certain amount of property each year free of estate/gift tax. Currently, you can give property worth $12,000 or less per person per year. A couple can give $24,000 a year tax free to one person. Tax-exempt gift giving works well for people who can afford it, and can be particularly advantageous for those who have several children, grandchildren, or other objects of their affection. (See Chapter 16, Section D.)

Making gifts of portions of a family business or other business assets like stock options, can, in the right circumstances, significantly reduce or eliminate estate taxes. This use of gift-giving is discussed in Chapter 28, Section B.

2. Create an Estate Tax-Saving Trust

You can use a number of different types of trusts to save on overall estate taxes, depending on your circumstances and desires. We discuss these trusts in detail in Chapters 18 through 23. If you individually, or you and your spouse together, have an estate exceeding $2 million, be sure to read those chapters carefully to determine whether you can use one or more of these trusts. You should make your final decision only after consulting an experienced estate planning lawyer.

F. THE FEDERAL INCOME TAX BASIS OF INHERITED PROPERTY

Though it's not strictly speaking an estate tax matter, the question of how inherited property is valued, for the purpose of calculating gain or loss from subsequent sale, is closely related. It is a tax question, and it can apply to property you leave. Because this issue matters to so many people, we discuss it here.

Let's start with a definition. The word "basis" means the value assigned to property from which taxable gain or loss on sale is determined. The concept of a property's basis is a tricky one, not made any easier by the fact that "basis" is not defined in the tax laws. When property is purchased, its basis is generally its cost. In fact, basis is often referred to as "cost basis." If you buy a painting for $5,000, for example, it has a basis equal to its cost—$5,000. If you sell the painting two months later for $16,000 (lucky you), your taxable profit is $11,000.

sale price	$16,000
minus basis–	$ 5,000
gain	$11,000

The original cost basis can be adjusted up, for certain types of improvements to property, or down, for reasons like depreciation. If you make what's called a "capital improvement" to a house, such as putting in a new foundation, the cost of the improvement is added to the basis of the property. Capital improvements, very roughly, last more than a year.

Example: Green Is Good, Inc., bought an old barn in which to design and make bicycles. The barn cost the company $270,000, so the company has a cost basis in it of $270,000. Over the next year, Green Is Good spent $230,000 for capital improvements to the barn, installing a new fire control system and a new roof.

Here's how the company determines the "adjusted basis"

original cost	$270,000
capital improvements	+$230,000
adjusted basis	$500,000

The company takes depreciation deductions for the barn on its income taxes of $30,000 over two years. The property's adjusted basis now becomes $470,000, since the deduction for depreciation lowers the adjusted basis of the property.

The barn is sold to T. Donald Bump (who plans to use the barn for a weekend getaway) for $600,000.

Green Is Good, Inc., determines its profit this way

Sale price	$600,000
Subtract basis	− $470,000
Profit	$130,000

T. Donald's cost basis in the barn is $600,000.

Now to move to the tax basis of inherited property. *Under federal tax law, the basis of inherited property is "stepped up" to its fair market value at the date of the decedent's death.* Actually, this is a simplification of the rule, which is that the basis of inherited property is adjusted *up or down* to the market value as of the date of death. However, the assumption that prices of property rise over time is so ingrained in our economic life, whatever the short- or medium-term fluctuations, that the term commonly used is "stepped-up" basis. And in practice, for property owned for any long period of time, the inheritor's basis—the net value of the property at death of the original owner—is almost always higher than that of the original owner.

Example: During the two years that T. Donald owned the barn until his death in 2006, he made no capital improvements to the barn. At the time of his death, when the barn was inherited by T. Donald Jr., it had appreciated in value to $800,000.

T. Donald Jr.'s basis in the barn is stepped up to:	$800,000
T. Donald Jr. sells the barn three months later for:	$750,000
Subtract basis	− $800,000
T. Donald Jr.'s loss:	($50,000)

The fact that the basis of property is stepped up at the owner's death to its fair market value means that it's almost always desirable to hold on to highly appreciated property until it can pass at death. That way, your inheritors obtain the advantage of the stepped-up basis rule. Thus, if T. Donald sold the barn a year before he died, when it was worth $780,000, he would have had to pay federal capital gains taxes (and possibly state taxes as well) on $180,000 ($780,000 sale price minus his $600,000 basis).

If T. Donald gave the barn to T. Donald Jr. during his lifetime, T. Donald Jr. would have had the same basis in the barn as T. Donald had—$600,000. Gifts made during life are not entitled to a stepped-up basis. Only transfers at death qualify for this desirable tax treatment.

BOTH HALVES OF COMMUNITY PROPERTY RECEIVE A STEPPED-UP BASIS

If you and your spouse own property in a community property state, both equal portions of that property will receive a stepped up basis to current market value when one spouse dies. The surviving spouse's share of the community property receives the same new share as the deceased spouse's share. If a couple bought a community property home for $80,000 that is now worth $700,000 when a spouse dies, each spouse's share is worth $350,000. The basis of each spouse's share, not merely the deceased spouse's share, is stepped up to that $350,000.

By contrast, in common law states, only the property owned by a deceased spouse receives a stepped up basis. No property of a surviving spouse receives a stepped up basis, even if that property was held in shared ownership with the deceased spouse.

STEPPED-UP BASIS RULES TO CHANGE IN 2010

Congress has changed the stepped-up basis rules for property inherited from a person who dies in 2010. In that year, inheritors will receive a stepped-up basis for inherited property worth a total of only $1.3 million. (Surviving spouses receive a stepped-up basis for an additional $3 million worth of property.) All property above the limit will carry the same basis as it had for the deceased person.

As discussed earlier, in 2011 the estate tax is scheduled to return. But it is not clear whether the stepped-up basis rules will also return. Congress will most likely reexamine the tax law, including what to do about the stepped-up basis rules, before 2010.

If Congress decides to continue the restrictions on the stepped-up basis rules after 2010, anyone who owns a significantly appreciated asset may face new, and daunting, estate planning problems.

Example: In 2006, Ricardo and Angelique, a frugal middle class couple, have amassed a combined estate worth $1,750,000. Each plans to leave his or her estate to the other; the surviving spouse will leave all the property to their daughter, Phaedra. They will use an AB trust. Because each spouse's estate is below the current minimum estate tax threshold of $2 million, no estate tax will be due on either's death. However, most of the estate consists of their house, which is fully paid for and worth $1,100,000, and greatly appreciated stocks. They bought the house

in 1965 for $48,000. Their total basis in stocks, currently worth $600,000, is $52,000. Thus their basis for $1.7 million of their estate is $100,000. If the stepped-up basis rules are repealed when the surviving spouse dies, Phaedra will lose a significant portion of her inheritance if she sells the house and the stocks.

Estate received by Phaedra	$1,750,000
Value of property with stepped-up basis	$1,700,000
Less stepped-up basis exemption	$1,300,000
Value of property Phaedra inherits with Ricardo and Angelique's basis	$400,000
Dollar basis (roughly) of that property	$24,000
Value of property subject to capital gains tax	$376,000

What could Ricardo and Angelique do now that would prevent Phaedra from possibly being subject to capital gains tax? Unfortunately, nothing that makes good sense. First, it is important to understand that the restricted stepped-up basis rules are not scheduled to become effective for some years, until 2010, and that Congress will surely revisit this issue before then. Second, because these restricted rules are so new, and not in effect yet, estate planners generally have not explored how to work with them, or around them. The best advice for now is: Do nothing. If you have a stepped-up basis problem in 2009, see an attorney.

G. STATE INHERITANCE AND ESTATE TAXES

There are two types of state taxes to consider when making decisions about how to leave your property: inheritance taxes and estate taxes. This section introduces each type.

1. State Inheritance Taxes

At one time, many states imposed inheritance taxes, but very few still do. The states listed below impose inheritance taxes on:

- all real estate owned in the state, no matter where the deceased person lived, and

- the personal property (everything but real estate) of residents of the state.

Inheritance taxes are imposed on the people who receive the property (the beneficiaries), rather than on the estate itself. Typically, beneficiaries are divided into different classes, such as "Class A: Husband or Wife," "Class B: Immediate Family," and "Class C: All Others." Each class receives different tax exemptions and is taxed at a different rate. Generally, the highest exemption and lowest rate goes to spouses, or "Class A."

STATES THAT IMPOSE INHERITANCE TAXES

Indiana

Iowa

Kentucky

Maryland

Nebraska (inheritance tax credited to county)

New Jersey

Ohio

Oklahoma

Pennsylvania

Tennessee

You can find the specific rules for each of these states in the appendix, at the back of this book.

If you live or own real estate in a state that imposes inheritance taxes, you may want to consider the impact of them. In many instances, the bite taken from an inheritance is annoying, but relatively minor. However, in some states, larger chunks can be taken, especially for property left to nonrelatives.

For example, Nebraska imposes a 15% inheritance tax rate on $25,000 left to a friend, but only 1% if it's left to your child. Many states impose no inheritance tax at all on property left to a surviving spouse. It's probably rare that someone would change the amount of property left to a beneficiary because of inheritance tax, but you should at least evaluate the issue if it applies.

2. State Estate Taxes

Even if your state does not impose inheritance taxes, your estate may face a state tax bill. Many states have adopted a new type of estate tax that is designed to replace revenue lost because of changes to the federal estate tax laws.

Before 2002, most states collected what was called a "pick up" tax from any estate large enough to pay federal estate taxes. This tax didn't increase the overall amount paid by the estate. Rather, under federal law, the state was entitled to a certain portion of the federal tax.

Congress changed this system in 2002. Under current federal law, all state "pick up" taxes were eliminated in 2005. To make up for the loss, many states have enacted a new estate tax that is not connected to the federal system. Many other states are likely to adopt similar laws soon.

The details of these new tax laws vary from state to state, but one important thing to keep in mind is that your estate may owe taxes to the state even if it is not large enough to owe federal estate tax. This could be true even if you use an AB trust to reduce federal taxes. (See Chapter 18.) If you leave an amount of property that exceeds your state's estate tax threshold, your estate will owe state tax even if no federal tax is due.

Example: Roy and Ann, who are residents of Rhode Island, make an AB trust. When Roy dies in 2006, his share of the couple's property is $900,000. That amount goes into Trust B, the deceased spouse's trust. Roy's estate is well under the federal estate tax threshold of $2 million for 2006, so it owes no federal tax. However, Roy's estate will owe tax to Rhode Island, because it imposes tax on estates worth $675,000 or more.

For more information about state estate taxes. If you live in a state that imposes estate tax, there's little you can do to avoid it, beyond moving to another state with more favorable tax laws. (Though there's no saying that state won't change its laws, too.) For most estates, the state tax amount won't be onerous. But if you are prosperous and want to know whether your estate may face this type of tax, see a good lawyer with up-to-date information about this rapidly changing area of the law.

3. Your Residence for State Tax Purposes

States that impose estate or inheritance taxes on residents do so on everyone "domiciled in the state." "Domicile" is a legal term of art. It means the state where you have your permanent residence, where you intend to make your home. Generally, it's clear where your domicile is. It's the state where you live most of the time, work, own a home, and vote.

Sometimes, however, it's not so clear. If you have homes in different states, there may be no decisive evidence of which state is your domicile. For example, several states, eager for tax revenue, claimed that Howard Hughes was domiciled there. A less dramatic and more common example is a person who divides his time between homes in two states. In some circumstances, it's quite possible that more than one state would assert the person was domiciled there.

Example: Rita retired and moved from New Jersey to North Carolina. However, she returns often to New Jersey to visit her children, keeps several bank and brokerage accounts in New Jersey, and never bothers to register to vote in North Carolina. New Jersey might claim, on her death, that Rita remained domiciled there and never transferred her domicile to North Carolina.

If you do divide your residence between two or more states, make sure you make it clear which state you are domiciled in. Normally, this means being sure that you maintain all your major personal business contacts and vote in the state you claim as your domicile. Obviously, if one state doesn't have estate or inheritance taxes and the other does, you might want to establish your domicile in the no-tax state. ■

16

GIFTS AND GIFT TAXES

We're used to thinking of gifts as a personal matter, not as an aspect of financial or estate planning. Up to a point, this is accurate; birthday or holiday presents don't normally have tax consequences. However, for a gift worth a substantial amount of money, the rules change. Currently, if you give more than $12,000 to one recipient in one year, the excess is subject to gift tax, unless the recipient is your spouse or another exemption applies.

Here we'll explore the federal gift tax rules, and the major ways gifts can be used to save on or eliminate gift taxes.

OTHER REASONS TO MAKE GIFTS

This chapter focuses on the gift tax and making tax-exempt gifts, but we're aware that many people, including those with estates over the estate tax threshold, are reluctant or unwilling to make big gifts simply to reduce their taxable estate. For them, the tax savings alone aren't worth the loss of the property given away. Making a large gift often involves many factors, with tax consequences being only one, often a relatively small one. Our focus on gift taxes and tax saving doesn't mean we're suggesting that these matters should be central to your decisions regarding making substantial gifts. Still, even if your primary motive in making a substantial gift isn't to save on taxes, why not take full advantage of the gift tax rules?

A. THE FEDERAL GIFT TAX: AN OVERVIEW

Gift tax is assessed against the giver of a gift. The value of the gift, for gift tax purposes, is the net market value of the property at the date of the gift. Net market value means the market price, less any debts owed on the property.

The recipient of a gift is not liable for federal gift tax, unless the giver failed to pay any tax actually due. Only in that case will the IRS go after the recipient for gift taxes.

1. The Annual Exclusion

Currently, federal law exempts from gift tax the first $12,000 you give to any person or noncharitable institution in a calendar year. Lawyers often call this "the annual exclusion." (I.R.C. § 2503(b).) The amount of the gift tax exclusion is indexed to the cost of living, rounded down to the closest thousand dollars. This means the cumulative increases in the cost of living must rise slightly more than 10% before the amount of the annual exclusion is increased to $13,000.

So if you give someone $25,000, the first $12,000 of that gift is exempt from gift tax, while the remaining $13,000 is not. Married couples can combine their annual exclusions, which means that they can currently give away $24,000 of property tax-free, per year, per recipient.

The annual exclusion can be extremely important. You can use it repeatedly over a number of years to reduce the size of your estate and hence your ultimate estate tax bill. Here are some examples of how the annual exclusion works:

- You give $8,000 to a cousin in one year: There are no federal gift tax consequences.

- You give $16,000 to the cousin in one year: $4,000 is subject to gift tax.

- You give $8,000 each to two cousins: None of the $16,000 is subject to gift tax.

- You give $7,000 each to two cousins, three years in a row: none of this $42,000 is subject to gift tax.

YEAR	ESTATE TAX EXEMPTION	GIFT TAX EXEMPTION	HIGHEST ESTATE AND GIFT TAX RATE
2006	$2 million	$1 million	46%
2007	$2 million	$1 million	45%
2008	$2 million	$1 million	45%
2009	$3.5 million	$1 million	45%
2010	Estate tax repealed	$1 million	top individual income tax rate (gift tax only)
2011	$1 million unless Congress extends repeal		55% unless Congress extends repeal

2. The Gift Tax Exemption

Aside from the annual gift tax exclusion, currently $12,000, there is a $1 million cumulative tax exemption for gifts. You can give away a total of $1 million during your lifetime without paying gift taxes. As the chart above shows, this $1 million exemption does not increase over the years, while the amount of the estate tax exemption has already risen above that amount. Even in 2010, the one year in which the estate tax will be repealed, the gift tax will still exist with an exempt amount of $1 million. For 2010 and thereafter (unless Congress changes the law), there will be a $1 million combined gift and estate tax exemption.

If you make more than $1 million worth of gifts in your lifetime, you will owe gift tax.

Example: In 2007, Elijah makes taxable gifts of $2 million. He must pay tax on $1 million. But in 2007, the personal exemption on death is $2 million. If Elijah had died in 2007 his estate would owe no taxes.

As this example demonstrates, the divergence of the gift and estate tax exemption is a matter only for the rich, and immaterial to most people. For the wealthy, it's not tax-wise to make gifts totaling more than $1 million during their lifetime (aside from any gifts made using the annual exclusion, currently $12,000).

3. Other Exemptions

Some types of gifts are completely exempt from federal gift tax:

- **All property one spouse gives the other, no matter how much it's worth.** (I.R.C. § 2523(a).) However, there's a different rule if the spouse receiving the gift is not a U.S. citizen. A U.S. citizen can give his or her noncitizen spouse up to $120,000 worth of property per year free of gift tax.

- **All property given to a tax-exempt charity.** (I.R.C. § 2522.)

- **Gifts made to pay for someone's medical bills or school tuition.** (I.R.C. § 2503(e).)

This final exemption has a couple of twists. First, the money must be paid directly to the provider of the medical service or the school. Gifts to pay for medical insurance, including payments to HMOs for amounts covering medical care, diagnosis, and treatment, are covered under this section. (I.R.C. § 213(d)(1)(D).) If you give the money to an ill person or student, who then pays the bill, the gift is not tax-exempt. Nor can you reimburse someone who has already paid a medical or tuition bill and have this be a tax exempt gift. Second, you cannot pay for a student's other educational expenses, such as room and board, and have this treated as a tax-exempt gift.

You can combine different gift tax exemptions.

Example: Victor gives $12,000 outright to his son, $50,000 to his wife, $20,000 to CARE (a tax-exempt charity), pays $17,000 for his grandson's tuition at college, and also pays $21,000 for a daughter's medical bills. All these gifts are completely exempt from federal gift tax.

FOREIGN GIFTS

Federal tax laws impose strict reporting and tax requirement on any U.S. citizen or legal resident who receives foreign gifts (any and all gifts made by a non-U.S. citizen) with a total value of more than $12,375 in one year. (The amount increases annually to reflect the rate of inflation.) Thus, if three residents of different countries each give you $5,000 within a year, you must report the full $15,000 received, and pay tax. Note that the rules for receiving foreign gifts are very different from those governing domestic ones: With foreign gifts, it is the recipient, not the donor, who must report the gift and pay tax. A foreign gift does not include payments made directly to a school for tuition or to a medical facility for bills for the benefit of a U.S. person.

The rules governing foreign gifts are new and complicated. If you receive, or expect to receive, large foreign gifts, see a tax expert.

---

4. When Gift Taxes Are Paid

If the IRS assesses gift taxes against you, as giver of a gift, you need not pay the taxes until and unless your total taxable gifts exceed the amount of the personal gift tax exemption for the current year. Instead, any tax imposed on the gifts you make eats up some of your personal exemption and thus reduces the amount that can later pass tax free. So people with estates below the estate tax threshold don't have to worry about actually paying gift tax. However, you must file a federal gift tax return for any gift over the amount of the annual exclusion (to repeat it again, currently $12,000) to a person per year (IRS Forms 709 or 709-A). And if you have a substantial estate, having made taxable gifts may cut into what you can leave free of estate tax.

Example: In the last ten years of her life, Sheila gives her two children a total of $300,000 over and above the $12,000 annual exemptions. These taxable gifts use up a portion of her personal estate tax exemption. Sheila dies in 2006 with an estate valued at $1,875,000. The amount of the personal exemption is $2 million.

To determine if Sheila's estate owes tax:

Size of estate	$1,875,000
Add taxable gifts	$300,000
Total taxable amount	$2,175,000
Subtract personal exemption	$2,000,000
Amount taxable	$175,000

B. WHAT IS A GIFT?

Before exploring more about gifts and estate planning, let's be sure you know what a gift is, legally.

Some transactions simply can't, by law, count as taxable gifts. For instance, you can perform services—from dispensing medical treatment to repairing a trombone—freely, without being held by the IRS to have made a taxable gift of the market value of your services. Similarly, you can lend property to someone, even for an extended period of time, and there's no legal gift.

Example: Grandpa Elijah has an old Rolls Royce that he lets his grandson Jacob drive. Indeed, Elijah has basically turned the car over to Jacob, although Elijah still pays for the car insurance. There is no gift—and would not be even if Jacob paid for the insurance, since Elijah remains the car's legal owner.

1. The Giver's Intent

In common understanding, a gift is the voluntary transfer of property made without receiving anything of value in exchange. (In legalese, anything of value is called "consideration.") In other words, a gift is a permanent transfer of property that isn't commercial in spirit.

From the point of view of the IRS, the crucial element in determining whether or not a gift is made is the giver's intent, which can be distinctly murky. For example, say you obtain a valuable painting from Frank. Did Frank intend to give you that painting, or lend it to you? Or was he hoping to sell it to you and wanted you to have it for a while before he mentioned the price?

Because someone's intent may not be obvious (now or in the future), it is an excellent idea to give a gift with a written statement explaining that it's a gift, so that the status of the transaction is clear. If there is no clear written evidence, the IRS doesn't know when you transfer something for less than its market value whether you intend to make a gift or you're just a poor businessperson. So, it does the only thing it can do—it looks at the "objective evidence" and demands gift tax if the transaction doesn't appear reasonable from a commercial (economic) point of view.

Example: Linda paid $15,000 to her niece for an office lamp and deducted the $15,000 as an expense of her small business. If the IRS questions this transaction and contends it was really a gift, Linda must convince the IRS that this was a bona fide commercial transaction— for example, that the lamp was a valuable antique—not a gift disguised as a purchase.

LOOKING DEEPER INTO GIFTS

For a fascinating discussion of the varied meanings of giving, read *The Gift: Imagination and the Erotic Life of Property,* by Lewis Hyde (Random House). The book brilliantly explores the spirit involved in giving and receiving a gift, from a Christmas present to creating a work of art, and how the giving spirit interacts with commercial culture.

---

2. The Recipient's Control Over the Gift

For a transaction to be a legal gift, the property must be delivered to and accepted by the recipient.

Example: Matt puts $11,000 into a drawer for Nina. There's no legal gift until Nina removes the money.

The giver must release all control over the property. If the giver retains any interest in the gift property, there is no legal gift.

Example: Sonya gives stocks she owns to her daughter, Misha, transferring the account into Misha's name. But Sonya continues to receive directly all of the dividends from the stocks. Legally, Sonya has not made a valid gift.

Gifts of real estate can be tricky. Some parents want to give a valuable house (aren't they all?) to a child, and structure the gift so that no gift tax is assessed. For example, a parent may take a mortgage on the property, with payments of $12,000 a year, and then forgive each year's payment when it becomes due. The IRS has disallowed schemes like this on the grounds that no legitimate mortgage existed. If you want to make a gift of real estate free of gift tax, see a lawyer.

Also, a gift of real estate will be disallowed, for tax purposes, if the giver held onto some important right over the property—for example, the right to receive rents from a small apartment building. To avoid this problem, you must comply with all applicable IRS rules.

If you give a tangible item (cash, an heirloom, pictures), the relinquishment of control necessary to establish a gift is usually easy to prove—the recipient gains unrestricted possession over the property. In other situations, the question of control may be more difficult to ascertain. For example, if a gift is contingent on a future event, that event must be determinable by some objective standard. "To Desiree, when she becomes 21," or "When she travels to Paris" is objective; "When she's happily married" is not.

Property you place in a revocable living trust isn't a gift because you retain full control over the property and can revoke the trust if you wish. The beneficiaries you name in the trust document have no current right to the trust property. Likewise, if you establish an irrevocable trust and retain the power to change who will benefit from it, even if you, yourself, are specifically excluded as a possible beneficiary, there's no gift.

Example: Roger, a wealthy older man, puts money in an irrevocable trust for his grandniece Olivia, to be used for her eventual college and possible graduate school costs. He appoints a trustee and gives her authority to alter the purposes for which the trust money can be spent. Roger also retains the right to substitute a new trustee. Because Roger still has so much control over the trust property, there has been no gift for gift tax purposes.

3. Common Kinds of Gifts

Here are some types of transactions that are legal gifts:

- Making an interest-free loan. Really? Yes. Federal law provides that an interest-free or artificially low-interest loan is a gift by the lender of the interest not charged. An "artificially low" interest rate is any rate below market interest rates when the loan is made. So, if you lend a friend $30,000 interest free, you are making a taxable gift of the interest you didn't charge. But because of the $12,000 annual gift tax exclusion discussed above, gifts of interest on most loans don't have gift tax consequences. For example, at a 10% simple interest rate, a single person can make an interest-free loan of $120,000 to a person without gift tax liability. A married couple could lend a person up to $240,000 interest free before the annual interest would exceed $24,000, the couple's combined annual gift tax exclusion.

- Handing someone cash, a check, or any tangible item, with the intention of making a gift.

- Transferring title to real estate, stocks, or a motor vehicle into another's name, without receiving anything of value in exchange. Remember that if you reserve the right to receive any income from the property, such as rent or dividends, no valid gift is made.

- Transferring property to an irrevocable trust you create to benefit another person. As mentioned above, the trust must have an objective standard of when the beneficiary will receive the property. An irrevocable trust means you can't change your mind and alter or terminate the trust once it is created. (By contrast, as we've mentioned, since a living trust is almost always revocable, naming someone as a beneficiary doesn't guarantee they will receive the property, so no gift is made.)

- Irrevocably assigning a life insurance policy to another. (See Chapter 12.)

- Forgiving a debt.

- Assigning a mortgage, court judgment, or other debt or loan owed you, without receiving fair compensation in return.

- Making a noncommercial transfer of your property into joint tenancy with another person. (Except for joint bank accounts; in that case, the rule is that a gift is made only when one depositor withdraws money deposited by the other.)

Partial gifts. Federal law authorizes "partial gifts." (I.R.C. § 2512(b).) These are gifts where you receive something of value back, but the gift is worth far more than what you received. Making a partial gift is a complex tax matter and you'll need to see a lawyer.

C. How the Federal Gift Tax Works

Before you can intelligently evaluate whether you want to use gifts as part of your estate plan, you need to thoroughly understand how the federal gift tax actually works. We touched on this above; now we present a more thorough treatment of this important subject.

Gift tax applies to all gifts made by U.S. citizens and residents, and also to gifts of property by nonresident aliens if the gift property is physically located in the U.S. The most obvious example is real estate in the U.S.

Here are the basics.

1. Gift Tax Payment and Rates

As we've discussed, currently if you give a gift worth more than $12,000, you must file a gift tax return, (unless the gift is exempt from tax) and the IRS will assess a gift tax against you.

The IRS requires that the amount of the gift tax be used to reduce the amount of your personal estate tax exemption. You cannot choose to pay gift tax now and "save" all of your personal exemption for later use.

> **Example:** Amber gives Beatrice an expensive car, worth $56,000; $12,000 is exempt from tax, so tax will be assessed on $44,000. Amber cannot simply pay the amount of the tax now and preserve the full amount of her personal exemption until her death. Rather, the IRS requires that she use up $44,000 of her personal estate tax exemption.

The estate/gift tax rates are graduated, so the higher the taxable value of the gift, the higher the gift tax rate that applies to it. (You can find the rate chart in Chapter 15, Section D.) Also, the tax rate is cumulative. This means that in determining the gift tax rate applied to a current gift, the value of all taxable gifts given (since January 1, 1977) must be added. Otherwise, large estates could be transferred at lower tax rates by piecemeal giving.

Example: Carol gives her niece $22,000 two years in a row. Each year, $12,000 of the gift is exempt from tax. Here are the gift tax consequences:

	Year 1	Year 2
Amount given	$22,000	$22,000
Amount taxed	$10,000	$10,000
Tax rate based on	$10,000	$20,000
Tax rate	18%	20%
Tax assessed	$1,800	$2,000

2. Gifts of Life Insurance Made Near Death

You can make almost any gift up to the moment you die without running afoul of IRS rules. However, a few types of gifts must be made at least three years before the giver's death, or the gifts are disallowed for estate tax purposes. A gift of a life insurance policy is the significant one in this category. If a life insurance policy is given away within three years of death, the IRS acts as if the gift were never made, and includes the full amount of the proceeds in the giver's taxable estate. (If you've already paid gift tax, that amount will be credited toward any estate tax due. I.R.C. § 2012(a).) This is for estate tax purposes only; it doesn't affect ownership of the policy, which remains with the recipient.

Disallowance of a gift of life insurance can result in a substantial increase in the size of the giver's taxable estate. The proceeds paid when the insured person dies are always worth much more than the value of the same policy given away before the insured dies. For example, a whole life policy that pays $300,000 at death might have a cash surrender value of only $50,000 two years or two days before the owner dies. (Gifts of life insurance are discussed in more detail in Section D4, below, and Chapter 12, Section E.)

GIFTS FROM A LIVING TRUST AND THE THREE-YEAR RULE

As trustee of your living trust, you can make gifts of living trust property directly from your trust at any time while you live. These gifts are not subject to the three-year rule. For a time, the IRS contended the three-year rule did apply here, but it never had much success in court. Finally, the Taxpayer Relief Act of 1997 explicitly provided that the three-year rule has no application to gifts made from a living trust. (I.R.C. § 2035(e).)

---

3. The "Present Interest" Rule

Under IRS rules, the annual gift tax exclusion applies only to gifts of what is called a "present interest." This means that the person or institution who receives the gift has the right to use it immediately. For the great majority of gifts, this is no problem. The receiver obtains full control when the gift is made. By contrast, gifts that someone can use only in the future, not when the gift was made, do not qualify for the annual exclusion. These are called gifts of a "future interest."

Example: Kim gives $10,000 outright to her friend Gayle and places another $10,000 in an irrevocable trust to benefit her friend Madeleine. Madeleine, age 32, can use principal from the trust only when she turns 35. The gift to Gayle is a gift of a present interest, because Gayle gets the money now. The gift to the trust for Madeleine is a gift of a future interest, because she has no right to the money when Kim gives it. So gift tax is assessed against the $10,000 Kim gives to the trust.

4. Gifts to Minors and the "Present Interest" Rule

Gifts to minors can qualify for the annual exclusion, even though the minor isn't given (indeed, by law, cannot be given) full present access to or control of the gift property. Federal law (I.R.C. § 2503(c)) provides that in order to make a gift to a minor that qualifies for the annual exemption, three conditions must be met:

1. The gift, and any income it produces, must be used or retained in trust, or an UTMA account, for the minor's benefit.

2. The remainder of the gift must go outright to the child when she or he reaches age 21. (The gift can go outright to the child when she or he is 18 or older, up to 21.)

3. If the child dies before reaching the age to receive the gift outright, the remainder of the gift must be paid to his or her estate.

5. "Crummey" Trusts and the Present Interest Rule

To get around the present interest rule for gifts to adults or to children or grandchildren where the giver does not want the property turned over when the child becomes 21, lawyers invented a crafty device called a "Crummey" trust (so called because it was judicially approved in the case of *Crummey v. Commissioner,* 397 F.2d 82, 1968). For one of a number of reasons, a giver may not want a recipient to become the owner of a gift, but still wants to get the annual exclusion for the gift. One example is a gift to an irrevocable trust to pay for trust-owned life insurance on the giver's life. A gift to a trust is not generally a gift of a "present interest." So in order to obtain the annual exclusion, beneficiaries of the

trust are given the right, for a limited time—as little as a few days—to accept (in legalese, to "withdraw") the gift. But they don't withdraw the gift, so it lapses and the gift becomes owned by the trust. Because the beneficiaries had the legal right to take the gift, it now qualifies as a gift of a "present interest" and gets the $12,000 exclusion.

 Crummey trusts are tricky. If Crummey trusts seem fuzzy to you, don't feel alone. They are used only with more complicated estates where outright gifts are not desired. Crummey trusts must be created by a lawyer.

6. The Federal Gift Tax Return

You must file an IRS gift tax return when your regular income tax return is filed (normally, April 15) if you:

- have made nonexempt gifts over the amount of the annual exclusion to any person or organization during the previous taxable year, or

- have made gifts over the amount of the annual exclusion to a tax-exempt organization during the previous taxable year. No tax is assessed for such tax-exempt gifts, but the IRS still requires you to file a return. Who knows why?

The IRS does not require you to file a gift tax return for gifts between spouses (unless the recipient is not a U.S. citizen and the gift exceeds $117,000) or for gifts for educational or medical expenses, no matter how large the gift.

D. Using Gifts to Reduce Estate Taxes

For people with larger estates, making tax-exempt gifts while living, either to individuals or charities, can be a significant part of their estate plan.

SOME THOUGHTS ON GIFT-GIVING AND TAXES

Estate planners have developed a number of ways to use gifts to reduce, or even eliminate, estate tax for many people who would otherwise face a tax bill. Before plunging into this subject (game might be a better word), take stock of what you really feel about making gifts now. Will giving property to your children or grandchildren enhance their lives? Or are they not yet ready to handle or appreciate your generosity? For example, helping a 21-year-old get an education or the head of a new family buy a house may be a truly great gift. By contrast, you may not want your money spent by a young person on a two-week vacation in Las Vegas or an expensive car. (But then, doesn't every kid merit a convertible?)

Many people make substantial gifts primarily for personal reasons, but with the awareness that they're obtaining estate/gift tax benefits, as well. Using gifts totaling up to $1 million, as well as annual exclusion gifts, to reduce the size of your estate when you die, can be desirable if three things are true:

- your estate may owe estate tax (see Chapter 15)

- the property you want to give has not greatly appreciated in value since you acquired it (if it has, it's better, for tax reasons, to transfer it at death; see Section E, below), and

- you don't need all of your assets and income to live on.

This last concern, of course, requires an evaluation of how much money and property you think you'll need (or want) now and in the future, as well as what your resources are, including income from retirement plans, Social Security, savings, and investments. Some people, who may not want to use up any of their principal for gifts, may decide to use some of their income for gifts.

Example: Mr. and Mrs. Tureba, in their 70s, have four children. The Turebas have an estate totaling $1,140,000: a house worth $275,000 (all equity), stocks currently valued at $120,000, savings of $340,000, and business investments of $405,000. At first, the Turebas don't feel comfortable with the thought of giving away any of this property. However, their incomes are substantially more than they need to live on. The figures are:

Retirement plan income	$32,000
Social Security	$12,000
Mrs. Tureba's part-time job	$8,000
Returns from investments	$56,000
Total Annual Income	$108,000

After completing a detailed budget (what fun), the Turebas figure they spend about $45,000 a year, and taxes claim another $30,000. In short, in addition to all the money and property they have already put aside, they're saving over $30,000 per year. Looking at the reality that this is likely to be more than they will ever need, the Turebas decide to give away $7,500 a year to each of their four children, rather than increase their savings. Over ten years this will result in their giving $300,000 to their children, all gift tax free.

THE TIMING OF GIFTS

For wealthy people who engage in extensive tax-saving gift giving, the timing of making gifts can be important. To briefly summarize what can fast become complicated, if the cumulative gifts made are over the estate tax threshold, it's advantageous to make taxable gifts near the beginning of the tax year. Although the gift tax is the same, no matter when the gift is made during the year, if you make a taxable gift in January, you do not have to pay the gift tax until April of the following year. In the meantime, the income from the gift goes to the recipient rather than increasing your taxable estate.

By contrast, charitable gifts are often given at the end of the tax year, so the giver can receive the income from the asset for most of the year, while obtaining the charitable tax deduction for that same year.

Example: Patti owns a successful small business, with an estimated net worth of $2 million. Her other assets are worth roughly $475,000. Patti intends to leave her business to her three children. To reduce the value of her eventual estate, she incorporates her business and starts giving her children stock. She can give each of her children stock worth $12,000 per year gift tax free—a yearly total of $36,000. For ten years she gives each child $12,000 worth of stock, transferring a total of $360,000 tax free.

This example assumes the worth of the company remained the same for ten years and that the gift tax exclusion remained at $12,000, unlikely in the real world. In practice, Patti would have to review the worth of her company yearly, and check out the gift tax law from time to time.

1. Using the Annual Exemption Repeatedly

Although the annual gift tax exclusion (to repeat, currently $12,000) may not seem like an immense sum, it can often be used over time to achieve substantial estate tax savings. The key is using the exclusion as fully as possible. It's a simple matter of multiplication. If you use the $12,000 annual exclusion for gifts to one person for five years, you've given away five times as much ($60,000) tax free as you would if you gave the same $60,000 to the same person in one year and qualified for only one $12,000 exemption. If you make $12,000 gifts to five recipients in one year, you've also given away $60,000 tax free. And obviously, it follows that if you make five $12,000 gifts to five people for five years, you've given away $300,000 tax free. (And since spouses can each make $12,000 gifts, giving as a couple multiplies your gift tax exemption by two.)

2. Some Types of Repeated Gifts Could Land You in Tax Trouble

The IRS scrutinizes complex repeat-gift programs to catch those that cross the line from clever to forbidden. Usually, the IRS catches illegal gift-giving programs when it audits an estate tax return. It then disallows gift tax exemptions for previous gifts, and hits the estate with a nasty tax bill for back gift taxes, interest, and penalties.

One area where you should tread very cautiously is making a gift that forgives a loan payment due you. For example, some parents have made large loans to their children, intending to forgive repayments of $12,000 a year. The IRS, skeptical of these arrangements to start with, has set out rules you must follow if you want to prove that your transaction is a bona fide loan, not a gift in disguise. The bottom line seems to be that if you are meticulous about paperwork, this strategy can be successful.

The IRS starts with the presumption that a transfer between family members is a gift. You can get around that presumption by showing that you really expected repayment and intended to enforce the debt. In making that determination, the IRS considers whether or not:

- the borrower signed a promissory note

- you charged interest on the loan

- there was security (collateral) for the debt

- there was a fixed date that the loan was due to be repaid

- the borrower had the ability to repay

- you demanded repayment

- the borrower actually repaid some of the loan

- your records or those of the recipient indicate that the transfer was a loan, and

- the transaction was reported, for federal tax purposes, as a loan.

Forgiving family debts. As you can see, there are a lot of hurdles to overcome if you want to legally forgive debts on a family loan. If you want to explore this further, see an expert attorney or accountant.

3. Giving Property That Is Likely to Appreciate

If you're prosperous and your estate will be subject to estate tax, it can make particularly good sense to give away property that you believe will appreciate substantially in the future, especially if it hasn't gone up in value much already. At first, this may seem a little complicated, but if you read what follows carefully, you'll see it really isn't.

Here is the basic idea. If property you own seems reasonably likely to go up in value substantially in the future, giving it away now not only excludes its present worth from your estate but also eliminates the value of its likely future appreciation from your estate.

Example: Brook, in her 60s, recently purchased some vacant land for $161,000 cash. The property is located in an area she believes will be ripe for development in a few years. She intends to leave this land to her niece, Laura, when she dies. If she waits to transfer the property until her death, then the market value of the property when she dies will be included in her taxable estate. But if Brook gives the land to Laura soon after buying it in 2002, all of its appreciation in value, as well as its current worth, won't be included in Brook's taxable estate.

The gift will be subject to gift tax. So $12,000 will be exempt from gift tax, but $149,000 won't be. Still, if Brook is right about the land increasing in value, the gift tax assessed will be far less than estate tax imposed on the appreciated property would be at Brook's death, for the obvious reason that the appreciated property will be worth more, and therefore taxed at a higher rate.

By contrast, it usually doesn't make sense to give away property that has already gone up in value, especially if you may not live long. The reason, as more fully explained in Section E, is that the recipient of a gift has the same tax basis in the property as the giver did (which is, very roughly, usually what the giver paid for the property). On the other hand, an inheritor obtains a basis that is stepped up to the fair market value of the property at the time of death. (These concepts are discussed in depth in Chapter 15, Section F.)

Example: Bill bought 1,000 shares of stock at $5 a share. It's now worth $30 a share and is still going up. If he gives it now to his daughter Betsy, her cost basis will be $5 per share. If he leaves it to Betsy upon his death, her stepped-up basis in the stock will probably be $30 a share or higher, depending on its market price when he dies.

This difference will be vitally important when Betsy sells the stock. If its cost basis is $5 a share and she sells it for $30 a share, she will have to pay capital gains tax on the $25 per share profit. By contrast, if the basis is stepped up to $30 because the transfer is made at death, and she sells the stock at $30 a share, she won't owe any capital gains tax.

4. Gifts of Life Insurance

In some situations, making a gift of life insurance can substantially reduce or eliminate federal estate tax. In fact, from a gift tax standpoint, giving life insurance can often be the most advantageous way to transfer a large sum out of your estate, since the gift normally has a low value for gift tax purposes. But because gifts of insurance policies can be such a good tax deal for the giver, special rules apply. The most important one is that the gift must be made more than three years before you die to be effective for estate tax purposes.

Gifts of life insurance are discussed in Chapter 12, Section E. As we've discussed above, the value of the gift of an insurance policy is always much lower than the proceeds paid in the event of the insured's death.

5. Gifts of a Family Business

Gifts of minority interests in a family business can result in significant estate tax savings. Currently, sophisticated estate tax planners play some very fancy games here. See Chapter 28, Section B.

6. Gifts to Minors

You can make a gift to a minor (a child younger than 18) during your life, as well as leave a minor property when you die. A minor cannot legally control any substantial amount of property in his or her own name. An adult must have that responsibility. If, while you are alive, you make a gift directly to a child, rather than to his or her parents or guardians, you have two choices.

Your options are to:

1. Give the money in a trust. If you, while living, make a gift to a minor using a properly drafted child's trust, you obtain the annual gift tax exclusion in the year the gift is made. (See Section C4, above.)

2. Appoint a "custodian" for the gift, under your state's Uniform Transfers to Minors Act (UTMA) or Uniform Gifts to Minors Act (UGMA). (UTMA, UGMA, Let's Call the Whole Thing Off.) The UTMA applies in all states but South Carolina and Vermont, where the UGMA applies. The UGMA provides only a device for making gifts to minors while you live, not for leaving property to them when you die.

Using either Act, you can, while you live, make a gift to a minor by naming an adult custodian for the gift property. (See Chapter 6, Section C.)

In most states, the custodianship must end when the child turns 18 or 21. Obviously, that satisfies the IRS age requirement that the minor must receive the gift outright by age 21. In Alaska, California, Nevada, Oregon, Pennsylvania, and Tennessee, however, for gifts you make to children during your life, you must be sure to provide that the recipient will receive the gift at some age between 18 to 21. These states' laws could be interpreted as extending the custodianship past age 21, if you don't provide otherwise.

Gifts to minors made while one is alive are often given primarily for personal reasons, not for gift tax savings. Your personal motives may override maximizing gift tax savings, or those motives may work harmoniously with gift tax rules.

Example 1: Oksana, who is quite prosperous, wants to be certain her grandson Viktor and granddaughter Marya will have enough money to attend college. Viktor is 12 and Marya is ten. Oksana wants to make the gift now, so she can take pleasure in knowing that her grandchildren know their educational future is secure. She creates an educational child's trust for each, to last until the child is 30, naming their father as trustee. Oksana realizes that by doing this, she will not obtain the annual gift tax exclusion for any money she gives the trust, because, as we explained, federal tax law requires the child to receive the money outright by age 21 for the exclusion to apply. But Oksana wants adult supervision of the trust until the children are 30, because she doubts that any 21-year-old is likely to be able to handle large amounts of money responsibly. Her concern over this issue overrides any consideration of tax savings.

Example 2: Biff decides to give an expensive thoroughbred horse worth $50,000 to his niece Brenda, age 16, who has loved horses since she was small. Biff makes the gift under his state's UTMA, which requires the horse to be legally turned over to Brenda when she becomes 21—which is fine with Biff. Biff names Brenda's mother, Josette, as custodian for the gift. They all know this is only technical, since Brenda will be, and wants to be, responsible for the horse.

Biff is not assessed gift tax on $12,000 of his gift. He is assessed gift tax on the remaining value of $38,000.

7. Making Taxable Gifts

If you are affluent, it might be to your family's financial advantage to make taxable gifts. This is a high-end strategy; it only makes sense for someone who has already used up all of her or his gift tax exemption of $1 million for previous taxable gifts. Then, you'll have to pay gift tax when you make new gifts.

The basic idea is that by making the taxable gift and then paying the tax from your property while you live, you'll wind up paying less overall gift and estate tax than if you didn't make the gift. If you don't make the gift, that property plus the amount you would pay in gift tax is included in your taxable estate. Because of the graduated estate tax rates, the overall tax bite can be larger.

To explore making taxable gifts, you'll need an expert. If making taxable gifts sounds confusing, that's only because it is. You need an expert to explore whether such a strategy is desirable for you. You'll probably have to crunch a lot of numbers, taking the following factors into consideration:

- the amount of money or property you can comfortably give away

- the gift tax on that gift

- the likely worth of your estate at death

- the effect of the increases in the estate tax exemption until 2010

- the scheduled repeal of the estate tax in 2010, and

- the possibilities of changes to the federal estate tax law.

Also, to prevent people from making taxable gifts as a deathbed tax ploy, the IRS includes any gift tax paid during the last three years of life in the decedent's taxable estate. (I.R.C. § 2053.) In other words, last-minute (or even last-year) gifts won't work to lower overall taxes.

E. WHEN NOT TO GIVE PROPERTY AWAY: TAX BASIS RULES

Much of this chapter has discussed why it is often advantageous, from an estate/gift tax point of view, to give away property before you die. But this isn't always the case. It's usually unwise to give away an asset (as opposed to leaving it at death) that has substantially appreciated in value since you purchased it, especially if you are older and likely to die before decades pass.

In order to understand why it is often better for the recipient to inherit appreciated property than to receive it during the giver's lifetime, you need to understand the tax concept of "basis." While we've discussed this concept in Chapter 15, Section F, it's so important that here we focus on how this applies to gifts.

The tax basis of property is the value (dollar figure) from which the IRS determines gain or loss on a sale. When you purchase property, its basis is generally its cost. In fact, basis is often referred to as cost basis. If you make major (capital) improvements to property—for example, adding a deck to your house—the cost of the improvement is added to the basis of the property.

The recipient of a gift takes the same basis in the property as the giver had. This is called the "carry-over" basis, in tax jargon.

Example: Lewella's basis in her house is $100,000 (net purchase price plus capital improvements). Lewella owns the house free and clear. The house now has a market value of $320,000. Lewella gives her house to Megan. Megan's (carry-over) basis in the house is $100,000. If Megan then sells the house for $320,000, her taxable profit is $220,000 ($320,000 minus her basis of $100,000).

Remember, the value of a gift for gift tax purposes is its present net market value. Thus, for property that has increased in value since the giver acquired it, there are two different valuations. The lower original purchase price—the basis of the property for the gift recipient—and the higher current market value, the figure used for the giver's gift tax. In the above example, the IRS assesses Lewella's (the donor's) gift taxes on the $320,000 market value, but the basis to Megan (the recipient) is $100,000.

Different basis rules apply to inherited property. These inherited property basis rules are more advantageous to recipients.

The tax basis for property a person inherits is the fair market value at the date of the original owner's death. So if the value of the property has gone up since the owner acquired it, the tax basis is increased (in taxese, "stepped up") from the deceased's basis to the value of the property at death.

Example: If Lewella dies and leaves her house to Megan, Megan's basis in the house is increased to its market value at Lewella's death, which is $320,000.

This stepped-up basis rule means there are major capital gains tax savings for the recipient if an asset that has appreciated in value is transferred at death instead of given to that recipient while the giver is still alive.

Example: Edward owns a Redon pastel painting, which he bought as an astute art student for $20,000. Sixty years later, an appraiser informs him it's worth $1.3 million. If Edward were to sell the painting, his taxable gain would be $1.3 million less his basis of $20,000. If he gives the painting away and the recipient sells it, the tax situation is the same—only now it's the recipient who owes capital gains tax on the profit.

By contrast, if Edward dies and uses his living trust to leave the painting to the same recipient, this beneficiary's stepped-up basis in the painting is $1.3 million. If the beneficiary promptly sells the painting, there's no taxable gain.

1. Special Rules for Community Property

If you're married and own community property (see Chapter 3, Section B, for a discussion of community property and a list of the eight community property states), another federal tax basis rule can be significant for any gift planning you consider. On the death of one spouse, the basis of each spouse's half of the community property is stepped up to the property's fair market value at the time of the spouse's death.

Example: Felicia and Max are residents of California, a community property state. They own a grand house in Malibu they bought decades ago for $100,000. The basis of each spouse's interest is $50,000, one-half the purchase price. When Felicia dies in 2007, the market value of the house is $8,000,000. Because of the stepped-up basis rule for community property, the federal tax basis of each spouse's half-interest in the house steps up to $4,000,000. If Max sells the house for $8 million shortly after Felicia's death, he will not owe any capital gains tax. The sale price equals the stepped-up basis of the house. In contrast, if the house had been sold before Felicia died, their profit would have been $7.9 million. Under capital gains tax law, $500,000 of the amount would be exempt because the profit is from sale by a couple of a home. So capital gains tax would be assessed on $7.4 million.

Again, what all this means is that there may be a considerable federal tax advantage for inheritors if a couple retains, until one of them dies, community property that has substantially increased in value since they purchased it.

2. State Tax Basis Rules

Estate planning decisions are rarely affected by state tax basis rules. In general, the impact of state tax basis rules on gifts or inherited property is minor, because the tax rates involved are relatively low in those states that impose gift and death taxes. If you want to explore your state's rules, you can either research that issue yourself (see Chapter 29, Section B) or consult an accountant or tax attorney.

F. Using Gifts to Reduce Income Taxes

If you are prosperous and are willing to give income-producing property to someone in a lower tax bracket while you are still alive, you can achieve some overall income tax savings in addition to the possible federal estate and gift tax savings discussed earlier in this chapter. With the current maximum income tax rate close to 40%, a gift to a person in a lower tax bracket, especially someone in the 15% bracket, will obviously result in less income tax being paid on income received from the property. Of course, you will not see the tax savings yourself, because you no longer own the property.

Be wary of giving property to children younger than 14. You might not obtain an income tax benefit for a gift to a child younger than age 14. The reason is that all income over $800 a year received by minors younger than 14 years, from any gift (whether from their parents or otherwise), is taxed, for federal income tax purposes, at the highest tax rate of their parents. ■

17

An Overview of Ongoing Trusts

An "ongoing" trust is a trust that is intended to operate as an independent legal entity for a long time, usually years or even decades, after the death of the person who establishes it (the grantor). Often, but not in all cases, an ongoing trust begins to operate as a separate legal entity only at the death of the grantor. An ongoing trust can be created in a will or in a living trust, or by a document making the trust operational while the trust grantor is alive. Once operational, an ongoing trust is irrevocable.

The two basic functions of ongoing trusts are to:

- save on estate taxes

- impose long-term controls on the management of trust property.

Some ongoing trusts serve both purposes, some only one.

Many people need only a simple probate-avoidance living trust, not an ongoing trust. By our terms, a living trust is not ongoing, because it functions as a separate entity for only a brief time after the grantor's death. By the end of this chapter, you should have a pretty clear idea of whether or not you need some type of ongoing trust.

This chapter explores basic features common to all ongoing trusts. Other chapters delve into some specific types of ongoing trusts, including:

- Estate tax-saving "bypass" trusts, including the popular AB trust (Chapter 18)

- Other estate tax-saving marital trusts, including a "QTIP" trust to postpone payment of estate taxes (Chapter 19)

- Charitable trusts (Chapter 20)

- Other estate-tax saving trusts, including generation-skipping trusts, irrevocable life insurance trusts, and grantor-retained interest trusts (Chapter 21)

- Combining ongoing estate tax-saving trusts (Chapter 23)

- Trusts useful to people with children from a prior marriage (Chapter 24)

- Trusts to impose controls over property (Chapter 25)

- Children's trusts or family pot trusts used to control property inherited by a minor or young adult (Chapter 6).

Ongoing trusts and medical bills. Many people would like to include a "catastrophic illness" clause or provision in any ongoing trust they create, to prevent trust assets from being used to pay medical bills if a trust beneficiary suffers a catastrophic illness. Often, couples are particularly concerned with preserving their trust assets from claims by medical providers or government agencies. At the very least, the couple doesn't want both members' assets used to pay for one's catastrophic illness.

Unfortunately, no simple trust clause applicable in all states will achieve this result. A provision properly geared to current federal laws and regulations, your state's specific laws, and your situation may provide some protection. But such provisions rarely, if ever, consist of a single clause or paragraph; indeed, they often go on for pages and require sophisticated knowledge of all applicable laws and regulations. An expert lawyer must prepare such provisions. It's absolutely essential to be up to date here.

A. TRUSTS TO REDUCE ESTATE TAXES

One goal of many ongoing trusts is to save on estate taxes. Most estates don't owe estate tax, but if you expect that yours will, there's good reason to want to cut the tax bill. Any federal estate taxes will take a substantial bite out of the property you leave behind.

As discussed in Chapter 15, tax laws passed in 2001 raise your personal tax exemption dramatically during the next years, finally phasing out all estate tax for the year 2010. However, appealing as it may be, no one can guarantee that we can all ward off the grim reaper until 2010. And there is another hitch to the new law. Unless Congress acts again to make the law permanent, the estate tax returns in 2011.

As a practical matter, most people will continue to prepare for the uncertain future with estate plans. This means having an effective plan in place for the present, and changing it when necessary. Any person owning property worth more than the personal estate tax exemption for the year of death will face hefty charges. The exemption is $2 million for the year 2006. (Again, see Chapter 15, Section A, for a discussion of the estate tax laws and a table listing the personal exemption amount for each year.)

Any individual with an estate over the estate tax threshold should explore tax-saving trusts. A couple with a combined estate that's likely to owe estate tax can use an ongoing AB trust that becomes operational after one member dies to achieve significant estate tax savings.

If you are afraid that reading about tax-saving trusts will overwhelm you, don't give up. You don't need to master the complexities of actually preparing most of these types of trusts. This book contains no forms for preparing your own estate tax-saving trusts. Except for basic AB trusts (see Chapter 18, Section C), these trusts are always complex and technical, and must be prepared by a lawyer.

Don't assume that estate tax-saving trusts aid only a handful of billionaires, or that they are somehow fraudulent or sleazy. That's simply not true. Many prosperous folks can take advantage of what these trusts offer, and they are perfectly legal.

If you have any doubts about the value of investigating estate tax-saving trusts, consider the following analogy: When you sit down each year to fill out your income tax forms, would it ever occur to you to just skip the personal exemptions and deductions you are entitled to and cheerfully send that money to the government? Well, that's exactly what you're doing if you prepare an estate plan that ignores the exemptions and deductions available through the use of estate tax-saving trusts.

We want to offer you sufficient information about major types of estate tax-saving trusts so you can decide whether it's worth your time and money to hire a lawyer to create one or more of them. Also, by reading the next six chapters, you should be able to tell whether a lawyer is providing helpful, accurate information and advice about estate tax-saving trusts or is primarily concerned with running up your bill.

B. Ongoing Trusts Used to Control Property

In addition to reducing estate taxes, ongoing trusts can also provide for the management and control of property you don't want to leave outright to someone. Property control trusts are particularly common when spouses have children from prior marriages. Often, each spouse wants to provide well for the other spouse. At the same time, each spouse doesn't want to leave everything outright to the other spouse, because each wants the bulk of his or her property to eventually go to his or her children. An ongoing trust can be used to achieve both these goals. (See Chapter 24.)

An ongoing trust to control property is also desirable or essential in other circumstances, including situations in which:

- You leave property to minors (or people who have been declared legally incompetent) who are not legally permitted to own substantial amounts of property outright.

- You believe the beneficiary can't handle money responsibly.

- The beneficiary has a disability and requires what's called a "special needs trust" to provide long-term support but not interfere with the beneficiary's eligibility for federal or state assistance.

- You decide you no longer want the burdens of managing your own property and want to turn that task over to someone else. For instance, someone who is old and ill may know that it's sensible to arrange for others to handle her finances. There are various methods to arrange for this, including preparing a durable power of attorney for finances. (See Chapter 26.) Sometimes people prefer a trust, however, because it is a more traditional legal form and the trust property will avoid probate on the grantor's death.

Property control trusts for each of these situations are discussed in Chapter 25.

C. Ongoing Trusts and Avoiding Probate

Property left in ongoing trusts doesn't automatically avoid probate. Most ongoing trusts become operational only when the grantor dies. So to avoid probate of property left in these trusts, ongoing trusts are usually incorporated as a part (a big part) of a living trust. By using a living trust, the property avoids probate after the person's death and goes straight into the now-operational ongoing trust.

> **Example:** Pilar wants to establish an ongoing trust to manage the property she intends to leave to her kid brother, Juan, who is 20 years her junior. She wants to create an ongoing trust because Juan, age 28, has always squandered whatever money he's acquired and shows no signs of change. Within her revocable living trust, Pilar creates an ongoing trust in which the trustee controls how and when money is given to Juan from the trust. This trust will become operational only after Pilar dies. Under the terms of the living trust, the property left to Juan will be transferred to the ongoing trust without probate.
>
> As long as Pilar lives, the living trust, and the ongoing trust contained in the living trust, are revocable. When Pilar dies, the ongoing trust becomes irrevocable and cannot be changed by anyone, including Juan.

All of the ongoing trusts discussed in the next chapters can be made part of a living trust, except ongoing trusts that become operational before the grantor dies. To say this metaphorically, just because an ongoing trust and a probate-avoidance living trust are technically different legal animals doesn't mean they can't drink at the same pond. We stress this here because it's important to understand you don't need to risk probate by creating an ongoing trust. We don't repeat this for each ongoing trust we discuss. These discussions are already complex enough.

D. WHAT ONGOING TRUSTS CAN'T DO

Expert estate planning lawyers can sometimes come up with truly ingenious plans to fit a family's particular needs and save on estate taxes. But some lawyers and financial planners push the line of what's legally safe. It's up to you to decide how safe or aggressive you want to be. But before betting a big estate on the cutting-edge theories of any estate planner—lawyer or not—it's wise to get a second, perhaps more conservative, opinion.

Those who believe trusts are truly lawyers' magic may seek or fall victim to what we call the "daydream" trust. In a daydream trust, the grantor wants to use an ongoing trust to:

- avoid all income and estate taxes

- shield the property from all creditors, and

- retain complete control over trust property or, at the very least, have full access to it in times of need.

It should come as no surprise that the daydream trust is just that—a fantasy. Tax rules do not allow people to escape legal responsibilities simply by use of a trust. You can't use a trust to escape responsibility for legal debts and obligations, including child support, alimony, court-ordered judgments, or any other legal debt.

Likewise, if you retain any control over your trust or benefit from it, the IRS will not let you use the trust to reduce your income taxes. For example, some tout trusts designed to save big money on income and estate taxes, while at the same time giving the grantor great powers over trust assets. The IRS looks askance at this.

E. WHEN ONGOING TRUSTS BEGIN AND END

Once an ongoing trust becomes operational, it is a legal entity separate from any person or organization. It is also, as we've stressed, irrevocable—that is, you can't change the terms of the trust. Before the trust takes effect, however, you can revoke or change it at any time—you're not bound by its terms. Most people don't want an ongoing trust to become irrevocable while they are alive. Understandably, they don't want to be locked into giving away some of their property during their life.

1. When an Ongoing Trust Takes Effect

A trust becomes operational as soon as it is effective in the real world as a legally distinct entity. As we've said, most often this happens at the death of the trust creator. Once an ongoing trust becomes operational, the trustee must obtain a taxpayer ID number for the trust, keep accurate trust financial records, and file an annual federal trust income tax return and any required state trust tax returns.

> **Example:** Alma, age 73, creates a living trust to avoid probate. As one component of this living trust, she creates an ongoing trust for her disabled daughter, with Alma's niece Maureen as trustee. Only when Alma dies does this ongoing trust for her daughter become operational and irrevocable. Then Maureen must handle the trust property and accompanying paperwork.

Occasionally, however, people want an ongoing trust to become operational and irrevocable during their lifetime. For example, charitable trusts are often set up this way. Such irrevocable trusts are operational as soon as the trust documents are signed and notarized. Trust property is promptly given to the charity, and the grantor retains certain rights to receive income from it. (See Chapter 20.)

There can be other reasons to make an ongoing trust operational during your lifetime, rather than at your death. For example, an irrevocable life insurance trust must be operational at least three years before the grantor's death to obtain estate tax savings. (See Chapter 21, Section B.)

2. How Long an Ongoing Trust Lasts

How long an ongoing trust lasts is defined in the trust document. While some trusts last for a set number of years, usually the end of the trust is triggered by a certain event. The trust may, for example, last until a surviving spouse dies; when that happens, trust property is distributed to the couple's children, and the trust ends. A trust for grandchildren may last until the youngest reaches age 30 or 35, or whatever age the grantor chooses, at which point the grandchildren receive all remaining trust property.

In most states, a legal rule called "the rule against perpetuities" requires a trust to have a set ending time or event. This rule prevents someone from tying up property for generations without that property ever being owned outright by anyone. For example, you can't leave property "first to my daughter, then equally to her children, then equally to their grandchildren," and so on. Generally, society has decided that there should be a finite period during which the instructions of a deceased person can control the disposition of property. At some time, some person has to own the property outright and be free to sell it or give it away. Several states, including

Alaska, California, Delaware, Idaho, Illinois, Maryland, South Dakota, and Wisconsin, have liberalized their rule against perpetuities statute. This matters to legal scholars, some of the very rich, and perhaps you, if you live in one of these states and, for some unusual reason, you would like to set up a trust that lasts for several generations.

The intricacies of the rule against perpetuities have baffled law students for generations. For practical purposes, the rule means you can legally tie up property only for people who are alive when you die. That means you can leave trust property for your grown children to use during their lives and specify that, at their deaths, the property goes outright to their children. But if you try to impose controls on your nonexisting great-grandchildren's freedom to use or dispose of the property, you risk running afoul of the rule against perpetuities.

Imposing controls for more than one generation. If you want to create controls on property for more than one generation, you'll definitely need an expert estate planning lawyer's advice to determine whether what you want is legally possible.

F. THE TRUSTEE

The trustee of an ongoing trust has serious responsibilities, and choosing a reliable trustee is a crucial part of creating an ongoing trust.

1. The Trustee's Duties

For any type of ongoing trust, the trustee must manage the trust property prudently and comply with any specific management instructions in the trust document.

> ### TERMINOLOGY NOTE
>
> When an ongoing trust is created as a component of a living trust, you are the original trustee. When you die, a person you've named as trustee for the ongoing trust manages it. Often, but not always, this person is the same as the successor trustee of your living trust. We refer to the person who manages an ongoing trust that becomes operational at your death simply as the "trustee."

The trustee's powers are usually set out in detail (sometimes many pages of detail) in the trust document. For example, the trustee may be given the specific power to sell trust real estate, or to buy or lease new real estate.

General legal rules also govern the trustee. Legally, the trustee is a "fiduciary," which imposes the standard of highest good faith and scrupulous honesty when handling trust business, unless the trust document itself declares a lesser legal standard. For example, unless it's specifically authorized in the trust document, the trustee may not personally profit from any financial transaction involving the trust.

The trustee of an ongoing trust will most likely engage in various business or financial transactions on behalf of the trust. For instance, the trustee will probably deal with banks or other financial institutions. The trustee may well be involved in other trust financial matters, from leasing trust property to dealing with the IRS. The trustee may also have to make investment decisions, or buy or sell trust property.

STANDARDS FOR ASSET MANAGEMENT

Traditionally, unless a trust specified a different standard, a trustee was required to manage trust assets under what is called the "prudent-person" rule. Essentially, this rule requires cautious investments, and prohibits all but the most conservative of stock market transactions. More recently, the stock market boom of the 1990s led a number of states to adopt laws, called the "prudent-investor" rule, permitting trustees to play the stock market "prudently," unless the trust itself imposes a more restrictive standard. Beneficiaries of a long-term trust can, of course, benefit if a trustee invests trust property wisely, or luckily, in stocks. (As Denis's wise brother put it, "It's easy to make money in a rising market.") But of course—and as we've seen—it's not obligatory that stock market prices rise. If the market falls drastically, or if the trustee doesn't pick winners, beneficiaries may wish more conservative investments had been chosen.

There's another serious potential problem here. Many irrevocable trusts, most prominently AB trusts, leave income from trust property to a life beneficiary, normally a spouse. There may be a lot less income if the trustee invests in stocks. Many stocks currently provide very little or no income (dividends); all the money is made if the stock price goes up and you sell. But a life beneficiary doesn't get any cash because a stock has increased in value, or even when the stock is sold for a profit. That profit goes to trust principal, not income.

With an AB trust, one standard way to handle this issue is to allow the trustee discretion regarding standards for investment. Normally, with an AB trust, the surviving spouse is successor trustee. She or he will probably invest to obtain a decent return on trust principal. (See Chapter 18, Section C.)

Trustee standard for property management. You may be concerned with what property management standard governs the trustee of your ongoing trust. Maybe you definitely do, or do not, want to allow investment or speculation in stocks. Or you may have concerns about balancing the interests of your spouse with your children regarding trust investments. (See Chapter 24.) If, for whatever reason, you want to define the property management standards that apply to your trustee, see an attorney to explore your alternatives and pin down the best standard for you.

Sometimes, the trustee's actual financial responsibilities can be rather simple. For example, if the trust primarily consists of a valuable house, the trustee has to be sure the house is properly maintained and perhaps decide when to sell it. But often the trustee's work is more difficult. If much of the trust money is invested, the trustee must decide whether the investments are reasonable ones—neither absurdly cautious nor too risky. If the trust property includes a business or a complex investment portfolio, managing the property can be quite a task. For this reason, it's normally permissible for a trustee to hire financial or investment advisors and pay for their advice from trust assets.

The trustee of an ongoing trust must also distribute trust income (or principal) to the beneficiaries as the trust document directs or permits. Sometimes this, too, is far from simple. If the trust document allows the trustee some discretion in whether or not to distribute trust income or principal on behalf of a certain beneficiary, it may not be easy for the trustee to decide what to do.

The trustee of an ongoing trust that becomes operational at the grantor's death is responsible for handling all trust paperwork—for example, getting the taxpayer ID number from the IRS and keeping accurate trust financial records. Professional help can be used here if, in the trustee's judgment, it's necessary. The trustee is also responsible for filing the annual trust income tax return (IRS Form 1041). If any federal tax is owed, the trustee must pay it from trust funds. Finally, the trustee must handle any required state income tax return.

Eventually, when the trust ends, the trustee must distribute any remaining trust property to the final trust beneficiaries.

Because of these responsibilities, most trustees of ongoing trusts are paid. The trust document often allows the trustees to pay themselves "reasonable compensation" or a set amount per hour from trust property. Of course, you can expressly prohibit pay for your trustee, but it's not wise. Are you sure you can rely on a person to do the work required of a trustee without compensation? And even if someone would do it, do you really think it's fair? After all, the trustee will be spending time on work you created by establishing your ongoing trust.

2. Choosing the Trustee

Obviously, if you create an ongoing trust, you must give serious thought to who will serve as the trustee. The two most important criteria your trustee should meet are that you completely trust the person and that he or she wants to do the job.

The trustee should also have some financial common sense. You may decide, in fact, that you want your trustee to have considerable financial expertise. For instance, you may want a trustee who understands the difference between a balanced, fairly conservative investment portfolio—say, a mix of income-oriented stock and bond funds—and much

riskier investment in someone's great idea for a new business or speculation in real estate.

If you can find all this in one person, fine, but remember—your trustee can always hire investment advisors. Someone you trust, and who is willing to do the job, can't be purchased.

Making this choice may also raise sensitive personal issues. For one thing, your trustee will have an ongoing relationship with the trust beneficiaries.

Example: Malik has three children from his former marriage. He wants to leave the income from his estate to his wife, Libby, during her life, and on her death, have his estate divided equally among his children. Who should be trustee of the ongoing trust he creates to achieve these goals?

Malik must carefully evaluate a number of factors:

- What is the relationship between Libby and his children?

- If Libby is the sole trustee, will she truly guard the trust principal for his children?

- If one of his children is the trustee, will that child be fair to Libby—or will he try to retain in the trust as much of the money as he can, regardless of what Libby needs?

- If Libby and one of Malik's children are cotrustees, can they get along?

- What will happen if they can't?

Different types of ongoing trusts raise different concerns about your choice of trustee. These issues are discussed in subsequent chapters, which cover various types of ongoing trusts.

3. Naming More Than One Trustee

Legally, you can name two, or even several individuals to serve as cotrustees. But before you do, make sure you have a compelling reason. Having two or more people serve as trustees for a trust that may last a long time can lead to serious conflict or confusion.

If you decide to appoint cotrustees, you must decide how they will share authority—whether each can act separately for the trust or all must agree in writing to act for the trust. But even more important, you must have complete confidence that all your trustees will get along. Do be cautious here. Sharing power and property can lead to unexpected results. If the cotrustees are prone to conflict, you may well create serious problems, and will be doing none of them a favor by having them share power.

If cotrustees can't agree, say, on how to manage trust property, the situation can get very messy. Your trustees could wind up in court. Not only would this probably waste trust money, but the end result might be much worse, and generate more animosity than if you had just picked one person to be trustee in the first place and let the chips fall where they may.

4. Trust Companies and Banks as Trustees

Would you and your beneficiaries be better served if a professional trustee (from a bank or private trust company) were named as a trustee? Generally, we believe not. Indeed, our strong preference is for you to select a person you know and trust to serve as trustee. A trustee should have good money sense and be reasonably knowledgeable about the financial world, but in most cases does not need to be an expert.

Banks can be very impersonal, perhaps paying little attention to trusts worth less than (many) millions, or treating a beneficiary as a nuisance. In addition, they charge overall management fees, and often additional fees for each tiny act, which can cost a bundle.

But if there is no person you trust who is willing to serve as trustee, and you want to create an ongoing trust, you'll have to select a financial institution as your trustee. Also, with certain complicated types of property, such as oil and gas interests, beneficiaries can benefit from professional management. Your best bet is probably to use a private trust company, a business that specializes in trust management. They tend to be smaller and less impersonal than banks, and more focused on trust management. If you're extremely cautious, you might even want to name another institution as an alternate trustee, just in case your first choice goes out of business or decides not to handle smaller trusts. But doing this means you have to make arrangements with two private trust companies—and this means extra work.

A possible compromise is to name cotrustees—an individual you trust and a financial institution. The hope is to get a measure of investment savvy but still have a real person in the mix. The reality may be less inviting. Many institutions won't accept a co-trustee arrangement. And whenever you appoint cotrustees, potential problems abound. (See Section 3, above.) Unless there's a financial institution you really feel comfortable with, a better bet is just to name an individual trustee, who can hire good financial advisors if needed.

5. Choosing a Successor Trustee

Since your ongoing trust will likely last a while, somewhere down the line your first choice may become unable to perform the job. So it's a good idea to give some thought to arranging for a successor trustee. You can simply name one or more successor trustees in your trust document. You can also authorize an acting trustee to name, in writing, additional successor trustees. The trustee would do this if—and only if—the trustee and any successor trustees you named are unable to serve. This should ensure that the position of trustee never becomes vacant. (If it did, there would have to be a court proceeding to name a new trustee.) Also, this ensures that any trustee will at least have been chosen by someone you trust.

Example: Shannon's living trust creates an ongoing trust for her two young grandchildren, to last until they reach age 35. She names the children's mother, Carolyn (her daughter), as the trustee and Carolyn's husband, Bill, as the successor trustee. She also includes in the trust document a provision allowing any trustee to name, in writing, additional successor trustees.

Carolyn dies a few years after the trust becomes operational, and Bill becomes trustee. He writes a document naming his brother Al, then Al's wife, Jane, to serve as trustees if he can't. Before either child is 35, Bill is killed in a car crash. Al then becomes the trustee.

⚠ An important and specific trustee power.
One of the powers given to a trustee is the power to allocate income and principal of the trust. You should be very specific about how you want the trustee to make these divisions. For instance, if you are an author and want your spouse to receive your royalties as trust income, the document must state this. The same is true for other property, such as reinvested dividends. If you don't spell out your intentions, state laws could defeat them. Various state laws define what is income and what is principal, in the absence of specific directions to the contrary. You could find your life beneficiary, most likely your spouse, unable to receive money you both thought was income.

G. Taxation of Ongoing Trusts

If an ongoing trust takes effect while you are alive, the property placed in the trust is a gift, subject to gift tax, unless the beneficiary is a tax-exempt charity. (See Chapter 16, Section A.) If the ongoing trust is created in a will or living trust and takes effect when you die, the property in the trust is part of your taxable estate; whether or not your estate will actually owe estate tax depends on its size, the year of death, and possibly other factors. (See Chapter 15, Section A.) In a few states, it is also subject to state estate tax.

From an income tax standpoint, it is rarely desirable to have an ongoing trust retain, for more than one year, income generated by trust property. Trust income tax rates are now higher than individual income tax rates. An ongoing trust is taxed on all income over $100 that it retains at the close of the tax year. If the trust distributes income earned in that year to a beneficiary, that income is taxed at the beneficiary's rate, not the trust's.

If a beneficiary's income tax rate will be lower than the trust's rate, the rule is simple: Trusts that retain income for more than one year pay more in income tax, and thus ultimately have less to distribute to the beneficiaries. So, in most cases, the trustee must feel that, for some non-income tax reason, it's vitally important that the trust accumulate income, assuming the trust authorizes it.

Current trust income tax rates begin at 15% for retained trust income and reach a top rate of 35% for retained trust income over $9,750.

TRUST INCOME TAX RATES

Retained Trust Income	Income Tax Rate
$100–$2,000	15%
$2,001–$4,700	$300 plus 25% of the excess over $2,001
$4,701–$7,150	$975 plus 28% of the excess over $4,701
$7,151–$9,750	$1,661 plus 33% of the excess over $7,151
Over $9,750	$2,519 plus 35% of the excess over $9,750

■

18

ESTATE TAX-SAVING BYPASS TRUSTS

A "bypass" trust is an ongoing trust designed to lessen or eliminate overall estate taxes. The most popular form of this trust, commonly called an "AB" trust, is used by couples with a combined estate exceeding the estate tax threshold. It sometimes goes by other names, such as a "marital life estate trust," "credit shelter trust," or "exemption trust."

Bypass trusts can also be used to impose restrictions on a beneficiary's rights to trust property. This type of trust is discussed in Chapter 24.

A. OVERVIEW OF BYPASS TRUSTS

Here are the basics of how a bypass trust works: You create an ongoing trust, either by will or within a living trust, that will take effect at your death. You name a beneficiary, usually your spouse, who has certain rights to the trust property during his or her life. This person is called, fittingly, the "life beneficiary."

The property you put into the trust is part of your taxable estate. As we have discussed previously, the tax laws passed in 2001 eliminate all federal estate taxes for one year only—in 2010. For this reason, estate planners continue to focus on avoiding death taxes.

Usually, when you use a bypass trust, no estate tax will be due at your death, regardless of the year. (We discuss this later.) That's good, but the main benefit comes when the life beneficiary dies. The key is that the life beneficiary never legally owns the trust property. This is true even if he or she had the rights to receive all income generated by the property, or to use it—if it's a house, for example. Because the life beneficiary never legally owns the property, it isn't counted as part of his or her estate, for estate tax purposes, when he or she dies.

When the life beneficiary dies, the trust property goes to the final beneficiaries you specify in the trust document, usually your children. No estate tax is taken out of the trust property when the life beneficiary dies. By contrast, if you had left your property to the life beneficiary outright, it would have been included as part of that beneficiary's taxable estate when he or she died.

The life beneficiary (again, this is usually your spouse) has only those rights to the trust property specified in the trust document. These rights can include receiving all trust income, using trust property—for example, living in the family home— or certain limited rights to spend trust principal for specific needs—for example, medical care and support.

Technically, it is the trustee who decides whether or not to spend trust principal for authorized needs of the life beneficiary. But in most tax-saving bypass trusts, the trustee and the life beneficiary are the same person. Still, the life beneficiary is never the legal owner of the trust property. She has no power to decide who receives it after her death.

Both couples (married or not) and individuals can create a bypass trust.

Example 1: Cecilia has been married to Lou for over 40 years. They have one grown child, Marietta, who is 37. Cecilia creates a bypass trust to become effective at her death. The trust will hold all her major items of property, both what's hers alone and her half of the assets she and Lou own together. She names Lou as life beneficiary. At Cecilia's death, he will have the right to receive all the income the trust property generates and to use the trust principal for basic needs like medical care for the rest of his life. When he dies, the trust property will pass outright to the final beneficiary, Marietta.

Example 2: Jefferson creates a bypass trust, naming his best friend, Isaac, as the life beneficiary. Isaac has the right to receive trust income, and also to live in the house the trust owns. Jefferson's trust document specifies that when Isaac dies, the property will be divided equally between Jefferson's children, the final beneficiaries.

To understand how bypass trusts actually save on estate taxes, you obviously need to know how those taxes work. (They are discussed in detail in Chapter 15.) Here we repeat three basic federal estate tax rules:

- Every person can leave a total at death, tax free, equal to the amount of the personal exemption. This amount is $2 million for 2006 and rises to $3.5 million in 2009. After that year, the tax is on track to be repealed—but this is not guaranteed. It's impossible to predict what Congress will do in the next few years. The personal exemption is available whether assets are left to one beneficiary or divided among many. The amount you can leave tax free is reduced if you made taxable gifts during life. (See Chapter 16.)

- Married people can leave any amount tax free to a spouse who is a U.S. citizen. (See Chapter 15, Section A.) In tax lingo, this is called the "marital deduction."

- If you leave property worth more than the amount of your personal exemption in the year of your death outright to someone other than your spouse (say, your brother) and a few years later he dies owning property worth more than his own exemption, estate tax will be levied twice on your property—once when you die and once when your brother dies.

Enter the bypass trust, where property is left for the use of a life beneficiary and then goes to a final beneficiary. Under U.S. tax law and IRS rules, if the life beneficiary never becomes the legal owner of the trust assets, property in the trust is subject to estate tax when the grantor dies, but is not taxed again when the life beneficiary dies—hence the name "bypass" trust.

Example: Continuing with Cecilia and Lou, from the example above, let's say Cecilia has property worth $2 million when she dies in 2006. Lou's estate is also worth $2 million when Cecilia dies.

If Cecilia had left her property outright to Lou, his total estate would be $4 million. If he were to die three years later, in 2009, his personal exemption would be $3.5 million. So $500,000 would be subject to estate tax. But because Cecilia used a bypass trust, no estate tax will be due on either's death. Cecilia's $2 million is the exempt amount in 2006, so no tax is due. And since Lou is never the legal owner of Cecilia's trust property, his estate remains at $2 million and so will not be subject to estate tax when he dies.

THE TAX BASIS OF AB TRUST PROPERTY INHERITED BY FINAL BENEFICIARIES

Final beneficiaries receive the property in an AB trust after the life beneficiary dies. The tax basis of that property for the final beneficiaries is its net market worth (its "stepped-up basis") on the date of death of the trust creator, not the date of death of the life beneficiary. (Income tax basis is defined and explained in detail in Chapter 15, Section F.) The point of an AB trust is to prevent the life beneficiary from having legal ownership of the Trust A property. Since she never owned the Trust A property, it cannot be included in her estate, and therefore is not entitled to a stepped-up basis equal to its worth on her death.

Example: Arnie leaves property worth $2 million in his Trust A when he dies in 2006. Brenda, his wife and life beneficiary, dies in 2008. The Trust A property is now worth $4 million. The tax basis to the final beneficiaries is $2 million.

Because of the increases in the amounts of the estate tax exemption through 2009, wealthy couples may face confusing choices regarding leaving property that may significantly increase in value over a few years. For instance, in the above example, Brenda dies in 2008, when the personal exemption is $2 million. Would it be desirable for Arnie to leave his property directly to Brenda, so that at Brenda's death it would receive a full stepped-up basis of $4 million? There's no clear answer to this question. It depends in part on how much other property Brenda owns, as well as on the capital gains tax rates for 2008 or whatever year the final beneficiaries sell Arnie's property. Plus, of course, who can know now what property will prove to be worth in 2008? If you own very valuable property, you'll want to consult an expert estate planner for help evaluating your choices.

B. IRS RESTRICTIONS ON BYPASS TRUSTS

All bypass trusts must comply with applicable IRS regulations. If yours doesn't, the estate tax savings you're after will be lost.

1. Right to Spend Trust Principal

The trustee cannot be given complete freedom to spend trust principal for the life beneficiary. If the trustee has such unlimited rights, the IRS will regard the life beneficiary as the legal owner of the trust property and impose estate tax on it when the life beneficiary dies.

The IRS does, however, allow the trustee to spend (invade) the trust principal for the life beneficiary's "health, education, support, and maintenance…in accord with his or her accustomed standard of living." (IRS Regulation 320.2041-1(c)(2).) Spending trust principal for these purposes is allowed because, according to the IRS, the need for these expenditures can be judged against an "ascertainable standard."

Example: Arlo leaves his property in a bypass trust with his wife Sirpa as the life beneficiary. Sirpa is the trustee and she has the right to invade trust principal for her health care, education, support, and maintenance. As trustee, she may sell trust property, invest it, or exchange it. For instance, if the trust includes a home, she could ordinarily sell it and buy a retirement condo with the proceeds.

By contrast, if the trust document says that trust assets can be spent for, say, the "comfort" or "well-being" of the life beneficiary, the IRS considers this an "unascertainable" standard. In that case, the trust assets will be regarded as legally owned by the life beneficiary and taxed at his death, even if no trust money was in fact ever spent for these purposes.

Example: Let's assume Arlo's trust gave Sirpa the right to spend principal for her comfort. Even if she never spends any of the principal for any purpose, the IRS will consider her the owner of the trust property and it will be subject to estate tax at her death.

This right to be able to spend trust principal for basic needs of the life beneficiary is crucially important to many couples. They want to conserve as much of their estate as possible for their children or other final beneficiaries, but they don't want the surviving spouse to risk running out of money for vital needs, such as health care or normal living expenses. A bypass trust document that is properly drafted—using the language acceptable to the IRS—eliminates this risk. The surviving spouse will have the right to use any amount of principal necessary for basic expenses, including medical care.

Example: Walter and Marjorie, a working couple in their late fifties, own shared property worth $2 million. They each draft a bypass trust for their half of the property, specifying that the income goes to the other spouse for life, with the assets then going to their children. Each includes in their trust language "powers," (in legal lingo) that give the survivor (as trustee) the right to spend trust principal for his or her health care, support, and maintenance.

Each spouse has taken advantage of their personal exemption instead of leaving all property to the survivor and wasting the exemption of the first spouse to die. No estate tax is due when the first spouse dies. They will also avoid any federal estate tax on the trust money when the second spouse dies. If their financial situation remains stable (or their wealth increases), the survivor may never need to spend trust principal. However, they have provided a security backup that allows the survivor to use all of the assets they both own if necessary.

You don't have to give the trustee the broad powers to spend principal that the law allows. In some situations, particularly second or subsequent marriages, one or both spouses may not want to give a surviving spouse the right to spend trust principal for support, and may even want to further restrict use of trust property. Normally, this is because a spouse wants to be sure trust property remains intact for her own children or other final beneficiaries. Indeed, you can forbid spending any of the trust principal at all. (See Chapter 24.)

2. The "5 and 5" Power

Another IRS rule allows you to give the trustee of a bypass trust what is called a "5 and 5" power. This authorizes the trustee to invade the trust principal annually for one or more beneficiaries, for any reason whatsoever, up to a maximum of 5% of the trust principal for all beneficiaries, or $5,000, whichever is greater. The trustee can be given authority to exercise this right for the life beneficiary, the final beneficiaries, or both. The trust document must specifically state which beneficiaries are eligible to receive trust property under the 5 and 5 power.

The 5 and 5 power is not in favor with many sophisticated estate planning lawyers. They reason that it's better to rely solely on a provision allowing the trustee to invade principal for the life beneficiary's health care, education, support, and maintenance, which protects the life beneficiary in case of real need. The risk of the 5 and 5 power is that it can allow the life beneficiary to use up, over the years, much or even all of the trust principal for any reason whatsoever.

One advantage of a 5 and 5 power, however, is that a final beneficiary, not just the life beneficiary, can benefit from it. If you think that one or more of the final beneficiaries (such as a child) may need money from the trust while the life beneficiary is alive, you can specify that the trustee can use the 5 and 5 power to benefit some or all of the final beneficiaries. (A "sprinkling trust" can also be used to benefit several beneficiaries. See Chapter 25, Section D.) For instance, if the trust document authorized it, a trustee might use the 5 and 5 power to spend some trust principal for the education of a final beneficiary, particularly if the life beneficiary would remain financially comfortable even after that money was spent.

The trustee does not have to exercise the 5 and 5 power. Each year it is up to the trustee to decide whether or not an eligible beneficiary should be given trust principal under this power. Normally there are no adverse tax consequences if the trustee doesn't exercise the 5 and 5 power.

C. AB Trusts: Bypass Trusts for Married Couples

For many couples who think their combined estate may be subject to estate tax, the ideal result can be simply stated: You want the surviving spouse to have access to the deceased spouse's property, if he or she needs it, but you don't want the surviving spouse to become the legal owner of that property, because then hefty estate tax may be due when the second spouse dies. You can achieve these goals with what's called an "AB" trust, which is simply a bypass trust for married couples. AB trusts can go by other names including "credit shelter trust," "exemption trust," or "marital life estate trust."

To summarize what we discussed in Section A, above, here's how it works: Each spouse creates an AB trust. (Usually, it's added onto a basic probate-avoidance living trust.) Instead of leaving his or her share of property outright to the survivor, each spouse leaves all, or at least the bulk, of his or her property to Trust A. When one spouse dies, the survivor gets only a "life estate" interest in all property of the deceased spouse that goes into the Trust A. The surviving spouse continues to have his or her separate revocable living trust, Trust B.

Each spouse names his or her final beneficiaries for his or her Trust A, who receive this trust's property when the surviving spouse dies. Most commonly, the final beneficiaries for both spouses are their children.

AB trusts involve some complexities and drawbacks, but they do work very well for many couples and families. Indeed, they are a standard component of most estate plans prepared by lawyers for couples with larger estates. For many older couples, the drawbacks amount to no more than relatively minor accounting and record-keeping hassles after one spouse dies, which they feel are well worth it to conserve up to hundreds of thousands of dollars worth of their property for their children or other final beneficiaries.

DO YOU NEED A LAWYER?

You may wonder whether or not it's wise to prepare an AB trust yourself, without the aid of an attorney. If you and your spouse have a combined estate worth $4 million or less, you may decide to go it alone. Couples in this situation can find forms and complete instructions for preparing an AB trust in the book *Make Your Own Living Trust*, by Denis Clifford or *Quicken WillMaker Plus* software (both from Nolo). The AB trust offered by these products is designed for couples who want to allow the surviving spouse the maximum legal rights over the trust property, while still gaining the estate tax-saving advantages of this type of trust.

You should consult a lawyer and should not use one of the trust products above if:

- You and your spouse expect to have a combined estate exceeding twice the estate tax threshold. Consult a good estate planning lawyer to explore more sophisticated options to reduce estate tax.

- You want to impose limits on the rights of the surviving spouse to use trust property. This includes many couples in second or subsequent marriages, who want to be sure the bulk of their property is preserved for children from prior marriages.

- You need a more complicated type of ongoing trust, such as a special needs trust for a disadvantaged child or a spendthrift trust for a child who can't properly manage money.

- You want to review all your estate planning options with an experienced attorney.

1. How an AB Trust Reduces Estate Tax

You may wonder why a married couple needs an AB trust. After all, because of the marital deduction, one spouse can leave the other an unlimited amount of money free of federal estate tax. But what happens when the second spouse dies? For couples with a combined estate exceeding the estate tax threshold, the result can be an estate tax trap.

For example, if spouses with a combined shared estate of $3 million—that is, each owns $1.5 million—leave their portion to each other, the surviving spouse will wind up with $3 million. Say the first spouse died in 2003, and the second in 2007 when the estate tax exemption is $2 million. When the second spouse dies, $1 million will be subject to estate tax (the $3 million minus the exemption).

Using an AB trust provides tax savings because the property in Trust A (the deceased spouse's share) is subject to estate tax only when the first spouse dies. If there is less than the personal exemption amount in that spouse's trust, no federal estate tax is due. And the Trust A property isn't subject to estate tax when the second spouse dies, because, as we've stressed, the second spouse never legally owns it.

Example: Arnold and Maggie share ownership of $3 million worth of property. (For the ease of both the authors and the readers, we will assume they both die when the personal exemption is $2 million.) Maggie dies first in 2007, and Arnold six months later in the beginning of 2008. If each leaves his or her property to the other, and the survivor leaves all their property to their two children, here are the tax consequences:

Without an AB Trust

On Maggie's Death:

Gross estate (1/2 shared property)	$1.5 million
Estate tax due (because of Maggie's personal exemption)	$-0-

On Arnold's Death:

Gross estate	$3 million
(his $1.5 million and $1.5 million inherited from Maggie)	
Arnold's personal exemption	$2 million
Estate tax due on $1 million	$345,800

Now let's look at what happens if Maggie and Arnold each create an AB trust in which each leaves his or her property in trust for the benefit of the surviving spouse for his or her life. When the second spouse dies, the trust property will be distributed to their children.

With an AB Trust

On Maggie's Death:

Gross estate (1/2 shared property)	$1.5 million
Estate tax due	$-0-
(again, because of Maggie's $2 million exemption)	

On Arnold's Death:

Gross estate	$1.5 million
Estate tax due	$-0-
(because of Arnold's $2 million exemption)	

Neat, isn't it? By using an AB trust absolutely no estate tax is paid. By contrast, without the trust, in this example, $345,800 must be handed over to the government in estate tax, instead of going to the children. What's more, owing tax also saddles the husband's executor (probably one of the children) with the hassle of having to file a federal estate tax return. And other costs may be involved if estate tax must be paid, such as appraisal fees. (However, with an AB trust, similar appraisal costs may have to be paid at the first spouse's death in order to divide the property between the now irrevocable Trust A and the surviving spouse's continuing, revocable Trust B.) Finally, because estate tax must be paid when Arnold dies, his assets may be tied up for nine months after his death (that's when the estate tax return is due) before what's left can be transferred to the children.

You can place whatever property you want in your AB trust. You can place all your separate property and your half of shared property, or any portion of either, in your trust.

If the Trust A assets appreciate substantially by the time the life beneficiary dies, this appreciation is not subject to any estate tax. The Trust A assets are subject to tax once, and only once—when the grantor dies.

Example: Isabel and Simon own shared assets totaling $2.4 million. They each draft an AB trust for their $1.2 million shares, with their children as the final beneficiaries. Isabel dies first, in 2006, and Simon lives for another six years, expertly investing the Trust A principal. At Simon's death, the Trust A property is worth $6.5 million. No estate tax is assessed against the Trust A property when Simon dies. The full $6.5 million is now distributed to the children with no estate tax ever paid on these assets.

2. Is an AB Trust Right for You?

AB trusts aren't for everyone. Before deciding to use an AB trust, you and your spouse should understand what you're getting into. Once one spouse dies, that spouse's Trust A becomes irrevocable; it imposes limits and burdens on the survivor's use of the deceased spouse's property that cannot be changed. There are other important considerations as well. Here are some guidelines.

a. Size of Your Estate

In our opinion, if you and your spouse have a combined estate worth more than $2 million, and you plan to leave all or the bulk to each other, you should seriously consider an AB trust. If both members of the couple die before 2009, estate tax would be assessed that could have been avoided by use of an AB trust. Even if both spouses survive past 2009, an AB trust is still smart for couples with a combined estate over $2 million. First, as of now, the personal estate tax exemption will revert to $1 million in 2011. By preparing an AB trust, you have a plan in place in case you're both alive when that $1 million limit reappears. Second, no one can predict how Congress may change the estate tax law between now and 2011. If Congress decides not to allow all the increases in the personal estate tax exemption currently scheduled through 2010, your AB trust will work with lower exemption amounts. And if the higher exemption amounts are allowed, you won't lose anything significant by having an AB trust. As we've explained, with an AB trust a surviving spouse can obtain any amount of the deceased spouse's Trust A principal needed for medical care or other basic needs.

b. Your Intended Beneficiaries

If you don't want to leave the bulk of your property for use of your surviving spouse, but want instead to leave substantial amounts of property directly to other beneficiaries, an AB trust won't accomplish your goals.

c. Restrictions on the Surviving Spouse

Couples under 45 rarely create an AB trust. Younger couples usually don't want to risk tying up one spouse's assets in a Trust A. If one spouse dies prematurely, the surviving spouse may well live for decades, and would likely be far better off inheriting the deceased spouse's property outright. The survivor will inherit everything estate-tax free, no matter what the amount, because of the marital deduction. That surviving spouse will probably have years to use the money—and to arrange for other methods of reducing eventual estate tax, if it still exists.

Similarly, couples where one spouse is considerably younger than the other and presumably will live much longer may not want an AB trust. Generally there's no need to burden the younger spouse with a trust designed to save estate tax when he or she is likely to live for many years.

Commonly, it's only as a couple reaches their 50s or 60s that they create an AB trust. But we've seen couples in their late 30s prepare AB trusts, because they want to be sure that they've done all they can to avoid any estate tax, or for other reasons, such as property control. (See Chapter 24.) They've considered and accepted the possibility that one spouse's property may be tied up in trust for decades of the surviving spouse's life.

d. Difficulty Dividing the Property

At the death of the first spouse, the couple's shared property must be divided into two legally separate entities. One share is owned by the surviving spouse's revocable living Trust B and is under the surviving spouse's complete control. The other share is placed in the deceased's Trust A.

When the first spouse dies, an estate lawyer or accountant must determine how to best divide the couple's assets between the now-irrevocable Trust A and the continuing Trust B of the surviving spouse. Under federal law, each item of the couple's shared property does not have to be divided 50/50 between the two trusts, but the total value of shared property in each trust must be equal. If state property ownership laws allow some flexibility in dividing shared property, you may obtain significant financial benefits when allocating assets between the two trusts. It takes an expert to decide on the best division, because different allocations have different tax consequences.

For example, what should be done with the family home? If full ownership of the house were placed in the Trust A, the house would be valued, for estate tax purposes, at its value on the death of the first spouse. By contrast, if the house were allocated to the surviving spouse, and she survives for many more years, the house would probably be worth more (given inflation) by the date of her death. Its increased value might result in the value of the survivor's estate exceeding the personal exemption amount or, if her estate were already well over that, in extra tax being paid because of the increased worth of the house.

But there can also be drawbacks to including the full value of a house in Trust A. If the trust owns a house, certain tax advantages are lost. For example, an individual has the right to sell a house and retain up to $250,000 profit (capital gain) without tax. An irrevocable trust has no such right. So if the house may be sold in the future, it can be costly, income tax-wise, to place it in Trust A. This just scratches the surface of the complexity of dividing a couple's property between the two trusts on the death of a spouse. Of course, not every case is complex, but the surviving spouse should at least check out the matter with an expert before actually dividing up the couple's shared property.

e. Duty to File Trust Tax Returns

The trustee of an operational Trust A must obtain a taxpayer ID number for the trust. The trustee must file an annual trust income tax return for that trust. This usually isn't a big deal, but like any tax return, it requires some work.

f. Complicated Record Keeping

After the first spouse dies, the surviving spouse must keep two sets of books and records, one for her own property, including property in Trust B, and one for Trust A property.

g. Potential Family Strife

No matter what age you are, an AB trust works best when all involved—both spouses and all final beneficiaries—understand and agree on the purposes of the trust. Again, these goals are to save on overall estate tax and at the same time give the surviving spouse the maximum allowable rights to use trust income, and principal if necessary. Without this agreement, serious conflicts may develop between the surviving spouse and the final beneficiaries. This can be particularly true when there are children from a prior marriage.

If there is any potential for conflict between the surviving spouse and the final beneficiaries of the trust, an AB trust may well provoke or aggravate it. After all, in theory at least, there is an inherent conflict of interest between the life estate beneficiary and the final beneficiaries. The final beneficiaries may want all the trust principal conserved, no matter what the surviving spouse needs. On the other hand, the surviving spouse may want or need to use up most or even all of the trust principal for health care, education, or maintenance.

Another conflict can arise if the surviving spouse becomes ill and can no longer serve as trustee. If a child who stands to eventually receive trust assets takes over as successor trustee, it's possible the child might be more concerned with preserving principal than with a parent's medical or other needs. We've heard of such situations, where it seemed to other family members and friends that a child disregarded his parent's basic needs and instead protected the trust principal for himself.

Conflicts can also occur if the final beneficiaries believe the surviving spouse, as trustee, is not managing the trust property well—for example, by investing in very speculative stocks or risky real estate deals. If this situation arises, there can be real trouble, possibly even a lawsuit.

An AB trust is less likely to create strife down the road if:

- Family members trust each other, are reasonably close, and are able to work out any conflicts that might arise.

- The final beneficiaries understand that taking the trouble to create an AB trust is a generous act; after all, the trust benefits the children, not the people who create the trust. The final beneficiaries receive much more of the couple's estate than they would have if the spouses had left property outright to the other.

- If Trust A allows the surviving spouse, as trustee, to spend trust principal for his support, health care, education, and maintenance, the final beneficiaries can be trusted to support the surviving spouse if he decides to spend trust principal for any authorized reason.

- The documents themselves are as clear as possible as to your intentions, leaving little or no room for interpretation.

FINAL BENEFICIARIES IN SECOND MARRIAGES

Couples in a second or subsequent marriage often want to name different final beneficiaries for each spouse's property. Each often wants children from a prior marriage as final beneficiaries. Fortunately, each spouse creates his or her own separate AB trust, so each has the right to choose the final beneficiaries for his or her own trust property. (This issue is discussed further in Chapter 24.)

---

3. How to Create an AB Trust

Normally, an AB trust is combined with a living trust. (See Chapter 17.) That way, when one spouse dies, the trust property first avoids probate, and then the irrevocable Trust A becomes operational.

Each spouse owns his or her distinct portion of the living trust property, which includes half of any community or co-owned property, and all that spouse's separate property. You can also leave any money left in an individual retirement plan—an IRA or profit-sharing plan, for example—to an AB trust. To do this with a 401(k) plan, however, you need a signed waiver from your spouse, otherwise federal law requires that you leave all funds in the 401(k) to your spouse outright. (See "Naming an AB Trust as the Beneficiary of Your Retirement Accounts," below.) When one spouse dies, that spouse's Trust A, containing whatever portion of his or her property was designated for the trust, becomes irrevocable. The surviving spouse, normally also the trustee, takes over management of the trust's property and must comply with all terms of the trust.

Meanwhile, the surviving spouse's Trust B (that is, her portion of the couple's original living trust) continues to be revocable, as long as she lives. The surviving spouse can amend her living trust to create whatever new provisions and beneficiary clauses seem appropriate. Or, she can leave her trust as it is. When she dies, the property in Trust B will go directly to whomever she named as the final beneficiaries in her living trust. The Trust A property will be distributed according to the original terms of the document.

4. Choosing the Trustee

We discussed how to select a trustee in Chapter 17, Section F. There are, however, some special considerations when you're choosing the trustee for an AB trust.

Most couples want the surviving spouse to serve as initial trustee of Trust A, which becomes operational when the first spouse dies. To do that, the trust document simply makes both spouses initial trustees of the AB trust. Because Trust A doesn't become operational until one spouse dies, only the surviving spouse will actually serve as trustee.

Example: Mark and Vera have three grown children and a combined estate worth approximately $2.9 million. In their shared living trust document, each creates an AB trust. Each specifies that all his or her property is to go into his or her Trust A at his or her death. The document names both spouses as cotrustees of the trusts.

Mark dies first. His property goes into Trust A, which is now operational. Vera is the sole trustee and will manage the property in Trust A. She also remains trustee for Trust B, a revocable living trust, which holds her own property.

Living trust documents normally also name a successor trustee for Trust A to take over management of the trust property if the surviving spouse becomes incapacitated. You may also want to name an alternate successor trustee.

If you don't want your surviving spouse to be trustee of your Trust A, you can name someone else. For example, your spouse may be infirm, not sensible about financial affairs, or simply uninterested.

If you wish, you can name more than one person to serve as cosuccessor trustees. For example, you might want to name your two adult children, or your spouse and one adult child, as cotrustees. (The potential pitfalls of naming cotrustees are discussed in Chapter 17, Section F.)

When selecting the successor and alternate successor trustees for an AB trust, ask yourself several questions about your choices:

- Does the person want to serve?
- Is the person capable of handling the trustee's duties?
- Would trust management duties create an undue burden on that person?
- Will the trustee be paid?
- Do you completely trust the person to manage the property as you would wish?

MANAGING TRUST A PROPERTY

The successor trustee of an AB trust is usually the surviving spouse. The successor trustee is often given discretion to manage the Trust A property as he or she thinks best. And the surviving spouse, having the right to income from trust property, will generally manage the property to provide at least significant income, and perhaps to maximize income potential.

This approach works fine when the final beneficiaries understand that the reason for creating the AB trust was to save on overall estate taxes, benefiting them, and that each spouse wants the other to have as much legal benefit from Trust A property as he or she wants. But if there's a potential for conflict between the life beneficiaries and the surviving spouse, problems can arise over how he or she manages Trust A property. The final beneficiaries may try to require that he or she invest in stocks, choosing long-term growth possibilities over shorter-term income.

Get help if you think there may be conflict between the life beneficiary and the final beneficiaries over management of your AB trust. To reduce the chance of conflict, you may want to be very specific in the trust document about the types of investments your successor trustee can make, or the nature and frequency of reports of the trust's finances that must be provided for the life beneficiaries. To best explore your options here, you need to work with an experienced estate planning attorney, who can fully explain the options available to you, and who can then draft a trust that has the best chance of achieving your goals. (These concerns are discussed further in Chapter 24, Section C.)

5. The Rights of the Life Beneficiary

Many couples want to make sure the surviving spouse has the broadest possible power over the trust property. As discussed in Section B, the trustee can be given all of the following rights:

- the right to distribute all trust income to the surviving spouse (and remember, the trustee and the surviving spouse are usually the same person)

- the right to control the trust property—that is, to use it (as with a house), or to buy or sell property, as long as principal is conserved

- the right to spend trust principal in any amount needed for the surviving spouse's "health, education, support, or maintenance, in his or her accustomed manner of living," and

- the 5 and 5 power (Section B, above).

However, you can place all kinds of restrictions on the rights of the life beneficiary to Trust A property. The only possible complication is that a surviving spouse in a common law state has the right to claim a certain portion (usually about one-third) of the deceased spouse's estate. As long as the surviving spouse has been left a substantial portion of your estate or is content with what she's inherited, there will be no problem. Even with these considerations, the rights to trust property can be fairly narrow.

> **Example:** Sam is in his 60s and is married to Diane. He has two adult daughters by his former marriage. Diane does not have children of her own. Sam's property is worth $1.1 million, consisting mainly of a residence and a stock portfolio. He also owns a life insurance policy that will pay $400,000 to Diane at his death. Diane has only $50,000 in assets. Sam wants to support Diane for her life and also preserve as much of his estate as possible for his daughters.

Sam prepares an AB trust for all his assets. When Sam dies, the income from property in Trust A will go to Diane for life; the principal will go to his daughters after Diane's death. Sam worries, though, that if he dies, Diane may remarry someone who'll push her to get at the trust principal. On the other hand, he doesn't want Diane to go without medical care she might need but can't pay for herself. So he names a daughter he trusts, not Diane, to be the successor trustee of Trust A. He also includes a provision in his trust that allows the successor trustee to invade the principal for Diane's health care only if all of her other assets are exhausted and the income from the trust is not sufficient. He feels that this is the best he can do for everybody, and hopes that his wife and children will agree.

Other still more restrictive provisions can be imposed if you wish. For example, the surviving spouse can be denied the right to invade Trust A principal for any reason. Or use of Trust A property can be strictly controlled—for instance, the surviving spouse can be given the right only to live in a house owned by the trust, not to sell it. Also, it's legal to provide that a spouse's benefits end if he remarries. If he remarries, the Trust A property is promptly turned over to the final trust beneficiaries. All these types of restrictions are discussed in depth in Chapter 24.

6. How Much Property to Place in an AB Trust

As we've discussed, if a couple has a combined estate that may be subject to estate tax, they'll want to take advantage of both of their personal estate tax exemptions by creating an AB trust and each leaving their own property in the trust. Doing this won't, however, necessarily eliminate all estate tax on the death of the first spouse. For example, if a couple has shared property worth $5 million, each one's share is worth $2.5 million. If a spouse's entire $2.5 million is placed in a Trust A, say in 2006, the part of it over the $2 million exemption could be subject to estate tax. So to reduce estate taxes further, each spouse may want to limit the amount in their Trust A to the personal exemption amount in the year of death, and leave the remainder outright to the surviving spouse or in another trust that will defer estate tax until the death of the second spouse. (See Chapter 19, Section A.)

a. Using a Formula Clause

If you are wealthy, with an estate worth several million dollars or more, many estate planners advise you not to leave all your property to your Trust A. Similarly, they recommend that you do not specify a dollar amount of property to be put in your Trust A. Instead, they recommend putting what's called a "formula" clause in the trust document. Essentially, the formula provides (in heavy legalese) that the worth of assets put in A trust is to equal the amount of the personal estate tax exemption in the year that the first spouse dies. Any property of the deceased above this amount is handled by other tax-avoidance methods.

A formula AB trust is useful only for people whose estates are likely to be over the estate tax threshold. If your estate is well under this threshold, you don't need a formula clause. If your estate is over the estate tax threshold, a formula clause ensures that you don't have to amend your AB trust as the amount of the personal exemption increases, or as your assets increase. As the exemption amount goes up over the next few years, a formula clause trust will always be current. This will also be so if Congress changes the exemption amounts in the future.

Example: Monica and Tony have a combined estate of $8 million, owned equally. They each create an AB trust, using a formula clause that provides that Trust A will contain the amount that results in no estate tax when the first spouse dies. The remaining assets go outright to the surviving spouse (or to the surviving spouse's Trust B). Monica and Tony don't have to worry about relatively minor changes in the estate tax law, and the survivor doesn't have to worry about paying any estate tax when the first spouse dies. If one of them dies in the year 2006, Trust A will hold $2 million, the amount exempt for that year. If the death is in 2009, the amount will be $3.5 million.

If you want to place more or less than the exempt amount in your Trust A, a formula clause is obviously not desirable. This is sometimes done with large estates to balance overall estate taxes. (See Subsection b, below.) A formula clause is necessary only if you want to place exactly the current exempt amount in your Trust A at your death.

Wealthy couples often combine a formula AB trust with other tax-deferral methods and postpone estate tax until later. Many couples simply do not want to pay any estate tax until they must—after the second spouse's death. They can accomplish this by each leaving no more than the exempt amount for the year of death in the Trust A, and all the rest to the surviving spouse. This property can be left to the surviving spouse outright or in another trust like a QTIP which qualifies for the marital deduction and defers tax until the second death. (See Chapter 19, Section A, for more on QTIP trusts.)

Using a formula AB trust can be desirable, no matter how much money the couple has, when it's likely that one spouse will long outlive the other. The deceased spouse leaves all property over the exemption amount to the surviving spouse free of estate tax. The surviving spouse will, hopefully, have many years, even decades, to use that money. The income and potential growth in value of the assets the spouse receives can far exceed any additional estate tax that eventually might have to be paid. Also, the surviving spouse can take other actions to lower any eventual estate tax, such as making regular tax-free gifts. (See Chapter 16, Section E.)

Finally, there can be other reasons to postpone estate taxes that may outweigh any higher overall tax costs. For instance, if an estate consists of property that is not liquid, such as a family-owned business or a valuable residence, it may be worth waiting and paying extra tax dollars at the second death to prevent having to sell assets to get cash for tax at the first death.

b. Placing More Than the Exempt Amount for the Year of Death in an AB Trust

In larger estates—and especially for older couples—it's sometimes sensible for each spouse to place assets worth more than the tax-exempt amount in an AB trust. The reason is those old graduated estate tax rates, which start at 45% and go higher for large estates. The larger the estate when it is taxed, the higher the percentage that will be lost to estate tax. This means for couples with substantial estates, overall estate tax can be lowered if some of their property is taxed when the first spouse dies.

c. Using a Disclaimer Trust

A disclaimer AB Trust allows the surviving spouse, as trustee of Trust A, to decide the worth of property placed in that trust. A "disclaimer" simply means that a beneficiary decides not to accept all or part of the property left to him or her. Anyone has a legal right to disclaim any gift property; no one can be compelled to accept an inheritance. The use of disclaimers in estate planning is discussed in depth in Chapter 22. Here, we'll examine only how disclaimers can be used with an AB trust.

The basic goal of a disclaimer AB trust is to ensure that property worth no more than the personal estate tax exemption for the year of the spouse's death is transferred to Trust A. Further, with the use of a disclaimer, the surviving spouse can decide to put substantially less than the exempt amount in Trust A.

Here's how it works: Each spouse leaves at least the bulk of his or her AB trust property to the other. Each spouse further specifies that his or her Trust A shall receive all trust property disclaimed by the surviving spouse. When the first spouse dies, the survivor assesses the overall financial situation, the amount of the estate tax exemption for the year of death, and the survivor's financial needs. Then the survivor decides how much of the deceased spouse's property to accept, and how much to disclaim.

Example: Wendy and Victor have a co-owned estate worth $7 million. They prepare a disclaimer AB trust. Wendy dies in 2006, leaving her $3.5 million estate to Victor. The estate tax exemption for 2006 is $2 million. Victor disclaims $2 million of Wendy's property, which goes in her Trust A. The other $1.5 million of Wendy's property is transferred to Victor free of estate tax, because of the marital deduction. (See Chapter 15, Section C2.)

Example: Ben and Jamulla get married. Each has been married before. Ben has an estate worth $1 million, while Jamulla's is worth $2 million. They prepare a disclaimer AB trust. Jamulla dies in 2007, when the estate tax exemption is $2 million. However, Ben decides to disclaim only $1 million of Jamulla's property, because he wants to obtain the other million outright. If Jamulla had children from her first marriage and they were the final beneficiaries of Trust A, they may not be excited about Ben's decision.

d. Spouses Who Own Different Amounts of Property

Spouses who don't own equal amounts of property need to take that difference into account when setting up an AB trust. Even if the total value of the couple's property is worth less than their combined personal exemptions, if the value of one spouse's separate property plus her interest in shared property adds up to an amount large enough to owe estate tax, that spouse has estate planning decisions to make. Does she want to place all her property in her Trust A when she dies, and have some estate tax paid on her estate? Or does she want to leave anything over the exempt amount to her husband, free of tax under the marital deduction?

To save money on estate tax, wealthy couples with different-sized estates can create AB trusts designed to equalize the worth of the two estates. This way, the wealthier spouse's estate tax rate is lowered, because the estate tax rate goes up as the value of the estate increases. Overall, the estate tax paid will be less.

Example: Joe has a $3 million estate; his wife, Nelda, has $800,000 in assets. Joe's estate plan places $2 million in his Trust A and leaves the remaining $1 million outright to Nelda. No estate tax is due on this $1 million because of the marital deduction. If Joe dies first, his estate pays no taxes. Nelda receives the $1 million, making her estate worth $1.8 million. The taxable estates of the two spouses have been equalized, and overall estate tax will be lowered or eliminated.

NAMING AN AB TRUST AS THE BENEFICIARY OF YOUR RETIREMENT ACCOUNTS

If you have substantial assets in your retirement accounts, you may want to leave those accounts to your AB trust to avoid or reduce estate tax on the funds. To accomplish this, you simply name your trust (technically, the trustee) as the beneficiary of the retirement plan.

Example: Jacques and Amanda have a shared estate worth $3 million. They want to leave their property in an AB trust to avoid possible estate taxes on the survivor's estate. The bulk of their wealth is in two retirement accounts: Amanda's 401(k) is worth $1.2 million; Jacques's profit-sharing plan is worth $.8 million. Each names their AB trust as beneficiary of their retirement account, so no estate tax is ever owed on the funds.

If you're thinking about using a retirement account as a significant source of funds for an AB trust, keep in mind that individual retirement plans (except Roth IRAs) are "wasting accounts." Once you reach age 70 1/2 you must withdraw a certain percentage of the account each year. So, if you live well beyond 70, you may withdraw most or even all the funds in the account before your death. Still, you may understandably be concerned about what happens to your retirement account money if you die prematurely or if, for any reason, your account contains significant funds at your death. If it worries you, you may want to learn more about naming your AB trust as the beneficiary.

Learn the rules about naming an AB trust as beneficiary. There may be additional paperwork to complete to validly name your AB trust as beneficiary of your retirement plan. For example:

- Federal law requires that all funds in a 401(k) or 403(b) plan be left outright to a surviving spouse, unless that spouse has given a written waiver of that right.

- Retirement accounts purchased with community property are co-owned equally by both spouses. If you want all funds in such an account to go to your Trust A, you need a written agreement called a "declaration of gift," from your spouse.

A thorough explanation of the applicable laws and rules can be found in *IRAs, 401(k)s & Other Retirement Plans: Taking Your Money Out*, by Twila Slesnick and John C. Suttle (Nolo.) This book provides detailed coverage of rules governing withdrawals of retirement funds by named beneficiaries after the plan creator dies. It includes an explanation of what happens if a trust is the beneficiary.

D. BYPASS TRUSTS FOR UNMARRIED PEOPLE

Anyone, whether married or not, can use a life estate bypass trust. In either case, the trust document names a life beneficiary to receive specified rights to the trust property, and final beneficiaries to receive the trust property when the life beneficiary dies.

You may want to consider a bypass trust if both of the following are true:

- You want to leave property to someone for his or her life only, then outright to others.

- You trust the life beneficiary or someone else to serve as the successor trustee of the trust after you die, while the life beneficiary lives. This trustee must protect the rights of both the life beneficiary and the final beneficiaries.

1. Unmarried Couples

An unmarried couple can achieve the same overall estate tax savings with a bypass trust as can a married couple. The terminology is different; the trust isn't usually called an AB trust, the term applied to a married couple's trust. Instead, the trust is sometimes simply called a bypass trust or a "life estate trust."

Of course, the marital deduction is not available for unmarried couples. Any amount one of you owns in excess of your personal exemption will be subject to tax when you die, unless you simply leave it to charity or you use another estate tax-saving trust, such as a charitable remainder trust. (See Chapter 20.) Still, the estate tax savings an unmarried couple can achieve by using bypass trusts can be substantial.

Example 1: Ira and Selma, an unmarried couple, have no children. They've been together for over 30 years, and all of their combined estate of $2.9 million is held in shared ownership. Ira has a much younger brother to whom he's very close. Selma is equally close to two nieces. Ira and Selma each leave the other his or her property in a bypass trust, rather than outright, and names his or her own relatives as final beneficiaries of each one's life estate trust. As a result, they avoid estate tax, and each ensures that his or her property will eventually go to the desired final beneficiaries.

Example 2: Antonio and Gina are an unmarried couple with two children. Their combined estates total $2.6 million. They wish to provide support for each other for life and then leave their assets to their children. If the first to die leaves a $1.3 million share outright to the other, then on the survivor's death, some estate tax may be due, depending on the year of death. However, if each of them creates a bypass trust with the other as the life beneficiary, the children will eventually inherit all the property tax-free. This is because by establishing a bypass trust, both Gina's and Antonio's personal estate tax exemptions are used.

Example 3: Shizue and Takanori each own property worth $1.4 million. After one of them dies, they want the other to have the use of and the income from the deceased partner's property. But each also wants to preserve the bulk of his or her estate for other beneficiaries. Each creates a bypass trust consisting of all his or her property, with income from the trust going to the other for life. Also, each authorizes the other to use any amount of trust principal for health care or basic maintenance. At the second death, remaining assets in the trust will go to their respective relatives.

Shizue dies first, in 2006, and then Takanori dies in 2007. The exemption amount for each year is $2 million.

On Shizue's death:

Gross estate	$1.4 million
Estate tax due	$-0-

(because of her personal exemption)

On Takanori's death:

Gross estate	$1.4 million
Estate tax due	$-0-

(because of his personal exemption)

Takanori never owned the $1.4 million left by Shizue in her life estate trust, so it bypassed his estate for tax purposes. At his death, those assets pass tax free to the relatives Shizue named in her trust document.

Now, let's look at what would have happened without a trust, if each had just left everything to the other. On Shizue's death, no estate taxes are due because of her personal exemption.

On Takanori's death, however, you can see how not using a bypass trust costs their inheritors several hundred thousand dollars:

Gross estate	$2.8 million
Personal exemption	$2 million
Estate tax	$267,800

The $267,800 saved by using the bypass trust will go, eventually, to their final beneficiaries.

The savings would be even greater if the value of the property went up before Takanori's death. For example, if Takanori lived 15 more years, the value of Shizue's bypass trust property might rise to well over $2 million. That appreciation would pass to the final beneficiaries without further tax, because the property was already taxed when Shizue died.

2. Single People

A single person, not a member of a couple, usually isn't concerned with providing for another person for her or his life, then having property go to other final beneficiaries. And there usually isn't any reason to look for tax savings through a trust, since there is no one other person the single person might combine his estate with, as there often is with a couple. Still, a life estate bypass trust can prove every bit as effective in saving on eventual taxes for final beneficiaries as it is for a couple.

Example: Gustav, a bachelor, leaves all of his property, worth $2.1 million in a bypass trust with his younger brother Ludwig as the life beneficiary. At Ludwig's death, the assets are to go to Gustav's favorite two nephews, Ludwig's sons.

If Gustav dies when the personal estate tax exemption is $2 million (from 2006 through 2008), $100,000 of his property will be subject to tax. In 2009 and 2010, there will be no estate tax assessed. No matter what the size of Ludwig's estate, no estate tax will be due when the trust property is turned over to Gustav's nephews, after Ludwig dies, because Ludwig never actually owned the property. ■

19

OTHER ESTATE TAX-SAVING MARITAL TRUSTS

Because estate tax laws treat the married and unmarried differently, we do too. This chapter covers tax-saving trusts available only to the legally married. Unmarried people—whether couples or single—can skip this chapter.

To save on estate tax, married couples can take advantage of several kinds of trusts other than the AB trust discussed in Chapter 18. This chapter covers some of the most popular and useful kinds, including:

QTIP Trusts. A QTIP trust allows a married person to name the surviving spouse as the life beneficiary of trust property. When the second spouse dies, the property passes to final beneficiaries named by the first spouse. In federal tax jargon, this type of trust is called a Qualified Terminable Interest Property trust. Usually, this obtuse moniker is shortened to "QTIP." So far, a QTIP trust sounds just like an AB trust, right? What's different for QTIPs is that, when the first spouse dies, all the property in the trust is exempt from estate tax, no matter how much it's worth. This is because under IRS rules, property in the QTIP trust qualifies for the unlimited marital deduction.

However, property remaining in the QTIP trust when the second spouse dies is included in that spouse's estate for estate tax purposes. So taxes are postponed, not eliminated. The principal reasons for using a QTIP are to avoid paying any estate tax when the first spouse dies, which makes more money available to the survivor, and perhaps more importantly, to retain some control over who finally gets the property. This can be a significant concern in second or subsequent marriages.

QTIPs are most often used if spouses have a combined estate exceeding the estate tax threshold. As discussed, the personal estate tax exemption is $2 million for 2006 through 2008, then becomes $3.5 million for 2009, after which it is eliminated for one year. (See Chapter 15, Section A, for a thorough discussion of estate taxes.) Couples with estates worth less than the personal exemption amount generally need only an AB trust. However, in second or subsequent marriages, even when an estate is under the estate tax threshold, many people choose a QTIP trust. This is because the trust can provide income and limited support for a current spouse and preserve the remaining assets for children of a former marriage. Some estate plans consist of just a QTIP trust for all of a person's assets.

QDOT Trusts. If you're married to a noncitizen and have an estate worth more than the estate tax threshold that you want to leave to your spouse, consider a QDOT trust. (Section B.) This trust lets you defer estate tax until the death of the second spouse. Property left in any other manner to a noncitizen spouse does not qualify for the unlimited marital deduction, so any amount over the estate tax threshold is taxed.

Marital Deduction Trusts. These types of trusts have been largely replaced by QTIP trusts. The marital deduction trusts provide the estate tax postponement of a QTIP, but unlike a QTIP, permit the surviving spouse to name the final beneficiaries, make gifts of principals, and accumulate income. (Section C.)

A. QTIP TRUSTS

The four basic purposes of a QTIP trust are to:

- Postpone estate tax on the estate of the first spouse to die until the second spouse dies.

- Leave money and property for the use (but not outright ownership) of the surviving spouse.

- Name final beneficiaries to receive the trust property at the death of the surviving spouse. (These beneficiaries are often children or grandchildren, including those from a prior marriage.)

- Allow for some after-death (lawyers call it "postmortem") flexibility. As we discuss below, your executor (the person in charge of carrying out the terms of your will) can evaluate the estate tax situation and choose whether or not a QTIP you've created should actually become operational.

Find a knowledgeable lawyer. To prepare a QTIP trust, you need an expert estate planning lawyer. Many complex issues can arise when actually preparing the trust, and mistakes can cost a bundle in estate taxes. The IRS regularly refuses to grant trusts QTIP status because they didn't conform to all applicable federal regulations. If that happens, estate tax isn't postponed, and the major benefit of a QTIP is wasted. (For tips on finding a good lawyer, see Chapter 29, Section A.)

1. How QTIP Trusts Work

As we've said, a QTIP trust is similar in many aspects to an AB trust. In each case, a spouse is the grantor—that is, the person who creates the trust. Each spouse can create a separate QTIP trust for his or her property, whether it's separately owned property, half of shared property, or both. With all QTIPs and most AB trusts, the surviving spouse is the life beneficiary. The original grantor gets to name the final trust beneficiaries—normally, his or her children—to receive his or her trust property when the surviving spouse dies.

The big difference between these two types of trusts is that with a QTIP, no federal estate tax is assessed against trust property when the first spouse dies—no matter how much that property is worth. With a regular AB trust, property above the amount of the personal exemption for the year of death is subject to estate tax when the grantor dies, unless it goes directly to the surviving spouse.

You can use an AB trust and a QTIP trust together. Indeed, using these two trusts for each spouse is the foundation of the estate plans of some wealthier people. When the first spouse dies, property worth up to the amount of the personal exemption for that year is placed in a formula AB trust and is exempt from estate tax. The deceased spouse's remaining property goes into the QTIP trust, which is also exempt from tax. (Combining these two types of trusts in an estate plan is discussed further in Chapter 23, Section A.)

Example 1: Li-shan leaves $2 million in a formula AB trust and $500,000 in a QTIP trust, with her husband as life beneficiary of both trusts. When she dies in 2006, no federal estate tax is due. The $2 million in the AB trust is exempt because Li-shan's personal estate tax exemption for 2006 is $2 million. Property in the QTIP trust is exempt because it qualifies for the unlimited marital deduction. (Any property left in the QTIP trust will be taxed when Li-shan's husband dies.) By contrast, if Li-shan had left the entire $2.5 million in the AB trust, with her husband as life beneficiary, $500,000 of the AB trust would have been subject to estate tax when Li-shan died.

Example 2: Bernice, who is married to George, has an estate worth $2.6 million. She creates both a formula AB trust and a QTIP trust for her remaining assets. Using both trusts, she is able to use her personal estate tax exemption and postpone all taxes. If she left the entire $2.6 million in a QTIP trust, no estate tax would be due when she died, but the whole amount would be subject to tax at her husband's death. She would never use her personal exemption, and the estate tax savings the exemption offers would be lost.

QTIPs AT A GLANCE

- A QTIP trust creates a life estate for the surviving spouse, who is entitled to:
  - use trust assets, such as a residence, for her lifetime
  - receive trust income regularly, and
  - spend trust principal to the extent allowed by the trust document.
- In the trust document, the grantor names final beneficiaries, who will inherit the QTIP trust assets when the surviving spouse dies.
- No estate tax is assessed when the grantor dies.
- When the surviving spouse dies, the full net value of the property in the QTIP (as of that date) is included in her taxable estate.
- The QTIP assets do not go through probate after the death of the surviving spouse.

2. Long-Term Tax Consequences of QTIP Trusts

It's vital to understand that estate tax on QTIP trust property is not eliminated. As long as we have estate tax, when the second spouse dies, tax must be paid on all property in that spouse's estate. Under current tax law, this includes the full net worth of all property in the QTIP, valued as of the date of the surviving spouse's death.

Example: Sheila leaves property worth $2 million in a QTIP, with Atah, her husband, as life beneficiary. No tax is due at her death.

Atah has an estate of $1 million of his own and his total estate, now including property in the QTIP, is $3 million. He dies in 2006 when his personal exemption is $2 million. The $1 million in the QTIP (or whatever the amount is at the time) will be taxed.

Because all of the value of QTIP property is included in the taxable estate of the second spouse to die, the tax rate will almost always be higher than if the first spouse had left that property by other methods, including making use of her own personal exemption.

Example: Gregor leaves $500,000 in an AB trust and creates a QTIP trust for his wife, Natalie, with his children as final beneficiaries. When Gregor dies $2 million is placed in the QTIP. Natalie's separate estate is worth $1 million, and now her total estate will be $3.5 million ($1 million + $2.5 million = $3.5 million.) The tax rate on this sum will be higher than the rate that would have been applied to Gregor's total estate of $2.5 million.

If the property in the QTIP trust increases in value during the surviving spouse's life, that increase is subject to estate tax when that spouse dies. Again, this is not true for property in an AB trust. With an AB trust, the value of the trust property for tax purposes is determined only once, at the date of death of the grantor spouse.

Example: Ivan creates a QTIP trust with property that is worth $2 million when he dies. By the time his wife, Olga, dies two years later, the value of the trust property has risen to $3.6 million. This total 3.6 million is included in Olga's taxable estate.

3. Who Can Benefit From a QTIP Trust

QTIPs are popular with some estate planners. But why, given the possible tax drawbacks just discussed? Most importantly, because some wealthier couples decide that postponing tax payment until the second spouse dies is worth any eventual tax cost. They strongly do not want to have any of their estate eaten up by tax when the first spouse dies, even if more taxes are paid in the long run. Moreover, it's far from clear, usually, that it will cost more in the long run. With a QTIP, a surviving spouse who outlives the other by a significant period of time—say a few years or more—will receive income from all the deceased spouse's property, without having had any taken out to pay estate tax. This money the surviving spouse receives from the trust property may exceed any additional tax paid on that spouse's death.

But why use a QTIP instead of leaving property outright to the surviving spouse? Because one spouse or both prefers the control a QTIP provides—the power of the original grantor to name the final beneficiaries for the trust. A unique advantage of a QTIP trust is that it allows you to have the trust property treated, tax-wise, as if the surviving spouse inherited it outright using the marital deduction, and simultaneously allows you to impose controls over this property and specify who eventually inherits your share.

Finally, because each member of a couple can create separate AB trusts and QTIPs, neither spouse must sacrifice his or her personal estate tax exemption. Rather, the usual plan, as we've said, is for each spouse to create a formula AB trust to use his or her personal estate tax exemption, and a QTIP trust to postpone payment of estate tax on any additional property.

QTIPs are commonly used when one spouse in a second marriage is older and more affluent than the other. Typically, the wealthy spouse wants to provide adequate financial resources during the other

spouse's life, but also wants the trust property to go to kids from an earlier marriage after the surviving spouse's death. An AB trust alone won't work well here, because it depends on each spouse owning a significant part of the couple's property (as is usually the case in long-term marriages). But a QTIP does the job nicely. A full 100% of the wealthier spouse's property is available for the surviving spouse's use, as life beneficiary, because no estate tax is levied when the first spouse dies.

Example: Sam, who is in his late 70s, has assets worth $2.3 million when he marries Angela, his second wife. She has very little property of her own. If Sam dies before Angela does, he wants to be sure she is provided for, but he also wants to ensure that his children from his previous marriage are the final beneficiaries of his property.

Sam feels that Angela may need all the income his $2.3 million could provide. For this reason, he does not want to create only an AB trust for his estate, part of which may be taxed on his death. Also, Sam does not want to leave Angela money outright (which he could do, tax free, because of the marital deduction) because he wants to preserve his property, to the extent possible, for his children.

So Sam creates a QTIP trust, containing all of his assets, that will become effective at his death. Angela is the life beneficiary. Sam designates his children as the trust's final beneficiaries, to receive all that's left when Angela dies. No tax will be due at Sam's death (if Angela is still alive) because all property in a QTIP trust takes advantage of the unlimited marital deduction. Income from the trust property will go to Angela for her life. Also, if he chooses, Sam can specify that trust principal can be used for Angela's "support, education, health, or maintenance" in any amount. Or, at the other extreme, he can greatly restrict invasion of the principal, to try to ensure that it's conserved for his children. (See Section 4, below.)

If you are in a second or subsequent marriage, you may be concerned with balancing the interests and needs of your current spouse and your children from a former marriage. (See Chapter 24.) Exactly how these needs sort out depends on each situation; there is more than one good way to use a QTIP trust in estate plans.

Example: Sol is married to Rosalie and has two children from a previous marriage. His estate is worth $3 million. He creates a QTIP trust of $2 million to take effect at his death. All of the income from the trust will be paid to Rosalie for her lifetime, and at her death the assets of the trust will go to his children.

Sol also leaves $500,000 outright to each child. No estate tax will be due on this $1 million because of Sol's personal estate tax exemption.

Thanks to the marital deduction no tax is due on the $2 million in the QTIP trust. At Rosalie's death, the trust principal—the amount as of the date of her death—will be counted as part of her taxable estate.

4. The Surviving Spouse's Rights

The surviving spouse must receive the sole right to all income from property in the QTIP trust. Also, the surviving spouse must have the right to require that the trustee sell non-income-producing property and invest the sale proceeds in income-producing assets. If the spouse doesn't have these rights, the IRS will rule that the QTIP property doesn't qualify for the marital deduction.

a. The Right to Receive All Trust Income

The surviving spouse must receive all of the income from an operational QTIP trust. There are no exceptions to this rule. The trustee (who is usually the surviving spouse) must distribute all income periodically (at least annually) to the spouse, and cannot accumulate income in the trust. If the surviving spouse becomes incapacitated, the trustee must spend the income for the spouse's benefit.

As long as the surviving spouse lives, the trustee of a QTIP trust cannot spend any of the principal or income from the trust for the benefit of anyone else. In general, this rule protects both the surviving spouse, who receives a continuing income, and the final beneficiaries, who are to later receive the trust principal.

But occasionally it can be troublesome. For example, suppose the surviving spouse remarries or earns a very large amount of money and no longer really needs the trust income. The spouse might want to end the trust and have its principal distributed to the final beneficiaries. Can't be done. A QTIP trust cannot end until the second spouse dies.

Or suppose that one of the final beneficiaries really needs some money from the trust, and the surviving spouse wants to give it. Officially, the trust's income, as well as the principal, cannot be spent directly on anyone else during the surviving spouse's lifetime. If the surviving spouse wants to help out, she must do so indirectly. Since all trust income is hers to do with as she wishes, once she receives some income, she can give it to the needy final beneficiary. But this is a legal gift, subject to gift taxes. Also, she won't be able to channel any of the principal to the final beneficiary.

Example: Alice creates a QTIP trust to become operational at her death, with the income going to her husband, Mark. He has no rights to spend trust principal. At Mark's death, the assets of the trust will pass to her five children from two previous marriages.

Mark has a substantial estate himself, and several years after Alice dies, he remarries a very wealthy woman. But the income from the trust must continue to go to him. Meanwhile, Alice's oldest son, Edward, has business trouble and desperately needs money to keep afloat. Because the trustee cannot obtain any of the principal of the QTIP trust for the son's benefit, even though Mark wants this, the business fails. This is hardly what Alice would have wanted. (Of course, Mark can give the income from the trust to the son, after he receives it, but he cannot touch trust principal.)

Defining income and principal. When any beneficiary, such as a spouse, will serve as trustee, make sure that your trust document spells out what is income for the trust and what will be principal. If you don't, state law will do it for you and may defeat your intentions. For instance, in some states, dividends that have automatically been reinvested will be treated as principal. The spouse may need those dividends for living expenses. Discuss this with your lawyer.

b. The Right to Demand That Trust Property Produce Income

You can put any kind of property into a QTIP—a house, furniture, money, stock, even a business—but, as mentioned, the surviving spouse has the right to demand that any non-income-producing property be converted into a form of property that does produce income. So if the trust includes a safe deposit box full of gold coins or a collection of valuable antique chairs, the surviving spouse can demand they be sold and the profits invested in income-producing property.

Example: Gretchen creates a QTIP trust and names her husband, Lloyd, as the life beneficiary. The trust assets consist of stocks, bonds, a residence, and a vacation home. After Gretchen's death, Lloyd decides that the income is not enough for him to live on in the manner he's used to. Using his authority as trustee, he sells the vacation home and invests the proceeds in property that yields income, such as bonds.

SUMMARY: IRS REQUIREMENTS FOR A VALID QTIP TRUST

In order to qualify as a valid QTIP trust under federal law (I.R.C. § 2056(b)(7)), the trust document must specify all of the following:

- All income from the trust must be distributed to the surviving spouse at least annually.

- The spouse can demand that the trust property be converted to income-producing property.

- No one, not even the surviving spouse, may spend principal for the benefit of anybody but the spouse.

- The executor of the deceased spouse's estate must elect, on the deceased's federal estate tax return, to have the trust be treated as a QTIP.

---

5. Powers That May Be Given to the Surviving Spouse

Now we move on to powers a grantor is allowed by the IRS to include in a QTIP, but that are not mandatory.

a. The Power to Spend Trust Principal

As we've stated, a surviving spouse must receive all the income from property in a QTIP trust. There is no flexibility here. But when it comes to permitting the spouse to spend (invade) principal, it's a different story—you have great flexibility.

Because the surviving spouse is considered, for estate tax purposes, the owner of all property in the QTIP, you can give her the right to invade trust principal for her benefit for any reason she wants, for any amount she wants. (This is another way in which a QTIP trust differs from an AB trust.) However, it's unusual to grant such broad power to spend trust principal. After all, this, in effect, leaves the property outright to the surviving spouse. If that's what you want, just do it directly, and no estate tax will be imposed at your death because of the marital deduction. Most QTIP trust grantors want to impose some restrictions on the surviving spouse to protect the principal for the final beneficiaries.

Sometimes, the surviving spouse is given no right to spend trust principal, period. In other situations, the right to invade principal is defined very specifically and narrowly, such as for emergency health care only. Or the trust document may limit the right to spend trust principal to the IRS "objective need" standard, allowing invasion only when necessary for the surviving spouse's "education, health, support, or maintenance." (IRS Reg. 20.2041-1(c)(2).)

If the surviving spouse has the right to spend trust principal, there's an inherent risk of conflict between the spouse and the final beneficiaries, so the trust document creating the trust should be very specific about the spouse's rights. The last thing you want is a fight over what assets can and cannot be used, or what standard the spouse must meet to justify spending principal.

The surviving spouse frequently serves as trustee of a QTIP trust. If, however, broad invasion powers are granted, you may want to name a disinterested party as trustee or cotrustee, to avoid or at least reduce the chances of hostility and conflict between the beneficiaries.

⚠ Keep an eye on the estate tax threshold.
As mentioned above, many people, especially those in second or subsequent marriages, create a formula AB trust (see Chapter 18), the A trust holding the personal exemption amount and any assets remaining over the exemption going into a QTIP for the spouse. Often, the exemption trust (the A trust) imposes strict controls on the surviving spouse, particularly restricting invasion of the Trust A principal. If you are planning such an approach, it is crucial that you pay close attention to the rising personal exemption rate. (See Chapter 15, Section A.) Remember that in a formula trust, the amount that will fund the exemption trust automatically adjusts to the estate tax threshold in the year of death. For midsized estates, this could result in a disaster for the surviving spouse. Suppose, for example, that you have a total estate of $2 million and die in 2008. By that time, the exemption amount will be $2 million and nothing whatsoever will be left to fund the QTIP. If you have already created such a plan—and many people have under the old tax laws—you will probably want to amend it to allow enough available funds for your spouse.

b. The "5 and 5" Power

The "5 and 5" power is a distinct right that allows the spouse to get $5,000 or 5% of the trust principal, whichever is greater, each year. There are no restrictions on how the surviving spouse can spend this money.

The surviving spouse does not have to use this 5 and 5 right in any given year. But if it is not used in a particular year, that year's right is lost. In other words, the right does not accumulate from year to year.

Example: Isabelle is the trustee and life beneficiary of a QTIP trust established by her late husband. The trust document includes a 5 and 5 power. If she doesn't exercise this right this year, she cannot take an extra 5% or $5,000 out of the trust principal next year.

The 5 and 5 power is not currently used much by sophisticated estate planners; it is usually better to use more controlled methods of allowing the surviving spouse access to the trust principal. (This is discussed in Chapter 18, Section B.)

c.   The Power to Distribute Trust Property Among Beneficiaries

One of the most important features of a QTIP trust is the power of the original grantor to control who gets the trust assets when the surviving spouse dies. Often, a grantor specifies that the assets go to his or her children. But a trusted spouse who survives many years after the other spouse's death may be in a far better position to know just which individuals in a group of final beneficiaries designated by the grantor need more than others, or which ones don't really need an inheritance at all. With a QTIP trust, the grantor can choose the group of possible final beneficiaries, but let the surviving spouse decide how much each one actually inherits. The surviving spouse formally makes this decision in her living trust or will. In legal terms, this is called giving the spouse "a limited power of appointment" over the assets in the trust.

Example: Sara is married to Emmanuel, nine years younger than she is. Sara fully trusts Emmanuel and is confident he loves her family. Sara has two children, Alison and Lori, from a prior marriage. When Sara prepares her QTIP, Alison has two young children (and wants more) and Lori is single. Sara wants to provide for her own children but also leave direct gifts to her grandchildren.

She specifies that her children and grandchildren will be the final beneficiaries of her QTIP trust. She provides that each daughter will receive 30% of the trust property, and that the remaining 40% shall be divided among all her grandchildren when final distribution of the trust assets is made. She doesn't want to specify the precise divisions now because there may be (she hopes) additional grandchildren. And if Emmanuel survives her by a considerable time, she believes he will be in a far better position to decide how much money should be given to each grandchild. So she gives Emmanuel authority to make the decision regarding actual distribution to the grandchildren.

Allowing the spouse to make such a decision can produce a fair and just distribution—one that may not have been foreseeable when the trust was created. One child may have completely dedicated himself to the family business, another may have special needs, and yet another child may have amassed such wealth that he needs less than the others. However, granting this power to the spouse is not very common in QTIPs. Most grantors want absolute control over who the final beneficiaries are. But if you have complete confidence in your spouse's judgment, granting this power can be sensible, especially when some desired beneficiaries are very young (or even unborn) when the trust is prepared.

6. The "QTIP Election"

A unique aspect of QTIPs is that the executor you name in your will must elect, on your federal estate tax return, to place property you left in a QTIP into that trust. Your executor has the final say here. You cannot require that he elect QTIP tax treatment for your property. If your executor doesn't properly make the QTIP election, no valid QTIP trust exists, period.

The QTIP election itself amounts to marking the correct box on the estate tax return and then listing the property that is to go into the trust. Seems simple, but it has surely been done wrong. In one case, an executor hurriedly filed an estate tax return, forgot to mark the box and then sought IRS permission to file an amended return electing a QTIP. Nope, said the IRS, which sometimes seems to take special delight in denying proposed QTIP trusts eligibility for the marital deduction.

Deciding how and whether to make the QTIP election can be difficult. The executor has several choices:

- not to elect the QTIP

- elect that all property the deceased left in the (possible) QTIP trust actually be treated as QTIP property, or

- elect to have only a portion of the trust property treated as a QTIP—for example, the executor can elect to have 60% of the trust property treated as a QTIP and 40% not. That 40% may then be subject to estate tax at the first death.

These options make possible a great deal of strategic after-death tax planning. Key tax decisions can be made in light of current circumstances rather than being frozen years before. But in some family situations, it can require the wisdom of Solomon (not to mention high-quality tax advice) to decide which election option to take.

For larger estates, this QTIP election is sometimes used to equalize the value of each spouse's estate. For example, sometimes it makes estate tax sense to choose not to elect a QTIP and allow the deceased spouse's possible QTIP trust property to be included in the taxable estate. If electing the QTIP would result in the surviving spouse's estate being much larger than that of the first spouse to die, higher overall estate tax would be paid. So in such a case, after the first spouse's death, the executor might elect to go ahead and pay any estate tax assessed against that deceased spouse's property, because the tax rate is lower on this amount of property than it would be if this property were combined, for estate tax purposes, with the surviving spouse's.

This means the surviving spouse must accept tax payments now in exchange for overall tax savings later. Usually, the surviving spouse is the executor and is in charge of making this decision. But if the surviving spouse isn't the executor, and the two disagree, there can be a real power struggle.

Another option is for the executor to elect to have only a percentage of the deceased spouse's property receive QTIP treatment. This is called a partial QTIP election. This, too, can be used to lower overall estate tax. Any percentage of the trust property not elected for QTIP treatment usually remains in the trust for the surviving spouse's benefit, but it does not receive QTIP estate tax treatment. Estate tax is paid on the portion not elected. In this case, two separate financial records must be kept—one for the trust property that is QTIP property and another for property that is not.

 Directing QTIP property to someone other than the surviving spouse. If you want to direct in your will or living trust that any unelected QTIP property goes to someone other than the surviving spouse, you'll need to consult an expert estate planning lawyer. The law in this area is complicated and unclear.

Making a partial QTIP election, instead of a full one, can make a big difference, tax-wise.

Example: Ben has an estate worth $2 million. He is married to Gloria and has children from a first marriage. Gloria has her own property worth $2 million. Ben leaves his $2 million in a QTIP for Gloria, with the income to go to her and the assets to go later to the children from his first marriage. Ben dies in 2007, when the personal exemption is $2 million. At Ben's death, if the executor elects the full QTIP, these are the tax consequences:

On Ben's death:

Ben's gross estate	$2 million
QTIP property	$2 million
Tax due	-0-

Gloria dies in 2009 when the personal exemption is $3.5 million.

On Gloria's death:

Gloria's gross estate	$4 million
Amount subject to estate tax	$500,000

Now suppose that the executor elects to have only 50% of Ben's property qualify for QTIP tax treatment.

On Ben's death:

Ben's gross estate	$2 million
Property given marital deduction for half of QTIP treatment	$1 million
Tax due	-0-

On Gloria's death:

Gloria's gross estate	$3 million
Amount subject to estate tax	-0-

By electing to have only half of the trust property qualify for the QTIP, money is saved for the final beneficiaries. Electing a full QTIP would cause Gloria's estate to be taxed when she dies.

A number of issues can contribute to the decision your executor makes regarding the QTIP election. One factor is simply that circumstances may have changed (indeed, they always do, according to the Buddha and Heraclitus) since you prepared the QTIP trust. Your original estate plan may not be the most financially desirable one after your death.

Example: Steve has an estate worth about $1 million. He drafts a QTIP trust for $900,000 of his assets and leaves $100,000 outright to his son Zack. His wife, Esther, has property of her own worth about $200,000. She will get the income from both trusts, and the principal from both will go to Zack upon Esther's death.

Several years later, Esther inherits property worth $2 million, raising the value of her own estate to $2.2 million. Steve neglects to revise his estate plan. When Steve dies, if the QTIP trust goes into effect, Esther's estate will now be worth over $3 million for tax purposes—well over the amount of the personal exemption until the year 2009.

Let's assume Steve dies in 2007 so his personal exemption is $2 million. His executor looks at the whole picture and decides not to make a QTIP election at all. This means that $900,000 will still go into trust subject to the exact terms of the QTIP.

The property will be subject to estate tax immediately, but no tax is due because of Steve's personal exemption. Esther will still get the income from the trust, and Zack will still inherit the principal when she dies.

Making a partial QTIP election has significant drawbacks, however. An executor can make a partial QTIP election only in terms of a percentage or fraction of the total property originally left for the QTIP. For example, a trustee can elect to have 40%, or 63%, or one-third of the total property originally left for the QTIP actually qualify for QTIP tax treatment. What the executor can't do is name specific assets to be included in or excluded from the QTIP. The IRS simply doesn't allow that kind of maneuvering. The executor can of course decide what assets he or she wants to exclude, figure out the percentage and then take out those assets to make up the excluded amount, but it must be reported as a fractional percentage, not as specific items of property.

The real world consequences of a partial QTIP election can be difficult. For example, there can be much paperwork if two-thirds of your house is owned by a QTIP trust and one-third owned by another trust. Also, it can complicate matters like real estate tax or refinancing. Because of the complexities, many sophisticated estate planners do not usually recommend partial QTIP elections.

7. The Reverse QTIP Election

A "reverse QTIP election" is a special legal procedure designed to avoid losing the personal exemption because of another tax imposed on gifts and bequests that skip generations. (See Chapter 21, Section A.) Without a reverse QTIP election, as long as estate tax exists, all assets that are left by a grandparent to a grandchild (skipping the middle generation) or in other generation-skipping plans are subject to an extra tax, called the Generation-Skipping Transfer Tax or GSTT.

Sometimes a QTIP trust leaves the trust principal, at the death of the surviving spouse, to the grantor's grandchildren or other beneficiaries more than one generation away. When this happens, the law considers the surviving spouse (the life beneficiary) the one transferring the property for GSTT purposes. This means that an inheritance worth up to the amount of the surviving spouse's GSTT exemption can go to the grandchildren GSTT-free. However, when the first spouse's executor makes a reverse QTIP election, the first spouse who died is legally the person who makes the eventual transfer to the grandchildren. This preserves that first spouse's GSTT exemption and allows the second spouse to transfer another amount to grandchildren free of the Generation-Skipping Transfer Tax.

This reverse QTIP election relates only to generation-skipping trusts and the Generation-Skipping Transfer Tax. It is an entirely separate matter from the basic QTIP election, where the executor decides whether or not to use a QTIP, and if so, how much property to actually place in the QTIP trust.

8. Planning for a QTIP

You must plan for and create a QTIP trust document before you die. No one has any authority to create one for you, and obtain its estate-tax postponing advantages, after you die.

A vital decision you must make is who will be the trustee, or trustees, of your QTIP trust. The trustee usually is your surviving spouse, but a grown child or someone else entirely can serve. Above all, choose the person you trust the most—and, of course, one who is willing to take the job.

If you plan to choose your spouse, ask yourself these questions: Do you fully trust your spouse to protect the trust principal, your final beneficiaries' inheritance? Do your final beneficiaries feel the same way? If the answer is "no," or you're not positive, perhaps a child should serve as cotrustee. Or, if you believe one of your children (and not your spouse) has the wisdom to best balance the needs of the surviving spouse against the final beneficiaries' rights to their eventual inheritance, you may want to name the child as sole trustee.

Obviously, there's no one-size-fits-all answer when it comes to choosing the trustee. A good lawyer may be able to help, by focusing your attention on your personal situation, but the final decision is definitely yours. (Choosing a trustee is discussed in Chapter 17, Section F.)

Remember also that the executor of your will has the authority to decide whether or not property in the trust should actually receive QTIP treatment. So it's common to have your QTIP trustee be the same person as your executor.

Since by law you cannot deny the executor the power to decide whether or not to elect QTIP tax treatment for property you include in your QTIP trust, it's obviously vital that you have an executor you trust completely to make the best judgment in light of the interests of all trust beneficiaries—life beneficiary and final beneficiary.

B. TRUSTS FOR NONCITIZEN SPOUSES: QDOTs

If you are married to someone who is not a citizen of the United States, property you leave to that spouse is not entitled to the unlimited marital deduction. In plain English, as long as estate tax exists, you cannot leave your noncitizen spouse an unlimited amount of money free of federal estate tax. The rule applies even if the noncitizen spouse is a legal resident of this country. Congress wanted to prevent noncitizen spouses from inheriting large amounts of money and then leaving the country with no U.S. estate tax ever being collected.

What can you do if you want to leave a large estate to a noncitizen spouse? First, it may make excellent sense to have the noncitizen spouse become a U.S. citizen. Usually this is possible, given some time. If, for whatever reason, a spouse doesn't obtain U.S. citizenship, there is one very important estate tax exemption that can be used by a citizen spouse for property left to a noncitizen spouse.

The personal estate tax exemption is available to each spouse, no matter who inherits the property. (See Chapter 15, Section A, for a table listing the amounts for each year.) So a citizen can leave her noncitizen spouse property worth up to the amount of her personal tax exemption in the year of death free of federal estate tax. Any amount over that left outright by a U.S. spouse to a noncitizen spouse is subject to estate tax.

However, all property, no matter how much it's worth, left by one spouse to a noncitizen spouse in what's called a "Qualified Domestic Trust" (QDOT) is allowed the marital deduction. (I.R.C. § 2056(A).) The federal estate tax that would otherwise be assessed on property in a QDOT is deferred until the noncitizen spouse dies. QDOTs are used only by spouses with an estate exceeding the estate tax threshold, because only these estates must pay federal estate tax.

 The rules governing QDOTs, estate tax, and noncitizen spouses are complicated. The U.S. has estate tax treaties with some countries that allow you to choose between the provisions of the treaty or the provisions discussed here. If you're married to a noncitizen and have an estate worth more than the estate tax threshold, you must get expert help with your estate plan.

Strict federal laws govern QDOT trusts. For example, if any trust principal is distributed to the noncitizen spouse during her life, estate tax is assessed on the amount distributed. So if the trust pays $150,000 from principal for a spouse's new boat, that amount is immediately subject to estate tax. There is a special exemption from estate tax for QDOT principal distributions to the noncitizen surviving spouse in cases of "hardship." The IRS defines hardship as an immediate need relating to health, maintenance, education, or support that cannot be met with other reasonable means.

For instance, if $150,000 were paid to the spouse from the QDOT for medical care (instead of a boat), the full amount would be exempt from estate tax if no other reasonable means of paying for this care were available. This is decided on a case-by-case basis. It's pretty awful to have the IRS so intimately involved in your daily living, but QDOTs can lead to such a situation.

Income the noncitizen spouse receives from the QDOT trust is taxable as regular income. Of course, this is true for any person, whether a U.S. citizen or not, for income received from any ongoing trust.

When the surviving noncitizen spouse dies, the QDOT trust assets are subject to estate tax. The tax is based on the value of the assets in the trust when the noncitizen spouse dies. Any increase in value in the trust property during the life of the surviving spouse is subject to estate tax on that spouse's death, unlike property in an AB trust.

GIFTS TO NONCITIZEN SPOUSES

Under a special gift tax regulation, a citizen spouse can currently give up to $120,000 per year (adjusted annually for inflation), free of gift tax, to a noncitizen spouse while both are living. (IRS Reg. 2523(i)(2).) By contrast, if both spouses were citizens of the U.S., they could give any amount to each other, free of gift tax. (See Chapter 16, Section A.) While the annual $120,000 exemption for gifts to noncitizen spouses is more limited than for gifts to citizen spouses, it is still a substantial amount. A U.S. citizen with an estate that's likely to owe estate tax should consider making large annual gifts to the noncitizen spouse.

A valid QDOT trust must meet all of the requirements of any trust that qualifies for the marital deduction, including:

- The surviving spouse must be entitled to receive all income from the trust.

- The QDOT trust must be "elected" by the executor of the grantor's estate on the estate tax return.

In addition, the QDOT must also meet the following special requirements:

- At least one of the trustees of the trust must be either a U.S. citizen or a U.S. corporation. Thus, the surviving spouse cannot be the sole trustee.

- The trust must comply with applicable IRS regulations. These regulations impose special security requirements (such as posting a bond or providing a letter of credit when the trustee is an individual) on QDOTs in excess of $2 million.

Example: Juan, a U.S. citizen, has an estate worth $2 million. He is married to Maria, who is a legal resident of the United States but not a citizen. Juan's estate plan includes an outright bequest to Maria of the amount that is exempt from federal estate tax because of Juan's personal exemption. The remaining assets will go into a QDOT trust for Maria's benefit during her life, and will be distributed, at her death, to their children. Juan appoints his brother Ricardo, who is a U.S. citizen, to serve as cotrustee with Maria of the QDOT trust. (Juan could also use a U.S. bank or other institution as a cotrustee.)

At Juan's death, his executor makes the election for the QDOT trust on Juan's federal estate tax return. No estate tax is due at this time because of the personal tax exemption and the QDOT trust. Maria will receive all of the income from the trust for her life and may receive necessary principal for her support. If she receives principal, it will be subject to estate tax upon distribution. At Maria's death, the assets remaining in the trust will be taxed.

The QDOT rules have one opening that is an incentive to a noncitizen spouse to become a U.S. citizen. If the spouse becomes a citizen before the deceased spouse's estate tax return is filed (generally, nine months after the death) or before any distribution of principal is made to the noncitizen spouse, property in the trust will receive the full marital deduction, and assets may be invaded during the spouse's lifetime without paying estate tax. The trust is no longer a QDOT, and the remaining assets will be subject to tax only when the surviving spouse dies.

A unique and extremely helpful aspect of a QDOT trust is that it doesn't necessarily have to be created before the grantor's death. If someone who is married to a noncitizen prepared a trust before the

federal QDOT law went into effect in 1988, or just didn't know about the law, the surviving noncitizen spouse can request of the IRS that the estate plan be "reformed" to meet the guidelines of a QDOT trust. For example, if a citizen simply left all property outright to a noncitizen spouse, the spouse can request the creation of a QDOT trust and obtain an estate tax deferment for the property.

C. MARITAL DEDUCTION TRUSTS

Before 1981, when the IRS authorized the use of QTIP trusts, a marital deduction trust (I.R.C. § 2056(b)(5)) was the mainstay of estate plans for many couples. These trusts are similar to QTIP trusts in that taxes on trust property can be postponed until the death of the surviving spouse, and the surviving spouse is the life beneficiary of the trust. Before QTIP trusts, they were the only way to obtain the full marital deduction and retain control of the property during the life of the surviving spouse. In the past, these trusts were especially used to manage business affairs of the husband when the wife had no knowledge or interest in them.

Today, the QTIP trust has replaced these other trusts in popularity, but marital deduction trusts are still very useful in situations where one of their special features is desired.

You may want to create a marital deduction trust if:

• You want your spouse to be able to give away trust principal to someone else (such as a child) during the spouse's lifetime.

• You want your spouse to choose who will inherit trust property after the spouse's death.

• You want the trust to hold property that is non-income producing. In one type of trust, the spouse cannot demand that the property be sold to produce income, as can the spouse under a QTIP trust.

- The trust will hold property such as a business and will need to reinvest the income, rather than pay it regularly to the surviving spouse.

Get help with a marital deduction trust. Marital deduction trusts are quite technical and must comply with applicable tax law and IRS rules. These trusts must be drafted by experts experienced with this type of trust.

Like a QTIP, one spouse creates a trust, naming the other spouse the life beneficiary. Trust property qualifies for the marital deduction, so no estate tax on property in the trust is paid when the first spouse dies. The trust property that remains when the second spouse dies is included in the taxable estate of the surviving spouse.

There are two types of marital deduction trusts. Let's look at each.

1. Power of Appointment Trusts

A "power of appointment" trust names the spouse as the lifetime beneficiary. As in a QTIP trust, the spouse is entitled to receive trust income and can require that trust property be converted to income-producing property. But to use this type of trust, you must give your surviving spouse either the right to invade the trust principal for any reason or to name the beneficiaries (including the spouse's own estate) that will receive the trust property at your spouse's death or during his or her life. This is called a "power of appointment." (See also Chapter 25, Section F.) This is in direct contrast to a QTIP trust, where you can, and normally do, limit the right to invade principal and you name the final beneficiaries.

The flexibility of invading principal and giving gifts of principal can be very attractive. When you prepare your trust, it may not be at all clear whether your surviving spouse will need access to the trust principal. Perhaps one or more of the final beneficiaries will genuinely need some of the trust principal while the surviving spouse is alive. One way to handle these uncertainties is to create a power of appointment trust and give the spouse power to make gifts of principal.

Example: Peter drafts a power of appointment trust for his wife, Lisa. Lisa will receive all income from the trust and can choose who will inherit the assets at her death. During her life, Lisa is authorized to give trust principal to each of their two children.

After Peter dies, Lisa is quite well off from other sources, but one of their children loses his job, and he and his family are threatened with eviction from their recently purchased home. Lisa decides to distribute $30,000 of trust principal to the child, bailing him out of this crisis.

This gift is a taxable event for estate tax purposes. Since the trust property will be part of Lisa's taxable estate, she will use part of her personal estate/gift tax exemption by making this distribution. Even if the estate tax disappears after 2009, gift tax may be due on the amount. (See Chapter 16, Section A, for an explanation of the unified gift and estate tax system.)

The spouse doesn't have to have both an unlimited power to invade principal and a power to name beneficiaries. Just one of the powers, such as the power to choose who inherits trust property, is all that is required.

If you give your spouse the right to name final beneficiaries of the trust property, you can then limit any powers to invade principal. For instance, the document could name only certain people (like the children) who could receive principal. Or, you can choose not to grant the power to invade principal to anyone, including the spouse.

The surviving spouse does not have to use the powers granted by the trust document. For example, you can designate the final beneficiaries, and if your spouse does nothing to change them, the property will pass to those you have chosen.

2. Estate Trusts

An "estate" trust is a special type of marital deduction trust requiring that when the surviving spouse dies, all remaining trust principal must go into his or her estate. This means that the surviving spouse gets to choose the final beneficiaries, such as by will or within a living trust. Also, the estate trust property will go through probate on the death of the surviving spouse. What makes this trust special is that the trust property can be, and remain, non-income-producing. In all of the other trusts that defer taxes because of the marital deduction (including QTIP trusts), this is not possible.

Example: Suzanne's property holdings include several acres of woodland and a small house by a river. Suzanne grew up spending much happy time on this land (and in the river) and she wants to be sure the land is preserved for her children, if possible. As it is now, the land is not income producing, and the house has no electricity and only rudimentary plumbing. Suzanne doesn't want the property improved or sold, so she leaves the land in a marital deduction estate trust. Specific directions in the trust document state that the land may not be sold while the trust lasts.

The other feature of this type of trust is that when the trust property does produce income, it does not have to be paid out to the spouse. At the trustee's option, the income can be accumulated, increasing the amount of the trust principal. If this occurs, income is taxed at the trust's higher tax rate. But for some purposes, this disadvantage may well be offset by allowing for business growth or other investment purposes.

Example: Arturo owns a large auto repair business with his brother, Sol. He leaves his share in an estate trust with his wife, Gilda, as life beneficiary. No tax is due because of the marital deduction. Sol will serve as trustee and manage the firm, reinvest income, and guide the business growth. Gilda directs by her will that at her death, the trust property will go to their children. ■

20

CHARITABLE TRUSTS

If you want to make a gift, especially a substantial one, to a charity, using a charitable trust may allow you to do it in a way that gives you significant tax benefits. As you'll see, there are several charitable trusts to choose from, and all can offer real financial advantages.

Even after Congress passed the Tax Relief Act of 2001, estate tax savings can still be important. (See Chapter 15 for a detailed discussion of estate taxes.) And although the Act lowered the highest income tax brackets, a little extra income tax relief is always welcome. Besides offering estate and income tax advantages, estate planners see charitable trusts as a good tool for both being generous and providing retirement income.

That said, if your basic estate planning goals are to pass on your property to family or friends, leave a few minor charitable gifts, and pay less estate tax, then a charitable trust is probably not for you. The income tax and estate tax breaks charitable trusts can offer probably won't make up for the amount of property that must be given to a charity instead of your family.

A. AN OVERVIEW OF CHARITABLE TRUSTS

There are two basic types of charitable trusts, each with its own obtuse name:

- charitable remainder trusts, including popular pooled charitable trusts (I.R.C. § 664), and

- charitable lead trusts (IRC §§ 664 and 671).

These trusts have certain features in common:

They can become operational while you are alive. To gain the maximum tax advantages, most people create charitable trusts during their life, in their highest income-producing years. A basic purpose of these charitable trusts is not simply to make a gift to a charity, but also to provide some

income, often later on in life (or other benefits) to you or to someone else you choose.

They are irrevocable. Once you create a charitable trust and it becomes operational, it is irrevocable. You cannot change your mind and regain legal control of the property you have given to the trust.

Only tax-exempt charities are eligible. In order to obtain the tax benefits, you must make your gift to a charity that is approved by the IRS. Normally, this means a charity that has gained tax-exempt status under Section 501(c)(3) of the Internal Revenue Code. The IRS maintains a long list of acceptable public charities, which include educational institutions, research organizations, and well-known organizations like United Way or CARE. Usually, the easiest way to determine whether the charity you want to make a gift to is an approved organization is to check IRS's public charities list in IRS Publication 78. You may be able to find a copy of Publication 78 in your local library's reference section; it's not currently available online. Or, you can call the IRS at 800-829-1040 to ask whether a particular organization is tax exempt.

You get an income tax break. The value of the charitable gift is deductible from your income tax. (See Section B, below.)

Now let's take a quick look at the two kinds of trusts.

1. The Basics of Charitable Remainder Trusts

With a charitable remainder trust, you give property to an irrevocable trust and name an income beneficiary and a final beneficiary. The final beneficiary is always the charity.

The income beneficiary can be (and often is) yourself, but it can be your spouse, mate, child, or anyone else. There can be more than one income beneficiary. This person (or persons) receives a set payment from the trust or a set percentage of the worth of trust property for the term defined in the trust. For example, the income beneficiary might receive 7% of the value of the trust per year, or a fixed sum of $8,000 per year. However, you cannot give the income beneficiary the right to receive all trust income, except in certain situations if the income beneficiary is your spouse.

You state, in the trust document, how long the income beneficiary will receive income from the trust property. This payment period can be a set number of years, or until the income beneficiary dies. At most, the income beneficiaries can have only the right to receive trust income during their lives. They never legally own the trust property, and it can never be included in their taxable estates.

The charity itself is usually the trustee of the trust property. As trustee, the charity is responsible for making proper payments to the income beneficiary. Usually, the charity converts any non-income-producing property, such as raw land or artwork, into income-producing property.

Money received by the income beneficiary may be subject to gift tax. If an income beneficiary is anyone other than you or your spouse, the payments from the trust are considered a taxable gift from you to that person. Currently, if more than $12,000 in income is received per year, you will be assessed gift tax on the excess over $12,000 and will have to file a federal gift tax return. (See Chapter 16 for more information about gift taxes.)

Establishing a charitable trust can give your inheritors an estate tax break. When the trust assets become solely owned by the charity—that is, when the income beneficiary's interest ends—they are no longer part of your taxable estate.

Charitable remainder trusts are discussed in more detail in Section C, below.

2. The Basics of Charitable Lead Trusts

With a charitable lead trust, the charity receives income from the trust property for a set period of time. Then the trust property goes back to you or someone else you named to receive it. In other words, the process is the reverse of that used with charitable remainder trusts.

Charitable lead trusts are not as widely used as charitable remainder trusts. They are discussed further in Section D, below.

3. Selecting a Trustee for a Charitable Trust

You can serve as trustee of your own charitable trust, or you can choose someone else. Most people choose the charity itself to serve as trustee. In fact, most large public charities insist on serving as trustee. They want to manage all gifts made to them, including yours. Large charities have experienced investment staff, and many people prefer to turn management and investment of trust property over to them.

A larger charity can also offer you other services. It may assist you in preparing the trust document, and it may administer the trust free of any charge for the trustee's services. And while you probably can't impose investment decisions over the charity serving as trustee, you can direct where you want the trust property to go after the income beneficiary's interest ends. For instance, if the trust will benefit a school, you could probably require that the property be used only for scholarship purposes in a certain field or to enhance the library's facilities and holdings.

Matters can be different if you're making a gift to a smaller, less-established charity. Its cause may be noble, and its staff dedicated, but that's far from a guarantee of investment experience and sophistication. So with a small or new charity, you may decide that it's wisest to name yourself as trustee, to better manage your property. But check to be sure the charity will allow it; even some small charities insist on serving as trustee of a charitable trust, or that you use an investment firm of their choice.

KNOW YOUR CHARITY

Many people make gifts to charities they know well, whether from publicity or personal experience. If you don't know the charity, investigate it thoroughly, including its history, annual financial reports, and current management.

You can check out particular charities on the Internet. For example, www.guidestar.org offers analyses of more than 650,000 charitable organizations. You may also want to visit www.give.org. There, you can find lots of information to help you evaluate charities, including a booklet published by the Better Business Bureau called *The Wise Giving Guide*.

Before you agree to let the charity serve as trustee, do two things:

Work with a lawyer knowledgeable in charitable trusts. An experienced lawyer should be able to help you clarify what your income requirements are and what, if any, risk you might incur if the charity is trustee. You need to know whether the charity you have chosen has a good investment record—one that will protect your income interest. The lawyer should also be able to suggest other possible trustees, aside from yourself—perhaps a corporate trustee, like a private trust company.

Investigate the charity's management style and investment staff. If the charity is the trustee, you can't control what the trust assets are invested in, so it's vital that you have confidence in the charity's investment personnel. Who in the charity will actually be doing the trustee work? Does that person seem open and easy to talk to? Do you feel confidence in her judgment and sympathies? How sophisticated is the potential trustee, and her staff, in money and investment management?

Don't choose the charity to be the trustee unless you are confident that the organization, and the people in it who will actually manage your trust and its property, will protect the income beneficiary's interests. Any trustee, including a charitable organization, has what's called a "fiduciary duty" to do what's best for all the trust beneficiaries. But you want to rely on real people you actually trust, not abstract legal rules.

NAMING A BACKUP CHARITY

To protect the income tax savings of a charitable trust, consider naming another tax-exempt charity as a backup beneficiary, or provide in the trust document that the trustee can choose another charity if this need arises. In the unlikely event that the chosen charity becomes defunct or loses its IRS tax-exempt standing, this ensures that there can be no (retroactive) loss of any income tax deduction. It also ensures that the charitable gift can never be subject to estate tax, because there will always be a valid, tax-exempt charity entitled to receive the trust property when the income beneficiary's term ends.

B. THE INCOME TAX DEDUCTION

You may get substantial income tax advantages by creating a charitable trust. That's because over time, you can deduct the full value of the gift to the charity from your income tax. The fact that a charitable remainder trust makes payments to you or some other beneficiary for many years doesn't change this basic rule.

Where things get tricky, though, is in determining the actual value of the gift to the charity for income tax deduction purposes. The value of your gift to charity is not simply the value of the property when you give it to the trust. With a charitable remainder trust, the IRS deducts from this value the estimated value of the income beneficiary's right to receive payments from the trust property.

Things are reversed in a charitable lead trust. The income tax deduction is the estimated value of the income the charity will receive. (See Section 1, below.)

Once the IRS determines the worth of a gift to a charitable trust, you are entitled to deduct 100% of this amount. But this deduction cannot be taken in a single year. Rather, you can deduct a certain percentage of the amount in the year the gift is made, and deduct the rest over the next five years.

The amount of the first year's deduction depends on how the IRS classifies the charity and on your annual income. The most you can possibly deduct is 50% of your adjusted gross income for the first year. For a gift to a charity to be eligible for the 50% deduction, that charity must be classified by the IRS as a "public" charity and the gift must be a cash gift. Most widely known charities meet this requirement, such as schools, churches, the Salvation Army, the American Cancer Society, and many environmental organizations.

Many private foundations, however, do not meet this public charity requirement. If your gift is made to one of these charities or you donate appreciated assets, you can take an income tax deduction of only up to 30% of your adjusted gross income the first year, and the rest over the next five years. To determine whether your charity makes you eligible for the 50% or 30% deduction, contact the IRS.

Example: Christopher creates a charitable remainder trust, with the charity CARE as the final beneficiary. He names himself as the income beneficiary. The IRS will determine the worth of his gift, for income tax purposes, by subtracting the value of his retained interest in the income from the trust principal. If the value of the gift is less than 50% of his income for the year, he may deduct the entire gift that year.

If, instead, Christopher had given the money to a tax-exempt foundation not in the IRS 50% category, he would have been able to deduct only up to 30% of the amount of his income on that year's tax return. In either case, he can deduct the rest of his gift over the next five years. And in either situation, the deductions save enormously on income taxes.

REPLACING THE DONATED MONEY FOR YOUR INHERITORS

If you want to donate large sums to charity but are afraid that your inheritors might need the money, you are in luck if you are in good health. Many people take the money saved by the income tax deduction and purchase life insurance to cover the money "lost" by the gift to the charity. You can then remove the life insurance from your estate for estate tax purposes. (See Chapter 12, Section E, and Chapter 21, Section B.)

---

1. Determining the Value of a Gift to a Charitable Remainder Trust

If you make an outright gift to charity, the income tax deduction permitted by the IRS is the gift's value at the time you make it. For example, if you write a $100,000 check to the Audubon Society, you're entitled to a $100,000 income tax deduction.

By contrast, if you make a gift to a charitable remainder trust while you are alive, determining the amount of your tax deduction is more complicated.

The IRS determines the value of the charitable trust gift from tables that estimate your life expectancy (or that of whoever is the income beneficiary), current interest rates, and what the charity is expected to receive—that is, how much principal will be left—when the income beneficiary's interest ends. The more the charity is expected to get, the bigger the tax deduction; the larger the expected return to the income beneficiary, the lower the deduction.

> **Example:** Zola, who is 80 years old, creates a charitable remainder trust. She gives $800,000 in trust to her favorite charity, Save the Children, and retains the right to receive income equal to 6% of the trust principal annually for her life. After her death, the charity will receive all remaining trust property outright.
>
> Curt, who is 40 years old, creates the same kind of trust, with the same amount of property and the same retained income rights. Under IRS rules, the value of Zola's gift to the charity is worth substantially more than Curt's, which means she can take a larger tax deduction. The reason is that Curt, who is just 40, will (under life expectancy tables) live much longer than 80-year-old Zola, so the trust will pay out much more money to Curt than Zola.

Because IRS calculations are influenced by prevailing interest rates, the precise worth of a gift to a charitable remainder trust depends on when the gift is made. Many large, experienced charities have professional staff members who will figure out your actual tax deduction for you. Otherwise, to determine the actual amount, you need to see an expert who has the most current IRS tables. You could dig up the tables yourself, but figuring out how to use them, interweaving estimated interest rates, your life expectancy, and the value of the charity's interest is definitely not easy; indeed, for the uninitiated, it's close to impossible.

2. Giving Appreciated Property to a Charitable Trust

One of the most useful features of a charitable trust is that it provides a method to turn highly appreciated assets into cash without paying any capital gains tax up front. If you donate a non-income-producing asset to a charitable trust, the charity can convert it into an income-producing one. Though a charity isn't legally required to do so, it surely will if the asset—say an appreciated house or painting—isn't producing any, or much, current income. And whatever the profit from such a sale, no capital gains tax is assessed; charities are simply not liable for capital gains tax.

Here's how it works: You donate an appreciated asset to the charity, using a charitable remainder trust. The charity sells it for its current market value. The charity retains all the money received, without any subtraction for capital gains tax. As the grantor, you benefit in two ways. First, you get a tax deduction based on the sale price (the current value) of the asset. Second, the income you receive from the trust property will be based on this amount—which will obviously be higher than if capital gains tax had to be paid out of the sale's profits.

> **Example:** Toni owns stock currently worth $300,000, which she paid $20,000 for 20 years ago. She creates a charitable remainder trust, naming the Red Cross as the beneficiary. She funds her charitable trust with the stock. The Red Cross sells the stock for $300,000 and invests the money in a safe mutual fund. No taxes are paid. Toni, as the income beneficiary, will receive income from this $300,000 for her life.
>
> Technically, there is a capital gain (profit) of $280,000 on the stock sale—that is, the sale price less Toni's original $20,000 purchase price. Had Toni sold the stock herself, she would have had to pay the capital gains tax.

Toni's trust document specifies that her annual income from the charitable trust will be 7% of the value of the trust property (currently $300,000). The IRS calculation of Toni's income tax deduction will also start from a gift worth $300,000.

Capital gains tax may enter the picture when you begin receiving income payments from the charity. Part of your payments will be considered a return of capital—that is, a return of a portion of your gift—and part will be taxed as capital gains. But any tax owed will be spread over a long period of time. Large charities will send you a year-end statement breaking down what, if anything, is taxable and how.

C. A CLOSER LOOK AT CHARITABLE REMAINDER TRUSTS

There are different types of charitable remainder trusts. Each one offers different advantages and drawbacks. The four main types are:

- **Annuity trusts.** These pay the income beneficiary a fixed amount each year.

- **Unitrusts.** These pay the income beneficiary an amount equal to a percentage of the trust assets each year.

- **Charitable gift annuities.** These are similar to annuity trusts but less complicated. The charity sets the amount of income that you receive.

- **Pooled income trusts.** These let you contribute to an existing charitable trust and receive income for a set time.

1. Charitable Remainder Annuity Trusts

This type of trust provides a fixed dollar amount of income every year (an annuity) to the trust's income beneficiary, regardless of the value of the trust assets.

When creating the trust document, you name the income beneficiary—often yourself—and the term of the annuity period—often your lifetime. You also state the precise dollar amount of annual income that the life beneficiary must receive throughout this period.

Once you have established the set yearly payment, and the trust is operational, you can't change that figure. For instance, if you create a trust worth $250,000 and specify that the charity pay you $13,000 a year for the rest of your life, you can't subsequently say, "Oops, I forgot about inflation. How about $18,000 a year?"

Since January 1, 1998 you can, theoretically, make the payments as high as 50% of the value of the trust. However, the law requires that the charity must actually receive at least 10% of the original gift at the end of the term. If the payment is set too high, it would require spending principal, possibly using up much of the gift before the payment term is over. Obviously, this defeats your desire to make a gift to the charity. And there are practical limits. First, the higher the set payments, the lower your income tax deduction. Second, a charity is unlikely to accept a gift, particularly if it must serve as trustee, where it is likely, or even possible, that much of the trust property will be consumed before the charity gets anything.

The advantage of this type of trust is that if the trust somehow has lower-than-expected income—for example, during a period when interest rates are extremely low—the income beneficiary still receives the same annual income. The trustee must invade the trust principal, if necessary, to make the payments. This can't be done with other types of charitable remainder trusts.

If you create a charitable remainder annuity trust, you don't obtain a hedge against inflation. Payments from an annuity trust remain the same, even if there's significant inflation or the trust assets significantly increase in value.

You cannot give additional assets to a charitable remainder annuity trust after it's operational. (IRS Reg. 1.664-2(b).) Once the trust is created and funded, that's it. Of course, you could create a new, second trust, and many people do, but this is a fair amount of bother, especially with subsequent record keeping. So you should carefully decide, before creating a charitable remainder annuity trust, how much money you want to put in it and how large an annuity you want.

There are income tax advantages to using an annuity trust. The same property contributed to an annuity trust has a higher value for income tax deduction purposes than if placed in a charitable remainder unitrust. (See Section 2, below.) If you are not concerned about inflation and wish to reduce your estate tax and income tax, an annuity trust is often a better choice than a unitrust.

CHARITABLE REMAINDER ANNUITY TRUSTS AT A GLANCE

- You create and fund the trust, with appreciated assets if possible.

- You take an income tax deduction, the amount of which is calculated according to IRS rules.

- The trustee (usually, the charity) converts all trust property into income-producing assets. No capital gains tax is due on the sale profits.

- The trustee pays a set amount to the income beneficiary for the annuity period.

- At the end of the annuity period, trust assets go outright to the charity. The value of these assets is not subject to federal estate tax.

---

2. Charitable Remainder Unitrusts

With this popular form of a charitable remainder trust, the trustee pays income each year from the trust to an income beneficiary—again, usually the grantor. But instead of a fixed amount, the income beneficiary gets a percentage of the current value of the trust property. For example, the trust document could specify that the income beneficiary receives 7% of the value of the trust assets yearly. Each year, the trust assets must be reappraised to obtain a current worth figure. If the value of the trust assets increases because of wise investment decisions by the trustee (or simple good luck), the payments received by the income beneficiary also increase. It is in the charity's interest to have the principal grow as much as possible so it will receive more at the end of the term.

Similarly, because the income beneficiary receives a fixed percentage, not a flat dollar amount, if inflation pushes up the dollar value of the assets, the payments to the income beneficiary go up accordingly. So a charitable remainder unitrust can serve as a hedge against inflation, in contrast to an annuity trust, where payments remain fixed no matter how rampant inflation becomes.

The payment to the trust income beneficiary must, under IRS rules, be at least 5% of the value of the trust assets each year and not over 50%. But here again, practical considerations, such as the grantor's desire to make a gift to charity, and the charity's willingness to accept and manage the trust property, mandate that the percentage be reasonable. It cannot be so excessive that it consumes all the trust property during the income beneficiary's period of payment. The IRS requires that a minimum gift of 10% of the original assets go to the charity.

In certain situations, the trust document can direct that the income beneficiary be given all the income from the trust:

- if the spouse of the grantor is the income beneficiary, or
- if the trust property is the grantor's residence or family farm.

If you create a charitable remainder unitrust, you can transfer more property to the trust later, if the power to make additional gifts was expressly included in the original trust document. (IRS Reg. 1664-3(b).)

Here's an example of how a charitable remainder unitrust can provide income tax relief, reduce estate tax, and provide other benefits:

Example: Felix, age 60, earns a very comfortable salary and owns assets worth $3 million. Much of his property consists of his home and stock that he bought years ago. The stock has appreciated substantially in value; it cost $600,000 and is now worth $1.6 million. It currently pays little in dividends.

If Felix sells the stock and buys income-producing assets, he'll be obligated to pay capital gains tax on his profit from the sale. Setting up a charitable remainder unitrust offers one way to avoid this tax and guarantee income later, when Felix retires. Felix establishes a charitable remainder with himself as the income beneficiary for life and his alma mater, his state's university, as the final beneficiary. Felix funds the trust with the stock.

For income tax purposes, his donation to the charity is the full market value of the stock, less the IRS deduction based on his retained interest, age, and current interest rates.

The $1 million profit on the sale of the stock is not taxed. The trustee reinvests the entire $1.6 million into investments that pay well. The trust document requires income to be paid to Felix at 6% of the trust value annually for life. This figure will be $96,000 the first year; it will change each year as (if) the value of trust assets changes. Obviously, if the value of the investment increases, Felix will receive more money. And equally obviously, it's desirable that the charity make wise investments to increase the odds that the trust principal will increase.

So far, Felix has avoided paying capital gains tax while turning an asset that paid little income into one that pays him much more. His income tax deduction will be almost $400,000, more than enough to buy life insurance to replace the gift amount for his inheritors, if he is healthy. He can then remove those proceeds from his taxable estate. (See Chapter 12, Section E, and Chapter 21, Section B.)

But there is even more good news. Felix has also reduced his estate to a level where much less estate tax may be due at his death. Felix has given money to the school for its eventual use instead of giving it to Uncle Sam. And he has a guaranteed income for life.

If Felix lives for 15 years while receiving income from this trust, the trust should pay him at least $96,000 x 15, or $1,440,000. If the trustee invests the original $1.6 million wisely, that principal amount should also increase significantly in 20 years. If the principal increases, Felix will obviously receive more than $96,000 a year.

CHARITABLE REMAINDER UNITRUSTS AT A GLANCE

- You create and fund the trust, with appreciated assets if possible.

- You take the income tax deduction.

- The trustee (usually, the charity) converts all assets into income-producing assets. No capital gains tax is due on any profits from the sales.

- The value of the trust property is redetermined annually.

- The trustee pays a percentage of the revalued trust assets to the income beneficiary annually.

- At the income beneficiary's death, trust assets go outright to the charity. The value of these assets is not subject to estate tax.

---

3. Charitable Gift Annuities

Charitable gift annuities are becoming increasingly popular, especially with educational institutions. They are nothing more than charitable remainder trusts with a different name.

Charitable gift annuities are very simple trusts. You contact the charity, say your alma mater, and inform them of your intentions to make a donation in the form of a charitable gift annuity. Their staff, with great enthusiasm, will furnish you with the information you need and forms to fill out. You and the charity sign a contract setting out the terms of your donation, including the amount and duration of the payments made to the income beneficiaries you have named, usually you and your spouse. The charity handles everything, including setting the percentage it will pay to the beneficiaries. All you have to do is to transfer the assets to the charity, usually appreciated stock.

This type of arrangement works well for those who are less wealthy, but still wish to make a contribution. Some charities will set up an annuity with as little as a $10,000 gift. They figure your tax deduction for you and you just sit back and receive your income payments. With the tax savings and income payments combined, you will probably recoup the donated amount within several years.

CHARITABLE GIFT ANNUITIES AT A GLANCE

- You donate assets to the charity, often appreciated stock.

- You take an income tax deduction for the present value of the gift less the income you will receive.

- The charity pays you an amount of money each year; this amount is determined in the initial contract.

- At your death, the assets you donated belong to the charity.

---

4. Pooled Income Trusts

A popular type of charitable remainder trust is a pooled income trust, which allows people of more modest means to take advantage of charitable income tax deductions, donate to their favorite charity, and receive an income for a set period. You don't set up your own pooled income trust; the charity does it. You simply donate to the charity. It pools your donation with other money it's been given and manages all the money in one big trust.

Not every charity offers pooled income trusts, but most large ones do. Many universities and museums have established them for their loyal supporters. If a pooled fund is available, the charity will surely be delighted to discuss it with you, and help set up the paperwork.

Pooled income trusts operate very much like mutual funds. You contribute money, bonds, or stocks to the charity. (Highly appreciated stock is desirable because, as we've discussed, the charity can sell it for its present market value and pay no capital gains tax.) The charity pools a number of individuals' donations, invests the money, and pays interest to the donors according to its earnings. You can specify that your earnings be retained until you reach a certain age, such as retirement age of 65 or 70, with payments to start then. The charity receives what remains of your gift after your death. If invested wisely, chances are the charity's share will have appreciated in value significantly by then.

You cannot give tangible property—from real estate to jewelry—to a pooled trust. It's not permitted under federal law. This is not true for other types of charitable trusts.

In a pooled charitable trust, the charity is always the trustee—you have no option here. If you don't think that a charity will manage your gift well, its pooled income charitable trust is simply not for you.

Pooled income trusts can be attractive for many reasons. The charity does all of the work of setting up the trust and managing the assets. Also, unlike other charitable remainder trusts, you can easily add amounts to the trust after the initial contribution. So if you don't have a large portfolio or cash to donate at one time, you can still build a nice retirement income and at the same time benefit a good cause, by donating smaller amounts over the years.

A deduction from your income tax is allowed every time you make a donation. The amount of the deduction is figured by using the IRS tables to value the charity's remainder interest. (See Section B1, above.)

Example: Yuki is a businesswoman in her 40s with a salary of $80,000 a year. She is not married and has no children. She wants to support her favorite museum and also plan for her retirement. Yuki contributes $10,000 to a charitable pooled fund managed by the museum and takes her income tax deduction, the exact amount of which is determined by the IRS tables. A year later she does the same thing.

She keeps this up for 20 years, adding more in high-income years and less in years when she has unexpected expenses. By age 65, when she needs the income, her pooled shares, having been well managed by the fund, are worth around $400,000. She will receive whatever income this amount generates.

Yuki has accomplished both of her goals—giving a substantial amount to charity and providing a retirement fund for herself.

CHARITABLE POOLED INCOME TRUSTS AT A GLANCE

- You contribute assets to a charity that has established a pooled trust.

- You take an income tax deduction.

- The charity combines your assets with other contributions in a fund.

- The fund pays income to you, based on the fund's income on all pooled gifts.

- You can make additional gifts. If so, you take further income tax deductions.

- The fund keeps paying you for life, based on your total contributions.

- At your death, the assets you contributed go outright to the charity.

⚠️ **Carefully check out pooled charitable trusts.** The pool must meet strict federal requirements in order for your contributions to be tax deductible. (I.R.C. §§ 170(f)(2)(A), and 642(c)(5).) The rules dictate who can serve as trustees and how contributions are combined and invested. If you are dealing with a "brand name" charitable pool, you should be safe. If not, and your own investigations have not reassured you that the charitable pooled trust you're considering fully complies with federal law (and this may not be easy to determine), you may want to take all the information you can gather about the trust to a good tax advisor.

THE VERY WEALTHY DONOR

People of enormous means don't get all of the tax benefits from charitable giving that most of us would. This is because income tax deductions are phased out when the donor's overall income is sky high.

This was pointed out in an article by David Flaum in the Memphis, Tennessee, *Commercial Appeal*, after Mr. and Mrs. James Barksdale (think Netscape) donated $100 million to the University of Mississippi for literacy programs in the state. The Barksdales are extremely generous people and have poured money into charity. But income tax deductions for their gifts are minimal, if they exist at all. The savings for them will be in estate tax if it still exists, probably at the highest rate, which of course should be substantial.

When you read about some of these huge donations that the very wealthy make, the donor may not just be playing a tax game, but may also be motivated to do good.

D. A CLOSER LOOK AT CHARITABLE LEAD TRUSTS

A charitable lead trust works in reverse fashion from any form of charitable remainder trust. In a charitable lead trust, the charity initially receives a set amount of income from the trust for a set period, usually a number of years. If the charity's income from the trust property drops below the set level, the charity can invade the trust principal to pay itself the set amount. At the end of the period, the trust principal goes to the final beneficiaries named by the grantor. Usually, the final beneficiaries are the grantor's surviving spouse or children.

There are two basic types of charitable lead trusts:

- **Unitrusts.** Here, a set percentage of the trust's net worth is paid to the charity for a period of years. The actual amount paid can vary over the years, as the trust assets are reappraised each year.

- **Annuity trusts.** With these trusts, the grantor provides that a set dollar amount is to be paid to the charity each year.

Charitable lead trusts do not offer all the tax advantages of charitable remainder trusts, but they do offer some of the same income tax advantages. For instance, if you donate appreciated property to a charitable lead trust and the charity sells it, no capital gains tax is assessed. Also, tax law allows you an income tax deduction of the amount that the charity is expected to receive, based on IRS tables.

Charitable lead trusts that become operational while the grantor lives are rarely used, because they involve a significant income tax drawback: Income from the trust paid to the charity (during the set payment period) is taxed to the grantor, because the assets will revert back to him or his inheritors later. So the grantor must pay income tax on income the charity, not he, receives. This can effectively cancel out the original tax deduction. Not a highly desirable state of affairs. Still, these types of trusts are occasionally used, mainly by the very wealthy. They can make sense if you have highly appreciated assets that you want ultimately to remain in the family, not be given to charity.

Example: Clark, a wealthy industrialist in his early 50s, wants to take advantage of every tax break he can find. He and his wife have many assets that will let them continue to live very well when they retire.

With the help of his lawyer, Clark creates a charitable lead trust, funded with real estate that he long ago paid $100,000 for and which is now worth $2 million. He chooses as the income beneficiary a research institute for the cure of Parkinson's disease and sets the income payments to the institute at 8% of the trust assets a year. At Clark's death, the trust assets are to go to his children.

The trustee sells the real estate and invests the proceeds in mutual funds. Clark avoids a large capital gains tax that would have been assessed if he personally sold the property, because the charity isn't taxed on the sale. Clark takes an immediate income tax deduction of the charity's projected income from these assets, based on the IRS tables that consider his life expectancy and interest rates. He knows he will have to pay tax on the income the charity obtains from these assets, but he hopes the gain he's achieved from avoiding capital gains tax will cancel out this drawback.

Even more important to him, Clark is able to leave the trust property to his children. Also, he feels satisfaction that he has contributed to the possible cure of a horrible disease.

It's impossible to say exactly how much income tax Clark will pay on what the trust earns during his life, because it depends on how long he lives and on income tax rates. Let's say Clark lives for 25 more years. If the trust earns 8% a year, that's $80,000. At current top rates, income tax the first year would be $24,800, although the rate does decrease for the very wealthy over the next few years.

Naming a child's trust as the final beneficiary of a charitable lead trust. When children or young adults are the final beneficiaries of a charitable lead trust, it can be a good idea to create a child's trust to receive the trust principal, in case the children are not old enough or responsible enough to handle the money when the charitable term ends. (Child's trusts are discussed in Chapter 6, Section C.) If children are the final beneficiaries, one child may need more money than the others, so a "family pot" trust may be advisable. Professional help here is a must.

When the final beneficiaries don't need their inheritance right away, a charitable lead trust created upon the death of the grantor can occasionally be useful. It can let you save on estate tax, give to charity, and still (eventually) benefit your family or other beneficiaries. If a charitable lead trust becomes operational on the grantor's death, any negative income tax consequence to the grantor is avoided. The grantor won't be earning any more income. (Death solves that concern.) The purpose of the trust becomes the reduction of estate tax. The value of the charity's income interest for the period of years is not included in the taxable estate. Even though we are supposed to have no more estate tax by 2010, this is not a sure thing. Congress must vote again on this law to make it permanent. As we all know, the needs of the federal budget are not predictable, and people are proceeding with these trusts.

Example: Rachel directs in her living trust that upon her death, a charitable lead trust of $4 million be established for a period of 15 years. During those years, income payments will go annually to her favorite charity. At the end of the period, the remainder will go to her niece. The charity's interest in the trust is calculated using the IRS tables. This amount is deducted from the taxable value of Rachel's estate and could save the estate a bundle.

CHARITABLE LEAD TRUSTS AT A GLANCE

- You create and fund the trust, with appreciated assets if possible.

- You take an income tax deduction.

- The trustee converts all trust property into income-producing assets.

- Income goes to the charity for the set period.

- You pay income tax on trust income paid to the charity.

- At the end of the set period, all trust property, including appreciation, goes to the beneficiaries you chose.

- At your death, the amount the charity received is removed from your estate for estate tax purposes.

E. TYPES OF CHARITABLE TRUSTS: A COMPARISON

TYPES OF CHARITABLE TRUSTS

	Charitable Remainder Annuity Trust or Gift Annuity	Charitable Remainder Unitrust	Pooled Income Trust	Charitable Lead Trust
Primary goals	Income tax and estate tax savings; fixed income for life	Income tax and estate tax savings; hedge against inflation	Income tax and estate tax savings; income (possibly for retirement)	Income tax and estate tax savings (though they can cause significant tax disadvantages); preservation of trust assets for final beneficiaries
Property you can transfer to trust	Money or tangible property	Money or tangible property	Money and stocks	Money or tangible property
Transfer additional property later?	No	Yes	Yes	Yes, if permitted in original trust document
Income tax deduction available to you	Larger than with unitrust, because IRS values the charity's share higher	Smaller than with annuity trust, because IRS values the charity's as less	Yes	The value of charity's income interest for set period
Trustee	Anyone you choose, including yourself or the charity	Anyone you choose, including yourself or the charity	The charity only	Anyone you choose, including yourself or the charity
Income beneficiary	You or anyone else you name	You or anyone else you name	You or anyone else you name	The charity
Final beneficiary	The charity	The charity	The charity	You or beneficiaries you name
Income paid to income beneficiary	Fixed dollar amount each year, even if trust principal must be used	Fixed percentage of trust assets each year	Interest earned from donor's contribution to the pool	Fixed dollar amount or percentage of trust assets, whichever you specify in trust document

21

OTHER ESTATE
TAX-SAVING TRUSTS

I ndividuals or couples with very large estates can use a number of different types of trusts to save on estate taxes. For this chapter's purposes, "very large" means, for a couple, that even if they use an AB trust, one or both of their estates will be over the estate tax threshold. (See Chapter 15, Section A.) The tax-saving trusts described in this chapter can be used by anyone, whether married, in an unmarried couple, or single.

These trusts, however, are complicated. You'll need a lawyer to prepare the trust documents.

A. GENERATION-SKIPPING TRUSTS (GSTT TRUSTS)

People who want to leave substantial property to their grandchildren may find themselves confronting an unexpected beast—the "generation-skipping transfer tax" (GSTT). This tax applies, in *addition* to any estate tax, to property worth more than the GSTT exemption that you leave to third-generation beneficiaries, such as your grandkids. One way to both reduce overall estate tax and escape the GSTT is to use a carefully funded generation-skipping trust, also called a GSTT trust.

A GSTT trust provides income to one generation of beneficiaries (called the middle or second generation) and then leaves the trust property outright to the next, or third, generation. (This makes it a type of bypass trust, introduced in Chapter 18.) One of the income beneficiaries—such as a child—usually serves as trustee. The main benefit of a generation-skipping trust is that the trust property avoids further estate tax when the second generation dies, because that generation never owns the property outright. In addition, if the trust property is worth less than the GSTT exemption amount (discussed below), the property avoids the GSTT when the third generation receives it. In the right situation, these trusts can save a family a bundle on overall taxes.

IF ESTATE TAX DISAPPEARS

As discussed in Chapter 15, the federal estate tax is slated to be repealed for the year 2010 and perhaps beyond that, if Congress acts to extend the repeal. Even if there's no more estate tax, some people will still choose to set up trusts for grandchildren. Their children may not need so much property or they may not want their children to inherit from them for any number of personal reasons. Therefore, generation-skipping trusts will probably always be with us.

There are no estate tax savings when the person from the older generation dies. All property in the trust is subject to estate tax at that point. But this type of trust works to transfer the funds tax free when the middle generation dies. This middle generation never legally owns the trust property. That means the property in the generation-skipping trust isn't subject to estate tax when the trust property is turned over to the third generation.

> **Example:** Alex, a grandparent, establishes a generation-skipping trust of $3 million to take effect at his death. His children, the middle generation, receive the income generated by the trust property while they are alive. They're called the income beneficiaries. When Alex's children die, no estate tax is assessed against the trust principal. The entire amount is turned over to his grandchildren, who are termed the final beneficiaries.

Use of a generation-skipping trust is not limited to your direct descendants. It can be used anytime you have beneficiaries in two subsequent generations and, of course, a sizable amount of money you're willing to tie up for a generation.

Example: Monroe, who has a lot of money, decides to leave $2 million to his niece and her three children in a generation-skipping trust. His niece, the middle generation, receives trust income for her life. When she dies, the trust ends and the property is distributed equally among her three children (the third generation). No estate tax is assessed at her death, because she didn't legally own the trust property.

You must keep in mind the limits of this tax break, however. As mentioned above, any property placed in this type of trust that exceeds the GSTT exemption in the year of the trustor's death is subject to a hefty generation-skipping transfer tax. The GSTT rate is the highest rate on the federal estate tax scale at the time the tax is applied, when the middle generation dies. (The GSTT is defined in I.R.C. § 2611, which refers to several other I.R.C. sections as well.)

The GSTT exemption is currently $2 million. It rises at the same rate as the personal estate tax exemption. (See Chapter 15, Section A, for the rate chart.) Members of a couple can each transfer their personal GSTT exemption amount free of GSTT. However, the GSTT exemption is not automatically available. To claim it, your executor must file for the exemption using federal estate tax forms. If your executor does not make this filing, you will lose all the benefits of the exemption.

This is complicated stuff, but it is important to remember that we are talking about two different taxes here—and two separate personal exemptions. For example, let's say you have an estate worth $4 million and it's the year 2007, when the exempt amount for each tax is $2 million. This means you can leave $2 million estate tax free and $2 million that will escape the GSTT if you and your executor file the correct IRS forms.

If you leave $2 million outright to your children and put $2 million in a GSTT trust with income to go to your children and the final property distribution to go to your grandkids, estate tax will be due on the trust amount when you die. But no additional estate tax will be due on the trust property when your children die, no matter how much it's worth, because they never actually owned the property. In addition, because the trust is within the GSTT exemption, money can be distributed to the grandchildren without paying that tax.

Getting help. As you can see, GSTT trusts are tricky. We provide only an overview of the subject. If you decide a generation-skipping trust is desirable, you absolutely need an expert in the field.

Fussy actuarial rules apply if you create a GSTT trust to benefit your "nonlineal" descendants—that is, anyone except children, grandchildren, and so on—to determine which generation they are in. Basically, the rules provide that a "generation" occurs every 25 years, except the "child" generation starts when a beneficiary is over 12-1/2 years younger than the grantor.

Example: Shanto leaves money in a trust that will pay income for life to his friend Lolly, who is 15 years younger than he is. At her death, the principal will go to Lolly's children. This is a generation-skipping trust, and Lolly will be considered a member of the "child" category.

ONE WAY THE RICH STAYED RICH

Before the adoption of the generation-skipping transfer tax, when Congress put a limit on the right to pass money to one's grandchildren free of estate tax in the middle generation, people with many, many millions (even billions) of dollars would leave the bulk, or perhaps all, of their property in generation-skipping trusts. Estate taxes were, of course, due when the trust grantor died, but no taxes at all would be assessed when the middle generation died. These types of trusts enabled the very wealthy to escape all estate tax in every other generation. And the income from a trust of many millions normally proved quite sufficient for the middle generation to live an affluent lifestyle. (Couldn't you survive well on the income from, say, $200 million?) Since Congress created the GSTT in the 1980s, there is no tax advantage in creating a generation-skipping trust worth more than the GSTT exemption.

---

1. Is a Generation-Skipping Trust for You?

You must have a substantial estate—usually at least a couple of million dollars (individually) before a generation-skipping trust could make sense. With a generation-skipping trust, the middle generation can have the right to receive all trust income, but only restricted rights to spend principal. So you want to be sure that your immediate family will be well provided for at your death before you create a generation-skipping trust that will benefit the third generation, usually your grandchildren.

> **Example:** Abigail is a widow with two children and four grandchildren. Each of her children is established in a successful career and is quite prosperous. Abigail has an estate of $4 million. She decides to leave $1 million outright to each of her children and create a generation-skipping trust for the remaining $2 million. This trust will become operational on Abigail's death. The trust will pay all income to Abigail's children, equally, during their lifetimes. When one child dies, all trust income will go to the surviving child. When the surviving child dies, the trust assets will be divided equally among Abigail's grandchildren, with no additional estate tax due. If she dies after 2005, no GSTT tax will be due because of her GSTT exemption.

a. Will Your Spouse Need Your Property?

Trusts paying income to children and then leaving assets to grandchildren are desirable only if your spouse is already fully provided for—from his own property, other property you leave for his benefit, or both. Your spouse could also receive income from the trust, and have a limited right to invade principal, but if spousal need is a real concern, a GSTT is probably not what you need.

However, when the financial picture is quite secure, a generation-skipping trust can certainly save on overall estate taxes.

> **Example:** Roberta and Byron own shared property worth $3.2 million. Neither has any separately owned property. Thus, each one's estate is worth $1.6 million, half the total. Each spouse creates the same estate plan: $600,000 is left in an AB trust, with the surviving spouse having maximum powers to spend trust principal for health care or other needs.
>
> Each spouse feels that with their own $1.6 million as well as income from the AB trust,

they are sufficiently protected economically. So each spouse leaves the remaining $1 million of his or her estate in a generation-skipping trust for their children and grandchildren.

b. Will Your Children Need Your Property?

If you establish a generation-skipping trust, your children (the second generation) will not have outright ownership of any of the trust property (principal). They can serve as trustees and receive trust income. And, if expressly allowed by the trust document, they can spend trust principal deemed necessary by the trustee for their "health, education, support, or maintenance." (This is the IRS "objective" standard for invasion of trust principal by life beneficiaries. See Chapter 18, Section B.)

What this amounts to is that, for most people, a generation-skipping trust makes sense only if you're sure your children (the middle generation) will be financially comfortable without unrestricted access to the assets in the trust. If this isn't the case, you'll probably want to simply leave them the property outright. Also, if members of the middle generation are reasonably young and may survive you by decades, you may not feel secure tying up a lot of money in such a way that they can reach it only in limited circumstances.

2. Creating Two Generation-Skipping Trusts

Each member of a couple (married or not) can transfer the personal exemption amount in a generation-skipping trust free of GSTT. Thus, a wealthy couple can create two generation-skipping trusts for their children and grandchildren, placing quite a lot of money in the trusts.

In second or subsequent marriages, each spouse may want to create a generation-skipping trust for her or his own children from a prior marriage, and for their children's children.

3. How the GSTT Works

Any gift of trust property to a beneficiary two generations down, no matter how it is made, is subject to the GSTT. As we've said, the GSTT rate is steep; it's the highest rate on the federal estate tax scale at the time the tax is applied.

If the amount in the original trust or gift exceeds the GSTT exemption amount at the grantor's death, the GSTT applies to the overage when the property or money is actually distributed to the third-generation beneficiary.

a. When the GSTT Is Assessed

The GSTT, if applicable, is assessed when the final beneficiaries of a generation-skipping trust receive their property. Usually, this happens only after the middle generation dies. Two other types of transfers are also subject to the GSTT.

A "direct skip" is an outright gift to someone two (or more) generations down. For instance, if you leave $4 million outright to a grandchild, the GSTT exemption amount of that gift avoids the GSTT. The rest is taxed at the highest estate tax rate. Also, the entire $4 million is included in your taxable estate, and so is subject to estate tax at your death. So the property is taxed twice.

Sometimes, a generation-skipping trust directs or permits payment to a beneficiary two generations removed from the grantor, while the middle generation is still alive. This is a "taxable distribution" and any such payments will be taxed under the GSTT, if the amount in the trust originally exceeded the personal exemption amount.

b. How the GSTT Is Assessed

As just discussed, the generation-skipping transfer tax will be due when the income (middle generation) beneficiary dies and the trust property goes to the final beneficiaries. In tax lingo, this event is called a "taxable termination."

However, whether or not a generation-skipping trust is subject to the GSTT is determined earlier, when the grantor dies—that is, when the trust becomes operational. If the amount in the trust at the time the grantor dies is less than the exempt amount, then all property in the trust is exempt from the GSTT tax. The tax will not apply when the trust assets are eventually distributed to the grandchildren, even if the worth of the trust assets has increased significantly by that time.

> **Example:** Frank is a widower with two children and four grandchildren. His total estate is worth $3 million. He sets up a generation-skipping trust of $1 million to take effect at his death. This $1 million is included in Frank's taxable estate when he dies. Frank has directed that all estate tax due on his death be paid from his other assets, not from property in the generation-skipping trust. So the full $1 million goes into the trust.
>
> The trust will pay the income to his children for their lifetimes. When they die, the principal goes to the grandchildren. When the children die, the property in the trust is worth $3.5 million. No GSTT is assessed, because the amount in the trust when Frank died did not exceed his exemption.

The amount of money in the trust, for GSTT purposes, is determined after any estate tax assessed on, and payable from, the amount left in trust has actually been paid.

> **Example:** Abigail funds her generation-skipping trust with her entire estate of $3 million. The income will go to her children for their lives, and when they die the assets will go to her grandchildren. She dies in the year 2007 when the personal exemption is $2 million. Estate tax will be due on the extra $1 million at Abigail's death. So the amount of her property left to go into the generation-skipping trusts will be less than $3 million after the tax is paid, and the GSTT calculation will be based on that reduced amount.

Determining in advance the exact tax rate that will be applied to property placed in a generation-skipping trust is not easy, especially when some of this property will be used to pay some portion of the grantor's estate tax. To really understand how this works means deciphering tax concepts like "inclusion ratios" and "applicable fractions." (The intrepid may wish to study I.R.C. §§ 2601 and 2602.) For regular affluent folks, a certified public accountant (CPA) or lawyer with estate tax experience is essential here.

4. Options With Generation-Skipping Trusts

You have some flexibility when you set up a generation-skipping trust. Sometimes, trust income is made available to the grandchildren—for example, for their education—while their parents (the middle, income generation) are still alive.

In addition, other estate planning devices can be useful in combination with a generation-skipping trust. Most common is use of an AB trust. (See Chapter 18, Section C.) Sometimes, the generation-skipping trust is combined with leaving property outright to a surviving spouse or a marital deduction trust such as a QTIP trust. (See Chapter 19, Section A.)

If you are married and wealthy, you must use care to take advantage of each spouse's GSTT exemption. A couple could simply leave their money outright to each other and lose one GSTT exemption, as well as one personal estate tax exemption.

Example: Arto doesn't want his spouse, Riki, to worry about estate tax or trust documents at his death, so he puts off taxes by leaving everything outright to her under the marital deduction. They both want their waterfront home (which they own together) to go eventually to their favorite granddaughter, Allie. Arto dies in 2006 and no tax is due because of the marital deduction. No estate tax forms or GSTT forms are filed

When Riki dies in 2008, the home is worth $4 million. If she leaves it to Allie, the GSTT will rear its head. If Arto had put his share of the house into a GSTT trust for Allie, no GSTT would ever be due.

Even when using an AB trust plan, when grandchildren are final beneficiaries, you can lose part of the GSTT exemption.

Example: Oscar and Gertie each leave the exact amount of the personal exemption in an AB trust that will eventually go to grandchildren. They do this by using a formula clause that will fund the trust with the amount of the exemption in the year of their death. (See Chapter 18, Section C.) They leave the remainder of their estates outright to each other. Oscar dies first in 2006, when the personal exemption is $2 million. His GSTT exemption is not automatic, however, and will be lost if Gertie, his executor, doesn't file the correct forms. This could result in a big GSTT bill when Gertie dies.

In many cases, the loss of the GSTT exemption can be avoided simply by submitting the proper forms to claim it. This is especially crucial as the amounts of the personal estate tax exemption and the GSTT exemption increase each year. When no estate taxes are due, many people may forget that they may still need to deal with property now owned or controlled by a spouse and eventually going to grandchildren. Both spouses should plan in advance to take full advantage of their GSTT exemptions.

In other circumstances, loss of the GSTT exemption can be avoided by using a QTIP trust (see Chapter 19 for details on QTIP trusts). When property is left to a spouse in a QTIP trust, for estate tax purposes, the surviving spouse is the owner of the property. But for GSTT purposes, the law allows the executor to make what is called a reverse QTIP election. This is simply a request to make the first spouse the owner of property (or part of the property) that will go to grandchildren, for GSTT purposes. The executor can make a partial election that will make sure each spouse uses his or her personal GSTT exemption. (See Chapter 19, Section A6.)

Example: Oscar leaves $2 million in the year 2007 in an AB trust with income to Gertie and assets to his grandchildren upon his death. He leaves a remaining $1.5 million in a QTIP with income to Gertie and the assets to be divided at Gertie's death among his children and grandchildren. The QTIP assets are considered Gertie's property for estate tax purposes. But his executor makes a reverse QTIP election for the entire amount of the QTIP property that will go to the grandchildren.

Although this portion will still be part of Gertie's property for estate tax, Oscar is considered the one eventually transferring the property to the grandchildren for GSTT purposes, and it will be exempt from the GSTT tax. And Gertie's GSTT exemption is still available for property she leaves to the grandchildren. Both spouses have used their GSTT exemptions.

B. IRREVOCABLE LIFE INSURANCE TRUSTS

After your death, all the insurance proceeds paid from a policy you owned are included in your taxable estate. (See Chapter 12.) If the payout is large, it may push the value of your estate over the federal estate tax threshold. So finding a way to remove life insurance proceeds from your taxable estate can save your inheritors a bundle in estate tax.

One way to remove life insurance proceeds from your estate is to use an irrevocable life insurance trust. This trust is a legal entity you create that becomes operational while you are alive. The trust becomes the owner of life insurance you previously owned as an individual or of a new policy purchased in the trust's name. Because the policy is owned by this legally independent trust, you are not the legal owner of the insurance proceeds, which therefore are not included in your taxable estate. Normally, the beneficiaries of the policy remain the same as they were before you set up the trust.

Irrevocable life insurance trusts aren't for everyone who faces estate tax, or even most of them. Indeed, simply giving the policy to someone you trust is normally a better approach. (See Chapter 12, Section E, for a discussion of the advantages and drawbacks of giving away your life insurance policy.) Life insurance trusts are for those who don't want the risks involved in giving their policy outright to another person. For instance, when the beneficiary of the life insurance isn't yet mature enough to be trusted with ownership, an irrevocable life insurance trust can be very desirable.

Get help. If you want to create or explore using a life insurance trust, see an experienced lawyer before you trundle off to your insurance company. In addition to the complexities of any irrevocable trust, there are potential problems unique to a life insurance trust.

1. IRS Requirements

Strict IRS requirements govern irrevocable life insurance trusts. To gain the estate tax savings this type of trust can offer, you must conform to these rules.

a. The Trust Must Be Irrevocable

The life insurance trust must be absolutely irrevocable. If you retain any right to revoke or amend the trust, or affect the insurance policy in any way—such as by naming a new beneficiary—the IRS will consider you to be the legal owner of the policy. That means the proceeds will be included in your taxable estate.

b. You Cannot Be the Trustee

Remember that the purpose of this trust is to remove the life insurance from your estate. You cannot control the trust, so you cannot be trustee. If you try to retain any rights that a trustee must have, the IRS will say you still own the policy.

Your spouse can be trustee, but you must be careful with this arrangement. You'll need expert legal help to make sure that the spouse is not given certain powers or too much power that might make him or her the legal owner of the policy. You want to keep the proceeds out of both of your estates, not just your own.

You can name your grown child, another relative, a friend, or even an institution to serve as trustee. No matter whom you choose, you'll have more control over the trustee than you would over someone to whom you gave an insurance policy outright, because you create the trust document that establishes the trustee's powers.

Example: Pilar is the divorced mother of two children, in their 20s, whom she has named as beneficiaries of her universal life insurance policy. It will pay $500,000 at her death. In addition to the insurance policy, Pilar has an estate of $3 million. She wants to remove the proceeds of the policy from her estate. If she doesn't, $1.5 million of her total estate will be subject to federal estate tax if she dies before the year 2009.

But Pilar has a problem. Although she loves her kids dearly, neither child is sensible with money, and she doesn't trust them enough to give her policy to them outright. She fears they might fail to make the premium payments, or possibly even cash in the policy in a time of financial desperation. She wants to be sure the policy is kept in force until her death, so that all the proceeds—far more than the cash-in value of the policy—will be distributed to her children on her death.

Pilar decides to create an irrevocable life insurance trust for the policy and to name her sister, Julianna, the person she's closest to, to be the trustee.

Even aside from the crucial fact that Pilar trusts Julianna, there's no real reason for Pilar to worry about Julianna cashing in the policy. If Julianna did that, she wouldn't receive the cash surrender value herself; the trust, not Julianna owns the property. The cash-in money would remain in the trust until Pilar's death.

c. The Trust Must Exist for at Least Three Years Before Your Death

You must establish the operational trust at least three years before your death. If the trust has not functioned for at least three years when you die, the trust is disregarded for estate tax purposes and the insurance proceeds are included in your taxable estate.

This three-year rule is crucial. It means that if you want to establish an irrevocable life insurance trust, you should do so promptly. Clearly, it would be unfortunate to create an irrevocable life insurance trust and die before the end of the three-year period, negating all estate tax savings the trust offered.

The reason for this three-year rule is that the estate tax savings offered by an irrevocable life insurance trust (or any transfer of life insurance ownership) can be so substantial that the IRS wants to prohibit last-minute transfers of life insurance, in anticipation of death. Three years seems like a pretty long "last minute," but lengthy or not, the rule exists. If you want to create an irrevocable life insurance trust, do it soon. You gain no benefits from waiting.

2. Paying Insurance Policy Premiums

One major concern when creating an irrevocable life insurance trust is how future premium payments to the insurance company will be made. If you set up the trust, you cannot directly make the payments through the trust, or the IRS will consider you to have retained some control or interest in the policy. This means, as we've warned before, that all the proceeds payable on your death will be included in your taxable estate.

At least two payment options are available to you. First, you can give money to the beneficiaries each year so that they can make the payments themselves. Of course, you'll have to trust the beneficiaries to spend that cash on policy premiums. Second, you can include what are called "Crummey" trust provisions (so named because someone named Crummey was the first to have this type of trust validated) in your irrevocable life insurance trust.

Here's how Crummey trust provisions work: The trust document provides that each year, each trust beneficiary has the right to receive up to $12,000 from the trust property ($12,000 is currently the maximum that can be given to a beneficiary, per year, free of gift tax). Usually, the beneficiaries have a deadline, say January 15, to claim their money for the year.

Each year, you give up to $12,000 per person to the trust. Now things get tricky. Each year the beneficiaries decline to accept this money. By doing this, the gift is converted from a "future interest" (not eligible for the annual gift tax exemption) into a gift of a "present interest"—which means it qualifies for this exemption. (This distinction is discussed in Chapter 16, Section C.) The trustee uses this declined money to pay that year's insurance premium. Any balance left over after the year's premiums have been paid is saved in the trust for future premium payments.

You should be aware that the IRS has made no secret of its distaste for Crummey trust provisions. So far, the Crummey method has remained legal, but the IRS may well find a new avenue of attack in the future. If the Crummey provision fails down the line, the gifts to the beneficiaries will be taxable, and not subject to the annual exclusion. Even so, gifts for the amount of a premium are small when compared to the eventual proceeds.

If neither of these methods provides enough cash to pay the yearly insurance premium, or you consider the Crummey provisions too complicated and risky, what can you, the grantor, do? Perhaps you could purchase a single-premium policy, so there's no worry about future payments. Another approach is simply to give money to the trust and be assessed gift tax on it.

3. When Circumstances Change

Sometimes tricky personal concerns arise when preparing or living with an irrevocable life insurance trust. For example:

- What happens if you get married, divorced, or have a child after setting up an irrevocable trust? Legally, it's up to the trustee to decide who the beneficiaries of the policy should be. Of course, a trustee who cares for you will probably revise the insurance beneficiaries as you want. For example, the trustee could add your new child as a beneficiary.

- Suppose you get divorced, and your ex-spouse is one of the beneficiaries of the life insurance policy and also of Crummey trust provisions you created to pay the premiums? Here's where matters can get very touchy. If the trustee simply removes the ex-spouse as a beneficiary of the policy, the ex-spouse could claim the trustee was really acting under your control. This could cause the entire trust to fail for estate tax purposes. With personal complexities like these, you must see a lawyer.

C. GRANTOR-RETAINED INTEREST TRUSTS: GRATs, GRUTs, AND GRITs

Names to the contrary, this section is not about lifting weights or Southern cooking. Here, we discuss three types of irrevocable estate tax-saving trusts. Their common feature is that you keep either income from trust property, or use of that property, for a period of years. Then the trust ends and the property goes to the final beneficiaries you've named. These trusts can let you make a gift to people you love, save on gift taxes, and save again on estate taxes. A good deal.

Some people will now ignore these trusts because of the steady reduction in estate tax. (See Chapter 15, Section A, for the estate tax rate charts.) However, as the law now stands, gifts will be subject to tax for an indefinite period of time. (I.R.C. § 2502(a)(2).) The result of this is that these trusts could actually become more important because they are, in effect, a discounted gift. In the past, the IRS has scrutinized these discounted gifts, and we can't say what the future holds. All we can do is give you current information. See a lawyer before you delve into one of them.

These types of trusts are called:

- Grantor-Retained Annuity Trusts (GRATs)

- Grantor-Retained Unitrusts (GRUTs), and

- Grantor-Retained Income Trusts (GRITs).

These trusts are for people who have enough wealth to feel comfortable giving away a substantial hunk of property. If you believe you'll want or need full control over all your property until you die, they are not for you.

1. Overview of GRATs, GRUTs, and GRITs

GRATs, GRUTs, and GRITs vary in some important aspects—such as how payment to the grantor is determined—but all have much in common. Here is how these trusts work to save on gift and estate tax.

You start by placing property in one of these trusts. You can be, and usually are, the initial trustee of your trust. You also retain some interest in that property for a set period. The retained interest can be income generated from the trust property, or the right to use that property—such as living in a trust-owned house. You name final beneficiaries, who will receive the trust property when this period ends or at your death, whichever comes first.

Once established, the trust is irrevocable—you can't change your mind and take back any property from the trust. No matter how much you may need that property, it can never again be yours outright.

For gift tax purposes, the value of the gift you make to the trust is determined when the trust is established. This value never changes. You hope that while you have a retained interest in the trust property, the value of that property will increase significantly. If you outlive the trust period and the property is turned over to the final beneficiaries before your death, this increase in value will never be subject to gift tax or estate tax. The only taxes ever assessed on the transaction are the gift taxes when the property is first placed in the trust. And because you no longer own the property at your death, the entire amount is excluded from your taxable estate.

Because you have retained an interest in the property—such as receiving income from the trust—the value of the gift, for gift tax purposes, is reduced; it is less than the property's market value. The gift tax is assessed on the value of the gift to the final beneficiaries, according to complex IRS tables.

The annual gift tax exclusion is not available, because the gift is not one for present use by any beneficiary but rather for use in the future. However, when you make your gift to the irrevocable trust, no gift tax must actually be paid, unless you have already used up your gift tax exemption by making previous taxable gifts. (See Chapter 16, Section A.)

As you'll see, the trick here is for you to survive the trust period (set by you in the trust document), so that the trust property is turned over to the final beneficiaries during your lifetime. If you do, the remaining value of the trust property will not be counted in your taxable estate. If you don't, the trust assets, complete with all appreciation in value, are included in your taxable estate. You gain nothing, estate tax-wise, and the money and time spent drafting the trust and administering it will have been wasted.

Both married and single folks can use a grantor-retained interest trust. Because estate tax breaks for single people are few and far between, a grantor-retained interest trust can be an attractive tax-avoidance technique for a wealthy single person.

Here's a rough example to show you how these trusts work. We'll get into more precise details soon enough.

Example: Phyllis, age 65, creates a GRIT (that's a grantor-retained income trust). She funds it with her house, worth $400,000, and retains the right to live in the house for 15 years. She names her son as the final beneficiary. The value of the gift (her house) to the trust is determined when she creates the trust. Her right to live in the house for 15 years is her income value, what it would cost someone to occupy the premises for that period. This is subtracted from the $400,000 gift for tax purposes.

Phyllis survives the 15-year period she set. When she becomes 80, the house, now worth $725,000, is legally turned over to her son. Because gift tax was assessed on the $400,000 value of the house at the time the trust was created minus her retained interest, Phyllis has avoided paying gift tax on more than $325,000. Moreover, she has removed the house from her taxable estate, for the obvious reason that she's no longer the owner of it.

As you've probably already suspected, this trust sounds so terrific that it must have risks. When she turns 80, Phyllis will no longer own her house. If her son doesn't charge her rent, the IRS will consider him to have made a gift of the rent to his mother. The son may have to file a gift tax return. (See Chapter 16.) Worse, her son could decide to sell the house, leaving Phyllis out on the street. And, as we discussed above, if Phyllis does not survive the time period she set in the trust document, the whole gamble collapses, and nothing is achieved, tax-wise.

2. Grantor-Retained Annuity Trusts (GRATs)

Another method for saving on gift and estate tax is a Grantor Retained Annuity Trust—a GRAT. Again, the grantor passes property—usually money or stock—to a child or favorite person, pays a reduced gift tax, and removes the assets from the estate.

a. How GRATs Work

To establish a GRAT, you transfer some valuable asset, from cash to real estate to stocks to any property with significant value, to the trust. Under the terms of the trust document, the trustee (usually yourself) dips into the trust assets and pays you an annual fixed sum (an annuity) for a set term of years. At the end of this term, the remaining trust assets go to the final beneficiary, perhaps your child, as the trust document directs. (I.R.C. § 2702.)

The benefit of a GRAT results from the fact that the IRS values the gift to the final beneficiaries only when the trust is established, not when the remaining trust property is later distributed, as long as you outlive the trust period. Your retained interest greatly reduces the value of the gift for gift tax purposes, even though the final beneficiary will normally receive (at a minimum) the full amount given.

The IRS tables used to determine the gift tax value of a gift to a GRAT are nearly impenetrable to all but real experts. They take into account the term period, life expectancy, and the interest rates when the GRAT is created. Rather than bore and quite possibly confuse you with a detailed explanation of how valuation works, we'll simply say that it is one big reason you must see an expert if you want to set up one of these trusts.

Example: Hattie, a 60-year-old widow, has assets worth $2 million. She sets up a GRAT with $1 million. The trust will last for 15 years and will pay Hattie $40,000 a year during the term. At the end of the term, or when Hattie dies, whichever happens first, the remaining trust assets will go equally to her three children. The value of the gift to the trust for gift tax purposes is set by an IRS formula that first subtracts Hattie's annuity interest ($40,000 x 15 years, or $600,000) and then considers Hattie's life expectancy and the amount in the trust ($1 million).

After subtracting the $600,000 value of Hattie's retained interest, the gift is initially worth $400,000. But now the IRS tables take into account Hattie's life expectancy and the interest rates when the trust is created. As a result, the value of the gift for gift tax purposes will be less than $400,000.

GRATs AT A GLANCE

- You create and fund the trust, establishing the dollar amount of the annuity you will receive each year for the set period.

- The value of the gift, for gift tax purposes, is determined when you fund the trust.

- The trustee pays you an annuity annually.

- When the annuity term ends, trust assets go to the final beneficiary.

Now let's continue the above example, to see in more depth how a GRAT works.

Example: The value of the gift to Hattie's children, for gift tax purposes, is determined at the time she creates the trust. If Hattie has not used any of her gift tax exemption by making other taxable gifts, no tax payment will actually be due when she sets up the trust, because the gift is valued at an amount less than the gift tax threshold. Instead, the value of the gift is deducted from Hattie's gift tax exemption.

Over time, the assets in the trust may well appreciate in value. This increase in value is not subject to tax. So, the real gift to her children will be much more than the taxable value of the gift.

Suppose Hattie's $1 million trust yields an actual annual return of 7%. That means income of $70,000 for the trust during the first year. After Hattie receives her $40,000 annuity, the extra $30,000 of income increases the amount of money in the trust. If this goes on year after year, with the trust assets increasing in worth each year, the same 7% return obviously yields more than the initial year's $70,000. For instance, the second year the income will be 7% of $1,030,000. And so it goes. The $1 million not only stays intact for the children, but gradually increases without tax consequences.

The more benefit you retain from the trust property, the less the property is worth for gift tax purposes. It follows then that the younger you are, and the longer the term during which you will benefit from the gift, the lower the taxable value of the gift. Likewise, the higher the annuity payments to you, the lower the taxable value of the gift.

Example: Sudata funds a GRAT with $1 million, retaining an annuity of $40,000 annually. But this GRAT is for a period of only ten years, rather than 15.

Her total benefit is $40,000 x 10, or $400,000, rather than $600,000 for a 15-year period. The gift tax value of the gift to the final beneficiary is close to $600,000. (As we've said, the exact figure will be different, because of the IRS calculation tables.) That means a higher gift tax assessment.

If the value of the gift to the final beneficiaries exceeds the current estate tax exempt amount, or you make the gift after the estate tax is repealed, you will have to pay gift tax when the trust is funded.

Example: In 2007, Max places $3 million in a GRAT and reserves a $60,000 annuity for himself for ten years. This results in a total benefit to him of $600,000 and a gift (to the final beneficiary) worth roughly $2.4 million. (Again, the IRS tables must be used to determine the precise taxable value of the gift.) Because the value of the gift exceeds Max's gift tax exemption, Max will have to pay gift tax on roughly $1 million, the amount of the gift tax exemption in 2007.

b. Increasing the Tax Savings From a GRAT

A GRAT is an irrevocable trust, which means that usually it functions as a separate taxable entity. However, it can be constructed in such a way that all income and capital gain from the trust are taxed to you, the grantor. This is called making the GRAT a "grantor trust." This way, more money is eventually given to the final beneficiaries.

Example: Theo funds a ten-year GRAT with a stock portfolio. Language in the trust document makes it a grantor trust. During the ten-year period, income from the trust is taxed to him and not to the trust. Also, during the trust term, as trustee, he sells part of the stock and makes a hefty profit. But Theo, not the trust, personally pays the capital gains tax due. This allows the trust assets to grow in value, and at the same time, further reduces Theo's estate.

3. Grantor-Retained Unitrusts (GRUTs)

Don't you just love the jargon? Yes, it's bizarre, but you can comprehend it sufficiently so you can make an informed choice of whether you want to hire an expert for this. A grantor-retained unitrust, or GRUT, is very similar to a GRAT with this important difference: the income payment to you (the grantor) is not a fixed amount annually. Instead, the amount is equal to a percentage of the value of the trust assets for that particular year.

Each year, the new current value of the trust assets must be determined. Assuming a decent economy, in a well-managed trust, the worth of the assets should gradually increase over the years. In that case, the annual payments you receive would also get larger.

If the percentage payment is larger than the trust's earnings—for example, you're entitled to 8% of the trust's net worth, but the trust property earned only 5% this year—the rest comes out of the principal. Any trust income above the percentage set for you is added to the trust assets.

Just as with a GRAT, the gift tax value of the gift to the final beneficiary is established when the trust is created. The taxable value of a GRUT gift, for gift tax purposes, is determined by a complex IRS formula. The formula considers how much you can expect to receive over the set period, your age and life expectancy, and how long the trust is supposed to last. The older you are, the more valuable the gift; the longer the term of the trust, the lower the gift value.

Because your annual payment is based on the value of the trust property, a GRUT can give you some hedge against inflation. For example, say you have $1 million in a GRUT and get 7% of the value of the trust assets per year. If suddenly there's 20% annual inflation, the dollar value of the trust assets will, presumably, also increase by roughly 20%, to $1.2 million. Obviously, 7% of $1.2 million is a higher number than 7% of $1 million. But all you are really doing is keeping up with inflation. In real dollar terms, you receive the same amount, although you receive more (inflated) dollars. No such hedge against inflation is available to grantors of a GRAT. They receive a set dollar amount every year, period.

Example: Ravi, aged 60, has an estate worth $2.5 million. He puts $300,000 into a GRUT that will last for ten years. Then the trust assets go to his friend Monica. The trust specifies that during each year of the ten-year period, Ravi will receive 8% of the trust's net worth.

The first year, the trust pays out $24,000 to Ravi—8% of $300,000. If Ravi survives the ten-year period, Monica will likely receive more than $300,000, and surely far more than the value the IRS assigned the gift when the trust was created. In addition, Ravi will have removed the $300,000 from his taxable estate.

> ### GRUTs AT A GLANCE
>
> - You create and fund the trust, establishing the percentage return you will get each year for however many years you want the trust to last.
>
> - The value of the gift, for gift tax purposes, is determined when you fund the trust.
>
> - The trustee pays you the established percentage of assets each year.
>
> - Trust assets are appraised annually.
>
> - When the term ends, the trust is terminated. Trust assets go to the final beneficiary.

4. Drawbacks of GRATs and GRUTs

The potential benefits of a GRUT or GRAT are rarely worth the risks involved unless you are very wealthy. If you have $10 million, putting $2 million in a GRUT or GRAT makes more sense than putting $500,000 in one if you have $2 million. Also, an expert must set up the trust, which is complicated and expensive.

Whether or not the drawbacks are likely to affect you depends on your family and tax situation. You should be aware of these drawbacks and evaluate how they could affect you and your beneficiaries before you create one of these trusts.

a. You Lose Control Over Trust Assets

As we've already stressed, once a GRAT or GRUT is established and operational, you lose legal ownership of the trust property. You can't later on turn around and decide that the income you receive from the trust isn't enough, and insist on higher payments. Nor can you get the trust assets returned to you personally. Further, you cannot add to, or subtract from, the trust principal. Under IRS rules, the amount put in the trust must stay there, period. Practically speaking, this means that if you or someone in your family suffers a financial disaster, the trust property isn't available to help out.

Further, if you do survive the trust term, you lose all benefit from the trust assets because they go to the final beneficiary at the end of the set term. Suppose you live for another ten years after the trust ends. You may well have become accustomed to the payments from the trust—or worse, may need them for expenses, such as medical costs. But anything you receive from the trust property (after the trust ends) will have to be a gift to you from the final beneficiaries—if they choose to make it.

b. Estate Tax Savings Are Not Guaranteed

Usually the biggest concern when deciding whether to use a GRAT or GRUT is the possibility that you won't outlive the period you've set to receive income from the trust. If you die before the trust period ends, all the trust property is legally part of your estate. All your possible estate tax savings are lost.

If you are married, you can plan to defer taxes in such circumstances by having the trust assets go to your spouse. All property left to your spouse (if he or she is a U.S. citizen) can pass estate tax free under the marital deduction. If the surviving spouse is young and healthy, that spouse can make or revise her own estate plan to try to soften the estate tax blow when she dies.

But if the surviving spouse is elderly or in poor health and may not live long, or if you are single, your untimely death and the resulting addition of the trust property to your estate could mean higher estate taxes. In hindsight, another form of estate plan, such as a program of direct gift giving, would have been preferable.

5. Grantor-Retained Income Trusts (GRITs)

If you set up a GRIT, you receive all income from the trust assets for a set period. The assets go to the final beneficiary when you die or the term ends. GRITs were enormously popular before 1990. In that year, Congress took away any tax savings if the trust assets eventually benefit your family. "Family" includes your spouse, lineal descendants, ancestors, siblings, and spouses of any of these family members.

The law left one exception. The one remaining form of GRIT that can save on taxes and be used for family members is called a "residence GRIT."

a. Qualified Residence GRITs

You may still successfully use a GRIT that will ultimately benefit family members, if it is funded with only your personal residence and nothing else. (I.R.C. § 2702.) This personal residence may be either your primary residence or a vacation home. You can do this for both, but you will need two separate trusts, one for each house. If the vacation home is sometimes rented by others, to qualify for a GRIT, you must actually use it each year for the greater of 14 days, or 10% of the time it is rented. So, if it is rented for 180 days a year, you must personally use it for at least 18 days, 10% of 180 days.

Here's how the residence GRIT works. You put your residence into a trust for a set period, usually about ten years. Your retained "income interest" during the term is the right to occupy the residence. When the term of the trust ends, the property goes to the final beneficiary you named in the original trust document.

Again, in order to obtain your goal, the trick is to outlive the term of the trust. If you don't survive the term, the full current value of the house is included in your taxable estate and your attempt at a reduced value gift fails.

If you set up a residence GRIT, you are usually the trustee. The trust document gives you full control over management of the house—it's almost like retaining actual home ownership. Among other things, this means that you can still take an income tax deduction for mortgage interest and real estate taxes on the house.

When carefully drafted, the trust document creating your GRIT can allow you to make additional payments to the trust for mortgage payments, taxes, insurance, and improvements. The document should also give you freedom to sell the property and reinvest the proceeds in another home.

Possibly more important, you can also retain the right, under IRS rules, to sell a principal residence and reinvest sale proceeds of $250,000 without capital gains tax. You may be able to take the proceeds and convert the GRIT into a GRAT.

The taxable value of the gift to the residence GRIT—the residence—is based on an IRS formula that considers the term of years of the trust, your age, and current interest rates.

Example: Lucille, 55 years old, funds her GRIT with her primary residence, worth $1 million. The term of the trust is for 15 years, after which the residence will go to her son. The gift tax value of the gift to her son is figured by IRS formulas. In this case, Lucille's retained interest is worth about $750,000. So for gift tax purposes, the gift to the son is worth about $250,000.

If Lucille survives the 15-year term, her son will receive the house. Because the house will not be part of Lucille's taxable estate, the only tax assessed was on the $250,000 gift, when the trust was funded. (No tax would actually be paid, as long as Lucille hadn't already used up her gift tax exemption.)

b. "Reversionary Interests" in a GRIT

One of the major reasons for the popularity of house GRITs is that the grantor can retain certain reversionary interests. Many estate planners suggest that married couples include a specific type of reversionary interest clause in a residence GRIT. This clause directs that if one spouse dies before the end of the term, the house is to be returned to the spouse's estate and given to the surviving spouse, so the unlimited estate tax marital deduction can be used.

Example: Celeste puts her summer cottage in a GRIT that will last 15 years; at the end of that period, the cottage will go to her daughter, Anna. But Celeste keeps a reversionary interest in the cottage so that if she dies during the term of the trust, the cottage reverts to her estate instead of going to her daughter. This would result in the property actually passing to Celeste's husband, so no estate tax will have to be paid if Celeste dies during the term.

In the past, you could structure a GRIT so that you had the right to purchase back the property from the trust before the term ended. Because the IRS viewed you as the property's owner until the trust period ended, you had no taxable gain or loss on this purchase. This technique was widely used to give the final beneficiaries a cost basis in the residence of current market value. The IRS, however, was extremely critical of this procedure, and now prohibits the sale of the residence back to the grantor or the grantor's spouse. (See Prop. Treas. Reg. 25.2702-5.)

You will need expert help in drafting any kind of residence GRIT. You need someone who not only knows how to draft these GRITs, but also someone who is current on relevant law.

RESIDENCE GRITS AT A GLANCE

- You create the trust and fund it with your house. You retain the right to live in the house, or sell it and buy a new one.

- The value of the gift for gift tax purposes is determined when you transfer the house to the trust. It is reduced by your retained interest of living in the house.

- When the term ends, the trust is terminated and the final beneficiary receives the trust assets.

c. Drawbacks of Residence GRITs

As with all grantor-retained interest trusts, the flip side of the potentially big tax advantages of a residence GRIT are potentially big disadvantages. The drawbacks of a GRIT are essentially the same as for a GRAT or GRUT, covered above in Section C4. One drawback unique to a residence GRIT is that at the end of the trust period, you no longer own your home. If you want to stay, you will owe fair rent to the final beneficiaries. For the wealthy, paying rent is often just another good way to pass on money to their children without gift tax and also to reduce their estate, and consequently its tax. But for people with less money, it could surely be a burden.

REMEMBER KING LEAR

In a perfect world, a parent might create a residence GRIT for the benefit of a child or grandchild, who will lovingly allow the parent to continue to reside in the house until death. The child or grandchild would then, at the death of the parent, move in or sell the house.

Sadly, this is not always what happens. (Surprise—there's need and even greed in some families.) When several children are the final beneficiaries, they may decide to sell the property as soon as they become its legal owners. If they need the money and don't care what happens to the parent (the grantor), that parent could find herself losing a place to live.

Even if the parent is wealthy and could afford another house, a GRIT might make it easier for a well-meaning child to pack a parent off to a nursing home. After all, the child could rationalize, it's not even the parent's house any more.

Making another trust the final beneficiary of a residence GRIT can sometimes alleviate these potential problems, if you select a trustee who'll treat you honorably. Still, the trustee has a legal obligation to the final beneficiaries to produce the most income possible from the trust, which might necessitate selling the house. And if you can't trust your own kids, how can you be confident a separate trustee will be more reliable?

d. "Regular" GRITs

You establish a regular GRIT by giving property—any kind, such as stock, money, or land—and retaining the right to the income from the property for a set term. Congress eliminated the advantages of regular GRITs for direct family members, but not for other beneficiaries. In fact, nieces, nephews, and cousins, as well as friends, can still be final beneficiaries for GRITs funded with property other than a personal residence. This is one strategy unmarried couples can use—and indeed, benefit from—because they are not legally "family."

In a regular GRIT, you receive all of the income for a set term from the trust property. The gift tax value of the gift consists of what the final beneficiary is expected to receive at the end of the set term. As with all of the other grantor-retained interest trusts, the IRS values the gift property for tax purposes when the trust is established, and does not revalue it again when the property is distributed to the final beneficiaries. Your income interest is subtracted from the total worth of the property to determine the value of the gift. The IRS tables used for this calculation take into account current interest rates, your age, and the length of the term. The actual gift is usually substantially discounted for gift tax purposes.

Example: Joseph creates a ten-year GRIT for the benefit of his longtime companion, Al. He funds it with a stock portfolio worth $1 million. Because he will receive all of the income for ten years, the gift to Al in the GRIT is valued at much less than what Al will receive. For estate and gift tax purposes, the gift retains its original gift tax value no matter what the stock is worth ten years later, when Al becomes the owner (assuming Joseph is still alive). If Joseph doesn't survive the term, the full value of the trust assets as of the date of his death will be included in his taxable estate, just as if he had done nothing.

Like the other trusts discussed above, the shorter the term, the larger the taxable gift to the final beneficiary. But if you are in good health, and especially if you are single, regular GRITS still offer an attractive method of giving gifts, reducing the size of an estate and saving on taxes at the same time.

"REGULAR" GRITs AT A GLANCE

- You create and fund the trust, specifying how long it is to last. The trust beneficiary may not be a "family member."

- The value of the gift for gift tax purposes is determined when you fund the trust.

- The trustee pays you all income annually.

- When the term ends, the trust is terminated, and trust assets go to the final beneficiary.

---

6. Questions to Ask About a Grantor-Retained Interest Trust

If a GRAT, GRUT, or GRIT sounds appealing, you need to sit down with an estate planning expert and carefully assess your situation. An expert should compare using any of these trusts with other possible estate planning alternatives. Make sure you can answer these questions:

- How do the tax savings from this type of trust compare with simply giving the gift directly (with any gift tax assessed), or making the gift over a period of years, using the annual gift tax exclusion repeatedly and allowing the beneficiary to invest the money you give?

- What are the likely savings overall, taking into consideration possible capital gains tax paid by the final beneficiary if he sells the trust property?

- Given your age, health, and financial situation, and your feelings about money and security, can you risk parting with these assets irrevocably?

- Are you confident that present feelings about who you name as your final beneficiaries will remain the same for years?

- Is it better to create a grantor-retained interest trust and pay gift tax now (if necessary) on the gift property? Or is it wiser to hang on to the property and let your estate pay any estate tax due on this property after your death?

- Is a grantor-retained interest trust really desirable? Consider your overall financial picture and the possible alternatives, including:

  - the personal estate tax exemption, which increases each year and may be repealed after the year 2009

  - a program of tax-exempt gifts over a number of years

  - using an AB trust so both spouses' personal estate tax exemptions are used

  - QTIP trusts

  - charitable trusts, or

  - life insurance policies owned by others on your life.

Answering these questions, and other personal ones that will surely come up, is time consuming and requires a high level of expertise in estate planning. And remember that regulations concerning these discounted gifts change frequently, particularly the IRS interest tables. If your expert can't address all of your questions or thinks that you should leave all these decisions up to him, quickly find another expert who is genuine and simpatico. ■

22

DISCLAIMERS:
After-Death Estate Tax Planning

It may sound strange, but after you die, one or more of your beneficiaries may decline part or all of the property you left them. Refusing to take an inheritance is called "disclaiming" it. A beneficiary has the legal right under federal law (I.R.C. § 2518) to disclaim or refuse all, or any part, of a gift. If a beneficiary disclaims property, it goes to the person you specified in your trust or will to receive it if the primary beneficiary cannot or does not take it. In other words, the person who winds up with the gift is the alternate beneficiary for that gift, or, if you didn't name an alternate beneficiary, your residuary beneficiary.

You may wonder why anyone in our materially oriented society would be so unworldly as to refuse even some of an inheritance. It's not because the people who disclaim are noble or saintly. (They may be, but that's not what disclaimers are about.) The most common reason people disclaim gifts is to lighten their individual or their family's overall estate tax burden. Also, some people simply want property they could inherit to go instead to needier relations, without having to give it to them and being subject to gift tax. Disclaimers are an important tool in estates of any size.

A. ADVANTAGES OF DISCLAIMERS

Disclaimers can be an effective way for a beneficiary who already has plenty of property to pass a gift along to another person (usually a family member) who has less, and by doing so, save on estate and gift taxes.

1. Estate and Gift Tax Savings

Once an estate reaches a certain size, estate tax kicks in—and the tax is hefty. (See Chapter 15.) As we explained in that chapter, new tax laws slowly raise the personal exemption from estate tax until it disappears entirely for one year: 2010. But Congress must vote on this law again before then, and many estate planning experts believe that Congress will change the new law drastically or even repeal it.

No matter what happens with the estate tax laws, disclaimers will always be important for many who need or want to shift assets to a different heir after someone's death. If Congress does indeed do away with estate tax, disclaimers will still be crucial in avoiding gift tax, which is not slated to disappear.

Disclaimers reduce estate and gift taxes because, under federal tax law, any property disclaimed by a beneficiary is never legally owned by that person. That means it cannot be included in that beneficiary's taxable estate at death. In addition, no gift tax is assessed against the person who disclaims a gift (in effect, giving it to someone else), again because the person never owned it.

While estate tax still exists, disclaimers can be particularly useful when a primary beneficiary already has a large estate and receiving the gift would add significantly to his eventual tax bill. If the alternate beneficiary has much less wealth, then overall estate tax is reduced.

> **Example:** Roger, an elderly widower, has an estate worth $540,000. He leaves it equally to his two children, George and Carlotta, and provides that if one of them cannot or does not take his or her half, it will go to the other. When Roger dies, his middle-aged children are in very different financial shape. Carlotta is a prosperous clothing designer, with an estate of roughly $2 million. Her husband has a similar-sized estate. George hasn't fared so well financially. His real estate business (his latest enterprise) was marginal from its beginning, five years ago, and it has been in a serious slump over the past year. George has almost no savings or other assets and a child with special educational needs.

Carlotta and George are close. Carlotta decides to disclaim her half of her father's estate so the entire $540,000 goes to George.

Carlotta disclaims the gift not primarily to save on estate tax, but because she felt George needed it and she didn't. But a pleasant side benefit is that there will be a significant estate tax savings. If Carlotta had accepted her half, her total estate would have grown to over $2 million, potentially creating an eventual estate tax liability. As of now, George's estate is about $540,000—his inheritance. So his estate will not be subject to estate tax unless, of course, it increases significantly in value before his death.

Disclaimers can also be desirable if the primary beneficiary is older and may not live long, and the alternate beneficiary is younger.

Example: Barton dies in 2007 and leaves his estate of $1 million to his sister Elizabeth. She is in her late 70s and already has an estate worth $2 million. The alternate beneficiaries for Barton's estate are Elizabeth's two children, both in their 30s, with very little property.

If Elizabeth accepted the gift, her estate would total $3 million. If she were to die in the year 2007 or 2008 when the estate tax exemption is $2 million, $1 million would be taxed. If Elizabeth instead disclaims the gift, it will be divided between her two children and no estate tax will be due at her death.

Clearly, disclaiming property can result in substantial estate tax advantages. But unlike a bypass trust (see Chapter 18, Section A), which is established in advance to save on estate taxes, it's solely up to the beneficiary to decide whether or not to disclaim a gift. A beneficiary who is insecure, needy, or even a tad greedy may choose not to disclaim property, even though disclaiming might be the wisest choice in light of "objective" personal need and overall estate tax consequences. But after all, the gift was left to that beneficiary. Disclaiming may make sense from the entire family's point of view, but it's hard to see it as a moral obligation.

2. Fine-Tuning Gifts

Disclaimers can allow beneficiaries to make adjustments regarding who gets what, no matter how much an estate is worth. This can be done to equalize beneficiaries' financial positions. The power to disclaim can also help beneficiaries avoid problems of owning something together, having to come up with the money to buy out co-owners, or having to sell property that one of them loves.

Example: Tony, a bachelor, leaves his entire estate to his two nephews, Phil and Angelo, in equal shares. Each is the alternate beneficiary for the other's gift.

Among the assets at Tony's death is an ocean beachfront vacation home. Phil, with a sizable estate of his own, doesn't care about the ocean and spends his summers in the mountains. Angelo, on the other hand, is not as well-off financially and has vacationed every summer of his life at the beach cottage. Phil disclaims his one-half interest in the beach property, keeping it out of his already large estate (and paying no gift tax whatever) when it then goes to Angelo.

Disclaimers can also be used when a person wants the property to go to the next in line for the gift.

Example: Babette leaves her house to her three children, in equal shares. Her living trust provides that the alternate beneficiaries for each child's share are his or her children. When Babette dies, all three of her children are quite well off. Two intend to accept their share of the house. One child, Fritz, disclaims his share, because he decides it's wiser to let it pass to his children, who are in their early 20s and starting their careers (or, at least, starting to earn money). Fritz knows his children will find much security in the financial nest egg his disclaimer provides for each.

If Babette had specified that the alternate beneficiaries for the house were her other children, Fritz would not have disclaimed his share. He would not have wanted that share divided between his brother and sister, bringing no benefit to his children.

3. Adjusting for Unforeseen Circumstances

Disclaimers can also be a lifesaver under pressing circumstances. For instance, a person may be overgenerous or overoptimistic regarding his finances when he prepares his estate plan, and his financial situation at death may turn out to be worse than he anticipated. Beneficiaries can use disclaimers to achieve fair results—results the person would surely have wanted if he'd known how his finances would turn out.

Example: Sven, who's doing well in business, prepares a living trust that leaves $200,000 each to his three children and the rest of his estate to his spouse. Later, after some business setbacks and an extended illness, his wealth has dwindled. When Sven dies, there will be almost nothing left for his widow after the $600,000 is given to his children. The

children generously disclaim their inheritance so the money will go to their mother for her support.

This sounds good—indeed, ideal—but there is, of course, an obvious risk if a disclaimer is needed for this purpose. A child or any beneficiary may be unwilling to give up an inheritance, no matter what hardship that creates for someone else, even a parent. It would have been wiser for Sven to rewrite his living trust after his business reversals, simply leaving all his property to his wife.

B. COUPLES AND DISCLAIMERS

Couples, whether married or not, can sometimes cut their tax bills significantly by using disclaimers. It's common for each member of a couple to leave everything to the other, with the children named as alternate beneficiaries. The surviving mate, they hope, will pass the deceased person's property on to their children. Especially when spouses or mates are relatively young and don't have a big estate, this makes sense. Why tie up property in a trust when a surviving spouse may need that property for decades?

But a couple who had modest property holdings when they prepared their estate plan may turn out to be quite prosperous by the time one spouse dies decades later. In situations like this, the surviving spouse's ability to disclaim part of the deceased spouse's estate, and have it go directly to their children, can achieve substantial overall estate tax savings. (A surviving spouse can also disclaim property and have it go into a trust that benefits that spouse. See Section C4, below.)

Example: Boris and his wife Natasha created their estate plan while in their mid-50s, leaving all of their property to each other.

Each named their three children as alternate beneficiaries. By their late 70s, they own combined assets worth $2.8 million.

Boris dies first in the year 2006, leaving his $1.4 million share to Natasha. Natasha is not in good health. Natasha disclaims $800,000 of her inheritance, which means it will go directly to their children. She does this for two reasons. First, there's a possibility that Natasha may end up in a nursing home or need major health care. If so, her entire estate could be gobbled up with distressing speed. But the $800,000 she has disclaimed cannot be subject to claims from any of her health care providers.

The second reason for her disclaimer concerns estate taxes. As the chart below shows, in the year 2006 her disclaimer will allow her to receive the maximum amount possible from Boris and still not have her estate subject to estate tax when she dies.

	Without Disclaimer	With Disclaimer
Value of Boris's estate	$1.4 million	$1.4 million
Estate tax due	-0-	-0-
Value of Natasha's estate	$2.8 million	$2 million
Estate tax at her death	due on $800,000	-0-

Now suppose Boris and Natasha had the same size estate, but Boris died suddenly in his late 50s. Natasha might well decide not to disclaim any of Boris's estate. It could be ten, 20, or many more years before her death, and she may well want or need all the $1.4 million during her lifetime.

When a surviving spouse wants to disclaim an interest in property the spouses own together, that spouse can disclaim only that portion that was left to her by the deceased spouse. The other half of the property is and remains owned by the surviving spouse; obviously, no disclaimer of that portion is possible.

Example: Yaphet and Malika together own property worth $850,000. Yaphet also has well over $1 million in separate property. They each leave their half of the shared property to each other, with their three children as alternate beneficiaries. After Malika dies, Yaphet wants to disclaim all he can, so it will go to his children. He can disclaim only Malika's one-half share of their shared property, a total of $425,000. He cannot disclaim his own one-half share of that property (or, of course, his separate property), because that wasn't left to him by Malika—he owned it all along.

C. IRS Rules for Disclaimers

Federal law requires that a beneficiary's disclaimer must be "qualified." This means that it must meet certain rules set out in I.R.C. § 2518. If these rules aren't met, the person disclaiming will not avoid legal ownership of the property for estate tax or gift tax purposes, and the major purpose of the disclaimer will be lost. The IRS requirements are:

- The disclaimer must be in writing.

- A disclaimer by an adult must be completed within nine months of the death of the person leaving the property.

- A minor who has been left property must disclaim within nine months after reaching age 21.

- The person who disclaims property may not accept any benefit from the property before disclaiming it. (An exception exists for a surviving spouse; see Section 4, below).

- The person refusing the property may not direct where it then goes. The deceased person's will or trust document determines who receives the disclaimed property.

1. Putting the Disclaimer in Writing

A beneficiary who wants to disclaim inherited property—for whatever reason and whatever the type of property—is responsible for putting the disclaimer in writing. The beneficiary must deliver the written disclaimer to the person who is in control of the property at that time. This is usually the successor trustee of a living trust or the executor of a will.

> **Example:** In her living trust, Carla leaves a money market account to her son, Francisco, and another of roughly equal value to her daughter, Eva. The trust provides that if either child dies before Carla does, the money goes to the other. She names Francisco as successor trustee of her trust.
>
> At Carla's death, Eva is financially comfortable, but Francisco is struggling. Eva is also aware of the fact that her mother spent a large amount on her college and graduate education, while Francisco chose not to go to college. She wishes to disclaim so he can receive the money directly from Eva's estate without it being a taxable gift from her.
>
> As successor trustee, Francisco is bound by law to follow the directions in his mother's trust. If Eva calls him up and tells him to take her money, he can't legally do it. He needs the written disclaimer so he can follow the trust instructions and satisfy IRS regulations. Only when armed with the signed disclaimer from Eva will he have the power to change his mother's primary instructions and take

the money himself. (See Section D, below, covering complexities that can arise when a trustee of a living trust disclaims trust property or receives it by disclaimer.)

2. The Nine-Month Deadline

IRS rules require that a disclaimer must be made by adults within nine months of the death of the original giver—that is, the trust grantor or will writer.

Disclaimers by minors. A minor can disclaim a gift within nine months of becoming age 21. This raises some odd questions, such as who manages the property until the minor turns 21? What can be done with it? Who may benefit from the property during this time? The answers depend on state law. It's a very complicated legal matter. If you are the parent or guardian of a minor who has been left property and think it's possible the minor would want to disclaim that property at age 21, seek some good professional advice.

The nine-month period is designed to allow enough time for survivors to begin getting back on their feet emotionally and to get the information they need to make wise financial decisions.

> **Example:** Makoto dies suddenly in 2007, leaving a wife, Hanako, in her 60s, and two adult children. His will leaves everything to Hanako or, if she doesn't survive him, to the children. Makoto's elder son, Keiji, who is executor of the will, sees immediately that the estate is worth about $3 million, more than Hanako, who has substantial assets of her own, needs. When Keiji hires a lawyer to probate the will, the lawyer advises changing things around for tax purposes. But no one in the family wants to think about these issues shortly after Makoto's death.

The nine-month period gives the attorney time to draft a tax-savings plan and explain it to the family. Also, the family has a chance to look at the situation and assess who needs what, and when.

In the end, Hanako decides to disclaim the $2 million, the amount of the personal exemption in 2007. This allows Makoto's estate to use its entire personal estate tax exemption of $2 million, which now goes to the children as alternates. Now Hanako's total estate is smaller than if she'd inherited the $3 million, so the estate tax that will be due at her death will be lower or nonexistent. But it's not only tax savings that motivate Hanako. She believes her children need this money now, when they are working hard and trying to raise their own children. With the disclaimer, they get it, with no taxable gift having been made by Hanako.

3. No Personal Benefit

With one important exception, discussed below in Section 4, a beneficiary who wants to disclaim property cannot use or accept any benefit from the property, however brief the use or slight the benefit. One danger here is when a beneficiary takes a small benefit from a large gift. For example, if you receive rent from gift real estate for a short time and then decide you want to disclaim the entire gift, it's too late. The disclaimer will not be valid.

Also, a beneficiary who will receive any benefit from the property after the disclaimer cannot disclaim the property. For example, a beneficiary cannot disclaim property that then goes into a trust that pays, or even could pay, the beneficiary any income. For instance, if you were to disclaim a gift that goes into a family pot trust with 15 potential beneficiaries, including you, the disclaimer is not

valid. The property still goes to the next beneficiary in line, but the transaction is considered, legally, a simple gift, and you may be assessed gift tax if the property is valuable enough.

4. Special Rules for Surviving Spouses

There's one exception to the general rule that a beneficiary can't receive any benefit from disclaimed property. A surviving spouse who disclaims a gift can still receive some benefits from it. This makes possible some flexible estate planning.

One strategy is to arrange things so that a surviving spouse can disclaim money inherited from the other. If the property is disclaimed, it goes into an AB trust, with the surviving spouse as life beneficiary. That spouse can be given rights to receive income from the trust, invade the principal for health care and other basic needs, and use the trust property. When the second spouse dies, the trust assets go to the couple's children (or other beneficiary they chose). The IRS never considers the second spouse to die the legal owner of the disclaimed property, even though he may have benefited from that property.

> **Example:** Benjamin and Esther, in their 40s, own shared property worth $800,000. Each has an estate worth $400,000. In their estate plan, each leaves their property outright to the other.
>
> However, they worry about what will happen if they acquire considerably more valuable property but don't get around to revising their plan. Then there might be substantial federal estate taxes when the surviving spouse dies, and an AB trust might be desirable. (See Chapter 18, Section C.) On the other hand, the surviving spouse may need or want the entire estate, not just the right to get trust income or limited rights to invade

principal, as an AB would provide. How can Benjamin and Esther decide now what's wisest? The answer is, they don't have to.

Suppose their total estate is worth $4 million when Esther dies in 2007. Esther leaves her $2 million to Benjamin, subject to his right to disclaim. Any amount disclaimed would go into an AB trust. Benjamin could disclaim the entire amount. In other words, Benjamin could decide that his own estate of $2 million plus the income from Esther's trust is enough for him. The personal exemption is $2 million, so no tax will be due on Esther's death or on his. By using the disclaimer, both Esther's and Benjamin's estates take advantage of their personal estate tax exemptions, saving a significant amount in estate taxes and leaving more, eventually, to the children.

When the estates of the spouses are unequal, disclaimers can be used similarly, placing property where it's wisest for estate tax purposes. The goal is to equalize the value of both spouses' estates, or at least make them closer in size. The reason for this is that old graduated estate tax and the personal estate tax exemption. If one spouse has an estate of $4 million, and the other has nothing, they will pay more estate tax than if each spouse owned property worth $2 million.

Disclaimers used to equalize, or balance, spouses' estates are often used in combination with other estate tax saving devices, such as AB trusts or QTIP trusts. (See Chapter 18, Section C, and Chapter 19, Section A.)

Example: Guido, 70 years old, is married for the second time, to Sophia. Guido's assets total $4 million, and Sophia's financial worth is negligible. Guido wants to ensure that Sophia is taken care of in the case of his death, but he wants his estate to eventually pass to the children of his first marriage.

He creates a plan that will pay income to Sophia for her support from two trusts, one a formula AB trust worth the amount of his personal exemption in the year of death (see Chapter 18, Section C), and the other a QTIP trust consisting of his other assets. (Tax on property in a QTIP trust is deferred until the second spouse dies. See Chapter 19.) Guido directs that the income and then the principal of the QTIP trust be used up, if necessary, before paying Sophia income from the AB trust. At Sophia's death, the assets remaining in both trusts will go to Guido's children.

If Sophia disclaims any amount of the QTIP trust property, it will go into the AB trust. She remains entitled to receive the income from that trust if she needs it. However, the amount in the AB trust is subject to tax at Guido's death, instead of at Sophia's death, when the property in the QTIP trust could well be over her personal exemption amount. She may choose to disclaim part of the QTIP trust and pay less estate tax on the smaller disclaimed amount at Guido's death than a larger amount at her death.

D. DISCLAIMERS AND LIVING TRUSTS

You might help your inheritors by directly incorporating your wishes concerning disclaimed gifts into your estate plan.

1. Planning for Disclaimers

Even though disclaimers are expressly authorized by federal law, incorporating a specific disclaimer provision in your living trust or will can create a helpful guide for your beneficiaries. A clause permitting beneficiaries to disclaim gifts you leave tells them that you know about disclaimers and personally authorize them. A beneficiary who wants to make a disclaimer doesn't have to worry about going against your desires. Also, not all beneficiaries (or successor trustees or executors) know about disclaimers, so specifically authorizing them can be a good means of alerting your beneficiaries that they exist.

You can also specify who is to receive property that one of your beneficiaries disclaims. This would be desirable only if you don't want a disclaimed gift to go the alternate beneficiary. This might be the case if the alternate beneficiary is likely to be in the same financial position as the primary beneficiary, as can be the case with husband and wife.

Example: Chang, a widower, leaves his $500,000 estate to his son Tai, with Tai's wife, Claudia, as the alternate beneficiary. But Chang also provides in his living trust document that should Tai disclaim any property, it then goes to Chang's favorite nephew. When Chang dies, Tai's and Claudia's assets are quite large; neither needs the inheritance. By contrast, the nephew, who is just starting out in business, really needs the money. Tai disclaims the gift, and the $500,000 goes directly to the nephew.

Because Tai never owns the property, his own estate is not increased for estate tax purposes. Nor has he made a taxable gift by disclaiming the gift and letting it go to Chang's nephew.

If Tai had accepted the gift, he could remove it from his estate by subsequently giving it to the nephew. But this would mean Tai would be assessed gift tax on the amount of his inheritance.

2. Problems With Trustees Directing Disclaimed Property

As we've mentioned, the law does not allow a person who disclaims property to determine who will receive it instead. This can present problems for trustees when the disclaimed property is held in trust.

Many trusts do not allow the trustee to determine who receives any trust income or property. The beneficiaries and their shares are all specified in the trust document. But if a beneficiary is considering disclaiming property that will then go into a trust, and the beneficiary is a trustee that has any powers at all over the trust assets, expert advice is needed. For instance, a power to distribute trust principal if a child needs it could raise a red flag for the IRS. Even a power by the trustee to allocate income and principal might cause a disclaimer to fail.

Someone who both serves as the successor trustee of a living trust and inherits trust property may run into complications disclaiming property. The basic rule is that if you have any authority to direct where any of the disclaimed property will go, you can't disclaim it. For gift and estate tax purposes, it will be considered your own property and a gift from you to the person who receives it. To avoid this problem, you must either resign as trustee or decline the authority to direct distribution of trust property.

Example: Tsultrim and her husband, Yeshe, each create a living trust, providing that on a spouse's death, $1 million of that spouse's property goes directly into a trust for their children. Any remaining property goes outright to the surviving spouse. The surviving spouse will serve as trustee of the children's trust and have broad trustee powers, including the authority to distribute trust principal and income to the children if they need it.

Yeshe dies first. The couple's estate turns out to be larger than expected, so it would be desirable, from the overall estate tax viewpoint, for Tsultrim to disclaim the property Yeshe left to her and let it go into the children's trust. Estate taxes would be lower in the long run if some tax were paid on part of Yeshe's property at his death.

But as long as she serves as trustee of the trust for the children, Tsultrim can't disclaim any of the property Yeshe left her. That's because, as trustee, she has the authority to direct the distribution of property to the trust beneficiaries. To have a valid disclaimer, she will have to also disclaim this authority or resign as trustee altogether. Otherwise, every distribution to a child would be considered a gift from her and taxed accordingly.

If you anticipate that a disclaimer may make sense, you can include a brief letter or note in the envelope with your will or living trust alerting the executor or successor trustee to the law about disclaimers so they can make intelligent choices about their powers and get help from a tax advisor if necessary. In fact, you may want to suggest that the executor or successor trustee make no distributions whatsoever until all concerned have consulted a tax expert.

When you're preparing a living trust, be sure to discuss disclaimer possibilities with an estate planning expert, and be sure the trust document is drafted so that potential problems are eliminated, to the extent possible. For example, if your successor trustee would have to resign to make her disclaimer valid, it's vitally important that you name the right alternate successor trustee. ■

23

COMBINING ESTATE TAX-SAVING TRUSTS

If you have a large estate, you may want to use more than one tax-saving trust in your estate plan. There are no legal rules or even fixed customs regarding how to combine trusts. This chapter can give you a sense of the possibilities offered. Your individual situation and desires will determine what combination, if any, is right for you.

Combining estate tax-saving trusts requires a lawyer. Combining estate tax-saving trusts involves sophisticated, technical legal work. So it should come as no surprise that you must hire a lawyer to do the work. Indeed, to understand precisely how different options could work for you, you'll need to carefully discuss your situation with a lawyer. Your legal bill will probably be substantial. But then, you must have considerable wealth before it's worth combining different trusts, and doing so can (presumably) save you and your inheritors a bundle. A good lawyer's cost is probably well worth it.

A. COMBINING TWO ESTATE TAX-SAVING TRUSTS

One or both members of a couple, especially in second or subsequent marriages, may want to combine a "formula" AB trust with a QTIP trust. (See Chapter 18, Section C, for information on AB trusts and Chapter 19, Section A, for more on QTIP trusts.) The spouse who creates the trusts names the other as life beneficiary of both trusts. Each trust's final beneficiaries, also named by the spouse who creates the trusts, receive that trust property when the life beneficiary dies. If the spouse who created the trusts survives the other, all his or her property goes, via the trusts, directly to the final beneficiaries.

By combining these two trusts, you can achieve several desirable goals:

- You make use of your personal estate tax exemption with the AB trust.

- If your spouse survives you, all of your property over the amount of the personal exemption in the year of your death is placed in the QTIP trust and qualifies for the unlimited marital deduction. So no federal estate tax is paid on your death.

- Your surviving spouse, as life beneficiary, has restricted rights to spend principal of Trust A, which conserves trust assets for the final beneficiaries. Restrictions are also normally imposed on the rights of the surviving spouse to spend principal of the QTIP trust. Under IRS rules, the surviving spouse must be given unrestricted rights to all trust income generated from assets in the QTIP trust.

- You determine who will ultimately receive all property in your AB and QTIP trusts, after your surviving spouse dies.

Example 1: Malcolm, age 61, has been married to Sadie, age 47, for four years. He has three children from a former marriage. Sadie has a small estate of her own, consisting of savings worth $50,000. Malcolm, on the other hand, owns his house and various investments worth a total of $3 million. He also owns a life insurance policy that will pay $200,000 to Sadie at his death.

Although his children seem to accept Sadie, Malcolm senses uneasiness among them about whether they'll actually receive the inheritance they've been expecting from him. What might happen if Sadie survives Malcolm by 20 or 30 years: A remarriage? A sudden urge to seek thrills and bet fortunes at the racetrack?

Wanting to take care of everybody, if possible, and also to create no hard feelings, Malcolm creates the following plan.

If Sadie survives him, upon his death his property will be divided into a formula AB trust, which will contain property worth the amount of the personal exemption at the year of his death and a QTIP trust for the rest of his property. Sadie is the life beneficiary of both trusts, to receive all trust income. She has no rights to spend either trust principal. When Sadie dies, the property in both trusts will go to Malcolm's three children in equal shares.

Malcolm names Sadie and his daughter Hilda, the most levelheaded of his children and the one who gets along with Sadie the best, to be cotrustees of both trusts.

Example 2: Carla has assets worth $2.5 million; her husband Peter's property totals $200,000. Carla is 73, Peter is 66. Carla has two children by a previous marriage. She wants to be sure her estate will avoid estate tax no matter when she dies. She also wants both to preserve her estate for her children and to help Peter to live a comfortable life, if he survives her.

Carla creates a formula AB trust and a QTIP trust. Peter is the life beneficiary of both trusts, and her children are the final beneficiaries. Carla dies in 2007, when the personal estate tax exemption is $2 million. That amount of her property is placed in the AB trust. The other $500,000 goes into the QTIP trust.

The property in the AB trust is tax free under the personal exemption. The amount in the QTIP is tax free under the marital deduction when Carla dies. When Peter dies, this amount (let's assume it has grown to $700,000) is part of his estate, for estate tax purposes. Peter's own estate is $200,000. The combined total, $900,000 will be well under the estate tax threshold.

LEAVING ALL PROPERTY OVER THE EXEMPT AMOUNT OUTRIGHT TO THE SURVIVING SPOUSE

Many couples, particularly in first marriages, have no need for a QTIP trust. Commonly, these couples share ownership of most or all of their property and want the same people, usually their children, to eventually inherit their property. These couples have no desire for the primary purpose of a QTIP trust, to guarantee that a spouse controls final disposition of her or his property. Rather, a spouse simply leaves all property over the exempt amount outright to the other spouse, trusting that spouse will do what's best for everyone.

Example: Miles and Suno, in their early 50s, have been married over 25 years. They have two children and substantial assets (all co-owned) worth over $4 million. Their estate plan consists of preparing a living trust in which each creates a formula AB trust, and a direction that any property above the formula be left outright to the surviving spouse.

No estate tax will be paid when the first spouse dies. The amount in the AB trust is tax free under the personal exemption. The balance left to the surviving spouse is tax free under the marital deduction.

While both Miles and Suno want their children to eventually inherit their property, neither wants or feels the need to impose on the other the restrictions of a QTIP trust. If one spouse dies prematurely, the other may survive for decades. Why limit this spouse's right over the deceased spouse's property?

B. COMBINING A CHARITABLE TRUST WITH OTHER ESTATE TAX-SAVING TRUSTS

If you want to leave some of your property to causes you care deeply about, you may be eligible for some tax breaks. For example, gifts made to tax-exempt charities through a charitable trust are exempt from estate tax. (See Chapter 20.) The other potential benefits from using a charitable trust are that you take an income tax deduction on the worth of the property you give to charity and you also avoid paying capital gains tax if the charity sells appreciated assets you gave it.

Unless you are extremely wealthy or don't want to leave anything to family or friends, however, you may understandably be reluctant to give or leave significant assets to a charity. Fortunately, you can make a charitable gift, but do it in such a way that the value of the property donated is replaced in your estate. That way your other beneficiaries receive almost as much as they would have without the charitable trust.

How can you make this magic happen? In the right circumstances, by creating both a charitable trust and an irrevocable life insurance trust. (Irrevocable life insurance trusts are discussed in Chapter 21, Section B.) You buy a policy payable to your noncharity beneficiaries, and transfer that policy to the trust. The proceeds of the life insurance policy will be roughly equal to the amount your individual beneficiaries would have inherited from you if you hadn't made the charitable gift. And because you've established the life insurance trust, the proceeds from the policy won't be included in your taxable estate.

Here's a summary of how you might use a life insurance trust to replace money "lost" to individual beneficiaries because of a charitable gift:

1. You make a gift to charity through a charitable trust.

2. You create the life insurance trust. You fund it, for the purpose of making premium payments, with the income tax-savings you obtained by making the charitable gift. This means there is no significant actual cost to you to create and fund the trust. You choose a life insurance policy that will pay out, at your death, more or less the same amount that you gave the charity.

3. You include "Crummey provisions" in your life insurance trust document. These clauses allow gifts you make to the trust to qualify for the annual gift tax exclusion. (See Chapter 21, Section B.) Otherwise, if you gave money directly to the trust, it wouldn't qualify for the exclusion.

4. Your gift money remains in the insurance trust until the trustee spends it on insurance premiums. The net effect is that you have indirectly paid the insurance proceeds (you can get in trouble with the IRS if you pay them directly).

Example: Aldo has four children and an estate worth $3 million. He funds a charitable trust with land currently worth $400,000. He bought the land for $170,000. The charity sells the land and buys stock that will provide payments to him for life. The charity will take what remains of the trust assets at his death.

When he creates the trust, Aldo obtains a significant income tax deduction. Also, by giving the land to charity, he avoids capital gains tax on the increase in value of $230,000 when the land is sold and converted to income-producing assets. And by removing $400,000 from his estate, he saves on estate tax, lowering his taxable estate to $2.6 million.

The property Aldo has given to charity would have gone to his children. But if he had kept the property, it might have been subject to estate tax, depending on the year of his death. If he chooses, he can give the payments made to him from the charity directly to the children as gifts.

Aldo creates an irrevocable life insurance trust. He buys and transfers to the trust a life insurance policy for $400,000—very roughly, the amount "lost" to his children because of his charitable gift. Aldo gives the trustee the amount of the premiums each year, which his children may withdraw. They refuse these "gifts" and the trustee pays the premiums.

If you are in reasonably good health (and especially if you're young), replacing the donated assets by life insurance is usually the preferred choice. If you are elderly, in poor health, or not insurable for any reason, you can try other replacement methods.

Example: After Aldo establishes his charitable trust, he discovers that he is ill and that insurance on his life would be too costly, if available at all. He still sets up an irrevocable trust for his children and donates money to it. The money he donates to the trust is subject to gift tax, but the trustee purchases assets he and Aldo hope will greatly appreciate in value. Depending on the expertise of the trustee and some luck, the money each child would have received but for the charitable gift may eventually be recouped.

C. COMBINING THREE DIFFERENT ESTATE TAX-SAVING TRUSTS

For larger estates, you may even want to make use of several different estate tax-saving trusts. For instance, you could use a formula AB trust for property worth up to the exempt amount at death with a generation-skipping trust and a charitable trust.

Example: Guillermo and Maria, a couple in their late 70s, have an estate worth $12 million, owned equally. They want to leave their property to their children and to some friends and charities.

Each creates a formula AB trust, leaving property to the surviving spouse for life, and then to various final beneficiaries. Also, each creates a generation-skipping trust, leaving $1 million in each trust for their grandchildren. (See Chapter 21, Section A, for information on generation-skipping trusts.) Each also creates a charitable trust, funding it with $900,000. All property of the first spouse to die, after all these gifts are made, goes outright to the surviving spouse.

Guillermo dies in 2007. At Guillermo's death, $2 million, the amount of the personal exemption for 2007, is placed in his AB trust and $1 million goes into his generation-skipping trust. The charitable trust receives $900,000, with Maria receiving 6% income from this trust property for her life. Guillermo's remaining wealth goes outright to Maria. She might want to do some additional estate planning, to minimize estate taxes on her death.

D. USING ONGOING TRUSTS AND GIFT-GIVING TO REDUCE ESTATE TAX

Ongoing trusts can be combined in a number of ways to reduce estate tax for the wealthy. You can leave gifts to your spouse, children, grandchildren, and to charities, all by using different trusts. Here's an example of combining a generation-skipping trust, a charitable remainder unitrust, an irrevocable life insurance trust, an AB trust, and a QTIP trust, all in one estate plan.

Example: Doris is 65 and married to Ted, her second husband. She has two children from her first marriage, both of whom are financially comfortable, and six grandchildren. Doris's estate is worth $7 million; Ted has a much smaller estate of $160,000.

If she dies first, Doris wants Ted to continue to live in the affluent style they've enjoyed, but she also wants most of her assets to go eventually to her children and grandchildren. She also wishes to contribute a sizable portion of her estate to charity. First, she sets up a charitable remainder unitrust of $1 million. (See Chapter 20, Section C.)

Ted and Doris will receive income from the trust annually. Next, she takes an income tax deduction based on the value of her gift to the charitable trust. Using the money saved on income tax, she purchases life insurance and funds an irrevocable life insurance trust. The beneficiaries of the life insurance are her children; they will receive an amount roughly equal to the amount she gave to charity. Proceeds from the life insurance trust will not be included in her estate for estate tax purposes.

Doris also establishes a formula AB trust, with Ted as the life beneficiary. When Ted dies, this trust's assets will be shared by her children.

Next, she establishes a generation-skipping trust of $1 million, with income paid to her children during their lives. This trust may be subject to federal estate tax when Doris dies, but not when the middle generation (her children) dies. When they die, this trust's assets will be distributed to the grandchildren tax free.

The remaining property in Doris's estate will go into a QTIP trust, with all income to Ted for life, and the assets to her children at his death. The trustee, one of Doris's children, can use the principal of this trust for Ted's medical care or basic support if the trustee decides it is needed.

Finally, during Doris's life, she also adopts a plan of giving gifts from her present income to keep her estate from increasing and eventually resulting in more estate tax. She gives $12,000 annually, gift tax free, to each of her two children, their spouses, and the six grandchildren. This is a total of ten people, so $120,000 a year is given away tax free. (See Chapter 16, for more about making gifts.) ■

24

PROPERTY CONTROL TRUSTS FOR SECOND OR SUBSEQUENT MARRIAGES

In many second or subsequent marriages, one or both spouses may feel truly conflicted about estate planning. On one hand, a surviving spouse may well need use of, or income from, the deceased spouse's property, or may even need to spend some of that property, to live as comfortably as before. On the other hand, if a spouse has children from a former marriage, he or she may want to be sure that the bulk of his or her property eventually goes to those children. A spouse may not want the other spouse to wind up with complete legal control of his or her property. A surviving spouse who controls the property of the deceased spouse could decide to leave the deceased spouse's children nothing. These kinds of concerns—which can be dicey at the best of times—become even more complicated if your current spouse and children from a former marriage don't get along.

This chapter discusses basic estate planning options for couples in second or subsequent marriages. (From here on, we use the shorthand "second marriage" to refer to any marriage after the first, whether it's the second or the seventh.) The focus is on trusts, particularly what we call a "marital property control trust." This type of trust imposes controls over your property after your death, so that the surviving spouse has some use of it, or income from it, but never owns it outright. The property goes to your children when the surviving spouse dies. By placing restrictions on the surviving spouse's rights to trust property, you can feel confident that most or all of the trust principal will remain intact for your children. Marital property control trusts are, of course, no guarantee that family conflicts and tensions will be eliminated or even reduced. But they can achieve at least some control over your assets, and give you the comfort that you've done your best to provide for your spouse and your children.

Marital property control trusts can also be used to save on estate tax. (See Section E, below.)

This chapter focuses exclusively on concerns of spouses in second marriages, because for many people this is a central concern of their estate planning. But trusts imposing property controls can be useful in many situations, not just those involving second marriages. (See Chapter 25.)

UNMARRIED COUPLES

This chapter talks in terms of subsequent marriages and surviving spouses, because most people who do this type of estate planning are married. But the principles apply equally to unmarried couples with children from previous relationships.

A. EVALUATING YOUR SITUATION

Tolstoy began *Anna Karenina* with the famous sentence, "Happy families are all alike, each unhappy family is unhappy in its own way." Whether families involving second marriages are happy or not, each is certainly unique in its own way. With a "blended" (or not so blended) family, you have to make a realistic appraisal of your unique situation to do sensible estate planning. Here are some factors to consider:

Your financial status. You'll need to take into account the value of property you and your spouse each own separately, and the value you own together.

The relationship between you and your spouse. Here, you'll need to think carefully about your needs and expectations, and those of your spouse. For example, do one or both of you depend on an income from or property of the other? Is one of you significantly younger? Is one or both of you in bad health? What expectations do you each have regarding inheriting the other's property and what do you each want to do with the property you own?

Do you have a prenuptial agreement? A "prenup," as a prenuptial or premarital agreement is commonly called, is a legally binding agreement made before marriage that covers property rights—what's his, what's hers, what's theirs—during the marriage and after it ends, whether by divorce or the death of one spouse. (A "postnup" is a similar type of agreement that's made after marriage, though it may be subject to more restrictions than a prenup.) Prenups can override most state marital property laws. However, in many states, you can waive spousal inheritance protections only if you comply with detailed requirements at the time you write and sign your contract. (In addition, you can't use a prenup to waive rights to child support and, in some states, you can't give up the right to alimony. Of course these issues usually come up during a divorce, not while making an estate plan.)

⚠ If you have made a prenup or a postnup. Marital property agreements can affect or even control a spouse's inheritance rights and ability to leave property. If you have a prenup or postnup, be sure that your estate planning documents—your will, any trusts, and all beneficiary designations—are consistent with the terms of your marital contract.

📖 If you want to learn about prenups. This potentially touchy subject is sensitively and thoroughly explored in *Prenuptial Agreements: How to Write a Fair & Lasting Contract*, by Katherine E. Stoner and Shae Irving (Nolo).

Legal constraints controlling how you can leave your property. Various circumstances may restrict what you can do with your property at death. For instance, if you have a prenuptial agreement, you can't unilaterally change it when planning your estate. Your spouse must consent to any changes you want to make to that agreement.

Similarly, if you have a 401(k) plan, by federal law your spouse must receive all funds in the account when you die, unless your spouse waives that right in writing.

Also, in common law states, your spouse has a legal right to inherit a certain portion of your property (usually one-third to one-half), no matter what you want. (See Chapter 3, Section C.) In most states, this right can be waived.

What are your relationships with your children? Just as you must consider the needs and expectations of your spouse, you must think about your relationship with each of your kids. For example, what do you feel about leaving property to your children, particularly if you have children from your present marriage as well as from a former partnership? What do you think your children need or deserve? Do you want to leave each of them an equal amount of property?

And the final problem, how do you reconcile all these concerns in your estate plan? You must decide how to balance and apportion the property you leave to your spouse with property you leave to your children, as well as any other beneficiaries you want to name.

There are a number of legal devices you can use to carry out your desires. You can simply leave some property outright to your spouse and other property outright to your children. But often the pie doesn't seem quite big enough for that. A spouse may want to leave property for the use of a surviving spouse for life, then to children from former marriages. The most commonly used device to accomplish this is the "marital property control trust," discussed below in Section B. Other devices that can be used or adapted for second-marriage estate planning include making gifts while living (see Chapter 16, Section D), using a QTIP trust (see Chapter 19, Section A), and making gifts of minority interests in family businesses (discussed in Chapter 28, Section B).

B. HOW A MARITAL PROPERTY CONTROL TRUST WORKS

A marital property control trust is in some ways similar to an AB trust (discussed in Chapter 18, Section C) but there are also important differences. The surviving spouse is the life beneficiary of the marital property control trust. However, the survivor's rights to use trust property, to receive trust income, and spend trust principal, are as limited as you choose. Indeed, these rights can end if the surviving spouse remarries.

With an AB trust that is intended only to save on estate tax, the surviving spouse is usually granted the maximum rights to use or spend trust property allowed under IRS rules. In marked contrast, with a marital property control trust, specific restrictions, expressly set out in the trust document, are imposed on the surviving spouse. The purpose of restricting the surviving spouse's rights is to protect the trust principal, so that it remains intact (or at least close to intact) until the surviving spouse dies, or perhaps remarries. Then the trust property goes outright to the grantor's children from a prior marriage or other final beneficiaries the grantor named.

> **Example:** Lisi and Greg get married in their late 30s. Lisi has a child from a prior marriage; Greg has two children from his prior marriages. Lisi and Greg have a child together, Dory. Lisi and Greg are now in their early 50s, and decide it's time to prepare their estate plan.
>
> Lisi owns separate property worth $700,000, and Greg owns separate property worth $410,000. Together they own a house that cost $320,000. Each contributed half the down payment for the house, and they share mortgage payments equally. Also, they own other shared assets worth a total of $375,000.
>
> Each spouse creates a marital property control trust. The other spouse, as life beneficiary, has these rights in the trust property:

1. to remain in the house for life
2. to receive the income from any trust property, and
3. to spend trust principal only for medical costs that can't be paid for from other resources.

> Each spouse names the final beneficiaries for his or her trust. Lisi decides that her final beneficiaries are Dory and her daughter from her prior marriage, who will share her trust's principal 50/50. Greg, who is not close to his children from his prior marriage, names them and Dory as his final beneficiaries. Dory will receive 70% of his trust property and the other two children will equally share the remaining 30%.

Because the purpose of a marital control trust is to preserve assets for your final beneficiaries, it's immaterial whether or not those assets will be subject to estate tax. You may want to create this type of trust even if your estate is well under the estate tax threshold.

> **Example:** Benny and Belle marry when they are in their late 50s. Benny has two children, ages 26 and 24, one each from two prior marriages. Belle has one child, age 19, from her prior marriage. Benny has an estate worth roughly $425,000; Belle's is worth $623,000. Neither estate is at all near the estate tax threshold.
>
> Because neither spouse has enough property to be securely self-sufficient if the other dies first, each creates a marital property control trust, allowing the other spouse income for life from the trust but absolutely no right to invade trust principal. This way, they've each ensured that their estate will remain intact, to be received by their child or children after the surviving spouse dies.

> ### HOW TO SET UP A PROPERTY CONTROL TRUST
>
> A marital property control trust usually is combined with a living trust to avoid probate. In that case, the marital property control trust remains revocable, as a component of the living trust, as long as you live and are mentally competent. After your death, your living trust property is transferred to your marital property control trust, without probate proceedings. At that point, your marital property control trust becomes irrevocable.

Getting help. Because of the complexities involved in setting up this type of trust, you'll need to work with a good lawyer. (See Section F, below, for more information.)

C. RESTRICTING THE SURVIVING SPOUSE'S RIGHTS OVER TRUST PROPERTY

You may impose a wide variety of restrictions on your surviving spouse's rights over the property in your marital property control trust. For instance, the surviving spouse may be given the right to receive income from the trust, but no right whatsoever to spend trust principal. Or you can name someone other than the surviving spouse to be the trustee of the trust. This obviously keeps one source of real-world power from the surviving spouse. If someone else is the trustee, there's presumably less chance that the surviving spouse will get more than the trust document allows.

Example: Leticia, in her 70s, marries Ben, also in his 70s. Leticia has been married twice before, and has one grown child from each marriage, a daughter, Lindsay, and a son, Kevin. Her estate consists of her condo, worth $595,000 (all equity), and savings of $580,000. Ben owns much less, about $40,000 in savings and stocks. He also receives a modest pension plus Social Security.

Leticia wants her property to eventually go to her two children, equally—but if she predeceases Ben, she doesn't want him thrown out on the street. She places her house and savings in a marital property control trust. She appoints Lindsay as trustee.

The trust document gives Ben the right to remain in the house, with all its current furnishings, for his life. If he leaves it for more than four consecutive months, whether to move to some tropical paradise or a nursing home, the house and furnishings can be sold or rented if the trustee decides that's desirable. Thus, Leticia leaves it up to Lindsay to decide what should happen to the house if Ben vacates it for more than four months. Leticia doesn't want to require that the house be turned over to her children in these circumstances. She just wants to protect her children, and not have the house empty or rented out by Ben. Leticia fully trusts Lindsay to make a wise decision if this matter comes up.

Ben also is to receive $15,000 per year from the income generated by the money in the trust. If the trust's annual income is lower than $15,000, Ben receives that lesser amount. If the income exceeds $15,000, Ben can be given any portion of the additional income if Lindsay, the trustee, determines he needs it for basic needs, such as health care or everyday expenses.

Each marital property control trust involves the unique circumstances of the couple and final beneficiaries involved. There are no set rules dictating what's right. You must try to foresee the future needs of your spouse and balance those needs with your desire to protect most, if not all, of the principal for your children or other final beneficiaries.

Here are some examples of the controls that can be placed on the surviving spouse's right to trust property:

- Someone other than the survivor can be named as trustee.

- The survivor can live in a house owned (or partially owned) by the trust, but has no right to sell it.

- The survivor can live in a house and can sell it, but only for the purpose of buying another residence, and then only with the approval of all trust beneficiaries.

- The survivor can live in a house but cannot sell it or rent it. And if the survivor moves into a nursing facility and remains there for more than a set time, the house must be turned over to the trust's final beneficiaries.

- The survivor (who is not the trustee) will be paid trust income only as the trustee determines is necessary for medical care or other basic needs.

- The survivor may drive a valuable car owned by the trust, but can sell it only with consent of at least one final beneficiary.

- The survivor must follow specific directions set out in the trust document, down to how he can use many items of trust property and care for valuable items such as antiques.

- If the surviving spouse remarries, the trust ends and the trust property goes to the final beneficiaries.

If your spouse and children don't get along, you may need to face the possibility that you will not be able to create a trust that will make all of them happy. In this case, you simply have to arrive at a resolution that seems the most wise and fair to you.

Example: Dottie and Sam have been living together for six years. Dottie is in her 50s and is the sole owner of a prospering women's clothing company. She owns, free and clear, a house worth $290,000, which she bought over 25 years ago. Her business is worth perhaps $500,000. (It's usually fairly hard to determine the market value of a small business, because often there is no actual market for it.) Her other assets total $130,000, so her total estate is worth $920,000. Sam owns property worth $200,000 and receives a small Social Security allotment.

Dottie has no children. Eventually, she wants her property to go to her niece, Betsy, who works with her in her business. Sam wants his property to go to his two children.

Dottie decides that Sam might need income beyond his Social Security income and whatever his $200,000 may generate, to continue to live in the comfortable style they've enjoyed together. Also, she wants to keep her business intact—most of all, so that Betsy can eventually inherit it, but also so it can produce income for Sam. So Dottie creates a marital property control trust, with Sam as the life beneficiary. She names Betsy as trustee, because Betsy will manage the business, owned by the trust. Sam is entitled to:

1. live in their house for the duration of his life

2. sell it and buy another place, if Betsy consents, and

3. receive 25% of any profits from the clothing company (leaving the rest so the business can expand or maintain itself), or any income from other assets in the trust. When Sam dies, all the trust property goes to Betsy.

Sam also creates a marital property control trust that allows Dottie the income from his assets for her life but prohibits her from spending principal. When Dottie dies, Sam's property will be divided between his children.

Sam's children do not get along well with Dottie, so he's reluctant to appoint one of his children as trustee of his trust. He feels confident that Dottie would not abuse the position of trustee. So he names her to be trustee, with the provision that she must give both children copies of the trust's annual income tax return so they can see that the principal is not being spent.

D. The Role of the Trustee

Obviously, choosing the right trustee for a marital property control trust is vital. The trustee will have authority to manage the trust property and to make authorized payments to the surviving spouse. (The trustee often has considerable discretion regarding how to manage and invest trust property.) Further, the trustee may have some enforcement—or at least checking-up—responsibilities, to be sure that the surviving spouse's use of trust property complies with trust requirements. These duties can require diplomacy or tough decision making.

1. Heading Off Family Conflict

Choosing the trustee can be a difficult task, requiring some serious thought. If your current spouse and your children are on good terms or, better yet, really trust each other, you may not face much of a problem. Still, even when the nicest of people are involved, you should understand that there's an inherent potential for conflict between the surviving spouse and the final beneficiaries. The surviving spouse may want or believe she or he needs to spend trust property, including principal. The final beneficiaries clearly have an interest in preserving as much of the trust principal as possible. As you may have observed, even usually kind people can at times act in self-interested, and even mean-spirited, ways.

Whatever rules and restrictions you place over the surviving spouse's rights to trust property, it will be the trustee who must enforce them. So it's best if both you and all the beneficiaries have complete confidence in this trustee. If your surviving spouse or one of your children fits that bill, you're fortunate. But certainly it's not unheard of that children from a prior marriage don't really trust one's current spouse sufficiently to want him to be sole successor trustee. Similarly, the spouse will not want his rights—including, perhaps, such basic rights as where he can live—to be supervised by a child with whom he has a hostile relationship.

If you find yourself facing this situation, it will be no surprise that there's no magic solution that will please everyone. The best you can do is think long and hard about who is most likely to be fair to all involved, and to be seen by all as fair. If your spouse and children trust another family member—a sister, perhaps—choosing her to serve as trustee, assuming she's willing, may be the best solution. If the potential for conflict and mistrust between the surviving spouse and the final beneficiaries is severe, you may need to look for a more unconventional solution.

Example: Alberto is married to Miranda. Alberto also has a son, Francesco, age 23, from a prior marriage. To put it bluntly, Francesco and Miranda can't stand each other. What's worse, Alberto thinks neither of them is a particularly good money manager. Alberto discusses the trustee issue with Miranda and

Francesco (separately) and they all agree that a trusted friend, Benito, should serve as trustee. Francesco has known Benito for many years, likes him, and is relieved that Benito, not Miranda, will be the trustee. Because Benito is Alberto's age and may predecease Miranda, Alberto puts a provision in his trust that allows Benito to appoint another trustee if he can't do the job. Benito promptly names his wife, Carla, to step in if necessary.

Another possibility is simply to name whomever you feel will be fairest, even if that person is your spouse or a child mistrusted by others involved, and let the chips (and sparks) fall as they may.

2. Naming Cotrustees

It's rarely a good idea to name cotrustees for a marital property control trust. You may hope to reduce potential conflict by naming your spouse and one of your children to serve as cotrustees, but if they don't get along, it could make matters worse. The result could be a case of trustee gridlock, where each person's vote cancels out the other. Even a simple matter like payment of trust income could lead to a court battle, if the trustees don't agree what "income" is. And if your spouse and your child or children get along, why bother with cotrustees?

Instead, consider requiring that the trustee provide annual trust income tax returns to all trust beneficiaries, or even copies of all monthly trust bank account statements. This allows nontrustee beneficiaries to check up on the trust without risking cotrustee power struggles.

3. Naming a Financial Institution as Trustee

If you can't find any family member or friend you think would be a suitable trustee, you have a serious problem. Your last resort is to name a financial institution, such as a private trust company, to serve as trustee. As we've discussed, there can be real drawbacks to this. (See Chapter 17, Section F.)

Many financial institutions will not handle trusts with property worth less than $250,000 or even $500,000. This eliminates many marital property control trusts altogether. Also, financial institutions usually charge hefty fees for serving as trustees. Finally, these institutions can be quite bureaucratic and impersonal, especially when handling trusts that seem like small potatoes to them. So if you must name one as trustee, try to establish a personal relationship with someone you can trust in the institution first.

E. SAVINGS ON ESTATE TAXES

For couples in second marriages with combined estates exceeding the estate tax threshold, a marital property control trust can be used for dual purposes: both to impose controls over the surviving spouse's rights to trust property and to save on overall estate taxes. Although the new tax laws raise the personal exemption gradually and will supposedly phase out estate tax after 2009, there are no guarantees. (See Chapter 15.) Nobody really knows what to expect from Congress in the years to come, so saving on taxes is still very much a part of many estate plans.

Example: In 2007, Khosro and Maheen, a couple in their late 70s, have a combined estate worth $4 million, with each owning half. Their home and personal belongings are valued at $400,000, and savings and stocks total $3.6 million. Khosro has a child from his previous marriage and Maheen has two from hers. They have no children from their marriage.

Each spouse creates a marital property control trust for all of his or her property. The trust documents provide that trust income will go to the surviving spouse, who also will have use of the home. The principal will be maintained for their respective children. The surviving spouse is not given the right to spend trust principal, even for health needs. The surviving spouse will receive income from the deceased spouse's share of their stocks and savings. Khosro and Maheen both feel that when combined with the surviving spouse's own assets plus Social Security and retirement benefits, this amount of income will be sufficient.

Khosro and Maheen are also delighted that no estate tax will be due on either of their deaths, because each will make use of their personal estate tax exemptions. For 2007, the exempt amount is $2 million and will continue to increase. So no matter what year each dies in, their entire $4 million estate will pass tax free and intact to their children.

There is nothing particularly tricky about using a marital property control trust to achieve estate tax savings. Basically, you—or, more accurately, your lawyer—prepare the trust document, imposing whatever controls you want to over the surviving spouse's rights to trust property. The trust property is subject to estate tax when you die. If your estate is under the amount of the personal exemption for the year of death, all the trust property is exempt from tax. And because that property is never legally owned by your surviving spouse, it will not be subject to tax when he or she dies.

OTHER APPROACHES

What do you do if you are considering using a marital property control trust both for control and tax savings, and anticipate conflict between beneficiaries? Begin by realizing that there are no fixed rules here. You really do have to come up with your own individual solutions. For instance, instead of a marital control trust, you could buy an annuity or insurance policy with the proceeds going to the survivor and leave all other property to the children. Or, you could leave your children a hefty chunk outright and leave the rest in trust with your spouse as the life beneficiary and grant him, as trustee, fairly generous powers to spend trust principal. The principal may never be touched, but even if it is gobbled up, at least the children have already gotten something.

F. WORKING WITH A LAWYER

If you decide you want a marital property control trust, you'll need to have the trust document prepared by a good estate planning lawyer. There are too many options and possibilities for you to safely prepare one yourself. Also, there are no reliable self-help materials available. A good estate planning lawyer will have experience with other people in second or subsequent marriages, and may be able to offer helpful suggestions for resolving your particular problems. She can also draft trust language that clearly and unambiguously expresses what you want. With this type of trust, it's especially important to avoid any possibly unclear phrases in the trust document. You don't want to leave any opening for beneficiaries to fight over what you intended.

Although you will need a lawyer, you can still do much of the essential work yourself. (See Chapter 29, Section A.) After all, it's best not to wander into a lawyer's office and start discussing your situation at $200 or more per hour. Try to work out a tentative plan before your first visit.

The principal issues with a marital property control trust are practical, human ones: working out what's fair (as best you can) and deciding who will be best able to carry out your decisions as successor trustee of your trust. These concerns may be easy to state but, in real life, they can be quite difficult to resolve. The best advice we can give is to be candid with yourself. Try to face family and domestic realities, even if they're not all rosy and romantic. Once you've carefully thought about your situation, needs, and desires, write down your specific concerns and what, if any, special problems you anticipate. This should mean less time spent with a lawyer, thus reducing your fee—which likely will still be enough to make you blink. ■

25

TRUSTS AND OTHER DEVICES FOR IMPOSING CONTROLS OVER PROPERTY

In a number of situations, the right estate plan includes the use of an ongoing, irrevocable trust that imposes controls over beneficiaries' rights to trust property. One such situation—married people who want to ensure that their property eventually goes to their children from prior marriages—is discussed in Chapter 24.

We call the types of trusts discussed here "property control trusts." Here are some of the circumstances in which you might want to consider using one:

- One of your beneficiaries is a minor. (Children's trusts are discussed in Chapter 6, Section C.)

- A beneficiary is a young adult who is not yet mature enough to manage significant sums of money or property. (Also discussed in Chapter 6.)

- You want to leave money for a child's education.

- A beneficiary is disabled and will probably always need help managing property. These are called "special needs trusts." You can use one of these trusts to leave property to a beneficiary while also preserving his or her eligibility for government benefits.

- You believe a beneficiary is improvident with money, and his rights to trust property must be restricted for his entire life. These are called "spendthrift trusts."

- You want the trustee to decide how to distribute trust income or principal among several beneficiaries. These are call "sprinkling trusts." (For minor children, this type of trust is called a "family pot trust." See Chapter 6, Section C.)

- You want to authorize someone else to decide who will receive your property after you die. This is called a "power of appointment." While it's not technically a trust, it is used for property control purposes, and so we discuss it here.

A property control trust is a complex legal animal. You are trying to impose limits on what can happen with trust property in the future. But since the future cannot be foreseen, you're struggling with what is, at best, very difficult: How to create a trust document that will last for a long time and achieve what you want. Rather than worrying about coming up with a detailed plan now, you may decide to allow the trustee broad powers to decide how to use the trust property for a named group of beneficiaries.

Still, in spite of inherent uncertainties, the property control trusts discussed here have been effective over the years for many, many people. Generally, using one of these trusts is far more desirable than not doing anything to handle a difficult beneficiary situation.

Most of the property control trusts discussed here become operational only after your death. In some circumstances, however, a trust can become operational when it's initially created.

Property control trusts require a lawyer.
Most of the property control trusts discussed in this chapter must be prepared by a knowledgeable estate planning attorney. Usually, these trusts involve many uncertainties, and they can tie up property for decades. Drafting such a trust is not easy and cannot safely be done without legal help.

Nolo does provide a resource to help you prepare a property control trust for a disabled child. See Section B, below.

A. EDUCATIONAL TRUSTS

A relatively common type of property control trust is one created to help beneficiaries pay for college or other schooling. These trusts are rarely set up by children's parents—most parents just pay educational costs directly, out of their own pockets. Commonly, grandparents or other older relatives who want to help young relations use these trusts.

Creating an educational property control trust often involves resolving many rather difficult issues including:

When the trust becomes operational. If the beneficiaries are very young and you are unlikely to live until a child begins college, this is not a serious problem. You can arrange for the trust to become operational at your death. But if the children are older, near or at college age, you may want the trust to become operational now, while you live.

If you create the trust now, there can be significant gift tax consequences. However, Congress seems to be moving toward exempting educational expenses from taxes and we hope this will eventually apply to all gifts that pay for these expenses, including those placed in trust.

Also, if you want one of these trusts to become operational while you're alive, you must decide whether you will be the initial trustee and who will continue to serve after your death.

NEW ALTERNATIVES TO EDUCATIONAL TRUSTS

You may now place funds in tax-advantaged educational accounts to pay tuition and other school-related costs for young people, without the bother of a separate educational trust. See Chapter 13, Section B, for more information about these accounts.

How a beneficiary qualifies for benefits. There are many questions you'll need to ask yourself when deciding how trust money will be distributed to beneficiaries. For example, what education levels must a child reach to get payments from the trust? If, say, you decide that your grandchild must attend college full time to receive payments, what constitutes "full time"? What qualifies as a college? Your grandchild may discover another way to learn—for instance, apprenticing with a metal sculptor. Would the trustee have authority to approve the payment of trust benefits? What about graduate school?

If there's more than one (potential) trust beneficiary, other issues arise. For example, if one grandchild attends Columbia Medical School, while the other grandchild goes to a nontuition community college, their expenses will vary greatly. Can unequal payments be made to different beneficiaries? Lawyers call a trust where a trustee can pay different amounts of principal or income to different beneficiaries based on their needs a "pot" or "sprinkling" trust—all the dough is in one pot. By contrast, if you want each child to have the same amount of money, you could direct that this be done or set up separate trusts for each one.

Adding new beneficiaries. You'll want to consider what happens if new, potential beneficiaries are born after you die. For instance, if you're creating a trust for all your grandchildren, do you want the trustee to be able to make payments to any future grandchildren born after your death? If you do, accomplishing this is largely a matter of proper legal drafting of the trust document, by an expert lawyer.

What happens if no beneficiaries attend college? You should decide what happens to the trust money if none of the beneficiaries go to school. For example, can the trust income be used for grandchildren's "emergencies"? What kinds? What else might you want to do with the trust principal if it's not all spent on educational costs?

When the trust ends. You must decide when the trust will end. Often this happens when the youngest child reaches a certain age. You'll also need to think about what happens to any money left in the trust when it ends. You can set out a plan—such as outright distribution of the funds—or leave this up to the trustee.

If you think you want to create an educational trust, first try to tentatively resolve these questions and any others you think of. Write out your basic thoughts and resolutions of the issues. Then see an experienced estate planning attorney to have your trust prepared.

Example: Rada has two nephews, one who wants to be a doctor and another who lives his life for music. He sets up an educational trust that will pay all college and graduate expenses for both children, including room and board. He also specifies that education includes private music lessons, instruments, and supplies to further the career of his musical nephew. He names his brother, the father of the boys, as trustee. He gives the trustee discretion to decide what other expenses are educational. When the youngest nephew turns 40, the trust ends and any remaining amount is divided between them and distributed outright.

B. TRUSTS FOR PEOPLE WITH SPECIAL NEEDS

Parents or others who care about someone who is disabled by serious physical or mental problems can face difficult estate planning questions. Understandably, they want to provide for the disabled person, to the extent possible, for as long as that person lives. If the disabled person cannot be expected to manage property, the property must be left in a property control trust, usually called a "special needs trust." The trust document must be carefully drafted, so that the trustee has enough flexibility to deal with the beneficiary's medical or other special needs.

There's another important concern here. A child or other loved one with a disability often requires long-term assistance from government programs. Money and property left directly to people with disabilities may disqualify them from receiving government help. By creating a special needs trust, parents or others can provide for a disabled child without risking loss of federal benefits, including health care payments. The key to this kind of trust is that the child is not named as trustee, and has no legal control over trust assets. Instead, the parents choose a trusted adult to serve as trustee for the child. Because the child never owns the trust assets, they do not count when determining eligibility for federal benefits.

Trusts for disabled children. *Special Needs Trusts: Protect Your Child's Financial Future*, by Stephen Elias (Nolo) enables you to prepare the trust you need. Using the book's clear explanations, instructions, and forms, you can create a special needs trust for your child to help provide for him or her without jeopardizing public benefits.

1. Choosing the Trustee

A primary concern with a special needs trust is making sure you select a trustee, and successor trustee, who is willing and able to do the job. The trustee must be attentive to the disabled person's situation, discerning what is needed and providing for those needs to the extent possible. The trustee will need to be in close contact with the disabled person, so it is essential that the two get along. And finally, the trustee should have the savvy to deal with various institutions, including banks, doctors, hospitals, and government agencies.

2. How a Special Needs Trust Works

The trustee of a special needs trust can spend trust income or principal for a wide variety of the child's needs that are not covered by federal or state benefits. Government benefits—most notably Supplemental Security Income (SSI) and Medicaid—may be reduced if the trustee gives the beneficiary cash or pays for the beneficiary's food or shelter. This means that the trustee will make payments for the beneficiary, rather than to him.

SSI is administered by the Social Security Administration (SSA). To remain eligible for benefits, the beneficiary cannot have cash resources, which include bank accounts, stocks and bonds, and real estate (other than a home) worth more than $2,000. However, under SSA guidelines, the property in a special needs trust doesn't affect eligibility for Social Security assistance as long as the beneficiary cannot:

- control the amount or frequency of trust payments, or
- revoke the trust and use the property.

In other words, the beneficiary must have no rights to demand and receive money from the trust, either income or principal. Nor can the beneficiary simply revoke the trust and obtain the trust principal. All power over the trust principal, including payment of income or principal to the beneficiary, must be given to the trustee.

Local SSA offices have wide latitude in interpreting these guidelines. For example, some SSA offices may require that the trust document show that the trust creator didn't "intend" the trust property to be used as the primary source of aid or income for the disadvantaged person. Happily, a well-drafted special needs trust can avoid these problems.

See an expert. Because the government rules here are complex and can change suddenly, a distinct legal subspecialty has developed: lawyers who prepare special needs trusts. The truth is that you really need not only an estate planning expert, but also someone who is knowledgeable in drafting special needs trusts. (See Chapter 29, Section A, for a discussion of how to find the right lawyer for you.) Don't rely on a general practice lawyer, most of whom are not nearly knowledgeable enough to properly prepare this type of trust.

C. SPENDTHRIFT TRUSTS

A spendthrift trust is designed to minimize an unreliable beneficiary's ability to squander trust principal. The "spendthrift" beneficiary may be someone who simply has no head for money and could easily waste trust principal if controls weren't placed on his right to get at it. This type of trust is also used when a beneficiary might squander trust principal on drugs, alcohol, gambling, or some other compulsive behavior. Creating a spendthrift trust is an attempt to balance concern for the beneficiary with a realistic appraisal of his more wasteful or destructive impulses.

"Spendthrift" may sound like a harsh epithet to apply to a loved one, but sitting down to work out a good estate plan demands facing facts, even painful ones. If you want to help someone who is financially irresponsible, a spendthrift trust can be a very sound idea.

With a spendthrift trust, the beneficiary is never the trustee. The trustee can spend trust money for the beneficiary's needs or make payments directly to the beneficiary, as the trust document directs or permits. The beneficiary has no right to spend trust principal. Nor does he have the legal right to pledge trust principal, or future income expected from the trust, as security for a loan.

Example: Pierre wants to leave money to his son, Maurice, a charming fellow who's always spent money as if he were a millionaire. (He's not.) So Pierre creates an ongoing spendthrift trust for the benefit of Maurice, to take effect after Pierre dies. The trust will be managed by Pierre's prudent bourgeois brother Jean-Paul, who will dole out trust income to Maurice on the first of each month. If Jean-Paul predeceases Maurice, first Jean-Paul's wife, Anne-Marie (also quite prudent) and next their son Charles (a chip off the old block) will serve as trustee.

Under the terms of the trust, Maurice cannot obtain the trust principal or pledge his expected trust income to obtain credit. The trust will end when Maurice becomes 50, by which point Pierre hopes he'll have learned financial prudence. If not, Pierre simply accepts the risk that he'll waste the trust principal at that age.

At the extreme, a spendthrift clause can give the trustee power to cut off benefits, temporarily or even permanently, to a beneficiary who becomes uncontrollably self-destructive. Income withheld could be accumulated in the trust or paid to another beneficiary named in the trust document.

Giving the trustee this power, however, is rarely if ever wise. It imposes a troubling burden on the trustee, who must decide what behavior by the unreliable beneficiary is so bad that income may be withheld. Even if certain offending behaviors are spelled out in the trust document, it's the trustee who must actually determine whether the beneficiary's behavior justifies withholding income payments. How is the trustee to make this determination? Must he play detective, or hire a professional to spy on the beneficiary?

Perhaps the most that you can wisely do is to describe, in the trust document, specific, objective acts which, if undertaken by the beneficiary, would allow the trustee to withhold income payments. For example, the trust document could provide that if the beneficiary were convicted of certain types of drug offenses, payments could be withheld. But even here, is this really the wisest course? Even if the beneficiary were in prison (where access to drugs should be greatly reduced), wouldn't receiving income payments from the trust be a help? Having some personal cash could ease a prisoner's life in many ways, from purchasing canteen food to affording good legal representation.

A less draconian method is for you to direct the trustee to continue to make payments for the benefit of a beneficiary who's become obviously self-destructive (such as paying his rent, food bills, or other basic needs) but withhold direct payments to that beneficiary. This still imposes on the trustee the burden of evaluating the beneficiary's behavior, with all the difficulties that involves. But sometimes imposing such a burden is necessary, particularly when the beneficiary's behavior could become (or already is) truly dangerous.

In other situations, you may decide that the trustee must make regular (monthly or quarterly) payments to the beneficiary, regardless of the beneficiary's behavior. These payments can be defined in the trust document as all of the trust income, a set amount, or a percentage of trust income. If you choose this option, you must accept the risk that the beneficiary won't spend the money wisely. No trust can prevent a beneficiary from squandering money once it's in his pocket.

The rigidity of some spendthrift trusts can be a problem down the road. What happens if the beneficiary needs more money than the monthly payment allowed? Does the trustee have the power to spend trust principal if the beneficiary becomes ill and lacks funds to pay medical bills? Or suppose the beneficiary sees the error of his wasteful ways and decides to settle down and go to dental school. Can the trustee use the principal to pay the beneficiary's tuition? You may decide to allow the trustee to spend trust principal for the beneficiary, either for specific needs or as the trustee determines is desirable.

D. SPRINKLING TRUSTS

Perhaps the most flexible property control trust of all is termed a "sprinkling" or "discretionary" trust. Under either lingo, this type of trust gives the trustee authority to "sprinkle" both the income and principal of the trust between named beneficiaries. (Sometimes this is called allowing "sprinkling" powers.)

A sprinkling trust differs from other trusts, including all other trusts designed to control property, in that you don't specify what property each beneficiary gets, or when. Rather, you leave money in the trust and name the group of possible beneficiaries. The trustee determines which of these beneficiaries will receive payments from trust income or principal, and how much. You can specify when the trust should end, and what happens to any money left in the trust, or you can leave these matters to the trustee.

In the trust document, however, you can give the trustee rules to follow. For instance, the trustee could be allowed to spend trust principal only for a beneficiary's educational or medical needs. Or a trustee might have the power to pay out only trust income, not principal. Or he could have the power to give no more than 20% of the trust principal to any one beneficiary in any one year.

Usually the trust document provides that if the trustee decides it's best, income may be accumulated in the trust instead of being handed out to any beneficiaries. However, the income tax rate applied to retained trust income may well be higher than the rate applied to trust income received by beneficiaries. (See Chapter 17, Section G.) So it's unlikely that a trustee would decide to retain trust income beyond

one tax year and thus effectively cost the beneficiaries money in higher taxes.

By law, you must name an independent ("disinterested") trustee—that is, a trustee who has no financial interest in how the trust money is distributed, but is dispassionate enough to hand out money as it's genuinely needed. Thus, a surviving spouse normally should not serve as trustee of a sprinkling trust. (See Section 3, below.)

1. Adding Sprinkling Powers to an AB Trust

If you create an AB trust, you may want to give your trustee the power to use trust income or assets for the final beneficiaries, probably your children. A sprinkling AB trust can be appropriate for a couple with a large estate, when the surviving spouse has plenty of assets and may not need or want regular income payments. Creating "sprinkling powers" in an AB trust can accomplish two important goals:

Helping other beneficiaries. You can take care of possible needs of other beneficiaries, such as your children, during the surviving spouse's life. At an extreme, for example, if a wealthy surviving spouse marries someone even wealthier, the trustee can choose not to pay anything at all to that spouse, but to spend (or save) all the trust income and assets for the children or other named beneficiaries.

More commonly, one child may need more money for education or support than another. When the beneficiaries are young, a sprinkling trust allows great flexibility over the years and makes the assets available when necessary.

Income tax savings. If your surviving spouse will be well off, you can achieve income tax savings by channeling some trust income to beneficiaries in lower tax brackets, such as adult children or children older than 14 with low incomes. (Income over $850 paid out to children 13 or younger is taxed at their parents' rates.)

Example: Akira and Mariko have a shared estate totaling $4 million. They have two young children, and Akira also has a teenage son by a former marriage.

Akira drafts a sprinkling formula AB trust, directing that the maximum amount of property exempt from estate tax in the year of his death be placed in the trust. His remaining property will go into a QTIP trust, with his wife as life beneficiary and Akira's three children as the final beneficiaries. (See Chapter 19, Section A, for a discussion of QTIP trusts, which are used to defer payment of estate tax.) If he dies first, the trustee of the AB trust will have the power to sprinkle both income and principal to Mariko and to any of the children for their support for the rest of Mariko's life. Upon Mariko's death, the remaining assets will be distributed to Akira's children. The trust document specifies that this division shall take into consideration how much from the trust has been previously paid to each, with the goal of equalizing the totals.

Akira accomplishes several purposes with this trust plan. He takes advantage of his personal estate tax exemption and defers all estate tax on his remaining property until Mariko's death.

Akira also makes funds available early on for his teenage son, who will be facing college and perhaps graduate school expenses. And if Mariko doesn't want some or all of the income, she can always disclaim it (see Chapter 22, Section A), building a larger trust principal for the children to inherit later.

2. Other Uses of Sprinkling Trust Provisions

Sprinkling trust provisions can be used in a wide variety of property control trusts. For example, if you want to leave property for minor children or young adults, you may create a "family pot trust." This is a kind of sprinkling trust, where you choose to let the trustee decide, according to the actual needs and circumstances of the children, how much money to pay to each child. (See Chapter 6, Section C.)

Similarly, a grandparent may create a sprinkling trust for grandchildren or, for that matter, for adult children. Indeed, sprinkling trust provisions can work well in any situation where a number of beneficiaries may need payments from the trust for a long period of time, and you have complete confidence in the trustee.

3. Choosing an Independent Trustee

No matter the type of sprinkling trust, a key to making one work well is to appoint a disinterested, independent trustee—someone you trust completely. Because a sprinkling trust is intended to operate over a lengthy period, you also need to select at least one successor trustee, and often an alternate successor trustee, with similar care.

An "independent" trustee means a trustee who cannot benefit from the trust—that is, is not a beneficiary of any kind. Even someone who is named as an alternate beneficiary (or fourth alternate, for that matter) cannot serve. If the trustee has a financial interest in the trust, the IRS may consider her to be the legal owner of all the trust property and include it in her taxable estate when she dies, which is definitely not what you want.

The surviving spouse cannot be the trustee of a sprinkling AB trust. As the life beneficiary, the surviving spouse obviously has an interest in trust payments. Indeed, normally, he receives all trust income during his life. But creating a sprinkling trust means there are other possibilities. Allowing the surviving spouse to be the trustee in this situation means the IRS will regard him as the legal owner of all trust property. That property will be included in his taxable estate when he dies, defeating the purpose of an AB trust.

You need a trustee who, although he or she has no financial interest in how the trust money is distributed, is personally interested in the welfare of the beneficiaries and will remain alert to their financial needs. A sprinkling trust, by its very nature, can create conflict among the beneficiaries. After all, they may all think they need money—and a lot of it—from the trust, so the trustee may have some serious personal as well as financial issues to handle. If you can't find a legally independent but emotionally involved person who'll do the job, and someone you fully trust, a sprinkling trust isn't for you.

E. TRUSTS TO MANAGE YOUR OWN PROPERTY

If you tire of coping with your property and financial affairs, you can arrange for someone else to manage them. One method is for you to put your property in a trust, to be managed by a trustee for your benefit. The trustee would have the authority to spend any amount of trust income or principal for you. You can define as carefully as you like in the trust document what standard of living you expect. (Of course, there must be sufficient assets in the trust to pay for that standard of living.)

Unlike the other trusts discussed in this chapter, there's no need to make this type of trust irrevocable. Indeed, there are real drawbacks if you do so. The trustee would have to obtain a trust taxpayer ID, maintain trust financial records, and file an annual

trust income tax return. None of this would benefit you. And, obviously, if you changed your mind, you would have no legal power to end the trust and regain control of the trust assets.

If the trust is revocable, you should make yourself one of the trustees. If you don't, under IRS regulations the tax requirements applied to irrevocable trusts will apply to your revocable trust as well. One simple way to avoid this problem is for you to name yourself and some other person as cotrustees, and provide in the trust document that either trustee may act for the trust. The other person, as cotrustee, in reality becomes the sole manager of the trust property. But as long as you remain one of the official trustees, no tax reporting obligations are imposed on the trust.

You can also use other devices to allow another person to manage your property for you. One method is to give another person authority, using a document called a durable power of attorney for finances, to manage your property. It's always a good idea to create a durable power of attorney for finances as part of your estate plan. (See Chapter 26, Section B.)

If you have transferred property to a living trust, there is no need to create any other device to handle that trust property in case you become incapacitated. A standard clause in a well-drafted living trust authorizes your successor trustee to take over management of your trust property, if necessary, for your benefit as long as you live. If this happens, the living trust remains revocable, if you regain the ability to manage your affairs.

F. POWERS OF APPOINTMENT

A "power of appointment" is simply the power to determine how someone's assets are distributed after his or her death.

Example 1: In her living trust, Anita authorizes her husband, Frederico, to distribute all her property among her children as he wishes, if he outlives her. If he doesn't outlive her, Anita grants the same authority to her brother, Marcello.

Example 2: Malcolm, a widower, has two children: Veronica, age 24, and Jamal, age 22, who has a serious drug problem. Malcolm certainly doesn't want to leave any property outright to Jamal if he's still using drugs when Malcolm dies. On the other hand, Malcolm hopes Jamal will see the light and cease using drugs, so he surely doesn't want to cut Jamal out irrevocably. So in his living trust he creates a power of appointment in his best friend, Ted. Ted will decide, after Malcolm's death, if Jamal can be given property outright because he has been clear from drugs for a specified period of time. (Of course, determining this may not be easy.) If Ted decides Jamal still suffers from drug addiction, then the property left for Jamal will go into a trust for him, managed by Ted.

There can be a number of wise reasons to use a power of appointment. One reason is that you are unsure, when you prepare your estate plan, exactly who you want your beneficiaries to be. You don't want to create a sprinkling trust, because the trustee normally has the power to distribute trust money only among beneficiaries named in the trust document. If you trust someone—a spouse, brother, or friend—completely, it may make sense to postpone the choice of beneficiaries, and what property beneficiaries will receive, until later.

Example: Jason and Beverly, an elderly couple, have a substantial estate. They leave large specific gifts to family and some friends. Each also intends to leave one-third of his or her estate to benefit minority grade school students. Rather than selecting the beneficiaries for this education gift, each provides that their daughter Celia has a power of appointment to distribute the property to whatever organizations she decides will best carry out their parents' goals.

1. Kinds of Powers of Appointment

There are two kinds of powers of appointment: "general" and "special" (also called "limited"). A general power of appointment can have adverse estate tax consequences, while a limited power of appointment does not.

With a general power of appointment, you name a person to distribute your property to the beneficiaries she chooses—including herself. You can define a set time period for this decision to be made, or leave it open.

Authorizing a general power of appointment is rarely a good idea. Under IRS rules, the person who has a general power of appointment will have the full value of the property subject to that power included in her taxable estate at her death. This is true even if she never gives any property to herself, had no intention of doing so, and in fact gave it all to someone else. The practical effect is that as long as estate tax exists, this property is subject to estate tax twice—once when you die and once when the person to whom you gave the power of appointment dies.

Example: In his living trust, Martin gives his wife Helen a general power of appointment over property worth $800,000. Martin's total estate is worth $3 million, so it is subject to federal estate tax if he dies before 2009. Helen's estate is worth $2 million, aside from the property subject to the general power of appointment. Shortly after Martin's death in

2006, Helen gives the entire $800,000 to their three children. Nevertheless, when Helen dies in 2008, that $800,000 is included in her taxable estate, because she had the power to give all this money to herself if she had chosen to. So the $800,000 has been included in two taxable estates, which is clearly undesirable.

By contrast, a special or limited power of appointment is restricted as you see fit. Most importantly, the person who has the power cannot give the property to himself, use it to pay his creditors, or leave it in his estate. This eliminates the double estate tax problem of a general power of appointment.

Typically, if you give someone a limited power of appointment, you specify which people (beneficiaries) the holder of the power can give property to. For instance, the person appointed can be given only the right to divide property among your four children. Or, as another example, you might direct the person to give at least 15% of your property to each of the children, with the remaining 40% to be distributed among them as the person with the special power of appointment determines.

Example: Woody sets up an AB trust, leaving the income from the trust to his wife, Janet, and the principal to their three children upon Janet's death. He includes a limited power of appointment authorizing Janet to direct how the trust assets will pass to the children, if she so chooses. Janet lives for 20 years after Woody's death and receives the income from the trust. During that time, Sarah, one of the children, gives birth to a severely disabled child. The other children are all financially well-off and don't, in Janet's opinion, need money from the trust.

Janet considers what Woody would want if he were alive and could make the decision.

Then, in her will, she exercises her limited power of appointment, by leaving 75% of the trust property outright to Sarah, with the understanding that Sarah will use the money primarily for her disabled child's needs. The other 25% of the trust property is divided between their other two children.

Watch out when using limited powers of appointment and disclaimers. With a limited power of appointment, problems can arise if the person given the power also wants to use a disclaimer at the grantor's death. If one disclaims (refuses) property that then goes into a trust, the one disclaiming cannot then direct where the disclaimed property eventually goes. So disclaiming is inconsistent with having any power of appointment, even a limited one. (See Chapter 22, Section C.) See a good estate planning lawyer if you think this problem might come up.

2. Limited Power of Appointment in QTIP Trusts

Limited powers of appointment are also occasionally included in QTIP trusts. As discussed in Chapter 19, a QTIP trust is basically a device to defer estate tax until the death of a surviving spouse, while allowing the first spouse to die to name the final beneficiaries for his estate.

When a surviving spouse is given a limited power of appointment over QTIP trust property, the surviving spouse simply has some control over the final distribution of the assets in the QTIP trust, within the limits the grantor imposed. The grantor can choose the final group of beneficiaries, such as his children, and allow a spouse to determine the amounts received by each one. The grantor, then, still controls who the final beneficiaries are—just not how much each receives.

Example: Gert leaves $2 million in a QTIP trust with the income going to her much younger husband, Raphael, for his life. She gives him a limited power of appointment to choose at his death how much each of her four children by a previous marriage will receive of what is left. Raphael may benefit for many years from the trust, and he may adjust the final outcome according to the children's needs. But if he remarries (and Gert expects, or suspects, that he might), the trust terms prevent him from shifting these assets to his new bride or to anyone else.

G. Combining a Property Control Trust With Estate Tax-Saving Trusts

Sometimes one or more property control trusts is combined with one or more tax-saving trusts as the central part of the overall estate plan.

Example: Parnell, in his 60s, has an estate worth $5 million. He recently married Moira, who has little property of her own. He has two children from his prior marriage—a daughter, Maeve, who he worries cannot handle money, and a son, Padraic, who is severely disabled. Parnell wants to leave some property for Padraic's needs, while also ensuring, as best he can, that Padraic will remain eligible for the government medical and rehabilitation services he now receives. Parnell also wants to provide for Moira if she outlives him, and leave some property on her death to Padraic and Maeve.

After working with an expert lawyer, Parnell decides to create three trusts:

1. A special needs trust for Padraic, to be funded with the amount of the personal estate tax exemption in the year of Parnell's death. (He will want to revise this plan as the estate tax exemption goes up, and certainly if estate tax disappears.)

2. A QTIP trust for the remainder of his property, to provide income for Moira and postpone estate tax on the balance of his estate. Maeve and Padraic are the final beneficiaries of this trust and will share the trust property equally when Moira dies. Parnell specifies that Padraic's share of this property will be added to his special needs trust.

3. A spendthrift trust Parnell creates for the property Maeve will eventually receive from the QTIP trust when Moira dies.

Parnell still has many matters he must resolve. For example, who should be trustee of the QTIP trust? Can Moira invade the trust principal? Who is the trustee of the spendthrift trust? How long will it last? Can the trustee decide that Maeve has become financially responsible and turn the trust principal over to her? With Padraic, Parnell faces the problems involved in creating any special needs trust.

Parnell also has to decide what he'll tell his family members about his estate plan. Moira surely needs to know about the QTIP, but how much does he want to tell his children? If he's not on good terms with

Maeve, maybe he doesn't want to tell her about the spendthrift trust. But letting her discover this only after he dies could be very hurtful. Parnell decides he will write Maeve a letter, explaining his estate plan, and why he's decided it's best to leave her property in a spendthrift trust. Parnell knows Maeve has a fierce temper. He hopes that by writing her, he'll lessen the chance of a screaming fight between the two of them, Parnell being no saint himself. But if Maeve has some time to reflect on Parnell's plan, perhaps they can discuss it later, without rancor. Parnell also informs Padraic that he's created a special needs trust to try to protect him over the years. ■

26

INCAPACITY:
Making Medical and Financial Decisions

We tend to think of estate planning as something we do now to arrange for handling important matters when we die. This definition has the advantage of being concise, but it's a bit too simple. As we grow older, many of us face the stern reality that before we die we may not be mentally or physically competent for some period of time, perhaps an extended period. A thorough estate plan must consider this possibility.

This chapter discusses how you can best ensure that your rights, dignity, and wishes will be protected if you ever become incapable of making or communicating decisions regarding medical treatment. It also covers how you can name someone to handle your finances if you can't manage them yourself.

If your health deteriorates and you become unable to make financial or medical decisions, another adult must have legal authority to make these for you.

There are two ways you can deal with this possibility:

Do nothing. If you don't make any arrangements in advance and you become incapacitated, a judge will appoint someone (called a conservator, guardian, custodian, or curator, depending on the state) to make decisions for you. Court proceedings for incapacitated people are almost always undesirable, unless there's no other option. These proceedings are costly, time-consuming, and expose to public concern what most people prefer to keep private.

If you suffer a medical emergency and are incapacitated and haven't prepared documents covering your medical care, that care will be determined according to hospital protocol or a doctor's decisions made after discussion with your immediate family members. You may get care that is very different from what you would have wanted.

With finances, people sometimes simply ignore the requirement of court proceedings—for example, a son might sign his ill father's name to the father's retirement check. Unfortunately, there's an unpleasant legal term for this act: forgery. Ignoring the law isn't wise, and it's often not practical either. Over an extended period of time, it's almost impossible to adequately manage another's affairs this way.

Create legal documents controlling how your affairs should be handled if you become incapacitated. Using medical directives, you can provide binding instructions concerning use of life-sustaining medical technology and other types of treatment; you can also appoint someone to enforce your wishes and make any other medical decisions for you that you can't make yourself. And with a durable power of attorney for finances, you can authorize someone to manage your financial affairs, and specify any limits or directions as to how your property should be handled.

Financial planning for long-term medical care. When planning for incapacity, you should also consider the possibility that you may need long-term health care, either at home or in a nursing facility. These matters are discussed in detail in *Long-Term Care: How to Plan and Pay for It*, by Joseph Matthews (Nolo).

A. MEDICAL DECISIONS

The increasing use of life-sustaining medical technology over the last decades has raised fears in many that our lives may be artificially prolonged against our wishes. The right to die with dignity, and without the tremendous agony and expense for both patient and family caused by artificially prolonging lives, has been addressed and confirmed by the U.S. Supreme Court, the federal government, and the legislatures in every state.

This individual right can also provide protection in a situation where doctors might wish to provide a patient with less extensive care than he or she would like. For example, a doctor may be unwilling to try experimental treatments or maintain long-term treatments on a patient who the doctor feels has slim chances of recovering (or, worse, couldn't pay the bill).

The United States Supreme Court has held that every individual has the constitutional right to control his or her own medical treatment. The Court also stated that medical personnel must follow "clear and convincing evidence" of a person's wishes—even if those wishes are directly opposed by the patient's family. (*Cruzan v. Director, Missouri Dept. of Health*, 497 U.S. 261 (1990).)

1. The Importance of Putting Your Wishes in Writing

In recognition of the legal right to control one's own medical treatment, every state authorizes individuals to create simple documents stating their wishes concerning medical care. The directions expressed in the documents will be followed if you are no longer capable of communicating to medical personnel your choices regarding life-prolonging and other medical care.

It is important to note that many of these documents take effect only if you are diagnosed with a terminal condition or in a permanent coma. Your

documents do not come into play if you are able to communicate your wishes in any way or are only temporarily unconscious, as with general anesthesia.

Writing down your medical care instructions can help alleviate your fears, whether worries about unwanted medical treatment being administered to you or desired medical treatment being withheld. It can also help relieve family members from having to make agonizing decisions about what kind of treatment you would want. This can be particularly important when family members have different ideas about what care you should receive. Also, doctors and hospitals have their own rules and beliefs about what is proper medical treatment, and even if your family knows your wishes and tries to assert them, medical personnel are not necessarily bound to follow them without a valid health care document.

2. Types of Medical Care Documents

There are two basic documents that allow you to direct your medical care, both grouped under the broad label "health care directives." You need to prepare both. First, you need a "declaration," a written statement that you make directly to medical personnel that spells out the medical care you do or do not wish to receive if you become incapacitated. (A declaration can go by various names, including Medical Directive, Advance Health Care Directive, or Directive to Physicians. It may also be called a "living will," but it bears no relation to a conventional will that you use to leave property at death.) A declaration functions as a contract with your treating doctors, who must either honor your wishes for medical care, or transfer you to other doctors or a facility that will honor them.

Second, you'll want what's often called a "durable power of attorney for health care," called a Designation of Health Care Surrogate or Patient Advocate Designation in a few states. In this document you appoint someone you trust to be your "attorney-in-fact" (sometimes called your "agent" or "health care proxy") to see that your doctors and health care providers give you the kind of medical care you wish to receive. In most states, you can also give your attorney-in-fact broader authority to make decisions about your medical care—excluding, of course, matters you covered in your declaration.

An increasing number of states combine both documents into a single form.

IF YOUR STATE FORMS ARE NOT DETAILED ENOUGH

When it comes to medical care documents, there are many differences in the forms and formats used by different states. Some state laws say that a specific form must be followed for a declaration to be valid. However, since the Supreme Court ruled in the *Cruzan* case that every individual has a constitutional right to direct his or her own medical care, the most important thing to keep in mind is that your directions should be clear and in writing.

If you feel strongly about a particular kind of care—even if your state law or the form you get does not address it—include your specific thoughts about it in your document. If you are using a state form that does not adequately address your concerns, write them in on the form with the additional request that your wishes be respected and followed.

---

3. What You Can Cover in Your Medical Care Documents

As mentioned above, your health care declaration is the place to write out what you do and do not want in terms of medical care if you become unable to speak for yourself. You don't need to become a medical expert to complete your documents, but it will help you to become familiar with the kinds of medical treatments that are commonly administered to patients who are seriously ill. These include:

- blood and blood products
- cardiopulmonary resuscitation (CPR)
- diagnostic tests
- dialysis
- drugs
- respirators, and
- surgery.

In addition to the treatments listed above, you may want to give some thought to the issues of pain medication, food, and water. The laws of most states assume that people want relief from pain and discomfort and specifically exclude pain-relieving procedures from definitions of life-prolonging treatments that may be withheld. Some states also exclude food and water (commonly called nutrition and hydration) from their definitions of life-prolonging treatments. But there is some controversy about whether providing food and water, or drugs to make a person comfortable, will also have the effect of prolonging life.

If you feel adamant about not having your life prolonged, you may choose to direct that all food, water, and pain relief be withheld, even if your treating doctor thinks those procedures are necessary. Again, under the U.S. Constitution, you are allowed to impose these instructions even if your state's law is restrictive, and your doctors are bound to follow your instructions or transfer you to another provider who will. You should be sure to name an attorney-in-fact to oversee your wishes, so that there will be someone available to lobby on your behalf.

On the other hand, you may feel concerned about how much pain or discomfort you'll experience during a final illness. In this case, you may prefer to have your life prolonged rather than face the possibility that discomfort or pain will go untreated. Obviously, it's an extremely personal choice. You're free to leave the instructions that feel right for you.

To make an informed decision about which procedures you do and do not want, as well as others that might pertain to your particular medical condition, it may be a good idea to discuss your medical care document with your physician. He or she can explain medical procedures more fully and can discuss the options with you. You will also find out whether your doctor has any medical or moral objections to following your wishes. If your physician does not agree to follow your wishes, consider finding a doctor who will.

Even when you have specified your wishes in medical care documents regarding life-prolonging medical treatment and comfort care, certain decisions may still be difficult to resolve:

- when, exactly, to administer or withhold certain medical treatments

- whether or not to provide, withhold, or continue antibiotic or pain medication, and

- whether to pursue complex, painful, and expensive surgeries that may serve to prolong life but cannot reverse the medical condition.

To deal with situations like these, your durable power of attorney for health care allows you to appoint someone who understands your wishes and who you trust to make these decisions in accordance with your wishes and in your best interest. To provide some guidance, your power of attorney may authorize the appointed person to:

- give, withhold, or withdraw consent to medical or surgical procedures

- consent to appropriate care for the end of life, including pain relief

- make decisions about any issues you have not covered in your declaration

- hire and fire medical personnel

- visit you in the hospital or other facility even when other visiting is restricted

- have access to medical records and other personal information, and

- get any required court authorization to obtain or withhold medical treatment if, for any reason, a hospital or doctor does not honor your written instructions.

You can also use your durable power of attorney to provide any other specific instructions you have for your attorney-in-fact.

Example: Sara is seriously ill, faces major surgery, and knows that, at a minimum, she will be unable to make all her own medical decisions. She prepares a durable power of attorney for health care, delegating to her sister, Kerry, the authority to make health care decisions for her. To make sure that her own wishes are complied with, she inserts several restrictions regarding Kerry's power. Specifically, Sara wants to be sure she is operated on by Dr. June Lee at Mattan Hospital. So, in defining her attorney-in-fact's authority, she includes the following clause:

"My attorney-in-fact shall comply with my stated desire that all surgery performed on me be done at Mattan Hospital, 134 Ridge Road, Linda Vista, California, by Dr. June Lee, unless Dr. Lee is unable to perform such surgery."

MAKING A DO NOT RESUSCITATE (DNR) ORDER

If you state in your health care declaration that you do not wish to receive life-sustaining treatment, you may also want to prepare a simple form called a Prehospital Do Not Resuscitate (DNR) order. A DNR order is used to alert emergency medical personnel that you do not wish to receive cardiopulmonary resuscitation (CPR) in the event of medical emergency. This means that if you are anywhere outside of the hospital—for example, at home—and you collapse, the paramedics who respond to the emergency call will not attempt to restart your heart or your breathing. If you are already in a hospital, you can ask your doctor to place a DNR order in your medical record.

DNR orders are sometimes used by people who:

- have a terminal illness

- are at increased risk of cardiac or respiratory arrest, or

- oppose the use of CPR under any circumstances.

In addition to preparing a DNR form, you will probably want to get a Medic-Alert bracelet or medallion to wear so that your wishes will be obvious to medical personnel. You can obtain a bracelet or medallion by calling the Medic Alert Foundation at 800-432-5378.

4. When Your Health Care Directives Take Effect

Your health care directive takes effect when you no longer have the ability, or capacity, to make your own health care decisions. Essentially, lacking capacity means that:

- you can't understand the nature and consequences of the health care choices that are available to you, and

- you are unable to communicate your own wishes for care, either orally, in writing, or through gestures.

Practically speaking, this means that if you are so ill or injured that you cannot express your health care wishes in any way, your directive will spring immediately into effect. Usually, this happens only if you are diagnosed as close to death from a terminal condition or if you are permanently comatose. If there is any question about your ability to understand your treatment choices and communicate clearly, your doctor (with the input of your health care proxy or close relatives) will decide whether it is time for your health care directive to become operative.

In some states, it is possible to give your health care proxy the authority to manage your health care immediately. If your state allows this option, you may prefer to make an immediately effective directive for any of several reasons, including:

- Allowing your proxy to put your document into effect quickly, without first having a doctor confirm that you are incapacitated. This may be particularly important if you are not under the care of a doctor with whom you have an established, trusting relationship.

- Keeping control in the hands of your proxy. You may feel that your proxy, not a doctor, is the best person to decide that you can no longer direct your own medical care.

- Asking your proxy to step in early and make decisions for you even if you still have the capacity to make your own choices. You may want this if illness, exhaustion, or other circumstances leave you feeling that you'd like someone to trust to deal with your doctors and make treatment decisions for you.

Making an immediately effective document will not give your proxy the authority to override what you want in terms of treatment; you will always be able to dictate your own medical care if you have the ability to do so. And even when you are no longer capable of making your own decisions, your proxy must always act in your best interests and try diligently to follow any health care wishes you've expressed in your health care directive or otherwise.

Finally, to ensure that your document takes effect and your wishes are followed if your need for care arises unexpectedly, you should place copies of your health care documents with several people, including your regular doctor, your health care proxy, and at least one other trusted relative or friend.

5. Choosing an Attorney-in-Fact or Proxy

There are a number of things to consider when choosing your health care attorney-in-fact or proxy. Most important, of course, is to choose someone that you trust to do the job right, if it becomes necessary. And a very difficult and painful job it may be. Your attorney-in-fact may be faced with confusing medical choices and opinions, under grave circumstances. Certainly no simple guide exists telling attorneys-in-fact how to handle what real life may throw at them, or how to cope with the emotions that can arise when trying to act in the best interests of an incapacitated and possibly dying loved one. This is not a choice to be made without serious reflection.

Here are a few other things you should think about. Appoint someone who:

- is likely to be present when decisions need to be made—most often, this means someone who lives nearby or who is willing to travel and spend time at your side during your hospitalization

- would not easily be swayed or bullied by doctors or family members who disagree with your wishes, and

---

HEALTH CARE DOCUMENTS AND HIPAA

If you've recently visited a doctor, you know there's a law requiring patients to sign forms regarding medical privacy and the release of medical information. This federal law is called "HIPAA," the Health Insurance Portability and Accountability Act. Some lawyers have argued, or worried, that HIPAA requirements apply to your agent's powers under your health care directive, and that you must prepare special HIPAA release forms to give your agent the authority to take over your health care decisions for you. Fortunately, this is not the case. Your health care power of attorney authorizes the person you name as your agent to obtain the medical information necessary to put your document into effect and carry out your wishes. As stated by the California Medical Association:

"CMA has received calls from physicians and other caregivers who have heard rumors that existing Advance Health Care Directives are invalidated by HIPAA's privacy rule, and that patients need to fill out new HIPAA-compliant ones. This is simply not true. . . . Nothing in the privacy rule regulations changes the way in which an individual grants another person power of attorney for health care decisions. The U.S. Department of Health and Human Services has confirmed on its website that state law regarding health care powers of attorney continues to apply."

Some states have begun to add HIPAA authorizations to their health care power of attorney documents, but doing so actually goes beyond what the law requires. You needn't be concerned about HIPAA. What's vital is that you prepare your health care documents and select the right person to enforce your medical instructions and make other health care decisions for you if necessary.

- is capable of understanding your medical condition and any proposed life-prolonging measures.

It is also a good idea to appoint a backup or replacement attorney-in-fact in case your first choice is unable or unwilling to serve. Make it clear, however, that the second person is only an alternate. It is not wise to appoint coproxies: having two people make decisions would only complicate the process.

 Do not appoint your doctor or other health care provider as attorney-in-fact. Although your doctor is an important person for your proxy to consult concerning health care decisions, you should not appoint your doctor as your attorney-in-fact or proxy. The laws in most states specifically forbid treating physicians and other health care providers from acting in this role—to avoid the appearance that they may have their own interests at heart and so may not be able to act according to your wishes.

6. Where to Get Medical Care Forms

Some states require residents to use a specific form designed for that state. In any case, it's always a good idea to use your state's form, because doctors and hospitals will be familiar with it.

You do not need to consult a lawyer to prepare your state's medical care forms. The forms are usually simple and can be obtained, free or for a nominal fee, from a number of sources, including:

- local senior centers
- local hospitals (ask to speak with the patient representative; by law, any hospital that receives federal funds must provide patients with appropriate forms for directing health care)
- your regular physician
- your state's medical association

- The National Hospice Palliative Care Organization provides free health care directive forms for every state. You can order your state's forms by calling 800-658-8898 or you can download forms from the website at www.nhpco.org.
- *Quicken WillMaker Plus* (software from Nolo) contains forms for all states except Louisiana, and thorough instructions to help you complete them. California residents can also use *Living Wills & Powers of Attorney for California*, by Shae Irving (Nolo).

7. Finalizing Your Medical Care Documents

After completing the documents directing your medical care, there are just a few steps you must take to make them valid and binding.

Signing your documents. Every state law requires that you sign your documents—or direct another person to sign them for you—as a way of verifying that you understand them and that they contain your true wishes. If you are physically unable to sign them yourself, you can direct another person to sign them for you.

You must sign your documents, or have them signed for you, in the presence of witnesses or a notary public—sometimes both. (This depends on your state's law.) The purpose of this additional formality is so that at least one other person can attest that you were of sound mind and of legal age (at least 18) when you made the documents.

 Keep documents up to date. The laws on medical care forms can change, so a particular form which was the right one in your state several years ago may by now have been replaced by a different, usually more complete form. In most states, documents you completed while an old law was in effect remain valid. Nevertheless, you should review your health care documents every few years, to be sure that your documents reflect your present wishes, and that you have the form with which doctor's and other health care providers are most comfortable.

Making and distributing copies. After you complete your health care documents, you should keep the originals where your attorney-in-fact can easily find them if the need arises. Ideally, however, you should also make an effort to make your wishes for your future health care widely known. Give copies of your documents to:

- your attorney-in-fact
- any physician with whom you now consult regularly
- the office of the hospital or other care facility in which you are likely to receive treatment
- the patient representative of your HMO or insurance plan
- close relatives, particularly immediate family members—spouse, grown children, siblings
- trusted friends, and
- clergy or lawyer, particularly if you are in regular contact with a member of the clergy or lawyer but you do not have a family member who lives nearby.

KEEPING TRACK OF COPIES

Keep the original of your medical directive in an easily accessible place in your home, where your attorney-in-fact can quickly locate it.

You should also keep a list of all the people and places that have copies of your medical directive. Then, if you change the terms of the directive, you will be able to retrieve each of the copies or have them destroyed.

---

8. Changing Your Mind—And Documents

You can change any type of medical care document as long as you are of sound mind. Therefore, neither your decisions about health care nor your appointment of an attorney-in-fact are final decisions. Anytime you wish to change the terms or attorney-in-fact, however, you must prepare a new document and finalize it properly—according to the formalities that must be followed in your state. You should also make sure that all copies of the document you made earlier are destroyed.

Review your medical care documents occasionally to make sure they still accurately reflect your wishes for your medical care. Advances in technology or changes in health care attitudes are two of the kinds of changes that may cause you to revise your view about the kind of medical care you want.

In addition, you should consider making new documents if:

- you move to another state, or
- the attorney-in-fact or proxy you named to supervise your wishes becomes unable to do so.

B. FINANCIAL DECISIONS

A durable power of attorney for finances allows you to name someone you trust (called your attorney-in-fact) to handle your finances if you can't. Every state recognizes this type of document. If you become unable to manage your finances and you haven't prepared a durable power of attorney, your spouse, closest relatives, or companion will have to ask a court for authority over at least some of your financial affairs. This procedure—called a conservatorship or guardianship proceeding—can be time-consuming and expensive. (See Section C, below.) In contrast, preparing a durable power of attorney is simple and inexpensive—and if you do become incapacitated, the document will likely appear as a minor miracle to those closest to you.

1. Granting Authority to Your Attorney-in-Fact

Any power of attorney arrangement depends upon trust and understanding between you and the person you appoint to handle your affairs. You can help make this relationship work by putting specific instructions in your document regarding financial actions you do and do not wish the attorney-in-fact to take. Your attorney-in-fact has only the financial authority you grant him or her in the document. Normally, an attorney-in-fact has authority to handle all regular financial matters, such as depositing checks and paying bills. Beyond the basics of routine financial maintenance, it's up to you to decide what you want to authorize.

THE ATTORNEY-IN-FACT'S DUTIES

Commonly, people give an attorney-in-fact broad power over their finances. But you can give your attorney-in-fact as much or as little power as you wish. You may want to give your attorney-in-fact authority to do some or all of the following:

- use your assets to pay your everyday expenses and those of your family

- buy, sell, maintain, pay taxes on, and mortgage real estate and other property

- collect benefits from Social Security, Medicare, or other government programs or civil or military service

- invest your money in stocks, bonds, and mutual funds

- handle transactions with banks and other financial institutions

- buy and sell insurance policies and annuities for you

- file and pay your taxes

- operate your small business

- claim or disclaim property you inherit or are otherwise entitled to

- represent you in court or hire someone to represent you, and

- manage your retirement accounts.

Whatever powers you give the attorney-in-fact, he or she must act in your best interests, keep accurate records, keep your property separate from his or hers (unless you specify otherwise in the power of attorney document), and avoid conflicts of interest.

While you may want to define and limit your attorney-in-fact's authority in some matters, you obviously can't foresee every financial concern that might arise. So it's vital that you choose someone you trust, and who has sound financial judgment, to be your attorney-in-fact. While this doesn't have to be the same person as you choose as attorney-in-fact for health care, it's sensible to name the same person for both roles unless you strongly believe someone else should handle your money. If you do name different people for these two jobs, be sure they can work well together.

In your document, you can specify whether or not you want your attorney-in-fact to be paid for taking care of your finances. (An attorney-in-fact is always entitled to reimbursement from your assets for any expenses he or she incurs on your behalf, but you may decide to authorize additional compensation.) In many family situations, the attorney-in-fact is not paid if the duties won't be complicated or burdensome. If your property and finances are extensive, however, and your attorney-in-fact will need to devote significant time and energy to managing them, it seems fair that you provide compensation for the work. Most importantly, discuss and resolve this issue with your proposed attorney-in-fact before you finalize your document.

As with health care directives, you can change the attorney-in-fact or any other provision of your durable power of attorney for finances any time, as long as you are of sound mind.

Powers of attorney and Medicare. If you're concerned about protecting your assets from the reach of a nursing facility or from Medicare, see an attorney who specializes in asset preservation. Federal law prohibits transferring assets within three years of applying for Medicare, so an expert attorney is a must.

2. When Your Durable Power of Attorney for Finances Takes Effect

There are two kinds of durable powers of attorney for finances: those that take effect immediately, and those that don't become effective unless a doctor (or two, if you wish) certifies that you are incapacitated. Which to choose depends, in part, on when you want your attorney-in-fact to begin handling tasks for you.

If you want someone to take over some or all of your financial tasks now, you should make your document effective as soon as you sign it. Then, your attorney-in-fact can begin helping you with your finances right away—and can continue to do so if you later become incapacitated.

On the other hand, you may feel strongly that your attorney-in-fact should not take over unless and until you are incapacitated. In this case, you have two options. If you trust your attorney-in-fact to use his or her authority only when it's absolutely necessary, you can go ahead and make your durable power of attorney effective immediately. Legally, your attorney-in-fact will then have the authority to act on your behalf—but, according to your wishes, won't do so unless he or she ever decides that you can't handle your affairs yourself.

If you're uncomfortable making a document that's effective immediately, you can make what's known as a "springing" power of attorney. It doesn't take effect until a physician examines you and declares, in writing, that you can't manage your finances.

There are some real inconveniences involved in creating a springing power of attorney. First, your attorney-in-fact will have to go through the potentially time-consuming and complicated process of getting the doctors' statements.

This may be made even more difficult by HIPAA. Unlike health care documents, it's unclear whether or not HIPAA rules apply to durable powers of attorney for finances. Without a valid HIPAA release, a doctor might refuse to prepare a statement for your agent that confirms your incapacity.

Second, though it's not too likely, some people and institutions may be reluctant to accept a springing power of attorney, even after your attorney-in-fact has obtained the necessary doctors' statements and your document is perfectly legal. A bank, for example, might question whether you have, in fact, become incapacitated. These hassles could delay your attorney-in-fact and disrupt the handling of your finances.

If you truly trust your attorney-in-fact (and you should), you may find that it makes more sense to create a document that's effective immediately and then make clear to your attorney-in-fact when he or she should take action under the document. Ultimately, of course, the decision is yours—and you should choose the option that feels most comfortable to you.

 See a lawyer for a springing durable power of attorney for finances. If you truly aren't comfortable granting someone immediate authority over your finances, you should see a knowledgeable lawyer to make sure you obtain a properly drafted springing document. The lawyer can make sure that your document includes all the necessary legal language, including a valid HIPAA release.

3. Finalizing Your Durable Power of Attorney for Finances

After you've completed your durable power of attorney for finances, you must observe certain formalities to make it legal. But these requirements aren't difficult to meet.

You must sign your durable power of attorney in the presence of a notary public for your state. In some states, notarization is required by law to make the durable power of attorney valid. But even where law doesn't require it, custom does. A durable power of attorney that is not notarized may not be accepted by people your attorney-in-fact needs to deal with. A handful of states also require you to sign your document in front of witnesses. Witnesses must be mentally competent adults, and your attorney-in-fact may not be a witness. Some states impose additional witness requirements as well and a few require your attorney-in-fact to sign the power of attorney or a separate consent form before taking action under the document.

Finally, if your document grants power over real estate, you must put a copy of your document on file in the land records office of any counties where you own real estate. This process is called "recording," or "registration" in some states. (You don't have to record your document until it takes effect. This means that if you make a springing power of attorney, your attorney-in-fact can record the document later, if you ever become incapacitated.) In just two states, North Carolina and South Carolina, you must record your durable power of attorney for it to be durable—that is, for it to remain in effect if you become incapacitated.

How to find the forms you need. You can use *Quicken WillMaker Plus* (software from Nolo) to prepare a durable power of attorney for finances that is valid in your state. If you live in California, you can also use the book *Living Wills & Powers of Attorney for California*, by Shae Irving (Nolo).

WHAT TO DO WITH THE SIGNED DOCUMENT

If your power of attorney is effective immediately, give the original, signed and notarized document to the attorney-in-fact. He or she will need it as proof of authority to act on your behalf.

If the durable power of attorney won't become effective unless you become incapacitated (a springing durable power of attorney), keep the notarized, signed original yourself. Store it in a safe, convenient place that the attorney-in-fact can reach quickly, if necessary. Your attorney-in-fact will need the original document to carry out your wishes.

You may also wish to give copies of your durable power of attorney to the people and institutions your attorney in fact will need to deal with—banks or government offices, for example. If the document is already in their records, it may eliminate hassles for your attorney-in-fact later. If you're making a springing durable power of attorney, however, it may seem premature to contact people and institutions about a document that may never go into effect. It's up to you.

DURABLE POWERS OF ATTORNEY FOR FINANCES AND LIVING TRUSTS

Many living trusts provide that the successor trustee is to manage the trust property if the grantor becomes incapacitated. Even if you use a durable power of attorney to appoint someone (your attorney-in-fact) to handle your property if you become incapacitated, property in your living trust still remains subject to your successor trustee, not the attorney-in-fact. This division is typically only one of terminology, not substance, because most people appoint the same person to handle both jobs.

Some people who plan to transfer all of their property under a living trust ask why they need bother with a durable power of attorney for finances at all. The reason is that you're likely to receive income, even if you become incapacitated, from pensions, Social Security, and other sources, and you will need a durable power of attorney for finances to handle this money, and maintain your personal bank account, pay bills, and so on.

C. GUARDIANSHIPS AND CONSERVATORSHIPS

If you are concerned about a person who is already incapacitated and unable to make decisions, most of the advice in this chapter will not apply to you. At that point, the person can no longer create valid legal documents or delegate responsibility for decisions to others. If the person made no durable powers of attorney or living trust, financial institutions, government agencies, health care providers, and bureaucrats of every variety may either refuse to take action regarding the person's affairs—or may take action with little regard for the person's wishes.

In this situation, you'll probably have to go to court to ask a judge to appoint you or another relative or friend to act on the person's behalf. There are procedures in every state to do this. Some states have only one legal category, usually called guardianship; others have a second category that is often limited to financial matters and called conservatorship.

In general guardianship proceedings, the legal question is whether or not a person has become "incompetent"—that is, unable to handle his or her own affairs. In many states, this requires that medical evidence of incompetence be presented to the court. In more limited proceedings to establish only a financial conservatorship (see below), the court can act if it finds that the person is unable to handle financial affairs even though not completely legally incompetent.

When appointing a guardian or conservator, a judge follows certain preferences established by state law. Most states give preference to the incompetent person's spouse, adult children, adult siblings, or other blood relatives. (In a few states, a judge may give highest priority to a registered domestic partner.) Judges have some flexibility in choosing the guardian; the judge may use his or her discretion to pick the best person for the job. Without strong evidence of what the incapacitated person would have wanted, however, it is unlikely that a nonrelative would ever be appointed over a relative who wanted the position. Because of this, guardianship or conservatorship proceedings can cause great heartache if an estranged relative is chosen as conservator over the person's partner or close friend.

In conservatorship or guardianship proceedings, a person has a right to appear in court with an attorney and to consent or object to all proposed authority. In many states, if the person does not have an attorney, the court may appoint one. Similarly, any change in the conservator or guardian's authority requires an additional court order to which the person can consent or object. The conservator or guardian is accountable to the court and will be held responsible for any mismanagement of the person's property.

In some states, it is possible to handle conservatorship proceedings without the assistance of a lawyer if no one challenges the need for the conservatorship and its scope. More complicated guardianship procedures, however, do require the assistance of a lawyer, particularly if the person alleged to be incompetent, or anyone else, does not agree that the guardianship is needed or that the person seeking to be guardian is not the right person for the job.

1. Financial Conservatorship or Guardianship

A conservator or guardian can be appointed by a court solely to protect a person's property—savings, real estate, investments, and other assets. He or she can also conduct daily financial affairs, such as paying bills, or arrange for services when the person is unable to do so. This type of limited management assistance is appropriate when the person is still capable of caring for himself or herself personally, but because of disorientation or disability is unable to responsibly carry out financial tasks. In this situation, the conservator or guardian does not have power over the person's personal conduct, but has authority over financial or other affairs as the court orders.

An advantage of a limited conservatorship or guardianship is that it leaves the person free to make many important decisions independently: where to live, with whom to associate, what medical care to receive. Nonetheless, it is still a court process in which a judge makes a ruling, occasionally against the person's will, that gives another person authority over some parts of his or her life. It is therefore a procedure to be used only if voluntary procedures such as making a durable power of attorney are no longer possible.

2. Full Guardianship

Full guardianship is an extreme measure that severely restricts the legal rights of a person based on a court's finding of incompetence. It reduces that person's legal status to that of a minor, with no control over her or his own money or property, decisions about medical care or institutionalization. A person under full guardianship even loses the right to vote.

If a person retains some degree of orientation and capability, a legal finding by a court that he or she is incompetent can be emotionally devastating and, in fact, self-fulfilling. The person deemed legally incompetent may well give up the will to care for himself or herself and become much less competent than before. Obviously, seeking a full guardianship is a very serious step, to be taken when a person's mental condition leaves no other choice. ∎

27

Body and Organ Donation, Funerals, and Burials

People facing the grief and reality that someone they love has died face other immediate problems: disposing of the body and arranging the ceremonies desired to mark the death. It's hard to even talk directly about a body once life has left it; the word "corpse" sounds unfeeling, and "cadaver" is worse. Statutes often refer to a dead body as "the remains," a word technically accurate and almost as disturbing. Perhaps it's because many of us don't like to contemplate death that the language we have invented for it can be awkward. But, however it is described, the reality is the same: a body must, somehow, be removed from the place of death and disposed of. And if desired, commemorative ceremonies need to be carried out.

Most people die in hospitals or nursing homes. These institutions want a dead body removed quickly. So it's nearly inevitable, if no planning has been done, for family or friends to turn to "professionals"—funeral homes. Often they do it without reflection or much knowledge of what the traditional funeral establishment offers or what it charges for its services. This passive approach often means family and friends pay far too much for a funeral they don't even like—and worst of all, for funeral goods and services that don't suit the person who has died.

Grief, guilt, sorrow, religious conviction, doubt, or whatever survivors are feeling often leave them distraught and confused. In these circumstances, expenses can seem trivial. However, we believe it's no slight to the deceased, or to the feelings of those who survive, to suggest that nothing is gained by needless costs. Funerals can be expensive. A funeral trade journal has estimated the average cost of a conventional U.S. funeral between $4,700 and $8,000. It's one of the most expensive items the average American family ever purchases. To many, including these authors, this is a huge and unnecessary cost to comply with the biblical injunction: "Remember, man, thou art dust and to dust thou shall return."

A. Making Your Own Choices

More and more people are reflecting on what they want to happen to their bodies when they die. They are making choices that have emotional meaning for them and save their families needless expense.

Broadly viewed, there are four choices available (we don't cover some of the more esoteric options, such as cryonics/body freezing):

Donating the entire body to a medical school. This must be arranged beforehand. If you do this, the school uses the body for studies and then, usually, the body is cremated, and the remains are buried or scattered. However, family members or friends can request that the body be returned when the study is complete—usually within a year or so. Even if a person opts for whole body donation, that donation may be refused at death for any of a number of reasons, requiring survivors to make other plans.

Donating specific body organs to an organ bank. If you donate organs, the rest of the body is normally returned to those responsible for cremation or burial, which means that someone still must arrange for its disposal.

Arranging a traditional funeral service conducted by a commercial funeral home. This includes cremation or body burial.

Arranging a simple funeral service, without embalming of the body. You can do this independently or with the help of a funeral or memorial society.

Planning for the immediate, practical aspects of your death is essential to make sure your wishes are carried out. To take one example, if you wish to donate body parts or organs, it's almost essential to authorize it, in writing, before your death. Similarly, if you want a nontraditional funeral, such as cremation with your ashes scattered over the sea, it may not happen unless you arrange the details yourself. (Each state has rules governing how and where ashes may be scattered, though it's legal in every state to scatter or bury ashes on private property as long as you have the landowner's permission.) Even for a traditional commercial funeral, planning is desirable. Costs for death goods and services vary widely—for example, caskets are commonly marked up from five to ten times their wholesale costs. So comparison shopping can often result in big savings.

In our view, there's really no good reason to plan how to save money on probate fees or estate taxes and then toss a chunk of it away on an overpriced funeral. Equally important, there's no reason to dread thinking about what kind of death notice and ceremonial service will be fitting, if you want them. Once you've decided what is appropriate, you need to convey your intention to others, preferably in a written declaration. This kind of planning can achieve much more than saving money. It provides survivors with essential guidance, and offers you peace of mind that you've made arrangements to your liking.

B. LEAVING WRITTEN INSTRUCTIONS

You should put your wishes regarding the disposition of your body in writing. Under most states' laws, written burial instructions left by a deceased person are binding, assuming, of course, the instructions don't violate state laws on body disposition. Even where laws do not specifically require that a deceased person's instructions be followed, they almost always are. You can also ensure that your wishes are followed by joining a local funeral or memorial society. (See Section F2, below.)

Written instructions are sometimes included in a will. But relying on this exclusively is not the best choice, because it may take time to locate and read a will—and dead bodies are most often disposed of quickly. A better approach is to prepare your

instructions in a separate document, and to also include them in your will.

Keep the instructions in a safe and readily accessible place, known to whomever will have the responsibility for implementing them. Or simpler yet, give a copy to the person you've chosen to be responsible for carrying out your desires. If you've joined a funeral society or chosen a mortuary make sure it has a copy of your wishes.

If you don't leave legally binding written instructions, your next of kin (the closest family relation) will have legal control over the disposition of your body. This can pose insoluble problems if a friend or partner knows you wanted a specific type of disposition that the next of kin opposes. Without legally binding written instructions, the friend or partner is powerless to prevent the next of kin from controlling the disposition.

More help with final arrangements. Nolo offers two excellent resources to help you decide on final arrangements—from burial or cremation to memorial ceremonies—and leave instructions for loved ones. Nolo's *Quicken WillMaker Plus* software lets you use your computer to prepare a final arrangements letter that makes your wishes clear. Or, if you prefer to use a workbook, *Get It Together: Organize Your Records So Your Family Won't Have To,* by Melanie Cullen with Shae Irving, provides a complete system to help you organize all your important paperwork and personal information, including instructions for final arrangements, for your survivors.

┌───┐
│ **ABOUT DEATH CERTIFICATES**   │
│   │
│ Whenever a person dies, a physician must │
│ complete a death certificate shortly after │
│ the death and file it with the appropriate │
│ governmental agency, often a local registrar │
│ of health. Those responsible for winding up a │
│ deceased person's affairs will need certified │
│ copies of the death certificate to transfer certain │
│ types of property to inheritors. For example, │
│ to collect money from a pay-on-death bank │
│ account or to end a joint tenancy of real estate, │
│ the inheritors need a certified copy of the death │
│ certificate. To wind up a probate-avoidance │
│ living trust, the successor trustee will often need │
│ several copies of the death certificate. For │
│ information about obtaining copies of a death │
│ certificate, see Chapter 31, Section E. │
└───┘

C. DONATING YOUR BODY OR ORGANS

If you want to leave your body, or parts of it, for medical research or instruction, you have two choices:

• you can leave your entire body to medical science, usually a medical school, or

• you can donate certain body organs or tissues to transplant facilities.

You cannot do both. Medical schools generally won't accept a body from which any part has been removed, except sometimes for eye transplants.

The procedure for donating a body to a medical school is simple. Contact the school, see if it accepts bodies for instruction and study, and if so, what legalities and forms it requires. Medical facilities are legally prohibited from paying for bodies, but many will absorb the cost of transporting a body—at least within certain distance of the institution.

Many, but not all, medical schools won't accept bodies that are too old or too diseased, or if death occurred during surgery. So it's important to have a backup plan if you're thinking about body donation. You can call the National Anatomical Service at 800-727-0700 to find out more about body donation in your locale.

The other option, donating body organs, is also a generous and useful act. There is a great need for many types of organ donations. Heart transplants get the most publicity, but many more organs, tissues, and bones can and are being transplanted, including middle ear, eyes, liver, lungs, pancreas, kidneys, skin tissue, bone and cartilage, pituitary glands, and even hip or knee joints. A gift of a vital organ is one of the most precious and loving acts one can make. We know this well, as we have a friend who was saved from blindness by a cornea transplant.

To authorize organ donation, it's a good idea to obtain a donor card and carry it with you at all times. In most states, you can use your driver's license for this purpose; the motor vehicles department will give you a card to carry and perhaps a sticker to place on the front of your license. In addition, your health care directive is often a good place to state your wishes regarding organ donation. An increasing number of states are providing a place on their official forms for such instructions. Also, after your death, your immediate family can consent to donating your organs—unless you've left instructions to the contrary.

Time is truly of the essence for the successful removal of donated body parts, so if you want to have organs removed on death you should make arrangements beforehand, and discuss your intentions with family and friends. Most people put off making these arrangements, no matter how intensely they may want to donate their organs. With donation of body parts, procrastination may result in your intentions being frustrated because they cannot be carried out fast enough.

D. DEATH NOTICES

When someone dies, one of the first things that most families do is notify others. For close friends and relatives, phone calls normally work. But what about notifying the many other people whose lives have been touched by the deceased, such as former neighbors, golf partners, sailing or bowling friends, retired business associates, and other friends? Doing this promptly is important, as many of these people will wish to attend one or more of the events that usually occur very soon after death, such as a wake, lying-in, funeral, or memorial ceremony. And other people will wish to communicate with the family and extend their sympathy.

In many communities, notification is handled by a local newspaper, with either a death notice or an obituary.

Death notices generally must be paid for, and consist of small print listings of the date of death, names of survivors, and location of any services.

An obituary is a news item, usually prepared by the staff of the newspaper. It runs in standard type, contains a small headline—for example, "Former Local School Principal Dies"—and is free. In small towns, many local newspapers prepare obituaries for a large percentage of people who die, giving more space to those who were locally prominent. In large metropolitan papers, however, very few people's deaths are sufficiently newsworthy to qualify for obituaries, and even fairly prominent people have their deaths recorded in the paid death notices, if at all.

Death notice information must be submitted to newspapers promptly. This can raise a real problem for survivors. Just when they are beset by difficult emotions and serious practical problems, someone has to call in to the newspaper office with details of the dead person's life and survivors. Newspapers are commonly very understanding and provide a lot of help, but it still can be difficult. Common problems involve remembering or locating dates, parents' full names, details of key events, correct spellings for clubs, and other affiliations, to mention just a few.

One solution to this problem is to prepare your own death notice. This might sound a bit macabre, but it will probably only take you a little while, and those who are later spared the task will surely be appreciative. Just look at the appropriate newspaper, follow the general form it uses, and write one out.

What about an obituary? At least for many local newspapers, you can help write the news story about your death in advance. The paper will have a form on which you can list all relevant biographical information, including your education and employment history, civic responsibilities, names of children, and so on. If this form is filled out in advance, it can be given to the paper immediately after death, and will be used to write the news story. In addition to completing this form, however, you may want to actually try your hand at writing your own obituary, leaving blank your date of death. Does this sound weird? Well, yes, a little, but remember, if you don't do it, someone you love may have to deal with a reporter precisely when there will be far more pressing practical and emotional concerns occasioned by your death. To get an idea of what an obituary should look like, read a few in your local paper. In our experience, if a family submits a well-written, factual obituary immediately after a person's death, a local newspaper is likely to use a good part of it, or at least echo its major themes.

E. SERVICES AND CEREMONIES FOLLOWING A DEATH

Many people wish to have input about the ceremonies held after their deaths. You may have a favorite church, synagogue, or temple where you would like the service held, or a particular priest, pastor, rabbi, or monk to conduct it. You may know how you want the service to be conducted. Of course, in many religious and spiritual communities, the broad outlines of rituals that accompany a death are well-established. Usually, however, when it comes to the particular prayers to be read and songs to be sung, there's room for personal choice. If the service won't be held by a religious institution, individual input becomes more urgent. It's sad to attend, as both of us have, funerals of good friends held in a commercial funeral home where not one personal word was said.

If you have specific ideas about ceremonies you want held after your death, the best way to make sure your wishes will be carried out is to put them in writing. Simply include a brief statement as part of your final instructions. (See Section B, above.)

F. Funerals

For funerals, you have two basic options: use a commercial funeral home or make arrangements in advance through a nonprofit funeral or memorial society.

1. Commercial Funerals

The traditional American funeral, as provided by a commercial funeral home or mortuary, normally includes the following:

- The funeral director takes care of the paperwork required for death and burial certificates.

- The funeral home removes the body from the place of death and embalms it.

- The embalmed body is shown at an open casket ceremony, or there is a closed casket. Many funeral parlors have their own chapels and encourage all services to be held there, rather than in churches.

Funerals are always products of culture. Our own culture, which studiously avoids contemplating death, is also made nervous by trying to decide what type of funeral is appropriate. In some ages, expensive funerals and burials were scorned as ostentatious, wasteful, and the norm was a simple, dignified, and inexpensive service. In other times, as in 17th-century England, expensive funerals and grand tombs were in vogue for those with status and wealth.

There is no one American cultural tradition concerning funerals and burials. Most Americans do hold ceremonies when a person dies, of course, and many ethnic and religious traditions are deeply ingrained, such as the Jewish custom of burial within 24 hours, the Buddhist practice of sitting with the body for several days, or the Irish wake. But, generally speaking, for those not close to their ethnic roots, there's still a significant cultural vacuum. As should come as no surprise, that vacuum was filled by business.

Before the Civil War, burials in America were most often simple affairs—a religious ceremony, a plain pine box, and quick burial. Undertakers did not exist until roughly the 1860s; originally they practiced some other trade, often carpentry. During the Civil War, bodies of dead soldiers were embalmed so they could be shipped home for burial. Next, undertakers emerged as a distinct trade; they later evolved into funeral directors and began to proclaim themselves professionals. The plain pine box was transformed into a luxurious coffin. Funerals became theater, and their cost rose accordingly. Embalming the dead body and showing the embalmed remains became standard funeral parlor practice—a practice that obviously adds substantially to the cost of burial, and one not used (and indeed regarded as barbaric) in most other countries. The funeral industry also developed a rationalization for embalming. It claimed that viewing the embalmed body is useful for the living, because seeing a lifelike body enables the viewers to cope with their grief. The term they invented for this is "grief therapy." Some funeral homes also offer "after care" help to a widow or widower, sometimes including support groups and professional therapists.

As many people sense, there's something odd, as well as expensive, about traditional American funerals. This shift in attitude was originally sparked by Jessica Mitford's book *The American Way of Death* (Simon & Schuster), a pioneering examination of commercial American culture in one of its more rapacious and grotesque areas. Written with wit and grace, Mitford's book (now over three decades old, but still influential) raised many questions about American funeral customs. As a result of her book and the efforts of many others, many beneficial legal changes have occurred.

Legal reform has aided the growth of funeral and memorial societies, which, in turn, have introduced real price competition into the commercial funeral business. Now some commercial funeral homes have begun to advertise less expensive funerals. So, if you do want to patronize a traditional funeral parlor, shop around for the best prices on costs and services. Mortuaries are legally required to give those who ask a detailed price list of their goods and services.

a. Embalming

One great expense of a traditional funeral is embalming the body. Generally, state law doesn't require embalming unless the body will be transported by common carrier, such as a commercial plane, or county health officials order embalming as a protection against the spread of contagious disease (a very rare event). There are those who claim that embalming is a necessary health measure, but there's little evidence to support this. If a body must be preserved for a short time, refrigeration is at least as reliable, and far cheaper.

In embalming, preservative and disinfectant fluid is injected into the arterial system and body cavities, replacing blood. Embalmed bodies aren't preserved for eternity, though medical science can do this for exceptional reasons (keeping Lenin's body on display,

for example). Generally, an embalmed body begins to decompose rapidly within a few weeks.

By embalming the body, a funeral parlor can preserve it sufficiently to allow open-casket viewing of the body at a funeral service, a popular practice with some Americans. How one feels about this is, of course, a private matter. The important point is to realize that open-casket viewing—and embalming— are far from inevitable practices. The choice is up to survivors or to you, if you make plans for your own burial.

b. Costs

The major factor in the total cost of a funeral—and the item most grossly marked up—is the price of the casket. Not surprisingly, funeral directors generally urge as expensive a casket as possible. Anyone who's ever been casket shopping can tell you it's a bit like visiting a car dealership. There's always a larger, fancier model available, with more expensive options. The question all too often becomes not how much a casket costs, but how much you are willing to pay. In most facilities, rental caskets are available for those who wish to be cremated or who choose not to purchase a casket.

The cost of a traditional funeral can easily add up to many thousands of dollars. In addition to the casket, there's normally a charge for each extra, and there are a lot of possible extras, including flowers, special burial clothing, additional limousines, clergyman's honorarium, music, and cards. Also, watch out for fraudulent fees, such as "handling" charges or AIDS body handling costs.

Flowers have become traditional at American funerals. A significant percentage of all flowers sold by commercial florists in America are sold for funerals. Not surprisingly, the florist industry resists any attempt to cut back on the practice of sending flowers to funerals. Some people prefer that money that would have been spent on flowers be given to a particular charity. Sometimes funeral notices or announcements state "Please Omit Flowers." Whether flowers are a beautiful and moving statement or an unnecessary expense is a choice each person can make; again, the point is to realize that there's a choice.

Finally, transporting a body from a distant place of death, or to a distant burial place, is particularly expensive. If you must arrange for the return of a body from a distant place of death, consult a customer service representative of the airlines to make sure you get the most affordable rates.

2. Funeral Societies

Funeral societies are private, nonprofit organizations, open to any who wish to join. They are devoted to the concept of simple, dignified burial services for a reasonable cost. There's usually a small fee for joining. Members are entitled to the burial programs offered through the society. Funeral societies don't generally employ their own morticians, or own their own cemeteries; rather, they have contracts of varying types with cooperating local mortuaries and crematoriums. The societies make a price list of goods and services available, and members choose the mortuary and service they would like. After a death, the society ensures that only the services selected are performed and billed for.

Specific policies, funeral costs and options vary somewhat from organization to organization, but the basics are common to all. Dignified, simple funerals can be arranged for hundreds of dollars, not thousands. Members are concerned not only with reducing the excessive costs, but at least equally with what they believe are the excesses and lack of spiritual values inherent in many commercial funerals. As the literature of the funeral societies notes, in the traditional funeral the emphasis is on the dead body—lying in an open casket, embalmed, often painted, rouged, or otherwise altered cosmetically in the belief that the embalmer's skills will make a more lifelike body, and that viewing a lifelike dead body is a sign of respect or affection.

Funeral societies want new members and readily provide information on their programs, services, and membership rules, as well as the names of all cooperating mortuaries. If you move, there's a good chance you can transfer your membership to another society; there are funeral societies in most urban areas of the United States.

There are hundreds of funeral societies throughout the U.S. To locate one near you, check the phone book or contact:

Funeral Consumers Alliance
33 Patchen Road
South Burlington, VT 05403
800-458-5563
www.funerals.org

G. Cremation

Cremation means the burning of the body. Cremation is common in many parts of the world and is now used for roughly half the deaths in the U.S. It's opposed by certain religions, such as Muslims, and Greek and Jewish Orthodox creeds. Catholics used to require the permission of their local bishop to be cremated, but the Catholic Church no longer bans cremation outright.

Be careful if you make a direct arrangement with a profit-making cremation organization. Some have been known to rip off customers, charging for "handling," "transportation," or "disposal" fees. Regular fees commonly are $1,000 or more for a "basic" cremation, plus possible additional charges of $350 to $700 for scattering the ashes, and $1,500 to $20,000 for putting the ashes in an (attractive) container.

Despite the risk of excessive costs, it is possible to arrange for a sensibly priced cremation. By law in many states, a crematory cannot require that a casket (rather than a bag) be used in cremation. This makes sense, as it seems particularly needless to pay for an expensive wood casket that is almost immediately burned. Cheaper wood caskets are often used, by custom, if no contrary directions are given.

Whether and how ashes can be scattered depends on state law. Scatterings were rare a few generations ago, but there has been a marked increase in their number as the number of cremations has grown. Cremated remains can be removed from the place of cremation or inurnment and disposed of by scattering by the person with the legal right to control the remains. Once again, leaving specific instructions regarding your wishes is a sound idea. A permit may be required for scattering in some locations. However, as noted earlier, in all states it's legal to scatter or bury cremated remains on private land, as long as the landowner approves. The crematory or mortuary involved should be able to handle any necessary paperwork involved in scattering or burying ashes.

H. BURIALS

A body must be disposed of in a lawful way. Unless it's cremated and the ashes scattered or kept in an urn or in a licensed columbarium (a building in which urns and ashes may be kept) it must be buried somewhere. Often this means the remains must be buried in a cemetery (graveyard, if you prefer the more descriptive word).

In this country, there's a wide variety of cemeteries, including profit-making ones, large mutually owned ones, church burial grounds, small co-ops, municipal ones, and national cemeteries, in which most veterans and their spouses are entitled to free burial.

Most American cemeteries, however, are private businesses. You have to buy your way in. Private cemeteries are normally separate businesses from funeral homes, although they often have working relationships with one another. Sometimes, though, they compete, and some cemeteries sell caskets. Usually, the fact that private cemeteries are separate means only that there's one more transaction to arrange—buying a burial plot. This purchase can often be arranged through a funeral society or a funeral home. If there's a specific cemetery you desire, you should be sure the funeral home or society can arrange for that particular purchase. Also, you might save money if you select your own cemetery, as prices can vary significantly.

Probably the best known private graveyard in the world is Forest Lawn Cemetery in Los Angeles. Evelyn Waugh's justly famous satire of Forest Lawn, *The Loved One,* hasn't diminished the success of this cemetery. Many people still choose (or their relatives choose) to be buried in its "splendor." Depending on how much splendor is desired, this can be quite expensive indeed.

Cemetery costs, like everything else, are going up. The minimum cost includes:

* the plot
* the coffin enclosure, which normally consists of a vault or grave liner of concrete and steel. Cemetery owners sometimes say vaults are required to prevent the land bordering the grave from eventually collapsing. Although this danger is often nonexistent or exaggerated, yearly vault sales have recently been estimated to amount to nearly one-half billion dollars. Many vaults are bought through a funeral director, although they are usually cheaper if bought from a cemetery.
* opening and closing the grave, and
* upkeep.

Many cemeteries sell "perpetual care," which they claim means that the grave will be attended "for eternity." This sounds pretty grandiose until you realize that graves don't require much care—what this really means is that the grass will be cut. And even this task doesn't amount to much in many modern urban cemeteries, which have eliminated the use of headstones, substituting plaques that are planted flush to the ground, so as not to interfere with the power mower.

If you haven't got enough to worry about, you could worry about what will happen when we run out of cemetery land. It'll take a while, surely, although one expert suggests that in only 500 years, at the present rate of graveyard growth, all the land in the United States would be graveyards.

Finally, if there's to be a headstone or plaque, why not create your own epitaph? It's your last opportunity for self-expression.

Among our favorite epitaphs are:

Cast a cold eye, on life, on death. Horseman, pass by!

—Yeats

and the classic:

On the whole, I'd rather be in Philadelphia.

—W.C. Fields

 More information about making your own final arrangements. How to arrange for funeral/burial yourself, with organizational help, is discussed in *Quicken WillMaker Plus* (software from Nolo). You may also want to read the highly regarded book, *Caring for the Dead: Your Final Act of Love*, by Lisa Carlson (Upper Access Books). ■

28

FAMILY BUSINESS ESTATE PLANNING

If you own an interest in a small business, whether as a sole proprietor, partner, shareholder in a closely held corporation, or member of a limited liability company, estate planning can get complicated fast. If a substantial part of your estate is a profit-making business of significant value, you'll need to look into three broad areas:

- operation of the business after your death
- estate tax concerns, and
- avoiding probate.

FORMING A BUSINESS TO SAVE ON TAXES

Even if you're not now a small business owner, you may wonder whether you should create a business simply to take advantage of special tax breaks applicable to family businesses. Would, say, a "family limited partnership" save your inheritors money? Be careful here. First, of course, your estate must be large enough so that estate tax will likely be paid on your death. Second, simply labeling assets a "family business" does not make them so in the eyes of the IRS. There must be significant and legitimate nontax reasons for creating the family limited partnership, and the partnership must be operated as a business. This means that profits must be distributed (roughly) according to legal ownership. If the person who creates the limited partnership continues to treat the business assets as if they were solely his or her own, the IRS will include the full value of the business in that individual's estate at death. In other words, a family limited partnership cannot be run solely as an estate-tax-avoiding scam. For example, turning your stock portfolio into a "family limited partnership" is unlikely to convince the IRS that there's any legitimate partnership business. However, a family business that combines, say, a stock portfolio and commercial real estate, might be acceptable to the IRS. In the right circumstances—with sound legal advice and a family business that passes IRS muster—establishing a family limited partnership can definitely offer estate tax savings.

Specialized legal work. Estate planning for the small business owner requires the assistance of an attorney experienced in the field. Here we can give you only a broad-brush introduction to the major concerns.

A. OPERATION OF THE BUSINESS

The death of the sole or part owner of a small business is likely to seriously disrupt that business. If no planning has been done, the disruption can be catastrophic, sometimes resulting in the failure of the enterprise. You need to have a sound succession plan. Who will take over the business? Will family members run it? (Roughly 80% of all U.S. businesses are family owned. The second generation takes over about 30% of these businesses, but only 10% of the third generation continues on.) If someone else will run the business, how will family members or other inheritors be paid for your interest?

1. Keeping Ownership in the Family

Obviously, to keep business ownership in the family, one or more family members must be willing and able to run the business. If they are, and you're the sole owner of your business, your main concerns are probably about dealing fairly with all your close family members. (See Section 2, below.)

But if you share ownership of a business, you must consider the rights of the other owners, even if there are capable family members who want to inherit your share. Commonly, a partnership agreement, corporate bylaws, or a shareholders' agreement, or the operating agreement of a limited liability company (LLC) controls the disposition of a deceased owner's interest in the business. You need to create a business estate plan that is in harmony with the documents that restrict your options.

Agreements between co-owners of a business normally cover the right of the surviving owners to buy the deceased owner's interest. One standard provision gives the surviving owners a "right of first refusal," allowing them to buy the interest for the price offered by an outside would-be purchaser. If there is no outside offer, another provision may provide a method for determining the value of the deceased owner's interest in the business. A related issue here is whether the surviving owners must buy out the deceased owners' share, or simply have the option to do so.

The agreement should also state how buyout payments will be made. Often the agreement allows the surviving owners to pay for a deceased owner's share over months or years. Particularly if the business is a corporation, determining the most desirable payout process can involve sophisticated tax planning.

Arranging to buy out a deceased owner's share necessarily involves practical financial problems. Will the business really have the money to make the payments? What happens if it doesn't? If the surviving owners aren't required to buy out a deceased owner's share, what happens if they decide not to? The inheritors can try to sell that share, but, if it's a minority share they may not find an outside buyer. Then what?

In the absence of an owners' agreement, the rights of the surviving owners are determined by the laws of the state where the business is located. It is not sensible to rely on these laws, since they are highly unlikely to fit the needs of you or your family. Much better to work out an agreement beforehand.

For information on how to draft a business agreement to cover sale and valuation issues, see these Nolo books:

Business Buyout Agreements: A Step-by-Step Guide for Co-Owners, by Anthony Mancuso and Bethany Laurence

Form a Partnership: The Complete Legal Guide, by Denis Clifford and Ralph Warner

Form Your Own Limited Liability Company, by Anthony Mancuso, and

Incorporate Your Business: A Legal Guide to Forming a Corporation in Your State, by Anthony Mancuso.

2. Treating Family Members Fairly

If you have more than one child, and some will run the business and some won't, you may have to resolve some difficult fairness issues. Do you want to leave all your children roughly the same amount? If so, what's the best way to leave the business and your other assets so that all your children are treated equally? If you don't want to leave equal shares, do you want to explain your decision to your children, in your estate planning documents or elsewhere? There certainly aren't any rules here; you have to figure out what works best for you and your family.

Example: Dante and Grace own a thriving construction business. This corporation is roughly 80% of their net worth. They have five children. After Dante and Grace die, two of the children, Steve and Patricia, will take over the business. The other three aren't interested in working in it. How can Dante and Grace achieve their goal of leaving each of their children an inheritance of roughly the same value?

One possibility is to leave the business to Steve and Patricia, and divide the remaining 20% of the estate among the other three children. The difference would be made up by the proceeds of life insurance. But the cost of life insurance turns out to be prohibitive. So Dante and Grace consider leaving the business (and the rest of their estate) equally to all five children. Only Steve and Patricia will have any voting or management powers in the business.

Of course, this leaves the other three children without control over the bulk of their inheritance. Also, what if Steve and Patricia can't agree about management decisions? They've had some nasty fights in the past.

Dante and Grace strongly believe it's in all the children's best interests to keep the business going. The best hope for this is to have Steve and Patricia run it. So Dante and Grace decide to leave equal shares to all five, with only Steve and Patricia having management powers in the business. The other children will share equally in all profits from the business, including any profits made from an eventual sale of the business.

Dante and Grace amend the corporation bylaws to require that if Steve and Patricia have a dispute they can't resolve themselves, they must try mediation and, if that fails, compulsory arbitration. Dante and Grace aren't thrilled with their plan, but feel it's the best they can do. They will talk with each child to explain why they've made their decision, and how they'd like the business to work.

Other complicated issues can arise if several children will be—or already are—involved in running the business. How do you determine who will have key leadership roles in the business? How do you structure your estate plan so that your wishes will be carried out? Do all the children involved understand and accept your plan? If one or more doesn't, how can you best diminish the potential for conflict? All sorts of worries can come up when planning for a family business and more than one child. We've had people ask us what will happen if one of their children gets divorced. Others worry because their children don't get along, but each wants to run the business. All we can say is (yet another) truism—do the best you can. And remember, once you're gone, your estate planning can, at best, impose limited control over what happens to your

family business. You need faith that the children you selected to manage your business will do a good and fair job. You can't control all the "what ifs."

3. Sales to Outsiders

What happens if no family member wants to carry on your business? Or there's no one you believe is capable of running it? If it's a sole proprietorship, it must be sold. If it's a shared ownership business but no co-owners are willing or able to buy your share, your inheritors would likely seek to find an outside buyer for their interest. In any case, how can you try to maximize your children's inheritance?

It's rarely desirable to simply close down or sell a business as soon as its owner dies, unless it's a one-person service business. Even if your beneficiaries do not want to participate in running the business over the long term, you'll want them to have some flexibility in the timing of the sale—which means the business must be capable of continuing in a profitable fashion for a while. One way to achieve at least short-term continuity is for key employees, the owner, and the future owners to agree in writing that these employees will stay around and continue to run the business for a period of time after the owner's death, perhaps in exchange for some portion of the eventual sale proceeds. Another way to accomplish this is to incorporate the business and make the key employees officers of the corporation and minority stockholders, perhaps through a stock-option plan. Of course the officers can still quit at any time, but they are less likely to do so if they have an ownership interest in the business.

B. REDUCING ESTATE TAXES

Family business owners often dread estate taxes. Will these taxes eat up the business? Will it have to be sold to raise cash to pay the estate taxes? What can be done to lower them? Happily, there are a number of legal methods owners can use to reduce or avoid estate taxes on a family business.

1. No Special Estate Tax Exemption for Family Businesses

Until 2004, a family business could receive an estate-tax break under federal law, allowing an estate of up to $1.3 million to be transferred free of tax. This exemption was combined with—not in addition to—the personal estate tax exemption. So it was useful even when the personal estate tax exemption was $1 million, because a business owner could transfer an extra $300,000 worth of business property, without estate tax. Now this tax break has been rendered meaningless, because the personal estate tax exemption has risen to $2 million. Congress made no similar increase to the family business estate-tax law, so whatever benefits it once conferred are gone.

2. Special Rules for Valuing Business Real Estate

Real estate used in a family trade or business or as a family farm can be valued for estate tax purposes at its value for the present use, rather than at its "highest and best" use. For example, a family farm doesn't have to be valued for its (possibly much higher) worth as a potential location for a shopping center or subdivision, but can be valued on the basis of its worth as a farm. This valuation rule can provide a real break for family businesses. Currently the value of the real estate can be reduced up to a maximum of $870,000 of the difference between "present use" and "best use." This figure is indexed to annual changes in the cost of living so it will rise in future years.

Several requirements must be met for the rule to apply:

- The value of the family business or farm must be at least 50% of the overall estate.
- The value of the real estate of that business must be at least 25% of the overall estate.
- The owner must leave the family business to a family member.
- The deceased or a family member must have used the real estate for the business in five of the eight years preceding the decedent's death.
- There are restrictions on the sale and use of the real estate for ten years (and in some cases 15 years) after the estate tax break. During this time, the family must agree to notify the IRS if the property is sold or no longer used for the business and may be required to repay some or all of the estate taxes if the ownership or use of the real estate changes.

3. Deferring Estate Tax Payments

If a family business, including a family farm, is part of a taxable estate, estate taxes due can be paid over a period of years, rather than within the nine months of the owner's death, as otherwise required. The basic rule is that estate taxes assessed against the value of a small business or family farm can be deferred for five years and then paid in ten annual installments. In other words, the final payment isn't due until 15 years after the owner's death. The principal Internal Revenue Code restriction here is that the value of the small business must exceed 35% of the total estate or 50% of the taxable estate.

> **Example:** Andrew dies in 2006 owning Shortstop Shipping, which has a net worth of $2.6 million. The total net value of his estate is $3.8 million. The personal estate tax exemption for 2006 is $2 million. The remaining $1.8 million is taxable. The taxes due are postponed for five years, then paid off over the next ten.

Significant income tax savings are permitted for corporate stock redeemed to pay estate taxes assessed against family businesses or farms.

4. Gifts of Minority Interests in the Business

Family business owners who face estate tax may be able to reduce or eliminate that tax liability by giving away minority interests in the business before death. Gifts are usually made to children or grandchildren.

The value of a minority interest in a business is reduced for gift tax purposes: whatever the interest would be worth if it were part of majority control of the business, that interest is worth significantly less as minority ownership. This is called a "valuation discount."

Two separate discounts are normally involved. The first is based on the fact that minority owners do not have voting control over the business. Minority owners cannot manage, sell, or liquidate the business, or distribute money to owners. So outside buyers will not pay the same price for minority interests as for majority ones. This is called a "discount for minority interest." The second discount is allowed if the basic small business agreement (partnership agreement, corporate bylaws, or operating agreement) restricts the sale of interests to family members or other narrow group, as many family businesses do. The interest cannot simply be sold to any willing buyer. This is called a "discount for lack of marketability."

The two combined discounts can range roughly from 20% to 60%. There are no statutory rules or IRS regulations governing how valuation discounts are determined. So calculating them is not easy. This is an area where owners may benefit from "aggressive" accounting and hiring "expert" appraisers. But even without skirting the edge of legality, substantial discounts are reasonable, and you can achieve significant estate tax savings.

> **Example:** McWilson is the sole owner of the DaaDee Corp., which has 50,000 shares of stock. By the best estimate of McWilson and his accountants, if all shares were sold, they would sell for $2 million. So, at first glance, each share seems to be worth $40. But if the shares are split between minority and majority shareholders, the valuation differs. McWilson takes a 25% valuation discount for the minority shares. Each minority share is valued at $30.
>
> In 2005, McWilson gives 10,000 shares to each of his two daughters. (In his living trust, he leaves the remaining stock to them equally.) For gift tax purposes, the minority shares are valued at $30. Realistically, each

share transfers $40 worth of assets; after all, each daughter will eventually own 50% of the business, and there won't be any distinction then between majority and minority shares. Nevertheless, "reasonable" discounts for minority shares are legal.

If the value of a discounted share of a family business that's given away exceeds the annual gift tax exempt amount (currently $12,000), a gift tax return must be filed. The gift tax return, IRS Form 709, now contains the question "Does the value of an item given reflect… a valuation discount?" If so, the giver must provide an explanation of the factual basis for the discounts and the amount of discount taken.

Under current tax law, the IRS has only three years to challenge a gift or gift valuation disclosed on a gift tax return. After three years have passed, the IRS cannot go back and reopen the valuation issue. So if you make a gift of discounted stock in a family business, file a gift tax return, and then three years pass, you can be sure that, after you die, the IRS can't attack the legality of that gift or the way you valued it.

You need a lawyer for gifts of minority interests. If you have a large estate and you want to obtain possible estate tax benefits by giving interests in a business to family members (or anyone else), you must see a lawyer. This is a very tricky and rapidly changing area of the law. In the right circumstances, you can achieve significant estate tax savings. But the IRS is not fond of discounted gifts of a family business, and scrutinizes them closely. You must do it right, and that requires working with a lawyer who knows this subject.

PHONY BUSINESSES DON'T FOOL THE IRS

Just a reminder that gifts of discounted interests in a family business work only if the business is legitimate. Some wealthy folks have tried to create family limited partnerships for their vacation homes or investment portfolios. The IRS has refused to accept valuation discounts with these kinds of alleged businesses. Currently the IRS is aggressively litigating a series of cases, claiming the family businesses are shams.

The lawsuits now in progress between the IRS and various inventive givers (and their sly estate tax advisers) should resolve the limits of a valid family business, for gift discount purposes. Some extremes are already clear. A family "business" created a few days before death, for the sole purpose of reducing estate taxes by giving away discounted minority interests, is not a valid business. Also, the enterprise must be run as an independent business. The primary owner must keep separate business records and can't mix up cash from the business with personal accounts.

With a family limited partnership, the limited partners (the children or grandchildren who receive minority interests) do not have to be actively involved in the business. But again, the basic rule is that the business itself must exist. Some very pricey lawyers are busy right now trying to turn "exist" into "anything goes." It's not likely to be in your or your family's interests to be on the cutting edge of this fight.

---

5. Gifts of Stock Options

This tax-reduction ploy is useful only for some top corporate executives who receive stock options as part of their compensation. A stock option is the right to buy a certain amount of stock for a set price in the future.

Example: C. Hardriver receives the right to buy 2,500 shares of stock in Workamorte at $35 a share. Two years later, the stock is selling at $55 a share. Hardriver can exercise the option and buy 2,500 shares at the option price of $35 a share. If Hardriver promptly sells the stock, he makes a profit of $20 per share.

Under IRS rules, only certain types of stock options can be given to family members or family trusts. The IRS has no rules on how to value stock options for gift tax purposes. Very low values can usually be put on them. After all, if the stock never reaches the option price, the option isn't worth anything at all.

Example: Jean-Francois, CEO of Blow-Em-Up Movie Productions, receives the right to buy 10,000 shares of company stock at $50. The stock is selling for $42 when he receives the option. American males suddenly tire of watching stuff explode on movie screens. The stock falls to between $13 and $18 and stays there. Obviously, Jean-Francois will not exercise his stock option.

Many major U.S. corporations have stock-option plans that allow top employees to give options to children, grandchildren, or family trusts. Because the option can be valued so low, the worth of the gift is usually under the annual gift tax exclusion, and no gift tax is assessed. Even if some gift tax is assessed, it is often far below the eventual worth of the option. If the stock price rises significantly, the recipient can make a bundle.

Example: Holly, President of Cashotronics, Inc., has the option to buy 2,000 shares of the corporation stock at $70 a share. The corporation is privately held, and there is no market for the stock. However, Holly is sure the company will go public soon, and then the stock will be worth much more.

She gives her option to her adult son, D.J. With the aid of a costly accountant and more costly lawyer, Holly values the option at $4 a share, or a total of $8,000. Since this is under the annual gift tax exclusion, no gift tax is assessed. Three years later, the company goes public, and the market stock price is $160 a share. D.J. exercises the option, buys 2,000 shares at $70 and immediately sells them. His profit is $90 a share, for a total of $180,000.

Gifts of stock options are fancy, high-end stuff, raising many tricky problems. Complicated income tax rules govern taxation of any profits from exercise of the option and subsequent sale of the stock. The stock plan itself must meet complex IRS regulations. Obviously, an expert lawyer is needed here, which is not news to the wealthy folks who benefit from this perk.

6. Family Business Estate Tax Freezes

A few lawyers still push a sophisticated, on-the-edge (or over it) tax-saving technique called a stock "freeze" for family corporations. It was a common practice until 1987, when Congress enacted restrictive (and confusing) provisions controlling attempted estate freezes.

Estate planning lawyers no longer consider estate freezes desirable for most family businesses. However, a few small loopholes remain, which might work for family business owners if the facts are just right.

Essentially, a freeze involved the creation of two classes of stock for the company: preferred stock (with voting rights to control the business) and common stock (with no voting rights). The owners would give shares of common stock, given as low a value as possible, to their children or grandchildren. They kept all preferred voting stock. Now, for the key: All subsequent appreciation in the worth of the business (if any) was attributed to the common stock. Thus the value of the business, for the controlling owners, would be "frozen" as of the date they gave away the common stock. Because this stock was legally owned by the children, none of the appreciation (nor the worth of the common stock given away) was included in the taxable estate of the owner.

Congress attempted to eliminate this ploy. If a lawyer proposes such a freeze to you, be sure you understand exactly why he thinks it is legal. Why would the IRS accept the lawyer's scheme?

C. Avoiding Probate of a Family Business

It's often disastrous for a small business to become enmeshed in probate. Not only is probate costly, but worse, it normally ties up the business under court control for a long time, often over a year. It can be burdensome, even destructive, to have to seek a probate court's approval for business decisions. Would you want a judge supervising your business for months or years? You can plan to avoid probate of your business interest by using either joint tenancy or a living trust. For a number of tax and ownership reasons discussed in detail in Chapters 9 and 10, a living trust is usually the best choice.

Although most business owners should plan to avoid probate, that's not best for everyone. If your business has many debts and creditors' claims, probate may be desirable, because it provides a convenient forum for having those claims resolved. (See Chapter 8, Section D, for more on this.) These problems are unusual.

1. Individual Ownership

For most solely owned businesses, a living trust works fine. The living trust allows the business to be transferred to its new owners promptly, without any risk of loss of control while you live.

Example 1: Sam is the sole owner of a New York restaurant. The business is not incorporated. Sam conducts the business under his name "dba [doing business as] The Manhattan Bar and Brasserie," and has filed the appropriate business and tax forms with city licensing agencies. Sam will leave the business to his son, Theodore. Sam creates a living trust and names Theodore to inherit the restaurant. Sam lists the restaurant on Schedule A of the trust: "The restaurant dba The Manhattan Bar and Brasserie...[street address]... and all assets, supplies, accounts receivable, good will, or other property of the business." Of course, when Theodore inherits the business, he'll need to complete a new "dba" form.

Example 2: Natalie is sole owner of the Stay-Potted plant store. She wants to leave her interest in the store as follows:

30% to her close friend Donna

25% to her niece Cindy, and

15% to each of her three brothers (totaling 45%).

After investigating her options, she decides to incorporate and then transfer the stock of the corporation into a living trust. The trust document provides that each of the beneficiaries receives the percentage of stock she's specified. Natalie also prepares the appropriate corporate records, according to the corporation's bylaws, to approve her actions. She decides she won't worry about management and continuity of the business after she dies. It's up to her beneficiaries. If they agree to run the business and can run it—fine. If that doesn't work out, they can sell the business.

2. Shared Ownership Businesses

Living trusts also work well if you own your business together with others. Your ownership agreement should specifically permit each owner to transfer her interest to a living trust. If the document does not provide for this, you should amend it so that it does. Then, each owner creates her own living trust, consistent with any requirements of the ownership agreement (such as the right of surviving principals to buy out the deceased's share), and transfers her interest in the business to that trust. The trust then works like any other probate avoidance living trust, as explained in Chapter 9. The business property transferred to the trust is listed on Schedule A, for example as:

"The grantor's shares in the Zeeet Corporation"

"The grantor's partnership interest in the Alphonse-Benjamin partnership"

"The grantor's interest in the "Go Giants!" Limited Liability Company."

Then, any business asset transferred to the living trust with a document of title must be reregistered in the trustee's name.

Example: Vikki and Sloane each own one-half of the stock in Go-Get-'Em, Inc., which owns two apartment houses. Vikki and Sloane each create a living trust for their business interests. Each must do the following to transfer his or her share of the business into the living trust:

- prepare the appropriate corporate records and resolution authorizing and approving the transfer, and

- prepare new corporate shares, listing the living trust (technically, the trustee of the trust) as owner. ■

29

USING LAWYERS

Some readers will decide that with the aid of this book and other Nolo resources, they can do all of their own estate planning, without a lawyer. Others will conclude that they need the help of a lawyer to safely plan their estate. If you're in the second group, read this chapter for our views on how to find an estate planning lawyer, if you don't already know of one, and how to evaluate a lawyer and what level of expertise you'll need.

We also discuss doing some legal research on your own. Even if you'll definitely need a lawyer, that doesn't prohibit doing some legal research yourself, going deeper into one or more topics than this book does. After all, the more you know about the broad legal issues involved in estate planning and the particular legal tools you are considering using in your plan, the more likely you are to make good choices—and the lower your eventual legal bill should be.

Of course, you don't have to do any legal research at all. It does take effort. You may conclude that you have gone as deep into advanced estate planning as you want by reading and understanding this book. That surely is a reasonable response. After all, unless you really are ready to invest a fair number of hours climbing the estate planning learning curve, you won't acquire enough expertise to creatively challenge and debate a lawyer's technical recommendations.

A. HIRING A LAWYER

If you do determine that you want an expert's assistance, obviously you don't want to hire a lawyer at random and say "Tell me what to do." As an intelligent consumer, you not only want to gain at least as much knowledge about your problem as you conveniently can, but you also want to invest sufficient time to be sure the person you hire is honest, knowledgeable, and provides good service for your dollar.

Your estate plan should express your intentions. No one else can know those intentions. Sometimes, when people think, or fear, that they need a lawyer, what they are really doing is longing for an authority figure (or believing that one is required) to tell them what to do. Keep in mind that only you can decide who should get your property, and how and when they should get it. An estate planning expert is your paid advisor and legal technician, not your mentor.

1. What Kind of Expert Do You Need?

The first question to decide is whether you need a lawyer, or if you will be better served by a financial expert such as an accountant or financial planner. Don't just assume a lawyer is your best choice. For example, questions about federal estate taxes or how to calculate tax basis rules on the sale of appreciated property can often be better answered by an experienced accountant. Similarly, for some financial decisions, such as what type of insurance to buy to fund a small business buyout, you may be better off talking to a financial planner. But for most estate planning concerns, you do need to see a lawyer. In the estate planning context, there are basically three categories of lawyers:

- general practice lawyers
- estate planning specialists, and
- highly specialized lawyers working in one very difficult aspect of estate planning.

Which type is right for you depends on your estate planning concerns and need. Let's look at each type of lawyer in more detail.

a. General Practice Lawyers

General practice lawyers handle all sorts of cases; they don't specialize in estate planning. If your needs are basic, such as a garden-variety living trust or will, or a check of some provision of your state's laws, a competent attorney in general practice should be able to do a good job at a lower cost than more specialized attorneys.

Similarly, if your small business needs to customize its partnership agreement, LLC operating agreement, or corporate bylaws to allow for surviving owners to buy out the shares of a deceased owner from his or her inheritors, a general practice lawyer should do fine.

b. Estate Planning Specialists

For any type of sophisticated estate planning work, you need to see a specialist. Estate planning, as this book may have convinced you, is often a complex matter, and to do a good job, a lawyer needs to be absolutely up to date on estate tax law and regulations, the rules governing ongoing trusts and numerous other matters. Whether your concern is to establish an ongoing trust for estate tax savings, handle issues raised by a second marriage, set up an ongoing gift-giving program while you live, or any one of many other possible complicated matters—you need an expert.

An expert may charge relatively high fees, but a good one is worth it. Most general practice lawyers are simply not sufficiently educated in estate planning to handle complex matters.

c. Highly Specialized Lawyers

These lawyers specialize in a particularly difficult aspect of estate law. For example, to prepare a "special needs" trust for a disabled person, a lawyer must be current on complex federal and state regulations regarding trust property and eligibility for government benefits. Even most estate planning experts don't have sufficient expertise for this. Also consult a specialized estate planning lawyer if you want to try to protect your, or your spouse's, assets from the cost of medical care for catastrophic illnesses or disabilities, or if you own property in two or more countries and need an attorney who's expert at multinational estate planning.

Unfortunately, finding a lawyer with the specialized skills you need may not be easy. In some states, such as California, state bar associations certify lawyers as expert estate planners, but even this does not guarantee that they are competent in one of the very specialized areas of estate planning. You simply have to seek until you find a lawyer with the experience you need.

2. Locating a Lawyer

How do you find a lawyer? Ours is such a lawyer-ridden society that it's unusual if one hasn't already found you. There is certainly a growing surplus of lawyers. The difficulty, of course, is not just finding a lawyer, but retaining one who is trustworthy and competent, and who charges fairly. In addition, as noted above, many readers will need to find an estate planning expert, not just a general practitioner who says "No problem" when you ask if she can prepare, say, sophisticated tax-saving trusts. A few words of advice on how you can find a good lawyer may be helpful.

When looking for a good lawyer, especially an estate planning expert, personal routes are the traditional, and probably best, method. If a relative or good friend who has good business and financial sense has found an estate planning lawyer she recommends, chances are you'll like him too. Failing this, check with people you know in any political or social organization you're involved with, especially those with a large number of members over age 40. Assuming they themselves are savvy, they may well be able to point you to a competent lawyer who handles estate planning matters and whose attitudes are similar to yours.

Another good approach is to ask for help from a lawyer you are personally acquainted with and think well of, even if she doesn't work in the estate planning area. Very likely she can refer you to someone trustworthy who is an estate planning expert.

Also, check with people you respect who own their own small businesses. Almost anyone running a small business has a relationship with a lawyer, and chances are they've found one they like. Again, this lawyer will probably not be an estate planning expert, but he'll likely know one, or several.

Another approach is to try the Martindale-Hubble law directory. Martindale-Hubble's series of books, available in most public libraries, lists lawyers by towns or cities they practice in, and also identifies estate planning specialists. For each lawyer or firm listed, you'll get some information about qualifications and experience. Martindale-Hubble tends to list established and establishment lawyers, so the fees they charge will not be at the lower end of the spectrum. You can also find Martindale-Hubble on the Web at www.martindale.com.

If you are a member of a legal insurance plan, you may be offered sophisticated estate planning assistance from a referral panel member at a reduced fee. Some of these referrals may be to excellent lawyers. In our experience, however, too often lawyers who sign up to do cut-rate work are not the best alternative. Excellent lawyers, particularly good estate planning experts, tend to have lots of work, and don't need to cut fees to gain clients.

Also, be cautious when dealing with bar association referral panels. Never assume a listing on a referral panel is a seal of approval. Although lawyers are supposed to be screened about their specialty to get on these panels, screening is usually perfunctory. Often the main qualification is that the lawyer needs business.

HOW MANY LAWYERS DOES A COUPLE NEED?

Sounds like a light bulb joke, right? Unfortunately, it isn't. Most couples can safely use one lawyer for both spouses' estate planning. However, if there's a potential conflict between different spouses' desires, then perhaps each needs a separate lawyer. For example, in a second or subsequent marriage, if children from one or both spouses' prior marriage(s) don't get along with the other spouse, each spouse may want a separate attorney. (And if you're considering a prenuptial agreement, you'll need the advice of separate lawyers to ensure its validity.) Or, say, the estate lawyer is a good friend of one spouse and the other spouse's children are suspicious that somehow they'll get cheated of their inheritance—or if one spouse can be extremely domineering— each spouse may sensibly decide they want independent advice regarding their estate planning. In this case, choosing two lawyers can be a form of insurance against possible later claims of undue influence or unfair representation by a single attorney. Happily, in real life few couples will decide their interests are, or could be, so conflicting that each must pay for a separate lawyer.

As you already know, lawyers are expensive, and expert lawyers are even more expensive. Lawyer's estate planning fees usually range from $150 to $500 per hour, with experts at the higher end of the scale. While fancy office trappings, dull clothes, and solemn (or aggressive) demeanor are no guarantee (or even a good indication) that a particular lawyer will provide top-notch service in a manner with which you will feel comfortable, this conventional style does almost always ensure that you will be charged at the upper end of the fee range. At Nolo, our experience tells us that high fees and quality service don't necessarily go hand in hand. Indeed, many of the attorneys we think most highly of tend to charge moderate fees (for lawyers, that is), and seem to get along very nicely without most stuffy law office trappings.

Keep in mind that in any field, including estate planning, there are good high-priced experts and bad ones. It's all too easy to get a mumbo-jumbo speaking lawyer who confuses you at first, and enrages you later, when you receive an exorbitant bill. Don't be afraid to keep looking until you find a lawyer you like. Many people who have had unhappy experiences with lawyers (and we all know some) wish they had done so.

HIRING A LAWYER TO REVIEW YOUR ESTATE PLANNING DOCUMENTS

Hiring a lawyer solely to review a will or living trust you've prepared from a Nolo resource sounds like a good idea. It shouldn't cost much, and seems to offer a comforting security. Sadly though, it can be difficult or impossible to find a lawyer who will accept the job. The reason is that many lawyers feel that by reviewing a document for a relatively small fee they become just as legally responsible for a client's entire estate plan as if they did all the work from scratch. Or, put more directly, many lawyers see every client as the instigator of a future malpractice claim, or at least a source of later hassles, and simply don't want to get involved for a modest fee.

To counter this mentality and help provide self-helpers with the coaching and advice they often need, Nolo has advocated unbundling legal services. The idea is that a customer should be able to contract with a lawyer for only the services wanted and the lawyer should have no broader liability beyond providing those services competently. With new phone law services, and lawyers who are setting up businesses to provide advice only, this approach is sure to be more common soon. But in the meantime, if you have trouble finding a lawyer who will help you help yourself, all you can do here is to keep trying to find a sympathetic lawyer. It should help if you are prepared to pay a decent fee so that the lawyer can take the time necessary to carefully review your work.

3. Evaluating a Lawyer

Personally evaluate any lawyer you've been referred to before you agree to hand over your estate planning work. Don't hesitate to question the lawyer, no matter how expert he or she is considered to be. To ask good questions, you need to have done some preparation; you should have at least a rough general idea of what you want to accomplish. Also, you need enough information (gleaned from this book or other sources) to pose intelligent questions and evaluate the lawyer's answers.

It's important that you feel a personal rapport with your lawyer. You want one who treats you as an equal. (Interestingly, the Latin root of the word "client" translates as "to hear, to obey.") When talking with a lawyer on the phone or at a first conference, ask specific questions that concern you. If the lawyer answers them clearly and concisely—explaining, but not talking down to you—fine. If the lawyer acts wise, but says little except to ask that the problem be placed in his or her hands, watch out. You are either talking with someone who doesn't know the answer and won't admit it (common), or someone who finds it impossible to let go of the "me expert, you peasant" way of looking at the world (even more common). You need a lawyer who's open and sympathetic to people who want to actively participate in handling their own legal affairs.

Be sure you've settled your fee arrangement—in writing—at the start of your relationship. Depending on the area of the country where you live, generally, we feel that fees for a general practice lawyer in the range of $150 to $250 per hour are reasonable in urban areas, given the average lawyer's overhead. In rural counties and small cities, excellent general help may be available for a little less. Expert estate planning lawyers usually cost more, sometimes a lot more. In addition to the amount charged per hour, you also want a clear commitment from the lawyer concerning how many hours the work will take.

B. Doing Your Own Research

Learning how to do your own estate planning research can provide real benefits. Of course, legal research isn't for everyone. You have to have the energy, patience, and ability to enter new mental areas, as well as the desire to do so. But for the intrepid, not only are you likely to save money on professional fees, you'll gain at least some sense of mastery over an area of law that concerns you.

Once you understand some research techniques, some aspects of estate planning law can be fairly easy to research. For example, to answer questions concerning technical aspects of state laws affecting wills or probate avoidance, you probably need only to check the relevant statutes of your state to find the provision you need.

If you decide you want to do your own research, how do you go about it? Begin by finding a good law library or a computer with an Internet connection.

1. Using a Law Library

There's often a law library in your principal county courthouse. The quality of these libraries varies a lot from state to state and county to county. County law libraries are normally supported by tax dollars or by the fees paid to file court papers. In our experience, county law librarians have been sensitive and generally most helpful and courteous to nonlawyers who want to learn to do their own legal research. However, some county law libraries don't have adequate resources for many types of legal research. And, of course, we can't vouch for every law librarian in the country.

If your county library is not adequate, your best bet is a law school library. Those in state colleges and universities supported by tax dollars are almost always open to the public, at least during certain hours.

Once you've found a good law library, you need an introduction to how they work. If you can't hire your own law librarian, the best book explaining how to do your own legal work is *Legal Research: How to Find & Understand the Law*, by Stephen R. Elias and Susan Levinkind (Nolo). It shows you, step-by-step, how to find answers in the law library, and is, as far as we know, the only legal research book written specifically for nonprofessionals.

Even with the assistance of a sympathetic law librarian and a good research aid, digging into the law can be intimidating at first. We urge you to stay with it. After a while—perhaps sooner than you anticipate—you'll understand the materials and how you can use them.

2. Legal Information Online

Another way to approach legal research is to use a computer. If you want information about current estate planning issues, such as a recent court decision or a new statute, you'll probably be able to find it somewhere on the Internet. Many public libraries now offer online access, if you're not connected at home or work.

Finding legal information on the Internet. The Nolo website offers extensive materials on estate planning and is a great place to start your online research. You can find us at www.nolo.com. There are also many other legal sites on the Web.

3. How to Approach Research Problems

There's no one standard method for approaching a legal research question. Sometimes, it's prudent to start from the general and move towards the specific. But rather than lay out a number of possible approaches, none of which may work for you, we'll simply refer you again to *Legal Research,* which explores these matters in far greater depth and clarity than any summary could.

4. Basic Research Sources

Sometimes a good way to dive into legal research is to do some background reading in a good book about a certain aspect of estate planning. This reading can provide an overview of the law applicable to your concerns, possibly provide some initial answers, and refer you to more specific sources.

There are several categories of estate planning background books. In reading these resources, please remember that they are written by estate planning attorneys, for attorneys, and often have predictable prejudices against a do-it-yourself approach. You may need to ignore an author's attitude, or, worse, struggle through wads of legalese, to get to solid legal information.

- **Overall estate planning.** There are many books covering estate planning in general. One of the best is *The CCH Estate Planning Guide,* by Kess and Westlin (Commerce Clearing House).

- **How-to-do-it estate planning books for lawyers.** Many states have estate planning books designed to show lawyers how it's done. These books contain specific clauses and forms for wills or trusts, and many other hands-on materials. For example, in California, the Continuing Education of the Bar (CEB) publishes several useful estate planning books, including *Drafting California Irrevocable Inter Vivos Trusts, Drafting California Revocable Inter Vivos Trusts,* and *California Will Drafting.* Comparable books in New York include:

  - *Drawing Wills,* by Jule Stocker and Harold Schwartzberg (Practicing Law Institute)

  - *Income Taxation of Estates and Trusts,* by Arthur Michaelson and Jonathan Blattmachr (Practicing Law Institute).

In other states, the best way to locate this type of book for your state is to ask the law librarian or look up "Estate Planning," or a more specific heading, in the library catalog.

- **Treatises on one area of estate planning law.** For example, for federal estate taxes there's *Federal Estate & Gift Taxes: Code & Regulations* (CCH). For trusts there's *Revocable Inter Vivos Trusts*, by Howard Zolitsky (Tax Management Inc.), and *Federal Taxation of Trusts*, by Joel Miller (Prentice Hall). And there are also a number of popular self-help tax guides. ∎

30

AFTER YOU COMPLETE YOUR ESTATE PLAN

I f you are serious about planning your estate, you'll eventually get the job done. What next? Up to you. A sigh of relief? A celebration? Maybe gather those you love, break out your favorite beverage, and offer a toast "To Life!"

But although your big job is complete, you've still got some more to do—storing your documents safely, and making any necessary future revisions to your plan. This chapter discusses what you may need to do after you've completed your planning documents.

A. STORING YOUR ESTATE PLANNING DOCUMENTS

Completing an estate plan means that you have created some important documents: a will, probably a living trust, quite possibly an ongoing trust, or even several, as well as other forms, such as a durable power of attorney for health care, and one for finances. And perhaps you've signed a joint tenancy deed, business ownership documents, or written instructions for your funeral or donations of body parts. Obviously, you want to keep all these documents in a safe place, where you, and your executor or trustee, can readily find them. It's no big secret how to accomplish this. Any secure place can be used for storage: a safe in your house or office, or even a drawer in your home desk or file cabinet.

Some people use a bank safe deposit box. If you do this, you must make sure that your executor or successor trustee will have ready legal access to that box when it's needed. Check with your bank to see what it requires to allow your executor or trustee to get documents from the safe deposit box. Also check with them to make sure the safe deposit isn't sealed, under state law, when one owner dies. (Some states that have estate or inheritance taxes require this.)

While you may want to keep at least some of your estate planning documents private while you live, you also surely want them to be promptly accessible to whoever will handle your affairs at your death. This is especially true for documents that deal with your wishes as to organ transplants and funeral or burial instructions, which must be immediately available. So once you have settled on a storage place, let the person who will wind up your affairs know what you've decided and how to obtain the documents.

What about making copies of your estate planning documents? You may have to produce copies of your living trust for financial institutions, such as a brokerage company, where you have an account you want placed in trust. Whether or not to make copies for personal reasons is up to you. Often people do want copies to give to their executor or successor trustee, family members, or friends. If you do need or want copies:

- Photocopy the documents you want people to see or have. These copies are not legal originals, because they are not signed by you. A photocopy of your signature doesn't make a document a legal original.

- Never sign a copy. If you do, it could legally qualify as a "duplicate original." If you later decide to change, amend, or revoke the document, you have to change each duplicate original as well.

- To be extra safe, mark "copy" in ink on each page. This isn't legally required, but it ensures that no one can claim a copy is an original.

B. REVISING YOUR ESTATE PLAN

Estate plans shouldn't be changed frequently. If impromptu changes ("I'll show her; I'll cut her out of my will") occur often, you have an underlying family or personal problem to examine. Major life events, however, call for estate planning changes. If any of the following events occur, you should review your plan:

- **You sell or give away any property you've specifically mentioned in your will or living trust.** Estate planning transfer devices, such as wills or living trusts, don't become binding until your death. So what happens if you dispose of property but don't change your will or trust? For example, what happens if your will leaves your son your 1988 Chevy, but by the time you die, you've already sold it and purchased a 2005 Buick? To summarize what can be a complicated area of law: if you leave someone a specific piece of property (say the Chevy) but you no longer own it when you die, that beneficiary is out of luck. The fact that you own a Buick doesn't help the beneficiary. Lawyers call this "ademption"; people who don't inherit the property in question are often heard to use an earthier term.

- **You get married.** If you don't update your will, your new spouse will have the right to inherit a share of your estate, as determined by state law.

- **You get divorced.** In some states, a divorce ends a former spouse's right to inherit under a will. In other states, it doesn't. Also, property left to a divorced spouse using other estate planning devices may not be affected by a divorce. For example, under federal law, divorce does not automatically cancel the rights of an ex-spouse who had been named as beneficiary of a 401(k) or other employer-sponsored retirement plan. The employee must fill out a form naming a new beneficiary.

- **The birth of a child.** The rule here is similar to that for marriage.

- **A beneficiary dies.**

- **Your financial situation changes significantly.**

- **You move to a new state.** It is particularly important to review your estate plan if you are married and move from a common law property state to a community property state or vice versa. (See Chapter 3, Section D, for a detailed discussion of the issues that may concern you.)

- **You acquire significant property.**

- **You want to change the successor trustee of your living trust, or the executor of your will.**

- **You want to change the personal or property guardian you have named for your minor children.** If you have established a child's trust, you'll need to revise your plan if you want to change the person or institution you have named as trustee, or custodian for a gift under the UTMA.

If you do decide to change your estate plan, you must decide whether you need, or want, to create entirely new documents or simply modify your existing ones. Which route is better depends both on how complex your changes are and the estate planning document involved.

1. Living Trusts

Living trusts can be revised fairly easily:

- **Transferring additional property to your trust.** If you just want to transfer more property to the trust, there should be no problem. A well-drafted living trust has a clause permitting additions of property to the trust after it has been created (called an "after-acquired property" clause). If your trust has such a clause, you can add property by listing it on the trust schedule and taking title to that property in the trustee's name. If you only add property to a trust schedule, you do not need to have the trust notarized again.

You don't have to name a new beneficiary for this new trust property. If you don't, it will go to the residuary beneficiary of your trust unless you've provided that "all property" on the trust schedule goes to some other beneficiary.

- **Amending the trust document (not just a property schedule).** For changes that don't necessitate a new document, you can make a formal amendment to your trust. Changes by amendment can include adding or deleting beneficiaries, changing gifts, or naming new successor trustees. You must sign and date the amendment and have it notarized.

- **Making a new trust document.** If you're making wholesale changes to your trust, you'll need to revoke the old trust and prepare a new one, reflecting your current intentions. This is the least desirable method, but is sometimes necessary. You'll have to get the new trust document notarized. Worse, you'll have to reregister property in the trustee's name, as trustee of the new trust as of the date of creation (notarization) of this trust. That's a lot of work.

2. Wills

There are only two ways to change a formal witnessed will:

- prepare a formal witnessed codicil to the will, or
- destroy the old will and make a new one.

    Let's briefly examine each procedure.

a. Make a Codicil

A codicil is a formal legal method for making changes to a will that has already been drafted, signed, and witnessed. A codicil is a sort of legal "P.S." to the will. It must be typed or printed, with a formal heading. The text of the codicil then identifies the date of the original will and sets out the change made. Following is a sample codicil, without the necessary signature, date, and witness clauses.

CODICIL TO WILL OF BETH THOREAU

1. I leave $3,000 to my friend Al Smith.

2. I leave my silver tea set to Bertha Weinstock, and revoke my gift of that tea set to Mary Warbler, now deceased.

3. In all other respects I reaffirm my will dated August 23, 2004.

A codicil must be typed, signed, dated, and witnessed just like a will. Because of this requirement, it can make more sense to prepare an entirely new will, especially if you are using a computer will program. It won't take you any longer to prepare a new computer-generated will than a codicil, and the signing and witnessing requirements for both are the same.

You must sign and date a codicil in the presence of the same number of witnesses who watched you sign the original will, who are told that it's a codicil to your will and then sign their names. The witnesses don't have to be the same people as those for the original will, though it's a good idea to use the original witnesses if they're available. Sample codicil forms can be found in *Nolo's Simple Will Book,* by Denis Clifford.

b. Make a New Will

If you want to significantly revise your will, it's better to draft a new will and revoke the old one than to use a codicil. A will that has been substantially rewritten by a codicil is an awkward document and can be confusing. The relationship of the codicil to the original will provisions may not always be clear.

If you make a new will, be sure to revoke your old will. You can do this by:

- destroying the will itself (and all copies, if you can get your hands on them)—rip 'em up and throw 'em out, and

- stating in the new will that you revoke all previous wills you have made.

Technically, either one of the acts listed above is sufficient, but we strongly recommend that you do both things.

3. Joint Tenancy

If you've established a joint tenancy, are you stuck with it? No. In almost all states, one joint tenant can transform the joint tenancy into a tenancy in common, which eliminates the right of the other co-owners to automatically inherit. (See Chapter 10, Section G.) However, it takes agreement of all the joint tenants to allow any one to become the sole owner of the property. If all joint tenants agree to end a joint tenancy, they can sign a document (a deed, for real estate) transferring the property into whatever new form of ownership is desired.

Changing a joint tenancy. If you want to transfer your share of joint tenancy property into tenancy in common and the other owners don't consent, you'll need to see a lawyer to learn the procedures required in your state, unless you live in California. In the Golden State, *Deeds for California Real Estate*, by Mary Randolph (Nolo), shows you how to do this.

4. Pay-on-Death Accounts

You can amend or revoke a pay-on-death account at any time. You can change a beneficiary simply by deleting the old one and entering a new one on the financial institution's registration form; sometimes a new, separate form must be completed. You can also end the pay-on-death account simply by closing it or by spending all the money the account contains. If the account is empty when you die, obviously the beneficiary gets nothing.

You cannot safely revoke a pay-on-death account by leaving the property to someone else in your will. Under the law of the great majority of states, a beneficiary under a pay-on-death account prevails over someone who was left the same property by will.

5. Insurance

If you are the owner of an insurance policy, you can cancel the policy or change the beneficiary of that policy. If you are not the legal owner of the policy, you have no right to cancel the policy or change the beneficiary, even if the policy insures your own life.

6. Ongoing Trusts

Most ongoing trusts, whether for estate tax saving, property control, or both, do not become irrevocable until the grantor's death. Some, however, such as many charitable trusts or life insurance trusts, become irrevocable upon creation. Once an ongoing trust has become irrevocable, by definition it can't be changed or revoked. Until an ongoing trust is irrevocable, it can be freely changed or revoked by the grantor. ■

31

AFTER A DEATH OCCURS

When someone who has created an estate plan dies, someone else (or several someones) must take actions to carry out the deceased person's plan. This is not a book that covers after-death work in depth. That's a subject for another big book. Indeed, Nolo offers just such a book: *The Executor's Guide: Settling a Loved One's Estate or Trust*, by Mary Randolph. Translating legal procedures and jargon into coherent English, the book enables executors and successor trustees to gain a clear understanding of what their jobs actually entail—which isn't terrifying, once the law has been demystified.

This chapter simply offers you summaries of the basic tasks someone may have to handle after a person dies.

A. WILLS

When the will writer dies, the person named as executor is responsible for carrying out the terms of the will. This includes handling probate—normally, by hiring a probate lawyer—and then, once probate is completed, distributing property governed by the will to the beneficiaries named in that document.

If an ongoing trust (including a child's trust or family pot trust) is created in the will, the executor is often also named as trustee of that trust, and so can have continuing duties of managing the trust property. If property is left to a minor under the Uniform Transfers to Minors Act, the executor must turn that property over to the custodian for that gift.

Some executors have additional responsibilities. If a federal or state estate tax return must be filed, it's the executor's legal responsibility to see this is done. (See Section D, below.) Also, in wealthier estates, if a QTIP trust is part of a deceased spouse's estate plan, the executor must decide whether or not to "elect" to have estate tax on the trust property postponed until the surviving spouse dies. (See Chapter 19, Section A.)

B. PROBATE-AVOIDANCE LIVING TRUSTS

With a living trust designed solely to avoid probate, the successor trustee is responsible, after a grantor dies, for carrying out the terms of the trust. This basically means transferring the trust property to the beneficiaries named in the trust.

1. Who Serves as Trustee

With a living trust for a single person, the successor trustee takes over promptly once the trust creator dies.

With a basic shared trust made by a couple, the surviving spouse serves as trustee after one spouse's death. (AB trusts are discussed below, in Section C.) After the surviving spouse dies, the successor trustee is in charge.

If more than one person is named in the trust document as successor trustee, they all serve as co-trustees. This does not, however, mean all trustees must agree on all decisions. Whether each trustee must formally agree on any action taken with regard to the living trust property, or whether one trustee can act independently, depends on the terms of the trust document.

If more than one successor trustee is named, but cannot serve, the other remains as trustee. The person named as alternate successor trustee does not take over unless all the people named as successor trustees cannot serve.

A trustee can resign at any time by preparing and signing a written resignation statement. The ex-trustee should deliver the notice to the person who is next in line to serve as trustee. With a well-drafted living trust, any trustee, including the last acting trustee, can appoint someone else to take over if no one named in the trust document can serve.

Usually, it's the last, or alternate, successor trustee who names someone else to act as trustee. The appointment must be in writing, signed, and notarized.

2. Winding Up a Single Person's Living Trust

Normally, the job of the successor trustee of a single person's living trust is simply to transfer the trust property outright to the designated beneficiaries. Only if the successor trustee is also trustee of an ongoing trust created in the living trust are continuing duties required of her.

Unless there are explicit directions in the trust document, it is not the trustee's responsibility to sell or manage living trust property.

> **Example:** Elliot's living trust leaves his house to his children, Clarence and Grace. After Elliot dies, Jamie, the successor trustee, deeds the house from the trust to Clarence and Grace. They can do with it what they wish— live in it, rent it, or sell it. Jamie cannot sell the house and divide the proceeds between the beneficiaries—that's not his decision to make.

Usually, after the grantor dies, the living trust continues to exist only as long as it takes the successor trustee to distribute trust property to the beneficiaries. In many cases, a living trust can be wound up within a few weeks after a grantor's death. But if an ongoing business is involved, it may take longer. (See Chapter 28, Section C.)

No formal termination document is required to end a living trust. Once the trust property has been distributed, the trust ends.

3. Winding Up a Shared Living Trust

Coping with what happens when one grantor dies is more complex for a successor trustee who's in charge of a shared living trust. The successor trustee (usually the surviving spouse or mate) must divide the living trust property into two portions. Each portion goes into a new trust entity, as provided for by the original trust document.

- **Deceased spouse's property.** One new trust contains the deceased spouse's share of the living trust property. The terms of this new trust cannot be changed, and the trust cannot be revoked. Property is promptly distributed to its beneficiaries by the successor trustee unless the grantor provided for its ongoing management, as would be the case for property left to a minor.

- **Surviving spouse's property.** A separate trust which, as a practical matter, is usually a continuation of the original living trust, contains the surviving spouse's trust property. This trust usually includes any of the deceased spouse's share of the living trust property that is left to the surviving spouse. The surviving spouse remains free to amend the terms of this trust, or even revoke it.

Though this may sound complicated, it often isn't. If, as is common, much of the trust property is left to the surviving spouse, that spouse may have little to do beyond distributing a few items to the deceased's other beneficiaries.

When all the property in the deceased spouse's trust has been distributed to the beneficiaries, that trust ceases to exist. No formal termination document is required. In contrast, the surviving spouse's trust remains revocable.

> **Example:** Edith and Jacques create a basic shared living trust to avoid probate. They transfer their major asset, their home, which they own together, to the trust, and name each other as beneficiaries. Edith names her son as alternate beneficiary.
>
> When Jacques dies, Edith inherits his half-interest in the house. Jacques' trust then ends its existence. Edith's trust remains in effect, and revocable.

Because of the way the trust document is worded, Edith doesn't have to change her trust document to name a beneficiary for the half-interest in the house that she inherited from Jacques. Both halves, now consolidated, will go to her son at her death. She may, however, want to amend the trust to make her son the primary beneficiary and name someone else to be alternate beneficiary.

When the surviving spouse dies, the successor trustee named in the trust document takes over as trustee. The process of winding up the surviving spouse's living trust is the same as that for an individual trust.

4. Property Left to Children

Living trust property left for a child's benefit is normally left in a child's trust, family pot trust, or through the Uniform Transfers to Minors Act. With any of these, the successor trustee must turn the child's property over to the adult manager of the child's property—the trustee of a child's trust or family pot trust, or the custodian of an UTMA gift. If the successor trustee serves in one of these capacities as well, she must manage the property until it is turned over to the child.

C. ONGOING TRUSTS FOR ESTATE TAX SAVINGS OR PROPERTY MANAGEMENT

As we've discussed, an ongoing trust is one that is irrevocable, usually becoming so on the grantor's death, and generally functioning for an extended period of time. Some ongoing trusts are created in a will, but more often an ongoing trust is combined with a living trust. First, the trust property avoids probate. Then the ongoing trust becomes operational

and may well last for years or decades. As we discussed in the chapters covering ongoing trusts, the successor trustee's job will be much more complex here than with a simple probate-avoidance trust.

As an example, let's consider an AB trust created as part of a living trust and see what happens when one spouse dies. (See Chapter 18, Section C.) The purpose of this type of trust is to save on overall estate taxes. Both spouses are the original trustees. When a spouse dies, the surviving spouse becomes sole trustee, and the living trust splits into two trusts: the irrevocable Trust A (of the deceased spouse) and the revocable Trust B (of the surviving spouse).

The surviving spouse, as trustee, must first distribute any living trust property the deceased spouse left outside of Trust A to specifically named beneficiaries. Then the trustee must establish and maintain the ongoing Trust A.

A major task here is to figure out how best to divide the couple's property (all that was in the original AB trust) between the ongoing Trust A and the surviving spouse's Trust B. Property must be clearly labeled as being owned either by Trust A or by Trust B. Any allocation of equally owned shared trust property is valid, as long as each trust gets 50% of the overall total worth of the AB trust property. Each specific item of property does not have to be split, with half going to each trust. For example, a house, worth (net) $300,000 can be placed in Trust A, as long as other property with a total worth of $300,000 is placed in Trust B.

Dividing AB trust property. Deciding how to divide AB trust property on the death of a spouse often requires the services of a lawyer or tax accountant. These decisions can have long-term tax consequences, and you can save yourself and your inheritors hassle and expense by getting good advice.

The surviving trustee must prepare two new printed or typed trust schedules. The first lists all property transferred to the irrevocable Trust A. The second lists all property transferred to the surviving spouse's revocable Trust B. The trustee needs to describe the property in enough detail that the IRS, and eventually the final beneficiaries, can tell what property is in each trust.

Establishing the ongoing irrevocable Trust A may require some reregistering of title of some of the deceased spouse's living trust property. For example, if the surviving spouse decides that it is wisest to put all of a shared ownership house in Trust A, a new deed should be prepared to reflect this, listing the trustee of the ongoing trust as the new owner.

Example: Moira and Joseph O'Sullivan created the Moira and Joseph O'Sullivan Living Trust. In that trust, each created an AB trust. Joseph dies. Moira, with the help of an accountant, divides the living trust property between her now separate Trust B and the newly operational Trust A for Joseph's property. Property with documents of title transferred into Trust A must be reregistered into the name of the trustee of this new trust. Thus the property would be registered as held by "Moira O'Sullivan, as trustee of the Joseph O'Sullivan Trust A."

An operational Trust A needs a federal taxpayer ID number. The surviving spouse must keep appropriate trust financial records and file a federal trust tax return for Trust A every year. Annual state trust tax returns may also be required, in states with income taxes.

As trustee, the surviving spouse manages the property in Trust A and receives any income it generates. Management can include making sensible investment decisions, which may necessitate the hiring of a professional investment advisor.

The surviving spouse's Trust B goes on as before. It remains revocable and can be changed at any time. The surviving spouse does not need to file a tax return for this trust.

After the death of the surviving spouse, the successor trustee winds up both trusts by distributing all property of both trusts to each trust's final beneficiaries. The successor trustee must file a final tax return for Trust A. The successor trustee files a closing tax return for the second spouse and may also manage any property left in a child's trust or a family pot trust.

D. PREPARING AND FILING TAX RETURNS

It is the responsibility of an executor to file federal estate and state death tax returns, if one or both must be filed because of the value of the deceased's estate. If most or all property is left by a living trust, however, it's the successor trustee who files any tax returns due. (Of course, the executor and successor trustee are usually the same person.)

A final federal income tax return (and state return, if there's a state income tax) must be filed for the deceased. Legally, this is the responsibility of the executor of the deceased's will. Also, a final federal trust income tax return (and state tax return, if one is required) must be filed for Trust A after both spouses die.

If a federal estate tax return must be filed (see Chapter 15), it is due nine months after the decedent's death. As we've discussed, estate tax matters can get quite sticky. For instance, for federal estate tax purposes, property can be valued as of the date of death or as of six months after death. The executor will need professional help, and is entitled to pay for it out of the deceased's assets.

The IRS publishes a helpful set of instructions for the estate tax return, *Instructions for Form 706*. Another useful IRS publication is *Introduction to Federal Estate and Gift Taxes* (Publication 950). You can download these publications for free from the IRS website: www.irs.gov.

E. TRUSTEE'S REPORTS TO BENEFICIARIES

Generally, a trustee is not legally required to make any report of trust income, transactions, or any other aspect of trust management to any beneficiary. There are some exceptions:

- The trustee of any ongoing trust may be required by the terms of the trust to give reports, such as copies of the trust's annual federal trust tax return, to all the trust beneficiaries.

- A few state's laws require the trustee to distribute an annual report to the beneficiaries. For example, Washington law requires distributing "a written itemization of all current receipts and disbursements made by the trustee." (Wash. Rev. Code § 11.106.020.) In most family situations, these laws have little or no impact, because beneficiaries trust the trustee, and don't insist on these legal rights.

- A number of states have laws requiring the successor trustee to notify beneficiaries or a state agency when the trust creator dies. We recommend that a successor trustee notify beneficiaries no matter what state the trust's creator lived in. (See Chapter 9, Section C2.)

HOW TO OBTAIN A DEATH CERTIFICATE

An executor will need at least several copies of the death certificate. One quick way to obtain them is to ask the mortuary or other institution involved in disposition of the body. Otherwise, there are a couple of ways you can obtain them yourself. You can write the vital statistics office or county health department in the county where the decedent died. Call the office first to find out where to send your request and how much money to enclose.

These days, however, it's often easier to find forms and instructions online. Many county websites offer death certificate request forms that you can print out and send; others allow you to submit your request electronically and pay by credit card. To find out your options, go to the official website of the county where the death occurred. You can usually find it by using this formula, substituting the state postal abbreviation for "XX":

www.co.[COUNTY_NAME].[XX].us.
For example, you can find the website for King County, Washington at www.co.king.wa.us.

F. COLLECTING THE PROCEEDS OF A LIFE INSURANCE POLICY

How to collect insurance proceeds after the insured person dies is not, strictly speaking, part of estate planning, but nevertheless people want to be sure their beneficiaries know how to collect these proceeds. Normally, this isn't a problem—they can be collected soon after the insured person's death by submitting an insurance company claim form and a certified copy of the insured person's death certificate to the company. The beneficiary may also have to file a copy of the policy, and proof of identity as the named beneficiary, if the insurance company requires it.

Although this is normally routine, there can be several flies in the ointment. In some states with state estate or inheritance taxes, insurance proceeds above a certain amount cannot be released until the tax officials approve. If the insured person owned the insurance policy, the insurance proceeds will be part of her taxable estate, and the state tax officials must first be satisfied that the estate has other sufficient assets to pay state death taxes before they authorize release of the proceeds to the beneficiaries.

In other instances, some companies have been known to delay payments for months, so that they can collect interest on the money for a longer time. If this happens to you, a letter to the insurance commissioner of both your state and of the one where the company is headquartered (with copies to the offending company) will normally pry the money loose pronto.

G. OBTAINING TITLE TO JOINT TENANCY PROPERTY

The major benefit of joint tenancy is the "automatic right of survivorship." But obviously, the words on a deed to real estate or certificate of title to a car don't magically change on the day one joint tenant takes that last breath. Until someone acts, the legal title will not be changed to the survivor's name. What "automatic right of survivorship" means in this context is that compared to most legal tasks it's possible to transfer title to the surviving owner fairly easily, quickly, and cheaply, without probate. This is true for all joint tenancies, whether of real estate or personal property.

To get the deceased owner's name off the ownership document, so that the surviving joint tenants are on record as legal owners, they must:

- establish that the joint tenant has died by filing a copy of the death certificate with the appropriate government official or recorder of title, and

- file a document establishing that the surviving owners are sole owners to the property.

The surviving owners can hire a lawyer to do this, but this is normally unnecessary, because the procedures are routine. If you hire a lawyer, however, be sure the fee charged is a reasonable hourly one. An unfortunate practice in many states is for a lawyer to propose charging one-third of what the probate fee would be to transfer joint property to the survivors. Usually, this is far too high a fee; the work is neither complicated nor time-consuming.

For example, to terminate a joint tenancy in real estate, you need to file a certified copy of the deceased's death certificate and a form called "Affidavit of Death of Joint Tenant," or something similar, with the county office of property records (often called the "County Recorder" or "Registry of Deeds"). The affidavit is a standard legal form, available in many office supply stores. On this form, you state that a joint tenant has died. In some states, such as California, you don't need to complete a new deed. After you record (file) the affidavit and death certificate and any deed required, you can transfer or sell title to the property by signing a deed as "surviving joint tenant."

Tax liens. In some states that have state death taxes, tax liens (legal claims) may be imposed on all of a deceased person's property, and title cannot be transferred until the liens are removed. Removing them may involve posting a bond, filing a final inheritance tax return, or otherwise satisfying the tax authorities that taxes will be paid. It can be a major hassle for the surviving joint tenant. You'll need to locate the governmental agency that imposes and releases these tax liens, and see what is required to release them.

Federal estate taxes. Joint tenancy property can also be liable for a proportionate share of a deceased's federal estate taxes, if the estate is large enough to owe them. (See Chapter 15.) The taxes due will depend on the size of the taxable estate, which probably won't be determined for some time. But if the surviving owner must wait until the full amount of estate taxes are known (or even worse, paid) before obtaining clear title to the joint tenancy property, the practical advantages of the right of survivorship are severely diminished. After all, one purpose of a right of survivorship is to obtain clear title fast. Fortunately, the IRS will usually allow prompt transfer of joint tenancy property if there's an estimate of the value of the property in the estate and clear indication that there are enough other assets to pay off all estate taxes. The proof required that all taxes due can be paid from the remaining taxable estate will vary depending on the size, complexity, and liquidity of the estate. ■

32

SOME ESTATE PLANS

This chapter presents eight different estate plans, each serving the needs of a person or couple in a different situation. As we stated at the beginning of this book, we don't believe that it makes sense to rely on a formula plan. Instead, you need a personal plan. And due to the changes in your own circumstances or changes in the laws—the estate tax laws, in particular—you may need to update your plan in the coming years. The purpose of this chapter is to illustrate how the estate planning methods discussed in this book can be assembled into a coherent plan.

A. A Prosperous Couple in Their 60s and 70s

Robert and Teresa Casswell are a prosperous married couple. He's 68, she's 72. Both are retired and live comfortably on their savings, assets, and retirement payments. They live in a common law property state and share ownership of all their property equally. The Casswells have four grown children.

Their property. A house worth $850,000 (all equity; they paid off the mortgage years ago), a summer home worth $225,000 (again all equity), stocks and mutual funds worth $1.5 million, cash savings of $360,000, works of art valued at $125,000, jewelry valued at $50,000, and miscellaneous personal property worth a total of $150,000. Their total estate is worth $3,260,000. Of course, they hope the value of their estate will increase by the time either of them dies.

Their estate planning goals. Robert and Teresa each want to leave most of their property to the surviving spouse and then to their four children in equal shares. Each wants to be sure that the survivor has sufficient income and assets to continue to live the affluent kind of life they've had together. They also want to leave smaller gifts to friends, relatives, and charities. They also want to plan to avoid probate and reduce estate taxes to the extent feasible.

Their plan. Robert and Teresa decide to establish a living trust to avoid probate. As part of that trust, each spouse creates a disclaimer AB trust to reduce overall estate taxes. With a disclaimer AB trust, the surviving spouse (as trustee) can decide how much of the deceased spouse's property to inherit outright, and how much to place in Trust A. The couple understands and accepts that the surviving spouse might choose to put less than the maximum exempt amount in Trust A.

Each spouse names their four children as the final beneficiaries of his or her AB trust.

In their living trust, each spouse also leaves several personal gifts to friends and charities. The successor trustee for the trust, after both spouses die, will be the Casswells' eldest daughter, a stable, savvy woman who lives near them and is respected by the other children. They have discussed this with her and mentioned it to the other children; happily, none of the others objected.

After working out these basic ideas about how they want their disclaimer AB trust to work, the Casswells hire a lawyer to help draw up the necessary documents, including basic backup wills, health care directives, and a durable power of attorney for finances.

B. A Wealthy Couple in Their 70s

Rabia and Alfonso have been married for over 35 years. Rabia is 70, Alfonso is 79. They have two grown children in their early 40s. Rabia has one child, in his late 40s, from a former marriage.

Their property. Rabia and Alfonso's shared estate has a total net worth of $8.3 million. In addition, Rabia has separate property—a rental house worth $180,000 that she inherited from her mother and owns free and clear.

Their estate planning goals. Because Rabia and Alfonso have a large estate, they want to save on estate taxes, leave much of their property for the eventual use of their two children, and also make a gift to charity. Also, Rabia wants to leave a gift to her son from her prior marriage.

Their plan. Each spouse's share of their common property is $4,150,000. Rabia, of course, has an additional $180,000 of her separate property.

First, they create a living trust to avoid probate of their property.

Next, each spouse decides to leave property in an AB trust, with their two children as the final beneficiaries. This way, each spouse makes use of his or her own personal estate tax exemption.

Then, each spouse decides that they have enough money to create a generation-skipping trust of $1 million (less any portion of estate taxes due paid from this sum). For Alfonso, this trust is relatively simple. His two children will be the middle generation, and their children (his grandchildren) the final generation. But Rabia wonders if she should also include her son from her first marriage, and his children, as beneficiaries of her generation-skipping trust.

After some reflection and soul-searching, she decides not to. Her son doesn't get along very well with one of her other children, so having both be beneficiaries of the same trust could become problematic. Rabia decides, instead, that she will leave her son a substantial amount of money outright. So, as a part of her living trust, Rabia leaves an outright gift of her separate property home (worth $180,000) and $320,000 from her shared property to her son, a total gift of $600,000. In the trust document, she directs that no estate taxes be paid from this gift.

Finally, each spouse creates a QTIP trust for any property left over after their other trusts have been funded, or gifts made. Using a QTIP trust postpones estate taxes on the property until the second spouse dies. Alfonso names his two children to divide equally all money in his QTIP trust. Rabia distributes the property held by her QTIP trust to her final beneficiaries differently: 40% to each of her children

with Alfonso, and 20% to her son from the earlier marriage.

Alfonso and Rabia complete their estate plan by each preparing a simple will, health care directives, and a durable power of attorney for finances.

C. A SINGLE MAN IN HIS 60s

Dick Daughterty, a bachelor, wants to leave some of his property to his sister, some to her three children, and much to many friends.

His property. Dick has personal possessions worth $75,000, jewelry worth $25,000, a limited partnership interest worth $160,000, stocks worth $47,000, and savings of $45,000. He doesn't own any real estate. His total estate is worth $352,000.

His estate planning goals. Dick is most concerned with who gets his property, not how they get it. He spends considerable time evaluating exactly who gets what, making several lists and numerous revisions before he settles on a plan.

Dick definitely doesn't want his estate to have to pay probate fees. Because his estate is well below the estate tax threshold, he doesn't have to worry about federal taxes.

His plan. Dick creates a probate-avoiding living trust. In his trust, he specifies the many beneficiaries he's chosen, identifying each item of property that goes to each. Then he transfers all his property, except his savings account, to the living trust. He writes the Office of the General Partner for the limited partnership and instructs it to reregister his ownership interest in his name as trustee of his trust.

Dick changes his savings account into a pay-on-death account and names his three best friends as equal beneficiaries of the account.

Next, he prepares a basic will, although, at present, none of his property will be transferred by will. His will covers the possibility he may subsequently acquire property that he isn't able to transfer to his trust before he dies.

Then he prepares his health care directives and durable power of attorney for finances. He names his best friend, Al, to be his attorney-in-fact for both, and another friend, Jacqueline, to be alternate attorney-in-fact for both if Al can't serve. Dick is particularly concerned about health care decisions. If he's incapacitated, he wants to be treated by his personal doctors. If he needs to be hospitalized, he wants to be taken to a specific local hospital. And he does not want life support technology used to artificially extend his life if he has a fatal, irreversible disease. So he drafts a health care directive that incorporates all his specific desires, making them legal and mandatory.

Finally, Dick prepares his funeral plan and instructions and gives them to Al, to ensure they're carried out.

D. A YOUNGER COUPLE

Mark Ryan and Alicia Lopez are married. He's 43, she's 32. They have two young children. Mark is employed as a carpenter; Alicia works part-time as a proofreader for a publisher. They live in Texas, a community property state.

Their property. They own their house (heavily mortgaged) in joint tenancy. It's their only major asset. They also own two cars, an old Ford and an older Toyota station wagon, the well-used furnishings of their home, personal possessions such as clothing, books, and electronic equipment, and two savings accounts—one shared account containing $18,000, and another containing $6,000 in Mark's name, an account he had before they were married.

Their estate planning goals. Mark and Alicia's main concern is providing for their children's care, both financial and personal, if both parents die. With total assets worth less than $150,000, they don't need to worry about federal estate taxes. And because their house is owned in joint tenancy, their major asset will avoid probate, unless they die simultaneously.

Their plan. Mark and Alicia decide they don't want to create a probate-avoiding living trust now, as they don't have a lot of property and, statistically, are unlikely to die for many years. They prepare a will leaving all their non-joint tenancy property, except Mark's savings account, to each other. In their wills, they name their children as alternate beneficiaries, to receive all property covered by the wills and the house, in case both parents die simultaneously.

Mark and Alicia learn, to their mutual surprise, that they disagree on what should be done with Mark's $6,000 savings account. Alicia believes it should be handled like all their other property; indeed, she points out that Mark can easily convert the account to community property by simply depositing it in their joint account. Mark states that he wants to keep exclusive control over the account, as his own separate property. Further, he wants to leave it to his brother, Herb, a struggling woodworker whom he is close to. Alicia, who has long felt Herb was a no-goodnik, becomes upset that Mark wants to hold out on his own children. After all, if Mark died, she and the kids would need every cent they could get their hands on. As Mark starts to get angry, Alicia realizes they need to slow down and talk it out.

It takes a couple of days, but finally they arrive at a compromise. Mark will transfer $3,000 of his account into their shared account. He can leave the other $3,000 to Herb in his will.

Only after they resolve this issue do Mark and Alicia approach the subject they agree is most important: providing for their two children as best they can if the unlikely occurs and they die simultaneously. They agree on who should be the children's personal guardian, named in their wills—Alicia's sister Joan, who is willing to do the job.

They also name Joan as the children's property guardian. They decide that some life insurance is necessary, at least until their savings increase and the children are older. They decide to purchase $150,000 term life policies on each of their lives, realizing that because both of them work and the family needs two incomes to get by, it's not enough just to insure Mark's life.

Each establishes a family pot trust in both their wills. If both parents die, the insurance proceeds will be paid to the trust and managed for the children's benefit until they become 18.

Finally, Mark and Alicia each prepare health care directives and a durable power of attorney for finances, each naming the other to make health care or financial decisions in case he or she becomes incapacitated, with Joan as the alternate attorney-in-fact.

E. A SINGLE WOMAN IN HER 30S

Anne Clark is a single woman who works as an attorney for the Public Defender's Office in Los Angeles. Anne's primary concern is providing for her eight-year-old daughter, Tina.

Her property. Anne's estate consists of money market savings of $90,000, a 403(b) retirement account presently worth $55,000, personal possessions (including her car) worth $80,000, and term life insurance with proceeds of $400,000 payable upon her death. She does not own any real estate.

Her estate planning goals. Anne's goal is simple: to be sure her daughter is cared for if anything should happen to Anne.

Her plan. Anne's first concern is who will raise Tina if she cannot. Tina's father now has a second family, and has shown little interest in Tina for several years. To obtain court-ordered child support Anne has twice had to threaten legal action. There is no person who, in Anne's opinion, would be ideal to raise Tina. Anne's older sister says that she'd accept the job, but she's not enthusiastic about it. Plus she lives in New Jersey and has three children and an unstable husband to cope with. So Anne talks to her best friend in Los Angeles, Frederick, about the possibility of caring for Tina. He declares that he'd be pleased to take on the job; he's single, likes Tina, and has always wanted a child.

In her will, Anne names Frederick to be Tina's personal guardian. She includes in the will a detailed statement of why Frederick would be in Tina's best interest, including the reasons why Tina's father is not suitable for the job. Anne also prepares a detailed letter, requesting that Frederick be named as Tina's custodian if Anne becomes incapacitated and unable to care for Tina herself. While not binding, the letter should be persuasive to a judge if something happens to Anne before her death and a custody conflict arises.

Without any other good choice as a backup, Anne names her sister as alternate personal guardian. She's relieved to recall that it's highly improbable that both she and Frederick would be unable to care for Tina.

Anne is healthy and active, so she doesn't have to make a complicated estate plan. Her two most important assets—the life insurance proceeds and 403(b) money—will pass outside of probate. Anne names Tina as the beneficiary of both assets. For each, she creates an UTMA account, naming Frederick as custodian for any funds Tina receives from either account. Similarly, she makes her money market account a pay-on-death account, naming Tina as the beneficiary through an UTMA account.

She leaves her personal possessions to Tina by her will, having decided that she doesn't have to worry about further probate avoidance: Her will property is not very valuable, and she's unlikely to die for decades. In her will, she creates a Uniform Trust for Minors account for any property left to Tina, with Frederick as the custodian.

Because she lives in California, Anne can choose an age Tina must reach up to 25 for terminating any UTMA accounts. Anne decides that the accounts will end when Tina becomes 21, not wanting to impose restrictions over Tina past the age when she will (Anne hopes) be graduating from college.

Finally, Anne creates health care documents and a durable power of attorney for finances, in each case naming Frederick to act for her if she cannot.

F. A WIDOW IN HER 80s

Ida Grant, a widow, lives in California. She wants to leave the bulk of her estate to her one child, Carla. She also has a four-year-old Irish terrier, which she loves and wants to provide care for after she dies. Finally, she wants to make a number of small gifts to friends and charities.

Her property. Mrs. Grant's estate consists of a house that she and her husband bought in 1947 for $8,000. It now has a market value of $460,000. Mrs. Grant has household furnishings worth $20,000, a car worth $5,000, stocks worth $70,000, and savings of $80,000. She lives primarily on interest from her savings and Social Security.

Her estate planning goals. Mrs. Grant values simplicity. She wants to transfer her property by the simplest means possible, but she also wants to avoid probate.

Her plan. Mrs. Grant considers transferring her house into joint tenancy with her daughter Carla, whom she trusts absolutely, because this seems to provide the simplest probate-avoidance transfer method. However, Mrs. Grant learns there will be serious tax disadvantages if she uses joint tenancy. The IRS will require that a gift tax return be filed because Mrs. Grant is giving a half-interest in the house to her daughter. No tax will actually be paid now because the house's worth is under the gift/estate tax threshold, but still, it's a hassle to prepare and file the tax return.

Mrs. Grant decides to use a living trust for her house. This allows the house to avoid probate. She names Carla as the trust's beneficiary and successor trustee. She then signs and records a deed transferring the house from herself to herself as trustee of her trust. When listing the house as part of the trust property on the trust schedule, Mrs. Grant includes "all household furnishings," so her daughter will receive this property outside of probate as well.

Mrs. Grant wants to provide care for her dog. When she investigated this possibility, she learned that trusts for animals are legal in California. But she decides to handle the matter informally. Mrs. Grant discussed her concern with Carla, who is far from being a dog lover. Carla suggested that the dog, and a sum of money necessary to care for it, be left to Betty Planquee, a good friend who has said she would accept the responsibility.

Mrs. Grant learns that under California law she can transfer property worth less than $100,000 by her will free of probate. She has her savings in a money market account. She changes that account to a pay-on-death account, naming her daughter as beneficiary, and so avoids probate of that account. Then, using a backup will, she leaves stocks to close friends:

- "I leave my stock in A Corp. to my good friend and longtime veterinarian, Arthur Pedronnzi.

- I leave my stock in B Corp. to my good friend and faithful gardener, William Service.

- I leave my stock in C Corp. and my dog Cherry Blossom to my friend Betty Planquee."

The residuary clause of her will provides, "I leave all my remaining property subject to this will to my daughter, Carla." Under this clause, any property that remains subject to her will after the stock gifts are made, such as her car, goes to Carla. Because the total amount of property transferred under her will is less than $100,000, no probate is required.

Mrs. Grant doesn't name any alternate beneficiaries. She wants to keep her will simple, and decides that if any of her friends die before her, she wants that money to go to Carla under the terms of the residuary clause. And she doesn't even want to consider the possibility that Carla could die before she does.

Mrs. Grant also prepares a health care directive and a durable power of attorney for finances, naming her daughter Carla in both as her attorney-in-fact, to act for her if she becomes incapacitated and can't make medical or financial decisions herself.

G. A Couple in Their 60s, in a Second Marriage

Miriam and Ira Bloom are a married couple in their 60s. They live in New Jersey. It's the second marriage for each. Miriam has one child, now 32, from her first marriage; Ira has two, who are 33 and 36, from his first marriage.

Their property. Miriam and Ira share ownership of a $200,000 condominium apartment ($160,000 equity), savings of $80,000, stocks worth $55,000, and miscellaneous furnishings worth approximately $15,000. Each separately owns a car worth roughly $10,000. Ira owns, as his separate property, real estate worth $340,000 ($250,000 equity), partnership interests worth $80,000, and savings of $40,000. Miriam owns a coin collection worth $5,000 and mutual funds worth $185,000.

Their estate planning goals. Both Miriam and Ira want to provide for each other, but each also wants to ensure that their children from their prior marriages are well provided for. Ira's total estate is now worth $535,000. Miriam's is worth $355,000. Neither's estate is large enough to be subject to federal estate taxes, but they do want to avoid probate fees.

Their plan. Miriam and Ira agree that each will leave their shared ownership property outright to the other. Any New Jersey state inheritance taxes assessed against either's estate will be paid from this shared property. Each one's separate property will be left in an AB trust for the other spouse, with the property in the trust to go ultimately to the deceased spouse's children. Then they see a lawyer to draw up the trust document. The surviving spouse will be the trustee of whichever Trust A becomes operational (containing the separate property of the deceased spouse). Each spouse fully trusts the other to manage his or her trust property, and is confident he or she will conserve the trust principal for their children. But both spouses know that their children are somewhat mistrustful of this arrangement. So the spouses agree that the surviving spouse will send the deceased spouse's children yearly reports of the trust's financial status (a copy of the trust's annual tax return will suffice) to reassure them that the property isn't being squandered.

Because one of Ira's children still needs financial support for education, he places $20,000 of his separate savings in a pay-on-death bank account for her, so she will get money without delay if he dies before she graduates. If the daughter completes her education with Ira's help before he dies, he can then, if he wants to, revoke the informal bank account trust and place the account in his living trust.

The Blooms also each execute health care directives and durable powers of attorney for finances, naming the other spouse as the attorney-in-fact.

Finally, the Blooms prepare simple basic wills.

H. An Unmarried Couple in Their 40s

Pat and Mercedes have lived together for 13 years. They have no children. They have a written living-together contract, stating that they share ownership of their house and household goods. They've also recorded a deed to the house as tenants in common, with each owning half. In their agreement they've provided that all other property of each is his or her separate property.

Their estate planning goals. Each wants to leave his or her interest in the house and furnishings to the other, and other items to family and friends. Each wants to avoid probate of all their property. Neither's estate will be subject to federal estate taxes. Finally, each wants to ensure that the other can make medical and financial decisions if one becomes incapacitated.

Their plan. They decide to create a living trust with three distinct property listings: one for their shared property and one for each one's separate property.

Each leaves his or her interest in the their shared property (the house and furnishings) to the other. They prepare and file a deed transferring ownership of their house into their names as trustees of their shared trust. Then, each leaves gifts of their separate property to the beneficiaries they've chosen. They both complete all paperwork necessary to transfer property to the trust.

Each also prepares a basic will and leaves all property subject to those wills (none right now) to the other.

Finally, Pat and Mercedes each prepare a health care directive and a durable power of attorney for finances, naming the other as attorney-in-fact. ■

GLOSSARY

Part of the hold that the legal profession has over us has to do with its use of specialized language. It is easy to be intimidated and uncomfortable when we don't know what lawyers and judges are talking about. It is only beginning to dawn on many of us that legal language is sometimes consciously, and occasionally even cynically, used to keep us intimidated, and that the concepts behind the obtuse language are often easily understandable. We'd rather use only plain English throughout this book and eliminate legalistic jargon altogether, but unfortunately we are stuck with a legal system that often creaks into motion best when "magic" (sometimes four-syllabic) words are used. (Lawyers call such words "terms of art.")

If you don't find a confusing term defined here, try Nolo's online legal dictionary at www.nolo.com. Or try a standard dictionary, but be sure to read the entire definition, as specialized legal meanings are often listed last. As a last resort, try *Black's Law Dictionary*, available in all law libraries.

Definitions in quotes and with the symbol (B.) following are taken from Ambrose Bierce's *The Devil's Dictionary*.

AB trust. As used in *Plan Your Estate*, a trust giving a surviving spouse (or mate) a life estate interest in property of a deceased spouse or mate. This type of trust is designed to save on eventual estate taxes by giving a surviving spouse (or member of an unmarried couple) the income from the property of the first spouse to die (not the property itself). It can also be called a "credit shelter trust," "marital life estate trust," "spousal bypass trust," or an "exemption trust."

Abatement. Cutting back certain gifts under a will when it is necessary to create a fund to meet expenses, pay taxes, satisfy debts, or take care of other bequests that are given a priority under law or under the will.

Abstract of trust. A condensed version of a living trust, which leaves out the key parts of what property is in the trust and who are the beneficiaries. An Abstract of Trust (also called a "Certification of Trust") is used to prove, to a financial organization or other institution, that a valid living trust has been established, without revealing specifics of property or beneficiaries the person who created the trust wants to keep private and confidential.

Accumulation trust. A trust where trust income is retained, and not paid out to beneficiaries until certain conditions occur.

Acknowledgment. A statement in front of a person who is qualified to administer oaths (e.g., a Notary Public) that a document bearing your signature was actually signed by you.

Ademption. The failure of a specific bequest of property to take effect because the property is no longer owned by the person who made the will at the time of his death.

Administration (of an estate). The court-supervised distribution of the probate estate of a deceased person. The person who manages the distribution is called the executor if there is a will. If there is no will, this person is called the administrator. In some states, the person is called "personal representative" in either instance.

Adopted child. Any person, whether an adult or a minor, who is legally adopted as the child of another in a court proceeding.

Adult. Any person 18 or older.

Affidavit. A written statement made under oath.

Annuity. Payment of a fixed sum of money to a specified person at regular intervals, usually for life.

Assign. To transfer ownership of something.

Augmented estate. A method used in a number of states following the common law ownership of property system to measure a person's estate for the purpose of determining whether a surviving spouse has been adequately provided for. Generally, the augmented estate consists of property left by the will plus certain property transferred outside of the will by gifts, joint tenancies, and living trusts. In the states using this concept, a surviving spouse is generally considered to be adequately provided for if he or she receives at least one-third of the augmented estate.

Autopsy. Medical examination of the body of a deceased person to determine the cause of death.

Basis. This is a tax term that has to do with the valuation of property for determining profit or loss on sale. If you buy a house (or a poodle) for $20,000, your tax basis is $20,000. If you later sell it for $35,000, your taxable profit is $15,000. A **stepped-up basis** means that you have been able to raise this basic amount from which taxes are computed.

Beneficiary. A person or organization who is legally entitled to receive gifts made under a legal document such as a will, trust, pay-on-death account, or retirement plan. Except when very small estates are involved, beneficiaries of wills receive their benefits only after the will is examined and approved by the probate court. Beneficiaries of living trusts receive their benefits outside of probate, as provided in the document establishing the trust. A primary beneficiary is a person who directly and certainly will benefit from a will or trust. A contingent beneficiary is a person who might or might not become a beneficiary, depending on the terms of the will or trust and what happens to the primary beneficiaries. For example, a contingent beneficiary might get nothing until and unless the primary beneficiary dies, with a portion of the trust corpus still remaining.

Bequest. An old legal term for a will provision leaving personal property to a specified person or organization. In this book it is called a "gift."

Bond. A document guaranteeing that a certain amount of money will be paid to those injured if a person occupying a position of trust does not carry out his or her legal and ethical responsibilities. Thus, if an executor, trustee, or guardian who is bonded (covered by a bond) wrongfully deprives a beneficiary of his or her property (say by blowing it during a trip to Las Vegas), the bonding company will replace it, up to the limits of the bond. Bonding companies, which are normally divisions of insurance companies, issue a bond in exchange for a premium, usually about 10% of the face amount of the bond.

Bypass trust. Any trust that creates a life estate for a life beneficiary, with the trust principal going to the final beneficiary when the life beneficiary dies.

Charitable trust. Any trust designed to make a substantial gift to a charity, and also achieve income and estate tax savings for the grantor.

Children. For the purposes of *Plan Your Estate*, one's children are: (1) the biological offspring of a will maker, (2) persons who were legally adopted by a will maker, (3) children born out of wedlock if the will maker is the mother, (4) children born out of wedlock if the will maker is the father and has acknowledged the child as being his as required by the law of the particular state, or (5) children born to the will maker after the will is made, but before his or her death.

Child's trust. A trust created for a minor child, or young adult.

Codicil. A separate legal document, which, after it has been signed and properly witnessed, changes an existing will.

Common law marriage. In a minority of states, couples may be considered married if they live together for a certain period of time and intend to be husband and wife.

Community and separate property. Eight states follow a system of marital property ownership called "community property," and Wisconsin has a very similar "marital property" law. Very generally, all property acquired after marriage and before permanent separation is considered to belong equally to both spouses, except for gifts to and inheritances by one spouse, and, in some community property states, income from property owned by one spouse prior to marriage.

Conditional gift. A gift which passes only under certain specified conditions or upon the occurrence of a specific event. For example, if you leave property to Aunt Millie provided she is living in Cincinnati when you die, and otherwise to Uncle Fred, you have made a "conditional gift."

Conservator. Someone appointed by a court to manage the affairs of a mentally incompetent person.

Contract. An agreement between two or more people to do something. A contract is normally written, but can be oral if its terms can be carried out within one year and it doesn't involve real estate. A contract is distinguished from a gift in that each of the contracting parties pledges to do something in exchange for the promises of the other.

Creditor. As used in this book, this means a person or institution to whom money is owed. A creditor may be the person who actually lent the money, or he may be a lawyer or bill collector who is trying to collect the money for the original creditor.

Curtesy. See **Dower and curtesy.**

Custodian. A person named to care for property left to a minor under the Uniform Transfers (or Gifts) to Minors Act.

Death taxes. Taxes levied on the property of a person who died. Federal death taxes are called "estate taxes." State death taxes (if any) go by various names, including "estate tax" and "inheritance tax."

Debtor. A person who owes money.

Decedent. A person who has died.

Deed. The legal document by which one person (or persons) transfers title (recorded ownership) to real estate to another person or persons. If the transfer is by a grant deed, the person transferring title makes certain guarantees or warranties as regards the title. If the transfer is by quitclaim deed, the person transferring does not make any guarantees, but simply transfers to the other persons all the interest he has in the real property.

Descendant. A person who is an offspring, however remote, of a certain person or family.

Devise. An old English term for real estate given by a will. In this book, it is called a "gift."

Disclaimer. The right to refuse to accept property left to you by trust or will. A disclaimer AB trust allows the surviving spouse to disclaim any trust property left to him or her by the deceased spouse, sending the disclaimed property to the deceased spouse's Trust A.

Domicile. The state, or country, where one has his or her primary home.

Donor. One who gives a gift. A **donee** is one who receives a gift.

Dower and curtesy . The right of a surviving spouse to receive or enjoy the use of a set portion of a deceased spouse's property (usually one-third to one-half) in the event the surviving spouse is not left at least that share and chooses to take against the will. Dower refers to the title which a surviving wife gets, while curtesy refers to what a husband receives. Until recently, these amounts differed in a number of states. However, since discrimination on the basis of sex is now illegal in most cases, states generally provide the same benefits regardless of sex.

Durable power of attorney. A power of attorney which remains effective even if the person who created it (called the "principal") becomes incapacitated. The person authorized to act (called the "attorney-in-fact") can make health care decisions and handle financial affairs of the principal.

Encumbrances. If property is used as collateral for payment of a debt or loan, the property is "encumbered." The debt must be paid off before title to the property can pass to a new owner. Generally, the value of a person's ownership in such property (called the "equity") is measured by the market value of the property less the sum of all encumbrances.

Equity. The difference between the current fair market value of your real and personal property and the amount you owe on it, if any.

Escheat. We put this in here because it's one of our favorite legal words; it means property that goes to a state government because there are no legal inheritors to claim it.

Estate. Generally, all the property you own when you die. There are different ways to measure your estate, depending on whether you are concerned with tax reduction (the taxable estate), probate avoidance (the probate estate), or net worth (the net estate).

Estate planning. What this book is about—the art of continuing to prosper when you're alive, then dying with the smallest taxable estate and probate estate possible, and passing your property to your loved ones with a minimum of fuss and expense.

Estate taxes. Taxes imposed on your property as it passes from the dead to the living. The federal government exempts a set dollar amount of property (between $1.5 million and $3.5 million, depending on the date of death). Taxes are imposed only on property actually owned by you at the time of your death. Thus, estate planning techniques designed to reduce taxes usually concentrate on the legal transfer of ownership of your property while you are living, to minimize the amount of such property you own at your death.

Estate tax threshold. The dollar value of an estate at which estate tax may be due.

Executor. The person named in your will to manage your estate, deal with the probate court, collect your assets, and distribute them as you have specified. In some states this person is called the "personal representative." If you die without a will, the probate court will appoint such a person, who is called the "administrator" of the estate.

Final beneficiaries. People or institutions designated to receive life estate trust property outright upon the death of a life beneficiary.

Financial guardian. See **Guardian of the minor's property.**

Formula AB trust. A trust funded with an amount no larger than the personal federal estate tax exemption as of the year of death.

Funding a trust. Transferring ownership of property to a trust, in the name of the trustee.

Funeral. "A pageant whereby we attest to our respect to the dead by enriching the undertaker, and strengthen our grief by an expenditure that deepens our groans and doubles our tears." (B.)

Future interest. A right to property which cannot be enforced in the present, but at some future time.

Generation-skipping trust. An estate tax-saving trust, where the principal is left in trust for one's grandchildren, with one's children receiving only the trust income.

Gifts. As used in *Plan Your Estate*, any property you give to another person or organization, either during your lifetime, or leave by will or living trust after your death.

Gift taxes. Taxes levied by governments on gifts made during a person's lifetime.

Grantor. The person who establishes a trust; also sometimes called a "settlor" or "trustor."

Grantor retained income trusts. Various types of trusts where the grantor retains some interest in the trust property during his life.

Guardian of the minor's property. Termed "property guardian" in this book, this is the person you name in your will to care for property of your minor child not supervised by some other legal method, such as a minor's trust. Also sometimes called "the guardian of the minor's estate," or "financial guardian."

Guardian of the person. An adult appointed or selected to care for a minor child in the event no biological or adoptive parent (legal parent) of the child is able to do so. If one legal parent is alive when the other dies, the child will automatically go to that parent, unless the best interests of the child require something different, or (in some states) the court finds the child would suffer detriment.

Health care directive. A document in which you state your wishes regarding health care in case you are ever unable to speak for yourself and/or name a trusted person to see that your wishes are carried out.

Hearse. "Death's baby carriage." (B.)

Heirs. Persons who are entitled by law to inherit your estate if you don't leave a will or other device to pass property at your death.

Holographic will. An unwitnessed will that is completely handwritten by the person making it. While legal in many states, it is never advised except as a last resort.

Incidents of ownership. All (or any) control over a life insurance policy.

Inherit. To receive property from one who dies.

Inheritance taxes. Taxes a few states impose on property received by inheritors from a deceased's estate.

Inheritors. Persons or organizations who inherit property.

Instrument. Legalese for document; often used to refer to the document which creates a trust.

Insurance. "An ingenious modern game of chance in which the player is permitted to enjoy the comfortable conviction that he is beating the man who keeps the table." (B.)

Inter vivos trusts. See **Living trusts.**

Intestate. To die without a will or other valid estate transfer device.

Intestate succession. The method by which property is distributed when a person fails to distribute it in a will. In such cases, the law of each state provides that the property be distributed in certain shares to the closest surviving relatives. In most states, these are a surviving spouse, children, parents, siblings, nieces and nephews, and next of kin, in that order. The intestate succession laws are also used in the event an heir is found to be pretermitted (not mentioned or otherwise provided for in the will).

Irrevocable trust. Means what it says. Once you set it up, that's it. Unlike a revocable, probate-avoidance trust, you can't later revoke it, amend it, or change it in any way.

Issue. Legalese for one's direct descendants—children, grandchildren, etc.

Joint tenancy. A way to take title to jointly owned real or personal property. When two or more people own property as joint tenants, and one of the owners dies, the other owners automatically become owners of the deceased owner's share. Because of this "right of survivorship," a joint tenancy interest in property does not go through probate.

Lawful. "Compatible with the will of a judge having jurisdiction." (B.)

Lawyer. "One skilled in circumvention of the law." (B.)

Legacy. "A gift from one who is legging it out of this vale of tears." (B.)

Letters testamentary. The term for the document issued by a probate court authorizing the executor to discharge her responsibilities.

Life beneficiary. A person who can receive use of trust property, and benefit of trust income for his or her life, but who doesn't own the trust property itself (the "principal") and has no power to dispose of the trust property upon his or her own death.

Life estate. The right to use trust property, and receive income from it, during one's lifetime.

Life insurance trust. An irrevocable trust that owns a life insurance policy to reduce the size of the original owner's taxable estate.

Liquid assets. Cash or assets that can readily be turned into cash.

Living trusts. A trust set up while a person is alive and that remains under the control of that person until death. Also referred to as an "inter vivos trust," a living trust is an excellent way to minimize the value of property passing through probate. This is because it enables people (called "grantors") to specify that money or other property will pass directly to their beneficiaries at the time of their death, free of probate, and yet also allows the grantors to continue to control the property during their lifetime and even end the trust or change the beneficiaries if they wish.

Living will. See **health care directive.**

Marital deduction. A deduction allowed by the federal estate tax law for all property passed to a surviving spouse. This deduction (which really acts like an exemption) allows anyone, even a billionaire, to pass his or her entire estate to a surviving spouse without any tax at all. This might be a good idea if the surviving spouse is relatively young and in good health.

Marriage. A specific status conferred on a couple by the state. In most states, it is necessary to file papers with a county clerk and have a marriage ceremony conducted by an authorized individual in order to be married. However, in a minority of states called "common law marriage" states, you may be considered married if you have lived together for a certain period of time and intended to be husband and wife.

Mausoleum. "The final and funniest folly of the rich." (B.)

Minor. Persons under 18 years of age. A minor is not permitted to make certain types of decisions (for example, enter into most contracts). All minors are required to be under the care of a competent adult (parent or guardian) unless they qualify as emancipated minors (in the military, married, or living independently with court permission). This also means that property left to a minor must be handled by a guardian or trustee until the minor becomes an adult under the laws of the state.

Mopery. Not genuine legalese, but a humorous facsimile, such as "indicted on two counts of mopery."

Mortgage. A document that makes a piece of real estate the security (collateral) for the payment of a debt. Most house buyers sign a mortgage when they buy; the bank lends money to buy the house, and the house serves as security for the debt. If the owners don't pay back the loan on time, the bank can seize the house and have it sold to pay off the loan.

Net taxable estate. The value of all your property at death less all encumbrances and your other liabilities.

Next of kin. The closest living relation.

Ongoing trust. Any trust that is designed to be irrevocable and be operational for an extended period of time.

Pay-on-death designation. A method of providing, on a property account form, who will inherit what remains of that property when you die. Most commonly used for bank accounts.

Personal property. All property other than land and buildings attached to land. Cars, bank accounts, wages, securities, a small business, furniture, insurance policies, jewelry, pets, and season baseball tickets are all personal property.

Pour-over will. A will that "pours over" property into a trust. Property left through the will must go through probate before it goes into the trust.

Power of appointment. Having the legal authority to decide who shall receive someone else's property, usually property held in a trust.

Power of attorney. A legal document where you authorize someone else to act for you. See also **Durable power of attorney.**

Pretermitted heir. A child (or the child of a deceased child) who is either not named or (in some states) not provided for in a will. Most states presume that people want their children to inherit. Accordingly, children, or the children of a child who has died, who are not mentioned or provided for in the will (even by as little as $1) are entitled to a share of the estate.

Probate. The court proceeding in which: (1) the authenticity of your will (if any) is established, (2) your executor or administrator is appointed, (3) your debts and taxes are paid, (4) your heirs are identified, and (5) your property in your probate estate is distributed according to your will (if there is a will).

Probate estate. All of your property that will pass through probate. Generally, this means all property owned by you at your death less any property that has been placed in joint tenancy, a living trust, a POD account, or in life insurance.

Probate fees. Because probate is so laden with legal formalities, it is usually necessary to hire an attorney to handle it. The attorney will take a substantial fee from the estate before it is distributed to the heirs.

Property control trust. Any trust that imposes limits or controls over the rights of beneficiaries, for one of a number of reasons. These trusts include:

Special needs trusts designed to assist disadvantaged persons with special physical or other needs;

Spendthrift trusts designed to prevent a beneficiary from being able to waste trust principal;

Sprinkling trusts which authorize the trustee to decide how to distribute trust income or principal among different beneficiaries.

Proving a will. Getting a probate court to accept the fact after your death that your will really is your will. In many states this can be done simply by introducing a properly signed and witnessed will. In others, it is necessary to produce one or more witnesses (or their affidavits) in court, or offer some proof of the will maker's handwriting. Having the will maker and witnesses sign an affidavit before a notary public stating that all will-making formalities were complied with usually allows the will to "prove" itself without the need for the witnesses to testify, or other evidence.

QDOT trust. A trust used to postpone estate tax, when a U.S. citizen spouse leaves more than the amount of the personal estate tax exemption in the year of death to a non-U.S. citizen spouse.

QTIP trust. A marital trust with property left for use of the surviving spouse as life beneficiary. No estate taxes are assessed on the trust property until the death of the life beneficiary spouse.

Quasi-community property. A type of property that may be owned by married couples who have moved to California, Idaho, or Washington. (A similar form of property, called "deferred marital property," exists in Wisconsin.) Laws in these states require all property acquired by people during their marriage in other states to be treated as community property at their death.

Real estate. A term used by *Plan Your Estate* as a synonym for the legalese "real property."

Real property. All land and items attached to the land, such as buildings, houses, stationary mobile homes, fences, and trees are real property or "real estate." All property which is not real property is personal property.

Recording. The process of filing a copy of a deed with the county land records office. Recording creates a public record of all changes in ownership of property in the state.

Residual beneficiary. Can have various meanings, including: a person who receives any property left by will or trust not otherwise given away by the document; a person receiving the property of a trust after the life beneficiary dies.

Residue, residuary estate. All property given by your will or trust to your residuary beneficiary after all specific gifts of property have been made—that is, what's left.

Right of survivorship. The right of a surviving joint tenant to take ownership of a deceased joint tenant's share of the property.

Rule against perpetuities. A rule of law that limits the durations of trusts (except charitable ones). The workings of the rule are very complicated, and have baffled law students for generations. Very roughly, a trust cannot last longer than the lifetime of someone alive when the trust is created, plus 21 years.

Separate property. In states which have community property, all property which is not community property. See also **Community and separate property.**

Spouse. In *Plan Your Estate*, your spouse is the person to whom you are legally married.

Successor trustee. The person (or institution) who takes over as trustee of a trust when the original trustee(s) have died or become incapacitated.

Surviving spouse's trust. Where a couple has created an AB trust, the revocable living trust (Trust B) of the surviving spouse, after the other spouse has died.

Taking against the will. The ability of a surviving spouse to choose a statutorily allotted share of the deceased spouse's estate instead of the share specified in his or her will. In most common law property states, the law provides that a surviving spouse is entitled to receive a minimum percentage of the other spouse's estate (commonly one-third to one-half). If the deceased spouse leaves the surviving spouse less than this in, or outside of, the will, the surviving spouse may elect the statutory share instead of the will provision ("take against the will"). If the spouse chooses to accept the share specified in the will, it is called "taking under the will." See **Dower and curtesy.**

Taxable estate. The portion of your estate that is subject to federal or state estate taxes.

Tenancy by the entirety. A form of marital property ownership, with a right of survivorship between spouses; similar to joint tenancy.

Tenancy in common. A way for co-owners to hold title to property that allows them maximum freedom to dispose of their interests by sale, gift, or will. At a co-owner's death, his or her share goes to beneficiaries named in a will or trust or to the legal heirs, not to the other co-owners. Compare **Joint tenancy.**

Testamentary trust. A trust created by a will.

Testate. Someone who dies leaving a valid will, or other valid property transfer devices, dies "testate."

Testator. A person making a will.

Title. Document proving ownership of property.

Totten trust. Another term for a pay-on-death bank account.

Transfer-on-death. Refers to the right to name a beneficiary in a document of title that allows the beneficiary to receive the property quickly, outside of probate. In most states, securities (stocks and bonds) can be registered in TOD form. In some states, you can register vehicles in this way or create tranfer-on-death deeds for real estate.

Trust. A legal arrangement under which one person or institution (called a "trustee") controls property given by another person (called a "grantor" or "trustor") for the benefit of a third person (called a "beneficiary"). The property itself can be termed the "principal" of the trust.

Trust corpus or res. Legalese (in Latin, no less) for the property transferred to a trust. For example, if a trust is established (funded) with $250,000, that money is the corpus or res.

Trust merger. Occurs when the sole trustee and sole beneficiary are the same person. Then, there's no longer the separation between the trustee's legal ownership of trust property from the beneficiary's interest, which is the essence of a trust. So, the trust "merges" and ceases to exist.

Trustee. The people or institutions who manage a trust and trust property under the terms of the trust.

Trustee powers. The provisions in a trust document defining what the trustee may and may not do.

Uniform Transfers (or Gifts) to Minors Act. A series of state statutes that provide a method for transferring property to minors.

Usufruct. Included because it's another of our favorite legal words, meaning the right to use property, or income from it, owned by another.

Will. A legal document in which a person states various binding intentions about what he or she wants done with his or her property after death.

■

APPENDIX

STATE INHERITANCE TAX RULES

INHERITANCE TAXES

Following are the rules for each state that imposes inheritance taxes:

INDIANA

Class A: Spouse, parents, children, grandchildren

Class B: Sibling, nieces and nephews, son- or daughter-in-law

Class C: All others

Taxable Amount			Tax Rate		
			Base Tax	Plus %	of Amt Over
Class A					
0	to	25,000	0	+ 1%	0
25,000	to	50,000	250	+ 2%	25,000
50,000	to	200,000	750	+ 3%	50,000
200,000	to	300,000	5,250	+ 4%	200,000
300,000	to	500,000	9,250	+ 5%	300,000
500,000	to	700,000	19,250	+ 6%	500,000
700,000	to	1,000,000	31,250	+ 7%	700,000
1,000,000	to	1,500,000	52,250	+ 8%	1,000,000
1,500,000	And Over		92,250	+ 10%	1,500,000
Class B					
0	to	100,000	0	+ 7%	0
100,000	to	500,000	7,000	+ 10%	100,000
500,000	to	1,000,000	47,000	+ 12%	500,000
1,000,000	And Over	107,000		+ 15%	1,000,000
Class C					
0	to	100,000	0	+ 10%	0
100,000	to	1,000,000	10,000	+ 15%	100,000
1,000,000	And Over	45,000		+ 20%	1,000,000

Exemptions

1. Spouse: All tax

2. Child younger than 21 at death: $10,000

3. Child older than 21 at death: $5,000

4. Parents: $5,000

5. Other Class A: $2,000

6. Class B: $500

7. Class C: $100

IOWA

Class 1: Spouse

Class 2: Parent, child, lineal descendant

Class 3: Sibling, son- or daughter-in-law, stepchild

Class 4: All others

Taxable Amount			Tax Rate
Class 1			No Tax
Class 2	0	to 5,000	1%
	5,000	to 12,000	2%
	12,000	to 25,000	3%
	25,000	to 50,000	4%
	50,000	to 75,000	5%
	75,000	to 100,000	6%
	100,000	to 150,000	7%
	150,000	And Over	8%
Class 3	0	to 12,500	5%
	12,500	to 25,000	6%
	25,000	to 75,000	7%
	75,000	to 100,000	8%
	100,000	to 150,000	9%
	150,000	And Over	10%
Class 4	0	to 50,000	10%
	50,000	to 100,000	12%
	100,000	And Over	15%

Exemptions

1. Each son and daughter: $50,000

2. Father or mother: $15,000

3. Any other lineal descendant: $15,000

4. Any estate not exceeding $10,000

KENTUCKY

Class A: Spouse, parent, children (including adopted children and stepchildren), grandchildren, siblings, half-siblings

Class B: Nephew, niece, half-nephew, half-niece, daughter-in-law, son-in-law, aunt, uncle, great-grandchild

Class C: All others

	Taxable Amount			Tax Rate
Class A	As of June 30, 1998 inheritance tax was effectively eliminated for all Class A inheritors. See the exemptions listed below.			
Class B	0	to	$10,000	4%
	$10,001	to	$20,000	5%
	$20,001	to	$30,000	6%
	$30,001	to	$45,000	8%
	$45,001	to	$60,000	10%
	$60,001	to	$100,000	12%
	$100,001	to	$200,000	14%
	$200,001	And Over		16%
Class C	0	to	$10,000	6%
	$10,001	to	$20,000	8%
	$20,001	to	$30,000	10%
	$30,001	to	$45,000	12%
	$45,001	to	$60,000	14%
	$60,001	And Over		16%

Exemptions

1. Class A   All tax
2. Class B $1,000
3. Class C $500

MARYLAND

Class 1: Spouse, grandparent, parent, children or stepchildren, other lineal descendants, brothers, sisters

Class 2: All others

	Taxable Amount	Tax Rate
Class 1	All Amounts	0%
Class 2	All Amounts	10%

Exemptions

1. All property that passes to a corporation owned solely by relatives listed in Class 1
2. Property administered under small estates law

NEBRASKA

Class 1: Spouse, parent, child, son- or daughter-in-law

Class 2: Uncle, aunt, niece, nephew, or their descendants or spouses

Class 3: All others

	Taxable Amount			Tax Rate
Class 1	0	to	10,000	No Tax
	10,000	And Over		1%
Class 2	0	to	2,000	No Tax
	2,000	to	60,000	6%
	60,000	And Over		9%
Class 3	0	to	5,000	6%
	5,000	to	10,000	9%
	10,000	to	20,000	12%
	20,000	to	50,000	15%
	50,000	And Over		18%

Exemptions

1. Spouse: All tax
2. Class 1: $10,000
3. Class 2: $2,000
4. Class 3: $500

NEW JERSEY

Class A: Spouse, registered domestic partner, parent, grandparent, children, stepchildren, direct descendants

Class B: Sibling, daughter- or son-in-law

Class C: All others

	Taxable Amount			Tax Rate
Class A				No Tax
Class B	0	to	1,100,000	11%
	1,100,000	to	1,400,000	13%
	1,400,000	to	1,700,000	14%
	1,700,000	And Over		16%
Class C	0	to	700,000	15%
	700,000	And Over		16%

Exemptions

1. Class B: First $25,000

2. Life insurance proceeds: All tax

3. Pension to surviving spouse: All tax

OHIO

Taxable Amount			Tax Rate			
			Base Tax	Plus %		of Amt Over
0	to	40,000	0	+	2%	0
40,000	to	100,000	800	+	3%	40,000
100,000	to	200,000	2,600	+	4%	100,000
200,000	to	300,000	6,600	+	5%	200,000
300,000	to	500,000	11,600	+	6%	300,000
500,000	And Over		23,600	+	7%	500,000

Tax credit

Lesser of $13,900 or amount of tax

OKLAHOMA

Class 1: Parent, child, child of spouse, descendant

Class 2: All others

	Taxable Amount			Tax Rate
Class 1	0	to	10,000	0.5%
	10,000	to	20,000	1.0%
	20,000	to	40,000	1.5%
	40,000	to	60,000	2.0%
	60,000	to	100,000	2.5%
	100,000	to	250,000	3.0%
	250,000	to	500,000	6.5%
	500,000	to	750,000	7.0%
	750,000	to	1,000,000	7.5%
	1,000,000	to	3,000,000	8.0%
	3,000,000	to	5,000,000	8.5%
	5,000,000	to	10,000,000	9.0%
	10,000,000	And Over		10.0%
Class 2	0	to	10,000	1.0%
	10,000	to	20,000	2.0%
	20,000	to	40,000	3.0%
	40,000	to	60,000	4.0%
	60,000	to	100,000	5.0%
	100,000	to	250,000	6.0%
	250,000	to	500,000	13.0%
	500,000	to	1,000,000	14.0%
	1,000,000	And Over		15.0%

Exemptions

(Taxable amount begins after taking applicable exemption)

1. Spouses: All tax

2. Other Class 1: $175,000

PENNSYLVANIA

Class A: Grandparents, parents, lineal descendants, widower or widow of child, spouse of child

Class B: Siblings

Class C: All others

	Taxable Amount	Tax Rate
Class A	All Amounts	4.5%
Class B	All Amounts	12%
Class C	All Amounts	15%

Exemptions

1. Spouse: All property
2. Life insurance proceeds
3. Social Security death payments
4. Employment benefits
5. Family exemption

TENNESSEE

Class A: Spouse, child, lineal ancestor or descendant, sibling, stepchild, son- or daughter-in-law, adopted child

Class B: All other

Taxable Amount	Tax Rate		
	Base Tax	Plus %	of Amt Over
$440,000	$30,200	9.5%	$440,000

Exemptions

(Taxable amount begins after taking applicable exemption)

Classes A and B: $600,000 ■

INDEX

CATALOG

...more from Nolo

	PRICE	CODE

BUSINESS

	PRICE	CODE
Becoming a Mediator: Your Guide to Career Opportunites	$29.99	BECM
Business Buyout Agreements (Book w/CD-ROM)	$49.99	BSAG
The CA Nonprofit Corporation Kit (Binder w/CD-ROM)	$69.99	CNP
California Workers' Comp: How to Take Charge When You're Injured on the Job	$34.99	WORK
The Complete Guide to Buying a Business (Book w/CD-ROM)	$24.99	BUYBU
The Complete Guide to Selling Your Business (Book w/CD-ROM)	$24.99	SELBU
Consultant & Independent Contractor Agreements (Book w/CD-ROM)	$29.99	CICA
The Corporate Records Handbook (Book w/CD-ROM)	$69.99	CORMI
Create Your Own Employee Handbook (Book w/CD-ROM)	$49.99	EMHA
Dealing With Problem Employees	$44.99	PROBM
Deduct It! Lower Your Small Business Taxes	$34.99	DEDU
Effective Fundraising for Nonprofits	$24.99	EFFN
The Employer's Legal Handbook	$39.99	EMPL
Federal Employment Laws	$49.99	FELW
Form Your Own Limited Liability Company (Book w/CD-ROM)	$44.99	LIAB
Home Business Tax Deductions: Keep What You Earn	$34.99	DEHB
How to Create a Noncompete Agreement (Book w/CD-ROM)	$44.95	NOCMP
How to Form a California Professional Corporation (Book w/CD-ROM)	$59.99	PROF
How to Form a Nonprofit Corporation (Book w/CD-ROM)—National Edition	$49.99	NNP
How to Form a Nonprofit Corporation in California (Book w/CD-ROM)	$49.99	NON
How to Form Your Own California Corporation (Binder w/CD-ROM)	$59.99	CACI
How to Form Your Own California Corporation (Book w/CD-ROM)	$34.99	CCOR
How to Get Your Business on the Web	$29.99	WEBS
How to Run a Thriving Business: Strategies for Sucess & Satisfaction	$19.99	THRV
How to Write a Business Plan	$34.99	SBS
Incorporate Your Business	$49.95	NIBS
The Independent Paralegal's Handbook	$34.99	PARA
Legal Forms for Starting & Running a Small Business (Book w/CD-ROM)	$29.99	RUNSF
Legal Guide for Starting & Running a Small Business	$34.99	RUNS
LLC or Corporation?	$24.99	CHENT
The Manager's Legal Handbook	$39.99	ELBA
Marketing Without Advertising	$20.00	MWAD
Mediate, Don't Litigate	$24.99	MEDL

Prices subject to change.

	PRICE	CODE
Music Law (Book w/CD-ROM)	$39.99	ML
Negotitate the Best Lease for Your Business	$24.99	LESP
Nolo's Guide to Social Security Disability	$29.99	QSS
Nolo's Quick LLC	$29.99	LLCQ
Nondisclosure Agreements (Book w/CD-ROM)	$39.95	NAG
The Partnership Book: How to Write a Partnership Agreement (Book w/CD-ROM)	$39.99	PART
The Performance Appraisal Handbook	$29.99	PERF
The Small Business Start-up Kit (Book w/CD-ROM)	$24.99	SMBU
The Small Business Start-up Kit for California (Book w/CD-ROM)	$24.99	OPEN
Starting & Running a Successful Newsletter or Magazine	$29.99	MAG
Tax Savvy for Small Business	$36.99	SAVVY
Workplace Investigations: A Step by Step Guide	$39.99	CMPLN
Working for Yourself: Law & Taxes for Independent Contractors, Freelancers & Consultants	$39.99	WAGE
Working With Independent Contractors (Book w/CD-ROM)	$29.99	HICI
Your Crafts Business: A Legal Guide (Book w/CD-ROM)	$26.99	VART
Your Limited Liability Company: An Operating Manual (Book w/CD-ROM)	$49.99	LOP
Your Rights in the Workplace	$29.99	YRW

CONSUMER

How to Win Your Personal Injury Claim	$29.99	PICL
Nolo's Encyclopedia of Everyday Law	$29.99	EVL
Nolo's Guide to California Law	$24.99	CLAW

ESTATE PLANNING & PROBATE

8 Ways to Avoid Probate	$19.99	PRAV
Estate Planning Basics	$21.99	ESPN
The Executor's Guide: Settling a Loved One's Estate or Trust	$34.99	EXEC
How to Probate an Estate in California	$49.99	PAE
Make Your Own Living Trust (Book w/CD-ROM)	$39.99	LITR
Nolo's Simple Will Book (Book w/CD-ROM)	$36.99	SWIL
Plan Your Estate	$44.99	NEST
Quick & Legal Will Book	$16.99	QUIC
Quicken Willmaker: Estate Planning Essentials (Book with Interactive CD-ROM)	$49.99	QWMB
Special Needs Trust: Protect Your Child's Fianancial Future	$34.99	SPNT

FAMILY MATTERS

Building a Parenting Agreement That Works	$24.99	CUST
The Complete IEP Guide	$34.99	IEP
Divorce & Money: How to Make the Best Financial Decisions During Divorce	$34.99	DIMO
Do Your Own California Adoption: Nolo's Guide for Stepparents and Domestic Partners (Book w/CD-ROM)	$34.99	ADOP
Every Dog's Legal Guide: A Must-Have Book for Your Owner		

	PRICE	CODE
Get a Life: You Don't Need a Million to Retire Well	$24.99	LIFE
The Guardianship Book for California	$39.99	GB
A Legal Guide for Lesbian and Gay Couples	$34.99	LG
Living Together: A Legal Guide (Book w/CD-ROM)	$34.99	LTK
Living Wills and Powers of Attorney in California (Book w/CD-ROM)	$21.99	CPOA
Nolo's IEP Guide: Learning Disablities	$29.99	IELD
Prenuptial Agreements: How to Write a Fair & Lasting Contract (Book w/CD-ROM)	$34.99	PNUP
Using Divorce Mediation: Save Your Money & Your Sanity	$29.99	UDMD

GOING TO COURT

	PRICE	CODE
Beat Your Ticket: Go To Court & Win! (National Edition)	$21.99	BEYT
The Criminal Law Handbook: Know Your Rights, Survive the System	$34.99	KYR
Everybody's Guide to Small Claims Court (National Edition)	$26.99	NSCC
Everybody's Guide to Small Claims Court in California	$29.99	CSCC
Fight Your Ticket & Win in California	$29.99	FYT
How to Change Your Name in California	$34.99	NAME
How to Collect When You Win a Lawsuit (California Edition)	$29.99	JUDG
The Lawsuit Survival Guide	$29.99	UNCL
Nolo's Deposition Handbook	$29.99	DEP
Represent Yourself in Court: How to Prepare & Try a Winning Case	$34.99	RYC
Win Your Lawsuit: A Judge's Guide to Representing Yourself in CA Superior Court	$29.99	SLWY

HOMEOWNERS, LANDLORDS & TENANTS

	PRICE	CODE
California Tenants' Rights	$27.99	CTEN
Deeds for California Real Estate	$24.99	DEED
Every Landlord's Legal Guide (National Edition, Book w/CD-ROM)	$44.99	ELLI
Every Landlord's Tax Deduction Guide	$34.99	DELL
Every Tenant's Legal Guide	$29.99	EVTEN
For Sale by Owner in California	$29.99	FSBO
How to Buy a House in California	$34.99	BHCA
The California Landlord's Law Book: Rights & Responsibilities (Book w/CD-ROM)	$44.99	LBRT
The California Landlord's Law Book: Evictions (Book w/CD-ROM)	$44.99	LBEV
Leases & Rental Agreements	$29.99	LEAR
Neighbor Law: Fences, Trees, Boundaries & Noise	$26.99	NEI
The New York Landlord's Law Book (Book w/CD-ROM)	$39.99	NYLL
New York Tenants' Rights	$27.99	NYTEN
Renters' Rights (National Edition)	$24.99	RENT

IMMIGRATION

	PRICE	CODE
Becoming A U.S. Citizen: A Guide to the Law, Exam and Interview	$24.99	USCIT
Fiancé & Marriage Visas (Book w/CD-ROM)	$44.99	IMAR
How to Get a Green Card	$29.99	GRN

	PRICE	CODE
Student & Tourist Visas	$29.99	ISTU
U.S. Immigration Made Easy	$44.99	IMEZ

MONEY MATTERS

	PRICE	CODE
101 Law Forms for Personal Use (Book w/CD-ROM)	$29.99	SPOT
Bankruptcy: Is It the Right Solution to Your Debt Problems?	$21.99	BRS
Chapter 13 Bankruptcy: Repay Your Debts	$36.99	CHB
Credit Repair (Book w/CD-ROM)	$24.99	CREP
Getting Paid: How to Collect form Bankrupt Debtors	$29.99	CRBNK
How to File for Chapter 7 Bankruptcy	$29.99	HFB
IRAs, 401(k)s & Other Retirement Plans: Taking Your Money Out	$34.99	RET
Solve Your Money Troubles	$29.99	MT
Stand Up to the IRS	$29.99	SIRS
Surviving an IRS Tax Audit	$24.95	SAUD
Take Control of Your Student Loan Debt	$26.95	SLOAN

PATENTS AND COPYRIGHTS

	PRICE	CODE
All I Need is Money: How to Finance Your Invention	$19.99	FINA
The Copyright Handbook: How to Protect and Use Written Works (Book w/CD-ROM)	$39.99	COHA
Copyright Your Software (Book w/CD-ROM)	$34.95	CYS
Getting Permission: How to License and Clear Copyrighted Materials Online and Off (Book w/CD-ROM)	$34.99	RIPER
How to Make Patent Drawings	$29.99	DRAW
What Every Inventor Needs to Know About Business and Taxes (Book w/CD-ROM)	$21.99	ILAX
The Inventor's Notebook	$24.99	INOT
License Your Invention (Book w/CD-ROM)	$39.99	LICE
Nolo's Patents for Beginners	$29.99	QPAT
Patent, Copyright & Trademark	$39.99	PCTM
Patent It Yourself	$49.99	PAT
Patent Pending in 24 Hours	$29.99	PEND
Patenting Art & Entertainment: New Stategies for Protecting Creative Ideas	$39.99	PATAE
The Public Domain	$34.99	PUBL
Trademark: Legal Care for Your Business and Product Name	$39.99	TRD
Web and Software Development: A Legal Guide (Book w/ CD-ROM)	$44.99	SFT

RESEARCH & REFERENCE

	PRICE	CODE
Legal Research: How to Find & Understand the Law	$39.99	LRES

SENIORS

	PRICE	CODE
Long-Term Care: How to Plan & Pay For It	$21.99	ELD
Social Security, Medicare & Goverment Pensions	$29.99	SOA

SOFTWARE

**Call or check our website at www.nolo.com
for special discounts on Software!**

	PRICE	CODE
Incorporator Pro	$89.99	STNC1
LLC Maker—Windows	$89.95	LLP1
Patent Pending Now!	$19.99	PP1
PatentEase—Windows	$349.00	PEAS
Personal RecordKeeper 5.0 CD—Windows	$59.95	RKD5
Quicken Legal Business Pro 2006—Windows	$109.99	SBQB6
Quicken WillMaker Plus 2006—Windows	$79.99	WQP6

Special Upgrade Offer

Save 35% on the latest edition of your Nolo book

Because laws and legal procedures change often, we update our books regularly. To help keep you up-to-date, we are extending this special upgrade offer. Cut out and mail the title portion of the cover of your old Nolo book and we'll give you 35% off the retail price of the NEW EDITION of that book when you purchase directly from Nolo.

This offer is to individuals only.

Call us today at 1-800-728-3555

Prices and offer subject to change without notice.

Order Form

Name

Address

City

State, Zip

Daytime Phone

E-mail

Return anything you buy directly from Nolo for any reason and we'll cheerfully refund your purchase price. No ifs, ands or buts.

☐ Check here if you do not wish to receive mailings from other companies

Item Code	Quantity	Item	Unit Price	Total Price

Method of payment

☐ Check   ☐ VISA   ☐ MasterCard

☐ Discover Card   ☐ American Express

Subtotal	
Add your local sales tax (California only)	
Shipping: RUSH $12, Basic $9 (See below)	
"I bought 3, ship it to me FREE!"(Ground shipping only)	
TOTAL	

Account Number

Expiration Date

Signature

Shipping and Handling

Rush Delivery—Only $12

We'll ship any order to any street address in the U.S. by UPS 2nd Day Air* for only $12!

* Order by noon Pacific Time and get your order in 2 business days. Orders placed after noon Pacific Time will arrive in 3 business days. P.O. boxes and S.F. Bay Area use basic shipping. Alaska and Hawaii use 2nd Day Air or Priority Mail.

Basic Shipping—$9

Use for P.O. Boxes, Northern California and Ground Service.

Allow 1-2 weeks for delivery. U.S. addresses only.

For faster service, use your credit card and our toll-free numbers

Call our customer service group
Monday thru Friday 7am to 7pm PST

Phone   1-800-728-3555

Fax   1-800-645-0895

Mail   Nolo
         950 Parker St.
         Berkeley, CA 94710

Order 24 hours a day @
www.nolo.com

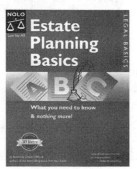

Remember:

Little publishers have big ears.
We really listen to you.

Take 2 Minutes
& Give Us
Your 2 cents

Your comments make a big difference in the development and revision of Nolo books and software. Please take a few minutes and register your Nolo product—and your comments—with us. Not only will your input make a difference, you'll receive special offers available only to registered owners of Nolo products on our newest books and software. Register now by:

PHONE
1-800-728-3555

FAX
1-800-645-0895

EMAIL
cs@nolo.com

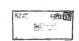

or **MAIL** us
this registration card

fold here

Registration Card

NAME _____ DATE _____

ADDRESS _____

_____

CITY _____ STATE _____ ZIP _____

PHONE _____ E-MAIL _____

WHERE DID YOU HEAR ABOUT THIS PRODUCT? _____

WHERE DID YOU PURCHASE THIS PRODUCT? _____

DID YOU CONSULT A LAWYER? (PLEASE CIRCLE ONE)   YES   NO   NOT APPLICABLE

DID YOU FIND THIS BOOK HELPFUL?   (VERY)   5   4   3   2   1   (NOT AT ALL)

COMMENTS _____

_____

_____

WAS IT EASY TO USE?   (VERY EASY)   5   4   3   2   1   (VERY DIFFICULT)

We occasionally make our mailing list available to carefully selected companies whose products may be of interest to you.

❑   If you do not wish to receive mailings from these companies, please check this box.

❑   You can quote me in future Nolo promotional materials.
     Daytime phone number _____.

NEST 8.0

Nolo *in the* NEWS

"Nolo helps lay people perform legal tasks without the aid—or fees—of lawyers."

—USA TODAY

Nolo books are ..."written in plain language, free of legal mumbo jumbo, and spiced with witty personal observations."

—ASSOCIATED PRESS

"...Nolo publications...guide people simply through the how, when, where and why of law."

—WASHINGTON POST

"Increasingly, people who are not lawyers are performing tasks usually regarded as legal work... And consumers, using books like Nolo's, do routine legal work themselves."

—NEW YORK TIMES

"...All of [Nolo's] books are easy-to-understand, are updated regularly, provide pull-out forms...and are often quite moving in their sense of compassion for the struggles of the lay reader."

—SAN FRANCISCO CHRONICLE

- - - - - - - - - - - - - - - fold here - - - - - - - - - - - - - - -

```
┌─────────────┐
│             │
│   Place     │
│ stamp here  │
│             │
└─────────────┘
```

Nolo
950 Parker Street
Berkeley, CA 94710-9867

Attn: NEST 8.0